19.95

The Arab World Competitiveness Report 2002-2003

WORLD
ECONOMIC
FORUM

COMMITTED TO
IMPROVING THE STATE
OF THE WORLD

New York • Oxford

Oxford University Press

2003

The views expressed in this report reflect the opinions of the authors and do not necessarily reflect the position of the World Economic Forum.

The Arab World Competitiveness Report 2002–2003 is published by the World Economic Forum where it is a special project within the framework of the Global Competitiveness Programme.

Professor Klaus Schwab
President

From the Global Competitiveness Programme:

Dr. Peter K. Cornelius
Director

Jennifer Blanke
Economist

Fiona Paua
Economist

From the Center for Regional Strategies:

Frédéric Sicre
Managing Director

Alexandre Theocharides
Associate Director, Middle East

Fouad Ghanma
Regional Manager, Middle East

Daniel Camara
Regional Manager

We thank Friedrich von Kirchbach, Mondher Mimouni, and Jean-Michel Pasteels from the International Trade Centre for their contribution of the detailed trade tables and charts.

Thanks also to Ibrahima Djeinabou Barry, Gonçalo Domingos Felicio, Henri de La Grandville, Catherine Vindret, and Kenichi Watanabe for invaluable research assistance.

Special recognition to Jafar Haydar for his beautiful cover calligraphy, signifying "The Arab World".

Thank you to Pearl Jusem and her team at DBA Design for the great interior graphic design and layout.

The terms *country* and *nation* as used in this report do not in all cases refer to a territorial entity that is a state as understood by international law and practice. The term covers well-defined, geographically self-contained economic areas that may not be states but for which statistical data are maintained on a separate and independent basis.

The views expressed in this report reflect the opinions of the authors and do not necessarily reflect the position of the World Economic Forum.

Oxford University Press

Oxford New York
Auckland Bangkok Buenos Aires
Cape Town Chennai Dar es Salaam Delhi
Hong Kong Istanbul Karachi Kolkata
Kuala Lumpur Madrid Melbourne
Mexico City Mumbai Nairobi Sao Paulo
Shanghai Singapore Taipei Tokyo Toronto

Copyright © 2003 by the World Economic Forum

Published by
Oxford University Press, Inc.
198 Madison Avenue
New York, New York 10016
www.oup.com

Oxford is a registered trademark of Oxford University Press

ISBN 0–19–516170–X

9 8 7 6 5 4 3 2 1

Printed in the United States of America on acid-free paper.

Contents

iv

Special thanks to the following institutions for their invaluable support in the Executive Opinion Survey process:

Algeria

Arab Communication Consult

Bahrain

Economic Development Board

Jordan

Ministry of Planning of Jordan

Kuwait

Kuwait Investment Authority

Lebanon

Conexus Consulting
Etudes & Consultations Economiques

Morocco

Foreign Investment Department

Qatar

Ministry of Foreign Affairs of Qatar

Saudi Arabia

Council of Saudi Chambers of Commerce and Industry

Tunisia

Institut Arabe des Chefs d'Entreprises

United Arab Emirates

The Executive Office, Dubai

Preface

Klaus Schwab
President, World Economic Forum

In recent years, the delicate political climate in the Middle East has often overshadowed critical discussions related to economic and social development in the Arab world. The region's economic fragility has been compounded over the past year by the economic backlash following the September 11 attacks. In this context, this *Report* focuses on the challenges facing the Arab world in improving its competitiveness at a particularly critical time.

Recent economic trends demonstrate the extent to which these challenges should not be understated. Income per capita has been steadily declining in several countries for the past two decades. In the Arab world as a whole, growth in real per capita income grew by only 0.5 percent per year between 1975 and 1998, compared to the global average of more than 1.3 percent. In fact, the only region that has had slower growth over the same period is sub-Saharan Africa. A number of the root causes of this economic stagnation are well known. The United Nations Development Program's recent *Arab Human Development Report* (2002), has identified a number of key challenges, including the "freedom deficit," the "women's empowerment deficit," and the "human capabilities/knowledge deficit." All of these deficiencies must be tackled head-on if competitiveness is to be restored to the region.

The twenty-two Arab economies of the Middle East and North Africa region possess two-thirds of the world's oil reserves, and this has been a clear strength in past years. However, Arab countries will find it challenging to create enough jobs to absorb new entrants to the labor force, which is expanding at more than 3 percent per year. This is increasingly critical, given that the changing demographics of the region are intensifying the need for job creation and educational systems that cater to the needs of the market and to the rapidly evolving global economy. Further, how will Arab countries have the resources to upgrade their economic infrastructure, or meet the health, housing, and other needs of their growing populations?

The responses to the present challenges have been quite diverse. It is encouraging to see that a number of countries in the region have made considerable headway in stabilizing, reforming, and opening up their economies. This sets the benchmark for other countries throughout the region in creating environments conducive to growth and development. Growth can be further harnessed by putting into place the fundamentals required to move from resource-based economies to knowledge-based economies. One important step in this direction is greater integration into the world economy. The Internet and new technologies also offer enormous opportunities for the region. In this respect, United Arab Emirates and Jordan serve as valuable examples of successful public-private partnerships to harness these new tools. The great potential of information and communications technologies as enablers for growth and development is specifically explored in this *Report*.

The World Economic Forum is very proud to present the first edition of the *Arab World Competitiveness Report*. As a supplement to our *Global Competitiveness Report 2001–2002*, this *Report* puts the economic challenges facing countries in the Arab World in an international context. This *Report* highlights the prospects for growth among countries in the Arab world and, more important, reveals the obstacles to competitiveness. Through in-depth analyses of regional trends and detailed country profiles for a number of countries in the region, it is our goal that the *Report* serve as a guide to policymakers and business executives alike. The results of the Executive Opinion Survey lend depth to the analysis by providing a snapshot of how leaders of the business communities in the countries perceive present competitiveness and future prospects.

We extend our gratitude to all the committed business leaders who responded to our Survey. My appreciation goes to Peter K. Cornelius, who has been charged with heading the Global Competitiveness Programme under which this *Report* is published, and to his team, Jennifer Blanke and Fiona Paua. I would also like to thank Alexandre Theocharides, associate director for the Middle East, and his team, Daniel Camara and Fouad Ghanma. Together with the *Global Competitiveness Report* and special reports on other regions, the *Arab World Competitiveness Report* is part of a family of research studies that truly mirror the increased integration of the world economy. Finally, we extend a very special thanks to the partners of the *Report* for their support in this worthwhile venture. This *Report* will serve as the intellectual foundation for the first Arab World Competitiveness Meeting. We also hope that it will have a wide distribution and long-standing positive impact in the Arab world.

Map of the Arab World

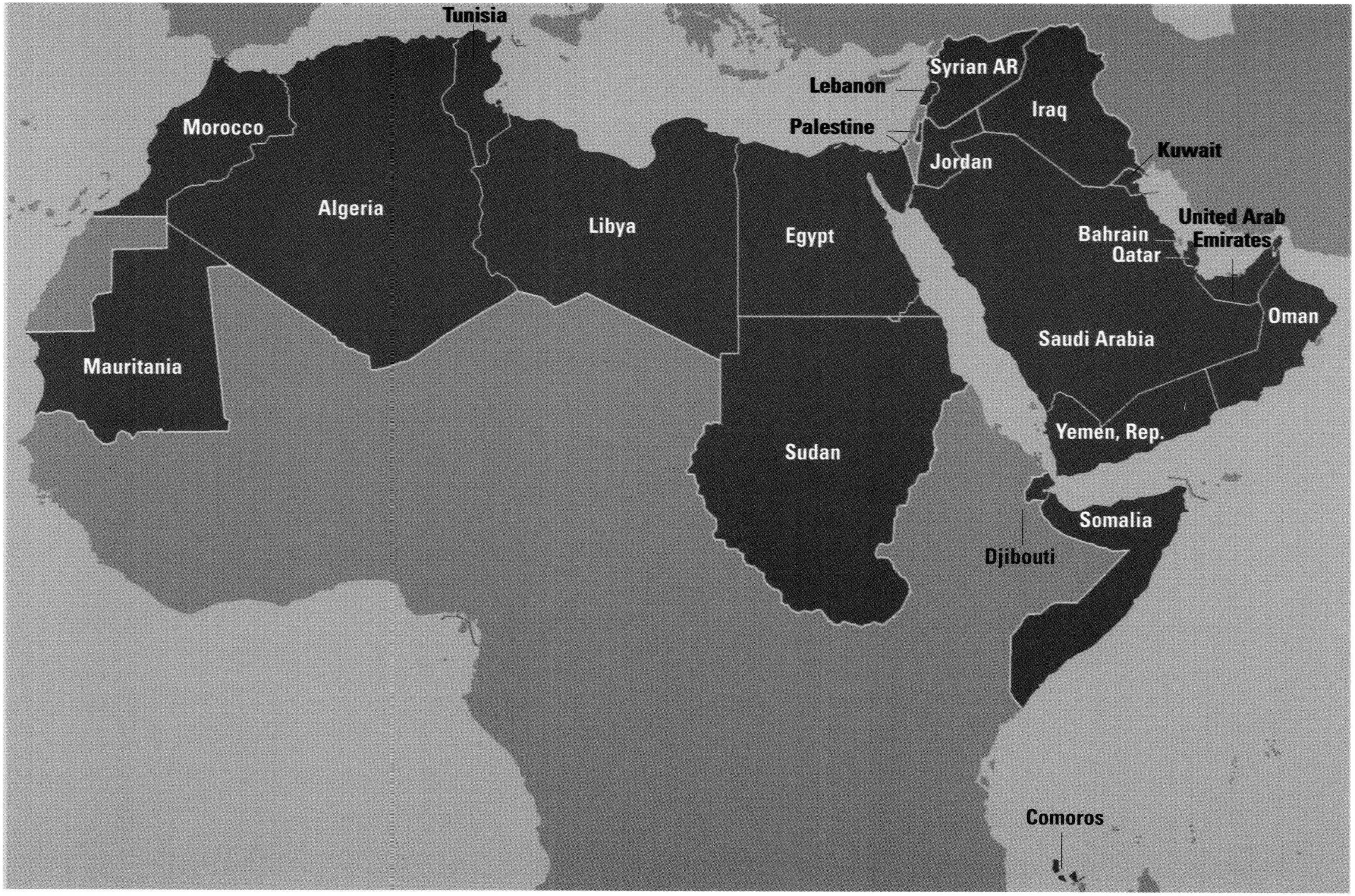

Tunisia

Morocco

Algeria

Mauritania

Libya

Egypt

Sudan

Lebanon

Palestine

Syrian AR

Jordan

Iraq

Kuwait

United Arab Emirates

Bahrain

Qatar

Saudi Arabia

Oman

Yemen, Rep.

Somalia

Djibouti

Comoros

Executive Summary

Peter K. Cornelius

The *Arab World Competitiveness Report 2002–2003* (AWCR) represents the first systematic benchmarking exercise for the region, combining broad macroeconomic and political analyses with analyses of country competitiveness. Published under the umbrella of the World Economic Forum's Global Competitiveness Programme, this *Report* has been produced as a companion volume of the *Global Competitiveness Report* (GCR). As such, the underlying approach of the AWCR is largely consistent with the GCR, defining competitiveness as "the set of institutions and economic policies supportive of high rates of economic growth in the medium term." Unlike the GCR and other regional reports, however, the AWCR does not attempt to rank individual countries according to their international competitiveness, mainly because of important data limitations.[1] Nevertheless, some Arab countries, namely Jordan and Eygpt, are also included in the GCR and thus serve as an anchor in the sense that they provide important hints as to where other countries, which are not ranked in the main report, broadly stand on an international scale.

The Arab world had been at the epicenter in the last three decades when the tectonic plates supporting the structure of global politics started to grind—precisely where the region is today. Indeed, the AWCR comes at a critical time. The global economy is wrestling to achieve a sustained recovery, and several countries in the Arab world have been hard-hit by the recent decline in economic activity. For several countries, namely those in the Gulf region, the main economic channel precipitating decline has remained the curtailment of oil production in line with falling demand. However, with economic integration, especially with the European Union (EU), having gathered momentum in recent years, other economic channels, such as nonenergy trade and capital flows, have become increasingly important. Moreover, the security situation in the post-September 11, 2001 period continues to have an important bearing on economic activity in several countries, primarily through depressed receipts from tourism. The hardest-hit economies, of course, are the West Bank and Gaza, where the ongoing conflict has led to a sharp contraction of output and a massive increase in unemployment.

With recovery in the industrial countries expected to be delayed into the final quarter of 2002 and early next year, the World Bank forecasts real output in the Arab region to expand by less than 3 percent this year, significantly less than in the two preceding years.[2] A moderate recovery is expected for 2003, but this expectation is predicated on a number of critical assumptions, notably an increase in world demand, the normalization of tourism receipts, and an improvement in the terms of trade. World Bank forecasts are more or less in line with those of other institutions, although some organizations, including the International Monetary Fund, are even more cautious.

While the short-term outlook for the Arab world remains clouded with substantial uncertainties, this *Arab World Competitiveness Report* is primarily concerned with the region's ability to achieve sustained economic growth over the medium and long run. That this ability is severely impeded by a wide range of structural factors becomes immediately clear when one looks at the Arab world's growth performance over the last few decades relative to other regions. While the current slowdown has much to do with lower oil production and the deteriorating security situation, it is also consistent with the trend of decline in real incomes per capita in most Arab states over the last ten years. Economic activity in the Arab world surged during the oil boom of the 1970s, and fell along with the sharp decline in oil prices that occurred first in 1981 and again in 1986. It would have been hard for the oil-exporting countries to avoid a dip in economic activity during the 1980s. However, the region continued to stagnate in the 1990s. The question is, why?

Between 1975 and 1999, economic growth averaged 3.3 percent per year, which was basically in line with the world average. Because population growth remained very strong, however, per capita incomes stagnated in the final quarter of the last century—underperforming all other regions, in fact, except for sub-Saharan Africa. In several countries, including Iraq, Kuwait, Libya, and Saudi Arabia, GDP per capita actually fell during this period. It is estimated that around 12 million people, or 15 percent of the labor force, are currently unemployed, a number that could rise significantly over the next few years unless there is an upswing in economic growth that creates more jobs.

The current cyclical slowdown exposes the existing structural impediments even more. Several of these impediments have been highlighted in a recent United Nations Development Program report.[3] According to this Report, three major "deficits" prevent the Arab world from reaching its potential. Removing them requires, the report argues, rebuilding Arab societies based on the following:

- Full respect for human rights and human freedoms as the cornerstones of good governance, leading to human development.

- The complete empowerment of Arab women, taking advantage of all opportunities to build their capabilities and to enable them to exercise those capabilities to the full.

- The consolidation of knowledge acquisition and its effective utilization. As a key driver of progress, knowledge must be brought to bear efficiently and productively in all aspects of society, with the goal of enhancing human well being across the region.

Tackling the three deficits will deepen and improve the Arab world's social capital, which is determined by a wide range of factors including the level of education, workforce skills and attitudes, managerial talent, legal institutions and regulatory practices governing business, the level of trust, and the presence of networks. It will also accelerate the speed of technological progress, affecting the Arab world's transition from an economy that largely competes with basic factor conditions to one where competitiveness is increasingly achieved by harnessing global technologies for local production. Therefore reducing, and eventually eliminating, the three deficits constitute a necessary condition for the Arab world to move to a steeper growth trajectory in the future.

Knowledge, innovation, and technology are also shown to play a central role in the present *Arab World Competitiveness Report 2002-2003*. As our previous research has shown, technological advancement represents a key driver of national competitiveness and economic growth.[4] In the current research, technological progress has been found to be a function of a complex set of variables, including the level of education of a country's population, the mix of public and private institutions that support innovation, the diffusion of ideas across sectors, the inflow of ideas from foreign economies into the domestic economy, the availability of venture capital, and tax laws favorable to new start-ups.

A business environment that is conducive to entrepreneurship and private risk-taking, thus supporting innovation, also requires macroeconomic stability, well-managed public institutions, and well-functioning goods and factor markets. Moreover, there is substantial evidence that the degree of a country's openness and integration into the global economy represents an important driver of its competitiveness and economic growth prospects. A liberal trade regime expands trade and investment options, and allows countries to specialize in and export those products for which they have a comparative advantage, thus helping to improve the efficiency of resource allocation. Distortions may arise not only from trade restrictions, but also from exchange controls such as multiple exchange rates, bilateral payment arrangements, or surrender requirements. Restrictions on capital flows limit a country's access to foreign savings and may therefore affect its growth potential. (However, it is important to note that dismantling such restrictions can also involve considerable risks.) Finally, the combined influences of distance, geography, and costs of trade affect the way countries compete internationally. Upgrading a country's physical infrastructure, that is, the quality of roads, railroads, ports, air traffic, and so on, should be considered an important policy objective, because lack of improvement may lead to a plateau in productivity growth.

It is important, however, to distinguish between necessary conditions for growth and development, and true engines of development. Necessary conditions for development are, for example, basic infrastructure or low-to-moderate inflation. Without satisfying the minimum thresholds of these factors, development will never take place. Yet these factors alone are not sufficient for development. Engines of development, by contrast, are the true forces that propel an economy to higher levels of income. It is possible for an economy to be sound and stable, but to stagnate nevertheless, because the engines of growth are not working with sufficient power. In addition, to an extent we do not yet fully understand, it may be necessary to have several engines functioning simultaneously to complement one another.

Much of the current policy debate about the Arab world's competitiveness is about necessary conditions: resolving international conflicts and tensions, achieving macroeconomic stability, and creating better institutions. When considering longer-term development and competitiveness, growth engines should also be considered, however. The region has for too long pursued a one-dimensional growth strategy, making it far too reliant on capital accumulation as the single engine of growth.

Based on an approach that encompasses both necessary growth conditions and individual growth drivers, this Report identifies key impediments to economic development in individual countries. These impediments—and appropriate policies to remove them—are examined in individual chapters of this Report.

Peter Cornelius (World Economic Forum) and Andrew Warner (Harvard University) present an analytical framework in their chapter, "Engines of Growth for the Arab World." Their point of departure is that growth in the region has been highly disappointing. While in the 1980s the substantial slowdown could be attributed to a massive deterioration in the terms-of-trade in the oil-exporting countries, in the 1990s it became apparent that the poor growth performance largely mirrored the lack of restructuring. The chapter identifies preconditions for sustained growth in nine different areas, maintaining that these preconditions must be met in order to launch the economies in the Arab world on a steeper growth trajectory. Such preconditions include developing an improved macroeconomic environment, well-functioning financial markets, openness to trade, quality of government, rule of law, accessible and relevant education, infrastructure, eliminating or reducing corruption, and ushering in the new economy. Meeting these preconditions is no guarantee, however, that economic growth will actually accelerate on a sustained basis. For this to happen, the growth engine needs to run smoothly, fostering innovation and technological transfer and ensuring that it is easy to start a business.

That the region has remained highly susceptible to factors such as changes in energy prices and geopolitical events is reflected not least in the substantial short-term fluctuations of economic activity. As Xavier Sala-i-Martin (Columbia University) and Elsa V. Artadi (Harvard University) in their chapter entitled, "Economic Growth and Investment in the Arab World" show, however, this volatility masks the fact that the growth rate in the Arab world has actually tended to decline since the 1960s. Examining the reasons for this trend, Sala-i-Martin and Artadi focus particularly on investment, which, interestingly, increased in the second half of the 1970s and early half of the 1980s and has remained fairly robust since then. The answer to the puzzle of high investment/low growth lies in the quality of investment, the authors argue, emphasizing that private investment in the Arab region is both insufficient and inefficient. The slowdown of the growth process has very important implications for human welfare; as Sala-i-Martin and Artadi show, the distribution of income in the last two decades has not improved much, and little progress has been made in poverty reduction.

While the Arab world represents only 5 percent of the global population, it is a region with one of the fastest population growth rates. Over the last few decades, the Arab world's population has become substantially younger. As the United Nations Population Fund's Country Technical Services Team for Arab States write in their chapter entitled, "The Arab Population," it will take only about thirty years for the total population in the Arab region to double from its current level of around 290 million. With fertility rates and population growth rates expected to fall in the next few decades, it is forecast that in 2025 it will take around forty-three years for the population to double again. These figures are alarming and pose substantial challenges for the Arab world, especially when the limited capacity and availability of land and the scarcity of water resources are taken into account.

In his chapter "Structural Reforms in the Middle East and North Africa," John Page (World Bank) takes as his point of departure the "inward-looking, statist model of development" that had characterized most countries in the region until around the mid-1980s. Since then, many economies have embarked on a reform process designed to achieve the "Washington Consensus" of macroeconomic stability; that is, a higher degree of integration with the world economy and an expanded role for the private sector. In reviewing the reforms in detail, Page finds that although encouraging progress has been made in some areas, the list of unfinished economic policies remains long.

In his chapter entitled, "Fiscal Revenues in South Mediterranean Arab Countries: Vulnerabilities and Growth Potential," Karim Nashashibi (International Monetary Fund) reviews the fiscal revenue performance in these economies. He finds that revenues have been declining considerably over the last decade, mainly because of a fall in mineral receipts and trade liberalization. Given that trade protection is still higher than in other regions and must be reduced further, Nashashibi argues that there is an important need for countries to reform their income-tax systems and petroleum-product pricing, and to maintain flexible exchange rate policies.

Rodney Wilson (University of Durham) discusses "Arab Banking and Capital Market Developments." Financial systems, as numerous empirical studies have shown, help mobilize savings; allocate resources; facilitate the trading, hedging, diversifying, and pooling of risk; monitor managers and exert corporate control; and facilitate the exchange of goods and services. Examining the banking industry and bond and equity markets in the Arab world, he finds that many of these functions are not yet fulfilled. In several countries, financial markets have remained in their infancy, retarding economic growth. Wilson also examines Islamic finance, which may be a market segment where the Arab world has a competitive advantage; this has yet to be fully exploited, however.

In order to assess the prospects of increasing foreign direct investment (FDI) in the Arab world, Florence Eid (American University of Beirut) and Fiona Paua (World Economic Forum) examine FDI patterns in the Arab world from 1985 to 2000 in their chapter "Foreign Direct Investment in the Arab World: The Changing Investment Landscape." They find that despite a deteriorating FDI trend for most Arab world countries, the prospects appear favorable in light of recent reforms being undertaken in a number of countries to improve the investment climate. Moreover, these prospects will be enhanced further if governments sustain the momentum of these reforms, and implement additional improvements in three critical areas: public institutions, physical infrastructure and human resource development.

Analyzing the trade performance of the individual Arab states, Friedrich von Kirchbach, Mondher Mimouni, Jean-Michel Pasteels (all from the International Trade Centre) and Fiona Paua (World Economic Forum) find that in most countries, export diversification has remained low. In the Gulf countries in particular, exports continue to be heavily concentrated on hydrocarbon products. Factor-based specialization continues to comprise the bulk of Arab world exports, and few companies have been able to gain competitive advantage by absorbing new technologies and producing increasingly sophisticated products. As a result, many countries remain highly susceptible to external shocks. As the authors emphasize, a key challenge lies in putting in place a business environment that is conducive to entrepreneurship and risk-taking.

Ahmed Farouk Ghoneim (Cairo University) and Jürgen von Hagen and Susanna Wolf (both from the University of Bonn) focus their chapter more specifically on "Trade Relations between the EU and North Africa." Analyzing the economic implications of the Euro-Mediterranean Association Agreements, the authors discuss the main aspects governing these agreements, consider the competitiveness status and trends of the four Arab countries involved, and examine these countries' potential for attracting foreign direct investment and for boosting exports. One of the key conclusions of the chapter is that the Association Agreements represent challenges for the North African countries rather than panaceas; however, as Ghoneim, von Hagen and Wolf argue, the Agreements may also represent an important opportunity if they are used to anchor otherwise tough reform decisions and overcome the many supply-side problems that have limited these countries' integration into the world economy.

Paul Tempest (Windsor Energy Group and British Institute of Energy Economics) examines "The Hydrocarbon Sector" in the Arab states. As he discusses in his chapter, short-term prospects in the oil market point towards a temporary decline in the Arab region market share and a dip in the price of oil. In the longer term, however, Arab countries will continue to dominate oil production, with 60 percent of the world's oil reserves and 25 percent of the gas reserves, and representing 45 percent of the international trade in oil. However, while Gulf countries are shifting more of their oil and gas exports to the Asia-Pacific region, North African producers are seeking closer long-term integration with oil and gas importers in Europe. As Tempest argues, this shift will have not only economic, but also important geopolitical, consequences.

Soumitra Dutta (INSEAD), and Charles El-Hage, Karim Sabbagh, and Paola Tarazi (all from Booz Allen Hamilton) present a discussion called the "Challenges for Information and Communication

Technology Development in the Arab World." They identify three sets of issues that must be addressed to bridge the digital divide and to have new information and communications technologies (ICTs) serve as an enabler in future development processes. The authors stress that, first, the ICT environment must be upgraded by devising a clear and comprehensive development plan, incorporating ICT skills into the educational system, and enacting telecommunications laws and regulations that enhance competition. Second, Networked Readiness must be improved, and this can be achieved by improving ICT literacy, promoting access device penetration among citizens, and devising appropriate strategies to deliver e-government services and participate in e-commerce. Finally, Dutta, El-Hage, Sabbagh, and Tarazi offer counsel on ICT usage, suggesting that usage can be promoted by taking positive action among population groups less likely to use the Internet, promoting purposeful uptake of Internet technologies in the business community, and supporting online public services.

Telecommunications infrastructure plays a critical role in any ICT strategy, an issue discussed in detail by Scott Beardsley, Kito de Boer, Gassan al-Kibsi, and Luis Enriquez (all from McKinsey and Company) in their chapter entitled, "A Review of Telecommunications and Networked Readiness in the Arab World: Capturing the Opportunity." Three important findings emerge from their study. First, reform can be a powerful tool to improve the performance of the telecommunications sector and hence Networked Readiness. Second, telecommunications in the Arab world exhibits an access gap compared to the rest of the world, particularly in penetration, in part due to the limited reform undertaken in the region. Finally, tailoring reform to each country and management of regulation at a detailed level will be critical to success.

Education must be a key element in the development strategy of the Arab states. Failing to expand access and improve the quality and equitable distribution of education resources could have serious consequences, as Thomas J. Cassidy Jr. (Harvard University) argues in his chapter entitled, "Education in the Arab States: Preparing to Compete in the Global Economy." Such consequences include possible regional isolation from global knowledge, information, and technology, the key drivers of prosperity and economic growth. The most critical challenge is to match educational output with labor-

market and development needs, which requires sustained reform efforts in several areas. Redefining standards, redesigning curricula, rehab facilities, and installing computer networks in schools—all this is very important. But, as Cassidy argues, it might not be enough. Equally, if not more, important, is to change what people do and how they do it. Evidence from other countries suggests that educational reforms can be very taxing on the capacities of educational professionals, and it takes time, sustained effort, and a great deal of support to change people's behavior.

Finally, recognizing that standards of living are inextricably tied to the quality of the natural environment, Daniel C. Esty (Yale University), and Marc A. Levy and Andrew Winston (both from Columbia University's Center for International Earth Science Information Network, CIESIN), examine "Environmental Sustainability in the Arab World." Their analysis draws heavily on the Environmental Sustainability Index, a project initiated by the World Economic Forum Global Leaders for Tomorrow Environmental Task Force. Esty, Levy, and Winston find that, in general, Arab states lag behind in many important areas, and they foresee major problems with serious economic and social consequences unless corrective action is undertaken to address the challenges of environmental sustainability. As they stress, these challenges are not confined to the problem of water scarcity, but include alarming trends concerning air pollution, greenhouse gas emissions, population growth, and urbanization.

The chapters in this Report are largely data-driven and supported by an extensive appendix that provides key economic information on sixteen individual member states of the Arab League. Specifically, the data appendix provides recent economic and social indicators, as well as a detailed analysis of the export structure of these countries. Finally, the Report contains the responses to the Executive Opinion Survey that the World Economic Forum, with the assistance of local partners, conducted in ten countries in the region. While the Survey should not be considered as representative of all countries in the Arab region, it provides anecdotal evidence that supplements publicly available information.

Endnotes

1. A key limitation results from the lack of survey evidence. While the Survey was conducted in the first quarter of 2002, we were able to cover only ten countries, and in some of them the response rate remained relatively low. Although we decided not to use the results for a systematic ranking of countries, they may provide interesting anecdotal evidence, and the reader is encouraged to compare the Survey responses with those obtained by Aymo Brunetti, Gregory Kisunko, and Beatrice Weder and presented in, "Institutional Obstacles to doing Business: Region-by-Region Results from a Worldwide Survey of the Private Sector," World Bank Policy Research Working Paper no. 1759. Washington, D.C.: The World Bank, 1997. While their sample is even smaller (109 firms from the entire region), the results do suggest that governance is perceived to be rather poor, and to represent a substantial obstacle to business operations. See Nugent, Jeffrey B. "Dispute Resolution and Firms' Competitiveness in the MENA region." In *Globalization and Firm Competitiveness in the Middle East and North Africa Region*, Mediterranean Development Forum 3, edited by S. Fawzy. Washington, D.C.: The World Bank, 2002:76–118.

2. The World Bank. *Global Economic Prospects and the Developing Countries 2002*. Washington, D.C.: The World Bank, 2002.

3. United Nations Development Program. *Arab Human Development Report 2002. Creating Opportunities for Future Generations*. New York: United Nations Publications, 2002.

4. See John W. McArthur and Jeffrey D. Sachs. "The Growth Competitiveness Index: Measuring Technological Advancement and the Stages of Development." In *The Global Competitiveness Report 2001–2002*. New York: Oxford University Press, 2001:28–51.

Part 1

Chapters

Engines of Growth for the Arab World

**Peter K. Cornelius and
Andrew M. Warner**

This first competitiveness report on the Arab world appears at a time when growth in the region is slowing significantly. While the current slowdown has much to do with lower oil production and the deteriorating security situation, it is also consistent with the declining trend over the past two decades, with real incomes per capita falling in most Arab states. Economic activity in the Arab world boomed during the oil boom of the 1970s, and declined along with the sharp decline in oil prices that occurred first in 1981 and again in 1986. It would have been hard for the oil-exporting countries to avoid a dip in economic activity during the 1980s. The question worthy of attention is "Why has the region continued to stagnate during the 1990s?"

Right after independence, and especially during the oil-boom years, the implicit growth strategy of leaders of the Arab world was public investment financed with oil money and foreign aid. In no other region of the world were the big-push ideas of the development economists of the 1950s pursued with such vigor (and, it should be mentioned, financed with such largesse). There were notable achievements. Major improvements in irrigation were achieved in the Nile delta in Egypt and the Tigris and Euphrates delta in Iraq. Nasser's high dam at Aswan was merely the most dramatic of a host of infrastructure improvements. In addition, public health improvements were so dramatic that the region's population boomed, mainly through a substantial reduction in the death rate. The resulting population explosion, combined with improved conditions in agriculture, led to an urban explosion that created different problems down the line. But these should not obscure the fact that these urban problems were the by-product of significant achievements in public health and agriculture.

In spite of these achievements, one telling economic fact of the Arab world today is that while rates of investment in the region have long been among the world's highest growth rates are among the world's lowest (see the chapter by Sala-i-Martin and Artadi in this volume). Clearly, much of the capital has been diverted to inefficient uses. It has been a region with enormous "white elephants" and economic mirages. Part of the blame for low growth rates surely lies with the predatory state and the heavy administrative burdens imposed on private investors, as stressed by Sala-i-Martin and Artadi. It must also be remembered that no other region in the developing world has so much access to homegrown financial capital as the Arab world. Despite this, growth has been highly disappointing.

To put the growth and competitiveness of the region in perspective, we show three graphs. The first, Figure 1, shows real GDP per capita in Saudi Arabia in U.S. dollars. As the case of Saudi Arabia illustrates, much of the growth in the 1970s was driven by the tremendous increase in prices and exports of natural resources, such as oil. The line at the bottom of the figure shows exports of oil per person (also in U.S. dollars). A large part of the GDP decline of the 1980s must also be seen as caused by the decline in oil exports. The crucial competitiveness issue for Saudi Arabia is not that it had economic troubles in the 1980s, for that was to be expected given the decline in the oil market; the problem is that the Saudi economy has not developed a source of growth in the 1990s that is independent of the oil market. This is a problem caused by lack of restructuring and lack of alternative growth engines.

Many of countries in the Arab world suffer from a similar lack of restructuring. Natural resources are not a growth engine on their own and have not proven to be a catalyst for other sources of growth for the region as a whole, despite what many followers of big-push ideas claimed in the 1950s. Algeria represents one of the most dramatic examples in the Arab world: a boom in the 1970s was followed in the 1980s and 1990s by a long period of economic decline or stagnation. In Figure 2 it is clear that real incomes have not grown significantly in Algeria in the 1990s. In addition, it is also clear that Algeria has not managed to restructure exports into anything other than natural resources, since total exports are almost exactly the same as exports of natural resources (see the two lines at the bottom of Figure 2).

Figure 1. Saudi Arabia, GDP per Capita and Exports

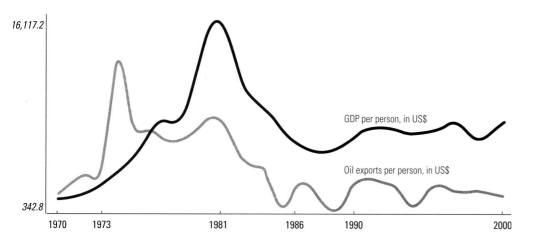

GDP per person, in US$

Oil exports per person, in US$

16,117.2

342.8

1970　1973　1981　1986　1990　2000

Figure 2. Algeria, GDP per Capita and Exports

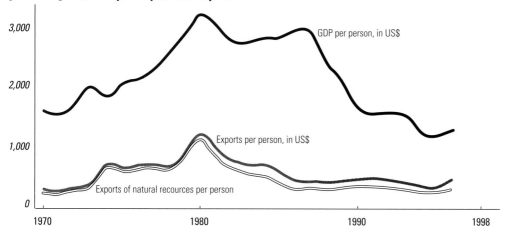

3,000

2,000

1,000

0

GDP per person, in US$

Exports per person, in US$

Exports of natural recources per person

1970　1980　1990　1998

Figure 3. Tunisia, GDP per Capita and Exports

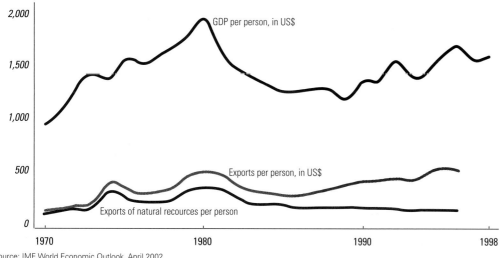

2,000

1,500

1,000

500

0

GDP per person, in US$

Exports per person, in US$

Exports of natural recources per person

1970　1980　1990　1998

Source: IMF, World Economic Outlook, April 2002

A closer look at the Arab world's 1990s growth rates shows that of all the countries, only Tunisia has managed to achieve a moderately high rate of economic growth. Tunisia's situation is depicted in Figure 3. One can see that exports peaked in 1980 (both total exports and natural resource exports); 1980 was also the high-water mark for GDP per capita in dollars. The rise in real GDP through 1980 is attributable both to the boom in trade and also, importantly, to the fact that the Tunisian exchange rate appreciated considerably during

this period, making output valued in Tunisian currency worth a lot of U.S. dollars. The decline in dollar GDP during the 1980s is, therefore, partly an actual decline in real incomes, but also partly an indication of the bursting of the exchange rate bubble of the 1970s.

In any case, it is clear that Tunisia experienced the classic boom and bust cycle of much of the Arab world during the 1970s and 1980s, a cycle that was driven by natural resource trade and commodity prices. Figure 3 shows that total exports from Tunisia begin to diverge from natural resource exports during the 1980s and that this trend accelerated during the 1990s. The boom in exports of light manufactures and garments from Tunisia to the European Union (EU) during this period was the main reason behind this divergence (for more details on export diversification see von Kirchbach et al. and Ghoneim et al. in this volume). In other words, the gap between the two lines depicting exports in Figure 3 is the Tunisian export boom, and this upward trend is associated with the rise in real GDP per capita in Tunisia during the 1990s. Of all the countries in the Arab world, Tunisia has managed to achieve, at least relatively, the greatest progress in restructuring away from natural resources; this progress explains to a considerable extent its improved performance in the 1990s.

The points we wish to stress in this chapter are the following. First, it is important to distinguish necessary conditions for growth and development from true engines of development. Necessary conditions for development are such things as roads and basic infrastructure or low to moderate inflation. Without satisfying minimum thresholds on these factors, development will never take place. Yet these factors alone are not sufficient for development. Engines of development, by contrast, are the true driving forces that propel an economy to higher levels of income. It is possible for an economy to be basically sound and stable but nevertheless stagnating because the engines are not working with sufficient power. To an extent we do not yet fully understand, it may be necessary to have several engines functioning simultaneously and complementary to each other in order to achieve sufficient power for development.

Regarding competitiveness in the Arab world, much of the current discussion in policy circles is essentially about necessary conditions: resolving international conflicts and tensions, macroeconomic stability, and better institutions. Discussions about longer-term development and competitiveness need to be complemented with discussions about engines. The region has for too long pursued a one-dimensional growth strategy that is far too reliant on capital accumulation as the single engine of growth.

Against this background, the rest of the paper is structured as follows. First, we discuss recent economic trends, focusing especially on economic growth, inflation, the structure of output, and global integration through foreign trade and investment. Next, we examine the extent to which the necessary preconditions for sustained economic growth are met. Finally, we analyze individual growth engines that are required to break the declining trend in economic growth and launch the Arab states on a steeper trajectory.

Recent Trends

This year, and probably for the immediate future, trends in the oil market and real and threatening international conflicts will dominate the economies of the Arab world. In the oil-exporting countries, the curtailment of oil production associated with OPEC agreements to limit global supply has depressed activity considerably; notwithstanding recent increases in oil prices, some countries are expected to suffer this year from declining per capita incomes. In the Mashreq countries and North Africa, the security situation has also had a significant impact on economic activity, including tourism, resulting in, among other things, higher unemployment. The most affected economy is, of course, the West Bank and Gaza, where economic activity is estimated to have declined by around 30 percent in 2001 and probably much more in 2002 in the wake of escalating hostilities that have resulted in widespread damage on physical infrastructure.[1]

While none of the Arab states has remained unaffected by the slowdown in global demand, the decline in energy prices, or the security situation in the region, it is important to note that recent economic trends in individual countries have been quite divergent (Table 1). Real output growth in Qatar, for example, averaged almost 8 percent a year in the period 1994 to 2001, around four times faster than in Saudi Arabia. In the Maghreb region, growth differentials during that period were somewhat smaller than in the Gulf region, but still significant. In Tunisia, real output expanded by around 5 percent per year compared with only around 0.5 percent per year in Libya.

Table 1. The Arab World: Real GDP Growth, 1984–2001 (in Percent)

	Average 1984–93	Average 1994–2001
Algeria	1.2	3.6
Bahrain	4.1	4.4
Egypt	3.9	5.0
Jordan	3.2	3.6
Kuwait	1.5	1.6
Lebanon	0.8	1.3
Libya	-0.5	0.5
Morocco	3.4	3.7
Oman	6.3	3.3
Qatar	0.7	7.6
Saudi Arabia	2.6	1.9
Syrian AR	3.1	2.9
Tunisia	4.0	5.2
U.A.E.	2.0	4.6
Yemen, Rep.	—	4.3

Source: IMF, World Economic Outlook, April 2002

Thanks to improved macroeconomic management, several countries have made encouraging progress in bringing inflation down to sustainable levels. In Egypt, where consumer price inflation averaged almost 20 percent per year in the 1980s, the rate of price increase fell to low single digits in the second half of the 1990s. A similar pattern can be observed in other countries such as Jordan, Lebanon, Morocco, Syria, and Tunisia. In some countries in the Gulf region, notably Bahrain, Oman, and Saudi Arabia, inflation has actually been negative in recent years; Yemen represents the only economy where the upward pressure on prices has remained relatively high.

As indicated above, the structure of output continues to be driven by resource extraction in many countries. In Saudi Arabia, the value-added contributed by the industrial sector to real output is still about 50 percent (Table 2). Services, by contrast, account for 43 percent. There is little information about the structure of output for many other countries in the Gulf region, but one may expect a similar structure of output to Saudi Arabia. Notable exceptions to this are Bahrain and United Arab Emirates, where the relative importance of the services sector has increased in recent years. While Bahrain has made considerable progress in becoming a regional banking center, the latter has made substantial efforts to become a new-technology knowledge hub. In other Arab countries, namely Egypt and Tunisia, the greatest contributions to GDP growth in recent years have come from services, which already account for more than half of the total value added. Tourism has remained particularly important for these two countries, accounting for more than 5 percent of GDP and more than 15 percent of their total foreign exchange

Table 2. The Arab World: Structure and Growth of Output (in Percent)

	Agriculture Value Added % of GDP, 2000	Agriculture Growth 1980–1990	Agriculture Growth 1991–2000	Industry Value Added % of GDP, 2000	Industry Growth 1980–1990	Industry Growth 1991–2000	Manufacturing Value Added % of GDP, 2000	Manufacturing Growth 1980–1990	Manufacturing Growth 1991–2000	Services Value Added % of GDP, 2000	Services Growth 1980–1990	Services Growth 1991–2000
Algeria	11	4.6	3	51	2.3	1	10	3.3	-5.7	38	3.6	2.7
Bahrain	—	—	—	—	—	—	—	—	—	—	—	—
Egypt	17	2.7	3.1	32	5.2	3.9	20	—	6	51	6.6	4.8
Jordan	2	6.8	-1.9	26	1.7	5.6	16	0.5	5.9	64	2.2	5.1
Kuwait	—	14.7	—	—	1	—	—	2.3	—	—	2.1	—
Lebanon	12	—	—	27	—	—	17	—	—	61	—	—
Libya	—	—	—	—	—	—	—	—	—	—	—	—
Morocco	15	6.7	-0.4	33	3	3.1	17	4.1	2.6	50	4.2	2.6
Oman	—	7.9	—	—	10.3	—	—	20.6	—	—	5.9	—
Qatar	—	—	—	—	—	—	—	—	—	—	—	—
Saudi Arabia	7	13.4	0.7	50	-2.3	1.5	8	7.5	2.7	43	1.3	2.2
Syrian AR	—	-0.6	—	—	6.6	—	—	—	—	—	0.1	—
Tunisia	13	2.8	2.1	28	3.1	4.5	18	3.7	5.4	54	3.5	5.3
U.A.E.	—	9.6	—	—	-4.2	—	—	3.1	—	—	3.6	—
Yemen, Rep.	17	—	5	40	—	7.9	11	—	4.5	47	—	-1.6

Source: World Bank, World Development Indicators 2002

earnings. The most advanced countries in terms of the transition towards services are Lebanon and Jordan, where the services sector already accounts for almost two-thirds of GDP.

The urgency of the transition away from natural resource-based production is particularly pressing for some countries. At current production levels, Bahrain's oil reserves are estimated to last only for another ten years, and United Arab Emirates' and Oman's not last much longer. The decline in income from the cessation of energy exports is considerable—around US$2,000 (in the case of Bahrain) to US$8,000 (in the case of United Arab Emirates) per head. Estimated oil reserves for Kuwait, Qatar, and Saudi Arabia are substantially larger; here the need for structural reform is based more on the need to develop an alternative source of growth rather that on an impending doomsday. Jordan, Morocco, and Tunisia also need to develop an alternate source of growth. As net oil importers their challenges are different, but not necessarily less complex.

The need for renewed growth in the Arab world is amplified by their strong population growth. From 1960 to 2000, Saudi Arabia's population expanded by around 4 percent per year, and today about 43 percent is younger than fifteen years. Around one-quarter of the Saudi population is noncitizens, with expatriates accounting for more than 50 percent of the workforce. In Qatar and the United Arab Emirates, the population has grown even faster; thanks to substantial inflows of foreigners, around 80 percent of the population is noncitizens, and expatriates account for around 90 percent of the population. In Egypt, the largest Arab country in population terms, the growth rate is lower, but at around 2.2 percent per year it is estimated that Egypt's population will have doubled between 1980 and 2015 (for a detailed discussion of the population dynamics in the Arab world, see the paper on the Arab population, prepared by Country Support Team for Arab States [CST] and the United Nations Population Fund [UNFPA]).

With the average age having fallen, the labor force in most countries has expanded even faster than the population (Table 3), and it is estimated that in some countries real output needs to grow by 5 percent and more in order to prevent unemployment from rising. However, few countries have achieved this target in the last few decades, and in several of them, notably Algeria, Kuwait, Libya, Saudi Arabia, and the United Arab Emirates, GDP per capita has actually shrunk.

Table 3. The Arab World: Long-Term Growth and Per Capita Incomes

	Population	Labor Force	Gross Domestic Product	Gross Domestic Product
	Annual Average Growth	Annual Average Growth	Annual Average Growth	Per Capita, Annual Average Growth
	1965–2000 (in Percent)	1965–2000 (in Percent)	1965–2000 (in Percent)	1965–2000 (in Percent)
Algeria	2.7	3.2	-0.3	-1.4
Bahrain	—	—	—	—
Egypt	2.2	2.4	5.6	3.3
Jordan	4.3	4.4	4.7	0.4
Kuwait	4.2	4.3	0.0	-3.9
Lebanon	1.9	2.5	—	—
Libya	3.6	3.2	0.5	-3.6
Morocco	2.2	2.6	4.2	1.9
Oman	3.9	3.8	9.5	5.0
Qatar	—	—	—	—
Saudi Arabia	4.3	4.8	4.6	-0.1
Syrian AR	3.2	3.3	5.7	2.3
Tunisia	2.1	2.8	5.0	2.7
U.A.E.	9.5	10.5	3.3	-3.9
Yemen, Rep.	3.2	2.8	—	—

Source: World Bank, World Development Indicators 2002

In some cases, the decline in per capita income has been quite dramatic; in Saudi Arabia, for example, it has halved since its peak in 1980. To be sure, economic developments in the oil-rich countries in the Gulf region have important implications for the rest of the Arab world (as well as beyond it). Apart from importing goods and services, the Gulf countries employ around 11 million people from abroad who send home around US$25 billion in remittances. A significant part of these flows go to other Arab countries, where they play an important role in recipient countries' balance of payments. In Egypt, for example, workers' remittances amounted to almost 3 percent of GDP; in Jordan this ratio was as much as 22 percent in 2000.

Whereas in Egypt, the world's fourth largest recipient of workers' remittances, employee compensation to nonresident workers have overcompensated outflows of investment income, in Jordan, Morocco, and Tunisia there are negative net income flows in their balance of payments. These net outflows mirror the countries' relatively high debt-service burden, with debt-to-GDP ratios ranging from around 55 percent in Morocco to around 90 percent in Jordan. In the

Gulf countries, by contrast, net income flows have generally remained positive thanks to these countries' considerable stock of portfolio and direct investment abroad, although in most cases the surplus has shrunk in the last decade.

Reflecting their geopolitical importance, some countries have benefited from substantial net transfers. Egypt, the largest recipient of development assistance, received around US$2 billion per year in the second half of the 1990s, with the United States representing by far the single largest donor country. In 2000, the United States alone provided US$735 million as economic grant aid (on a commitment basis), on top of US$1.3 billion of military grant aid.[2] In terms of GDP, Jordan has received even more foreign aid, amounting to close to US$600 million, or almost 8 percent of GDP, in 2000. By comparison, foreign aid to Morocco and Tunisia (controlled for their income levels) was significantly less, amounting to around 2 percent of GDP in 2000.

Foreign Trade

The countries of the Arab League are, of course, major players in the global economy when it comes to exports of fuels and hydrocarbons. In this sense, they are quite integrated. However, apart from commodity exports, the region has actually been relatively closed and inward looking. Measured by their export share in GDP, the nonfuel exporting countries of the Arab world still are fairly closed economies. This applies especially to Egypt, where the exports-to-GDP ratio has remained below 20 percent. The Maghreb countries are relatively more open, although their respective ratios are considerably lower than in many other developing countries, especially in Asia. Most countries have become more open over the last decade. One notable exception, however, is Egypt, where export growth has continued to fall short of GDP growth. In volume terms, Egyptian exports grew by just around 2 percent per year between 1980 and 2000, substantially slower than total output.

The Pan-Arab ideology of the Arab world has been a millstone around the necks of Arab economies since independence. The ideology has understandable historic roots in the backlash against the crusades and the European colonial experience. But in purely economic terms, the last thing an oil-dependent economy should want is to integrate with another oil-dependent economy. Unfortunately, Pan-Arabism and nationalism combined with the state-led development ideology of the 1950s has created some of the most closed and hermetic economies in the world.

Not surprisingly, therefore, relatively little progress in diversifying their product base has been made in the Gulf countries, as discussed in detail by von Kirchbach et al. in this volume. For example, fuels still account for around 90 percent of Saudi Arabia's exports, only marginally less than a decade ago. The highest concentration—and the least progress in diversification—is in Libya.

Somewhat more progress has been made in the non-oil exporting countries, although their export bases remain concentrated with regard to both their export goods and export markets.[3] Lack of product and market diversification continues to make these countries susceptible to external shocks, both in terms of export volumes and abrupt changes in their terms of trade. In light of these risks, some countries have taken further steps to liberalize their trade regimes and seek deeper trade integration both within the region and with third countries. As regards the latter, particular hope is attached to the EU Association Agreements that some countries recently signed.

Generally speaking, the Association Agreements the EU has thus far signed with Egypt, Morocco, and Tunisia cover a wide range of issues, including political, security, economic, and social and cultural. As far as foreign trade is concerned, a progressive elimination of tariffs is envisaged under the accords, representing a precursor to the countries' entry into the Euro-Mediterranean free-trade area to be established by the end of this decade. However, as the quality of products will have to be improved in order to compete successfully in the European market, the Association Agreements are widely regarded as part of a process to modernize industries in these countries.

Foreign Investment and Borrowing

Greater integration can also take place through capital flows, and especially foreign direct investment. How do foreign investors perceive the business environment in the Arab world? Do they find the Arab world attractive as a business location relative to other regions? And how has investor sentiment been affected by recent developments in the region? (These and other questions are addressed in detail later in this report; here we provide a brief overview of investment inflows to show that they are a possible reflection of market perceptions.)

Considerable caution needs to be taken, however, when interpreting the flow and stock data on international capital transactions. There can be a wide range of reasons why companies invest in a particular country.[4] According to the senior executives who participated in the World Economic Forum's most recent Global Opinion Survey, the three most important factors determining foreign direct investment (FDI) are: (1) the ability to repatriate capital and remit profits, (2) the predictability and reliability of government policies, and (3) their access to local markets. By contrast, other factors, such as investment incentives, low labor costs, or special tax incentives, appear to play a comparatively unimportant role.

Moreover, foreign direct investment may not be attracted by a favorable business environment, but instead may reflect a poor one. As has been argued in the context of Latin America, where FDI inflows have continued to surge despite a very negative investor sentiment vis-à-vis emerging markets in the wake of the Asian financial crises, the absence of well-functioning capital, goods, and labor markets may actually provide incentives for investors to extend the operational scope of the firm and internalize market functions.[5] In this sense, the firm can be thought of as a substitute for the market.

Investors are, of course, free to decide against investing in a particular country. For the Gulf states, it can be assumed that foreign investors are largely attracted by the natural resources in these countries. In absolute terms, Saudi Arabia represents by far the most important destination country in terms of its FDI inward stock, which is estimated to have amounted to more than US$28 billion at the end of the last decade. This amount is more than twice the total inward stock in all Gulf countries combined and around 50 percent of the total stock in the entire Arab world. The second most important FDI country is Egypt; Egypt is followed by Tunisia, where foreign investment is concentrated in tourism. However, in terms of the size of the individual economies a different picture emerges, with Bahrain enjoying by far the highest FDI/GDP ratio. Next is Tunisia, where inward stock is equal to about 50 percent of GDP; Saudi Arabia and Egypt's ratios are significantly lower. Nevertheless, at rates of around 20 percent, FDI still plays a larger role in the Arab world than in many countries in Asia and Latin America, including the Philippines, Thailand, Argentina, Brazil, and Mexico.

Portfolio investment, by contrast, has remained largely underdeveloped. At the end of 2001, there were just seventy-five domestic companies in Saudi Arabia listed on the stock exchange. In Morocco and

Table 4. The Arab World: Foreign Direct Investment Inward Stock (in US$ billion), 1980–2000

	1985	1990	1995	2000
Algeria	1.30	1.30	1.40	1.40
Bahrain	0.40	0.60	2.40	5.90
Egypt	5.70	11.00	14.10	19.00
Jordan	0.50	0.60	0.60	1.80
Kuwait	0.03	0.03	0.51	0.53
Lebanon	0.03	0.05	0.19	1.00
Libya	—	—	—	—
Morocco	0.40	0.90	3.00	5.80
Oman	1.20	1.70	2.20	2.50
Qatar	0.08	0.06	0.44	1.99
Saudi Arabia	21.80	22.50	22.40	28.80
Syrian AR	0.04	0.37	0.92	1.34
Tunisia	6.90	7.30	11.00	11.60
U.A.E.	0.48	0.75	1.77	2.64
Yemen, Rep.	0.28	0.18	1.88	0.89

Source: UNCTAD 2001

Tunisia, this number was even lower—fifty-five and forty-six, respectively. There were more than 1,000 domestic companies listed in Egypt, but the market has remained rather inactive, as reflected in the low value traded in terms of GDP and as a percentage of market capitalization.

While markets in government bills and bonds in the Arab world have become much more sophisticated in recent years, access to international debt markets has remained limited. By the end of March 2002, total outstanding international debt securities in the region was US$15.1 billion, or only about 3 percent of all outstanding international debt securities issued by developing countries at that date.[6] As a matter of fact, only three countries raised this entire amount, namely Lebanon, Qatar, and Tunisia. Lebanon accounted for the bulk, with almost US$10 billion outstanding at the end of the first quarter of 2002. Of this amount, only around US$1.5 billion was raised by financial institutions; the rest was raised by government and state agencies. In the case of Tunisia, the government was the only borrower, and in Qatar, corporate issuers owed one-third of the outstanding debt.

Although few Arab countries have actually borrowed in international bond markets, many more have been rated by the leading rating agencies. Lebanon, the most important borrower, currently has a B- from Standard and Poor's and a B2 from Moody's for its long-term sovereign debt issued in foreign currency (Table 4); these ratings are, relatively speaking, the lowest in the Arab world. Qatar, by contrast, enjoys

Table 5. The Arab World: Long-Term Bond Ratings (Foreign Currency) as of 30 June 2002

	Standard & Poor's	Moody's
Algeria	—	—
Bahrain	—	Ba1
Egypt	BB+	Ba1
Jordan	BB-	Ba3
Kuwait	A+	A2
Lebanon	B-	B2
Libya	—	—
Morocco	BB	Ba1
Oman	BBB	Baa2
Qatar	A-	Baa2
Saudi Arabia	—	Baa3
Syrian AR	—	—
Tunisia	BBB	Baa3
U.A.E.	—	A2
Yemen, Rep.	—	—

Source: Credit rating agencies

Table 6. External Loans of BIS-Reporting Banks to Individual Arab Countries, 1999–2001

Country	Amount Outstanding (in US$ million) at:		
	End-1999	End-2000	End-2001
Algeria	5,412	4,498	3,852
Bahrain	—	—	—
Egypt	6,784	6,899	6,677
Jordan	1,147	1,212	1,156
Kuwait	7,327	7,637	8,118
Lebanon	3,610	3,264	2,545
Libya	245	294	313
Morocco	6,762	5,822	5,334
Oman	3,879	3,708	3,622
Palestinian Authority	39	53	25
Qatar	6,333	6,103	5,181
Saudi Arabia	25,846	25,169	22,692
Syrian AR	533	498	465
Tunisia	3,236	3,868	2,650
U.A.E.	14,475	13,401	15,744
Yemen, Rep.	348	605	327
Total	**85,976**	**83,031**	**78,701**

Source: Bank for International Settlements Quarterly Review, June 2002

an A- and Baa, respectively. The least risky country in terms of a possible default on foreign-currency bonds, however, is perceived to be Kuwait, with ratings of A+ and A2, respectively.

Finally, loans from banks reporting to the Bank for International Settlements (BIS) have remained by far the most important source of capital inflows, although the total amount of cross-border debt arising from these inflows has largely stagnated in recent years (Table 6). By far the largest borrower is Saudi Arabia, with outstanding loans totaling US$22.7 billion at the end of 2001, followed by the United Arab Emirates and Kuwait. These three countries accounted for a large percentage of the total debt owed to BIS-reporting banks as of year-end 2001.

In sum, it appears that international financial integration has remained limited in most cases. Equity investment has remained impeded by underdevelopment of the financial markets, and few countries have borrowed in international debt markets. Cross-border borrowing from banks has remained the one of the most important ways of gaining access to foreign savings, but in recent years there have actually been net outflows, with repayments exceeding new borrowing.

International Rankings on Preconditions and Engines of Fast Growth

In the following sections we present comparative data on factors that favor growth. The data are presented in the form of indexes that are, in turn, averages of several component indexes. The factors we present are divided into ten necessary conditions for growth (i.e., preconditions for growth) and five engines of growth. These divisions are based on our reading of the main findings in current research on the determinants of economic growth, but inevitably reflect some personal judgment. The cross-country rankings are provided for seventy-five countries, corresponding to the countries included in the *Global Competitiveness Report 2001–2002*. Given the difficulties in collecting data in the Arab world, there are only two Arab countries included: Egypt and Jordan. However, our hope is that regulators in other Arab countries that are familiar with the condition of these two countries, or some third comparator country, will be able to make an assessment of where their country would rank if it were included in the rankings. Further editions of the *Arab World Competitiveness Report* will, it is hoped, stimulate further data collection in other Arab countries.

Table 7 outlines how the various indexes are calculated. The underlying data are normalized to a scale of one to seven, and then these normalized data series are included together in unweighted averages to form the final index. Table 7 shows the underlying

Table 7. Summary of the Data Behind the Calculation of Indexes Describing Growth Engines

Part One: Necessary Conditions for Growth		
Name of Index	**Components**	**Sources**
I. Macroeconomic Stability		
	Low government deficits	National Sources
	Low inflation	National Sources
	Exchange rate stability	2001 GCR Executive Opinion Survey
	Solvency of financial system	2001 GCR Executive Opinion Survey
II. Deep Financial Markets		
	Low interest rate spreads	National Sources
	High banking sector assets as percent of GDP	National Sources
	High financial risk rating	Institutional Investor
	High perceived sophistication of financial system	2001 GCR Executive Opinion Survey
	Developed equity markets	2001 GCR Executive Opinion Survey
III. Openness to International Trade		
	Low import tariffs	National Sources
	Low hidden import barriers	2001 GCR Executive Opinion Survey
	Low premiums on obtaining foreign exchange	2001 GCR Executive Opinion Survey
	Low export taxes	2001 GCR Executive Opinion Survey
IV. Quality of Government		
	Public expenditures not wasteful	2001 GCR Executive Opinion Survey
	Subsidies improve productivity	2001 GCR Executive Opinion Survey
	Highly competent personnel in public sector	2001 GCR Executive Opinion Survey
V. New Economy		
	Internet hosts	National Sources
	Computers per capita	National Sources
	Development of internet service providers	2001 GCR Executive Opinion Survey
	Telephone density	National Sources
	Level of public support for internet	2001 GCR Executive Opinion Survey
	Development of laws in support of new economy	2001 GCR Executive Opinion Survey
	Perceived quality of local internet service providers	2001 GCR Executive Opinion Survey
VI. Education		
	High years of schooling in population	2001 GCR Executive Opinion Survey
	High perceived quality of education	2001 GCR Executive Opinion Survey
	Companies invest in training	2001 GCR Executive Opinion Survey
VII. Infrastructure		
	High road quality	2001 GCR Executive Opinion Survey
	Efficient electrical generation	2001 GCR Executive Opinion Survey
	Fast international mail	2001 GCR Executive Opinion Survey
	High level of competition in provision of basic infrastructure	2001 GCR Executive Opinion Survey

Table 7. Summary of the Data Behind the Calculation of Indexes Describing Growth Engines (continued)

Part One: Necessary Conditions for Growth (continued)		
Name of Index	**Components**	**Sources**
VIII. Rule of Law		
	Independent judiciary	2001 GCR Executive Opinion Survey
	Ability to successfully litigate against government	2001 GCR Executive Opinion Survey
	Low legal costs	2001 GCR Executive Opinion Survey
	Governments honor commitments of previous governments	2001 GCR Executive Opinion Survey
IX. Red Tape		
	Senior management spends little time dealing with government officials	2001 GCR Executive Opinion Survey
	Administrative regulations are not burdensome	2001 GCR Executive Opinion Survey
X. Low Corruption		
	Low corruption in provision of trade permits	2001 GCR Executive Opinion Survey
	Low corruption in provision of utility connections	2001 GCR Executive Opinion Survey
	Low corruption in award of public contracts	2001 GCR Executive Opinion Survey
	Low corruption connected with tax payments	2001 GCR Executive Opinion Survey
	Low corruption connected to loan applications	2001 GCR Executive Opinion Survey
Part Two: Engines of Growth		
I. Start-ups and Entrepreneurship		
	Low administrative barriers to start-ups	2001 GCR Executive Opinion Survey
	Venture capital available	2001 GCR Executive Opinion Survey
	Loans available with low collateral	2001 GCR Executive Opinion Survey
II. Capital Accumulation		
	High national saving rates	National Sources
	High investment rates	National Sources
III. Low Taxes		
	Low VAT tax rate	National Sources
	Low top income tax rate	National Sources
	Low corporate profits tax	National Sources
	Tax system perceived to improve competitiveness	2001 GCR Executive Opinion Survey
IVa. Innovation		
	Highly rated research institutions	2001 GCR Executive Opinion Survey
	Businesses make R&D	2001 GCR Executive Opinion Survey
	Close collaboration between universities and businesses	2001 GCR Executive Opinion Survey
	Government supports research	2001 GCR Executive Opinion Survey
	High expenditures on R&D	2001 GCR Executive Opinion Survey
IVb. Transfer of Technology		
	Foreign direct investment brings new technology	2001 GCR Executive Opinion Survey
	Licensing pursued to obtain foreign technology	2001 GCR Executive Opinion Survey
V. Exports		
	Exports other than natural resources (average dollar value 1990–1997 per capita)	Center for International Data (2000)*

Source: *Robert C. Feinstein, "World Trade Flows, 1980–1997," University of California-Davis and National Bureau of Economic Research, March 2000.

data for each index and provides a brief description of the source. To a large extent, since we are dealing with factors for which there is no obvious hard data source, we rely on the perceptions of the survey respondents from the Executive Opinion Survey of the *Global Competitiveness Report 2001*. We take the mode of the distribution of the survey responses in each country. The mode will be an unbiased estimator of the true situation if the response errors are uncorrelated.

We present a brief summary of each factor below; each factor is followed by tables giving the cross-country rankings, organized into two lists. The first list includes ten factors that assist growth without necessarily actively promoting growth. In other words, poor performance on these factors would limit growth, but satisfactory performance on these factors is no guarantee of especially rapid growth. The second list includes the more dynamic factors that are at the core of theories in development that focus on the engines of fast growth.

List One: Necessary Conditions

I. Macroeconomic stability

While there is little disputing the proposition that a macroeconomic crisis can stop growth, few would argue today that stability alone would guarantee rapid growth. Traditionally, factors that would be included in an assessment of macroeconomic stability would be the following. The first factor would be high deficits (fiscal or current account), because high deficits always carry with them a question mark regarding financing. Further traditional indicators would be an overvalued exchange rate, which would suggest imminent devaluation. High inflation would forecast instability because of the drastic monetary measures that would be required to eliminate it. A final indicator of an imminent crisis would be a vulnerable banking system, since banks are susceptible to creditor panics (Table 8).

II. Deep financial markets

Growth requires financing. This may take the form of formal bank loans, issuing shares or bonds on equity or bond markets, or simply borrowing from friends. While there is some dispute about the relative importance of developed financial markets in the growth process and the extent to which the various types of financial markets can substitute for one another, there is little dispute that some minimal level of financial development is essential for growth. There is a belief that the more formal the financial market, the wider the scope of projects competing for funds. The more a country's savings flows through

healthy, competent banks, the better the economy is able to select and finance good investment projects. In economies with weak financial systems, people put less of their savings in banks and thus, less savings in the economy find its way to productive uses. However, if there are few profitable projects available in the economy for other reasons, having deep financial markets will not by itself achieve growth (Table 9).

III. Openness to trade

Openness to international trade is important for growth because capital equipment, particularly equipment that embodies the latest technologies, is produced in a variety of countries, and high import barriers can raise the cost of purchasing equipment and lower the returns on a variety of investment projects within an economy. This lower return can depress investment and growth. In addition, openness helps maintain competitive pressure on domestic industries to keep costs low, which helps consumers and other domestic businesses that rely on their products. Finally, openness is a way to expose the country to the latest products and technologies, and this has side benefits in promoting learning about new technologies. Openness facilitates the process of technology transfer and learning, which can drive new inventions and create value-added and growth, but which by itself, does not guarantee it (Table 10).

IV. Quality of government

All governments produce public goods that are inputs to production to some extent. In this sense, poor-quality government services can limit profitability and slow growth. The quality of government is important for growth because the government provides crucial services for industry, such as infrastructure, and a legal framework for resolving disputes and conducting business. Poorly chosen government expenditures simply waste tax revenues and thus impose unnecessary costs. In addition, slow and inefficient government services for routine tasks such as administrative record keeping, mail service, permits, and other small services can impose further unnecessary costs on businesses (Table 11).

V. New economy

Since the inception of the Internet and with the development and diffusion throughout the world of e-mail and a host of other related new technologies, a country will seriously limit the range of products and services it can engage in without Internet infrastructure. In this sense, information and communication technology infrastructure is a necessary condition for continued growth (Table 12).

VI. Education

Education provides direct learning and also teaches the capacity to learn, but by itself, education does not guarantee that the learning is applied to activities that create value-added. In this last sense, education is more of a necessary condition for growth than a process that creates growth (Table 13).

VII. Infrastructure

Western Europe has some of the highest-quality infrastructure in the world, but this does not make them growth tigers. As we move from poor to good infrastructure, infrastructure changes from something that limits production to something that is nice for consumption purposes, but no longer really limits production. The level where this transition begins is, of course, hard to precisely define. Few would deny that the destruction of basic infrastructure would bring production to a halt, as we see in war-ravaged regions. Many countries with rather mediocre infrastructure nevertheless have proven capable of fast growth, suggesting that the threshold is rather low. Yet in these countries most people complain bitterly about the poor infrastructure, suggesting that there are real constraints. Good infrastructure is important for growth for the same reason as low taxes. Efficient infrastructure tends to reduce costs and raise the net return on a broad range of investments. However, infrastructure is not sufficient for growth in any important sense. The desert roads that Kuwait and Saudi Arabia built to the desert did not by themselves bring higher economic output (Table 14).

VIII. Rule of Law

An efficient and reliable legal system is important for several reasons. Orderly and efficient bankruptcy proceedings facilitate an orderly shutdown of inefficient activities, and facilitate the transfer of resources to more profitable activities. Legal systems also offer businesses off-the-shelf procedures for resolving disputes and enforcing contracts. This makes business activity more efficient; it also facilitates investment and helps promote business relationships that do not rely on personal trust or family connections (Table 15 here).

IX. Low Red Tape

High levels of red tape are like a traffic jam that can really shut down an economy. We created this index by averaging perceptions of the overall burden of administrative regulations together with an assessment of the amount of time that senior executives typically spend with government officials (Table 16).

X. Lack of Corruption

A high level of corruption can impede economic activity by raising the costs of activities affected by corruption. Corruption further undermines growth by eroding trust in legal institutions and equity in the political process (Table 17).

List Two: Engines of growth

I. Start-ups and entrepreneurship

A good environment for start-ups can encourage growth by facilitating economic change. Active start-ups and entrepreneurship promote the development of new sectors in an economy. Capital and labor do not become stuck in old industries whose growth prospects are declining (Table 18).

II. Low taxes; small government

No matter the ideology about what constitutes the right mix between the public and private sector, it is indisputable that governments can only exist by levying taxes of some form, and that these create disincentives for the private sector. Governments also do not directly engage in activities that create value-added. Since the disincentives go in only one direction, lower taxes and smaller governments help promote investments to some extent. The potency of this effect is a contentious issue; however, it seems clear that lower taxes and smaller governments should be included as a possible engine to promote fast growth (Table 19).

III. Capital accumulation

Capital accumulation is a potential engine of growth because new equipment and more modern structures raise the productivity of workers. Higher productivity means higher wages and profits. This index is a simple average of the national savings rate and gross fixed capital accumulation, both in percent of GDP using data from 2000 (Table 20).

IV. Innovation and inward transfers of technology

Innovation and the adaptation of new technologies and products is a fundamental driving force behind growth, according to some of the more modern theories. This index is an average of data from the Executive Opinion Survey of the *Global Competitiveness Report* on the following: the level of technological sophistication, the level of innovation versus imitation in national enterprises, the extent of business collaboration with local universities, the extent of legal protection for intellectual property, the average level of business research and development, and the extent and nature of government support for research and development. The technology transfer index is based on survey data on the extent to which foreign direct investment in the local market is a vehicle for the transfer of technology, as well as on survey data on the extent to which licensing of foreign products is practiced in the local market as a means to obtain and work with foreign technologies. For countries that are not innovative leaders, we include an index for the extent to which they are adept at absorbing technology through technology transfer (Table 21).

V. Exports

Exports have been a crucial source of growth in the post-war period in Japan, Korea, Taiwan, Malaysia, and Indonesia, and, more recently, Mauritius and Tunisia. Table 22 below shows values of non-natural-resource exports per capita, averaged over the 1990s. Exports allow smaller economies to sell in much deeper and wider markets than the home market. For most economies, the global market is huge when compared to the domestic market. Therefore, increases in market shares that may seem trivial from the perspective of the world are big events from the perspective of the local economy. Moreover, market penetration on the global level is possible without price-cutting that would otherwise dampen profits, since the global price tends to be insensitive to changes in supply from smaller countries. Finally, exporting enables a country to achieve higher overall productivity by specializing in sectors where it is relatively more productive (Table 22).

Final Section

We conclude this chapter by highlighting the results for Jordan and Egypt from the previous list of growth engines and preconditions for growth. When looking at the list of necessary conditions for growth, the rankings of Jordan and Egypt stand out in three areas. Both countries obtain extremely low rankings on openness to international trade, development of Internet infrastructure and, especially, red tape. Indeed, Egypt ranks number 75 out of seventy-five countries regarding the burden of red tape. On most of the other factors, Jordan and Egypt tend to be ranked in the middle of the seventy-five countries. Taken at face value, these rankings suggest that the constraints on growth in these counties are related to continued isolation from the world economy and especially the tremendous burden of red tape.

When we look at the engines of growth, both countries have rather average rankings on most of the engines with the exception of innovation, where both rank near the bottom. On export structure, Tunisia stands out in the Arab world as having an

abnormally high value of exports other than natural resources. To the extent that we may take this limited sample as a preview of what we may expect to find if the Arab world engaged in a full-fledged competitiveness survey, factors such as a lack of global integration, a lack of absorption of modern information and communication technologies, and, especially, high levels of red tape, will likely emerge as the chief obstacles to higher growth and competitiveness in the region.

Endnotes

1. Our analysis is based on publicly available information. An executive survey was conducted in ten Arab countries between November 2001 and March 2002. The design of the survey basically followed that used for the *Global Competitiveness Report 2001*. The results of the survey are presented in the Part 3: Survey Responses. However, given the political developments in the region and the relatively low response rate in several cases, the results should be interpreted with a substantial degree of caution. Rather than taking the survey results as representative, the reader is advised to consider them as nothing more than anecdotal evidence. This Report includes most of the member countries of the Arab League, a region that accounts for roughly 280 million people. However, we do not include Comoros, Djibouti, Somalia, and Sudan, which will be covered by the forthcoming *African Competitiveness Report*. Moreover, we do not attempt to examine Palestine or Iraq, for which very little reliable information exists. Indeed, the lack of data is an important reason why Arab countries have remained under-researched compared with other parts of the world. This gap has recently narrowed, thanks to the United Nations Development Program's *Arab Human Development Report 2002*. It is the objective of this paper—and the entire *Arab World Competitiveness Report 2002–2003*—to continue to narrow the remaining gap.

2. See Economist Intelligence Unit, Egypt Country Profile 2001.

3. See Part 2: Country Profiles and Data Presentation.

4. For a review of the theoretical and empirical literature, see, for example: Moran, Theodore H. *Foreign Direct Investment and Development. The New Agenda for Developing Countries and Economies in Transition*. Washington, D.C.: Institute for International Economics, 1998.

5. See Hausmann, Ricardo, and Eduardo Fernandez-Arias. "Foreign Direct Investment: Good Cholesterol?" Working paper no. 417. Research Department, Inter-American Development Bank. Washington, D.C., 2000.

6. See Bank for International Settlements Quarterly Review, June 2002, Table 11.

Table 8. Macroeconomic Stability

Rank	Country	Score
1	Norway	6.2
2	Finland	6.0
3	Hong Kong SAR	6.0
4	Denmark	5.9
5	Singapore	5.9
6	Netherlands	5.8
7	Ireland	5.8
8	Trinidad and Tobago	5.7
9	Canada	5.7
10	Belgium	5.6
11	United States	5.6
12	Switzerland	5.6
13	Austria	5.6
14	United Kingdom	5.6
15	Greece	5.5
16	Spain	5.5
17	Estonia	5.5
18	Sweden	5.5
19	Portugal	5.5
20	Germany	5.5
21	France	5.5
22	Iceland	5.4
23	Argentina	5.4
24	Israel	5.4
25	Chile	5.3
26	Australia	5.3
27	New Zealand	5.3
28	El Salvador	5.3
29	Panama	5.2
30	Italy	5.2
31	Latvia	5.1
32	Slovenia	4.9
33	Brazil	4.9
34	Uruguay	4.9
35	Hungary	4.9
36	**JORDAN**	**4.9**
37	Costa Rica	4.8
38	South Africa	4.8
39	Peru	4.8
40	Mauritius	4.7
41	Philippines	4.7
42	Dominican Republic	4.7
43	Malaysia	4.7
44	Poland	4.7
45	Taiwan	4.6
46	Nigeria	4.6
47	Bulgaria	4.6
48	China	4.5
49	Venezuela	4.5
50	Korea	4.5
51	Lithuania	4.5
52	Thailand	4.5
53	Romania	4.4
54	Slovak Republic	4.4
55	Czech Republic	4.4
56	Jamaica	4.3
57	Bolivia	4.3
58	**EGYPT**	**4.3**
59	Russia	4.3
60	Mexico	4.3
61	India	4.2
62	Honduras	4.1
63	Vietnam	4.1
64	Ukraine	4.1
65	Sri Lanka	4.1
66	Guatemala	4.0
67	Bangladesh	4.0
68	Colombia	4.0
69	Japan	4.0
70	Paraguay	3.8
71	Indonesia	3.6
72	Ecuador	3.3
73	Nicaragua	3.2
74	Turkey	3.0
75	Zimbabwe	2.7

Table 9. Financial Depth

Rank	Country	Score
1	United Kingdom	5.7
2	Netherlands	5.6
3	Switzerland	5.6
4	Canada	5.4
5	United States	5.2
6	Hong Kong SAR	5.2
7	Taiwan	5.1
8	Japan	5.1
9	Norway	5.1
10	Ireland	5.1
11	Sweden	5.0
12	Finland	5.0
13	Australia	4.9
14	France	4.9
15	Singapore	4.9
16	Austria	4.9
17	Portugal	4.8
18	Belgium	4.7
19	Germany	4.6
20	Korea	4.5
21	Malaysia	4.5
22	Denmark	4.4
23	Italy	4.3
24	Israel	4.3
25	New Zealand	4.3
26	Thailand	4.3
27	Spain	4.2
28	Chile	4.2
29	Panama	4.2
30	**EGYPT**	**4.2**
31	Hungary	4.1
32	China	4.1
33	South Africa	4.0
34	Trinidad and Tobago	3.8
35	Indonesia	3.8
36	India	3.7
37	Argentina	3.7
38	Philippines	3.7
39	Estonia	3.7
40	Poland	3.6
41	Latvia	3.6
42	El Salvador	3.5
43	**JORDAN**	**3.5**
44	Uruguay	3.4
45	Paraguay	3.4
46	Greece	3.4
47	Slovenia	3.4
48	Czech Republic	3.4
49	Vietnam	3.3
50	Iceland	3.3
51	Nigeria	3.3
52	Brazil	3.2
53	Lithuania	3.2
54	Slovak Republic	3.2
55	Sri Lanka	3.2
56	Mauritius	3.1
57	Jamaica	3.1
58	Turkey	3.1
59	Romania	3.1
60	Dominican Republic	3.0
61	Honduras	2.9
62	Costa Rica	2.9
63	Colombia	2.9
64	Bangladesh	2.8
65	Mexico	2.7
66	Venezuela	2.7
67	Guatemala	2.6
68	Peru	2.6
69	Bulgaria	2.6
70	Russia	2.6
71	Nicaragua	2.5
72	Zimbabwe	2.4
73	Bolivia	2.4
74	Ukraine	2.3
75	Ecuador	1.9

Table 10. Openness to International Trade

Rank	Country	Score
1	Hong Kong SAR	6.9
2	Singapore	6.7
3	Canada	6.6
4	Finland	6.6
5	Netherlands	6.6
6	Switzerland	6.5
7	New Zealand	6.5
8	Belgium	6.5
9	Estonia	6.5
10	Austria	6.5
11	Denmark	6.5
12	France	6.5
13	Japan	6.4
14	Sweden	6.4
15	Germany	6.4
16	United States	6.4
17	Greece	6.4
18	Spain	6.3
19	Australia	6.3
20	Taiwan	6.3
21	Slovak Republic	6.3
22	United Kingdom	6.3
23	Ireland	6.3
24	Lithuania	6.2
25	Israel	6.2
26	Hungary	6.2
27	Latvia	6.2
28	Portugal	6.1
29	Italy	6.1
30	Mexico	6.1
31	Czech Republic	6.0
32	Norway	5.9
33	Turkey	5.9
34	Iceland	5.8
35	Chile	5.7
36	El Salvador	5.6
37	Poland	5.6
38	Trinidad and Tobago	5.6
39	Slovenia	5.6
40	Thailand	5.5
41	Uruguay	5.4
42	Malaysia	5.4
43	Jamaica	5.4
44	South Africa	5.4
45	Korea	5.3
46	Philippines	5.3
47	Argentina	5.3
48	Indonesia	5.2
49	Peru	5.2
50	Costa Rica	5.1
51	Guatemala	5.1
52	Romania	5.1
53	Honduras	5.1
54	Colombia	5.0
55	Mauritius	5.0
56	Paraguay	5.0
57	Bulgaria	4.9
58	Venezuela	4.9
59	**JORDAN**	**4.9**
60	Sri Lanka	4.8
61	Panama	4.8
62	Nicaragua	4.7
63	Bangladesh	4.7
64	Ukraine	4.5
65	Vietnam	4.5
66	Bolivia	4.4
67	Ecuador	4.2
68	China	4.1
69	Russia	4.0
70	Dominican Republic	4.0
71	**EGYPT**	**3.8**
72	Brazil	3.8
73	India	3.2
74	Nigeria	2.7
75	Zimbabwe	2.1

Part 1 Engines of Growth for the Arab World

Table 11. Quality of Government

Rank	Country	Score
1	Singapore	5.6
2	Finland	4.8
3	Hong Kong SAR	4.8
4	Ireland	4.2
5	Spain	4.1
6	Switzerland	4.1
7	Netherlands	4.1
8	Australia	4.1
9	Taiwan	4.0
10	Iceland	4.0
11	Hungary	4.0
12	Austria	3.9
13	New Zealand	3.9
14	Sweden	3.9
15	United Kingdom	3.8
16	Denmark	3.8
17	France	3.8
18	Canada	3.6
19	**JORDAN**	**3.6**
20	Estonia	3.6
21	Thailand	3.6
22	Trinidad and Tobago	3.6
23	United States	3.6
24	Belgium	3.5
25	Israel	3.5
26	China	3.5
27	Mauritius	3.4
28	Norway	3.4
29	Latvia	3.4
30	Germany	3.4
31	Chile	3.4
32	Korea	3.4
33	Slovenia	3.3
34	Vietnam	3.3
35	Slovak Republic	3.3
36	Malaysia	3.2
37	Mexico	3.2
38	South Africa	3.2
39	Japan	3.2
40	Bulgaria	3.2
41	Italy	3.2
42	Jamaica	3.2
43	**EGYPT**	**3.1**
44	Brazil	3.1
45	Indonesia	3.0
46	Russia	3.0
47	Lithuania	3.0
48	Panama	3.0
49	El Salvador	3.0
50	Peru	2.9
51	India	2.9
52	Poland	2.9
53	Sri Lanka	2.9
54	Czech Republic	2.9
55	Uruguay	2.8
56	Philippines	2.8
57	Costa Rica	2.8
58	Colombia	2.8
59	Nicaragua	2.7
60	Portugal	2.7
61	Turkey	2.7
62	Dominican Republic	2.7
63	Nigeria	2.7
64	Greece	2.6
65	Bangladesh	2.5
66	Argentina	2.5
67	Ukraine	2.5
68	Bolivia	2.5
69	Paraguay	2.4
70	Honduras	2.4
71	Romania	2.3
72	Guatemala	2.3
73	Ecuador	2.2
74	Venezuela	2.1
75	Zimbabwe	1.7

Table 12. New Economy

Rank	Country	Score
1	Finland	6.6
2	Iceland	6.5
3	Sweden	6.4
4	Singapore	6.4
5	United States	6.3
6	Norway	6.3
7	Denmark	6.2
8	Canada	6.2
9	Netherlands	6.2
10	Hong Kong SAR	6.2
11	Australia	6.1
12	Switzerland	6.1
13	Austria	6.1
14	United Kingdom	6.1
15	Germany	6.0
16	Taiwan	6.0
17	New Zealand	6.0
18	Ireland	6.0
19	Belgium	5.9
20	Estonia	5.9
21	France	5.9
22	Korea	5.9
23	Israel	5.8
24	Japan	5.8
25	Portugal	5.7
26	Spain	5.6
27	Italy	5.5
28	Slovenia	5.5
29	Czech Republic	5.4
30	Hungary	5.3
31	Slovak Republic	5.2
32	Chile	5.2
33	Malaysia	5.2
34	Uruguay	5.1
35	Greece	5.1
36	Latvia	5.0
37	Poland	4.9
38	Brazil	4.8
39	Argentina	4.8
40	South Africa	4.8
41	Mauritius	4.8
42	Costa Rica	4.7
43	Lithuania	4.7
44	Trinidad and Tobago	4.6
45	Turkey	4.6
46	Mexico	4.6
47	Jamaica	4.6
48	Venezuela	4.5
49	Panama	4.5
50	Bulgaria	4.4
51	Colombia	4.4
52	**JORDAN**	**4.3**
53	Thailand	4.2
54	Russia	4.2
55	Philippines	4.1
56	China	4.0
57	Dominican Republic	4.0
58	Peru	4.0
59	Romania	4.0
60	El Salvador	3.9
61	**EGYPT**	**3.8**
62	Ukraine	3.8
63	Ecuador	3.6
64	Paraguay	3.6
65	Bolivia	3.5
66	Guatemala	3.5
67	Indonesia	3.4
68	India	3.4
69	Sri Lanka	3.4
70	Honduras	3.2
71	Nicaragua	3.2
72	Zimbabwe	3.1
73	Vietnam	2.8
74	Nigeria	2.2
75	Bangladesh	2.0

Table 13. Education

Rank	Country	Score
1	Finland	6.2
2	Denmark	6.0
3	United States	6.0
4	Switzerland	6.0
5	Sweden	5.9
6	Norway	5.8
7	Austria	5.8
8	Netherlands	5.7
9	France	5.6
10	Japan	5.5
11	Belgium	5.5
12	Ireland	5.5
13	Canada	5.5
14	Australia	5.4
15	Iceland	5.4
16	Germany	5.4
17	Singapore	5.3
18	New Zealand	5.2
19	Taiwan	5.1
20	Korea	5.0
21	Israel	4.9
22	Estonia	4.9
23	Hong Kong SAR	4.9
24	Slovak Republic	4.8
25	United Kingdom	4.7
26	Czech Republic	4.7
27	Hungary	4.7
28	Slovenia	4.6
29	Poland	4.5
30	Spain	4.4
31	Romania	4.3
32	Malaysia	4.2
33	Greece	4.2
34	Italy	4.2
35	Latvia	4.2
36	Bulgaria	4.0
37	Trinidad and Tobago	3.9
38	Costa Rica	3.9
39	Lithuania	3.8
40	South Africa	3.7
41	**JORDAN**	**3.7**
42	Portugal	3.6
43	Uruguay	3.6
44	Russia	3.5
45	Philippines	3.5
46	Panama	3.5
47	Thailand	3.5
48	Argentina	3.4
49	Mauritius	3.4
50	Jamaica	3.4
51	Chile	3.4
52	Sri Lanka	3.2
53	Turkey	3.2
54	Ukraine	3.2
55	Mexico	3.1
56	Vietnam	3.0
57	**EGYPT**	**3.0**
58	China	3.0
59	Peru	2.9
60	Zimbabwe	2.8
61	Brazil	2.8
62	Colombia	2.8
63	Indonesia	2.7
64	Paraguay	2.6
65	Dominican Republic	2.5
66	Ecuador	2.4
67	El Salvador	2.3
68	Venezuela	2.3
69	India	2.3
70	Nigeria	2.3
71	Bolivia	2.0
72	Nicaragua	1.9
73	Honduras	1.9
74	Guatemala	1.7
75	Bangladesh	1.5

Table 14. Infrastructure

Rank	Country	Score
1	Germany	6.3
2	United States	6.3
3	Finland	6.3
4	France	6.2
5	Sweden	6.2
6	Netherlands	6.1
7	Austria	6.0
8	Canada	5.9
9	Iceland	5.9
10	Belgium	5.9
11	Switzerland	5.9
12	New Zealand	5.8
13	Australia	5.8
14	United Kingdom	5.8
15	Denmark	5.7
16	Hong Kong SAR	5.7
17	Norway	5.6
18	Spain	5.6
19	Singapore	5.5
20	Czech Republic	5.4
21	Israel	5.3
22	Chile	5.3
23	Portugal	5.2
24	Estonia	5.2
25	Korea	5.1
26	Italy	5.1
27	Argentina	5.1
28	Japan	5.0
29	Brazil	5.0
30	Hungary	4.9
31	Malaysia	4.9
32	Slovak Republic	4.8
33	South Africa	4.8
34	**JORDAN**	**4.8**
35	Thailand	4.8
36	Taiwan	4.8
37	**EGYPT**	**4.7**
38	Uruguay	4.6
39	Slovenia	4.6
40	Greece	4.5
41	Ireland	4.5
42	Poland	4.4
43	Latvia	4.4
44	Turkey	4.3
45	Venezuela	4.3
46	Lithuania	4.2
47	Dominican Republic	4.2
48	Trinidad and Tobago	4.1
49	El Salvador	4.1
50	Peru	3.9
51	Colombia	3.9
52	Indonesia	3.9
53	Zimbabwe	3.9
54	Panama	3.8
55	Jamaica	3.8
56	Ukraine	3.8
57	Mexico	3.8
58	India	3.7
59	Russia	3.7
60	China	3.6
61	Sri Lanka	3.6
62	Bulgaria	3.5
63	Guatemala	3.5
64	Philippines	3.5
65	Bolivia	3.4
66	Paraguay	3.4
67	Costa Rica	3.3
68	Honduras	3.2
69	Mauritius	3.1
70	Nigeria	3.0
71	Ecuador	3.0
72	Bangladesh	3.0
73	Vietnam	2.9
74	Nicaragua	2.8
75	Romania	2.7

Table 15. Rule of Law

Rank	Country	Score
1	United States	6.3
2	Israel	6.2
3	United Kingdom	6.1
4	Germany	6.1
5	Hong Kong SAR	6.1
6	Australia	6.0
7	Finland	6.0
8	Ireland	6.0
9	Switzerland	6.0
10	Netherlands	5.9
11	Denmark	5.9
12	Canada	5.9
13	Iceland	5.8
14	Austria	5.8
15	Belgium	5.8
16	Norway	5.7
17	South Africa	5.5
18	Sweden	5.5
19	Singapore	5.5
20	New Zealand	5.5
21	France	5.4
22	Portugal	5.3
23	Japan	5.3
24	Uruguay	5.3
25	Spain	5.2
26	Italy	5.2
27	India	5.1
28	Mauritius	5.1
29	Chile	5.0
30	Poland	5.0
31	Jamaica	5.0
32	**JORDAN**	**4.9**
33	Hungary	4.9
34	**EGYPT**	**4.7**
35	Estonia	4.7
36	Slovenia	4.7
37	Brazil	4.6
38	Trinidad and Tobago	4.6
39	Slovak Republic	4.4
40	Thailand	4.4
41	Mexico	4.4
42	Greece	4.4
43	Czech Republic	4.4
44	Philippines	4.4
45	Sri Lanka	4.3
46	Turkey	4.2
47	Argentina	4.2
48	Korea	4.2
49	Taiwan	4.1
50	Costa Rica	4.1
51	Bulgaria	4.0
52	Malaysia	4.0
53	Romania	4.0
54	Dominican Republic	3.9
55	Nigeria	3.9
56	Latvia	3.9
57	China	3.8
58	Colombia	3.7
59	Zimbabwe	3.7
60	Bangladesh	3.7
61	Vietnam	3.7
62	Indonesia	3.6
63	Panama	3.5
64	Lithuania	3.5
65	Venezuela	3.5
66	Russia	3.5
67	El Salvador	3.4
68	Honduras	3.3
69	Paraguay	3.1
70	Ukraine	3.0
71	Nicaragua	3.0
72	Guatemala	2.7
73	Peru	2.6
74	Ecuador	2.3
75	Bolivia	2.3

Table 16. Red Tape

Rank	Country	Score
1	Iceland	5.9
2	Finland	5.8
3	Singapore	5.8
4	Switzerland	5.8
5	Netherlands	5.7
6	Hong Kong SAR	5.6
7	Spain	5.3
8	Ireland	5.2
9	Sweden	5.1
10	United States	5.1
11	Trinidad and Tobago	5.0
12	Japan	5.0
13	Estonia	5.0
14	United Kingdom	5.0
15	Germany	4.9
16	Belgium	4.8
17	Czech Republic	4.7
18	Norway	4.7
19	Malaysia	4.7
20	New Zealand	4.7
21	Sri Lanka	4.6
22	Mauritius	4.6
23	Denmark	4.6
24	Chile	4.6
25	Israel	4.6
26	Peru	4.5
27	Slovenia	4.5
28	Canada	4.5
29	France	4.3
30	Austria	4.3
31	Taiwan	4.3
32	Korea	4.3
33	Poland	4.2
34	Argentina	4.2
35	India	4.1
36	Lithuania	4.0
37	Portugal	4.0
38	Jamaica	4.0
39	Hungary	3.9
40	Brazil	3.9
41	Australia	3.9
42	South Africa	3.9
43	Colombia	3.9
44	Uruguay	3.9
45	Romania	3.9
46	Philippines	3.8
47	El Salvador	3.8
48	Costa Rica	3.6
49	Greece	3.6
50	Vietnam	3.6
51	Bulgaria	3.6
52	Zimbabwe	3.6
53	Mexico	3.4
54	Venezuela	3.4
55	Nigeria	3.3
56	**JORDAN**	**3.3**
57	Dominican Republic	3.2
58	Russia	3.2
59	Italy	3.2
60	China	3.2
61	Latvia	3.2
62	Nicaragua	3.1
63	Bangladesh	3.1
64	Indonesia	3.1
65	Ecuador	3.0
66	Honduras	3.0
67	Paraguay	3.0
68	Turkey	2.9
69	Slovak Republic	2.8
70	Guatemala	2.8
71	Panama	2.8
72	Ukraine	2.7
73	Thailand	2.6
74	Bolivia	2.3
75	**EGYPT**	**1.8**

Table 17. Corruption

Rank	Country	Score
1	Iceland	7.0
2	Finland	6.8
3	Denmark	6.6
4	New Zealand	6.5
5	Singapore	6.5
6	Sweden	6.5
7	Canada	6.4
8	Australia	6.4
9	United Kingdom	6.4
10	Netherlands	6.3
11	United States	6.3
12	Hong Kong SAR	6.3
13	Norway	6.2
14	Chile	6.1
15	Japan	6.1
16	Israel	6.1
17	Lithuania	6.0
18	Belgium	6.0
19	Austria	6.0
20	Switzerland	5.9
21	Ireland	5.9
22	Taiwan	5.9
23	Germany	5.8
24	France	5.6
25	Spain	5.6
26	Italy	5.4
27	Hungary	5.4
28	Portugal	5.2
29	Estonia	5.1
30	Peru	5.1
31	South Africa	5.1
32	Trinidad and Tobago	5.0
33	Slovenia	4.9
34	Bulgaria	4.9
35	Slovak Republic	4.9
36	**JORDAN**	**4.8**
37	Jamaica	4.8
38	Malaysia	4.7
39	Uruguay	4.7
40	Mauritius	4.6
41	Costa Rica	4.6
42	Colombia	4.5
43	Latvia	4.5
44	**EGYPT**	**4.5**
45	Dominican Republic	4.4
46	Brazil	4.4
47	Mexico	4.4
48	Greece	4.4
49	Poland	4.4
50	El Salvador	4.3
51	Turkey	4.3
52	China	4.3
53	Korea	4.2
54	Russia	4.2
55	Thailand	4.2
56	Sri Lanka	4.2
57	Panama	4.2
58	Romania	4.1
59	Bolivia	4.1
60	Argentina	4.0
61	Venezuela	4.0
62	Guatemala	4.0
63	Czech Republic	4.0
64	Ecuador	3.9
65	India	3.7
66	Nicaragua	3.7
67	Honduras	3.7
68	Philippines	3.6
69	Vietnam	3.5
70	Zimbabwe	3.5
71	Indonesia	3.3
72	Ukraine	3.3
73	Paraguay	2.8
74	Nigeria	2.8
75	Bangladesh	2.1

Table 18. Start-up Conditions

Rank	Country	Score
1	Finland	5.8
2	United States	5.7
3	Sweden	5.6
4	Hong Kong SAR	5.4
5	Netherlands	5.4
6	Iceland	5.3
7	Israel	5.2
8	Switzerland	5.2
9	United Kingdom	5.2
10	Singapore	5.2
11	Canada	5.0
12	Norway	5.0
13	Denmark	5.0
14	Taiwan	4.9
15	Australia	4.8
16	New Zealand	4.8
17	Ireland	4.7
18	Germany	4.7
19	Belgium	4.7
20	Estonia	4.6
21	Hungary	4.4
22	France	4.3
23	Trinidad and Tobago	4.2
24	Poland	4.2
25	Portugal	4.2
26	Austria	4.2
27	India	4.1
28	**EGYPT**	**4.1**
29	Spain	4.1
30	Thailand	4.0
31	Brazil	4.0
32	South Africa	4.0
33	Sri Lanka	4.0
34	Japan	4.0
35	Korea	3.9
36	Malaysia	3.9
37	Panama	3.8
38	Italy	3.7
39	**JORDAN**	**3.7**
40	China	3.7
41	Slovenia	3.7
42	Chile	3.7
43	Czech Republic	3.7
44	Mauritius	3.6
45	Vietnam	3.6
46	Philippines	3.6
47	Zimbabwe	3.5
48	Indonesia	3.4
49	Jamaica	3.4
50	El Salvador	3.4
51	Latvia	3.4
52	Uruguay	3.3
53	Turkey	3.3
54	Dominican Republic	3.3
55	Lithuania	3.3
56	Greece	3.2
57	Nigeria	3.1
58	Paraguay	3.1
59	Argentina	3.1
60	Guatemala	3.1
61	Costa Rica	3.0
62	Venezuela	3.0
63	Nicaragua	2.9
64	Bangladesh	2.8
65	Colombia	2.8
66	Russia	2.8
67	Slovak Republic	2.8
68	Mexico	2.7
69	Peru	2.6
70	Ecuador	2.6
71	Bolivia	2.5
72	Ukraine	2.5
73	Bulgaria	2.4
74	Honduras	2.3
75	Romania	2.3

Table 19. Low Taxes

Rank	Country	Score
1	Hong Kong SAR	5.9
2	Singapore	5.0
3	Estonia	4.9
4	Nigeria	4.2
5	Taiwan	4.2
6	United States	4.2
7	Malaysia	4.1
8	Mauritius	4.1
9	Panama	4.0
10	Thailand	4.0
11	Ecuador	4.0
12	Dominican Republic	4.0
13	Bolivia	3.9
14	Guatemala	3.8
15	El Salvador	3.8
16	Japan	3.8
17	Honduras	3.6
18	Brazil	3.6
19	Philippines	3.6
20	Costa Rica	3.6
21	Indonesia	3.6
22	Nicaragua	3.5
23	**JORDAN**	**3.5**
24	Ukraine	3.5
25	Sri Lanka	3.5
26	Latvia	3.5
27	Ireland	3.5
28	India	3.4
29	Korea	3.4
30	Chile	3.3
31	Trinidad and Tobago	3.3
32	Jamaica	3.3
33	Hungary	3.3
34	United Kingdom	3.2
35	Australia	3.2
36	New Zealand	3.2
37	**EGYPT**	**3.2**
38	Bangladesh	3.2
39	Venezuela	3.2
40	Finland	3.1
41	China	3.1
42	Peru	3.1
43	South Africa	3.1
44	Lithuania	3.1
45	Spain	3.0
46	Mexico	3.0
47	Canada	2.9
48	Turkey	2.9
49	Slovenia	2.9
50	Czech Republic	2.9
51	Iceland	2.9
52	Colombia	2.9
53	Portugal	2.8
54	Vietnam	2.8
55	Austria	2.7
56	Poland	2.6
57	Israel	2.6
58	Netherlands	2.6
59	Argentina	2.6
60	Russia	2.6
61	Germany	2.5
62	Slovak Republic	2.5
63	Norway	2.5
64	Greece	2.5
65	Italy	2.4
66	Bulgaria	2.3
67	Romania	2.3
68	Sweden	2.2
69	Belgium	2.0
70	France	2.0
71	Zimbabwe	1.9
72	Denmark	1.8
73	Paraguay	—
74	Switzerland	—
75	Uruguay	—

Table 20. Capital Accumulation

Rank	Country	Score
1	Singapore	6.5
2	China	5.9
3	Korea	4.5
4	Mauritius	4.4
5	Malaysia	4.4
6	Slovak Republic	4.4
7	Hong Kong SAR	4.2
8	Honduras	4.1
9	Nigeria	4.1
10	Vietnam	4.1
11	Ireland	4.0
12	Japan	4.0
13	Trinidad and Tobago	4.0
14	Czech Republic	4.0
15	Slovenia	3.9
16	Hungary	3.8
17	Jamaica	3.7
18	Sri Lanka	3.7
19	Norway	3.7
20	Portugal	3.7
21	Switzerland	3.7
22	Spain	3.6
23	Latvia	3.5
24	Taiwan	3.5
25	Russia	3.5
26	Netherlands	3.5
27	Dominican Republic	3.4
28	Poland	3.4
29	Indonesia	3.4
30	**JORDAN**	**3.4**
31	Panama	3.4
32	Greece	3.3
33	Belgium	3.3
34	Austria	3.3
35	Estonia	3.3
36	Denmark	3.3
37	Ukraine	3.2
38	Chile	3.2
39	Thailand	3.2
40	Finland	3.1
41	**EGYPT**	**3.1**
42	India	3.1
43	Philippines	3.1
44	Australia	3.1
45	Germany	3.1
46	Turkey	2.9
47	Lithuania	2.9
48	Mexico	2.9
49	Paraguay	2.9
50	Iceland	2.9
51	France	2.9
52	Canada	2.8
53	Brazil	2.8
54	Italy	2.8
55	Ecuador	2.7
56	Peru	2.6
57	Sweden	2.5
58	New Zealand	2.5
59	Venezuela	2.5
60	Israel	2.4
61	Romania	2.4
62	United Kingdom	2.3
63	United States	2.2
64	Bolivia	2.2
65	South Africa	2.1
66	Bangladesh	2.0
67	Costa Rica	2.0
68	Argentina	2.0
69	El Salvador	1.9
70	Zimbabwe	1.9
71	Guatemala	1.8
72	Bulgaria	1.8
73	Uruguay	1.4
74	Colombia	1.4
75	Nicaragua	—

Table 21a. Innovation

Rank	Country	Score
1	United States	5.9
2	Finland	5.9
3	Israel	5.7
4	France	5.7
5	Netherlands	5.6
6	Germany	5.6
7	Switzerland	5.6
8	Taiwan	5.5
9	Sweden	5.5
10	Japan	5.5
11	Singapore	5.3
12	United Kingdom	5.3
13	Austria	5.3
14	Denmark	5.2
15	Canada	5.2
16	Belgium	5.1
17	Ireland	5.1
18	Australia	5.0
19	Iceland	4.9
20	Italy	4.9
21	Norway	4.8
22	Spain	4.7
23	Korea	4.5
24	New Zealand	4.4
25	Hong Kong SAR	4.3
26	Hungary	4.2
27	South Africa	4.2
28	Slovenia	4.1
29	Sri Lanka	4.0
30	Estonia	4.0
31	Brazil	4.0
32	India	3.9
33	Portugal	3.9
34	China	3.9
35	Malaysia	3.9
36	Costa Rica	3.8
37	Poland	3.8
38	Trinidad and Tobago	3.8
39	Czech Republic	3.8
40	Slovak Republic	3.7
41	Chile	3.7
42	Russia	3.7
43	Jamaica	3.7
44	Latvia	3.6
45	Uruguay	3.6
46	Panama	3.6
47	Thailand	3.6
48	Greece	3.5
49	Ukraine	3.5
50	Lithuania	3.5
51	**JORDAN**	**3.5**
52	Philippines	3.4
53	Mauritius	3.4
54	Indonesia	3.3
55	Argentina	3.3
56	Mexico	3.3
57	Colombia	3.3
58	Turkey	3.3
59	Vietnam	3.2
60	**EGYPT**	**3.2**
61	Zimbabwe	3.1
62	Nigeria	3.1
63	Venezuela	3.1
64	Bulgaria	3.1
65	Paraguay	2.9
66	Peru	2.9
67	Guatemala	2.8
68	El Salvador	2.8
69	Nicaragua	2.7
70	Ecuador	2.6
71	Romania	2.6
72	Bangladesh	2.5
73	Honduras	2.4
74	Bolivia	2.3
75	Dominican Republic	—

Table 21b. Transfer of Technology

Rank	Country	Score
1	Singapore	6.1
2	Malaysia	6.0
3	Hungary	5.8
4	Romania	5.8
5	Hong Kong SAR	5.7
6	United Kingdom	5.7
7	**EGYPT**	**5.6**
8	Netherlands	5.6
9	Poland	5.6
10	Brazil	5.6
11	Ireland	5.6
12	Australia	5.5
13	Chile	5.5
14	Israel	5.5
15	Taiwan	5.5
16	Belgium	5.5
17	India	5.5
18	Mexico	5.5
19	Thailand	5.4
20	Slovak Republic	5.4
21	Venezuela	5.4
22	Portugal	5.4
23	Italy	5.4
24	Canada	5.4
25	Czech Republic	5.3
26	Argentina	5.3
27	Spain	5.3
28	Austria	5.3
29	South Africa	5.3
30	Philippines	5.3
31	New Zealand	5.2
32	Estonia	5.2
33	Costa Rica	5.2
34	Turkey	5.1
35	Germany	5.1
36	Denmark	5.1
37	Sri Lanka	5.0
38	France	5.0
39	Korea	5.0
40	Nigeria	5.0
41	Iceland	4.9
42	Japan	4.9
43	**JORDAN**	**4.9**
44	Trinidad and Tobago	4.9
45	Vietnam	4.9
46	Norway	4.9
47	Greece	4.9
48	Switzerland	4.9
49	Jamaica	4.9
50	Indonesia	4.8
51	Mauritius	4.8
52	Peru	4.8
53	Latvia	4.7
54	Colombia	4.7
55	Panama	4.7
56	United States	4.6
57	Honduras	4.6
58	El Salvador	4.6
59	Sweden	4.6
60	Finland	4.6
61	Slovenia	4.5
62	Lithuania	4.5
63	Zimbabwe	4.4
64	China	4.4
65	Uruguay	4.3
66	Ecuador	4.2
67	Guatemala	4.1
68	Bangladesh	4.1
69	Russia	3.8
70	Bulgaria	3.8
71	Nicaragua	3.8
72	Ukraine	3.8
73	Paraguay	3.7
74	Bolivia	3.5
75	Dominican Republic	—

Table 22. Exports Per Person (excluding natural resources)

Rank	Country	Score
1	Singapore	97.6
2	Hong Kong SAR	96.9
3	Malaysia	46.3
4	Taiwan	35.0
5	Ireland	33.0
6	Belgium	30.6
7	Slovenia	29.3
8	Mauritius	28.8
9	Slovak Republic	27.2
10	Czech Republic	26.5
11	Netherlands	20.4
12	Switzerland	19.6
13	Korea	18.9
14	Thailand	18.7
15	Dominican Republic	18.2
16	Sweden	17.1
17	Tunisia	16.3
18	Lithuania	16.1
19	Germany	15.7
20	Hungary	15.6
21	Sri Lanka	15.2
22	Austria	15.0
23	Portugal	14.1
24	United Kingdom	13.7
25	Canada	13.5
26	Denmark	13.4
27	Italy	13.0
28	China	12.9
29	Croatia	12.6
30	Finland	12.1
31	Mexico	11.9
32	Philippines	11.8
33	France	10.6
34	Israel	10.4
35	Namibia	10.2
36	Romania	9.8
37	Bulgaria	9.2
38	Latvia	8.6
39	Spain	8.1
40	Indonesia	7.8
41	Poland	7.7
42	Vietnam	7.7
43	Japan	7.6
44	Jamaica	6.9
45	Haiti	6.9
46	Jordan	6.2
47	Turkey	6.1
48	Norway	5.8
49	Bangladesh	5.6
50	Botswana	5.6
51	United States	5.1
52	Costa Rica	4.9
53	Ukraine	4.6
54	Morocco	4.6
55	Uruguay	3.8
56	Greece	3.5
57	Nicaragua	3.5
58	India	3.5
59	New Zealand	3.3
60	Zimbabwe	3.1
61	El Salvador	2.7
62	Russia	2.7
63	Colombia	2.6
64	Honduras	2.5
65	Australia	2.4
66	Guatemala	2.0
67	Trinidad and Tobago	2.0
68	South Africa	2.0
69	Brazil	1.8
70	Bolivia	1.6
71	Chile	1.4
72	Argentina	1.2
73	Iceland	1.2
74	Venezuela	1.1
75	Peru	1.1
76	Panama	1.0
77	Ecuador	0.9
78	Paraguay	0.5
79	Nigeria	0.2
80	Estonia	—

Economic Growth and Investment in the Arab World

Xavier Sala-i-Martin and Elsa V. Artadi

Growth

The growth performance of the Arab world over the last twenty years has been disappointing. Figure 1 shows a measure of Arab world GDP per capita between 1960 and 2000.[1] After increasing at rapid rates between 1963 and 1980, GDP per capita stagnated over the following two decades. In fact, GDP per capita in the region as a whole was lower in the year 2000 than in 1980; the huge decline of the early 1980s was followed by a very moderate recovery, which has not yet helped the region reach the income levels of 1980. Of course, not all economies within the Arab world behave in exactly the same way. For example, whereas the pattern of GDP per

capita for oil-producing economies is similar to that of the group as a whole (the level is slightly higher for the oil countries than for the average country in the region, but the pattern over time is virtually identical), the non-oil producing countries grew almost continuously between 1960 and 2000 (see also Figure 1).[2] The rate at which GDP per capita increased, however, also seemed to slow after 1980.

The pattern of growth rates for the Arab world and differences between oil- and non-oil-producing countries are displayed in Figure 2. The first thing to notice is that the annual growth rate is highly volatile. The volatility is more pronounced for the oil countries, which shows that the growth rate depends, at least in the short run, on oil prices.

The short-term volatility, however, masks some well-defined medium- and long-term trends. For example, if we add a linear trend line to Figure 2, we see that it is negatively sloped, which suggests that the growth rate has had a tendency to decline over time. The negative trend of the growth rate over time applies equally to the oil and non-oil producing countries.

Figure 3 separates the annual growth rates into averages for five well-defined periods: the pre-oil-shock period (1963 to 1973), the oil-shock period (1974 to 1980), the period of steep decline in oil prices (1981 to 1985), the second half of the 1980s (1986 to 1990), and the 1990s (1991 to 2000). We notice that the annual growth rate of per capita GDP for the Arab region as a whole between 1963 and 1973 was much greater than 4 percent. The growth rate declined slightly to just above 3 percent between 1974 and 1980. Between 1980 and 1985 the growth

Figure 1. GDP per Capita (in US$)

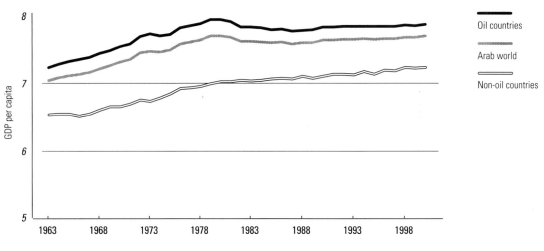

Oil countries

Arab world

Non-oil countries

Source: Authors' calculations

Figure 2. Annual Growth Rates (in Percent)

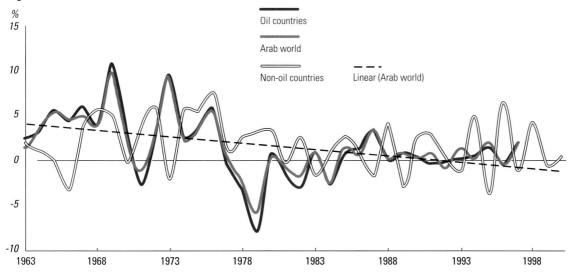

Oil countries
Arab world
Non-oil countries
Linear (Arab world)

Source: Authors' calculations

rate was negative 2 percent, and it never recovered the levels of the 1960s—in fact, the rate was below 1 percent for the rest of the 1980s and the 1990s.

As was the case for the level of GDP per capita, the growth rate was not uniform across all the Arab countries. For example, between 1981 and 1985, the growth rate for oil producers was negative, whereas that of the non-oil producers was slightly positive (given the superior weight of the oil producers in

Figure 3. Annual Growth Rates in the Arab World (in Percent)

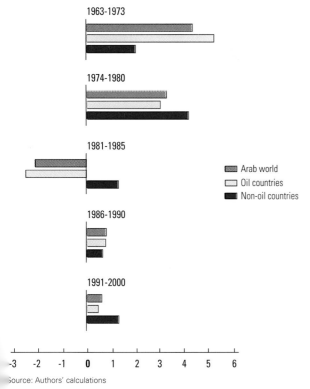

1963-1973

1974-1980

1981-1985

Arab world
Oil countries
Non-oil countries

1986-1990

1991-2000

-3 -2 -1 0 1 2 3 4 5 6

Source: Authors' calculations

overall Arab GDP, the aggregate growth rate for the region ended up being negative). Not surprisingly, the growth performance of the oil economies was vastly superior during the second half of the 1970s (when oil prices were high) and vastly inferior during the first half of the 1980s (when oil prices declined). In fact, the growth rate for the oil economies during this period was consistently lower than that of the non-oil countries, although neither of them was very high. Despite these differences, the medium-term behavior of growth rates is similar for oil and non-oil economies; that is, the extraordinary growth rates of the 1960s disappeared after the first oil shock.

The yearly correlations between each country's growth rate and the aggregate growth rate for the region are very low for some of the countries. This indicates that the short-term business cycle for different Arab countries is not highly synchronized. However, when we divide the period into five medium-term subperiods, we see that similar patterns arise.

Figure 4 shows the growth rates for the same five subperiods defined above for a sample of ten Arab countries (plus the aggregate Arab world numbers displayed in Figure 3). The growth rates are certainly not the same for every country, but the overall pattern is very similar: large growth rates for the two initial periods, a substantial reduction in the early 1980s (Oman was an exception; its growth rate was more than offset by the large negative growth rate of Saudi Arabia), and very small growth rates across the board for the second half of the 1980s and 1990s. The overall trend for the growth rates is clearly negative.

Figure 4. Annual Growth Rates for Selected Countries (in Percent)

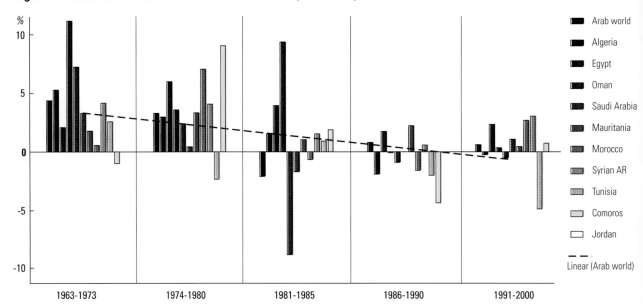

Source: Authors' calculations

In sum, despite the fact that the Arab world displays substantial heterogeneity in its economic growth performance, one common behavior requires analysis: the large growth rates of the 1960s and 1970s, which disappeared after 1980. For some countries, the growth rate became negative on average, and for others it declined but remained positive. Overall, however, we can say that the growth performance of the Arab world after 1980 was disappointing across the board.

Growth and the Distribution of Income and Poverty

The slowing of the growth process has very important implications for human welfare. For example, positive growth tends to increase the income of most social groups and "shift" the distribution of income to the right. Figure 5 estimates the distribution of income for the Arab region for select years between 1970 and 1998, using the methodology developed by Sala-i-Martin (2002). We note that income distribution improved substantially during the 1970s—growth led to improvements in the level of income for the majority of the population, rich and poor. We see that the "area under the distribution" and to the left of the US$1 a day line (that is, the "poverty rate") decreased substantially during this period. As the region's growth rate slowed, so too did the improvements in income distribution (in Figure 5, the distribution does not move much to the right between 1980 and 1998). Of course, this means that poverty rates did not decline much over the period of slow growth.

Over the last two decades, the world has witnessed spectacular reductions of poverty rates, thanks to the extraordinary growth performances of some of the largest economies of the planet: China, India, and Indonesia (Sala-i-Martin 2002). Figure 6 displays the poverty rates for the Arab world. We see that during the "high growth rate years" of the 1970s, there was a substantial reduction in poverty rates in the Arab region . The fraction of the population living on less than US$1 a day[3] went from 11 percent in 1970 to 2.4 percent in 1980. The fraction living with less than US$2 a day decreased from 30 percent in 1970 to 14 percent in 1980. The rapid reduction in poverty rates slowed down dramatically after 1980, when the aggregate growth rates also slowed down. By 1998, the US$1 a day poverty rate was still 1 percent (little change since 1980) and the US$2 a day rate was still above 5 percent.

Poverty levels in the Arab world are substantially lower than those in countries with similar levels of income. There are various reasons for that. One is that the public system in the Arab world has relatively effective safety nets because governments try to maintain social cohesion and an egalitarian society. Another reason is that Arab countries are marked by an important and cohesive system of private social responsibility under which families provide help to their members during hard times and income is redistributed through a religious charitable system. The dual Islamic practices of *zakat* and *sadaqa* encourage the rich members of society to donate a percentage of their income and

Figure 5. Arab World Distribution of Income (in Percent)

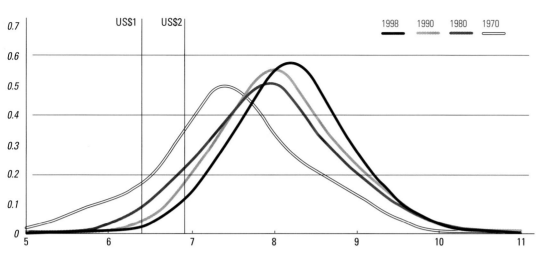

Source: Authors' calculations

wealth to the poor. *Zakat* fixes the donations to 2.5 percent of annual earnings; *sadaqa* allows some larger flexibility to the donor, but it can amount to substantial sums. Overall, the sums of money collected by charitable organizations to redistribute income and to deal with poverty are estimated to amount to large sums of money. All of this explains why poverty rates in the Arab world are low relative to its income levels. However, Figures 5 and 6 make it clear that the best way to reduce poverty over time is to increase the growth rate of the economy; poverty declined substantially over the period of high growth and progress slowed significantly during the period of low growth. From a welfare point of view, therefore, one of the key economic questions is: Why has the Arab world not grown much after 1980?

Investment

The first answer economists tend to give when exploring the economic success or failure of a country or an economic region is that the key determinant of economic growth is the investment rate: countries that grow quickly are countries that invest a substantial fraction of their GDP, and countries that fail to grow are countries that fail to invest. This explanation is partly based on economic theory. After all, the basic neoclassical growth model of Solow (1956) and Swan (1956) predicts that one of the key determinants of growth is the investment rate. Figure 7, however, shows that investment rates in the Arab world are not particularly low. The average investment rate over the period 1974 to 2000 is 24.6 percent, a rate higher than that of the OECD economies (22.9 percent) and only slightly lower than that of the successful economies of east Asia.

Figure 6. Poverty Rates in the Arab Region (in Percent)

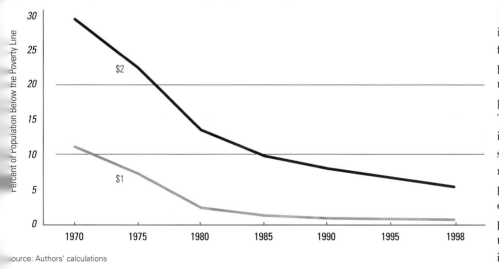

Source: Authors' calculations

Over time, we see that the investment rate in the Arab world increased substantially from 17 percent in the pre-oil-shock period to 27 percent in the post-oil-shock period. The interesting thing is that this rather large shift in the investment rate applies to both oil producers and non-oil producers. The puzzling fact is that the investment rate increased again to 28

Figure 7. Investment Rates (in Percent)

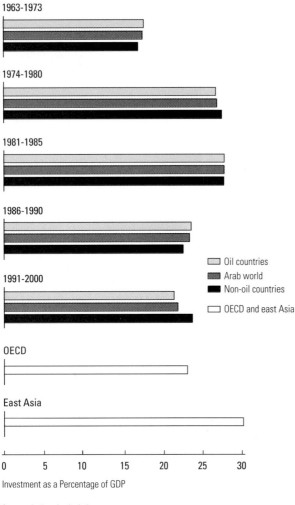

1963-1973

1974-1980

1981-1985

1986-1990

1991-2000

OECD

East Asia

Oil countries
Arab world
Non-oil countries
OECD and east Asia

0   5   10   15   20   25   30

Investment as a Percentage of GDP

Source: Authors' calculations

percent during the 1981 to 1985 period. We say this is puzzling because the growth rate became negative during this period. If the investment rate is a key determinant of the growth rate of an economy, why did the growth rate decline in the 1980s, a time in which the investment rates increased and remained high?

The investment rates declined slightly during the late 1980s and into the 1990s. Some analysts (UNDP 2002; Bisat et al. 1997) suggest that this reduction in the investment rate is responsible for the slow growth of the Arab region after 1980. We think that this is not the case, for two reasons.

First, we note that the reduction in the investment rate occurs five years after the overall growth rate falls dramatically (and even becomes negative). In particular, the investment rate achieves its highest level (27 percent of GDP) in the period 1981 to 1985, which is precisely the five-year period in which the growth rate was at is lowest level (-2.1 percent). One would

think that the high investment rates during the early 1980s were a response to—indeed a consequence of—the high growth rates of the 1970s (the Arab countries were trying to invest the proceeds of the good old seventies), rather than the cause of slow growth during 1981 to 1985 period. Similarly, the reduction in investment rates that followed the horrible first half of the 1980s was a consequence, not a cause, of the terrible growth performance of the first half of the decade.

Second, despite the small reduction in investment, rates remained high by international standards. Granted that the Arab world investment rate was not as high as rates in the "miraculous" countries of east Asia, but it was certainly comparable to those of the industrial countries of the OECD and far larger than those of the average developing country (see Figure 7). Moreover, investment rates in the Arab world during the late 1980s and through the 1990s remained higher than they had been in the 1960s, a period in which the region enjoyed much higher growth rates. If investment rates were higher in the 1990s than in the 1960s, why was the growth rate so much lower? Where was all this investment going during the 1980s and 1990s? Why didn't the large investment effort that was made after 1973 pay off in the form of higher growth rates?

We should point out that the investment-growth behavior of Arab countries is not particularly puzzling, because empirical growth economists have found that the investment rate is not robustly correlated with growth in a large cross section of countries. For example, Doppelhoffer et al. (2002) used a new methodology based on Bayesian Model Averaging to test the variables that are robustly correlated with growth and found, perhaps surprisingly, that the investment rate is not one of the successfully robust variables. Similarly, Easterly et al. (1993) and Easterly and Levine (2001) show that, while the investment rate changes little over time for most countries in the world, the growth rate is highly volatile. If investment rates do not move much across decades whereas growth rates do, it is not possible for investment to be an important determinant of growth. In fact, this empirical result is partially confirmed by our data for the Arab world: the growth rate falls dramatically after 1973, but the investment rate remains relatively constant over the same period. Thus, an initial answer to the question "where has Arab investment gone?" is that we do not know, but this is not especially puzzling because the investment-growth phenomenon we have described happens all over the world.

A clearer answer to the investment-growth question can also be found in the empirical cross-country growth literature. It is this: what matters for growth is not the overall level of investment, but its quality and efficiency. For example, Doppelhoffer et al. (2002) found that one of the robust determinants of the rate of economic growth is public investment. Perhaps the most surprising fact is that the sign of the partial correlation is negative! In other words, with aggregate investment and various other determinants of growth held constant, the larger the fraction of investment from the public sector, the smaller the growth rate of the country. Although this result might seem puzzling, there are, in fact, some economic explanations for it. Public investment, like all public expenditures, needs to be financed with distortionary taxes, and these tend to hurt economic growth. If public investment is productive, its overall effect on aggregate growth will depend on whether the positive effects on national productivity are larger than the negative effects arising from the distortionary taxes needed to finance it. This, of course, is true if public investment is productive. In reality, however, it is not uncommon for public investments to be inefficient or appropriated to the wrong sectors. Efficiently chosen, a project financed by the public sector could be very productive, but a project could be quite useless, for example, if the government makes investment decisions with the objective of political or private gain. However, even unproductive public investment still needs to be financed with distortionary taxes. Thus, when public investment projects in a country are predominantly unproductive, the overall effect is to reduce the growth rate.

This discussion is particularly relevant for the Arab world, because if we analyze the ratio of private investment to public investment, we see that it is unusually low. Figure 8 shows that, for the Arab world as a whole, the ratio is close to 2; that is, private investment is twice as large as public investment. The private/public ratio is slightly larger for non-oil economies than for oil economies in the region, but the overall ratio remains well below the levels of OECD economies (with ratios close to 6) or that of the rapidly growing east Asian economies (with ratios close to 5).[4]

The reforms of the 1990s have moved the Arab economies in the right direction, in the sense that the ratio of private to public investment has increased. For the region as a whole, the ratio increased from 1.6 in the 1980s to 2.4 in the 1990s. The non-oil countries were the ones that went further in reforming: the ratio increased from 1.8 to 3.0 whereas the non-oil

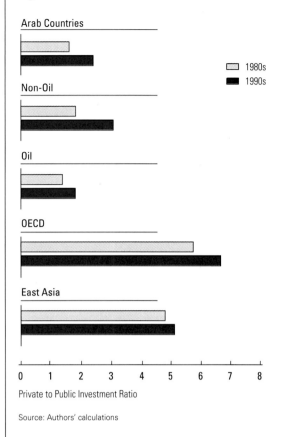

Figure 8. Private to Public Investment Ratio Over Time

Arab Countries
Non-Oil
Oil
OECD
East Asia

☐ 1980s
■ 1990s

Private to Public Investment Ratio

Source: Authors' calculations

economies increased from 1.4 to 1.7. It is interesting to see that the ratios of OECD economies also increased from 5.7 in the 1980s to 6.6 in the 1990s. Similarly, the ratios for east Asia increased from 4.8 to 5.1 over the same period. Hence, although reforms in the Arab world have gone in the right direction, they were not nearly large enough to put the private-to-public investment ratios at the levels of OECD or east Asian economies.

Despite large public-sector investments in the Arab world, infrastructures remain alarmingly inefficient. For example, according to the World Bank (1995), the percentage of unsuccessful telephone calls is 35 percent in Tunisia, 46 percent in Yemen, 50 percent in Lebanon, 57 percent in Morocco, and 60 percent in Jordan. Whereas the process of transmission and distribution of electricity suffers losses equivalent to 5 percent of output in OECD and east Asian countries, losses in the Arab world amount to 13 percent. These are hardly the numbers one would expect from economically competitive countries.

Inefficient Transmission of Savings to Investment

Private investment in the Arab world is both insufficient and inefficient. One of the reasons for investment insufficiency is that savings are not properly channeled by the financial sector to productive projects. Some of the blame must go to the government and its exceptionally high involvement in the financial sector. As in most of the developing world, the financial sector in Arab countries plays a smaller role than in rich industrial economies and, perhaps more important, the sector is almost completely dominated by the banking system. Capital markets are either underdeveloped or nonexistent. Most have low levels of trading and very few listed companies. Figure 9 shows three measures

Figure 9. Stock Market

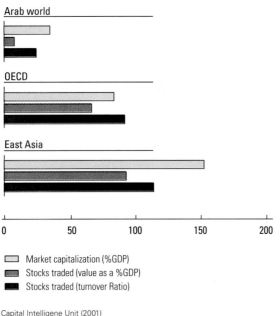

Capital Intelligene Unit (2001)

of the importance of capital markets: the market capitalization as a percentage of aggregate GDP, the value of stocks traded as percentage of GDP, and the turnover ratio. We notice that the three measures show the substantial underdevelopment of the Arab world relative to both industrialized economies of the OECD and high-growth economies of east Asia. For example, according to the Capital Intelligence Unit (2001), the stock market value of traded companies as a fraction of GDP is ten times higher in the OECD than in the Arab world and thirteen times higher in east Asia. The turnover ratio is four and five times larger, respectively. As an example, at year-end 1999, the Tunis Stock Exchange was comprised of only forty-four companies, of which thirteen were banks. Yemen has no stock market. There are two official stock exchanges in the United Arab Emirates, the Dubai Financial Market (DFM) and the Abu Dabi Securities Market (ADSM). The problem is that the DFM was set up in March 2000 and the ADSM

in November 2001. The lack of liquid investments in the Arab region has a direct negative effect on productive investment in the region, as it makes it difficult for entrepreneurs to raise capital to finance their potentially good ideas.[5] The fact that many large companies tend to be either public or in the hands of politically influential individuals has led to low repayment rates, and this fact has helped to impede the development of efficient bond and capital markets. The low levels of development of capital markets as well as of primary and secondary bond markets forces potential real investors into the hands of the banking system, which, as a result, has become immensely powerful, both economically and politically.

Despite their domination of the financial sector, banks are not efficient enough to play the critical role that they must in the process of economic growth and development. Lending remains predominantly short-term and trade-related; very little lending is directed at long-term productive investments. The lack of competition among banks leads to lack of innovation in lending. Despite recent efforts to liberalize and privatize the banking system, governments have protected the banks from competition by restricting entry at the local and international levels, and this has made them inefficient. In several countries, the state remains the dominant player in the banking system, owning a major proportion of the bank capital. An important fraction of the state-owned banks' business is financing housing at subsidized interest rates, which usually mean significant financial costs to the banks and, therefore, to the state. In some of the countries where banks are privately owned, public policy tends to select "privileged sectors" that enjoy credit at subsidized interest rates as well as recurrent debt forgiveness. While many countries have freed interests on deposits and lending, the legal failure to enforce collateral rights discourages financial intermediaries from lending to small businesses or clients that do not have long borrowing records, or, for that matter, political connections.

In sum, although the banking system is the most important part of the financial sector, its extraordinary inefficiency does not lead it to allocate national savings to their most productive uses. Without proper channeling of savings into productive and efficient investment, economic growth is impossible. Thus, continuing reform of the banking sector is a necessary process for the Arab world. These reforms must include the: (a) further elimination of abusive and inefficient regulation; (b) opening of financial markets to domestic and foreign entrants in order to promote competition, financial innovation, and modernization; (c) strengthening (public or private) of supervision to achieve sound corporate governance and accountability; (d) privatization of the remaining state banks, ensuring that the right incentives for sound commercial policies are in place (i.e., shifting commercial operations away from housing finance at subsidized interest rates to productive long-term investment); and (e) incorporation of the new technologies that are already changing the nature of the financial sector worldwide.

Inefficient Investment

Another source of low growth in the Arab world is the region's reduced overall economic efficiency. One measure of the overall evolution of the efficiency of an economy is the Total Factor Productivity (TFP) growth index. TFP growth measures the growth in the economy that cannot be accounted for by the measured increases in capital and labor. In other words, the part of overall economic growth that cannot be accounted for by increases in physical capital and labor must be accounted by the change in the overall efficiency of capital and labor. Figure 10 shows the evolution of TFP growth for a sample of Arab countries between 1975 and 2000.[6] The numbers are staggeringly low. With the exception of Egypt, Oman, Syria, and Tunisia, productivity growth in the Arab world has been negative; that is, the efficiency of the economy has markedly deteriorated.

Why is the productivity of investment in the Arab world so low? And why has it declined over time? Again, there is no unique explanation. We will highlight three reasons: political and social instability, a deteriorated business environment due to excessive public intervention and overregulation, and the low quality of human capital.

Political instability

War, violence, and social conflicts are and have been widespread throughout the Arab world during the period we are considering here. For example, Libya has had constant conflicts with Chad over the Aozou strip and has suffered U.N. sanctions for supporting terrorism. This is not the optimal political and social environment needed for productive investment to flourish.

In Algeria, the first-round success of the Islamic Salvation Front (FIS) party in December 1991 caused the army to nullify the results and crack down on the FIS. The FIS reaction resulted in continuous civil conflict with the state apparatus, which involved mass

Figure 10. Investment Efficiency

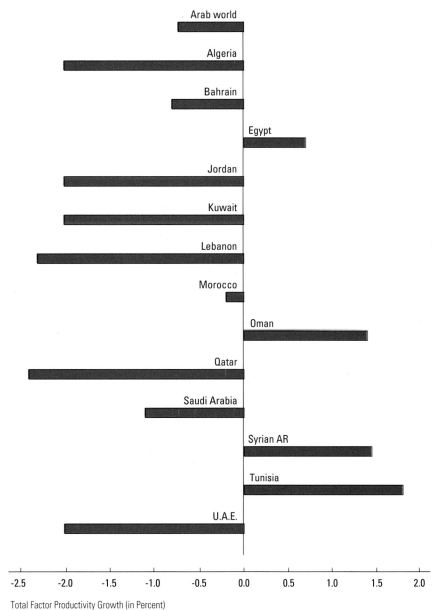

Total Factor Productivity Growth (in Percent)
Source: Authors' calculations

assassinations and widespread political violence. FIS's military arm, the Islamic Salvation Army, disbanded itself in January 2000 and many armed militants surrendered under an amnesty program designed to promote national reconciliation. Nevertheless, residual fighting continues.

Lebanon suffered a devastating sixteen-year civil war, which ended in 1991. Since then, the country has made progress toward rebuilding its political institutions and regaining its national sovereignty. The Lebanese have conducted several successful elections, most of the militias have been weakened or disbanded, and the Lebanese Armed Forces has extended central government authority over about two-thirds of the country. However, Hizballah (the radical Shi'a party) retains its weapons. Syria maintains about 25,000 troops in Lebanon, based mainly in Beirut, North Lebanon, and the Bekaa Valley. The Arab League legitimized Syria's troop deployment during Lebanon's civil war and in the Ta'if Accord that ended it. Israel's withdrawal from its security zone in southern Lebanon in May 2000, however, has emboldened some Lebanese Christians and Druze enough to demand that Syria withdraw its forces as well.

Territorial disputes between Iraq and Iran led to a very costly eight-year war between 1980 and 1988. In August 1990 Iraq seized Kuwait, but was expelled by U.S.-led, United Nations coalition forces during January and February 1991. Following Kuwait's liberation, the UN Security Council required Iraq to destroy all weapons of mass destruction and long-range missiles and to allow UN verification inspections. Sanctions remain in effect due to alleged incomplete Iraqi compliance with relevant Security Council's resolutions.

The Israel-PLO Declaration of Principles on Interim Self-Government Arrangements (the DOP), signed in Washington on 13 September 1993, provided for a transitional period, not to exceed five years, for Palestinian interim self-government in the Gaza Strip and the West Bank. Israel agreed to transfer certain powers and responsibilities to the Palestinian Authority, which includes the Palestinian Legislative Council elected in January 1996, as part of interim self-governing arrangements in the West Bank and Gaza Strip. A transfer of powers and responsibilities for the Gaza Strip and Jericho took place after the May 1994 Cairo Agreement on the Gaza Strip and the Jericho area. Additional areas of the West Bank followed suit. An *intifadah* broke out in September 2000; the resulting widespread violence in the West Bank and Gaza Strip, Israel's military response, and instability in

the Palestinian Authority are undermining progress toward a permanent settlement and contribute to the deterioration of the business environment that would be necessary for the two countries to regain the path towards steady economic growth.

The British withdrew from South Yemen (a protectorate they had created in the nineteenth century around the southern port of Aden) on 30 November 1967. Three years later, the southern government adopted a Marxist orientation. The massive exodus of hundreds of thousands of Yemenis from the south to the north (which had become independent from the Ottoman empire in 1918) contributed to two decades of hostility between the two states. The two countries were formally unified as the Republic of Yemen on 22 May 1990. A southern military bid to break away from the Union was defeated by the north in 1994.

These are just some examples of the political, military, and social conflicts that have plagued the Arab world during the last several decades. This kind of instability has direct implications on the level of income through destruction of productive capacity, but instability also has longer-term consequences, because it does not help create the business environment necessary for any economy to prosper. These conflicts have certainly deterred investment and slowed the process of economic growth and development in the Arab world.

Business environment

The weak business environment of the Arab region acts as another important constraint to the process of economic growth. Of course, the social and military conflicts that we described in the previous section contribute to the continued deterioration of the business environment. But violence is not the only problem. Potential investors in many Arab countries face a suffocating web of complex regulations, licensing, and other institutional obstacles that are often unclear and usually inconsistent with the rules that apply in the rest of the world. Most private investors are scared away by such cumbersome processes, and this leads to less entry and competition. This lack of competition, in turn, leads to a more inefficient and less innovative economic system.

Those investors not deterred by such opaque system participate in it at a very high cost. Egyptian entrepreneurs spend close to 35 percent of their time solving problems related to government regulation. Even Morocco (a country that has liberalized its economy more than its Arab neighbors) requires more than twenty documents and more than six months to register a new business. The easy way around the complicated bureaucratic process is often bribery, local corruption, and unhealthy incest-like relations between family-owned businesses and political power. Needless to say, this causes further deterioration in competition and the business environment.

Privatization and the separation of business and politics need to be a priority in the Arab world. Countries with large and inefficient public sectors (such as Algeria and Egypt) will, first, have to sell state-owned money-losing enterprises and, second, attract private investment by deregulating and lowering political and institutional barriers of all kinds. The evidence shows that there is no shortage of funding for privatization in the region. But there is a bottleneck in the inefficient banking system and the small or inexistent debt markets and stock exchanges. Countries with less burdensome public enterprise systems (such as Jordan, Lebanon, Morocco, Tunisia, and some Gulf countries) will have to concentrate on the second strategy—the reduction of excessive regulation, licensing requirements, and bureaucratic barriers that impede the normal process of business investment. Finally, an equitable, well-functioning legal system (including an effective judiciary) that supervises the economic process and guarantees transparency and justice is also critical in promoting economic investment and growth.

Human capital

Another important explanation for the lack of incentives for private businesses to invest in the Arab world is the low quality of human capital. The literature has emphasized the importance of human capital in the process of economic growth and development. Moreover, authors emphasize the complementarity between human and physical capital investment: if potential investors cannot hire a highly qualified and trained labor force, their investments will not deliver profits. It follows that investment in physical capital will not take place in economies with low-quality human capital.

Despite some improvements over the last two decades, enrollment rates in the Arab world remain well below that of the industrial countries: primary school enrollment remains

below 85 percent (compared to 100 percent in the OECD),[7] secondary school enrollment remains below just above 50 percent (again close to 100 percent in the OECD), and tertiary school enrollment remains below 15 percent (over 60 percent in the OECD).

But apart from low enrollments, perhaps the most important problem with human capital in the Arab world is the low quality of the education system and the fact that education remains unconnected to the needs of productive firms. An empirical confirmation of this fact is that in the Arab world, the educated suffer from high unemployment rates and declining real wages; the education system fails to teach Arab citizens how to adapt to a dynamic world of rapid technical change. The Arab education system does not prepare students for today's global world of knowledge and information technologies.

According to the International Telecommunication Union (ITU) (2001), the penetration of both computers and Internet access in the Arab world is small relative to that of east Asia and the OECD (see Figure 11). One possible reason, of course, is that prices are higher in the Arab world. For example, the ITU reports that off-peak Internet access costs close to US$35 per month in the Arab world, whereas the average cost is less than US$23 in the OECD and about US$13 in east Asia. The cost in the United States is less than US$7, whereas in Yemen, Internet access costs US$45, more than six times more. Another possible

Figure 11. Access to New Technologies

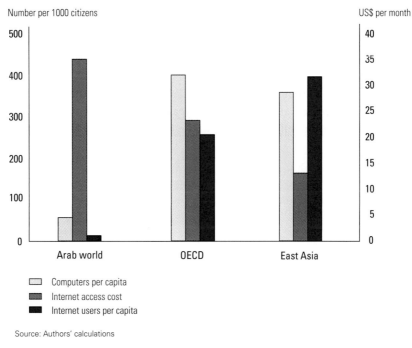

Source: Authors' calculations

reason for the low penetration of the Internet and computers is, of course, that people in the Arab world are not as trained to use new technologies as are people in the industrial nations.

The education system should be reformed so that students are not made to "learn things" but are taught "how" to learn. Only if future workers learn how to adapt in a changing technological and business environment will firms feel confident in the human capital of a nation. The reforms must bring together the education sector, the government, and the private business sector. Close coordination between firms and schools and universities is needed if education has to provide useful and productive services to the workers of the future.

The introduction of new technologies provides a unique chance for the Arab world to catch up, as it allows the countries to bypass old problems that have strangled the traditional sectors. In order to take advantage of the opportunities provided by the information technologies, these need to be introduced without the monopolistic and highly distorted structures that characterize other sectors. Interest groups may make it harder to reform old sectors than to introduce the right structures in new sectors. However, the chance to introduce the right structures is an opportunity not to be missed.

Conclusions

The Arab world has suffered a twenty-year growth slowdown. The decline in the investment rate in the region is probably a consequence, not a cause, of this slowdown. By international and historical standards investment has remained high, but this has not translated into higher growth rates. The reason is that what matters for growth is not the quantity of investment, but its quality. We have argued that there are two broad explanations for this "missing growth." First, too large a fraction of overall investment has been unproductive public investment. Second, the environment for private investment has been hostile for at least three reasons: (1) excessive political, social, and military conflicts throughout the region; (2) excessive government intervention, protection, and regulation (which suffocates the business environment and makes private investment expensive and, therefore, uncompetitive); and (3) inadequate human capital.

References

Bisat, Amer, Mohammed A. El-Erian, and Thomas Helbing. "Growth, Investment, and Savings in the Arab Economies." IMF working paper, 1997.

Capital Intelligence Unit. "National Banking Environment." 2001. Various issues for Jordan, Oman, Yemen, Bahrain, Qatar, Saudi Arabia, Tunisia, Egypt, the United Arab Emirates, Kuwait, Lebanon, and Morocco.

Demirguc-Kunt, Asli, and Ross Levine, eds. *Financial Structure and Economic Growth: A Cross-Country Comparison of Banks, Markets, and Development.* Cambridge, MA: MIT Press, December 2001.

Easterly, William, Michael Kremer, Lant Pritchett, and Lawrence H. Summers. "Good Policy or Good Luck? Country Growth Performance and Temporary Shocks." *Journal of Monetary Economics* 32,3(1993): 459–483.

Easterly, William, and Ross Levine. "It's Not Factor Accumulation: Stylized Facts and Growth Models." *World Bank Economic Review* (2001).

Doppelhoffer, G.,R. Miller, and X. Sala-i-Martin. "The Determinants of Economic Growth: A Bayesian Averaging of Classical Estimates (BACE) Approach." Mimeograph. Columbia University, August 2002. Forthcoming *American Economic Review* (2002).

Heston, A.R., Summers, and B. Aten. Penn World Table Version 6.0. Center for International Comparisons. University of Pennsylvania (CICUP), December 2001.

International Telecommunication Union. "World Telecommunication Development Report, 2001." ITU 2001.

Ravallion, M., Datt, G., and D. van de Walle. "Qualifying Absolute Poverty in the Developing World." *Review of Income and Wealth* 37 (1991):345–361.

Sala-i-Martin, Xavier. "Estimating Poverty Rates, Inequality, and the World Distribution of Income from Individual Country Distributions: 1970–1998." Mimeograph. Columbia University, March 2002.

Solow, R. "A Contribution to the Theory of Economic Growth." *Quarterly Journal of Economics* February (1956).

Swan, T.W. "Economic Growth and Capital Accumulation." *Economic Record,* 1956.

United Nations Development Program. The Arab Human Development Report. New York. 2002.

World Bank. *Claiming the Future: Choosing Prosperity in the Middle East and North Africa.* October 1995.

Endnotes

1. Arab world GDP per capita is constructed by aggregating World Bank or Heston et al. (2001) PPP-adjusted GDP data for each country and dividing it by aggregate population. Since the data are measured in PPP-adjusted units, it is strictly comparable across countries and, therefore, can in principle be aggregated. The countries used to construct this measure of Arab world GDP are: Algeria, Egypt, Kuwait, Oman, Saudi Arabia, Mauritania, Morocco, Syria, Tunisia, Comoros, and Jordan. Lebanon, Libya, the West Bank and Gaza Strip, Bahrain, Qatar, the U.A.E., Iraq, and Yemen have been excluded because of data limitations. For example, there is very little information available on the performance of the U.A.E. economy. In fact, the Central Bank published price-adjusted real GDP figures for the first time in 2000. Iraq's GDP data "disappeared" after the Gulf War.

2. Due to data availbility, only the following countries were included in the "oil producers" category: Algeria, Egypt, Kuwait, Oman, and Saudi Arabia. .

3. The original definition of absolute is attributed to Ravallion et al. (1991). These researchers used "perceptions of poverty" in the poorest countries to place the poverty line at US$31 per month. Later, the definition was changed to US$30.42, and it then was modified to US$1/day. The US$1/day poverty line was later adopted by the World Bank as the "official" definition of "absolute poverty." Another poverty line appeared in the literature that doubled the original figure to US$2/day. We use both definitions in this paper.

4. Again, there is substantial heterogeneity within the Arab world: the ratio for Morocco is seven whereas that for Tunisia is four. Both countries' ratios are close to those of the OECD and east Asia.

5. See Demirguc-Kunt et al. (2001) for an empirical and theoretical documentation and discussion of the negative impact that an underdeveloped financial system may have on growth.

6. The productivity estimates are our own, but they are similar to those estimated by other researchers and analysts, such as UNDP (2002) and Bisat et al. (1997).

7. In fact, primary school enrollment ratios in the Arab world are lower than those of the developing world as a whole.

The Arab Population

United Nations Population Fund (UNFPA)*

Acronyms and Abbreviations

AEGR — Average Economic Growth Rate

CCA — Common Country Assessment

CEDAW — Convention on The Elimination of All Forms of Discrimination Against Women

DHS — Demographic and Health Surveys

EMRO — East Mediterranean Regional Office of WHO

FGM — Female Genital Mutilation (also used as FGC)

FGC — Female Genital Cutting

GDP — Gross Domestic Product

GNP — Gross National Product

HIV/AIDS — Human Immunodeficiency Virus/ Acquired Immune Deficiency Syndrome

ICPD — International Conference on Population and Development

IDU — Intravenous Drug Users

IEC — Information, Education and Communication

IMR — Infant Mortality Rate

IUD — Intrauterine Device

JCGP — Joint Consultative Group on Policy

KAP — Knowledge, Attitudes and Practice

LBW — Low Birth Weight

MENA — Middle East and North Africa

MMR — Maternal Mortality Ratio

MSM — Male's Sex With Males

NGO — Nongovernmental Organization

OPT — Occupied Palestinian Territory

PAPCHILD — Pan Arab Project for Child and Maternal Development

RTIs — Reproductive Tract Infections

STIs — Sexually Transmitted Infections

SVAW — Sexual Violence Against Women

TBAs — Traditional Birth Attendants (DAYYATS)

UN — United Nations

UNAIDS — Joint United Nations Programme on HIV/AIDS

UNDAF — United Nations Development Assistance Framework

UNDP — United Nations Development Programme

UNESCWA (ESCWA) — United Nations Economic and Social Commission for Western Asia

UNFPA — United Nations Population Fund

UNICEF — United Nations Children's Fund

WHO — World Health Organization

WFS — World Fertility Survey

TFR — Total Fertility Rate (number of children born per woman)

Background

The Arab world is the cradle of civilization, witness to the rise of a number of kingdoms; one of the first was the Saba'a Kingdom in the South Arabian Peninsula (i.e., the Kingdom of Sheba in Yemen). Migrations in the area were dictated by periods of drought, with flows of people moving up along the Red Sea to the north of the Arabian Peninsula and North Africa, and down the Arabian sea to East Africa, south and east Asia, and up the Gulf.

The Babylonians in Iraq and Pharaohs in Egypt established great and durable civilizations in the region. For a long time, these civilizations had a significant role in the shaping of the political map of the region—up until Greek, Roman, and Persian civilizations replaced them; meanwhile, small Arab kingdoms with limited power emerged in between the two empires of Rome and Persia. It was at this time that Islam emerged, unifying the entire region and expanding in all directions: north and west to Europe, south in Africa, and east in South and Southeast Asia.

Under Islam, which, *inter alia,* mandated continuous education for both males and females, both Muslim and non-Muslim populations made advances in literature, the humanities, medicine and surgery, optics, navigation, chemistry, physics and algebra, and science and technology. The Arab world, through the Silk Road, a trading route that facilitated both commerce and the transfer of knowledge, was the link between Asia, Africa, and Europe.

*UNFPA Country Technical Services Team for Arab States (CST) Amman, Jordan

Currently, the Arab populations together number about 287 million, which constitutes about 5 percent of the global population. In general, most of the countries of the region are socially, culturally, linguistically, and demographically similar. Commonalities include high rates of marriage, a predominantly young age at marriage followed almost immediately by pregnancies that are too closely spaced; relatively high population growth rates; a large, young population; and, consequently, a high burden of dependency. High rates of illiteracy, particularly among women, are common. Also common is anemia related to pregnancy, including iron-deficiency, nutritional anemia, and protein energy anemia. The high reproductive patterns (summarized by early marriage, immediate pregnancy, closely spaced pregnancies, and anemia) usually lead to maternal depletion (from frequent deliveries) and spontaneous abortions, premature deliveries and/or underweight babies, and children with stunting and wasting. These in turn, lead to high infant, child, and maternal morbidity (i.e., illness or injury related to pregnancy or childbirth).

There are also differences between the Arab countries and populations. These include varied levels of development, unemployment, urbanization, per capita income, and population distribution and growth rates. In addition, Arab countries also vary greatly in what they perceive as their population problems, and on what population policies or strategies are needed to solve or mitigate these problems and attain sustainable human development.

In his 1973 theory of epidemiological transition, Abdul-Rahim Omran[1] explained demographic transitions in the Arab World. According to Omran, mortality is the major trigger of population change while fertility is a modifying factor. Omran argued that populations pass through three stages during the transition from high to low mortality and fertility, which are as follows.

1. **The Age of Pestilence and Famine**, where both mortality and fertility fluctuate at high levels due to frequent epidemics and crop failures caused by nature or civil wars and lack of order. These factors cause widespread infections and famine, low standards of living, and short life expectancies of thirty to forty years of age. Living examples of this stage are the Iraqi (due to sanctions) and Somali populations, each of which lost the majority of its age five and younger population to famine and infections. The remaining under-five population is threatened by long-lasting consequences, including stunting and wasting, which affect their general well-being and future learning capabilities.

2. **The Age of Receding Pandemics**, which follows the availability of health services including preventive medicine such as vaccinations and improved nutrition, particularly for women and children. This leads to a continuous decline in mortality while fertility remains at a high level or temporarily increases. As a result, life expectancy improves, ranging from fifty to more than sixty years as compared to thirty to forty years of age in the Age of Pestilence and Famine, and population growth rates increase. Many Arab countries are currently passing through this stage, while others have passed to the next stage.

3. **The Age of Degenerative and Man-Made Diseases**, which is associated with aging and industrial development such as stress and stress-related diseases, radiation injuries, cancers due to food additives, and environmental degradation and exposure to industrial and chemical waste leading to induced gene mutations. Fertility is relatively low and populations continue to grow, but at a low rate. The Gulf states are currently in this stage.

All societies usually pass through the above-mentioned process of demographic transition. However, the pace of change differs for each society, placing them at different points in the transitions. Consequently, the following general models have evolved:

1. **The Classical Model**, which accompanied the Industrial Revolution in Europe, extended over a long period of time and resulted in a substantive decrease in mortality and fertility (particularly in France, where fertility decline preceded mortality decline). Mortality (death) rates reached below 10 per 1,000 people and birth rates reached below 20 per 1,000 people;

2. **The Accelerated Model**, where emphasis was put on family planning services along with health services both preventive and curative. Consequently, both fertility and mortality declined at fast rates. Examples of this model are Japan and countries in Eastern Europe. Countries in Eastern Europe also resorted to induced abortions; and

3. **The Delayed Model**, which is currently taking place in developing countries. Mortality declines started after World War II, while fertility declines started much later, with only a few exceptions. The Arab countries belong to this model; there are high population growth rates due to the widening gap between high fertility and declining mortality. Such increasing growth rates are higher than the rate of economic development; thus, growth rates threaten

the living standards of the people. Being aware of this situation, Arab countries are increasingly adopting population policies and programs to bring about a balance between population growth, sustainable development, and the protection of the environment.

The Demographic Profile of the Arab Populations

Population growth

In the mid-twentieth century, the total population of the Arab region was estimated at about 76 million; this increased by an average annual growth rate of 2.5 percent, to reach more than 144 million in 1975 (almost doubling in twenty five years). The growth rate had increased to 2.7 percent between 1975 and 2000, and in 2000 the total population was estimated at about 284 million.

The population growth rate of 2.7 percent during the second half of the last century was very high compared to the world rate of less than 2 percent for the same period. This substantial population increase was a direct result of the effective lowering of mortality rates coupled with a young population and sustained high fertility patterns. Prompted by great political changes in the Arab region and lessons from the experience of the Western world that emphasized good health in general and control of mortality, Arab countries took measures aimed at raising the standard of living of their populations during the post–World War II period. Health, in general, and control of mortality were the primary foci of action. The United Nations (UN), working with specialized organizations such as the World Health Organization (WHO), facilitated the transfer of knowledge and resources that were first used to reduce mortality. Such declines were initiated and accelerated by progress in medicine (such as the use of antibiotics) as well as through national programs targeting infectious and parasitic diseases (and promoting the use of insecticides). The WHO was a leading agency in the initiation and implementation of such programs. Mortality levels of infants, children, women, and the population at large irreversibly declined; this resulted in a widening gap between the birth rate and the death rate and caused an accelerated population growth. By the late 1970s, the crude birth rate was about 42 births per 1,000 people (or more than 6 million births per year) and the crude death rate was 12.2 per 1,000 (1.8 million deaths per year), a net increase of more than 4 million people a year.

It is expected that the birth rate, and consequently the growth rate, will continue to be high in the twenty-first century. However, these rates are likely to decline due to social and economic changes that have resulted the increased use of contraceptives, among which is the improvement and expansion of the education of women and the population at large, empowerment of women, and male involvement in reproductive health. Accordingly, the average annual rate of population growth will decline for the first quarter to 2 percent. Between 2025 and 2050 it will decline to 1.3 percent, reaching a total population of about 470 million in 2025 and 654 million by mid-century.

Arab countries have realized that there are impressive gains to be had from improving health services and combating mortality. Crude death rates declined from 16.6 per 1,000 in the 1970s to 12.2 per 1,000 in the 1980s and 9.2 per 1,000 in the 1990s. This decline reached 8.9 per 1,000 in 1998 and is expected to continue its decline to 7.1 per 1,000 in the first decade of the twenty-first century. Currently, life expectancy in the Arab world ranges from a high of 74.9 and 79.3 years for males and females, respectively in Kuwait to as low as 39.4 and 41.6 for males and females, respectively in Djibouti. In terms of numbers of deaths, this leveled at about 11 million per decade for the 1980s and 1990s, and it is expected that this number will remain unchanged during the first decade of the twenty-first century.

Improvements in health services have led to an increase in life expectancy from 49.8 years in the 1970s to 57 years in the 1980s, 61.8 years in 1990, and 66 years in 2000. These reductions in numbers of deaths contributed to a substantial increase in population. With further improvements in health services, mortality rates will continue to decline, particularly in countries with high mortality rates like Djibouti (16.4), Somalia (18.1), Sudan (14.4), Mauritania (17.5), and Yemen (13.9). Unless balanced by effective family planning programs, declines in mortality rates will trigger high population growth rates and further population increases in these countries.

Because the health focus has been on prevention of diseases, sizable resources were not required to reduce rates of mortality. Reduced mortality rates were also achieved without significant improvements in populations' standard of living. Reducing mortality in the population at large, but particularly among infants, children, and women, was a universal aim—people reacted positively to preventive measures such as vaccination, which had a significant impact on the control of infectious diseases.

Post–World War II, mortality declines accelerated, and the improvement of women's health conditions caused some increase in the already high fertility levels in the region. This resulted in an additional increase in the rate of natural increase, causing the overall population growth to rise from 2.5 to 2.7 percent between 1950 and 1975, and between 1975 and 2000. However, in some countries, such as Tunisia, Egypt, Algeria, and Morocco among others, this rate could have been higher if there had been no initiatives to reduce fertility through nation-wide family planning programs.

The high population of youth also plays a crucial role in population growth. In the 1980s, those aged younger than fifteen years accounted for about 47 percent of the total population. More than 77 million in number, these people were well into their reproductive years by the mid-1990s. The population of youth numbered more than 100 million in the 1990s, and it is anticipated that for the first decade of the 2000s the number of those aged younger than fifteen years will be around 130 million.

An examination of the population pyramid or the age and sex distribution of the population reveals that, annually, the number of people entering their reproductive years is many times that of those completing their reproductive life. Consequently, in societies where marriage is almost universal and at a young age, the number of couples will continue to increase geometrically. This is referred to as "population momentum." It is worth noting that even if all these couples elected to produce on average of only 2.1 children per couple, which is considered a replacement level, the population would continue to grow simply because of the population momentum. To illustrate this, some 37 million women were in

Table 1. Population Size and Percentage Distribution by Subregion and Period

Subregion		Population Size (000)				
		1950	1975	2000	2025*	2050*
CATEGORY 1: Sudan, Comoros, Djibouti, Egypt, Somalia	F	33,523	60,168	109,096	167,653	221,274
	%	44	42	38	36	34
CATEGORY 2: Algeria, Morocco, Libya, Tunisia, Mauritania	F	23,089	42,808	77,583	111,407	134,038
	%	30	30	27	24	20
CATEGORY 3: Iraq, Jordan, O.P.T., Lebanon, Syrian AR	F	11,573	24,416.8	50,736	88,100	118,468
	%	15	17	18	19	18
CATEGORY 4: Bahrain, Kuwait, Oman, Qatar, Saudi Arabia, U.A.E. and Yemen, Rep.	F	8,337	17,077	46,959	102,418	180,362
	%	11	12	17	22	28
TOTAL	F	76,522	144,470	284,372	469,578	654,142
	%	100	100	100	100	100

Sources: United Nations Population Division. World Population Prospects. 1996, 1998, 2000, New York: UN
*Figures beyond 2001 are estimates based on projections.

Table 2. Annual Population Growth Rates by Period and Subregions

Subregion	Annual Population Growth Rates (in Percent)			
	1950–1975	1975–2000	2000–2025*	2025–2050*
CATEGORY 1: Sudan, Comoros, Djibouti, Egypt, Somalia	1.9	2.0	1.1	0.5
CATEGORY 2: Algeria, Morocco, Libya, Tunisia, Mauritania	2.4	3.0	3.5	2.6
CATEGORY 3: Iraq, Jordan, O.P.T., Lebanon, Syrian AR	3.0	2.9	2.2	1.2
CATEGORY 4: Bahrain, Kuwait, Oman, Qatar, Saudi Arabia, U.A.E. and Yemen, Rep.	2.9	4.0	3.1	2.3
TOTAL	2.5	2.7	2.0	1.3

Sources: United Nations Population Division. World Population Prospects. 1996, 1998, 2000, New York: UN
*Figures beyond 2001 are estimates based on projections.

Table 3. Estimated Population of Arab Countries Between 1950 and 2050 (000)

Country	Population Size				
	1950	1975	2000	2025*	2050*
Algeria	8,753.0	16,018.2	30,291.3	42,737.9	51,179.6
Bahrain	115.6	271.9	639.8	887.3	1,007.8
Comoros	172.7	318.6	705.9	1,326.9	1,900.1
Djibouti	62.0	210.0	632.1	800.9	1,068.0
Egypt	21,834.0	38,841.0	67,884.5	94,776.9	113,839.9
Iraq	5,158.3	11,019.7	22,946.2	40,298.0	53,574.2
Jordan	472.5	1,936.7	4,913.1	8,666.1	11,709.1
Kuwait	152.3	1,006.6	1,914.4	3,219.4	4,001.4
Lebanon	1,442.7	2,767.3	3,496.5	4,580.8	5,017.8
Libya	1,029.0	2,446.0	5,289.7	7,972.1	9,969.3
Mauritania	824.7	1,371.2	2,664.5	6,351.3	8,452.2
Morocco	8,953.0	17,305.0	29,878.4	42,002.1	50,361.2
O.P.T.	1,004.8	1,255.1	3,190.9	7,145.0	11,821.0
Oman	456.4	880.4	2,538.2	5,410.8	8,751.4
Qatar	25.0	171.2	565.4	754.1	830.8
Saudi Arabia	3,201.4	7,251.4	20,346.2	40,472.9	59,682.9
Somalia	2,264.1	4,134.1	8,777.9	21,192.2	40,935.7
Sudan	9,190.0	16,664.3	31,095.2	49,556.1	63,530.2
Syrian AR	3,495.1	7,438.0	16,188.8	27,410.5	36,345.5
Tunisia	3,529.6	5,667.5	9,458.7	12,343.1	14,075.8
U.A.E.	69.9	504.8	2,606.0	3,467.6	3,709.2
Yemen, Rep.	4,316.0	6,990.8	18,348.7	48,205.8	102,378.5
Total	**76,522.1**	**144,469.8**	**284,372.4**	**469,577.8**	**654,141.6**

Sources: United Nations Population Division. World Population Prospects. 1996, 1998, 2000, New York: UN
*Figures beyond 2001 are estimates based on projections.

Table 4. Distribution of Population in the Arab Region (in Percent)

Country	Distribution				
	1950	1975	2000	2025*	2050*
Algeria	11.4	11.1	10.7	9.1	7.8
Bahrain	0.2	0.2	0.2	0.2	0.2
Comoros	0.2	0.2	0.2	0.3	0.3
Djibouti	0.1	0.1	0.2	0.2	0.2
Egypt	28.5	26.9	23.9	20.2	17.4
Iraq	6.7	7.6	8.1	8.6	8.2
Jordan	0.6	1.3	1.7	1.8	1.8
Kuwait	0.2	0.7	0.7	0.7	0.6
Lebanon	1.9	1.9	1.2	1.0	0.8
Libya	1.3	1.7	1.9	1.7	1.5
Mauritania	1.1	0.9	0.9	1.4	1.3
Morocco	11.7	12.0	10.5	8.9	7.7
O.P.T.	1.3	0.9	1.1	1.5	1.8
Oman	0.6	0.6	0.9	1.2	1.3
Qatar	0.0	0.1	0.2	0.2	0.1
Saudi Arabia	4.2	5.0	7.2	8.6	9.1
Somalia	3.0	2.9	3.1	4.5	6.3
Sudan	12.0	11.5	10.9	10.6	9.7
Syrian AR	4.6	5.1	5.7	5.8	5.6
Tunisia	4.6	3.9	3.3	2.6	2.2
U.A.E.	0.1	0.3	0.9	0.7	0.6
Yemen, Rep.	5.6	4.8	6.5	10.3	15.7
Total	**100.0**	**100.0**	**100.0**	**100.0**	**100.0**

Sources: United Nations Population Division. World Population Prospects. 1996, 1998, 2000, New York: UN
*Figures beyond 2001 are estimates based on projections.

their reproductive years (i.e., aged fifteen to forty-nine) in 1980. This number reached 50 million in 1990 and 69 million by the year 2000. This number will continue to grow for years to come, particularly since the median age in the Arab world was 18 years of age in 1980, increased slightly to 18.4 years in 1990, and was 19.5 years by the year 2000.

With the decrease of fertility rates and population growth rates, it is expected to take longer for the Arab population to double. According to the prevailing rate between 1975 and 1980, it was estimated that the Arab population would double in twenty-two years. This duration for doubling had increased to thirty years by 2000, and is expected to reach forty-three years by the year 2025 and sixty-three years by 2050. However, in seven countries, the 1990 Arab population would double in twenty years or less. These figures are especially alarming when noting the limited carrying capacity of the land, the scarcity of water resources, and the decreasing areas of arable land, primarily due to population encroachment.

Population distribution

The Arab region, which is comprised of twenty-two countries, extends from the Arab Gulf in the east to the Atlantic ocean in the west. The total area is estimated at 14 million square kilometers. All Arab countries are members of the League of Arab States. Geographically, Arab countries can be grouped into four categories. These are:

a. The Nile Valley and the African Horn, which consists of Egypt, Sudan, Somalia, Djibouti, and Comoros;

Table 5. Estimated Annual Growth Rates of Arab Countries, 1950–2050 (in Percent)

Country	Annual Rate of Population Growth				
	1950–1955	1975–1980	2000–2005*	2025–2030*	2045–2050*
Algeria	2.1	3.1	1.8	1.0	0.5
Bahrain	2.9	4.9	1.7	0.8	0.4
Comoros	2.3	3.9	2.9	1.8	1.2
Djibouti	2.0	8.6	1.0	1.4	0.9
Egypt	2.5	2.4	1.7	1.0	0.5
Iraq	2.7	3.2	2.7	1.3	1.0
Jordan	6.9	2.8	2.8	1.5	1.0
Kuwait	5.4	6.2	2.6	1.1	0.6
Lebanon	2.2	-.07	1.6	0.6	0.1
Libya	1.8	4.4	2.2	1.2	0.6
Mauritania	1.8	2.5	3.0	2.4	1.3
O.P.T.	0.7	3.2	3.6	2.6	1.4
Oman	1.9	5.0	3.3	2.4	1.4
Qatar	6.7	5.8	1.5	0.6	0.3
Saudi Arabia	2.3	5.6	3.1	2.0	1.2
Somalia	2.2	9.0	4.2	3.0	2.2
Sudan	2.0	3.0	2.3	1.2	0.8
Syrian AR	2.5	3.1	2.5	1.3	0.8
Tunisia	1.8	2.6	1.1	0.7	0.3
U.A.E.	2.5	14.0	1.7	0.5	0.1
Yemen, Rep.	1.8	3.2	4.1	3.5	2.5
Total	**2.3**	**3.2**	**2.3**	**1.6**	**1.1**

Sources: United Nations Population Division. World Population Prospects. 1996, 1998, 2000, New York: UN
*Figures beyond 2001 are estimates based on projections.

b. North Africa, which includes Libya, Tunisia, Algeria, Morocco, and Mauritania;

c. Al-Hilal Al-Khasib (the Fertile Crescent), which covers Iraq, Syrian AR, Jordan, Lebanon, and the Occupied Palestinian Territory (O.P.T.); and

d. The Arab Peninsula and the Arab Gulf states, which are Saudi Arabia, Yemen, Oman, United Arab Emirates (U.A.E.), Qatar, Bahrain, and Kuwait.

According to year 2000 population estimates, the population of the first category was about 109 million, or 38 percent of the total Arab population. Countries in the first category have been in a declining trend; in 1950, the populations were 44 percent of the total, and it is expected that by the middle of the twenty-first century it will decline to 34 percent. In the year 2000, the North Africa group comprised about one-fourth (27 percent) of the Arab population. The trend for this group also indicates a decline, going from 30 percent in 1950 to a projected 20 percent in 2050). Countries of Al-Hilal Al-Khasib and those of the Arabian Peninsula and the Gulf together make up the total, with almost equal proportions (17 to 18 percent each). While population increases in Al-Hilal Al-Khasib were moderate in the twentieth century, in fifty years the population will remain at the same level. On the other hand, the declines in the proportion of the total population of the first two categories were compensated by the increase in the populations of the Arabian Peninsula and the Gulf (from 11 percent in 1950 to 28 percent in 2050).

Egypt, the largest country in the Arab world, had the largest population—about 28 percent of the 1950 total. Algeria, Sudan, and Morocco were the second largest in population size, with 11 to 12 percent each; followed by Iraq (about 7 percent); then Yemen, Tunisia, Syrian AR, and Saudi Arabia with 5 to 6 percent each. Lebanon, Jordan, Libya, Mauritania, and the O.P.T. together were about 7 percent, while Bahrain, Comoros, Djibouti, Qatar, and U.A.E. constituted less than 1 percent altogether.

Population growth rates increased in all Arab countries, but variations in mortality declines, sustained high fertility, and international migration (i.e., reasons behind the widening gap between birth and death rates) caused the population of some Arab countries to grow at faster rates than others. In most countries, the growth rate had increased during the early 1950s and/or late 1970s. Generally, the annual growth rates that prevailed in the early 1950s for most countries were about 2 percent or higher, with the exception of the O.P.T., where the rate was less than 1 percent. This was due to forced migration to Jordan (and was reflected in the high population growth rate of Jordan). Immigration, in addition to natural growth, caused the population to grow faster in Bahrain, Djibouti, Saudi Arabia, Qatar, U.A.E., Oman, and Kuwait. The decade of the 1970s, which saw a marked rise in oil prices, had the highest growth in population of the Gulf countries due to immigration.

High growth rates during the last quarter of the last century prevailed in Bahrain, Comoros, Djibouti, Iraq, Jordan, Kuwait, Oman, Saudi Arabia, Somalia, U.A.E., and Yemen. By the end of the twentieth century, the total population was estimated at 284 million. The population share each of Egypt, Algeria, Sudan, Tunisia, and Lebanon declined to about 24, 11, 11, 3, and 1 percent, respectively. These percentages are expected to decline further by the

Table 6. Trends of Age Structure of the Arab Region, 1950–2050 (in Percent)

Age Group	Distribution				
	1950	1975	2000	2025*	2050*
0–14	41.6	44.6	38.4	30.5	24.9
15–59	52.7	50.0	56.0	60.6	60.0
60 +	5.7	5.4	5.6	8.9	15.1
Total	**100.0**	**100.0**	**100.0**	**100.0**	**100.0**

Source: United Nations Population Division. The Sex and Age Distribution of the World Population, 1996 Revision. New York: UN, 1997

*Figures beyond 2001 are estimates based on projections.

middle of the twenty-first century. By that time, Egypt is expected to be less than one-fifth (17 percent) of the total, Algeria 7.8 percent, and Sudan 9.7 percent. Tunisia is projected to be about 2 percent of the total and Lebanon less than 1 percent.

Age structure

There have been changes to the age structure of the population of the Arab world at large since the middle of the last century. It is expected to continue to change due to the demographic transition (i.e., the Delayed Model), which started in some countries earlier than others. Mortality rates started declining after 1950, while fertility rates continued to increase or remain high. Consequently, the proportion of the population aged younger than fifteen increased. This increase was accompanied by a decrease in the population who were of working age and of those of older age. In some of the oil countries, however, the proportion of the population of working age had increased due to the immigration of workers; they were propelled by the increase in oil prices, which was followed by economic growth.

Table 7a. Trends of Population Age Structure in Arab Countries, Ages 0–14 (in Percent)

Country	Ages 0–14				
	1950	1975	2000	2025*	2050*
Algeria	40.1	47.6	34.8	23.6	19.7
Bahrain	42.3	43.0	28.2	20.3	18.2
Comoros	43.5	47.4	43.0	35.0	23.8
Djibouti	46.8	43.6	43.2	40.7	28.1
Egypt	39.7	40.0	35.4	24.1	20.1
Iraq	45.7	46.6	41.6	31.2	22.5
Jordan	45.7	47.2	40.0	30.8	22.5
Kuwait	36.1	44.4	31.3	22.9	19.7
Lebanon	34.2	41.2	31.1	21.3	17.5
Libya	41.9	46.0	33.9	24.1	20.1
Mauritania	41.7	43.3	44.1	40.3	27.2
Morocco	44.4	47.2	34.7	23.8	20.1
O.P.T.	45.7	46.1	46.4	39.3	26.7
Oman	42.3	44.3	44.1	38.8	26.8
Qatar	42.3	33.4	26.7	21.2	19.8
Saudi Arabia	42.0	44.3	42.9	35.1	23.1
Somalia	41.2	46.0	48.0	45.9	36.3
Sudan	43.8	44.6	40.1	30.7	22.7
Syrian AR	41.4	48.5	40.8	28.6	21.8
Tunisia	38.9	43.8	29.7	22.8	19.6
U.A.E.	42.3	28.2	26.0	19.5	18.6
Yemen, Rep.	42.3	50.9	50.1	46.7	37.0
Total	**41.2**	**44.2**	**38.9**	**31.2**	**25.3**

Source: United Nations Population Division. The Sex and Age Distribution of the World Population, 1996 Revision. New York: UN, 1997

*Figures beyond 2001 are estimates based on projections.

Table 7b. Trends in the Population Age Structure in Arab Countries, Ages 15–59 (in Percent)

Country	Ages 15–59				
	1950	1975	2000	2025*	2050*
Algeria	53.1	46.3	59.1	65.3	58.1
Bahrain	53.1	53.4	67.1	59.3	56.9
Comoros	51.1	48.3	52.8	59.4	64.0
Djibouti	49.8	53.0	51.2	53.1	66.1
Egypt	55.2	53.5	58.3	64.4	59.1
Iraq	49.9	49.3	53.8	61.3	62.4
Jordan	46.9	48.5	55.4	62.2	61.9
Kuwait	59.4	53.0	64.3	61.4	54.7
Lebanon	55.4	51.3	60.3	65.2	57.1
Libya	50.8	50.2	60.6	66.0	58.7
Mauritania	53.6	51.8	51.1	54.3	63.8
Morocco	51.0	47.6	59.0	65.0	59.3
O.P.T.	46.9	49.0	48.7	55.0	63.3
Oman	52.7	51.3	51.7	54.6	62.7
Qatar	52.1	63.5	70.2	57.1	59.5
Saudi Arabia	52.4	50.9	52.3	57.0	64.0
Somalia	54.1	49.1	48.1	50.2	58.0
Sudan	50.9	50.8	54.4	61.4	62.9
Syrian AR	51.7	46.2	54.4	63.7	60.2
Tunisia	53.1	50.4	61.9	63.7	55.9
U.A.E.	52.1	68.4	68.9	56.9	54.8
Yemen, Rep.	51.5	44.7	46.3	49.6	57.7
Total	**52.9**	**50.3**	**55.6**	**60.1**	**60.1**

Source: United Nations Population Division. The Sex and Age Distribution of the World Population, 1996 Revision. New York: UN, 1997

*Figures beyond 2001 are estimates based on projections.

Generally, fertility rates (number of children born per woman) started to decline as early as the late 1960s and 1970s in a few Arab countries, while an observed decline actually started in most countries in the 1980s. This decline caused an increase in the proportion of the population who were of working age. Using countries that completed the demographic transition as examples, it can be concluded that once fertility rates decline, the decline will continue as couples continue to have less children in order to hold on to the advantages gained from a smaller family unit. Thus it is expected that the fertility rates of the Arab world will continue to decline, with variable pace among the countries. Consequently, the proportion of children younger than age fifteen will start to decline, eventually reaching only about one-quarter of the total population, while the proportion of older-aged population will increase significantly to about 15 percent (about three times the current proportion). Therefore, there will be an aging problem in the Arab world, despite the postponement caused by delays in fertility decline compared to other regions.

Changes in the age structure of the Arab population have an impact on dependency levels. While the third quarter of the last century saw an increase in the dependency ratio due to declining mortality and high fertility rates, this ratio started to decrease in the last quarter due to fertility declines. This decline is expected to continue during the first quarter of the twenty-first century; after that it should level off or increase slightly. Increase in numbers and proportion of the elderly is expected to offset the decline in the number of children.

In 2000, only a few countries in the region had a proportion of children of less than one-third of the total population. Of these countries, only two (Lebanon and Tunisia) had this proportion because of low fertility. In other countries (Bahrain, Kuwait, Qatar, and U.A.E.), the low proportion of the children to the general population was influenced by immigration. By the year 2025, it is expected that in eight countries (Algeria, Egypt, Iraq, Jordan, Libya, Morocco, Sudan, and Syrian AR), less than one-third of the population will be younger than age fifteen.

Table 7c. Trends in the Population Age Structure of Arab Countries , Age 60+ (in Percent)

Country	Age 60+				
	1950	1975	2000	2025*	2050*
Algeria	6.8	6.1	6.0	11.1	22.2
Bahrain	4.6	3.6	4.7	20.4	24.9
Comoros	5.4	4.3	4.2	5.6	12.2
Djibouti	3.4	3.4	5.5	6.2	5.8
Egypt	5.1	6.5	6.3	11.5	20.8
Iraq	4.3	4.1	4.6	7.5	15.1
Jordan	7.4	4.3	4.5	7.0	15.6
Kuwait	4.5	2.6	4.4	15.7	25.7
Lebanon	10.4	7.5	8.5	13.5	25.4
Libya	7.3	3.7	5.5	9.9	21.1
Mauritania	4.7	5.0	4.7	5.5	8.9
Morocco	4.6	5.2	6.4	11.2	20.6
O.P.T.	7.4	4.9	4.9	5.6	9.9
Oman	5.0	4.4	4.2	6.6	10.5
Qatar	5.7	3.1	3.1	21.8	20.7
Saudi Arabia	5.6	4.8	4.8	7.9	12.9
Somalia	4.6	4.8	3.9	4.0	5.7
Sudan	5.4	4.6	5.5	7.9	14.4
Syrian AR	6.8	5.3	4.7	7.7	18.0
Tunisia	8.0	5.8	8.4	13.4	24.6
U.A.E.	5.7	3.4	5.1	23.6	26.7
Yemen, Rep.	6.2	4.4	3.6	3.6	5.3
Total	5.8	5.4	5.5	8.7	14.7

Source: United Nations Population Division. World Population Ageing. 1996, 1950–2050. New York: UN, 2002
*Figures beyond 2001 are estimates based on projections.

Mortality and fertility

Life expectancy is a powerful summary indicator of mortality of all ages, including infancy and early childhood, as well as old age. The high levels of mortality in almost all Arab countries in the early 1950s were reflected in the low levels of life expectancy. Females were expected to live in the neighborhood of forty years after their birth, while males were expected to live about two years less. Improvement in health conditions in particular, and living conditions in general, had an impact on life expectancy. Most of the countries added about ten years or more to life expectancy during the third quarter of the last century, and an additional ten years in the fourth quarter. Some countries, such as Iraq, Jordan, Oman, U.A.E., Saudi Arabia, and Qatar, added record numbers of years to life expectancy. As most of the countries had attained reasonable levels of mortality declines by the end of the century due to control of infectious and parasitic diseases (with, for example, high rates of vaccination against many infectious diseases), further declines in mortality and increases in life expectancy would require more inputs, but would lead to limited gains. By 2025, it is expected that gains will be around an additional five to seven years, with about half this gain in the next quarter.

Table 8. Trends of Life Expectancy in Arab Countries, by Gender (in Percent)

Country	1950–1955 Female	Male	1975–1980 Female	Male	2000–2005* Female	Male	2025–2030* Female	Male	2045–2050* Female	Male
Algeria	44.2	42.1	58.5	46.5	71.8	68.7	77.7	73.7	80.6	76.3
Bahrain	52.5	49.6	67.8	63.9	76.3	72.1	80.7	76.0	82.7	77.9
Comoros	42.0	39.5	53.0	49.0	62.2	59.4	72.2	69.4	78.0	74.5
Djibouti	34.5	31.5	44.6	41.4	41.6	39.4	48.5	47.5	64.5	62.0
Egypt	43.6	41.2	55.3	52.9	69.9	66.7	76.7	72.7	80.1	75.6
Iraq	44.9	43.1	62.3	60.5	66.5	63.5	76.2	72.4	79.8	75.6
Jordan	44.3	42.2	63.0	59.4	72.5	69.7	78.1	74.5	81.0	76.8
Kuwait	57.5	54.1	71.7	67.5	79.0	74.9	82.1	77.7	83.8	79.3
Lebanon	57.7	54.3	67.0	63.1	75.1	71.9	78.8	75.0	81.4	77.0
Libya	43.9	41.9	59.3	56.0	73.3	69.2	79.1	74.5	81.7	76.5
Mauritania	37.1	34.0	47.1	43.9	54.1	50.9	67.1	63.9	74.1	70.1
Morocco	43.9	41.9	57.5	54.1	70.5	66.8	76.9	72.7	80.3	75.6
O.P.T.	44.3	42.2	62.7	59.0	74.0	70.8	78.4	74.5	81.3	76.8
Oman	37.0	35.8	56.1	53.8	73.2	70.2	77.8	73.9	80.7	76.5
Qatar	49.3	46.7	67.6	63.5	72.1	69.4	78.0	74.2	80.9	76.8
Saudi Arabia	40.7	39.1	59.9	57.6	73.7	71.1	78.9	75.5	81.5	77.5
Somalia	34.5	31.5	43.6	40.4	50.5	47.4	61.0	57.9	69.9	66.7
Sudan	39.1	36.3	48.1	45.3	58.4	55.6	68.7	65.6	74.9	71.0
Syrian AR	47.2	44.8	61.9	58.3	73.1	70.6	78.3	75.0	81.2	77.0
Tunisia	45.1	44.1	60.6	59.6	72.2	69.6	78.1	74.4	81.0	76.7
U.A.E.	49.3	46.7	68.9	64.7	78.4	74.1	81.5	77.2	83.3	78.9
Yemen, Rep.	32.3	32.0	44.4	43.9	62.9	60.7	73.2	69.4	77.6	73.4

Source: United Nations Population Division. The Sex and Age Distribution of the World Population, 1996 Revision. New York: UN, 1997

*Figures beyond 2001 are estimates based on projection.

Despite improvements to the health services made available to the populations of Arab countries and the ensuing reductions in mortality, the crude death rate, infant and child mortality rates and, consequently, the maternal mortality ratio (MMR), remain extremely high. The crude death rate declined from 12.2 per 1,000 people in 1980 to 8.9 per 1,000 in 1998. Some countries experienced a greater decline than others; the decline depended on the level at base year and the age structure, as well as on economic resources. The infant mortality rate was 99 per 1,000 live births in 1980, and this declined to 69 per 1,000 live births in 1990 and 51 per 1,000 live births in the year 2000. Currently, only eight countries in the Arab world have rates of infant mortality below 30 per 1,000 live births, whereas five countries have rates of infant mortality exceeding 80 per 1,000 live births.

MMRs are also high in the Arab world. In addition to various forms of discrimination against women through their life cycle due to gender distribution of status and roles, the main reasons behind the persistently high infant and maternal mortality levels are pregnancies at a young age, pregnancies at a late age, and pregnancies that are too closely spaced. These three factors contribute to increased maternal depletion because there is no chance for the mother to regain

Table 9. Crude Death Rates and Infant Mortality Rates in 1980, 1990, and 2000 (Per 1,000 persons)

Country	Crude Death Rate 1980	1990	2000	Infant Mortality Rate 1980	1990	2000
Algeria	10.4	7.0	5.3	88	61	41
Bahrain	4.5	3.5	3.2	22	12	8
Comoros	—	—	9.0	—	—	67
Djibouti	19.4	16.4	13.8	132	112	94
Egypt	12.7	9.1	6.9	115	57	39
Iraq	8.7	6.7	5.1	77	56	37
Jordan	7.6	5.5	4.3	54	36	25
Kuwait	3.2	2.4	3.0	23	15	10
Lebanon	8.8	7.7	6.3	48	40	29
Libya	10.9	8.2	6.0	97	68	45
Mauritania	20.5	17.5	14.5	137	117	98
Morocco	11.4	8.3	6.2	97	68	45
O.P.T.	—	—	4.0	—	—	21
Oman	13.0	5.8	4.7	60	34	24
Qatar	4.9	4.3	4.6	38	26	19
Saudi Arabia	9.0	6.5	4.9	85	58	39
Somalia	22.3	18.1	15.0	143	122	103
Sudan	17.3	14.4	11.8	118	99	82
Syrian AR	8.6	5.7	4.3	59	39	28
Tunisia	8.5	6.4	5.5	71	44	32
U.A.E.	4.0	3.9	4.7	32	22	16
Yemen, Rep.	18.1	13.9	10.1	134	107	81

Source: United Nations Population Division. World Population Ageing. 1996, 1950–2050. New York: UN, 2002

Table 10. Crude Birth Rates (Per 1,000 Persons) and Total Fertility Rates (Number of Children Per Woman) in 1980, 1990, and 2000

Country	Crude Birth Rate			Total Fertility Rate		
	1980	1990	2000	1980	1990	2000
Algeria	40.6	34.9	30.2	6.4	4.9	3.7
Bahrain	30.9	24.8	19.6	4.6	3.7	2.9
Comoros	—	—	38.0	—	—	5.0
Djibouti	47.7	45.8	44.7	6.6	6.5	6.1
Egypt	39.1	30.8	24.5	5.1	4.0	3.0
Iraq	44.4	40.5	35.5	6.7	5.9	4.9
Jordan	38.2	38.8	32.8	6.8	5.5	4.3
Kuwait	34.6	25.7	21.0	4.9	3.5	2.8
Lebanon	29.3	29.6	23.2	3.8	3.4	2.8
Libya	45.6	43.4	39.7	7.2	6.7	5.8
Mauritania	46.5	46.0	43.8	6.5	6.5	6.2
Morocco	37.3	32.6	24.8	5.4	4.2	3.0
O.P.T.	—	—	39.0	—	—	5.6
Oman	47.7	43.2	40.8	7.2	7.1	6.5
Qatar	34.7	28.4	27.1	5.9	5.3	4.7
Saudi Arabia	43.2	41.8	40.9	7.3	7.1	6.5
Somalia	53.2	46.8	44.9	6.6	6.6	6.1
Sudan	45.9	43.3	39.6	6.6	6.3	5.6
Syrian AR	45.5	42.5	36.9	7.2	6.3	5.0
Tunisia	33.7	27.2	20.6	4.9	3.4	2.5
U.A.E.	26.7	20.3	20.7	5.2	4.3	3.5
Yemen, Rep.	52.7	49.8	43.5	7.7	7.3	6.2

Source: United Nations Population Division. World Population Ageing. 1996, 1950–2050. New York: UN, 2002

her strength and replenish lost protein and minerals; these factors are particularly pertinent since fertility rates have remained at high levels for a long time. The total fertility rate in Arab countries declined to only six children per woman in 1980. This rate declined further to 5.2 children per woman in 1990 and reached just below 4.2 children per woman by the year 2000, which is exactly double the replacement level of about 2.1 children per woman. However, the marital fertility rates are much higher than the total fertility rate. In 1990, there were only four Arab countries with total fertility rates not exceeding four children per woman; the number of such countries reached nine by the year 2000 (Algeria, Bahrain, Egypt, Kuwait, Lebanon, Libya, Morocco, Qatar, Tunisia, and the U.A.E.). On the other hand, the crude birth rate was in the range of 40 per 1,000 for most of the countries in 1980, and it remained at high levels (more than 30 per 1,000) during the following two decades.

Fertility declines were mainly due to the expansion of contraceptive use in a number of countries, while other factors, such as a rise in age at marriage, prevailed in other countries. Modern contraceptive prevalence rates are generally less than actual needs by a minimum of 18 percent. Ten countries have a modern contraceptive prevalence rate of 30 percent or more; only four countries have a modern contraceptive prevalence rate of 50 percent or higher. To reach a replacement fertility rate of 2.1 children per woman, it is estimated that a 60 percent prevalence rate of modern contraceptive use must be achieved. This translates to providing these services to about 42 million couples in the Arab world today, increasing to reach more than 50 million couples by the year 2005. Realizing this goal, however, would not mean a zero population growth. Because of population momentum, the size of the Arab population would continue to grow for another century, even below a fertility replacement level,

Table 11. Estimated Urban Population for Arab Countries in 1980, 1990, and 2001

Country	Urban Population (000)			Urban Population (%)
	1980	1990	2001	2001
Algeria	8,160	12,776	17,801	58
Bahrain	279	429	603	93
Comoros	90	147	246	34
Djibouti	239	408	542	84
Egypt	19,178	24,499	29,475	43
Iraq	8,488	12,027	15,907	67
Jordan	1,340	2,350	3,979	79
Kuwait	1,248	2,034	1,894	96
Lebanon	1,967	2,284	3,203	90
Libya	2,109	3,528	4,757	88
Mauritania	430	877	1,624	59
Morocco	8,000	11,917	17,082	56
O.P.T.	902	1,379	2,222	67
Oman	356	1,109	2,006	77
Qatar	196	407	534	93
Saudi Arabia	6,325	12,046	18,229	87
Somalia	1,441	1,734	2,557	28
Sudan	3,855	6,606	11,790	37
Syrian AR	4,066	6,061	8,596	52
Tunisia	3,323	4,726	6,329	66
U.A.E.	726	1,615	2,314	87
Yemen, Rep.	1,578	2,648	4,778	25

Source: World Urbanization Prospects, The 2001 Revision, Data Tables and Highlights; Population Division, Department of Economic and Social Affairs, United Nations Secretariat, New York, USA

before it might stabilize. The sooner Arab countries satisfy its people's needs for contraceptives, the sooner its population would stabilize.

Urbanization

Urbanization has occurred rapidly in the Arab world. In 1980, 44 percent of Arab populations were urban; this increased to 50 percent and 56 percent in 1990 and 2001 respectively. Currently, eight countries have an urban population of more than 80 percent and four countries have an urban population of less than 40 percent.

Education in the Arab World

Girl's education

Education remains one of the most powerful tools for gender equity and the empowerment of women. All Arab constitutions and laws affirm the equal right of women to education and highlight the equality of opportunity between sexes. Most Arab countries have even made primary education compulsory and free for the first few years. As a result, women in the region have made gains. Generally speaking, girls' school enrollment rates have been good. The percentage increase in enrollment among females between 1980 and 1990 was higher than that among males, but there are still education gaps, both between and within countries in the Arab region. Within countries, there are still large gaps between boys and girls in school enrollment and retention, between rural and urban residents, and between regions. With few exceptions, these gaps increase as we go higher on the education ladder.

While there is awareness of gender gaps in education and attempts to address them, the problem is often that of families exercising the right to education and of relevant authorities enforcing the laws of compulsory education. Underlying both factors is the state's inability to provide quality free education to all. There are concrete structural and institutional obstacles to girls' education that are related to the quality of education, as well as to facilities and policies. Additionally, there are obstacles related to the education system, such as textbooks and curricula, that reinforce stereotypes on gender distribution of labor, roles and status, and that perpetuate discrimination against women at all stages of their lives. There are generally not enough schools; a number of countries have had to adopt a double shift schedule. The quality of teaching and the relevance of the content of education also affect students' enrollment and retention.

While structural factors rank high among the obstacles to women's education, cultural perceptions, stereotypes, and traditional beliefs are also major obstacles. These obstacles are in people's minds. The beliefs—that boys should be educated before girls; that girls should not travel alone to schools; that investment in girls will be lost on them since at the end of the day they will "belong" to someone else; that educating girls will limit their chances of getting married because educated women are less submissive to the dictates of their husbands—all have adverse bearings on female empowerment. The limited employment opportunities for women might also prompt families to question the value of education as a means of developing a livelihood. Most unfortunately, in the minds of the members of some socioeconomic groups, a male child is an asset, while a female child is a liability.

Higher education

In addition to the school retention gap, the educational specialization of women in the Arab world reflects cultural biases initiated by the expected role of women. Generally, women tend, and are pushed, to specialize in the fields of education, the humanities (arts, languages), nursing, and domestic economics in accordance with their expected reproductive role and tasks, and less in the fields of natural sciences, engineering, computer sciences, and medical sciences, which are considered productive and masculine. It is also easier to keep professionals, in fields such as teaching, separate from men. On average, only 23 percent of all female students in tertiary education are in the scientific fields, compared to 61 percent of all males. Women are also often discriminated against in terms of receiving postgraduate education scholarships, due to scarcity of these fellowships and based on the assumption that they will ultimately get married and stop working, which makes women, in the minds of some, a 'losing educational investment.'

Similar gaps exist in vocational education, and while there has been a noticeable rise in the number of females enrolled in vocational training in the last twenty years, short-term vocational training for women tends to focus on traditional areas such as nursing, secretarial skills, hairdressing, and weaving and other household related skills.

Literacy

While the gender gap in school enrollment has narrowed slowly, illiteracy is still a resilient problem, more so among women than among men. It is estimated that around 70 million people, mostly women, are illiterate. One half of all women in the

Table 12. Adult Literacy Rates and School Enrollment in the Arab World

Country	Adult Literacy Rate 1995–1999		Primary School Enrollment Ratio 1995–1999 (Net)		Secondary School Enrollment Ratio 1995–1997 (Gross)	
	Male	Female	Male	Female	Male	Female
Algeria	73	54	94	91	65	62
Bahrain	87	73	96	98	91	98
Comoros	78	70	65	55	21x	16x
Djibouti	60	33	39	28	17	12
Egypt	64	38	94	89	80	70
Iraq	71	45	98	88	51	32
Jordan	93	81	86	86	52x	54x
Kuwait	95	83	89	85	65	65
Lebanon	91	77	—	—	78	85
Libya	87	67	97x	96x	95x	95x
Mauritania	60	33	61	53	21	11
Morocco	58	31	77	64	44	34
Oman	79	57	86	86	68	65
Qatar	84	81	96	92	81	79
Saudi Arabia	91	70	81	73	65	57
Somalia	36x	14x	13	7	10x	6x
Sudan	67	47	43	37	21	19
Syrian AR	91	73	96	92	45	40
Tunisia	76	53	97	94	66	63
U. A. E.	85	93	98	98	77	82
Yemen, Rep.	69	36	79	39	53	14

Source: UNICEF, The State of the World's Children Report, 2001

X indicates data that refer to years or periods other than that specified in the column heading, differ from the standard definition, or refer only to part of the country.

region are illiterate compared to about 30 percent of all men. Countries with lower GDP and GNP per capita have higher illiteracy rates and higher male/female education gaps. A review of illiteracy rates among those fifteen to twenty-four years old in the region reveals a lower rate among them than that of the whole adult population; this indicates an improvement in literacy rates. The absolute numbers of illiterates might not be dropping as fast, however. The link between curricula and teaching styles, on one hand, and the needs and realities of the life of older people, on the other hand, has been generally weak. Unless curricula are clearly linked to improving the lives of women and solving their problems, they will not see the benefit of literacy.

The Reproductive Health Profile of the Arab Population

Reproductive health—definition and approach

The consensus definition of reproductive health, ratified at the 1994 International Conference on Population and Development (ICPD), represents an important initial step in the process of transforming the approach to and service for reproductive health. Reproductive health is defined as "a state of complete physical, mental, and social well-being, and not merely the absence of disease or infirmity, in all matters relating to the reproductive system and to its functions and processes."

This definition constituted a real shift from the approach of previous population programs, where vertical family planning was promoted primarily to achieve demographic targets. Instead, the ICPD plan of action emphasizes the importance of providing family planning within and central to the context of comprehensive sexual and reproductive health care.

The shift in the sexual and reproductive health approach involves a shift in the thinking behind service provision. The new plan involves using a holistic, quality, client-oriented approach; ensuring that services are youth-friendly, female and male-friendly, and gender-sensitive; addressing the needs of men and women throughout their life cycles; and ensuring a perspective that acknowledges human rights, and women's rights, and reproductive rights. Thus, the basic elements, in fact the cornerstone, of gender, population, and development programs as well as reproductive health services and rights consist of:

1. Ensuring women's control of their own fertility. Women's rights are human rights, and family planning, reproductive, and sexual rights mean the right of any woman to control all aspects of her health, especially her own fertility. *This is the basis of her empowerment.*

2. Achieving the empowerment of women. While initiatives have concentrated on involving women in high-level positions, it is also very important to empower women who are in lower positions. *The principles of equality, justice, democracy, and sustainability are key aspects of empowerment.*

3. Achieving gender equality and equity. Equal opportunities for women and men require that they start out on a level playing field. When the status of women and men are unequal and they have unequal access to knowledge and resources in a community, special treatment and affirmative action for women may be needed before their "starting point" can be considered equal; this is positive discrimination. Gender equity connotes a sense of fairness or justice that should be applied to all gender issues. In an area such as reproductive health in which women bear the largest share of the costs, dangers, or burdens (physical, mental, social, economic, or otherwise), it is equitable that they should control more of the decision-making. Insisting on absolute equality is not always equitable.

4. Eliminating all forms of violence against women. Gender-based violence/violence against women, including sexual violence, is now recognized as a public health problem (WHO/EMRO, 1998) and an integral component of reproductive health (UNFPA, 1999).

Reproductive Health Status and Challenges in the Arab States

Improvements were recorded in the health status of infants and children and in life expectancy in all the countries of the Arab world; countries struck by wars and unrest had the most varying levels. Crude death rates have registered an impressive decline from 16.6 per 1,000 in the 1970s to 8.9 per 1,000 in 1998. During the last three decades, improvements in health services have also led to an increase in life expectancy of sixteen years (with variations among countries). Primary school enrollment reached 100 percent in most of the countries and adult literacy has significantly improved. Despite these gains, as discussed above, there remain some 70 million Arabs, mostly rural women, who are illiterate. This has a direct inverse relationship between fertility levels, the status of women, and general health. Fertility rates are falling, but not as rapidly as in Latin America and Asia. The average number of children per woman has dropped from 6.6 in 1950 to 4.2 today, but this number is still high by international standards. Knowledge of contraceptives has reached a high level in many countries, with usage rates averaging 40 percent of married couples. Estimated unmet needs stand at a minimum of 18 percent. However, maternal mortality is still too high, and is among the leading causes of death among women of reproductive age.

Although there have been marked improvements during the last decade, the Arab world faces many challenges in reproductive health and reproductive rights. These are discussed below.

Maternal Mortality

High maternal mortality is a key health challenge facing most Arab countries. The MMR varies significantly among Arab countries. Despite difficulties in measuring maternal mortality, data gathered in Table 13 show that more than half of the Arab countries have an MMR exceeding 75 per 100,000 live births, and as many as one-third have an MMR exceeding 200 per 100,000 live births. Only two Arab countries (Kuwait and the U.A.E.) have managed to reduce maternal mortality to a level that is low by international standards (not more than 5 per 100,000 live births), and have a high percentage of skilled attendants present at births (95 percent and above). The other Gulf countries of Oman, Qatar, and Saudi Arabia have moderately low levels (an MMR of between ten and twenty per 100,000 live births).

Of all the health statistics monitored by the WHO, maternal mortality shows the largest discrepancy between developed and developing countries. Women in developing countries are about thirty times more likely to die from pregnancy-related causes than those in developed countries. In this respect, most Arab countries fall in the category of developing countries.

Causes of maternal death

Ninety-nine percent of the approximately 585,000 maternal deaths each year are in developing countries,

Table 13. Maternal Mortality Ratio, 1990 to 1998, and Percentage of Births with Skilled Attendants in Arab Countries

Country	MMR 100,000 Live Births	% Births with Skilled Attendants	Country	MMR 100,000 Live Births	% Births with Skilled Attendants
Algeria	220	77	Bahrain	46	98
Comoros	570	52	Djibouti	740	—
Egypt	85	46	Iraq	310	54
Jordan	41	97	Kuwait	5	98
Lebanon	100	89	Libya	75	94
Mauritania	550	40	Morocco	230	40
Oman	19	91	O.P.T.	70–80	95
Qatar	10	97	Saudi Arabia	18	90
Somalia	1600	20	Sudan	550	86
Syrian AR	110	77	Tunisia	70	81
U.A.E.	3	99	Yemen, Rep.	350	43

Sources: MMR data from UNDP Arab Human Development Report 2002; percentage of skilled attended deliveries from The State of World Population Report 2001

including the Arab countries, where complications of pregnancy and childbirth take the life of about one out of every forty-eight women. Most of these maternal deaths could be prevented. Four common problems, all involving delays, greatly increase women's risk in childbirth: delays in recognizing a developing problem, delays in decisions to act, delays in arranging transport to a health facility, and delays in reaching health services. A community-based system for ensuring rapid transport to an equipped medical facility is a crucial factor in saving mothers' lives.

The leading causes of maternal mortality in developing countries are: sepsis, hemorrhage, eclampsia, obstructed labor, and abortion complications. In developed countries, most maternal deaths are due to hemorrhage from ectopic pregnancy, embolism, pregnancy-induced hypertension, and anesthesia complications.

The primary means of preventing maternal deaths, however, is to provide access to emergency obstetric care, including treatment of hemorrhage, infection, hypertension and obstructed labor. Life-saving interventions, such as referrals to medical centers, antibiotics, and surgery, are unavailable to many women in the Arab countries, especially those in rural areas. Access to health care ranges from 100 percent in the Gulf countries to 20 percent in Somalia. The lower the percentages of population with access to health care, the wider the gaps between rural and urban populations.

Maternal morbidity

MMR is only the tip of the iceberg of maternal morbidity. It is estimated that of 150 million pregnancies worldwide, 585,000 will end up as maternal deaths; 34 million with pregnancy-related complications; 20 million with serious disability; and millions of others with illnesses aggravated by pregnancy such as malaria, anemia, hepatitis, cardiac diseases, diabetes, tuberculosis, and other disorders. In the Arab world where maternal death ratios remain high, there is growing evidence that the extent of maternal morbidity may have been seriously underestimated. The scarcity of data in the Arab world on the magnitude and patterns of maternal morbidity is one of the obstacles to addressing this issue comprehensively. To a large extent, this concern is reflected in an increased effort by national and regional institutions in the Arab world to gather and analyze data pertaining to health determinants and the health of women.

Chronic diseases and malnutrition leave many women unable to meet the physical demands of pregnancy. Anemia, often the result of poor nutrition, affected 18 to 54 percent of pregnant women in the Arab world during the last three decades. Also, a woman's age and the number of previous births affect her chances of dying in childbirth.

Consequences of Infant and Child Mortality

Infants and children also suffer as a result of poor maternal health. The same factors that cause maternal mortality and morbidity, including complications and the associated poor management of pregnancy and childbirth, contribute to an estimated 8 million stillbirths and newborn deaths each year. Tragically, when a mother dies, her children are also more likely to die. With no healthy and empowered women, there can be no healthy children (Sadik, 1993).

Infant and child mortality

Table 9 shows that although infant mortality rates (IMR) vary greatly among Arab countries, there have been remarkable reductions in IMR everywhere except in Iraq, where sanctions caused a reversal and increase in IMR.

While Bahrain, Kuwait, Qatar, and the U.A.E achieved IMRs of less than 20 per 1,000 live births, Djibouti, Iraq, Mauritania, Somalia, Sudan, and Yemen still experience IMRs of 95 or higher per 1,000 live births. (For Iraq, this is despite the fact that the country had achieved a lower IMR before the Gulf War).

High fertility

As discussed earlier, the average number of children per woman in Arab countries has dropped from 6.6 in 1950 to 4.2 today, with wide variations among countries. This rate is still significantly higher than the average world total fertility rate (TFR) of 2.7. Table 14 below shows that there have been declines in fertility rates during the period 1978 to 1998 in all Arab countries, except in Somalia and Yemen; the latter has the highest fertility rate in the world. Yet only four countries have TFRs of less than three births per woman: Bahrain, Kuwait, Lebanon, and Tunisia.

Four proximate determinants affect the TFRs in the Arab world: age at the woman's first marriage, postpartum amenorrhea, induced abortion, and contraceptive use.

Use of Contraceptives

Contraceptive prevalence rates are not available for all the Arab countries; figures are available for only twenty countries. Of these, fourteen countries have a contraceptive prevalence rate (any method) of 30 percent or higher, and of these fourteen, only ten have a prevalence rate of modern methods of 30 percent or higher. This is compared to nine countries having a contraceptive prevalence rate (any method) of 50 percent or higher and only four countries having a prevalence rate of modern contraceptive use of 50 percent or higher. To reach a replacement fertility rate of 2.1 children per woman, it is estimated that a modern contraceptive prevalence rate of 60 percent is needed. Realizing this goal would not mean zero population growth. Because of population momentum, the size of the Arab population would continue to grow, even under a fertility replacement level, for another century before it might stabilize.

Table 14. Total Fertility Rates 1978 and 1998, Contraceptive Knowledge, and Prevalence of Use

Country	Total Fertility Rate 1978	Total Fertility Rate 1998	Knowledge of a Contraceptive Method (%)	Use of Any Contraceptive Method (%)	Use of Modern Contraceptive Methods (%)
Algeria	7.2	3.8	99.0	61.9	60.2
Bahrain	5.2	2.9	—	68.8	30.9
Comoros	—	5.8	—	21.0 *	11.4
Djibouti	6.7	5.8	—	—	—
Egypt	5.3	3.4	100.0	56.1	53.9
Iraq	6.6	5.3	—	13.7 *	10.4
Jordan	7.4	4.9	100.0	60.1	42.3
Kuwait	5.9	2.9	—	51.0	49.8
Lebanon	4.3	2.7	91.0	61.0 *	37.0
Libya	7.4	3.8	—	39.7 *	25.6
Mauritania	6.5	5.5	61.0	3.3 *	1.2
Morocco	5.9	3.1	99.0	65.0	53.9
O.P.T.	—	5.6	99.0	64.1 *	49.2
Oman	7.2	5.9	—	34.5	25.8
Qatar	6.1	3.7	—	45.2	32.9
Saudi Arabia	7.3	5.8	—	31.8 *	28.5
Somalia	7.3	7.3	—	—	—
Sudan	6.7	4.6	71.0	8.7	7.8
Syrian AR	7.4	4.0	78.0	36.1	28.3
Tunisia	5.7	2.6	99.0	70.2	61.6
U.A.E.	5.7	3.4	—	27.5	23.6
Yemen, Rep.	7.6	7.6	60.0	29.0	12.0

Sources: Fertility rate data from The State of the World Population Report 1999. Data on the Contraceptives Prevalence Rate for the year 2000 from UN World Population Monitoring Reproductive Rights and Reproductive Health: Selected Aspects 2002 (draft), and the source for countries denoted by "*" is from the UN World Contraceptive Use 2001 chart

Table 15. Reason for Using Contraception, Selected Arab Countries

Country	Year	Current Use of Contraception (in Percent)			Percentage of Use for Limiting
		Total	Spacing	Limiting	
Egypt	2000	56.1	11.4	44.7	79.7
Morocco	1995	50.3	17.2	33.1	65.8
Sudan	1990	8.7	5.0	3.6	41.4
Comoros	1996	21.0	11.8	9.2	43.8
Jordan	1997	52.6	18.2	34.3	65.2
Yemen, Rep.	1997	20.8	7.2	13.6	65.4

Source: United Nations Population Division. *World Population Monitoring 2002: Reproductive Rights and Reproductive Health: Selected Aspects* (draft). 2002, New York, USA

education of women, it is expected that the efficacy of modern contraceptives will further lower current fertility rates.

On average, unmet needs for contraceptives in the Arab world stands at a minimum of 18 percent. Table 16 below shows that the unmet need for contraceptives ranges from a high of 38.6 percent in Yemen to a 11.2 percent in Egypt.

Malnutrition

Nutrition is the fundamental pillar of human life, health, and development across the entire lifespan. However, women and children in the East Mediterranean region might be exposed to several

Table 16. Total Need and Unmet Need for Family Planning, Selected Arab Countries (in Percent)

Country	Year	Percentage of Currently Married Women with						Percentage of Total Need Satisfied for		
		Unmet Need for			Total Need for					
		Total	Spacing	Limiting	Total	Spacing	Limiting	Total	Spacing	Limiting
Egypt	2000	11.2	3.6	7.6	68.2	15.4	52.9	83.6	76.6	85.6
Morocco	1995	16.1	6.3	9.8	69.4	25.1	44.3	76.8	74.9	77.9
Sudan	1990	26.0	18.0	7.0	34.0	23.0	11.0	23.5	21.7	36.4
Comoros	1996	34.6	21.8	12.9	55.6	33.6	22.0	37.8	35.1	41.4
Jordan	1997	14.2	7.4	6.8	71.3	28.9	42.3	80.1	74.4	83.9
Yemen, Rep.	1997	38.6	17.2	21.4	59.4	24.4	35.0	35.0	29.5	38.9

Source: United Nations Population Division. *World Population Monitoring 2002: Reproductive Rights and Reproductive Health: Selected Aspects* (draft). 2002, New York, USA

A careful review of Table 14 shows that for a number of Arab countries, higher rates of modern contraceptive use should have resulted in lower total fertility rates than those observed. Age-specific fertility rates and age-specific modern contraceptive use indicate that in these countries, women who had at least three deliveries represent the higher proportion of contraceptive users. The data also indicate much lower rates of use of contraception among younger cohorts. In the majority of these countries, contraception is used mostly by women who have completed their family, rather than for child spacing (Table 15). In addition, discontinuous usage appears to be high, particularly with IUDs and hormonal contraceptives, indicating less than optimal quality of care. Equally, therefore, contraceptive failure rates are also relatively high. With recent improvements in the quality of care and

dietary deficiencies, including iron (very common in pregnant women and children), folic acid, and vitamin A.

Table 17 on the next page shows that between 6 and 19 percent of infants start their lives with low birth weight, which exposes them to higher risks of mortality and morbidity. Stunting of children younger than five years of age is still high in the region, and is a serious health challenge in Arab countries. Not surprisingly, poor and war-torn countries reflect high levels of moderate and severe stunting (Yemen, as high as 52 percent; Mauritania, 44 percent; and Comoros, Iraq, and Sudan higher than 30 percent); these same countries have the highest incidence of low birth weight.

Table 17. Children Younger Than Age Five with Low Birth Weight (LBW), Underweight, and Stunting, 2000 (in Percent)

Country	Infants with LBW	Underweight, Moderate and Severe	Underweight, Severe	Wasting, Moderate and Severe	Stunting, Moderate and Severe
Algeria	9.0	13.0	3.0	9.0	18.0
Bahrain	6.0	9.0	2.0	5.0	10.0
Comoros	8.0	26.0	8.0	8.0	34.0
Djibouti	18.0	18.2	—	12.9	25.7
Egypt	10.0	12.0	3.0	6.0	25.0
Iraq	15.0	23.0	6.0	10.0	31.0
Jordan	10.0	5.0	1.0	2.0	8.0
Kuwait	7.0	10.0	3.0	11.0	24.0
Lebanon	10.0	3.0	0.0	3.0	12.0
Libya	7.0	5.0	1.0	3.0	15.0
Mauritania	11.0	23.0	9.0	7.0	44.0
Morocco	9.0	10.0	2.0	4.0	23.0
Oman	8.0	24.0	4.0	13.0	23.0
O.P.T.	8.6	2.7	6.2	1.7	9.1
Qatar	—	6.0	—	2.0	8.0
Saudi Arabia	7.0	14.0	3.0	11.0	20.0
Somalia	16.0	26.0	7.0	12.0	14.0
Sudan	15.0	34.0	11.0	13.0	33.0
Syrian AR	7.0	13.0	4.0	9.0	21.0
Tunisia	8.0	4.0	0.0	1.0	8.0
U.A.E.	6.0	14.0	3.0	15.0	17.0
Yemen, Rep.	19.0	46.0	15.0	13.0	52.0

Source: UNDP Arab Human Development Report 2002

Reproductive Tract Infections (RTIs)/ Sexually Transmitted Infections (STIs) and Human Immunodeficiency Virus/Acquired Immunodeficiency Syndrome (HIV/AIDS)

WHO and Joint United Nations Programme on HIV/AIDS (UNAIDS) data indicate that an estimated 80,000 people became newly infected with HIV/AIDS in 2001, bringing the total number of people living with HIV/AIDS in the Arab world to 440,000. Sexual contact and intravenous drug use are the dominant modes of transmission. In some countries, HIV/AIDS has been caused by blood transfusions and renal dialysis. While Arab countries remain among the less affected globally, the number of infections in these nations continue to increase steadily; the fact that the epidemic is not yet visible in most Arab countries should not be taken as a sign that they face fewer challenges than any other country. With 16 million deaths from the disease worldwide, AIDS represents one of the most fatal diseases ever known. However, a decade after the first cases were identified, there is still no total government recognition of the presence of the epidemic in the Arab world.

The prevalence rates of AIDS, although still low, show alarming trends. According to regional experts, the HIV/AIDS situation in Arab countries seems to be at a critical turning point. The available data show that the Arab countries are not affected by the epidemic to the same degree as in other parts of the world. However, there are indications and trends that point to the fact that the epidemic has taken a dangerous turn in several countries. Pockets of infection have been revealed in groups of intravenous drug users in Bahrain, Oman, and Tunisia; HIV outbreaks have been registered in Egypt and Libya. It is essential to acknowledge the fact that the occurrence of HIV in one country inevitably leads to HIV in another one; no country is spared, as the human behaviors and social conditions that spread the virus are present in all Arab countries.

Table 18. Regional HIV/AIDS Statistics

Region	Adults and Children Living with HIV/AIDS	Adults and Children Newly Infected with HIV/AIDS	Percent Adult Prevalence of HIV/AIDS	Percent HIV Positive Women	Main Mode of Transmission
Sub-Saharan Africa	28.1 million	3.4 million	8.4	55	Hetero
North Africa and the Middle East	**440,000**	**80,000**	**0.2**	**40**	**Hetero, IDU**
South and Southeast Asia	6.1 million	800,000	0.6	35	Hetero, IDU
East Asia and the Pacific	1 million	270,000	0.1	20	IDU, Hetero, MSM
Latin America	1.4 million	130,000	0.5	30	MSM, IDU, Hetero
Caribbean	420,000	60,000	2.2	50	Hetero, MSM
Eastern Europe and Central Asia	1 million	250,000	0.5	20	IDU
Western Europe	560,000	30,000	0.3	25	MSM, IDU
North America	940,000	45,000	0.6	20	MSM, IDU, Hetero
Australia and New Zealand	15,000	500	0.1	10	MSM
Total	**40 million**	**5 million**	**1.2**	**48**	

Source: UNAIDS and WHO presentation, December 2001

MSM= male's sex with males; IDU= intravenous drug users; Hetero= heterosexual contact

Table 18 shows the status of HIV/AIDS in the Arab world in comparison to other regions. In the Arab world, heterosexual contact is the most common mode of transmission, accounting for 82 percent of reported AIDS cases. However, the role of intravenous drug use in transmitting the HIV infection is of growing concern in many Arab countries.

The countries of the Arab world most affected by HIV are Djibouti, Somalia, and Sudan. Studies report rates ranging between 1.6 percent and 3 percent of HIV positivity among pregnant women attending antenatal clinics in the three countries. Djibouti is the worst affected by the epidemic, with an adult prevalence rate of 11.75 percent. In most countries, infection is concentrated in specific groups of the population, such as intravenous drug users, migrants, and those who practice risky sexual behavior. Several other countries are now in a generalized epidemic, with the spread moving into every segment of the population. UNAIDS estimates that 40 percent of all HIV-positive adults are women, and local studies in Algeria revealed prevalence rates of 1 percent among pregnant women attending antenatal clinics. Studies on HIV among tuberculosis patients reported rates of 0.6 percent in Egypt, 4.8 percent in Oman, and 8 percent in Sudan as compared to 2.06 percent in Pakistan and 4.2 percent in Iran.

There is growing concern about the situation in the Horn of Africa, where a combination of poverty, population displacement, political instability, lack of security, as well as weak health structures are important contributing factors to the spread of the epidemic. In North Africa, there is concern about the rates of sexually transmitted diseases and migration patterns, urban-rural movements, and socioeconomic factors. In other countries, the focus is on specific groups at increased risk for infection through sexual or drug use behavior; a substantial number of cases have been reported among intravenous drug users in recent years. Across the region, young people and adolescents are a concern, as is the tendency towards the increasing proportion of HIV/AIDS cases among women.

Adolescents

The Arab Human Development Report 2002 indicates that the age structure of the Arab population is significantly younger than the global average. Thirty-nine percent of the population is younger than fifteen years of age; there are wide variations among Arab countries, ranging from 26 percent in the U.A.E to 50 percent in Yemen. New health issues that are associated with the youthful profile of the population have emerged. Among these issues is the persistence of early pregnancies, with their associated increased risks for morbidity and mortality. In spite of deeply entrenched cultural beliefs that preclude risky sexual behavior; there is nevertheless a need to further strengthen safe behaviors particularly in light of the youthful profile of the population, fluid population movement, and gender-related discriminatory customs and practices. Improvements in education about reproductive health, the welfare of young people, and the status of women, female adolescents, and girls require continual support.

Prevailing socio-cultural norms in most Arab countries, particularly among rural populations, still favor the early marriage of girls followed by an early pregnancy to prove the girl's fecundity. These factors are important determinants of the high level of morbidity and even mortality among adolescent girls. In North Africa and the Middle East, 15 to 30 percent of all adolescent births are unintended. In Bahrain, WHO data show that 18 to 20 percent of mothers got pregnant between the ages of eleven and fifteen years and about 43 percent between the ages of sixteen and nineteen years. In Oman, 16 to 18 percent of women had their first pregnancy at younger than fifteen years of age and almost 70 percent between the ages of fifteen and nineteen years; only 15 percent had their first pregnancy at the age of twenty years and older. A study in Saudi Arabia showed 45 percent of married women had their first pregnancy when they were younger than age twenty. The detrimental effects of early pregnancy and poor nutrition are passed to the next generation through low birth weight infants and the associated high mortality and morbidity levels.

As noted earlier, reliable information and data about morbidity patterns of adolescents in the Arab countries are relatively scarce. This scarcity of data is due to the absence of any attention to adolescents in conventional health programs. Quality of reproductive health services for adolescents is of considerable concern in Arab countries. Although adolescent reproductive health forms an integral part of general reproductive health care, adolescents have their own special needs. Health workers often lack the experience and special training to deal with adolescents, and they may be reluctant to provide reproductive health services, particularly contraceptive services, to young people.

Hereditary disorders

Consanguinity, though declining, is also common in most Arab countries, but especially in Jordan and the Gulf countries. In Bahrain and the U.A.E., it is estimated that almost 32 percent of currently married women younger than age 50 married a relative. There is an inverse relationship between the prevalence of consanguineous marriages and the educational levels of women. Recently, several studies in the Gulf countries revealed that the practice of consanguineous marriage rapidly declines with a higher level of education among girls. While almost

all adolescent girls that are married to close cousins are rural illiterate girls, the practices are reduced by almost 50 percent among girls whose families value university education, and who are university-educated. The prevalence of congenital anomalies in Bahrain and U.A.E. are among the highest in the world. Consanguineous marriages and pregnancies late in life are among the important causes. Genetic blood disorders, including sickle-cell anemia and thalassaemia, are common in most Arab countries mainly because of consanguinity. Blood testing has become a requirement prior to marriage in most Arab countries.

Conflicts and Wars

Data suggest that military conflicts, sanctions, and embargoes in countries such as Iraq, the O.P.T., Sudan, and Somalia further jeopardize the health of the most vulnerable groups, namely women and children. In Iraq, data suggest that MMR has increased from 68 per 100,000 live births in 1989 to 294 per 100,000 in 1999. IMR increased from 47 per 1,000 live births during the period 1984 to 1989 to 131 per 1,000 during the period 1994 to 1999. Incidence of low birth weight infants increased from 4.5 percent in 1990 to 24.8 percent in 2001.

In the O.P.T., United Nations Relief and Works Agency for Palestine Refugees in the Near East (UNRWA) data indicate that since the beginning of Intifadha (Uprising of Palestinian population against Israeli occupation) on 28 September 2000, there have been increases in the rates of stillbirth (47 percent); home deliveries (41 percent); and low birth weight (22 percent); drops in immunizations against measles, polio, hepatitis (10 percent) and tuberculosis (7 percent); skilled attendance for childcare (7 percent); the number of family planning acceptors (7 percent); and attendance for antenatal care (4 percent). Reports are that during closures and curfews, deliveries, infant deaths, and maternal deaths occurred at the checkpoints hindering access to health care.

Poverty

Poverty is multidimensional and the central challenge to development. People become ill because they are poor and they become poor because they are ill. According to the Arab Human Development Report 2002, the average economic growth rate (AEGR) in the Arab world is lower than the population average growth rate, and the AEGR is the lowest in the world after sub-Saharan Africa. Women and children are the groups most affected by poverty.

Figure 1. Antenatal Care Usage Rates Among Poor and Rich in 44 Countries (in Percent)

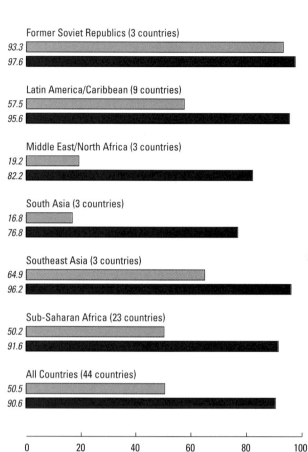

Figure 2. Rates of Attended Deliveries Among Poor and Rich in 44 Countries (in Percent)

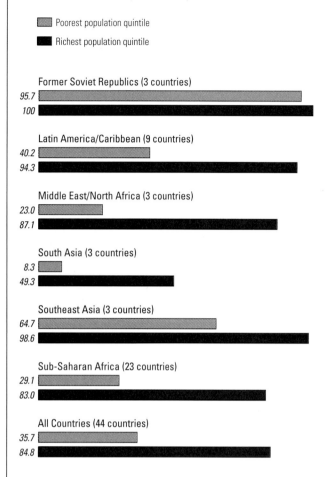

Source: Gwatkin, Davidson. The Evidence Base on Poverty and Reproductive Health (World Bank Presentation, September 2001). URL: http://wbweb5.worldbank.org/database/reprohealth/evidence.pdf

The presentation also showed that only 23 percent of all deliveries among poor populations of the Middle East and North African countries are attended by trained personnel (such as doctors, nurses, and midwives; this excludes traditional birth attendants (TBAs)). This percentage increases to 87.1 percent among rich populations of the Arab world, as shown by Figure 2.

Strengthening Governments' Ability to Formulate, Implement, and Monitor Population Policies and Programs

The population of the Arab world is young; almost 39 percent are younger than the age of fifteen. Annual population growth rates in most Arab countries exceed economic growth rates, and this greatly diminishes achievements in socioeconomic development, leading

to increased poverty and unemployment. Rapid population growth triggers rural to urban migration, depriving the agricultural sector of the labor force required to maintain agricultural production and prevent desertification. It also adds to problems in urban areas by increasing slum areas, unemployment, and crowding. Further, population pressure stimulates international migration, depriving countries of educated and qualified nationals. Curbing population growth contributes to maximizing the benefits of socioeconomic development and helps achieve a balance between the numbers of people and natural resources, thus minimizing the degradation of the environment.

Water is the most precious commodity in the Arab world. Available water resources, it is projected, are not sufficient to meet the needs of a rapidly growing population or that are created by irrigation and industry. The benefits of investing in population programs, including family planning, outweigh the costs involved. Savings realized in the lower costs of education, health services, housing, and sanitation as well as on basic food and other commodities could be invested in economic development.

There is increasing recognition among Arab governments and thinkers that high rates of population growth pose a major threat to economic growth, sustainable human development, quality of life, and the environment. Non-oil producing Arab countries are recognizing the need for adopting explicit population policies with quantifiable goals. Governments are establishing population commissions to research and formulate policies responsive to their specific population and economic development situations, and that are in line with prevailing cultural norms. Formulating responsive population policies and programs and monitoring their impact require a base of high-quality socioeconomic, demographic, and health data that are disaggregated by sex, age groups, geographic and administrative (local administration boundaries) levels, and socioeconomic groups. These data should be at macro, mezzo, and micro levels. The analysis, dissemination, and utilization of these data, particularly in target setting and in integrating population variables into development planning processes through appropriate models, needs to be institutionalized and supported. Almost all Arab countries, including the Gulf states, have established or are establishing population commissions or councils. The United Nations Population Fund (UNFPA) has provided technical support to these councils to ensure that staff has the required skills. Coordination between the various ministries and the inclusion of a population dimension in sectoral programs has been gaining recognition and support from Arab governments. These commissions are increasingly ensuring the participation of the private sector and nongovernmental organizations, particularly women's organizations, in policy formulation and coordinated policy implementation. Also important is according special consideration, by the Arab governments and donors, to gender issues and concerns and the empowerment of women in the policy formulation and implementation.

On the basis of the above realities and issues, UNFPA is now adopting a strategic approach to the policy development process for the Arab world that includes:

1. *Ensuring the availability of quality and disaggregated data by age groups, gender, small geographic areas, and socioeconomic groups through censuses; conducting dedicated socioeconomic, demographic and health sample surveys—both quantitative and qualitative; and keeping administrative records such as civil registration/vital statistics and health records, where such records can be collected. Emphasis is placed on the need for the data to be analyzed using causality analysis approaches; and disseminated and utilized in policy and program formulation, implementation, impact assessment, and intervention under a results-based approach;*

2. *Supporting population commissions with high-level representation from various ministries, the private sector, and NGOs, especially women's organizations and groups, and supporting the training of the staff of these commissions on policy research and formulation, program management and impact assessment, and on gender concerns and women's issues and programs;*

3. *Supporting the institutionalization, within ministries of planning, of the process of integrating gender analysis and population variables (as endogenous variables) into development planning and adjustment programs (such as the Sector Wide Approach, Common Country Assessment/United Nations Development Assistance Framework, and Poverty Reduction Strategy Papers) at national, sub national, and sectoral levels;*

4. *Ensuring coordination with, and participation of, the private sector and NGOs in the actual formulation of population policies and strategies and implementation of population and other development programs, including monitoring and evaluation;*

5. *Ensuring effective policy and program coordination between the donors, particularly the United Nations Joint Consultative Group on Policy (JCGP), and increased appropriation of funds by the governments.*

Strengthening Information, Communication, and Education Efforts to Foster Positive Changes in Attitude and Responsible Behavior Toward Population Issues

Traditionally in Arab societies, mothers and trusted women prepare their daughters for married life through a process of information and communication. This usually includes information related to home economics, sex education (instructing young girls to protect their virginity), pregnancy, child rearing, medicinal remedies, family planning, and the like. In addition, on sensitive or critical issues including the termination of unwanted pregnancies, younger and relatively inexperienced wives consult mothers and trusted elderly women. These are usually face-to-face private exchanges. Birth attendants are traditionally considered a trusted friend. However, wrong information, as well as many misconceptions are transferred through this process.

Family planning has its roots in the Arab culture and is supported by Islam. Men practiced *al-azl* (i.e., withdrawal) and women resorted to specific traditional methods for either avoiding or terminating unwanted pregnancies. That these traditional methods, including withdrawal, are still practiced today is evident from the various surveys conducted in the 1970s, 1980s, and 1990s. The surveys clearly indicated motivation, attitude, and practice of traditional family planning methods among the Arabs, albeit being relatively ineffective methods. For practical reasons, those practicing traditional methods (both males and females) should be included in the category of a gap in service or as unmet demand for effective and safe methods.

Data generated under the World Fertility Survey (WFS), Demographic and Health Survey (DHS), and the Pan-Arab Program for Maternal and Child Health (PAPCHILD) showed evidence of pregnancies that did not come to term. The relatively high proportions of these pregnancies along with pregnancies ending with stillbirths suggest induced abortion or maternal depletion resulting in spontaneous abortion or a stillbirth. A good proportion of women with these types of pregnancies could also be considered as part of the gap in service or as unmet demand. However, further research and study of this category is required to determine more accurately the real reason or reasons behind the interrupted pregnancies. Such studies should be of the qualitative socio-cultural type as opposed to quantitative demographic and health surveys.

Data also showed marriage at a young age, particularly for women (mean age between seventeen and twenty) coupled with a first pregnancy at a young age (to prove the fertility of the young wife), and preference for a male child. They also showed pregnancies that are closely spaced, particularly among women with lower parity.

Knowledge of family planning appears to be almost universal in most Arab countries. A good proportion of women indicated their preference for a smaller family size than the size they actually had; practice of family planning is not commensurate with the declared knowledge of family planning or desire for smaller family size. Clearly, there is a KAP (i.e., knowledge, attitudes, and practice) gap among the Arab populations. Some of the reasons given by women who know about family planning methods and desire a smaller sized family, but are not currently practicing any family planning method (modern or traditional), are related to the fear of health complications, unavailability of female health and family planning service providers, the prohibitive cost involved, fear of the husband or mother-in-law, lack of female empowerment, and misconceptions related to religion. Clearly, information, education, and communication (IEC) has contributed to knowledge of contraceptives, but it appears that the IEC provided did not effectively dispel many misconceptions about contraceptives, the permissibility of family planning in Islam, changing attitudes; nor was it effective in creating demand for family planning services. These failures point to the benefit of making family planning a woman's, rather than a couple's, responsibility, despite historical and cultural evidence of active male participation in avoiding pregnancy (*al-azl* [withdrawal]).

Strategic IEC approaches followed by the UNFPA in the Arab world include:

1. *Conceptualizing and implementing responsive socio-cultural studies with the objective of providing further insights into the issues raised above, particularly on the decision-making process within the family as it concerns pregnancies and family planning;*

2. *Utilizing the findings of these socio-cultural studies to adapt services according to the women's needs- and rights-based approach, which includes formulating messages directed at men, women, and couples along with "information batteries; that is to say well studied and articulated information packages/messages aiming at behavioral change" for dissemination through women community leaders (the concept of the trusted friend), folklore (songs, theatre, and so on), mass media (particularly television through soap operas and women's talk shows), and women's magazines;*

3. *Revisiting population education curricula so that they reflect the population issues of the countries and include concepts that are relevant to the daily lives of the families, particularly gender issues and female empowerment, as well as promote equal education;*

4. *Sensitizing political and religious leaders, primary school directors in rural areas, and community leaders by providing accurate information as well as scientific and religious arguments explaining the benefits of family*

planning to the mother, child, family, and society, and on the status of women in Islam with the view of arriving at gender equity and the empowerment of women;

5. *Providing traditional birth attendants, midwives, and reproductive health/family planning service providers with information and communication skills targeted at young people in general and at young couples and wives in particular, either prior to their first pregnancy or immediately after the marriage;*

6. *Changing the cultural attitude of male-child preference and that of the low value of a girl child, and toward female circumcision (practiced in some Arab African countries) with specific messages. These messages should be aimed particularly at men and also at mothers, since they raise the children and inculcate the existing value system in them. Television soap opera could play an important role in this area. Due attention should also be given to the elimination of gender stereotyped messages or roles in school textbooks and media;*

7. *Maintaining the confidence of users and new recruits by making the availability and quality of family planning care equal in priority to IEC efforts;*

8. *Highlighting family planning and glorifying women as contributors to the development of the nation equally with men, protectors of the health and development of children and the well-being of the family, and defenders of the nation by raising strong, healthy, educated, and positive thinking children;*

9. *Orienting population education to the target groups in conformity with the options of the educational policy of the countries, taking into consideration both the immediate and long-term concerns of the population policy.*

Improving the Reproductive Health and Well-Being of Men and Women: Effectively Meeting the Demand for Quality Care, Services, and Information for Safe Motherhood and Family Planning

In 1968, the International Community recognized the human right of individuals and couples to "freely and responsibly decide the number and spacing of their children and to have the information, education and the means to do so." The available data show (in addition to what has been mentioned under the IEC section) that fertility is affected primarily by four proximate determinants. These are the age of the woman at marriage, the number of abortions, the mean duration of postpartum amenorrhea, and contraceptive use. Efforts in socioeconomic development, effective IEC, and improving women's status (through education and employment) will lead

to marriage at an older age, particularly for women, and favorable conditions for making a smaller family the norm. Exclusive breast-feeding contributes to increasing the duration of postpartum amenorrhea and thus provides some protection against pregnancy during the first three months after delivery. This protection could be enhanced by the use of condoms or other suitable family planning methods that do not preclude breast-feeding.

The IEC together with health education and socioeconomic development should lead to demand for effective reproductive health and family planning services. Affordable, accessible, acceptable and gender-sensitive quality care in family planning services should be readily available to meet this demand. In addition to the mother's education, three aspects of childbearing have an important effect on child survival, namely: the mother's age at first birthing, the number of children she has previously borne, and the length of time between births. Of these factors, the birth interval appears to have the greatest impact on maternal health and child survival. Also, it is known that too many children can be as dangerous as having them "too close" together. Births to women who are younger than twenty years of age or older than thirty-five years of age are also known to increase the risks to both mother and child. These risks to life and health, summarized by "too close, too many, too old, or too young," hold true for all socioeconomic groups, although in each case the increase in risk is exacerbated by lack of awareness of factors affecting maternal and child health as well as by poverty.

The survival, protection, and development of a child are greatly threatened by the loss of the child's mother due to maternal mortality; without mothers, there are no healthy children. Increasing women's control over their own fertility is, therefore, a change that could clearly have a major impact on the health of mothers and their children. Individual choices about family size are made effective through fertility regulation and by means of effective contraception. Child survival is closely related to the reproductive behavior of the mother, especially in the context of the traditional family building process. The traditional reproductive pattern is characterized by an early start to childbearing, short birth intervals—usually only lengthened by prolonged breast-feeding—and, ultimately, by high parity. High mortality in infancy and childhood as well as maternal morbidity and mortality generally feature in this process. An analysis of reproductive patterns and identification of the direction and magnitude of fertility differentials is thus an essential step towards an understanding of the determinants of maternal and child health. It is on the basis of a clear understanding of these determinants that political commitments to policies and programs aimed at reducing infant, child, and maternal mortality and morbidity by supporting family planning efforts, could be guaranteed.

Available data show that contraceptive prevalence rates in the Arab world range from a low of 4 percent (Mauritania) to 64 percent (O.P.T.). The data also show that almost 25 percent of users depend on traditional methods including withdrawal, rhythm, and abstinence (i.e., male methods or methods with the husband's consent). Due to its relatively low rate of effectiveness, users of traditional methods could be classified as candidates (who have an unmet demand) for the use of modern and more effective contraceptives including implants, injectables, and surgical procedures. In addition, women at a high-risk age (i.e., outside the safe age range of twenty to thirty years) who are not practicing contraception should receive special attention for service delivery and information; delaying the first pregnancy after marriage by three to five years needs to be advocated. Equally, women who have experienced a recent stillbirth or abortion (induced or spontaneous) and who are not current users of contraceptives should receive special attention for reproductive health and family planning information, counseling, and service delivery.

Data indicate a curvilinear association between the number of living children and contraceptive practice. The proportion of women who use contraceptives in order to delay their first pregnancy is small; a sizeable proportion of women start using contraceptives only after having their second live child. Contraception use peaks among women with three or four live births, and it starts to decline among women with five or more living children. The data also indicate an inverted u-shaped pattern of contraceptives use with respect to the age of the mother. That is, use is lower among young women and older women than among women of intermediate ages. Thus women who are at higher risk of pregnancy complications, which adversely affects their own health and the well-being of the child, are least protected.

If both infant mortality rates and maternal morbidity and mortality rates are to be substantially reduced, concerted efforts must be made to promote the Safe Motherhood Approach (a WHO-led, and UNFPA, World Bank, UNICEF, USAID-supported initiative,

launched in 1987. The initiative seeks to reduce illness and death related to pregnancy by ensuring that women have the best chance of having a safe pregnancy and delivery and a healthy baby. The ingredients necessary for making motherhood safer include prenatal care, safe delivery, postnatal care, family planning, and good nutrition. Also essential, is information to raise awareness among pregnant mothers and their families about the importance of maternal health care and family planning services) within an integrated reproductive health approach. Protecting women under twenty years of age and women thirty-five years of age and older from the higher risks of pregnancy through effective contraception, and protecting women aged twenty to twenty-four years from the risks of pregnancy, or at least the risk of closely spaced pregnancies, should receive top priority. For this approach to be effective, there is a need for improving the application of the "contraceptives target setting model" (Bongaart's Model) by activating the age-specific features of the available models and by providing a wider mix of modern and long-acting methods, including surgical interventions. This should be coupled with further improvements in communication and information, maternal care, improved availability of and access to quality services and care, including obstetric emergency care, and joint efforts (strategic partnerships) with UNFPA, WHO, the United Nations Children's Fund (UNICEF), regional organizations, bilateral donors, and national programs.

In order to monitor the progress of the established goals and to introduce effective program interventions, record keeping and information should be emphasized. Specifically, data should be generated on current users through health administrative records that document age, age at marriage, number of children, dates of deliveries, methods previously used and their durations, current methods used and date of use, failure of methods, discontinuation, and abortions. Since, by definition, administrative records cover users only, demographic and health surveys should be implemented at four or five year intervals. These surveys will capture users as well as nonusers. Key information on nonusers, such as their ages, socioeconomic strata, parity, reasons for nonuse, and so on, are important for determining the characteristics of hard-to-reach individuals and couples as well as for identifying issues related to reasons for nonuse of contraceptives. The identified issues would point to the need for further program improvements in terms of availability, accessibility, affordability, acceptability, and gender sensitivity, and

care; refinement of the IEC message, and its wider dissemination. Surveys would also identify issues requiring further insights through sociocultural research.

Age-specific target setting that is based on accurate, recent, and disaggregated data contributes greatly to the efficacy of family planning programs in general and to the success of the Safe Motherhood Approach in particular. In addition, and subject to the availability of input data, age-specific target setting models could be utilized at sub national levels such as by administrative unit or by "urban" and "rural." A strategic advantage of calculating contraceptive requirements (i.e., target setting) by urban and rural is in being able to quantify the task of bridging the contraception gap between rural and urban populations. Data show that in most Arab countries, contraceptive prevalence rates in rural areas are half or less than rates for urban areas. It also shows younger age at marriage for women, earlier fertility, more closely spaced pregnancies, higher parity, economically less advantaged populations, and much less availability of services in rural areas as compared to urban areas. Target setting models also allow calculations of contraceptive requirements by source of service provider. This is advantageous as it quantifies the role of the government, the private sector, the nongovernmental organizations, and other sources. Quantification is also important for securing the required contraceptives sufficiently in advance (particularly for government; it involves budgetary appropriations, procurement, and distribution).

There is an acute need for strengthening governments' capabilities in contraceptives procurement and logistics. The timely quantification of needs by contraceptive method facilitates the management of family planning by providing the information required for deciding the size, gender, and distribution of family planning service providers as well as the necessary method-specific training of staff; this is in addition to providing the basis for effective monitoring of family planning achievements. Most important, it facilitates the undertaking, by national and/or international private sectors, of market segmentation studies and differentials in cost per socioeconomic group, and of feasibility studies for local production of specific methods. Furthermore, it guides those responsible for family planning information and communication in designing messages and campaigns for specific target groups and on specific methods.

The best available estimates (obtained in 1998) put the number of couples in the Arab world using contraceptives at about 28 million, or a contraceptive prevalence rate of about 40 percent. However, in order for the 1990 levels of infant, child, and maternal mortality rates to be reduced by 50 percent, and for total fertility rates to be reduced by one child per woman (from 4.2 children to 3.2 children between 2000 and the year 2010), about 56.2 million couples will need contraceptive protection by the year 2010. This means that contraceptive prevalence rates would have to grow from 40 percent in 2000 to 60 percent in the year 2010. Along with this increase, reliance on ineffective traditional methods by some 9 million couples in 2000 would have to gradually shift to reliance on modern and long-acting methods, including surgical interventions for those who have completed their desired family size.

Certain traditional practices in Arab African countries are harmful to women's reproductive health. Female genital mutilation (FGM), also commonly known as female circumcision, is such a practice. It is widely performed in Egypt, Sudan, Somalia, and Djibouti, and some reports suggest it is also known in Yemen and Oman. It is estimated that 31 million women have experienced FGM in Arab African countries. Both types of operations, clitoridectomy and infibulation, carry the risk of bleeding and infection which may lead to death or infertility. The effect on women's psychosexual health is also grave. Infibulation often causes obstructed labor, which may lead to vesico-vaginal fistulas. Other delivery complications are common, and they threaten the health and lives of mothers and their children. Use of intrauterine contraceptives and routine gynecological examinations are often made impossible by infibulation, thus reducing women's contraceptive choices; infibulation can also mask pelvic diseases. Governments, religious leaders and national women's groups, youth, and health professional organizations need to more actively publicize the health risks of FGM and dissociate the practice from all religions.

Strategic approaches followed by UNFPA for reproductive health care and family planning in the Arab world include:

1. *Strengthening the capacity and capability of governments to institutionalize the process of formulating, implementing, and monitoring responsive population policies, including gender and reproductive health/ family planning policies, with quantifiable goals and appropriating funds for implementing these policies;*

2. *Strengthening the capacity and capability of governments to formulate reproductive health /family planning programs with quantifiable goals, implementing these programs in collaboration with the private sector and nongovernmental organizations, and monitoring the implementation and achievements of these programs. Such programs should include the Safe Motherhood Approach, the reproductive and sexual rights-based approach, and should put emphasis on bridging the gap between rural and urban populations. It should also address men and the hard-to-reach groups;*

3. *Improving the process of contraceptives target setting at national, and preferably, also at sub-national levels and by age group and source (type) of service provider. This also includes ensuring the availability of family planning data (Management Information System);*

4. *Improving the management of family planning programs at central and provincial levels through training in logistics management and health education;*

5. *Improving the availability of quality family planning services and the accessibility, affordability, and acceptability of these services to rural and urban couples. Quality of care and gender sensitivity should be improved, including the availability of qualified women service providers and a wider range of contraceptive methods that are safe and long-acting;*

6. *Strengthening national capabilities and capacities for manufacturing and/or procurement as well as distribution and promotion, of contraceptives. This should also include community-based distribution, preferably by women community leaders, as well as cost recovery systems;*

7. *Improving coordination among donor agencies and encouraging joint programming, particularly with WHO, UNICEF, and the World Bank. Coordination with bilateral and multilateral donors should also be strengthened, and Arab donors should be identified and approached.*

Improving Gender Equity and the Status of Women

Especially women's access to and control of resources in order to ensure their full participation in population and development programs

Women make up 50 percent of the total population and, of course, 100 percent of all mothers. Less than half of women ten years or older in the Arab world are literate. The participation of women in the formal economic sector is limited. However, their contribution in the non-formal economic sector is vast, although usually not recognized because they generally work without pay. Women in the Arab world marry and have their first child at a relatively young age; they also have pregnancies too closely spaced, resulting in high parity, a situation that contributes to continuous maternal depletion and leads to higher rates of maternal mortality and morbidity. Women in most Arab countries endure their situation in silence.

It has been established that fertility is affected by a woman's level of educational attainment and gainful employment. Women with higher education have lower fertility rates and are in control of regulating their fertility; they are also better equipped to contribute effectively to the survival, protection, and development of their children than illiterate mothers. Governments should invest in the education of young girls and provide them with opportunities similar to young boys. Culturally, women's roles in the formal economic sector and in political life are extremely limited; positive discrimination in favor of women may be needed to achieve gender equality and equity, and to give women equal opportunities to participate in the economic sector and in political life. As in other societies, different forms of discrimination and violence against women are observed in the Arab world. While it is difficult to ascertain its magnitude, there is enough evidence that violence, including sexual violence, occurs against women. Many Arab countries have already ratified the Convention on the Elimination of all Forms of Discrimination Against Women (CEDAW), the majority with reservations, but ten countries still need to join the international community in ratifying the convention. In the Arab region, women are usually the best agents for social development. They are the ones who normally raise future generations and inculcate the value system of the society into children. Women, in addition to their reproductive role, also contribute in a vast way to development through their productive and community roles. They should be involved in conceptualizing programs aimed at enhancing their status in society and their contribution to development. Family planning services, along with family planning information and communication, are tasks that should increasingly be entrusted to women, particularly women service providers and women community leaders. Strategic approaches followed by UNFPA in the Arab world in promoting gender equity, population control, and development includes the following:

1. *Investing in the education of young girls, by giving them opportunities similar to those given to young boys; this holds a high yield return for the overall social and economic development of a nation;*

2. *Empowering women to have greater access to, and control of, resources including control over their bodies and regulating their own fertility;*

3. *Improving data collection, processing, analysis, dissemination and utilization of gender-specific information;*

4. *Encouraging women nongovernmental organizations (NGOs) to take active advocacy and action roles on issues related to women's rights, education, employment, health, and political participation, as well as the improvement of their status in society. Women's NGOs should be encouraged to play an active role in policy and program formulation, implementation, and assessment to ensure that women's concerns are adequately addressed. Women community leaders are in an excellent position to be the agents of social change. They can provide the women of the community with accurate information, counsel them, and distribute contraceptives. They can also put women in contact with reproductive health/family planning centers and follow up on dropouts. These women community leaders should be organized, trained, and supported;*

5. *Supporting national women higher commissions. These commissions should encourage the organization of women's NGOs, coordinate among the various entities active in socioeconomic and health services, and contribute to women's political agenda;*

6. *Making sure all developmental efforts are gender sensitive and address women's concerns. Sensitization of planners and policymakers on gender and women's issues, rights, and concerns should receive top priority.*

References

Cassels, Andrew. "Health Sector Reform: Key issues in Less Developed Countries." Journal of International Development. 1995 May-June; 7(3):329-347 and WHO, Forum on Health sector reform, discussion paper # 1, Geneva, 1995.

Davidson, Gwatkin. Presentation titled "The Evidence base on Poverty and Reproductive Health", (http://wbweb5.worldbank.org/database/reprohealth/evidence.pdf) The World Bank, Wash. D. C., USA, 11 September, 2001.

Future's Group International. "Implementing RH Services in an Era of Health Sector Reform." Occasional Papers, Washington D.C., 2000.

League of Arab States, and United Nations Economic and Social Commission for Western Asia (UNESCWA). "Proceedings of the Arab Population Conference." Amman, Jordan, 1993.

Ministry of Foreign Affairs. "Sector Wide Approaches for Health Development." The Hague, Netherlands, 1999.

Omran, Abdul-Rahim. *Family Planning in the legacy of Islam.* Routledge, London; United Kingdom: UNFPA, 1994.

Omran, Abdul-Rahim. *The Population of the Arab World: Current and Future.* New York: UNFPA, 1998.

Human Development Network, World Bank. *Safe Motherhood and the World Bank: Lessons from 10 years of Experience.* The World Bank, Washington D.C. June, 1999.

Sadik, Nafis. Briefing points to the drafting committee of the 2nd Amman Declaration on population and Development, Amman, Jordan: April, 1993.

Salm, A.P. "Promoting Reproductive and Sexual Health in the Era of Sector Wide Approaches." *Reproductive Health Matters.* 2000 May; 8 (15):18–20.

United Nations Development Program, and Arab Fund for Economic and Social Development. *Arab Human Development Report, 2002. Creating Opportunities for Future Generations.* Amman, Jordan, 2002.

United Nations Economic and Social Commission for Western Asia. *"Migration and Population Policies in the Arab Region."* United Nations, New York, N.Y., 2001. (E/ESCWA/POP/2001/5, 26 December 2001, Original: Arabic)

United Nations Population Fund. "Proposal on the Regional Population Strategy for the Arab World for the Decade 1994–2003." [Draft]. UNFPA Regional Country Directors Meeting, Amman, Jordan, 1–3 April 1993.

United Nations Population Fund. *Report of the International Conference on Population and Development, Cairo, Egypt, September 5–13, 1994, "Program of Action."* Adopted at the International Conference on Population and Development, Cairo, 5–13 September 1994. New York, October, 1994.

United Nations Population Fund. "The State of World Population, 1999." New York, 1999.

United Nations Population Fund. "The State of World Population, 2000." New York, 2000.

United Nations Population Fund. "The State of World Population, 2001." New York, 2001.

United Nations Children's Fund. "The State of Children and Women in the Middle East and North Africa Region." Amman, Jordan, 2001.

United Nations Population Division. *The Sex and Age Distribution of the World Population*, 1996 Revision. New York, 1997.

United Nations Population Division. *The World Contraceptive Use 2001*. New York: UN, 2001.

United Nations Population Division. *World Population Prospects*. 1996 Revision. New York: UN, 1998.

United Nations Population Division. *World Population Prospects*. 1998 Revision. New York: UN, 1998.

United Nations Population Division. *World Population Aging, 1950–2050*. New York: UN, 2002.

United Nations Population Division. *World Urbanization Prospects*. 2001 Revision Data Tables, and Highlights. New York: UN, 2002.

United Nations Population Division. *World Population Monitoring 2002, reproductive rights and reproductive health: selected aspects* (draft). New York, 2002. (presented to the Commission on Population and Development, Thirty-fifth session, 1–5 April 2002).

United Nations Relief and Works Agency for Palestine Refugees in the Near East (UNRWA). "UNRWA Health Report, 2001." Department of Health, 2001. HQs, Amman, Jordan.

World Bank. "Human Development Network, 2000. Population and the World Bank: Adapting to Change." Washington D.C., 2000.

World Bank Institute. "Reproductive Health and Health Sector reform: Linking Outcomes to Action." Washington D.C., 2000.

World Health Organization/Eastern Mediterranean Regional Office. "Demographic and Health Indicators for Countries of the Eastern Mediterranean." WHO/EMRO, 1998.

World Health Organization. "Primary Health Care Approaches for Preparation and Control of Congenital and Genetic Disorders." Geneva, Switzerland: WHO, 1999.

World Health Organization. "World Health Report 2000, Health Systems: Improving Performance." Geneva, Switzerland: WHO, 2000.

World Health Organization/Eastern Mediterranean Regional Office. "Adolescent Health, Report on the Inter-country Consultation on the Promotion of Health of Adolescent Girls Through Maternal and Child Health Programs." Alexandria, Egypt, : WHO/ EMRO, 1996.

World Health Organization. "World Health Report, 1999" Geneva Switzerland: WHO, 1999.

World Health Organization. "World Health Report, 2000", Geneva Switzerland: WHO, 2000.

World Health Organization. "World Health Report, 2001", Geneva Switzerland: WHO, 2001.

Endnote

1. Omran, Abdul-Rahim. *The Population of the Arab World: Current and Future*. New York: UNFPA, 1998:83–124

Structural Reforms in the Middle East and North Africa

John Page[1]

After more than twenty years of rapid economic growth, falling oil prices in the mid-1980s and an abrupt decline in investment and growth pushed Arab governments to rethink their basic frameworks for economic management (Page 1998; World Bank 1995).[2] The post-independence Arab socialist period left virtually all of the economies in the Middle East and North Africa (MENA) with an inward-looking, statist model of development that lost dynamism in the 1980s.[3] Beginning in about 1985, Arab governments—supported by the international financial institutions—shifted at varying rates toward policies designed to achieve the "Washington Consensus"[4] of macroeconomic stability, a higher degree of integration with the world economy, and an expanded role for the private sector.

This chapter surveys MENA's track record in implementing "structural reforms" intended to restore macroeconomic stability, increase international trade, and raise the volume and efficiency of private investment. The first section briefly summarizes the economic transition in MENA from a state-dominated, import-substituting industrialization to a more open, private sector-led model of development. It outlines several factors, including the high current level of public sector employment and its impact on poverty and income distribution, that may limit the political ability of MENA governments to accelerate the pace of economic reform. The second section describes macroeconomic management since the

late 1980s and highlights the reform experience of four key low- and middle-income countries (LMICs): Egypt, Jordan, Morocco, and Tunisia[5]. The third section examines multilateral trade policy reforms and the important regional trading arrangements of the European Union Mediterranean (EuroMed) Initiative and Arab Free Trade Area (AFTA). The fourth section looks at policy reforms designed to increase the volume and efficiency of private investment, including privatization and improvements in the investment climate. The concluding section presents an overall assessment of the structural reform process and outlines some priorities for the future.

A Region in Transition

It is conventional to describe the economies of Eastern Europe and the former Soviet Union as in "transition," that is, moving from heavily state-dominated and closed economic systems to ones based on private initiative, market forces, and greater integration with the rest of the world. In many ways, the low- and middle-income economies of MENA share these transitional characteristics. They have limited and declining integration with the world economy, large public sectors, and low levels of private investment. In an era of strong and rising oil prices and large intraregional flows of capital and labor, economic growth, worker remittances, and government employment combined in MENA to reduce income inequality and absolute poverty to very low levels by international standards, similar to those in Eastern Europe and Central Asia (Adams and Page 2002). But maintaining this achievement in a period of lower oil prices and growth represents both a challenge for, and a constraint on, economic policymakers in the Arab world.

Increasing isolation from the global economy

Over the last three decades, a striking feature of the MENA region has emerged: how little these economies have increased their integration with the rest of the world. Figure 1 shows changes in real trade ratios (exports plus imports as a share of GDP) from 1965 to 1998, a period of rapid expansion of the global economy. High-income countries have led the growth in real trade ratios since the mid-1970s. In the developing world, the lion's share of the growth in world trade has accrued to the economies of east Asia, Eastern Europe, Central Asia, and Latin America. Growth of real trade ratios in the MENA region—aside from oil-related volatility—has been weak. The major Latin American and east Asian

Figure 1. Changes in Real Trade Ratios

Source: World Bank, Global Development Indicators, 2001

economies (Brazil, Argentina, China, South Korea, Indonesia, Taiwan) have made consistent inroads into MENA markets, while MENA exporters have not significantly penetrated the markets of Latin America and east Asia. Nor are there significant links to the major economies in the rest of Africa or south Asia (Madani and Page 2002). International capital flows that exploded in the 1990s have similarly bypassed MENA (Page 1998).

In sum, the MENA region has been losing ground in terms of integration into the world economy. Figure 2 shows the speed of integration of Arab economies compared to those in other developing regions.[6] From the mid-1980s to the mid-1990s, the "median" country in MENA had a speed of integration that was just about the same as in sub-Saharan Africa, and well below other developing regions. In fact, during that period, even the top performing economies in MENA were reducing the extent of their integration with the rest of the world.

Public investment grew while private investment lagged

Public investment has consistently been higher in the Middle East and North Africa than in other developing regions. Of the nearly $55 billion in oil rents that flowed into the region during the 1970s, more than 90 percent accrued to the public sector (Page 1998). Even non-oil producers benefited from the boom. Between 1970 and 1990, public investment in Egypt, Jordan, and Syria was closely correlated

Figure 2. Speed of Integration

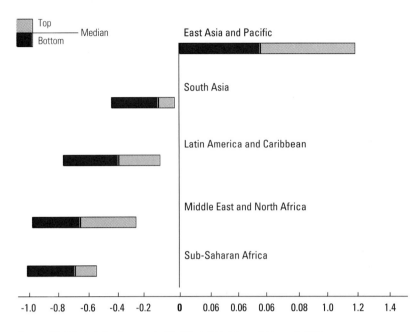

Sources: World Bank staff estimates using World Bank, Global Economic Prospects 1996

in MENA is high relative to other developing countries and, perhaps more important from a policymaker's perspective, the share of the total labor force employed by the state is also high (Page 2001). During the post-independence period, public sector salaries and benefits in MENA were established largely without reference to alternative wages in the private sector, and the public sector became the wage leader in the labor market. Civil service (and public enterprise) jobs paid better wages, offered more fringe benefits, gave better job security, and assured more social status than those in the private sector. In a number of MENA economies the government guaranteed public employment to university graduates, and frequently acted as "employer of first resort" for graduates at lower educational levels (Adams and Page 2002).

One result of this pattern of employment, wages, and benefits is that MENA countries are now endowed with one of the largest and, relative to their private sectors, best-paid public sectors in the world (see Table 1). The countries of MENA devote a larger share of their GDP (9.8 percent) to civil service salaries than any other region. They are the only grouping of countries, internationally, in which the

with aid flows from both Arab and non-Arab sources. During the 1970s and 1980s (with the exception of the socialist economies of Europe and Central Asia), MENA economies were the public investment champions of the developing world (World Bank 1995). As Arab governments encountered increasing fiscal pressure and intraregional aid flows from oil exporters diminished, MENA's public investment rate converged toward that of other LMICs.

Where MENA countries have historically lagged is in the rate of private investment. Until the late 1980s, private investment as a share of GDP in MENA was substantially below that for other LMICs. Low investment rates were not primarily due to low levels of private savings, but to a perceived lack of investment opportunities. Very substantial portfolio diversification by Arab investors took place outside of MENA during the 1980s. Despite modest increases in private investment during the 1990s, the region continues to lag behind east Asia and Latin America in private investment and to trail all developing regions except Africa in the rate of foreign direct investment.

A large and relatively well-paid public sector

Although it is no longer growing rapidly, the public sector continues to dominate MENA economies to an extent that is greater than in most other parts of the developing world. Both the share of total assets and the share of output produced in the public sector

Table 1. Central Government Wages, Early 1990s

Region	Number of Countries	Central Government Wages and Salaries as Percent of GDP	Average Central Government Wage as Multiple of per Capita GDP	Ratio of Public to Private Sector Wages
Africa	21	6.7	5.5	1.0
Asia	14	4.7	3.0	0.8
Europe and Central Asia	21	3.7	1.3	0.7
Latin America and the Caribbean	12	4.9	2.7	0.9
MENA	8	9.8	3.4	1.3
OECD	16	4.5	1.6	0.9
Overall	92	5.4	2.9	0.8

Source: Page 2001

**Table 2. Incidence of Poverty in the Developing World (in Percent)
Using International Standards of $1.00 or $2.00 per Person per Day, 1987–1998**

Region and Income	1987		1990		1993		1996		1998	
Per Capita, 2000	$1.00	$2.00	$1.00	$2.00	$1.00	$2.00	$1.00	$2.00	$1.00	$2.00
East Asia and Pacific (US$1,030)	26.6	67.0	27.6	66.1	25.2	60.5	14.9	48.6	14.7	48.7
Europe and Central Asia (US$2,300)	0.2	3.6	1.6	9.6	4.0	17.2	5.1	19.9	3.7	20.7
Latin America and the Caribbean (US$4,035)	15.3	35.5	16.8	38.1	15.3	35.1	15.6	37.0	12.1	31.7
Middle East and North Africa (US$1,975)	4.3	30.0	2.4	24.8	1.9	24.1	1.8	22.2	2.1	29.9
South Asia (US$450)	44.9	86.3	44.0	86.8	42.4	85.4	42.3	85.0	40.0	83.9
Sub-Saharan Africa (US$515)	46.6	76.5	47.7	76.4	49.7	77.8	48.5	76.9	48.1	78.0
World	28.3	61.0	29.0	61.7	28.1	60.1	24.5	56.1	23.4	56.1

Sources: World Bank, World Development Report 2000/01: Attacking Poverty; World Bank, Global Economic Prospects and the Developing Countries, 2000

ratio of public sector wages to wages in the private sector exceeds one (the MENA ratio is 1.3).

Public employment and worker remittances reduced poverty

Oil rents and the state-led model of development yielded some important benefits for MENA's citizens. By international standards, the LMICs of the MENA entered the last decade of the twentieth century with strikingly low levels of income poverty. MENA was the developing region with the lowest incidence of extreme poverty (defined as $1.00 per person per day) throughout the 1990s (see Table 2). Using an international poverty standard of $2.00 per person per day—perhaps more appropriate for MENA's average level of per capita income—the Middle East still remains a low poverty region; in 1998 about 30 percent of the region's population lived below the $2.00 per person per day line. Only the transitional economies of Europe and Central Asia had a lower incidence of poverty.

Despite slow economic growth and rising unemployment in the 1990s, MENA has been largely successful in holding the line with respect to increases in poverty-level income. In contrast to Europe and Central Asia, where poverty numbers have increased dramatically in the course of economic transition, continued high levels of government employment and substantial remittances from Arab workers migrating to the Gulf and Europe have caused poverty numbers in MENA to remain quite stable (Adams and Page 2002).

One consequence of slow growth and the labor market distortions introduced by the public sector has been the saddling of MENA economies with the highest recorded rates of unemployment internationally (World Bank 1996b). While unemployment is fundamentally a product of low economic growth rates and high population growth, governments are reluctant to exacerbate the problem by aggressive reform measures such as trade liberalization or privatization of public enterprises that employ large numbers of workers. In Algeria, Egypt, Jordan, Kuwait, Tunisia, and Yemen, fear of labor redundancies has slowed down privatization, particularly in the manufacturing sector. The case of Egypt was particularly dramatic. In 1994, textile workers in Kafr-al-Dawwar initiated a strike, filling the streets with mass demonstrations of more than 7,000 workers to protest privatizations proposed under an agreement with the IMF. This event is one that still influences the pace and depth of the Egyptian privatization program. Jordan's attempts to rationalize and reduce consumer subsidies and to privatize its railways have been met with similar episodes of civil unrest.

Macroeconomic Adjustment

In the mid-1980s, macroeconomic imbalances began to emerge in many MENA economies. Most undertook macroeconomic stabilization programs in the late 1980s and early 1990s and succeeded in restoring macroeconomic stability by the mid-1990s. This section examines the macroeconomic adjustment experience of four key MENA economies—Egypt, Jordan, Morocco, and Tunisia—and then attempts to place the extent of the region's macroeconomic adjustment in an international context using a composite index of macroeconomic stabilization.

Stabilization in Egypt, Jordan, Morocco, and Tunisia

Triggered by the regional economic slowdown, Egypt's twenty-year economic expansion ended in 1986, and by 1991 it had embarked on a difficult period of stabilization. Between 1991 and 2001 the overall budget deficit was reduced from 15.2 percent to 3.6 percent of GDP; the inflation rate fell from 15 percent to 3 percent; and the average current account balance during the period was 1.7 percent of GDP. Structural reforms designed to restore economic growth by opening the economy to greater competition and decreasing the role of government in economic activities, were also put in place. Gross domestic investment increased from 12 percent to 17 percent of GDP, and growth picked up in the late 1990s. Still, the performance of exports and foreign direct investment remained poor. Recent growth has been driven by domestic demand and has relied primarily on the accumulation of labor and capital, rather than on the growth of productivity. Further, despite modest gains in manufacturing, growth has come primarily from the expansion of nontradeables such as construction and services (World Bank 2001e).

At the beginning of its stabilization program, Egypt pegged its nominal exchange rate to the dollar. During most of the 1990s, external competitiveness suffered due to appreciation of the real effective exchange rate, an effect of the inflation differential between Egypt and its trading partners. In January 2001, the Central Bank implemented a new exchange rate policy, still in effect: the Egyptian pound is nominally pegged to the dollar, but is also allowed to float within a band. Under this "managed peg" system, a moving rate is established by the Central Bank based on the weighted average of all transactions made during the previous three weeks. The change in the exchange-rate regime has resulted in a substantial nominal depreciation of the Egyptian pound, but a depreciation that has also been moderated to some extent by administrative restrictions on foreign exchange transactions.

Jordan's economy was also hard-hit by the fall in oil prices. Foreign capital inflows and worker remittances from the oil-rich states fell dramatically in the late 1980s, and by 1988 Jordan faced a balance of payments crisis that was further exacerbated by dislocations associated with the Gulf War. Since 1989, Jordan has made considerable stabilization and adjustment efforts. The fiscal deficit was reduced from a high of 18 percent

of GDP in the period 1990 to 1991, to 7.8 percent in 1995. Inflation was maintained in the 3.0 to 3.5 percent range throughout the 1990s. The Jordanian dinar was devalued and pegged to the dollar, and tight monetary management (with accompanying high real interest rates) helped build foreign reserves from a low of less than two months of import coverage in the early 1990s to a high of more than five months by 1996. The current account remained essentially balanced throughout the second half of the 1990s. Between 1994 and 1996 there was a burst of renewed growth, fueled by an inflow of savings from returnees during and after the Gulf War. But the signs of a possible recovery reversed in 1997, as the construction boom that followed the Gulf War ran its course and unfavorable regional developments—including impediments to expansion of trade with neighboring countries—negatively affected the economy.

In 1983 Morocco, faced with negative growth rates and large macroeconomic imbalances unrelated to oil price fluctuations, began its stabilization efforts. The stabilization program was successful in restoring internal and external balance within five years; their budget deficit fell from 10.4 percent of GDP in 1984/1985 to 2.7 percent in 1991/1992, and the current account deficit dropped from 7.3 percent to 1.7 percent during the same period. Structural reforms focused on reorienting the economy away from pervasive state controls, and the economy responded with a period of positive growth in the latter part of the 1980s. However, by the early 1990s growth had slowed, due in part to unfavorable external shocks, including severe droughts. While Morocco continued to consolidate its stabilization efforts throughout the 1990s, growth remained poor—virtually stagnating in real per capita terms throughout the decade. The pegged exchange-rate regimes led to a real appreciation of the currency and a deterioration in external competitiveness. In April 2001, there was an effective nominal devaluation of the currency by 5 percent.

Tunisia followed a state-led model of development until the mid-1980s, when a set of factors—a poor crop year, growing financial imbalances, and the collapse of oil prices—precipitated a crisis. In 1987 the government initiated a series of economic reforms aimed at restoring macroeconomic stability, gradually liberalizing prices, trade and investment controls, and decreasing the emphasis on the public sector to free resources for the private sector. After an initial period of adjustment and continued low growth, the results were impressive by regional

Table 3. Average Annual Growth Rates of Real GDP in Egypt, Jordan, Morocco and Tunisia, 1980 to 1999

Country	Average Annual Growth Rates (in Percent)				
	1980–1984	1985–1989	1990–1994	1995–1999	Overall
Egypt					
Real GDP	7.46	3.94	3.12	5.48	5.00
Real per capita GDP	4.87	1.48	0.97	3.59	2.73
Jordan					
Real GDP	5.67	(-1.22)	5.28	2.24	2.99
Real per capita GDP	1.75	(-4.83)	(-0.41)	(-0.86)	(-1.09)
Morocco					
Real GDP	1.84	3.82	3.06	1.94	2.66
Real per capita GDP	(-0.37)	1.69	1.14	0.21	0.67
Tunisia					
Real GDP	4.57	2.54	5.03	5.17	4.33
Real per capita GDP	2.06	0.09	2.97	3.78	2.22

Sources: GDP growth rates from International Monetary Fund, International Financial Statistics Yearbook (various issues); Population growth rates from World Bank, MENA Live Database

standards. The Tunisian economy sustained growth rates of higher than 5 percent per year throughout the 1990s.

Table 3 presents average annual rates of real GDP growth in the four countries for the period 1980 to 1999. For three—Egypt, Jordan, and Tunisia—the impact of adjustment is evident in the deceleration in the rate of per capita income growth. The magnitude of the economic contraction experienced by Jordan is particularly striking; GDP growth per capita fell from 1.75 percent between 1980 and 1984 to –4.83 percent

between 1985 and 1989, and remained negative throughout the 1990s. In Egypt, income growth per person fell from nearly 5 percent between 1980 and 1984 to less than 1 percent between 1990 and 1994, before recovering to about 3.6 percent in the period 1995 to 1999. Tunisia faced the shortest adjustment period. While per capita income growth fell to nearly 0 percent between 1980 and 1984 as well between 1985 and 1989, it recovered to more than 3 percent on average for the decade of the 1990s. Morocco began the 1980s with five years of negative average per capita income growth (1980 to 1985) followed by positive, but decelerating, income growth per person during the following fifteen years.

Macroeconomic adjustment in international perspective

How well does the macroeconomic adjustment effort made by MENA economies stack up when compared with other parts of the developing world? Figure 3 shows the behavior, over time, of a composite index of economic management for seven MENA economies contrasted with five other regions. The index gives a broad measure of the quality of macroeconomic management by equally weighting performance on: (i) fiscal balance as a ratio to GDP; (ii) current account balance as a ratio to GDP; (iii) consumer price inflation; and (iv) the black market premium on the exchange rate in percent.

Conservative macroeconomic management and the willingness to carry through economic stabilization have resulted in very substantial gains in macroeconomic stability for MENA economies. While the 1990s saw a generalized improvement in macroeconomic

Figure 3. Composite Index of Economic Stabilization by Regions

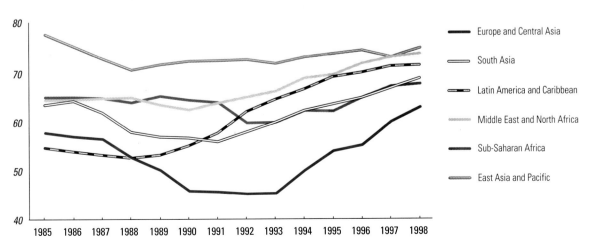

Source: World Bank Staff Estimates

management throughout the developing world, MENA's performance was particularly impressive. Between 1991 and 1998, MENA moved from a level of stability roughly similar to that of south Asia and sub-Saharan Africa to that of east Asia and the Pacific, traditionally the best performing regions in macroeconomic terms.

Trade Policy Reform—Going Global Slowly

MENA's lagging integration with the world economy is not surprising. Until recently—with the exception of the Gulf states and Lebanon—the region's trade regimes were quite closed by international standards. Quantitative restrictions on imports were pervasive, and tariffs were high. The net result of this structure of protection was that by the 1990s, domestic price structures in Arab countries differed substantially from international prices for similar goods. In 1990, MENA (excluding the Gulf states) ranked second only to Africa south of the Sahara in terms of the extent to which average domestic prices of traded goods diverged from the international prices of equivalent goods (Page 2001).

The region is shifting from widespread use of quantitative restrictions on trade (QRs) to tariff-based protection. Algeria, Morocco, Tunisia, Egypt, and Jordan have all reduced the coverage of their domestic manufacturing sector by QRs in the last five years. Nevertheless, an important agenda remains for eliminating nontariff barriers to trade. Syria and Iraq have failed to follow the regional trend in shifting from quota- to tariff-based protection. Despite the free trade agreements signed by Morocco and Tunisia with the European Union, all three economies in the Maghreb have maintained quota-based protection in a subset of "sensitive sectors" (Page and Underwood 1997). Similarly, Egypt and Jordan have not fully eliminated nontariff barriers to trade (World Bank, 1997).

Many MENA economies—including the relatively open ones of the Gulf Cooperation Council (GCC)—have government-granted monopoly rights in the distribution of imports. This discourages international access. These barriers to entry keep domestic and international prices from converging, and mute

Opening up to the world—multilateral trade liberalization

Beginning in the mid-1990s, Arab governments made modest efforts at multilateral trade policy reform. Many MENA countries were active participants in the Uruguay round of trade negotiations and, as World Trade Organization (WTO) members, have recently agreed to enter into a new round at Qatar. Progress in liberalizing trade and reducing anti-export bias in MENA has lagged behind that of east Asia, Latin America, and some of the transition economies of Europe and central Asia. Although tariff and tax reforms have been undertaken by most MENA countries since the 1980s, progress has been slow and uneven. The result has been that, throughout the 1990s, the unweighted tariff rate in MENA was higher than in any other region except for south Asia, and no significant reduction in average tariffs took place (see Figure 4).

Figure 4. Average Nominal Tariffs by Region 1980–1998 (in Percent)

Source: World Bank 2001a

the positive impact of trade reforms. Government and parastate procurement of goods and services is a significant part of the economy in every MENA country, and it discourages new entrants and foreign competition. Typical procurement rules in the region require that bids and contracts be secured by bonds or bank guarantees, which are themselves secured by cash or real property collateral. Contracts, receivables, inventory, design, software, and intellectual property generally cannot be used or leveraged.

Trade policy reform in Egypt, Jordan, Morocco, and Tunisia

Egypt's merchandise exports amounted to less than 3 percent of GDP in 2000. Part of this poor export performance is a result of policies that have sustained substantial anti-export bias in the incentive structure. Although average tariffs were reduced from 32 percent in 1988 to 28 percent in 1999, they remain high relative to the average of 18 percent for all lower middle-income countries. Additional taxes and charges add another 3 percent. Further, the tariff structure is not uniform. Effective tariffs for fully processed products are significantly higher than tariffs for semiprocessed products and raw materials, diverting resources away from exports to import-substituting sectors.

Bureaucratic obstacles, including customs procedures, administrative controls, and quality controls, not only increase protection to domestic producers but also hurt Egyptian exporters who use imported inputs. Temporary admission and duty drawback schemes do not function well, and there has been relatively little outward oriented investment in Egypt's free trade zones (FTZs). Lack of access to internationally priced inputs may help explain why Egypt, despite its proximity to European markets and relatively low labor costs, has not become part of the new global pattern of production in which multinational companies outsource the production of parts to other companies globally.

Jordan's external competitiveness is in part linked to factors outside its control, including progress in the peace process between Israel and the Palestinian Authority and the situation in Iraq, traditionally its largest trading partner. In the early 1990s, a round of unilateral tariff reductions (part of its stabilization program) reduced anti-export bias somewhat, but Jordan's traditional exports of potash, phosphates, and fertilizers continue to dominate export performance. By 1999, further reductions in tariffs and efforts towards fulfilling requirements for accession to the

WTO led to some improvement in the trade policy regime. Reforms have focused on improving the legal and institutional framework, including custom reforms, trade deregulation, measures to facilitate investment, and improvements in product standards.

After a period of relatively strong export growth in the late 1980s, Morocco's trade performance deteriorated in the 1990s, and it lost market share in most of its traditional products. Morocco continues to maintain high levels of protection; this limits its international competitiveness and results in significant anti-export bias. In the second half of the 1990s, tariffs—including a flat surcharge of 15 percent on manufactured goods—averaged 40 percent, and imports of "strategic" agricultural products, such as wheat, were subject to rates in excess of 100 percent, resulting in the production of agricultural goods in which Morocco has little comparative advantage.

Tunisia has had the most successful experience with FTZs in the region. These "offshore" manufacturing areas are characterized by duty-free access of imported inputs for export manufacturing, and a separate customs regime. Much of the dynamism in Tunisia's manufacturing sector has come from the expansion of firms in the FTZs that export mass manufactured goods to the European market. Tariff protection to import-substituting industry located outside the special customs zones has decreased over the 1990s but remains relatively high by international standards, and few backward linkages have developed between the export manufacturing sector and the rest of the domestic economy. Tunisia has also been successful in encouraging tourism, which is, globally, the fastest-growing services export. Current account transactions are liberalized, and restrictions on long-term capital flows are minimal. Tunisia, Morocco, and Algeria are also members of a nominal free trade area, the Maghreb Union, but they have made little significant progress in implementing its trade liberalization agreements.

The Euro-Mediterranean Agreements[7]

In 1995, Tunisia become the first country in the MENA region to sign a partnership agreement with the European Union (EU), followed by Morocco, Jordan, and Egypt.[8] These EuroMed agreements represent a dramatic potential departure from the slow pace of trade policy reform in MENA. The agreements set a well-defined time frame (twelve to fifteen years) and outline intermediate steps that will lead to a free trade area for nonagricultural products between each of the southern Mediterranean countries and the EU. Elimination of nontariff barriers takes effect upon signing the agreement, while tariffs are to be removed within twelve years. During the implementation period, the EU will continue its policy (which has been in existence since the early 1970s) of granting duty-free access to virtually all manufactured products exported by partner countries and of providing limited preferential access for their agricultural exports. The agreements also cover reciprocal rights of establishment for investors, and the Arab Mediterranean countries have agreed to adapt their regulatory framework to approximate that of the EU in the areas of competition, government procurement, subsidies, and technical standards.

In recent years, a body of analytical research has considered the likely impact on Arab economies of the EuroMed Agreements.[9] One message that emerges clearly from this literature is that the one-time welfare gains from these agreements by themselves are likely to be small. This is because even prior to the agreements, Arab Mediterranean countries already had free access to European markets in almost all industrial products and raw materials on a nonreciprocal basis. Thus, the potential for substantial near-term increases in manufactured exports to Europe appears slight, and any major benefits from the agreements will have to come in the form of improvements in the productivity of firms currently serving the domestic market.

The decline of import prices to European levels and the increased quality and variety of goods associated with liberalizing the import regimes of the Arab Mediterranean countries will significantly increase competitive pressures faced by a number of existing manufacturing industries (Page and Underwood 1997). While it is difficult to estimate precisely the impact of these price changes at the sector or individual firm level, simulations suggest that, in general, output gains in consumer products and light intermediates, particularly clothing, are likely.[10] Medium and heavy industries (machinery, chemicals) are generally projected to be negatively affected. Overall agricultural output would tend to fall in all economies, reflecting some import liberalization and limited access to the European market.

The architects of the agreements have attempted to cushion the impact of the tariff reductions on import-competing goods by allowing early reductions in tariffs for noncompeting imports, followed only late in the implementation period, by tariff reductions on locally manufactured goods. While this transitional protection of domestic producers may have made the agreements more politically palatable in the short run, it will

increase the adjustment problems of many firms in the medium term (Madani and Page 2002).

The Arab Free Trade Area (AFTA)

The Arab Free Trade Area was established in January 1998 by eighteen member states of the Arab League, with the goal of eliminating all trade barriers on goods of Arab origin between member countries by 2008. It is the first of many intra-Arab agreements to use a negative (as opposed to positive) list approach to negotiations; it also was the first to involve the private sector in monitoring implementation of the program, including such areas as customs administration and deregulation.

Effective implementation of the AFTA could lead to substantial reductions in tariffs and nontariff barriers between Arab countries, offering the potential for increased production sharing and intra-industry trade (Devlin and Page 2001). Difficulties in implementation, however, including the inability to agree on negative list items, have thus far limited the impact of the agreement and there is a risk that implementation will be delayed beyond the ten-year time frame set in the original accords.

Building a Basis for Private Investment

Historically, Arab governments have dominated their economies. While the public sector still looms large in the region's economies today (providing the vast majority of infrastructure and financial services in most economies and substantial fractions of industrial output in many), fiscal constraints, shifts in governments' economic philosophy, and increasing globalization of trade and investment flows have caused a shift toward greater reliance on private investment. MENA governments seeking to expand the role of the private sector have embarked on privatization programs and institutional reforms designed to improve the climate for private investment. Implementation of these programs, however, has often been delayed and inconsistent, as Arab governments have attempted to reconcile competing stakeholder interests and avoid job losses.

Higgledy-piggledy privatization

Privatization of state owned enterprises (SOEs) in MENA has been slow relative to other regions, especially Latin America and east Asia (see Figure 5). Although privatization programs in many of the region's major economies have been in place since the early 1990s, progress in implementation has been slow (see Figure 6). Globally, between 1990 and 1998, MENA's share of privatization transactions in

Figure 5. Privatization Revenues in Developing Countries, 1990–1997 (in US$ million)

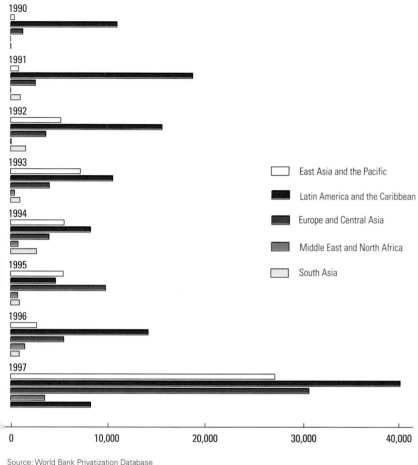

East Asia and the Pacific

Latin America and the Caribbean

Europe and Central Asia

Middle East and North Africa

South Asia

Source: World Bank Privatization Database

250 in Algeria, 100 in Egypt, 20 in Jordan, 100 in Morocco, 60 in Tunisia, and 70 in Yemen.

Within individual MENA economies, shifting political support and changing privatization strategies and techniques have characterized privatization efforts. The results have been mixed. Privatization programs have gained and lost momentum because investors have been unsure of governments' intentions with respect to the types of enterprises to be offered for sale, the methods of privatization, and the conditions of sale (including regulations).

Privatization efforts in Egypt, Jordan, Morocco, and Tunisia

State-owned enterprises continue to dominate Egypt's economy despite a privatization program that began in 1991. The public sector—including the public administration, service and economic authorities, and public enterprises—employs about 35 percent of the labor force and produces nearly 60 percent of nonagricultural output. Public enterprises still employ more than 1 million workers, and the state sector accounts for approximately two-thirds of Egyptian manufacturing.

After a tepid beginning, the government accelerated the pace of privatization substantially in 1996 when more than US$800 million in assets were privatized. The program for 1997 called for the sale of thirty-three companies to strategic investors, and initial public offerings (IPOs) for an additional twelve. Several highly-publicized transactions, including the sale of the nation's only brewery to a foreign investor, increased international awareness of the program. Public sector holding companies have undertaken a process of "quiet restructuring" since the late 1990s, streamlining operations and shedding redundant labor, mainly via early retirements. Since the inception of the program, this, together with privatizations, has resulted in a decline in the public industrial work force employed by the holding companies of about 50 percent (Carana Corporation 2001). But, progress has been uneven. The bulk of privatization transactions have been concentrated in three types of holding companies:

developing countries was less than 3 percent. The region has also lagged in offering new projects for the private provision of infrastructure (PPI). Through the end of 1998, MENA accounted for only 4 percent of all PPI projects worldwide.

The vast majority of privatizations in the 1990s took place in only three MENA countries—Egypt, Kuwait, and Morocco. Tunisia, which began its privatization efforts in 1986 (earlier than most MENA countries), failed to maintain the early momentum of its program and has sold few SOE assets since 1993. Jordan only recently (in 1997) offered for sale substantial numbers of shares in public sector companies. Algeria's privatization program—faced with growing political violence and the need to shift to the sale of larger SOEs—has stalled, while privatization efforts in Syria, Lebanon, and the majority of the GCC have yet to begin in earnest. The scope for potential privatizations in the region is quite large (see Figure 7).

Governments in various Arab countries have identified some 600 enterprises as privatization candidates:

Figure 6. Privatization Timelines in the Middle East and North Africa

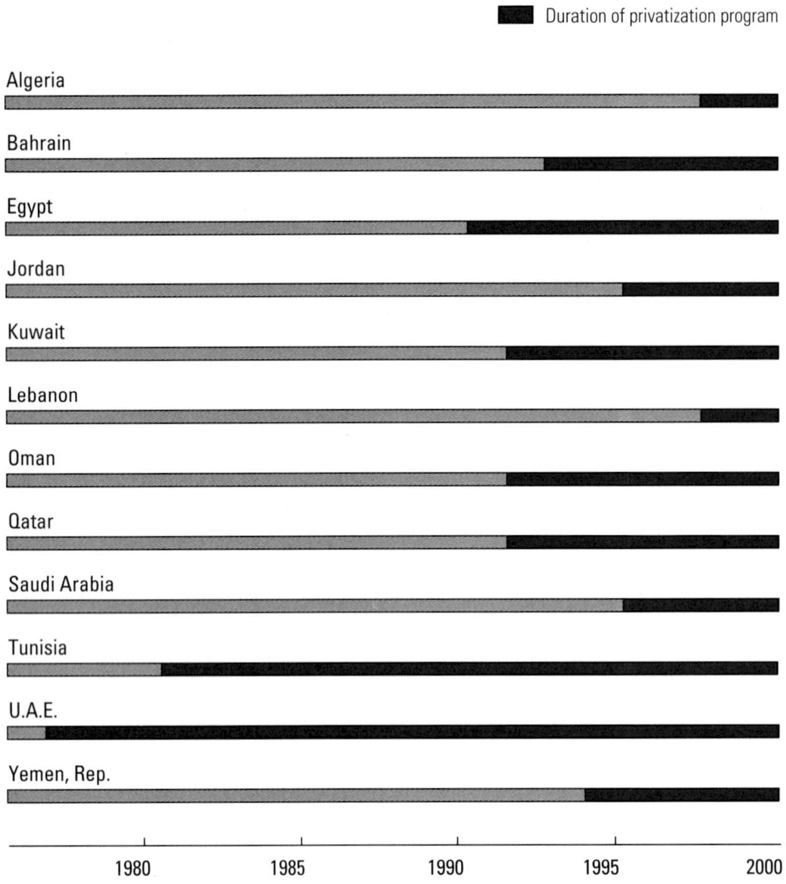

■ Duration of privatization program

Source: World Bank MENA Privatization Database

metallurgy, chemical industries, and food industries. The employment-sensitive textiles sector has remained largely outside the privatization program.

In 2001, the reported value of sales fell to US$317 million, the lowest figure in the history of the program, despite a large minority placement of the Helwan Cement Company. The program's declining momentum underlines a number of important problems remaining in Egypt's approach to privatization. These problems are as follows:

- Most transactions have consisted of minority placements through the capital market, liquidation or sale of assets, and employee ownership schemes. While these transactions have increased the momentum of the program and added to revenues, they have not fundamentally altered the governance structure of the public enterprises.

- The privatization program has followed no coherent strategy in identifying enterprises to be brought to market, relying instead on the decisions of the individual holding companies.

  Some holding companies have, therefore, attempted to retain their most profitable enterprises and privatize loss-makers that have elicited little investor interest.

- Initial steps to privatize telecommunications and power generation have proceeded slowly, and have required changes in legislation. Pricing issues and the regulatory regime have still not been fully addressed.

- Privatization of the major public financial institutions has lagged behind privatization efforts in the real sectors.

While Jordan's public sector is large—accounting for about 55 percent of total employment—state ownership in manufacturing and services is less pronounced than in most other MENA countries. State-owned enterprises are concentrated in infrastructure (transport, water, electricity, and telecommunications) and in phosphate mining and cement manufacturing. In addition, the Jordan Investment Corporation (JIC) holds minority shareholdings (mostly 10 percent) in sixty companies listed on the Amman Stock Exchange.

Until 1996, privatization efforts were ad hoc and decentralized among individual ministries and the JIC, with the result that only two hotels had been sold and the telecommunications company made corporate; this despite the announcement of several privatization initiatives by the JIC. In 1996, a central privatization authority was created as the privatization effort accelerated when 40 percent of the telecommunications company was offered for sale to an anchor investor; by 2000, 48 percent of the company was privatized. Further progress included a 33 percent sale of the Jordan Cement Company, the signing of a water management contract for Amman,

Figure 7. Potential and Completed: Privatization Values in MENA (in US$ million)

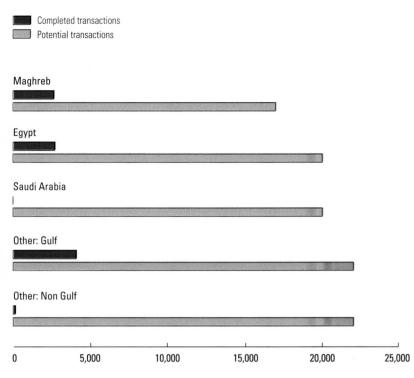

■ Completed transactions
▨ Potential transactions

Maghreb
Egypt
Saudi Arabia
Other: Gulf
Other: Non Gulf

0   5,000   10,000   15,000   20,000   25,000

Source: World Bank MENA Privatization Database

markets, including the Casablanca Stock Exchange, and by competitive bidding. The law does not mandate employment guarantees, but in some cases employees may be accorded preference in buying shares. Foreign investment in privatized firms is in general allowed, and economy-wide, there are no restrictions on foreign ownership. Between 1991 and 1997, fifty-four privatizations had taken place with a total asset value of US$1.22 billion; a target date for privatization of the end of 1998 was set for 114 public investments (seventy-seven companies and thirty-seven hotels).

A unique feature of the Morocco program was the creation in 1998 of privatization bonds. These public debt instruments had a maturity of three years and guaranteed bondholders preferential participation in future privatization transactions. The bonds proved extremely popular, raising nearly US$1 billion in revenues, and were converted into shares at the earliest possible opportunity in the context of the 1999 refinery privatization. The government issued a second round of bonds in 2000.

The SOE sector in Tunisia is extensive. State ownership in Tunisia is characterized by a complex web of minority shareholdings, subsidiary agreements, and ownership by state-controlled banks; widespread public investment was undertaken in virtually every area of production and services from independence in 1954 through the beginning of the 1970s. When privatization efforts began in the second half of the 1980s, enterprises in which the state had an equity share of more than 34 percent accounted for 31 percent of GDP and 40 percent of total investment. SOEs employed about 156,000 people, 13 percent of total employment.

Tunisia's privatization program was launched in 1986 as part of its larger effort at macroeconomic adjustment and structural reform. Between 1986 and 1994, approximately forty-five companies were privatized. The majority of these transactions consisted of private placements, and a number of unprofitable firms were liquidated. In 1994, a second legislative framework was enacted to permit the government to undertake privatizations through the sale of shares on

and divestiture of JIC shares valued at US$113 million in forty-four companies. Total privatization proceeds through 2001 were in excess of US$900 million. The Jordan Electricity Authority was made into a public shareholding company and it was decided to separate distribution from generation. A large pipeline of potential transactions has been identified, including the national airline, phosphate mining, water authorities, and state warehousing and distribution facilities, but these actions, while a major increase over previous efforts, still primarily reflect intentions to privatize rather than transactions completed, and Jordan has had difficulty finding strategic investors at an acceptable price.

There are about 800 state-owned enterprises and public/private joint ventures in Morocco across a wide range of sectors, including finance, industry, services, and agriculture. Together, they produce about 12 percent of GDP and employ 6 percent of the urban formal labor force. The privatization program was authorized in 1989 by an Act of Parliament, but did not begin in earnest until 1991. Morocco's institutional framework is among the most well defined in the region. A privatization minister is responsible for overall program implementation. Transactions are allowed to take place through the financial

the Tunis bourse, and to allow strategic investors to participate in large, sensitive transactions. This second phase of privatization has, for the first time, targeted larger more "strategic" companies. By the end of 1996, twenty-nine transactions had been completed from a list of forty-seven eligible companies. The flagship transaction was the sale of 20 percent of the shares of TUNISAIR, the national airline, via an IPO. In the late 1990s, sixty enterprises with total net assets of approximately US$1.5 billion were identified for sale, including key strategic companies such as cement plants and banks.

Tunisia's privatization program has several limitations that constrain its scope and speed of implementation, such as the following:

- The institutional framework for the program has changed several times since 1989;

- In an effort to minimize worker resistance, the government has refused to make public the enterprises to be privatized, and identification of the number and value of public enterprises eligible for privatization is made difficult by a maze of direct ownerships, cross-holdings, and mixed public/private ownership;

- The process by which transactions are carried out is not well understood, nor is it transparent;

- The government has required new owners to maintain existing staffing levels in privatized firms, and to avoid whole or partial closure of enterprises.

Each of these country cases underscores several aspects of privatization in the region. Few large transactions have caught the attention of potential investors. Governments have generally sold small portions of state-owned companies, in many cases retaining operating and managerial control, and there has been a reluctance to allow foreign strategic partners to invest in key industries. Failure to address pricing issues, as well as governments' marked reluctance to address over-manning in industries to be privatized, has limited the attractiveness of many infrastructure privatizations for potential investors.

Improving the climate for private investment

As it attempts to increase the volume and quality of private investment, the Arab world has a distinct advantage relative to many other parts of the developing world. Increased private investment in MENA can come mainly from regional sources. The considerable private assets of Arab nationals

held in OECD countries could be attracted back to individuals' own economies and to other Arab states. Some estimates place the level of savings of nationals held outside the region in the range from US$100 to 500 billion (Page 1998). For countries such as Egypt, Jordan, and Syria, the estimated total savings of nationals held abroad exceeds GDP. Private capital flows from the GCC to other MENA economies are also a potentially significant source of future private investment. Non-Arab portfolio and direct foreign investment may also play an important role. In all cases, however, the domestic investment climate—and a high degree of international creditworthiness—will be critical in determining the attractiveness to external capital of individual economies.

In surveys worldwide, investors say that institutions matter for investment.[11] Clear-cut rules, adequate enforcement, and consistency of the institutional framework in a market-oriented economy, are all important considerations in a business' investment decision. The structural reform period brought significant improvements to the institutional setting offered to private investors in the MENA region, but in the eyes of investors, significant shortfalls remain. While investment frameworks and licensing procedures have improved during the last fifteen years, the quality and discretionary power of the bureaucracy in implementing these changes is still seen as a major obstacle in many MENA countries.

By the mid-1990s, Tunisia was relatively successful in creating an "investor-friendly" investment code and a "one-stop shop" for investors. But the efforts of Jordan, Egypt, and Morocco had been less so. In Jordan, bureaucratic discretion in the interpretation of the investment code continued to present problems. In Egypt, while procedures were streamlined on paper, investors were impeded by slow bureaucratic approvals. In Morocco, private investors found that both the potential for discretionary treatment (in part caused by ambiguity in the investment codes) and slow bureaucratic processing greatly increased their cost of doing business. Further, investors felt that among public officials, the notion of providing services and facilities for businesses (such as water and telephone connections) had not completely replaced the past system of bureaucratic controls.

A complex regulatory maze survives in most countries of the MENA region; a web of regulations creates an environment of detailed interference in economic activity (Page et al. 1997). In this process, property rights are created, increased, diminished, and often extinguished by discretionary bureaucratic actions or failures to take action. Entry licensing and regulation, unpredictable and often predatory business and tax administration, problems of land titling, and lack of ability to collateralize property such as know-how, receivables and contracts, are cited in numerous surveys as major constraints to doing business in every MENA country (Page and Underwood 1997).

In general, entry regulations are very restrictive. For example, to enter Egypt's formal sector as a company, three types of approval are needed: incorporation, investment licensing, and establishment and operation licensing. A thicket of regulations impedes entry to Morocco, and a five-step process is involved in Jordan. Each involves one or more bureaucratic decisions with attendant costs. Most of MENA's company codes trace their origins to the interwar period French step in Jordan's process Code. While there has been some modernization, most codes are outdated. In addition, the promotion and registration of a limited liability company is everywhere a time-consuming and costly process.

In Morocco, a multiplicity of national and local regulations for establishing and operating businesses are compounded by ambiguities in their requirements and application. To set up (and to some extent expand) a business, entrepreneurs face an administrative gauntlet to complete all the formal steps. It typically takes six months or longer. Eleven principal steps are required to set up a business and as many as thirty-five separate documents may need to be completed and approved by central or local government agencies, as well as by state-owned utility companies. Agencies have wide latitude in determining their procedures; many of these procedures change often and are difficult to obtain information about. The approval process may require face-to-face negotiation with officials to whom the regulatory ambiguities give considerable discretionary power to decide what information is needed and on what criteria the decision will be made. The regulatory maze is obviously more of an obstacle for new, small entrepreneurs, who often lack training and resources. Yet, without the necessary registrations, licenses, or approval, access to the formal sector is denied.

Investors also care greatly about both the adequacy of the legal framework and the reliability of the judiciary. In MENA, perceived weaknesses with respect to recognition of property rights and contract enforcement contribute to a sense of insecurity and arbitrariness, and thereby reduce investment (Page et al. 1997).

Throughout the region, the formal court systems are viewed as slow, but specific concerns vary by country. In Egypt, while the court system is slow, investors tend to rely on a fairly good commercial arbitration system. In Lebanon, the main problem is the shortage of judges. Investors in Morocco cite concerns about reliable legal recourse, particularly with respect to enforcement of government contracts. Investors also express concerns that there is inadequate protection of intellectual property rights in the region. While by the mid-1990s Morocco and Tunisia had fairly good patent and trademark protection, protection of intellectual property rights was a serious concern for investors in Egypt, Jordan, Lebanon, and the Gulf countries.

New provisions for the establishment and governance of companies have been drafted in Egypt and Jordan. Most of the changes have been recommended to conform to European Community practices; the changes are primarily in the governance of joint stock companies, and provide increased minority protection, empower the supervisory board with authority often reserved to the general assembly of shareholders, and provide for the governance of holding companies.

Figure 8 summarizes the view of one international investment advisory firm regarding the investment climate across Arab countries (Economist Intelligence Unit 1999). None of MENA's economies approach "best practice" as defined by the investor-friendly regimes of a number of east Asian and Latin American countries, and there is substantial intraregional variation. Interestingly, Yemen, one of the poorest countries in the Arab League, ranks relatively well while, not surprisingly, the heavily statist economies of Algeria, Syria, and Iraq are poorly ranked. Among Gulf economies, Saudi Arabia trails several of its GCC partners, while Egypt and Tunisia marginally outperform their neighbors in the Mashreq and Maghreb, respectively.

An Unfinished Agenda

Clearly, the Arab world's record with respect to structural reform has been mixed. On the plus side, governments in the region have succeeded in restoring macroeconomic stability in the face of significant fluctuations in the price of oil and accompanying volatility in capital flows and remittances. Performance with respect to integration with the global economy has been less outstanding. Trade policy reform has proceeded slowly, but continuously, under the Uruguay round and may continue under the Doha round of negotiations in the WTO. The EuroMed agreements represent a

Figure 8. Investment Climate Ratings in MENA

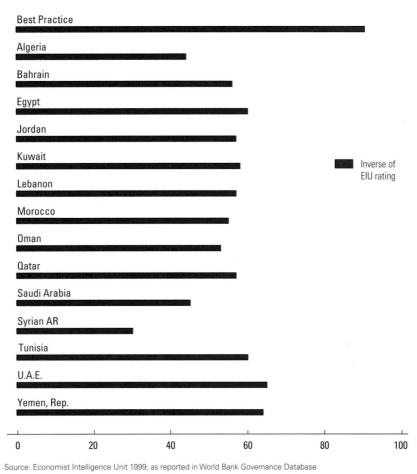

Source: Economist Intelligence Unit 1999, as reported in World Bank Governance Database

production-sharing among Arab economies, but its slow pace of implementation may doom it to irrelevance. Accelerating the pace of implementation of multilateral trade policy reform and of the two key regional trading agreements, EuroMed and AFTA, is key to increasing the productivity of existing industry and reducing the bias against non-oil exports.

But trade policy reforms alone are not sufficient to ensure increased competitiveness. MENA lags most in those areas of structural reform directly relevant to raising the volume and improving the efficiency of private investment. Privatization programs have lacked clear strategic focus, have been implemented on a stop-go basis, and have, in many cases, resulted in the transfer of ownership without an accompanying transfer of state control. Investor surveys continue to highlight substantial problems with MENA's investment climate, including lack of transparency, cumbersome regulations,

genuine opportunity to increase foreign competition in Egypt, Jordan, Morocco, and Tunisia, but to date the impact of the agreements has been limited primarily to liberalizing imports of noncompeting goods. AFTA offers substantial potential benefits, especially in promoting intraindustry trade and

problems with the definition and enforcement of commercial law, and weak public institutions. Privatization programs should be accelerated and refocused on improving performance in trade-related infrastructure and institutions (Page 2001).

Figure 9. Composite Structural Reform Index in Developing Regions

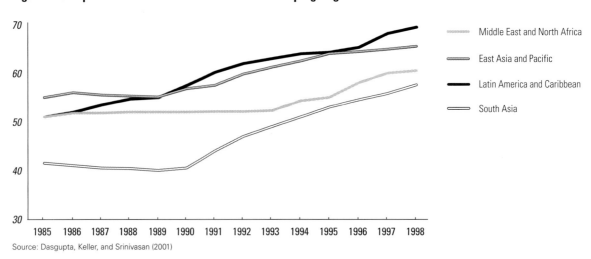

Source: Dasgupta, Keller, and Srinivasan (2001)

Complementary improvements in the investment climate, in terms of legal and regulatory reforms and their implementation, will also be required if Arab economies are to raise their levels of private investment.

Figure 9 attempts to place MENA's overall record of reform during the past fifteen years in an international context by summarizing composite index changes in structural policies. The index measures implementation of reforms in macroeconomic management, trade policy, and privatization/private sector development in MENA, east Asia, Latin America and south Asia.[12] The figure clearly shows that the Arab world was the last region to start a meaningful process of structural reform, and that there was little measurable change until the mid-1990s. Reform has also proceeded at a slower pace in MENA than in other regions, with the result that both Latin America and east Asia are further ahead of Arab countries today in terms of their economic policy frameworks than they were fifteen years ago; south Asia, in fact, has significantly closed the gap.

If Arab countries are to keep pace with their international competitors, the structural reform process in MENA will need greater focus, more consistent implementation and must proceed at a faster pace. But governments in the region find themselves caught between the need to accelerate structural reforms for increased investment and growth, and the fear of a backlash provoked by potential losses of jobs and incomes. While the key to resolving this conflict is clearly increasing growth, employment, and real wages, the majority of Arab governments have chosen to err on the side of caution in implementing the structural reforms required.

References

Adams, Richard and John Page."A Case of Pro-Poor Growth?: Poverty Trends in the Middle East and North Africa, 1970–2000." The World Bank, Washington D.C., 2001.

Brown, Drusilla, Alan Deardorff, and Robert Stern. "Some Economic Effects of the Free Trade Agreements between Tunisia and the European Union." In *Regional Partners in Global Markets: Limits and Possibilities of the Euro-Med Agreements*, edited by A. Galal, and B. Hoekman. Cairo: CEPR and ECES, 1997.

Carana Corporation. "Privatization in Egypt: Quarterly Review October-December 2001." Cairo: United States Agency for International Development, 2001.

Dasgupta, Dipak, Jennifer Keller, and T.G. Srinivasan. "Reform and Elusive Growth in the Middle East—What has Happened in the 1990s?" Paper presented at the MEEA Conference on Global Change and Regional Integration. London, 20–22 July, 2001.

Devlin, Julia, and John Page. "Testing the Waters: Arab Integration, Competitiveness and the EuroMed Agreements." In *The Dynamics of Open Regionalism in the Middle East and North Africa*, edited by S. Dessus, J. Devlin, and R. Safadi. Paris: OECD, 2001.

Economist Intelligence Unit. *Survey of the Middle East.* London: The Economist Newspaper, Ltd., 1999.

Hoekman, Bernard, and Denis Konan. "Rents, Red Tape, and Regionalism: Economic Effects of Deeper Integration." In *Catching Up with the Competition: Trade Opportunities and Challenges for Arab Countries*, edited by B. Hoekman and J. Zarrouk. Ann Arbor, Michigan: The University of Michigan Press, 2000.

International Monetary Fund (IMF). *International Financial Statistics Yearbook.* Washington, D.C.: IMF, 1991–1999.

Madani, Dorsati, and John Page."Challenges to Firm Competitiveness and Opportunities for Success." In *Globalization and Firm Competitiveness in the Middle East and North Africa Region*, edited by Samiha Fawzy. Washington, D.C.: The World Bank, 2002.

Morisset, Jacques, and Olivier Neso."Administrative Barriers to Foreign Investment in Developing Countries." Policy Research Working Paper 2848. Washington, D.C.: The World Bank, 2002.

Page, John, Joseph Saba, and Nemat Shafik. "From Player to Referee: The Changing Role of Competition Policies and Regulation in the Middle East and North Africa." Washington, D.C.: The World Bank, 1997.

Page, John, and John Underwood.Growth, the Maghreb and Free Trade with the European Union." In *Regional Partners in Global Markets: Limits and Possibilities of the Euro-Med Agreements*, edited by A. Galal, and B. Hoekman.Cairo: CEPR and ECES, 1997.

Page, John. "From Boom to Bust and Back? The Crisis of Growth in the Middle East and North Africa." In *Prospects for Middle Eastern and North African Economies*, edited by N. Shafik. London: MacMillan, 1998.

Page, John. "Getting Ready for Globalization: A New Privatization Strategy for the MENA Region?" In *State Owned Enterprises in the Middle East and North Africa*, edited by Merith Celasun. London: Routledge, 2001.

Rutherford, Thomas, Elisabet Rutstrom, and David Tarr. "A Free Trade Agreement Between the European Union and a Representative Arab Mediterranean County: A Quantitative Assessment." In *Catching Up with the Competition: Trade Opportunities and Challenges for Arab Countries*, edited by B. Hoekman, and J. Zarrouk. Ann Arbor, Michigan: The University of Michigan Press, 2000.

Van Gelder, Linda, and John Page. "Missing Links: Institutional Capability and Growth in the Middle East and North Africa." In *The State and Global Change: The Political Economics of Transition in the Middle East and North Africa*, edited by H. Hakimian, and Z. Moshauer. London: Curzon Press, 2001.

Van Gelder, Linda, and John Page "Globalization, Growth, and Poverty Reduction in the Middle East and North Africa, 1970–1999" paper presented at the Mediterranean Development Forum, Amman, Jordan, 2002.

Williamson, John. "What Washington Means by Policy Reform." In *Latin American Adjustment: How Much Has Happened?* Washington, D.C.: Institute for International Economics, 1990.

World Bank. *Claiming the Future: Choosing Prosperity in the Middle East and North Africa*. Washington, DC: The World Bank, 1995.

World Bank. *Egypt: Country Economic Memorandum*. Washington, D.C.: The World Bank, 1997.

World Bank. *Egypt, Social and Structural Review*. Report No. 22397-EGT. Washington, D.C.: The World Bank, 2001e.

World Bank. *Global Economic Prospects and the Developing Countries 1996*. Washington, D.C.: The World Bank, 1996a.

World Bank. *Global Economic Prospects and the Developing Countries 2001*. Washington, D.C.: The World Bank, 2001a.

World Bank. *Globalization Growth and Poverty: Building an Inclusive World Economy*. New York: Oxford, 2001d.

World Bank. *Hashemite Kingdom of Jordan: Poverty Assessment*. Report No. 12675 (2 volumes). Washington, DC: The World Bank, 1994.

World Bank. *Kingdom of Morocco: Poverty Adjustment and Growth*. Report No. 11918 (2 volumes). Washington, DC: The World Bank, 1994.

World Bank. *Kingdom of Morocco, Poverty Update*. Report No. 21506 (2 volumes). Washington, D.C.: The World Bank, 2001c.

World Bank. *Republic of Tunisia: Social Conditions Update*. Report No. 21503 (2 volumes). Washington, D.C.: The World Bank, 2000.

World Bank. *Will Arab Workers Prosper or be Left Out in the 21st Century?* Washington, D.C.: The World Bank, 1996b.

World Bank. *World Development Report 2000/2001: Attacking Poverty*. New York: Oxford University Press, 2001b.

Endnotes

1. The findings, interpretations and conclusions expressed in this paper are those of the author. They do not reflect those of the World Bank, its executive directors, or the countries they represent.

2. Throughout this chapter, the terms Middle East and North Africa and Arab world are used interchangeably to indicate countries of the Arab League, excluding those located in sub-Saharan Africa. In practice, much of the evidence and data are drawn from a smaller subset of those countries, primarily Algeria, Egypt, Jordan, Morocco, Tunisia, Yemen, and the Gulf Cooperation Council (GCC) countries—Saudi Arabia, Kuwait, Oman, Bahrain, Qatar, and the United Arab Emirates.

3. It is important to note that while Arab league countries share many similarities and can be discussed in large measure as a group, there are substantial variations in both policy frameworks and economic performance. For example, Lebanon has never relied on a state-led model of investment and growth, and the countries of the GCC have always remained relatively open to international trade.

4. The term "Washington Consensus" was used by Williamson (1990).

5. The experience of Egypt, Jordan, Morocco, and Tunisia will frequently be highlighted throughout this chapter. These are the major reforming low- and middle-income economies in the region; there is, therefore, a substantially larger body of evidence on structural reforms in these countries.

6. The speed of integration index is the average of changes in four indicators: the ratio of real trade to GDP, the ratio of foreign direct investment to GDP, institutional investor credit ratings, and the share of manufactures in exports (each expressed as standard deviations from the mean) over the period 1987 to 1996 (see World Bank [1996a]).

7. For a more detailed analysis, see Ghonheim, von Hagen, and Wolf in this volume.

8. Negotiations are currently underway or planned to extend the EuroMed agreements to other Arab countries including Algeria, Lebanon, Syria, and possibly Yemen.

9. This research is based on the use of computable general equilibrium (CGE) models to predict changes in output and incomes. Rutherford, Rustrom, and Tarr (2000) found that for Morocco, significant welfare gains come only from the increased market access that stems harmonization and mutual recognition of standards, rather than from changes to traditional border measures. Brown, Deardorff, and Stern (1997) conclude that the static welfare benefits for Tunisia from the EuroMed agreement will be small, although they postulate that over time, with capital mobility, the welfare gain will grow. Hoekman and Konan (2000) confirm these findings for Egypt.

10. Wood products and footwear are also positively affected in the Tunisian case.

11. See, for example, Morisset and Neso (2002).

12. The index uses as its measure of macroeconomic performance a measure of deviations from international purchasing power parity; for trade policy, data on average incidence of tariffs; and for privatization/private sector development, privatization revenues as a share of GDP and maximum marginal private and corporate tax rates. Europe and Central Asia and Africa are excluded due to lack of data. See Dasgupta, Keller, and Srinivasan (2001).

Fiscal Revenue in South Mediterranean Arab Countries:

Vulnerabilities and Growth Potential

Karim Nashashibi

Overview

Over the past few years, public finance in Southern Mediterranean Arab countries (SMCs) has experienced a structural deterioration. Fiscal deficits have edged upward, with particularly high levels in Jordan (9 percent of GDP), Lebanon (25 percent of GDP), and Morocco (7 percent of GDP). This deterioration has occurred against the backdrop of low growth, high unemployment, and high public debt levels, even in countries that had benefited from debt relief at the beginning of the decade, such as Jordan and Morocco. While expenditure rigidities have remained and high unemployment has stymied expenditure reforms, the major factor behind this deterioration appears to be a decline in the share of revenue in GDP as a result of a reduction in both nontax and tax revenue. The reduction in nontax revenue is due to some exhaustion of mineral wealth and diminished earnings from state enterprises because of privatization. Tax revenue has been affected adversely by trade liberalization, a narrowing of the tax base, and, in a number of countries, an appreciating real exchange rate. Of even greater concern is that these trends are expected to continue over the next few years, at a time when the SMCs will face major demographic pressures and the challenges of globalization.

This chapter focuses on government revenue in the SMCs by looking at underlying trends in various revenue categories; comparing their performance to a broad sample of middle-income countries; assessing their vulnerabilities; and identifying potential sources of growth and possible improvements in their existing tax systems.

Some Aggregate Indicators and Trends

Government revenue in some SMCs has decreased as a result of two opposing trends: a decline in nontax revenue in virtually all countries and a major tax effort resulting in higher tax revenue. While it is expected that nontax revenue will continue to decline, tax revenue is also beginning to decline because of trade liberalization. Given the rising demands for government expenditures stemming from demographic country profiles and trends—with a very young population and high rates of entry into the labor force—the SMCs can ill afford to have a decline in tax ratios, particularly in low growth, underperforming economies.[1] Consequently, the main challenges for the next few years will be to broaden the tax base, find new sources of tax revenue, and strengthen tax administration.

Government revenue in SMCs (25 percent of GDP) on average exceeds revenue from a broad sample of middle-income countries (Tables 1 and 3). This average conceals substantial rents accruing to most SMCs from mineral deposits. Nevertheless, this revenue performance has been relatively good in the Maghreb, with tax revenue (21.2 percent of GDP) exceeding the average in middle-income countries (20.3 percent of GDP), while the Mashreq countries' tax ratio (15.7 percent of GDP) was closer to the poorer countries in the comparator group (Bolivia, Indonesia, Philippines, and Thailand).

During the 1990s, government revenue in about one half of the SMCs increased (Tables 1 and 2). Four out of seven countries succeeded in raising their tax ratios. However, over the last two to three years, the tax revenue/GDP ratio has been declining in most SMCs, partly due to trade liberalization with multilateral tariff reductions, and in Morocco and Tunisia where the free trade agreements with the European Union (AAEUs) has been implemented. This trend will strengthen as other countries in the region also start implementing free trade agreements with the European Union (EU). Consequently, SMCs face a number of vulnerabilities, and, if current trends continue, virtually all SMCs will face a decline in overall government revenue and the prospect of higher budget deficits.

Table. 1 Southern Mediterranean Arab Countries: Central Government Revenue Structure, 1999–2000 (in Percent of GDP)

	Total Revenue	Tax Revenue	Nontax Revenue[1]	Taxes on Income, Profits, and Capital Gains of which: Total	Individual	Corporate	Social Security Taxes	Domestic Taxes on Goods and Services of which: Total	General Sales, Turnover or VAT[2]	Excises	Trade Taxes Import Duties	Property Taxes
Maghreb												
Algeria	29.9	11.5	18.4	3.9	1.0	2.8	0.0	5.1	3.3	1.7	2.5	0.0
Morocco	28.2	26.1	2.1	7.6	3.4	4.2	1.9	11.9	6.1	5.8	4.7	0.0
Tunisia	29.1	26.0	3.1	5.6	2.9	2.7	4.9	11.1	7.6	3.5	3.0	1.3
Average	29.1	21.2	7.9	5.7	2.4	3.2	2.3	9.4	5.7	3.7	3.4	0.4
Mashreq												
Egypt[3]	22.8	16.0	6.8	6.0	1.8	4.2	1.2	6.0	4.5	1.5	2.8	0.0
Jordan	26.7	15.9	10.8	2.7	1.1	1.6	0.3	8.1	7.2	0.9	4.7	0.0
Lebanon	18.3	12.3	6.0	2.0	0.6	1.4	0.0	1.6	—	1.6	7.5	1.2
Syrian AR	24.4	13.6	10.9	10.8	0.9	9.9	0.0	0.6	0.3	0.3	2.0	0.1
West Bank and Gaza[4]	23.4	20.7	2.7	2.0	1.5	0.5	0.0	11.5	9.1	2.4	7.1	0.0
Average	23.1	15.7	7.4	4.7	1.2	3.5	0.3	5.6	4.2	1.3	4.8	0.3
Overall Average	25.3	17.8	7.6	5.1	1.7	3.4	1.0	7.0	4.8	2.2	4.3	0.3

Sources: Data provided by the country authorities and IMF staff estimates

1. Including hydrocarbon revenue fees, dividends, and Central Bank profits, but excluding privatization receipts
2. Including VAT on imports
3. Fiscal year 1999/2000
4. Fiscal data are for calendar year 1999

Nontax Revenue

Nontax revenue includes income from state enterprises and mineral rents, proceeds from sales of assets, and fees and charges. In medieval times, these sources of revenue were the only source of government finance (*droits du seigneur*). Rulers would exploit their monopoly rights and territorial control to exact tolls from travelers and traders and levy rents on farmers. In modern times, as countries have transferred economic activity to their private sector and fostered competition, these kinds of revenue have dwindled—particularly in industrial countries—and are mostly limited to fees and charges. In OECD countries (Table 4), they average about 2 percent of GDP (1.2 percent in the United States) while they are somewhat higher in middle-income countries at 3.3 percent of GDP (Table 3). In the eight SMC countries considered, five have nontax revenue greater than 4 percent of GDP, and the average is 7.6 percent of GDP. Aside from fees and charges—which are small (less than 2 percent of GDP) but clearly desirable—this revenue accrues mainly from oil production (Algeria, Egypt, Syria, and Tunisia) and phosphates (Jordan

and Morocco). It also includes transfers from state monopolies on electricity and communications and profits from the central bank. For instance, central bank profit transfers in Egypt in 1999/2000 were 1.2 percent of GDP and substantially higher in the mid-1990s when Egyptian foreign exchange reserves had risen to US $20 billion.

Nontax revenue in SMCs has been declining over the last decade and should be expected to decline further in the next five years, possibly losing 1 percent of GDP in Morocco and Tunisia and 2 to 5 percent of GDP in the Mashreq, depending on the country. This decline results primarily from exogenous factors such as the depletion of mineral resources and decreases in oil and phosphate prices. Egypt and Tunisia have become net oil importers while Syria is expected to follow soon, although prospects for natural gas production in both Egypt and Syria have strengthened. Similarly, phosphate production in Jordan and Morocco has reached its limit and has suffered from stiff competition abroad and declining prices.[2] More recently, this decline has also reflected a policy shift toward scaling back the public sector

Table 2. Southern Mediterranean Arab Countries: Central Government Revenue Structure, 1989–1990 (in Percent of GDP)

| | Total Revenue | Tax Revenue | Nontax Revenue[1] | Taxes on Income, Profits, and Capital Gains of which: | | | Social Security Taxes | Domestic Taxes on Goods and Services of which: | | | Trade Taxes | |
				Total	Individual	Corporate		Total	General Sales, Turnover or VAT[2]	Excises	Import Duties	Property Taxes
Maghreb												
Algeria	37.3	16.3	21.0	5.0	3.1	1.9	—	7.8	7.5	—	2.6	—
Morocco	23.0	20.8	2.1	5.5	1.6	3.9	1.0	10.6	5.6	5.0	4.7	0.6
Tunisia	26.8	19.5	7.3	3.3	—	—	4.1	6.6	2.5	3.0	8.0	0.6
Average	29.0	18.9	10.1	4.6	2.4	2.9	1.7	8.3	5.2	2.7	5.1	0.6
Mashreq												
Egypt[3]	24.4	16.7	7.6	4.4	0.5	3.1	3.6	3.1	1.9	1.2	3.2	0.25
Jordan	27.1	14.4	12.7	4.3	1.0	3.3	0.0	4.5	0.0	4.5	4.4	0.81
Lebanon	14.1	9.2	4.9	1.3	—	—	—	0.8	0.0	0.8	5.1	—
Syrian AR[4]	22.5	16.9	5.6	6.8	—	—	0.0	6.9	—	6.9	1.3	0.34
Average	22.0	14.3	7.7	4.2	0.7	3.2	0.9	3.8	0.5	3.4	3.5	0.5
Overall Average	25.0	16.3	8.7	4.4	1.5	3.1	1.2	5.8	2.5	3.1	4.2	0.5

Sources: Data provided by the country authorities and IMF staff estimates

1. Including hydrocarbon revenue fees and dividends, but excluding privatization receipts
2. Including VAT on imports
3. Fiscal year 1989/1990
4. Average of calendar years 1989 and 1990

and introducing greater competition. Over the past few years, SMCs have introduced or accelerated privatization programs for public enterprises, and they have opened up the market for public utilities in which the state had a monopoly—particularly in telecommunication, electricity generation and distribution, and water provision and treatment. This change is expected to have a dual impact. On one hand, the stream of dividends from these state enterprises will stop after their privatization, which has already happened in Egypt, Jordan, Morocco, and Tunisia. On the other hand, and to the extent that privatization and greater competition raise efficiency and profitability, income taxes from these enterprises—and possibly sales and excise tax revenue—would increase, although such revenue would be realized only in the medium term. Also to the extent that privatization proceeds were used to reduce public debt, overall expenditures and budget deficits would fall because of lower interest payments.[3]

Over the next five years, however, nontax revenue are bound to fall with the modernization of the economy through the rise in privatization, greater competition, and a more optimal management of central bank

reserves. Nevertheless, there is a possibility of slowing down this decline by broadening and strengthening user charges for government services, including fees for higher education and some health services.

Income Taxes

Income taxes, both corporate and individual, have risen over the last ten years in SMCs as a result of the strengthening of tax administration and the expansion of private sector activities. Both individual and corporate income taxes ranging from 2.7 percent of GDP in Morocco and 4.2 percent of GDP in Tunisia compare favorably with most middle-income countries. On the other hand, in the Mashreq countries, individual income taxes average only 1.2 percent of GDP. This average cannot be attributed to an inadequate income tax system or low rates of taxation but to its very narrow base of taxation, which is limited to civil servants and salaried personnel in large enterprises and the financial sector where the tax is automatically deducted at the source. The government's inability to adequately tax other groups such as the business community, professionals, and wealthy individuals has not only limited government revenue but also resulted in major inequities. This

Table 3. Selected Middle-Income Countries: Consolidated Central Government Tax Structure, 1999–2000 (in Percent of GDP)

| | Total Revenue | Tax Revenue | Nontax Revenue | Taxes on Income, Profits, and Capital Gains of which: | | | Social Security Taxes | Domestic Taxes on Goods and Services of which: | | | Trade Taxes | |
				Total	Individual	Corporate		Total	General Sales, Turnover or VAT	Excises	Import Duties	Property Taxes
Estonia	33.7	30.1	3.6	6.0	3.8	2.2	10.7	13.3	9.6	3.4	0.0	0.0
Hungary	38.4	33.5	4.9	7.1	5.1	2.0	10.8	12.0	7.7	3.3	2.8	0.2
Latvia	31.7	27.0	4.7	3.3	1.0	2.3	10.3	12.8	8.9	3.5	0.6	0.0
Lithuania	25.1	23.9	1.1	3.5	2.3	1.2	7.4	12.3	8.9	3.3	0.6	0.0
Poland	36.2	32.7	3.5	8.9	6.2	2.7	10.1	11.6	7.6	3.9	1.8	0.0
Turkey	21.2	17.5	3.6	7.5	5.6	1.6	0.0	8.5	5.2	2.8	0.5	0.4
Indonesia	17.6	15.7	1.8	9.6	4.5	4.9	0.6	4.8	3.6	0.8	0.5	0.1
Malaysia	24.0	19.5	4.5	8.8	2.5	6.2	0.3	6.2	2.1	2.3	2.5	0.1
Philippines[1]	18.1	16.0	2.0	6.4	2.5	2.7	0.0	4.9	1.8	2.2	3.9	0.0
Thailand	17.6	15.7	1.9	5.4	2.3	3.0	0.3	7.6	3.7	3.6	2.2	0.2
Argentina	13.6	12.5	1.1	1.8	0.6	1.2	4.0	5.4	3.7	1.6	0.8	0.3
Bolivia	17.3	13.9	3.4	1.1	—	1.1	1.9	8.0	6.0	1.9	1.1	1.5
Brazil	24.5	19.8	4.7	3.9	0.3	1.5	8.6	5.4	2.1	1.9	0.6	0.0
Chile	22.9	19.0	3.9	4.1	—	—	1.4	10.6	8.5	2.1	—	0.0
Peru	17.2	14.9	2.4	3.4	—	—	1.4	8.5	6.4	2.1	1.6	0.0
Venezuela[2]	18.8	13.7	5.1	5.9	—	—	0.6	5.7	4.5	0.7	1.6	0.3
Unweighted Average	23.6	20.3	3.3	5.4	3.1	2.5	4.3	8.6	5.6	2.5	1.4	0.2

Sources: IMF, Government Finance Statistics; IMF, International Financial Statistics; and IMF, World Economic Outlook

1. Budgetary central government
2. Adjustment to tax revenue

situation is particularly evident in Lebanon and Syria, where individual income taxes are only 0.6 percent and 0.9 percent of GDP respectively, even though thriving business communities have been the driving economic force in these two countries.

A sustained effort at broadening the tax base and at modernizing the collection mechanism through computerization and enforcement of standard accounting practices should readily raise individual tax collections in Mashreq countries by 2 to 2.5 percent of GDP to reach the levels attained in Morocco and Tunisia. In turn, these two countries can aspire to reach the levels attained by Estonia (3.8 percent of GDP), Hungary (5.1 percent of GDP), Poland (6.2 percent of GDP), and Turkey (5.6 percent of GDP), keeping in mind that the OECD average for individual income taxes is 7.2 percent of GDP. Income tax reform is important in most SMCs not only to broaden the tax base but also to reduce excessive

marginal rates and to adjust thresholds. Typically, thresholds are not being adjusted for increases in income or inflation, which results in bracket creep toward the highest marginal rate.

Corporate taxation levels in both Morocco (4.2 percent of GDP) and Tunisia (2.7 percent of GDP) are quite respectable as they exceed the average for other middle-income countries (2.5 percent of GDP) and the OECD (2.6 percent of GDP). While both countries' tax yields are boosted by profits of state-owned enterprises that exploit mineral deposits, the tax ratios reflect, nevertheless, both the dynamism of the private sector (and the small share of public enterprises) and a well-performing tax system. Of all the middle-income countries in the comparator sample, only Indonesia and Malaysia have attained corporate income tax levels beyond 4 percent, but this level is essentially due to income taxes on oil production (Table 3).

Part 1 Fiscal Revenue in South Mediterranean Arab Countries: Vulnerabilities and Growth Potential

Table 4. Consolidated Central Government: Tax Structure for OECD Countries, 1995–1999 (in Percent)

| | Periods | Total Revenue | Tax Revenue | Other Revenue | Domestic Taxes on Goods and Services of Which: | | | | | Domestic Taxes on Goods and Services of Which: | | | International Trade Taxes[1] of Which: | | | Property Taxes |
					Total	Individual	Corporate	Social Security Taxes	Payroll Taxes	Total	General Sales, Turnover or VAT	Excises	Total	Import Duties	Export Duties	
Canada	1995–97	20.9	18.7	2.2	10.8	8.4	2.1	4.1	0.0	3.5	2.5	0.9	0.3	0.3	—	0.0
Mexico[2]	1995–98	14.6	12.6	2.0	4.4	—	—	1.8	0.0	8.4	3.0	1.5	0.6	0.6	0.0	0.0
United States	1995–99	20.1	18.6	1.4	11.0	8.8	2.1	6.5	0.0	0.7	—	0.6	0.2	0.2	—	0.2
Australia	1995–99	24.2	22.3	1.9	15.9	11.8	4.0	—	0.6	5.0	2.4	2.5	0.6	0.6	0.0	0.0
Japan		—	—	—	—	—	—	—	—	—	—	—	—	—	—	—
Korea	1995–97	19.8	17.0	2.8	5.7	3.5	2.2	1.7	0.0	6.5	4.1	2.3	1.3	1.3	—	0.4
New Zealand[3]	1995–99	35.0	31.8	3.1	21.3	15.7	4.0	0.0	0.3	9.1	6.3	1.9	0.9	0.9	0.0	0.2
Austria[4]	1995–99	37.2	34.5	2.7	9.1	—	—	14.9	1.6	8.9	—	—	—	—	—	0.0
Belgium[4]	1995–98	43.9	42.9	1.1	15.8	12.7	3.0	14.7	0.0	11.2	7.3	2.4	—	—	—	1.3
Czech Republic	1995–99	33.9	32.2	1.7	4.8	1.7	3.1	14.7	0.0	11.4	7.0	3.9	1.0	1.0	—	0.3
Denmark[4]	1995–99	38.8	33.7	5.1	14.8	11.4	2.2	1.5	0.3	16.0	9.7	3.8	—	—	—	0.7
Finland[4]	1995–98	32.0	27.5	4.5	9.2	7.5	1.8	3.7	0.0	13.8	8.2	4.6	—	—	—	0.6
France[4]	1995–97	41.1	38.3	2.8	7.5	5.7	1.8	17.5	0.5	11.6	7.9	2.7	—	—	—	0.8
Germany[4]	1995–98	31.6	26.7	4.9	4.7	4.1	0.5	15.2	0.0	6.6	3.4	3.0	—	—	—	0.0
Greece[4/5]	1995–98	22.4	20.2	2.2	7.7	4.0	2.3	0.5	0.0	12.8	7.6	4.7	—	—	—	0.9
Hungary	1995–99	38.4	33.5	4.9	7.1	5.1	2.0	10.8	0.1	12.0	7.7	3.3	2.8	2.8	—	0.2
Iceland	1995–98	30.3	25.9	4.4	6.8	5.7	1.0	2.7	0.0	14.6	9.4	3.4	0.4	0.4	—	1.3
Ireland[4]	1995–97	32.2	30.8	1.4	13.2	10.1	3.1	4.4	0.4	12.0	6.4	4.8	—	—	—	0.8
Italy[4]	1995–99	41.8	39.3	2.5	14.4	11.4	2.7	13.4	0.0	10.2	5.7	2.7	—	—	—	0.9
Luxembourg[4]	1995–97	41.7	39.9	1.7	14.1	8.5	5.1	10.8	0.0	10.9	5.9	4.5	—	—	—	2.9
Netherlands[4]	1995–97	45.8	42.8	3.1	11.6	7.6	4.0	18.7	0.0	10.5	7.0	2.9	—	—	—	1.3
Norway	1995–98	42.0	33.4	8.6	8.3	4.5	3.8	9.0	0.0	15.4	8.9	5.4	0.2	0.2	0.0	0.4
Poland	1995–99	36.2	32.7	3.5	8.9	6.2	2.7	10.1	0.3	11.6	7.6	3.9	1.8	1.8	0.0	0.0
Portugal[4]	1995–98	35.2	31.5	3.7	9.1	5.9	3.1	8.7	0.0	12.8	7.5	4.7	—	—	—	0.1
Spain[4]	1995–97	30.2	28.3	2.0	9.1	7.0	2.1	11.7	0.0	7.3	4.4	2.7	—	—	—	0.1
Sweden[4]	1995–99	39.6	34.5	5.1	4.9	1.9	2.9	14.2	2.1	11.4	7.1	3.8	—	—	—	1.8
	1995–99	23.0	22.1	1.7	3.3	2.5	0.8	12.5	0.0	5.5	3.4	1.8	0.2	0.2	—	0.6

Country	Period															
Turkey	1995–99	21.2	17.5	3.6	7.5	5.6	1.6	0.0	0.0	8.5	5.2	2.8	0.5	0.5	—	0.4
United Kingdom[4]	1995–99	36.2	33.9	2.3	13.7	9.8	3.9	0.0	6.2	11.5	6.8	4.0	—	—	—	2.5
Unweighted Average[6]																
OECD Total		32.5	29.4	3.1	9.8	7.2	2.6	8.5	0.2	10.0	6.2	3.2	0.8	0.8	0.0	0.7
OECD America		18.5	16.6	1.9	8.7	8.6	2.1	4.1	0.0	4.2	2.7	1.0	0.4	0.4	0.0	0.1
OECD Pacific		26.3	23.7	2.6	14.3	10.3	3.4	0.8	0.3	6.9	4.3	2.2	0.9	0.9	0.0	0.2
OECD Europe		35.3	31.9	3.3	9.3	6.6	2.5	9.8	0.2	11.2	6.9	3.6	1.0	1.0	0.0	0.8
EU 15		36.7	33.7	3.0	10.6	7.7	2.8	10.4	0.3	11.2	6.8	3.7	—	—	—	1.0

Sources: IMF, Government Finance Statistics; IMF, International Financial Statistics.

1. European Union countries do not report statistics on international trade taxes to Government Finance Statistics.
2. Total tax revenue shown is net of tax revenue transferred back to subcentral levels of government due to revenue sharing agreements.
3. Budgetary central government
4. European Union countries
5. Components of tax revenue are based on budgetary operations. Total tax revenue reported is net of transactions among entities within the central government
6. For each revenue classification, only countries for which data are available are included in the calculation

In the Mashreq countries, corporate income taxation is substantially lower than in other middle-income countries. In both Jordan and Lebanon, they amount to about 1.5 percent of GDP and mostly stem from the financial sector. Construction activities, other services, manufacturing, and agriculture hardly seem to be taxed. For Egypt, if we exclude the income taxation of the oil sector, the Suez Canal, and the Central Bank of Egypt, the ratio of corporate taxation would fall to 2.2 percent of GDP, which is still a respectable level. In Syria, most of the tax yield results from public enterprises (including the oil corporation) and is difficult to interpret because of monopolistic practices, multiple exchange rates, and opaque accounting procedures where losses and interest payment are often financed by commercial bank credit and capitalized. Overall, the private business sector in Syria incurs very little taxation. In addition, agricultural activities have been exempted from taxation in some countries (Jordan and Morocco) and generous investment laws—which often provide tax holidays for five to fifteen years—have eroded the tax base. Here, as in the case of individual income taxes, the major effort should be in broadening the tax base by reducing exemptions and modernizing tax administration. In this respect, Egypt, Jordan, Lebanon, and Syria should be in a position to raise their yield from corporate taxation by at least 1 to 2 percent of GDP.

Taxes on Goods and Services

Proceeds from sales taxes have increased markedly in virtually all the SMCs following the introduction of the value-added tax (VAT). The VAT yields, in relation to GDP, have exceeded all other government revenue in the countries that have introduced it (6.3 percent of GDP). The overall average for taxes on goods and services in SMCs (7 percent of GDP) is not far behind comparator countries (8.6 percent of GDP).

The most successful introduction of the VAT has been in the Maghreb countries, in Jordan, and in the West Bank and Gaza (WBG) (Morocco: 6.1 percent of GDP; Tunisia: 6.7 percent of GDP; Jordan: 7.2 percent of GDP; and WBG: 9.1 percent of GDP). These ratios exceed the average for middle-income countries (5.6 percent of GDP) and, in three countries, the OECD average (6.2 percent of GDP). In the WBG, under the unified invoice system and a single VAT rate established with Israel, the yield from the VAT (9.1 percent of GDP in 1999) was exceeded only by Denmark (9.7 percent of GDP) and Hungary (9.4 percent of GDP). Nevertheless, multiplicity of VAT rates in most SMCs and substantial exemptions limit tax yields below their potential. The introduction of a VAT in Lebanon and Syria is urgently needed to strengthen their public finance as it may bring 3 to 4 percent of GDP during the first year—possibly rising to 5 to 6 percent within a few years.

Excise taxes in SMCs are levied mostly on petroleum products, alcohol, and tobacco. In some countries, some construction material (cement, rebars) has been taxed as a proxy for property taxes. Excise taxes have declined in yield over the past decade with the introduction of the VAT and the phasing out of state monopolies. They still average 2.2 percent of GDP, slightly lower than in middle-income countries (2.5 percent of GDP), although, again, the Maghreb countries are doing much better (3.7 percent of GDP).

Much of the disparity in excise taxes in SMCs pertains to the pricing and taxation policy for petroleum products. In Table 5, domestic prices for gasoline, diesel fuel, and fuel oil are shown in relation to international prices at Mediterranean ports. Typically, gasoline prices include a substantial share of taxation, which should be used for infrastructure development and environmental cleanup. Unfortunately, in most countries, the taxes are used to subsidize diesel fuel (used in transport vehicles) and fuel oil (for electricity generating). Since consumption of fuel oil and diesel fuel far exceeds that of gasoline, this subsidization often results in an overall budget subsidy or quasi-fiscal expenditure. In Morocco and Tunisia, where two of the three products are taxed, the yield from excises is substantial, 5.8 percent of GDP and 3.5 percent of GDP, respectively. In the Mashreq, the WBG generates substantial excise revenue because it is the only country where all three products are taxed. On the other hand, Egypt, Jordan, and Syria heavily subsidize both diesel fuel and fuel oil, resulting in very low yields in excise taxes (1.5 percent of GDP, 0.9 percent of GDP, and 0.3 percent of GDP, respectively). This pricing policy also results in resource misallocation, energy waste, and greater environmental damage.

Excise tax yields also depend on the adjustment mechanism for petroleum prices. An automatic adjustment mechanism obviously protects the budget from subsidization or a decline in excise receipts, when international oil prices rise. This approach is followed in most OECD and middle-income countries. In Algeria, Lebanon, Morocco, and the WBG, a system has been established whereby petroleum prices are periodically adjusted to fluctuations in world prices. However, Algeria and Morocco departed from their

Table 5. Southern Mediterranean Arab Countries: Petroleum Product Prices (US$ per Gallon)

	Super Gasoline		Diesel Fuel		Fuel Oil	
	DP	DP/IP	DP	DP/IP	DP	DP/IP
Algeria	1.07	1.08	0.50	0.55	0.50	0.98
Morocco	3.17	3.20	2.02	2.22	0.70	1.37
Tunisia	1.94	1.96	1.15	1.26	—	—
Egypt[1]	0.90	0.91	0.38	0.42	0.14	0.28
Jordan[2]	2.05	2.08	0.56	0.61	0.32	0.62
Lebanon[3]	2.47	2.49	0.96	1.05	0.65	1.28
Syrian AR	1.54	1.56	0.47	0.52	0.10	0.20
West Bank and Gaza[4]	3.52	3.56	1.78	1.96	—	—

1. Based on the latest prices available. Prices are converted from US$/metric ton to US$ per gallon using conversion factor 0.0033
2. As of August 2001
3. Prices as last set, on September 19, 2001
4. Retail prices inclusive of all taxes as last set on September 21, 2001

DP–domestic prices in 2000 or latest prices; IP–ex-refinery price Mediterranean ports
IP 2000 averages (in US$ per gallon); gasoline: 0.99; diesel fuel: 0.91; fuel oil: 0.51

systems. When they did not increase their domestic petroleum prices in line with world prices, they incurred tax expenditures.

In the other SMCs, domestic price adjustments for petroleum products are purely discretionary, resulting in a buildup of subsidies when world prices are trending upward. Syria has not changed its petroleum prices since 1994; both Egypt and Jordan have sustained long periods without prices adjustment. In Jordan, a yearly net subsidy of 2.2 percent of GDP has been incurred over the last few years, but it was substantially reduced when domestic petroleum prices were raised by 15 percent of GDP in August 2001.

Clearly, a move toward automatic adjustment of petroleum prices would protect excise revenue from petroleum price fluctuations. However, the more important objective for Egypt, Jordan, and Syria—and to a lesser extent other SMCs—would be to reestablish relative petroleum prices to their international levels. There would also be merit in establishing a "reasonable" level of taxation, which is harmonized at the regional level to ensure avoiding cross-border smuggling and a competitive level playing field.

Taxes on International Trade

The worldwide trend of declining taxes on international trade is the result of continuous trade liberalization, World Trade Organization (WTO) accession, and a proliferation of free trade agreements. In OECD countries, customs duties yield only 0.8 percent of GDP in revenue while in middle-income countries, the average is 1.4 percent of GDP (Table 3). In emerging markets that have a large degree of openness, tariff revenue typically does not exceed 1 percent of GDP (Brazil: 0.6 percent; South Africa: 0.9 percent; and Turkey: 0.5 percent). Yet, most SMCs continue to have a high degree of protection (average tariffs are about 30 percent) and large reliance on custom duties with tariff revenues ranging from 2 to 7 percent of GDP (Table 1). Indeed, over the last decade, trade taxes have increased or remained constant in all SMCs, except Egypt and Tunisia.

In the Maghreb countries, the average most-favored nations (MFN) tariff is 31.2 percent and the trade restrictiveness index[4] is also high—particularly for Morocco and Tunisia that are considered emerging markets (Table 5). The tax yield is also high in both Morocco at 4.7 percent of GDP and Tunisia at 3 percent of GDP(Table 6). However, the effective import tariff (custom duties divided by import value) is a better indicator of real trade restrictiveness. It drops to 15 percent for Morocco and to 10 percent for Tunisia, signaling exemptions, the impact of free trade agreements, and an import composition skewed toward lower tariff bands.

In the Mashreq countries, Egypt, Lebanon, and Syria appear to be quite restrictive while Jordan and the WBG are more open and liberal.[5] Nevertheless, all of the Mashreq countries have custom receipts/GDP ratios that are out of line with world levels. The accession of SMCs to the WTO and integration with the global economy would inevitably entail further losses of tariff revenue in the range of 2 to 4 percent of GDP. This situation is already happening in Morocco and Tunisia with the implementation of the AAEUs, while Egypt and Jordan—which have already reached agreements with the EU—are likely to follow suit. This process should also entail some multilateral tariff reduction to maintain the preferential treatment of the EU within a 10 to 15 percent margin; otherwise, trade diversion is likely to reach significant proportions. Finally, for the first time, a Pan-Arab free trade agreement (greater Arab free trade area), which began implementation in 1998, has yearly reductions in customs tariffs among Arab countries. Yet, while this trade liberalization is ongoing on a number of levels, SMCs have not moved with concrete plans—with the exception of Tunisia—to make up for tariff revenue losses.

Table 6. Southern Mediterranean Arab Countries: Import Taxation, 1999–2000

	Trade Restrictive-ness Rating[1]	Average MFN Tariff[2]	Effective Imports Tariff[3]	Custom Duties (Percent of GDP)
Maghreb				
Algeria	7	23.7	13.5	2.0
Morocco	8	34.0	15.0	4.7
Tunisia	8	35.9	10.1	2.8
Mashreq				
Egypt[3]	8	30.2	15.1	2.8
Jordan	6	16.0	5.3	4.7
Lebanon	7	21.0	21.4	7.5
Syrian AR	10	35.0	7.2	2.0
West Bank and Gaza[4]	4	8.8	9.1	7.1

Source: IMF, Trade Policy Information Database
1. IMF restrictiveness rating, with 10 being the most restrictive
2. Includes other duties and import surcharges; observations are for the most recent year available
3. Customs duties on imports divided by the value of imports
4. Since the WBG is in a custom union with Israel, the index for Israel applies

Exchange Rate Regimes

Exchange rate overvaluation undermines tax revenue.[6] When the real exchange rate appreciates, import prices rise at a slower pace than the GDP deflator. Or, to put it differently, nontraded goods prices rise relative to traded goods prices. This reduces the tax yield in relation to GDP for all indirect taxes on traded goods, such as custom duties, VAT, and excises.

In those SMCs with fixed exchange rate regimes that have experienced a sustained real appreciation of their currency (Egypt, Jordan, Lebanon, Morocco, and Syria), the tax yield from traded goods has been lower than yields that could have been obtained if their exchange rate policy had protected their competitiveness. Conversely, the adoption of a flexible exchange rate regime, which avoids real appreciation (Algeria and Tunisia), can sustain tax yields on traded goods and facilitate trade liberalization. Currency appreciation, which has reduced the competitiveness and profitability of traded goods sectors, has also resulted in lower corporate income taxes and has generated pressure from exporters for tax exemptions. Both Egypt and Morocco have recently responded to these pressures (as well as to pressures on their external reserves) by devaluing their currency by about 34 percent and

5 percent, respectively. Nevertheless, these ad-hoc adjustments tend to be politicized, are difficult to carry out, and typically do not make up for past losses.

Looking Forward

The major areas of tax revenue vulnerability and growth potential in SMCs are summarized below.

Areas of vulnerability

a. Nontax revenue will continue to decline relative to GDP because of depletion of mineral resources, privatizations, and reduction in monopolistic profits with greater market access. On the whole, this healthy development is in line with the modernization of SMCs, but revenue losses may be substantial.

b. Most SMCs also need to reform their income taxes by lowering their marginal rates, particularly with respect to the individual income tax.

c. Custom duties will decline with further trade liberalization and removal of trade restrictions. This change will have a dual impact of lowering custom duties receipts and, during an adjustment period, lowering income taxes in sectors that have been protected and are now exposed to greater competition from imports. Estimates of tax revenue losses due to the implementation of AAEUs for Morocco and Tunisia range from 2 to 3 percent of GDP.

Areas of potential growth

a. There is scope for broadening and adjusting user charges for a number of government services (while improving quality), including for higher education and some health services.

b. Reform of the individual income tax that would broaden the base, strengthen tax administration, and eliminate exemptions could raise tax yields substantially.

c. The introduction of the VAT in most SMCs has been very successful. The reduction of the number of rates and elimination of some exemptions would further raise its tax yield in a number of countries. The introduction of VAT in Lebanon and Syria would substantially improve their public finance.

d. In those countries where petroleum products are subsidized, bringing their prices to international levels and adopting an automatic adjustment mechanism could reduce subsidies and increase excise tax revenue. Harmonization of petroleum product excises across SMCs would be the next step to avoid smuggling and ensure fair competition.

e. The negative impact of trade liberalization on competitiveness and the concomitant stream of income tax revenue will be exacerbated by the decline in customs duties receipts. This impact can be partly offset by the adoption of a flexible exchange rate policy (in those countries with a fixed exchange rate regime) to avoid any real appreciation of the exchange rate and to strengthen competitiveness.

Endnotes

1. To the extent that the number of entrants to the labor force rises faster than the population, the country may benefit from a demographic dividend provided that the entrants can be fully employed without a decline in real wages. However, to the extent that this trend results in higher unemployment and welfare payments, public expenditures are likely to rise faster than public revenues.

2. These limitations have been moderated by diversification into fertilizer production and other chemical derivatives.

3. There may also be an increase in net tax proceeds depending on the source of privatization proceeds (domestic or external) and on how they are spent by the government.

4. The IMF trade restrictiveness index combines average MFN tariff levels with trade restriction measures (import licensing, imposition of reference prices, etc.) to rank countries from 1–10 with 10 being the most restrictive.

5. In Syria, both the average tariff and the trade restrictiveness index are overstated. The average tariff has been set at a high level because customs valuations have been using appreciated exchange rates. That is why the effective tariff is much lower (7.2 percent) and the customs duties yield (2 percent of GDP) is the lowest (with Algeria) of all eight countries.

6. Karim Nashashibi and Stefania Bazzoni: Exchange Rate Strategies and Fiscal Performance in Sub-Saharan Africa, IMF Staff Papers, March 1994.

Arab Banking and Capital Market Developments

Rodney Wilson

Efficient banking and financial systems are important to promote long-term sustainable economic growth and competitiveness. Unfortunately, in the Arab world, banking and financial systems are often inefficient, which results in low savings rates, expensive borrowing, and a misallocation of capital with some businesses unable to obtain funding. Government intervention in finance has not helped; in some Arab countries, notably Syria and Egypt, the banking system is wholly or largely under state ownership. In those Arab states where banks are quoted companies, notably in the Gulf Cooperation Council (GCC) countries (Bahrain, Kuwait, Oman, Qatar, Saudi Arabia, U.A.E.), banking systems are more modern and sophisticated, with a good range of financial services on offer to retail clients.

This chapter highlights both the successes and shortcomings of Arab banking and capital markets. Commercial banking has had a long history in the region, dating back to the 1850s; the Cairo and Alexandria stock exchanges were the most developed in the Mediterranean by the 1880s. Given this rich historical experience, the present shortcomings were avoidable. Nevertheless the results of government-dominated financial services are all too apparent, with inadequately-funded and usually rather small nationally-focused businesses, and the complete absence of any Arab multinational companies with the exception of the Saudi Basic Industries Corporation (SABIC). Government bond markets are still underdeveloped and corporate bond issues are in their infancy, while stock markets are very limited in the value of active trading and the number of quoted companies compared to those in other emerging regions in Asia and Latin America.

Islamic finance is also examined. Although its quantitative impact remains limited in the Arab world, Islamic banks and managed funds have attracted savings and investments from market segments that conventional financial institutions have largely ignored. Arab countries are predominately Muslim, and although not everyone wishes to practice their beliefs through their financial dealings, many do, and Islamic finance has become a US$200 billion industry worldwide, with much of this capital coming from the GCC countries. Islamic finance is one market segment where the Arab World potentially has a competitive advantage, although it has yet to be fully exploited.

Bank Deposits and Lending in the Arab World

The development of banks in the Arab world can be assessed by the scale of deposit and lending activity, which partly reflects the size of particular economies and the extent to which financial intermediation plays a significant economic role. As Table 1 shows, Saudi Arabia accounts for the largest value of bank deposits, followed by Egypt and the U.A.E. Deposits in Lebanon are significant not only from domestic residents, but also from Lebanese expatriates and,

Table 1. Arab Bank Deposits, February 2002 (in US$ billion)

Rank	Country	Demand	Time	Total
1	Saudi Arabia	35.9	27.0	62.9
2	Egypt	5.4	50.9	56.3
3	U.A.E.	7.9	31.9	39.8
4	Lebanon	0.6	33.3	33.9
5	Kuwait	4.4	25.0	29.4
6	Syrian AR	10.3	17.9	28.2
7	Morocco	15.0	7.2	22.2
8	Algeria	6.8	11.2	18.0
9	Libya	7.2	3.6	10.8
10	Tunisia	2.8	6.2	9.0
11	Qatar	1.0	6.4	7.4
12	Oman	1.1	4.1	5.2
13	Bahrain	1.1	4.7	5.8
14	Jordan	1.2	3.5	4.7
15	Yemen, Rep.	0.3	1.5	1.8
16	Sudan	0.4	0.6	1.0
	Bahrain offshore	1.6	211.9	213.5

Source: IMF, International Financial Statistics

to a lesser extent today, other Arabs. The Bahrain offshore banking sector accounts for most deposits in the Arab world; however, most of these deposits come from other banks in the Arab region.

In Saudi Arabia, most deposits are in transaction accounts that earn no interest, as depositors are concerned with the Islamic prohibition of *riba* (interest). In countries where there has been significant inflation in the past and where high rates of interest are paid on time deposits because of currency uncertainties, time deposits predominate. In February 2002, the average time deposit rate in Saudi Arabia was 2.16 percent, but rates in Egypt averaged 9.3 percent and those in Lebanon 10.8 percent (IMF June 2002).

The distribution of Arab bank lending is shown in Table 2, with countries ranked according to the value of lending to the private sector. In so far as

Table 2. Distribution of Arab Bank Lending (in US$ billion)

Rank	Country	Government	Public Enterprises	Private Sector
1	Saudi Arabia	31.6	2.9	50.7
2	Egypt	21.0	9.7	44.2
3	U.A.E.	3.0	1.4	35.6
4	Kuwait	10.7	0.0	20.0
5	Morocco	6.2	0.0	17.6
6	Lebanon	15.6	0.0	14.7
7	Tunisia	1.0	0.0	11.7
8	Oman	1.1	0.0	7.9
9	Syrian AR	7.6	15.5	6.9
10	Jordan	0.7	0.4	6.7
11	Libya	1.0	10.3	5.1
12	Qatar	2.3	0.2	4.8
13	Algeria	3.6	6.7	3.6
14	Bahrain	0.3	0.0	1.9
15	Yemen, Rep.	0.3	0.0	0.6
16	Sudan	0.0	0.0	0.4

Source: IMF, International Financial Statistics

banks are lending to central governments there is little or no credit appraisal, because the banks are simply recycling deposits to cover budgetary deficits, often through compulsion. Much bank funding is employed in this manner in Saudi Arabia, Egypt, Kuwait, Lebanon, and Syria. This funding results in less finance being available for more productive purposes in the private sector. In Egypt and Syria a major portion of bank funding is allocated to public

sector enterprises, which also reduces the amount available for private business. Usually this credit is advanced on the directions of government rather than being based on business plans and revenue projections, which means less efficient financial intermediation. With economic liberalization and privatization, more Arab bank funding has being going to business in recent years, but in Egypt and Syria, the legacy of state planning and control of financial activity remains. Rates for private sector lending averaged 13.7 percent in Egypt in early 2002, reflecting the shortages of funding available once the demands of public sector enterprises and the central government were met.

Banking Development, Economic Growth, and Financial Reform

Despite extensive literature on the contribution of banking to economic growth, notably the work of Ross Levine (1997), no attempts have been made to assess that relationship in the Arab world. One problem is that because of the continuing significance of oil for the region and the increasing importance of gas, growth rates are still largely exogenously determined by energy prices, rather than reflecting domestic economic developments. These external factors are also important for Arab economies without oil and gas resources, as they benefit from remittances and aid from the oil-exporting countries, and these are affected by developments in global energy markets. Hence, the impact of banking size and structure is at best of limited significance for economic growth, though arguably it is of more importance for the non-oil economy, where it will affect future employment growth as the private sector develops.

Not surprisingly, the Arab country with the largest economy, Saudi Arabia, also has the largest bank deposits, and Egypt, the second largest economy, has the second largest bank deposits, as Table 1 shows. This finding simply suggests a relationship between the scale of financial intermediation and the size of Arab economies, rather than proving causation (Levine et al. 2000). Arguably, as retail banking is especially developed in the high-income GCC countries, the scale of financial intermediation may be a consequence of market growth, not its cause. Nevertheless the evidence from international empirical surveys of how efficient financial intermediation may promote development has some relevance for Arab countries, even though most are well beyond the early stages of development (Thiel 2001). The effect of financial intermediation on capital productivity through the selection and monitoring of investment is significant. Countries with developed banking systems such as Saudi Arabia and the U.A.E. have efficient services and industrial sectors. But Syria and Iraq, where the allocation of funding is determined politically rather than through the appraisal of business plans and revenue projections, do not have efficient services and industrial sectors.

During the 1990s, many Arab governments embarked on financial reform programs (El-Eriam et al. 1996), but these tended to involve macroeconomic stabilization rather than banking sector change even though the IMF has stressed the importance of efficient financial intermediation in the region (Camdessus 1996). The Appendix table gives some indication of the extent of financial reform. The major change for the banking sector has been the increasing use of interest rates as an instrument of monetary policy, which in practice has meant higher discount rates for central bank lending to the commercial banks and consequently higher borrowing and deposit rates for bank customers. In Egypt, the discount rate rose to 13 percent in the mid 1990s and it remains at 11.0 percent; in Lebanon, it was 30 percent in 1997 and 1998 and still remains at 20 percent (IMF 2002). The corresponding lending and deposit rates are 13.7 percent and 9.5 percent in Egypt and 16.76 percent and 10.82 percent in Lebanon (IMF 2002). Jordanian lending and deposit rates were 10.45 percent and 5.19 percent in December 2001.

The main objective of interest rate policy is to maintain exchange rate pegs, usually with the dollar. There are no restrictions on capital movements in the GCC states, and other Arab countries such as Algeria, Jordan, Lebanon, Morocco, Tunisia, and Yemen liberalized their international payments systems in the 1990s. Consequently, external deficits can result in exchange rate pressures, which are countered by raising interest rate differentials with those on dollar deposits. Syria has a much more controlled payments regime, which enables it to maintain fixed discount rates of 5 percent, deposit rates of 4 percent, and lending rates of 9 percent. However, the bureaucratic nature of its payments system is a significant deterrent to trade.

The cost of capital is generally lower in the Gulf, with deposit rates a mere 2 percent by February 2002, and with many Muslims not accepting interest because of the Islamic prohibition of *riba*. Lending rates were around 6 percent, with rates generally varying with dollar rates against which Gulf currencies are pegged.

The Saudi Inter-Bank Offer Rate (SIBOR) moves exactly in line with LIBOR, the London Inter-Bank Offer Rate on dollars.

Arab Bank Size

Most banks in the Arab world are largely focused on their national markets rather than multinational markets. Cross-border mergers and acquisitions are precluded in most Arab countries, as foreign banks are either prohibited from entering the market or constrained in the number of services they can offer, in order to protect local banks. As a consequence, even the largest Arab banks are small by international standards, and none are represented in the world's leading 100 banks measured by asset size. Indeed, the assets of the leading international banks such as Citigroup or HSBC exceed those of all Arab banks combined.

Of the leading twenty Arab Banks listed in Table 3, no less than fifteen are from the GCC countries, including the largest banks, the Bahrain-based Arab Banking Corporation and Saudi Arabia's National Commercial Bank. Measuring bank size in the Arab world is far from straightforward because many banks are government-owned and accounting procedures are varied. Technically the Commercial Bank of Syria, a state-owned banking monopoly, is the largest bank in the Arab world with assets of $66 billion, but as the valuation of its assets is open to different interpretations and the exchange rate conversion can be questioned, it is not included in the table.

The Arab Banking Corporation was founded in 1980 as an Arab joint venture owned by the governments of Kuwait, Abu Dhabi, and Libya. It provides commercial banking, treasury, Islamic, and retail services, and has an extensive network of branches in Europe and North America, with much of its business being generated from other banks. Like its rival the Bahrain-based Gulf International Bank, it represents the nearest Arab equivalent to the major international banks, with high visibility and transparency and the capacity to offer investment-banking services to large corporate clients, either on its own or through syndications (in the case of very large projects). The Arab Bank, originally a Jerusalem-based institution but now headquartered in Amman, is the other major Arab international bank, and its core customers are the Palestinian Diaspora. Most of the GCC banks provide a standard range of commercial banking services, trade finance being particularly significant. But in recent years, much of their focus has been on developing retail services. These services include personal finance, notably for

Table 3. Leading Arab Banks, 2001 (in US$ million)

	Bank	Assets	Loans	Deposits	Equity	Profits
1	Arab Banking Corporation	26,586	14,225	12,762	1,913	160
2	National Commercial Bank	26,530	10,340	20,900	2,272	—
3	National Bank of Egypt	23,623	—	—	1,048	139
4	Arab Bank Group	22,228	8,738	15,086	2,051	312
5	Saudi American Bank	20,595	8,973	15,913	2,240	603
6	Riyadh Bank	17,909	5,650	10,694	2,220	361
7	Gulf International Bank	15,232	3,309	4,759	1,194	101
8	National Bank of Kuwait	14,553	5,089	8,820	1,702	342
9	Al Rajhi Banking & Investment Corporation	13,798	—	10,080	1,792	411
10	Banque Misr	12,856	—	—	360	17
11	Saudi British Bank	11,179	4,272	8,410	1,055	221
12	Arab National Bank	10,771	3,944	7,006	898	130
13	Al Bank Al Saudi Al Fransi	10,668	4,474	8,950	1,073	225
14	National Bank of Dubai	8,889	1,959	6,848	1,261	123
15	National Bank of Abu Dhabi	8,788	5,542	5,862	958	166
16	Libyan Arab Foreign Bank	8,002	—	—	965	4
17	Qatar National Bank	7,797	5,235	5,876	1,294	145
18	Kuwait Finance House	7,713	—	—	779	167
19	Abu Dhabi Commercial Bank	7,246	4,457	4,830	1,121	168
20	Credit Populaire d'Algerie	6,935	—	—	312	5

Source: Middle East Economic Digest and The Banker July 2002

the purchase of vehicles, and debit card and other transaction services including money transfers. The retail banking market in Saudi Arabia is especially competitive despite the barriers to foreign entrants, as the local institutions vie for client business. The two wholly locally-owned banks compete with banks such as Saudi American and Saudi British in which Citibank and HSBC, respectively, have a minority stake. Retail banking services are on a par with the best in the world, with all banks providing cash machines and most providing online banking and even mobile phone banking. Service within branches is generally pleasant and efficient, and the banks have a good record in employing Saudi Arabian nationals, a major issue for other employers in the Kingdom where foreign nationals still outnumber local citizens in the workforce.

The weakness of Saudi Arabian and other GCC banks is their limited ability to provide financing for major projects. The banks' modest size and lack of investment banking experience means that financing for the major petrochemical and gas utilization projects has to be arranged through international banks. The development of the Saudi Arabia gas sector alone is expected to cost US$25 billion, which means lucrative financing opportunities for the banking

sector (Marks 2000). Rather than simply relying on syndicated loans, there is scope for more varied methods of project financing, including bonds and share issues, as well as private placements and the arrangement of floating rate notes. Islamic financing techniques of the type pioneered in Malaysia may also be attractive to local investors, although Islamic banks in the GCC have been reluctant to commit themselves to long-term funding.

The Arab Mediterranean countries have fewer modern banking systems than the GCC states, and between the 1960s and 1990s, the systems in Egypt, Algeria, Libya, and Syria were virtually frozen in a time warp. In Egypt, four state-owned banks dominate the sector— the National Bank of Egypt, Banque Misr, Banque du Caire, and Bank of Alexandria. Although Egypt embarked on a major privatization program in the 1990s, it has not been extended to the banking sector where resistance to change is high (Huband 2000). Egypt's banks are overstaffed and many employees would fear for their jobs if the banks became private sector companies. Information technology systems are basic in comparison to those in GCC banks, although more advanced than those in the Commercial Bank of Syria where most transactions remain paper based.

Since the 1960s much of the state sector bank dealings in Egypt have been with other state sector industries (Wilson 1983), but privatization is gradually changing this, with banks increasingly having to deal with more commercially-driven businesses. The state sector banks established joint venture undertakings from the 1970s to deal with foreign companies involved in Egyptian contracts; the major institutions included the Egyptian American Bank, a joint venture between American Express and the Bank of Alexandria, and Nationale Societe Generale Bank, a joint venture between Societe Generale and the National Bank of Egypt. These banks are now developing retail-banking services such as car finance, mortgages, and debit cards. Citibank provides card services in Egypt to clients of high net worth as well as telephone banking, but neither it nor the joint venture banks have the networks outside Cairo to serve the major portion of the Egyptian population.

The Opening up of the Arab Banking Sector

Competition is undoubtedly strengthened by the opening up of the financial sector to outside banks, but politically they are reluctant to return to a pattern of relationships associated with the colonial era when European-owned banks dominated in countries such as Egypt, Syria, Iraq, and Algeria. Pan-Arab ownership is one way forward, but would be best driven by commercial synergies rather than political agreement. Banks with full banking licenses to operate in one GCC country can establish branches in other GCC states, but so far, only the Gulf International Bank has taken advantage of this opportunity by establishing a branch in Riyadh. GCC banks, notably those based in Saudi Arabia, have the resources to open branches in Egypt, Syria, and the North African countries, but it may not be as effective a way of widening their operations as taking over existing banks in these countries. The opportunity for more branch expansion in the GCC itself is limited in scope, but by acquiring banks elsewhere in the Arab world, leading Saudi Arabian banks could use their retailing skills and technological experience to build new markets. Rebranding of the institutions taken over might not be necessary or appropriate, and existing staff could be retrained.

Some markets such as those of Bahrain, Qatar, Oman, and the U.A.E. are open to foreign banks and have major international banks represented, but much government business is conducted with local banks, some of which are partly government owned. The "national bank" model is still important in the Arab world, with virtually every state or emirate having its own national bank. Central banks have close relationships with these national banks, often

finding these relationships more comfortable than their relationships with foreign banks. Governments themselves exercise patronage through their national banks, and are reluctant to see the role of these institutions diminished. The national banks, for their part, are dependent on government for much of their business. The banks help to cover government spending deficits, usually by lending to the state and holding government paper. This practice does not encourage these banks to be innovative or to compete for private clients. As a consequence, the national banks are somewhat detached from the populations of their own countries (that they are supposed to serve) and they do not market their services effectively or cater for the needs of smaller- and medium-sized businesses. Furthermore, although most of the national banks have extensive correspondence relations with banks abroad, as they are too small to maintain more than a few offices at best in international financial centers, they lack any international strategy or vision.

Some Arab states have sought to capitalize on the obstacles to international banks' entering major Arab markets by encouraging the establishment of offshore financial centers in their jurisdictions. International banks are actively encouraged to set up in these centers and attract business from neighboring Arab counties, but not usually from the domestic market. Following the nationalization of banks in Egypt and Syria, Lebanon, with its emphasis on business freedom and a bank secrecy law became the major Arab financial center in the 1960s (Bridge 1975), a role that came to an end in 1973 with the civil war. The oil price rises and the barriers to entry in Gulf markets created an opportunity for Bahrain to take on a similar role as an offshore banking center from the mid-1970s, and within five years it played host to more than 100 international banks, including the largest Western international banks (Wilson 1981). By the 1980s, with less buoyant oil revenue and the Iraq-Iran and Gulf Wars, offshore banking business declined, but picked again up by the 1990s. Bahrain today is an established banking center with over US$210 billion in bank assets and where major international banks find it worthwhile to maintain a presence, as Table 4 shows. In addition to the fifty-two offshore banking units, Bahrain has thirty-four investment banks including Daiwa Securities, Merrill Lynch, and Nomura; thirty-eight representative offices; and seventeen brokers and investment advisors.

Abu Dhabi and Dubai are the other centers in the GCC with aspirations to becoming regional financial hubs, but they are unlikely to challenge Bahrain's preeminent position in banking. To date, Abu Dhabi has not been successful in getting the Saadiyat offshore zone off the ground, and Nomura withdrew from the public offering (Marks 2000). Dubai may be more successful with its international financial market, although its main services strength has been in distribution, with the success of the Jebel Ali duty-

Table 4. Major International Banks with a Presence in Bahrain

Bank	Country	Offshore Unit	Onshore Branch
ABN-AMRO	Netherlands	Yes	Yes
Arab Bank	Jordan	Yes	Yes
ANZ Banking Group	Australia	Yes	No
BNP Paribas	France	Yes	No
Bank of Tokyo-Mitsubishi	Japan	Yes	No
Citibank	U.S.	Yes	Yes
Credit Agricole Indosuez	France	Yes	No
HSBC	U.K.	Yes	Yes
JP Morgan Chase	U.S.	Yes	No
Korea Exchange Bank	Korea	Yes	No
Maybank	Malaysia	Yes	No
Standard Chartered Grindlays	U.K.	Yes	Yes

Source: Bahrain Monetary Agency, March 2002

free zone (the largest in the Arab world), up-market tourism, and its Internet and media cities. The U.A.E. is arguably overbanked, with twenty local and twenty-seven overseas banks, plus thirty representative offices. Much of this banking activity is sustained by relatively low labor costs, given the liberal policy adopted by the U.A.E. on work permits for expatriate bank employees, but in the longer term, takeovers and mergers seem inevitable as consolidation is needed to take advantage of economies of scale.

As international financial centers are important for financing major Arab projects, a number of Arab-owned or joint venture banks have been established to cater both for governments and major Arab corporate entities (Wilson 1998). These banks also provide asset management facilities and serve the Arab expatriate community. Five out of the six banks listed in Table 5 are in London, with the Union de Banques Arabes et Francaises based in Paris. These banks serve their affiliates in the Arab world, but are British and French institutions, and are regulated accordingly; they are not merely representative offices.

The Challenges of International Accountability

As the Arab world becomes increasingly integrated into the global economy, its financial institutions face numerous challenges, some arising from international economic governance and others that are market-driven. Of course, Arab banks have no obligation to report to international bodies such as the Bank for International Settlements (BIS) or to seek ratings from

Table 5. Major Arab Banks Based Internationally, (in US$ million)

Bank	Assets	Capital	Profit
Gulf International Bank	4,102	376	-27
National Bank of Kuwait	2,567	449	—
Union de Banques Arabes et Francaises	2,445	295	12
British Arab Commercial Bank	2,304	191	29
United Bank of Kuwait	2,062	193	21
ABC International Bank	2,050	314	21

Source: The Banker, July 2002

agencies such as Moody's or Standard and Poor's. Many increasingly do so, as those who adhere to the Basel Committee standards of capital adequacy or have low risk ratings can enjoy more favorable terms in their dealings with both international banks and other Arab banks. Accountability to national central banks no longer carries much weight, especially where economies are heavily indebted and are subject to foreign exchange restrictions or uncertainties about the sustainability of exchange rates. 'Lender of the last resort' support by central banks is in national currencies, not dollars or euros, but even small Arab banks are involved in trade financing.

The 1988 BIS Capital Accord of the Basel Committee on Banking Supervision stipulated an 8 percent requirement for capital in relation to risk-weighted assets, which most GCC-based banks were able to meet; the National Commercial Bank of Saudi Arabia fell just below the threshold. Three of the four major state-owned banks—the Commercial Bank of Syria, the Libyan Arab Foreign Bank, and Credit Populaire d'Algerie—all fall well short of requirements for the soundness of their capital assets; only the National Bank of Egypt and the Sahara Bank in Libya meet the Basel criteria.[1] Arguably, as the banks in Egypt, Syria, Libya, and Algeria are state-owned, the issue of financial soundness was less important, at least for local currency depositors. But for those with capital-to-asset ratios of less than 4 percent, privatization is not a feasible option without major prior restructuring.

Fortunately, the new Basel capital accord, which will be implemented in 2004, permits more flexibility.[2] Credit risks are to be weighted into different categories, with four rather than one category for corporate borrowings and account taken of operational risks such as computer failure, poor documentation, or fraud. Risk weights are to be refined with reference to assessments provided by credit rating agencies that will increase the incentive to be independently rated. Banks in the GCC, most of which are rated, will have little problem in complying with the new capital accord, but banks in Egypt, Syria, Libya, and Algeria will continue to face problems.

The position in Jordan, Tunisia, and Morocco is more favorable, as the leading banks in these countries, including the Jordan-based Arab Bank, do meet the 1988 Basel criteria for soundness and have been rated for many years. Jordan, Lebanon, and Yemen have also made formal commitments to the IMF to comply with its Financial Sector Assessment Program (FSAP) introduced in response to the Asian financial crisis of 1997. These countries are IMF borrowers, and adherence to FSAP implies adherence to Basel capital adequacy requirements as well as strengthening their capacity to monitor financial activity and promote transparency and integrity in financial reporting.

Arab countries that are members of the World Trade Organization (WTO) also have to adhere to the requirements of the General Agreement on Trade in Services (GATS). These countries are Egypt, Jordan, Morocco, Tunisia, and five out of the six GCC states (Saudi Arabia is still an applicant). Syria, Iraq, and Libya are not members, and Lebanon has observer status at the WTO but is not a member. Following the Doha meeting of the WTO in 2001, the WTO and the Arab Monetary Fund (AMF) signed an agreement on trade-related technical assistance and capacity-building for Arab countries (WTO News 2002). Although banking services are not specifically covered, trade financing is very relevant, and it is likely that this topic will be covered by the joint workshops that the AMF and the WTO have agreed to organize. Although GATS has no timetable for the opening up of markets for financial services, this topic is also likely to be on the agenda for future discussion within the joint AMF/WTO program.

Under the GATS agreement, WTO members are obliged in principle to offer to remove restrictions on inward investment by foreign banks in locally-incorporated institutions. However, the WTO Trade Policy Review for Pakistan in January 2002 set an interesting precedent in exempting the Islamic finance sector by using infant industry arguments (WTO 2002). There is no reason why similar arguments cannot be used for the forthcoming Trade Policy Reviews of Arab countries that host Islamic financial institutions.

Most Arab countries are resisting pressures from the WTO to open up their financial sectors to foreign banks, including countries such as the U.A.E. that already have a large number of foreign banks. Negotiators in the U.A.E. argue that as the country already has twenty domestic banks and twenty-seven foreign banks they have no room for further banks to enter, as the local population is only 3.3 million (*Gulf News* 9 July 2002). New talks with the WTO on its continuing exemptions from the provision to open its banking market started in July 2002 and are expected to last until 2005. Saudi Arabia's reluctance to allow foreign banks into its market is regarded as a major obstacle to its WTO membership, and it resents that higher hurdles are being imposed on it when existing WTO Arab members, including Egypt, Jordan, Kuwait, and the U.A.E., continue to be allowed exemptions.

Money laundering has not been a major problem historically for Arab banking, but as regulations concerning customer disclosure have been tightened in the West and in many offshore centers, some of those involved in international criminal activity have turned their attention to the Arab world. Those Arab countries that restrict foreign exchange dealings such as Syria are of little interest to money launderers, and state-owned banks in countries such as Egypt or Algeria are unlikely to be used given their bureaucratic procedures. In practice, it is the stable-currency countries of the GCC, with their absence of foreign exchange restrictions, which have proved the most attractive.

Although terrorist funding accounts for only a very minor portion of money laundering activity, post-11 September 2001 efforts have intensified internationally to curb illegal money transfers. The Paris-based Financial Action Task Force (FATF), the international organization responsible for the control of money laundering, has asked central banks and monetary agencies in the GCC to cooperate by establishing special units to monitor and control suspected transfers of illegal funds through the commercial banks. The U.A.E. has established a National Committee for Anti-Money Laundering that attended the FATF conference in Hong Kong in January 2002, and the FATF President has visited GCC countries and had discussions with relevant officials (*Gulf News* 11 June 2002). Although not full members of the FATF, GCC states are implementing its forty recommendations, and the U.A.E. Central Bank organized a conference during May 2002 on *hawala*, the informal system of transferring funds through money changers that accounts for a large proportion of the transfers between the Gulf and south Asia. Regulations have been tightened on the identity documents that those wanting to transfer funds must produce, although this change adds to transactions costs and penalizes poor migrant workers and their families trying to make a modest livelihood in the GCC. *Hawala* is prohibited in Saudi Arabia, but in other GCC states including the U.A.E., the emphasis is on licensing and regulation rather than prohibition (*Gulf News* 17 May 2002).

The Arab World's Competitive Advantage in Islamic Banking

The most distinctive contribution of the Arab world to global finance during the last forty years has been in Islamic banking. Although Islamic finance that avoids *riba* (interest), has been used since the early years of Islam, its modern application dates only from the early 1960s in Egypt when Ahmad El Naggar established an Islamic bank in the delta town of Mit Ghamr (Wilson 2001). It functioned as a credit union rather than a bank, but it proved very popular, attracting over 10,000 depositors in 1963 and rapidly expanding its operations by opening new branches. It was as a result of an agreement of the Finance Ministers of the Organization of the Islamic Conference in 1973 to found the Islamic Development Bank (IDB), however, that the Islamic finance movement really took off and came to the attention of the outside world. Although primarily a development assistance agency, the IDB has done much to promote Islamic banking worldwide by organizing conferences and workshops and encouraging research on how Islamic banking products can be developed to serve modern financing needs.

There is no return on current accounts in Islamic banks, but most offer debit cards and full checking facilities, and in the GCC many offer Internet,

telephone, and even mobile phone access to accounts. Unlike conventional bank savings deposits, which earn interest, those with Islamic banks are placed on a *mudarabah* basis, with account holders sharing in the profits of the bank that are declared annually (Wilson 1997). This profit-sharing is regarded as more just than interest-based returns, as the latter are usually adjusted in line with monetary policy changes, which are unrelated to the contract between a depositor and a bank. With profit-sharing, the depositor is much more closely involved with the bank, and shares in its risks. *Mudarabah* investment deposits are not usually guaranteed, so there is the possibility of capital loss, although in practice the main risk is of zero returns. Generally returns are competitive with those offered by conventional banks.

The financing facilities offered by Islamic banks are very different from those of conventional banks, the essential principle being that finance should be asset based. Sami Homoud, a Jordanian banker with much experience in trade finance, developed a type of mark-up financing, *murabahah*, whereby an Islamic bank can purchase a good on behalf of a client and then subsequently resell the good to the client for a premium (Usmani 2002). The return to the bank is justified by the ownership risk when it acquires and holds the asset, unlike the interest returns for conventional trade financing that relate only to the advance of money. *Murabahah* was the dominant form of Islamic financing during the 1970s and 1980s, partly because much of the banking business was trade finance, for which it was well-suited, but also because from the bank's perspective, it was relatively secure because it had ownership rights over the goods being financed.

During the 1980s and 1990s, *ijara* (leasing) and *ijara wa iqtina* (hire purchase) increased in popularity, with the beneficiary paying rental installments rather than interest to the Islamic bank (Lewis and Algaoud 2001). This type of financing was often for five years or longer, but given the stability of Islamic bank deposits, Islamic banks felt confident in having lengthening maturity mismatches between assets and liabilities. Even *murabahah* terms have been extended, with some Islamic banks in Bahrain offering revolving facilities involving multiple purchases and sales of assets over a two-year period. Islamic banks also offer project financing, one popular method being *istisna*, which involves the bank making payments for work completed on predetermined dates. This type of financing is especially well-suited for manufacturing enterprises.

The largest Islamic bank, as Table 6 shows, is the Al Rajhi Banking and Investment Corporation based in Riyadh. It is the fourth largest bank in Saudi Arabia and the ninth largest in the Arab world. Like other Saudi Arabian banks, it is very focused on the domestic retail market, vehicle and housing finance being of increasing significance. It has 375 branches, the largest network of any bank in Saudi Arabia. It is a quoted company on the Saudi Arabian stock exchange, and competes with the Saudi American Bank and the National Commercial Bank to be the most profitable bank in the Kingdom. The National Commercial Bank also provides Islamic deposit and financing facilities, but unlike Al Rajhi, is not exclusively Islamic.

The Kuwait Finance House is the second largest bank in Kuwait and has the highest return on capital. The second oldest Islamic banking institution in operation since 1977, it is well-run and respected. The Dubai Islamic Bank, established in 1975, is the oldest Islamic commercial undertaking, as the Mit Ghamr Bank of Egypt was superseded in 1971 by the Nasser Social Bank, a government-controlled institution run on a not-for-profit basis. Dar-Al-Maal-Al-Islami, although Geneva-based, is listed as an Arab Bank, as its chairman is Prince Mohammad Al Faisal Al Saud and much of its financing comes from the GCC. There are Faisal Islamic Banks in Egypt and the Sudan; its main rival group is Al Baraka, which is also based in Saudi Arabia.

Table 6. Major Arab Islamic Banking Institutions Ranked by Assets, 2000 (in US$ millions)

Rank	Bank	Equity	Assets	Profits
1	Al Rajhi Banking, Saudi Arabia	1,733	12,987	493.9
2	Kuwait Finance House	700	6,532	370.0
3	Dar-Al-Maal-Al-Islami, Geneva	215	3,530	-9.5
4	Dubai Islamic Bank	297	3,204	20.4
5	Shamil Bank, Bahrain	230	1,490	6.0
6	Jordan Islamic Bank	76	1,198	4.3
7	Qatar Islamic Bank	68	1,099	25.2
8	Abu Dhabi Islamic Bank	305	726	5.0
9	Qatar International Islamic Bank	45	576	9.3
10	Al Baraka, Bahrain	59	220	1.3
11	ABC Islamic Bank, Bahrain	42	195	4.0
12	First Islamic Investment Bank, Bahrain	129	193	20.5

Sources: Annual Reports of the banks and data from the Institute of Islamic Banking and Insurance, London

Note: All figures refer to year ending 31 December 2000, except for Dar-Al-Maal-Al-Islami data that refers to 1999

The success of Islamic banking is demonstrated by the enthusiasm of major international banks to offer Islamic financing facilities. In the 1980s some of the British overseas banks, such as Grindlays and Flemings, became interested in Islamic finance and developed products for their Muslim clients; the British banks were followed by Swiss banks such as UBS, Germany's Deutsche Bank, and ABN-AMRO of the Netherlands. Citibank, which since the 1990s had also offered limited Islamic financing, established a dedicated Islamic Banking Division in Bahrain in 1996; HSBC, which had provided Islamic financing facilities and asset management from many of its branches and subsidiaries in London and in the Arab world, opened its Amanah Finance Division in 2000, and centralized its Islamic banking operations in Dubai in 2001. HSBC has the most ambitious plans of any major international bank for Islamic finance, from Islamic mortgages in the United States to project finance and fund management products designed for GCC investors.

Competition from major international banks with strong brand names and a wealth of financial expertise poses a major challenge for the much smaller, dedicated Islamic banks. One reaction has been for some Islamic banks to reorganize their activities and attempt mergers. The Faisal Bank in Bahrain reorganized in 2000, and rebranded as the Shamil Bank. An attempt was made to merge the Al Baraka Bank in Bahrain with the Kuwait-based International Investor, but a clash of corporate cultures resulted in this plan being abandoned. The Arab Banking Corporation has widened its Islamic financing base by adding a dedicated Islamic asset management division in London to the Islamic banking operation it has run in Bahrain for over a decade.

Arab Bill and Bond Markets

Markets in government bills and bonds in the Arab world have become much more sophisticated in recent years, partly reflecting the growth of government debt and the consequent efforts to find more methods of funding it. Saudi Arabia, in particular, has been increasingly innovative in its funding, with a growing use of very short-term repurchase agreements or repos, while the Egyptian government has extended the maturity of government bonds to relieve short-term financial pressures.

Repurchase agreements are short-term loans in which treasury bills serve as collateral, which the lender receives if the borrower does not pay back the loan.

In the case of Saudi Arabia, repos are handled by the Saudi Arabian Monetary Agency (SAMA) through its transactions with the commercial banks, with the repos serving as their liquid assets. Transactions in repos average almost US$450 million a day in Riyadh, most being on an overnight basis, with SAMA deposits with the commercial banks amounting to US$1.1 billion in 2001 (SAMA 2001). Saudi Arabia's commercial banks finance a large part of the government's debt, with over US$31 billion outstanding as Table 2 shows. Development bonds account for most of this debt; bank claims on public sector enterprises, which amount to less than US$3 billion, are less significant in Saudi Arabia. Internal borrowing has enabled the Saudi Arabian government to be less reliant on international credit to cover budget deficits.

The Egyptian market in government securities includes treasury bills and bonds, housing bonds, and bonds issued to raise the capital of the state-owned commercial banks. Treasury bills amount to around US$6.5 billion, with maturities from 90 and 180 days up to one year, the longer-dated bills being predominant (Central Bank of Egypt [CBE] Annual Report 2000/2001). Most bonds are not traded, although the market has become more active in recent years with bonds worth around US$25 million traded in 2001. Bonds account for around half of government debt (around US$20 billion) and are largely held by the major state-owned banks. Only around 8 percent of Egyptian government bonds are traded in the financial markets. Bonds worth a massive US$10.4 billion were issued in March 2001 as part of an Egyptian government-refinancing package (CBE Economic Review 2000/2001). Banks hold few public sector securities, as most of these are held by the National Investment Bank, which is financed from national insurance contributions and post office savings.

In Lebanon, where post-civil war reconstruction has imposed large financial burdens, the government is indebted to the commercial banks for over US$15 billion, one-quarter of which is accounted for by short-term treasury bonds of under twelve months duration, while the remainder is largely accounted for by bonds of twenty-four and thirty-six months to maturity (Banque du Liban 2001). The securities designated as short-term bonds of three months maturity in Lebanon would usually be regarded as bills, but the average issuance of these rarely exceeds US$6 million. Most Lebanese long-term bonds are issued through the euro-dollar markets; the longest are fifteen-year bonds for US$400 million maturing in 2016 and yielding 11.7 percent. The value of total Lebanese government dollar bonds outstanding amounts to almost US$6 billion, and a further US$850 million has been issued in euro-denominated bonds (Banque du Liban 2002).

Some support for Lebanese bond issues has been political in nature. This ensures that the Lebanese pound is supported and that the economy does not fail, which would promote further domestic tensions that could have wider implications in the Arab world. Rafiq Al-Hariri, the Lebanese Prime Minister, has lobbied GCC governments to encourage bond purchases, and in June 2002 a new Lebanese euro-dollar bond for US$1 billion that matures in 2005 received subscriptions of US$500 million from Saudi Arabia, Oman, and Malaysia (*Gulf News* 1 June 2002). The proceeds are being added to the Central Bank of Lebanon's reserves to help defend the currency and enable the Central Bank to make essential foreign exchange available to the commercial banks.

Markets in corporate bonds are underdeveloped in the Arab world, although in Amman government agency debt is financed largely by securities described as corporate bonds, the value of which is around US$90 million (Central Bank of Jordan 2002). Dubai has aspirations to become the corporate bond center for the Arab world, with the creation of the Dubai International Financial Centre (DIFC) that is to be built by U.S.-based Turner Construction on 3.5 million square feet of land (*Gulf News* 8 July 2002). Clifford Chance, the international law firm, is drawing up laws and regulations to govern the center, and Phillip Thorpe has been appointed as chief commissioner of its regulatory agency (*Gulf News* 13 June 2002). Moody's, the ratings agency, is to locate its regional base in the center (*Gulf News* 7 July 2002) and the World Bank has indicated its willingness to raise US$100 million through a DIFC bond issue by the end of 2002 once the regulations are in place (*Gulf News* 13 May 2002). The 2003 annual joint meeting of the World Bank and the IMF will be held in Dubai, giving a boost to DIFC. The first bond issue is to be issued by the DIFC itself for US$300 million (*Gulf News* 2 June 2002).

At present most of the major projects in the GCC are financed through syndicated loans rather than through the issue of bonds. Dubai Aluminium raised US$900 million through a ten-year loan at fifty basis points over LIBOR in July 2002, and Qatar Fuel Additives Company raised US$300 million for refinancing, also on a syndicated loan basis (*Middle East Economic Digest* June 2002a). Local currency financing has also been through syndicated loans, such as the KD 114 million (US$368 million) loan in June 2002 for the Sulaibiya wastewater project in Kuwait (*Middle East Economic Digest* June 2002b). Bonds could have provided a fixed rate alternative for at least part of these financings, and as Saudi Arabia embarks on gas projects worth US$25 billion over the next ten years, the scope for corporate bond financing is considerable. Cross-border financing is well established in the GCC, especially with Bahrain's offshore banking role, but DIFC can play a similar role in corporate securities.

GCC investors are increasingly interested in floating rate notes, some of which are mistakenly called bonds, although they provide variable rather than fixed returns. These notes offer greater capital protection than equities, although the income varies with the market rates of interest. In July 2002, Shuaa Capital of Kuwait issued notes worth US$25 million at 200 basis points over LIBOR, with the Global Investment House of Kuwait as the lead manager. Unlike the syndicated notes for project financing that are held mostly by banks, this issue was aimed at private investors of high net worth.

Bahrain as a Center for Islamic Bills and Bonds

Bahrain has become the most important center for Islamic finance in the Gulf, with nineteen dedicated Islamic banks and finance houses controlling assets worth US$5.7 billion. The island hosts the General Council for Islamic Banking, which has taken over from the Jeddah-based International Association of Islamic Banks (Wilson 2001). The establishment of the Council was spearheaded by the IDB, and its membership of Islamic banks is growing rapidly. The IDB has also chosen to locate its Infrastructure Fund in Bahrain because of the island's position as an Islamic financial center. The Infrastructure Fund is a private equity fund that is being managed by the Emerging Markets Partnership of Bahrain. The IDB has also agreed to set up an International Islamic Rating Agency that will be located on the island. This agency will rate Islamic securities that should help ensure their international acceptability. Islamic and conventional banks that purchase and hold such securities will have a clear indication of the risks involved. This rating should enable them to compare risks versus returns for different categories of Islamic securities, increasing transparency and the potential efficiency of the market.

On 13 June 2001, the Bahrain Monetary Agency offered for the first time in the Arab world, government bills that were structured to comply with the *shariah* Islamic law. The bills were worth $25 million, and were in the form of three-month paper, referred to as *Sukuk Salam* securities (IIBI July 2001). Although the Malaysian government has offered Islamic bonds since the 1980s and Kuala Lumpur has a well-established secondary market for Islamic bonds, Islamic objections to trading in debt instruments precluded similar developments in the Arab world. *Shariah* advisors in Bahrain and the *Fiqh Academy* in Jeddah have approved the new securities, which are seen as distinctive from conventional *riba*-based bonds.

The *Sukuk Salam* securities provided a fixed return, equivalent to 3.95 percent at an annualized rate, for the first Islamic bill issue, which is not based on interest. The return has been calculated in relation to the real benefit the government expects to obtain on the funds, rather than with reference to market interest rates. The initial offer of bills on June 2001 worth US$25 billion was oversubscribed, with almost US$60 million being offered. The minimum subscription was fixed at US$10,000, which meant that relatively small financing houses could participate, as well as private investors seeking a nonbanking home for their dollar-denominated liquidity. The same minimum subscription limit was set for the longer-term *ijara* leasing securities worth US$100 million that were offered in August 2001. These were issued on 4 September 2001 and will mature in five years time. They offer a rental return of 5.25 percent per annum, guaranteed by the government of Bahrain (IIBI Oct. 2001).

The first Islamic bills matured on 12 September 2001, and a new issue was launched; this process has subsequently been repeated every three months. The September 2001 returns on the new issue of US$25 million were cut to 2.27 percent; and for the December 2001 issue, a rate of 2.00 percent was offered, which appeared to be nearer the equilibrium price with a more modest oversubscription (IIBI Feb. 2002).

The establishment of the Islamic money market in Bahrain will, it is hoped, result in the emergence of markets in longer term Islamic securities, notably bonds, with Bahrain playing a similar role in the GCC and west Asia as Kuala Lumpur plays in Southeast Asia. So far prospects look encouraging, and the Kuwait Finance House, the Bahrain Islamic Bank, and the Dubai Islamic Bank have jointly launched an Islamic liquidity center in Bahrain with each institution providing US$5 million.

Arab Stock Markets

Equity markets are underdeveloped in much of the Arab world, with the total stock market capitalization amounting to less than US$180 billion.[3] As Table 7 shows, Saudi Arabia is by far the largest stock market in the Arab world in terms of market capitalization, with Egypt and the U.A.E. competing for second position. Egypt has exchanges in Cairo and Alexandria and the U.A.E. has separate exchanges in Abu Dhabi and Dubai. But Saudi Arabia has a centralized electronic market that serves the whole Kingdom from Riyadh using online brokerage facilities offered by all the commercial banks.

In Saudi Arabia, an estimated 1.4 million shareholders deal in the shares of the country's seventy-six quoted companies. Although electronic trading has been operating since 1990, to reduce costs and to increase the efficiency of transactions a new real-time trading network, the *Tadawul* system, was introduced in July 2001. The *Tadawul* system has much greater capacity for electronic trading (*Middle East Economic Digest* Oct. 2001). There has been concern about the relatively high costs of share trading, company disclosure, and the division of regulatory responsibilities between SAMA and the Ministry of Finance and National Economy. At present the domestic Saudi Arabian banks, together with the Riyadh office of the Gulf International Bank, are the only licensed brokers. This restriction would change, however, under the new Capital Markets Law due to be passed in 2003 which will provide for the registration of specialist brokerage houses (*Middle East Economic Digest* June 2002). This change will permit greater competition and lower

Table 7. Arab Stock Market Capitalization and Performance

Rank	Country	Market Capitalization 31 December 2000, (in US$ million)	Percentage Change Year to 3 July 2002	Index
1	Saudi Arabia	67,171	13.94	NCFEI
2	Egypt	28,741	0.79	Hermes
3	U.A.E.	28,211	8.25	EMNEX
4	Kuwait	18,814	31.60	KSE
5	Morocco	10,899	-22.06	MADEX
6	Bahrain	6,624	1.19	BDE
7	Qatar	5,502	25.9	CBQ
8	Jordan	4,943	8.53	ASE
9	Oman	3,463	21.67	MSM
10	Lebanon	1,583	-4.48	BSI

Source: World Bank and Middle East Economic Digest July 2002

transactions costs, although initially it is expected that the major local banks will establish broking subsidiaries to service their existing clients.

The Capital Markets Law, which has been reviewed by the Supreme Economic Council under Prince Abdullah, also provides for a Capital Markets Authority that will take over regulatory responsibilities from SAMA and the Ministry of Finance and National Economy. Its functions will be similar to those of the United States Securities Exchange Commission, although the exact model adopted will resemble more the Malaysian Securities Commission that regulates the largest stock market in the Muslim world.

An estimated 85,000 Saudi Arabian investors have assets worth more than US$700 billion in the West, mostly in financial securities, including equities (Borland 2001). Some of these funds have been repatriated since 2001, partly reflecting disillusionment with the performance of U.S. equities and worries over financial disclosure after Enron and WorldCom, as much as due to the political aftermath of 11 September 2001. As a result, share prices have risen significantly in Saudi Arabia since the summer of 2001, with even greater rises recorded for Kuwait. The main problem for Saudi Arabian investors in the local market is the limited range of shares on offer, with shares in the banks accounting for over one-third of market value and around one-quarter of share trades. Industrial shares account for around 40 percent of market value, but this is dominated by SABIC, with the Arabian Fertiliser Company the only other quoted industrial stock to record significant trading. Privatization of major companies, such as the airline Saudia or companies in the telecommunications sector, would help the market grow, but there is no timetable for such moves.

The Egyptian stock exchange lists 1,072 companies, and the markets in Cairo and Alexandria are integrated as a single market for transactions purposes (CBE Economic Review 2000/2001). This exchange has more companies quoted than for all other Arab markets combined, but the majority are small companies, with relatively little trading in their shares. The major quoted companies include cement producers, construction firms, hotel chains, and investment companies. Although many medium-sized businesses in Egypt have been privatized, some of which are now quoted on the stock exchange, privatization has not extended to the airline Egyptair or utilities such as electricity and water. Mobile communications companies are quoted, notably

MobiNil and its smaller rival Orascom Telecom, but fixed-line telephones are still a state monopoly.

The government in Egypt has taken a number of measures to develop and activate the stock market, mostly involving amendments to the Capital Market Law of 1992. Commissions for brokerage were reduced in 2000, and in 2001 arbitration procedures were made more transparent (CBE Annual Report 2000/2001). Listed companies are now allowed to issue bonds as well as other types of financial securities to diversify their funding sources. The efficiency of the market is not the major constraint, however; the major constraint is government economic policy. The state itself limits the capacity of the market to develop. It diverts pension contributions to the National Investment Bank, rather than encouraging private provision, which limits the supply of funds, and it refuses to privatize major companies that would increase the demand for equity capital.

The Arab Managed Fund Industry

Saudi Arabia has the largest managed funds industry in the Arab world, accounting for more than half of the total value of funds managed (Al-Shaikh 2000). The other markets of significance are Kuwait, the U.A.E., and to a much lesser extent, Egypt, where their twenty-one managed funds are worth around US$1 billion (CBE Economic Review 2000/2001).

In Saudi Arabia, the funds are offered by the major commercial banks to their existing clients, usually being cross-sold to depositors who are encouraged to take on equity exposure. The Islamic stress on participatory finance and avoiding *riba* (interest) has made those with savings more predisposed toward equity financing, and the higher potential returns usually gained over the medium- to longer-term for those taking some risks with their capital have also proved attractive. The National Commercial Bank pioneered managed funds in the Kingdom, offering the open-ended Al-Ahli Short Term Dollar Fund in 1979. This fund, however, invests largely in time deposits with U.S. banks, dollar-denominated commercial paper, and certificates of deposit; hence its income is interest-derived and the only exposure is default risk.

The success of the banks in marketing managed funds is illustrated in Table 8; by 2001, almost 175,000 Saudi Arabian residents had invested in this way. Until recently, most of the funds were invested abroad, mainly in U.S. equities. But since 2000, the expansion and favorable performance of the local stock market has encouraged more domestic investment, a trend

that has become more pronounced with the large fall in stock prices quoted on the NASDAQ and the New York Stock Exchange and that was exacerbated by the events of 11 September 2001. Eleven equity funds had invested wholly in Saudi Arabia by 2001; the largest was the Al-Ahli Saudi Equity Fund first offered by the National Commercial Bank in 1992. Around 60 percent of its assets are accounted for by bank stock, with industrial stock being worth one-fifth of the portfolio.

The National Commercial Bank accounts for more than half of the managed fund market in Saudi Arabia, a position it has strived to hold onto. The other major banks are trying to catch up, notably the Al Rajhi Banking and Investment Corporation, which is the second largest fund provider, although its share

Table 8. Managed Fund Growth in Saudi Arabia

Year	1992	1995	1998	2001
Number of funds	52	71	114	139
Number of subscribers	33,162	33,051	70,216	174,639
Foreign assets, (in US$ billion)	1.9	1.9	3.7	5.2
Domestic assets, (in US$ billion)	1.4	1.5	2.8	6.9

Sources: Saudi Arabian Monetary Agency, Thirty-Seventh Annual Report, 2001, op. 314; Saudi Arabian Monetary Agency, Quarterly Statistical Bulletin, Third Quarter 2001:95.

is only 11 percent of the market (Al-Shaikh 2002). The latter, as an Islamic bank, solely offers funds that are acceptable in accordance with the *shariah* law. Investments are screened for compliance; companies involved in alcohol or pork production or distribution are excluded, as are conventional banks dealing in interest. The Al-Rajhi Local Share Fund has been the most successful domestic Islamic fund since its launch in 1992; this prompted the National Commercial Bank to launch the Al-Ahli Saudi Trading Equity Fund in 1998, which is also screened for *shariah* compliance. This fund cannot invest in shares in conventional banks, but ironically, more than 15 percent of its portfolio is accounted for by investment in its banking rival the Al Rajhi Corporation.

Twenty-six Islamic funds were offered in Saudi Arabia at the end of 2001 and six of the funds, including the largest, were global funds investing mainly in the West.[4] The National Commercial Bank offered one exclusively Northern American Fund, the Al-Ahli US Trading Equity, and an exclusively European fund, the Al-Ahli European Trading Equity. The three Asian

Islamic funds marketed to Saudi Arabian investors focus on Japan and Hong Kong quoted shares. Three so-called balanced Islamic funds are offered, promising investors both income and capital growth, but these are also focused on the West, as are the three small capital and technology funds. This leaves only seven Saudi Islamic funds concentrating on emerging markets, and five of these invest within the Kingdom. It is perhaps ironic that Islamic funds are more exposed in Western markets than are conventional funds, although this can be explained largely by the predominance of emerging market shares in conventional banks, and these are excluded from *shariah*-compliant portfolios because such banks deal in *riba* (Wilson 2001–2002).

Although much of the investment in Saudi Arabia goes abroad, there are important reasons why many investors choose to invest at least some of their funds domestically, apart from patriotism. If investors have future anticipated liabilities in riyals, then they will also want to have assets denominated in local currency. The banks or fund promoters also have an advantage in their local markets because they can manage the funds themselves given their knowledge of their own market, rather than relying on international banks or fund-management groups (Al-Shaikh 2000).

No-interest Islamic funds accounted for 43.2 percent of all managed fund investment in Saudi Arabia as of March 2001; these funds are increasing rapidly in importance and may account for over half of the total by 2003 (Al-Shaikh 2002). Of the total managed fund investment in March 2001 of US$10.7 billion, Islamic funds were worth US$4.62 billion. Within the National Commercial Bank, the trend toward Islamic funds is especially marked, with a 57 percent increase in assets managed in accordance with *shariah* law in 2001, while assets in conventional funds fell by 32 percent over the same period. Islamic managed funds in the National Commercial Bank alone amounted to US$4.73 billion by the end of 2001, more than the March 2001 total for all banks in the Kingdom. Islamic funds account for three-quarters of all National Commercial Bank managed funds.

Conclusion

The Arab world offers a wealth of banking and financial experience, and many institutions offer a quality of service that compares favorably with the best internationally. Not surprisingly the banks in the GCC are the most developed in the region, while those in the Mediterranean Arab countries that remain under state ownership have often failed to develop a more

client-friendly ethos. Financial markets are also more developed in the GCC, and although they are far from integrated, banks regulated in one GCC country can open branches in others, and cross-listing of company stock is also permissible. Bahrain plays a regional role as a banking center and a very major role in Islamic finance in particular, and the Dubai International Financial Centre is well placed to be a regional market for securities trading.

The GCC is likely to become increasingly integrated as a result of its customs union agreement that comes into place in January 2003, and with plans for a common currency by 2010, it is possible to envision a single market for capital with different specialist centers, but with dispersed distribution of services. Elsewhere in the Arab world, foreign exchange pressures are likely to result in continued currency restrictions and controls on capital movements, which is likely to limit the prospects for wider Arab financial integration.

Political risk perceptions are also important, because it has prompted much Arab capital flight and discouraged capital inflows from the OECD countries. The Arab world as a whole attracted less than US$3.6 billion in direct investment flows in 2000, just 0.3 percent of the investment in developing countries; meanwhile, Western portfolio investment in Arab financial markets has been minimal. At the same time, Arab investments in the EU alone amounted to US$365 billion, and total Arab funds invested in the OECD countries possibly exceeds US$1.3 trillion (*Gulf News* 16 December 2001). Clearly such imbalances cannot be corrected in the short term, but greater regional cohesion and the development of Arab banks and financial markets can facilitate a more equitable balance in the longer term.

Despite some progress with financial reform, a number of key challenges confront Arab policy makers. Egypt, Iraq, Libya, Sudan, and Syria have not formally accepted Article VIII of the IMF that prohibits payment restrictions, multiple currency practices, or discriminatory currency arrangements (although in the case of Egypt most of these practices have ceased). Privatization remains a major challenge. State sector managers and bank employees concerned about their job security resist privatization of state-owned banks, but the purpose of banks is to serve their clients efficiently, and not simply to preserve employment. Foreign ownership is also a contentious issue, and it would be unrealistic to expect much progress in this area given the vulnerability of local banks to foreign takeovers. Easing restrictions on Arab ownership could be an initial step that would promote banking consolidation in the region.

In the monetary sphere, greater central bank independence would be desirable, especially as interest rates are already largely determined by economic factors. Central banks should not simply bail out banks that get into difficulty as a matter of course, because this reaction introduces moral hazard problems. Deposit protection insurance may be one way forward. The regulation of Islamic banking in the region is largely ad hoc; greater consistency is needed, with advice taken from the new Islamic Financial Services Board, the Islamic Development Bank, and the Accounting and Auditing Organisation for Islamic Financial Institutions, AAOIFI (Aziz 2002). The regulation of securities markets should be handled by separate securities commissions as is proposed in Saudi Arabia, rather than by the central banks. Governments themselves should raise more of their debt finance through these markets rather than relying on bank lending, which crowds out advances to the private sector. Autonomous state corporations can issue their own securities in these markets as a move toward privatization.

Back in 1994, David Cobham suggested that the major priority for Arab policy makers should be to upgrade their banking and financial institutions rather than developing organized financial markets (Cobham 1995). Here a case is argued for a more balanced approach to reform, including the development of capital markets (Caprio 2000); building on the achievements of the 1990s; and drawing on Arab best practices, especially in the area of Islamic banking and finance.

Appendix: Banking Systems and Monetary Regulation

Country	Domestic Ownership*	Foreign Ownership	Interest Rates	IMF Foreign Exchange Acceptance**
Algeria	State	No	Fixed	1997
Bahrain	Private	Yes	Variable	1973
Egypt	State	JV***	Variable	No
Iraq	State	No	Variable	No
Jordan	Private	Yes	Variable	1995
Kuwait	Private	No	Variable	1963
Lebanon	Private	Yes	Variable	1993
Libya	State	No	Fixed	No
Morocco	Private	No	Variable	1993
Oman	Private	Yes	Variable	1974
Qatar	Private	Yes	Variable	1973
Saudi Arabia	Private	JV***	Variable	1961
Sudan	Private	No	Variable	No
Syrian AR	State	No	Fixed	No
Tunisia	Private	No	Variable	1993
U.A.E.	Private	Yes	Variable	1974
Yemen	State	No	Variable	1996

Notes: *Predominate ownership; for example, in states such as Egypt a smaller private bank operates and in some GCC countries the state has minority ownership of some local banks

**Acceptance of Article VIII, sections 2, 3, and 4, prohibiting payment restrictions, multiple currency practices, or discriminatory currency arrangements

***Joint ventures with minority foreign bank ownership

References

Al-Shaikh, Said Abdullah. "The Mutual Funds Market in Saudi Arabia." NCB Economist 10, 2 (March/April 2000):5–12.

Al-Shaikh, Said Abdullah. "The Mutual Funds Market in Saudi Arabia." NCB Market Review and Outlook (1 February 2002): 4–6.

An Introduction to Short-Term Savings through Mutual Funds. Jeddah: National Commercial Bank. 1999:3.

Al-Ahli Long-Term Mutual Funds. Achieve Your Long-term Investment Goals. Jeddah: National Commercial Bank, 2000: 10.

"Arab funds in EU Put at About $365 Billion." Gulf News, 16 December 2001, Dubai edition.

Aziz, Zeti Akhtar. "Setting the Standards for Regulation." Islamic Banker 76 (May 2002):9–13.

"Banks Invited on QAFAC Financing." Middle East Economic Digest 21 (21 June 2002a).

Banque du Liban. Monthly Bulletin. February 2002:10, 17.

Banque du Liban. Quarterly Bulletin. Second Quarter. 2001: 21–22.

Borland, Brad. "Outward Flows, Inward Investment Needs in the GCC." Arab Banker (Autumn 2001):49–51.

Bridge, John. "Financial Growth and Economic Development: A Case Study of Lebanon." University of Durham, PhD thesis, 1975. (See especially Chapter 6).

Camdessus, Michael. "The Challenge for the Arab World in the Global Economy: Stability and Structural Adjustment." Address by the managing director of the IMF at the annual meeting of the Union of Arab Banks, New York, N.Y., 20 May 1996. <www.imf.org/external/np/sec/mds/1996/mds9608.htm> (1996).

Caprio, Gerard. "Long-term Finance." In Financial Markets and Growth in the Mediterranean: the Next Steps. <www.worldbank.org/mdf/mdf1/steps.htm>.

Central Bank of Egypt. Annual Report. 2000/2001:22–23, 60–63.

Central Bank of Egypt. Economic Review. 2000/2001:20–22, 29.

Central Bank of Jordan. Monthly Statistical Bulletin. May 2002: 50–52.

Cobham, David. "Financial systems for developing countries with particular reference to Egypt, Iraq, Jordan, Lebanon and Syria." In Development of Financial Markets in the Arab Countries, Iran and Turkey, edited by. Cairo: Economic Research Forum for the Arab Countries, Iran and Turkey, 1995:9–31.

"DIFC Plans Dh 1.85 Billion Bond," Gulf News, 2 June 2002, Dubai edition.

El-Eriam, Mohammad A., Sena Eken, Susan Fennel, and Jean-Pierre Chauffour. Growth and Stability in the Middle East and North Africa. IMF Middle East Department Paper, March 1996:31–38.

"Gulf States and Malaysia Buy Lebanese Eurobond," Gulf News, 1 June 2002, Dubai edition.

Huband, Mark. "Country Focus: Egypt—Broader Sweep Given to Decision-Making." Supplement. Financial Times Survey of Middle Eastern Banking and Finance 2000.

Institute of Islamic Banking and Insurance (IIBI). New Horizon (July 2001):22.

Institute of Islamic Banking and Insurance (IIBI). New Horizon (October 2001):18.

Institute of Islamic Banking and Insurance (IIBI). New Horizon (February 2002):17.

International Monetary Fund. "International Financial Statistics." Washington, D.C.:

International Monetary Fund. "International Financial Statistics." Washington, D.C.: June 2002:45, 51, 53.

Marks, Jon. "Gulf Door Begins to Open." The Banker (September 2000):.

Levine, R. "Financial Development and Economic Growth: Views and Agenda." Journal of Economic Literature 35 (1997):688–726.

Levine, R., N. Loayza, and T. Beck. "Financial Intermediation and Growth: Causality and Causes." Journal of Monetary Economics 46 (2000):31–77.

Lewis, Mervyn K., and Latifa M. Algaoud. Islamic Banking. Cheltenham, U.K.: Edward Elgar, 2001:56–58.

"Moody's Eyes Regional Base," Gulf News, 7 July 2002, Dubai edition.

"Saudi Arabia Gets Tough on Money Crime," Gulf News, 17 May 2002, Dubai edition.

Saudi Arabian Monetary Agency (SAMA). Thirty-Seventh Annual Report. 2001:118.

"Stock Markets Point the Way." Middle East Economic Digest 21 June 2002c.

"Sulaibiya Finance Agreed." Middle East Economic Digest 21 June 21,2002b.

"Tadawul Gets Mixed Reviews." Middle East Economic Digest 5 October 2001.

Thiel, Michael. "Finance and Economic Growth: A Review of Theory and Empirical Evidence." European Commission Directorate General for Economic and Financial Affairs, Economic Paper 158, July 2001.

"Thorpe Named as DIFC Chief Commissioner," Gulf News, 13 June 2002, Dubai edition.

"Top Companies to Guide DIFC," Gulf News, 8 July 2002, Dubai edition.

"U.A.E. Lauded for Steps Against Illegal Money," Gulf News, 11 June 2002, Dubai edition.

"U.A.E. Rules Out Plan for More Foreign Banks," Gulf News, 9 July 2002, Dubai edition.

Usmani, Muhammad Taqi. An Introduction to Islamic Finance. New York: Kluwer Law International, 2002:37–68.

Wilson, Rodney. Banking and Finance in the Arab Middle East. New York: Macmillan, 1983:49–56.

Wilson, Rodney. Banking and Finance in the Middle East. London: Financial Times Publications, 1998:65–67.

Wilson, Rodney. "The Evolution of the Saudi Banking System and its Relationship with Bahrain." In State, Society and Economy in Saudi Arabia, edited by Tim Niblock. London: Croom Helm, 1981.

Wilson, Rodney. Islamic Finance. London: Financial Times Publications, 1997:26.

Wilson, Rodney. "Islamic Mutual Funds Unveiled." Institute of Islamic Banking and Insurance New Horizon (December 2001–January 2002):8–9.

Wilson, Rodney. "Three Decades of Modern Islamic Banking." Arab Banker (Autumn 2001):38–41.

"World Bank Plans to Raise $100 Million Through DIFC," Gulf News, 13 May 2002, Dubai edition.

World Trade Organization. Trade Policy Review Pakistan. Press release no. TPRB/185, January 2002.

WTO News. Press release no. 293, 3 May 2002. <www.wto.org> (2002).

Endnotes

1. According to data compiled by *The Banker*, July 2002

2. Secretariat of the Basel Committee on Banking Supervision. "The New Basel Capital Accord: An Explanatory Note." Bank for International Settlements, January 2001.

3. Saudi Arabian Monetary Agency (SAMA). Thirty-Seventh Annual Report. 2001:107–110. The market capitalization has remained stable in relation to GDP since the early 1990s. See Henry Azzam, "Gulf Capital Markets: Development Prospects and Constraints." In Development of Financial Markets in the Arab Countries, Iran and Turkey. Cairo: Economic Research Forum for the Arab Countries, Iran and Turkey, Cairo, 1995:185–186.

4. "List of all Known Islamic Funds." Failaka International, Inc. Updated monthly. <http://www.failaka.com/Funds.html> See also the list in: Institute of Islamic Banking and Insurance. New Horizon (October 2001):10–11.

Foreign Direct Investment in the Arab World:

The Changing Investment Landscape

Florence Eid and Fiona Paua

Examining the global flows of capital reveals startlingly low levels of foreign direct investment (FDI) inflows to the Arab world. According to the recently released *Arab Human Development Report* (UNDP 2002), the Arab world has received less than 1 percent of the total net flow of global FDI over the 1975 to 1998 period. Noting that the Arab world remains "comparatively cut off from financial globalization,"[1] the Report moreover highlights that there has been "a steady reduction" of FDI net flows during this period: from 2.6 percent of the total net flow of global FDI in the 1975 to 1980 period, to 0.7 percent in the 1990 to 1998 period.

That the region has received such a small proportion of FDI flows—and that these flows have been declining—has significant implications for the development prospects of the region. Foreign direct investment, which refers to capital[2] provided by an investor in one country to an enterprise in another country to acquire a long-term interest, usually amounting to 10 percent or more of voting stock, is considered important to development because of its significant potential benefits to developing countries.[3] FDI is considered a desirable means of ushering in resources—capital, technology, and other skills—that can facilitate the higher levels of productivity required for economies to transition to higher levels of development.

According to the findings of a recent study on FDI by Sadik and Bolbol (2001), however, not only has the Arab world experienced a trend of declining FDI

net flows, but, equally noteworthy, the technological spillovers arising from FDI are apparently not yet visible. The challenge for Arab world governments regarding FDI is, therefore, two-fold: first, how can FDI flows be increased? And, equally important, how can the benefits from FDI be more fully captured?

This chapter seeks to address these two questions in two parts: first, with an examination of the historical FDI flows to the Arab world; and second, through an assessment of the investment climate in the specific countries in the region. The latter entails a review of recent reforms in selected countries, as well as an analysis of relevant responses from the *Arab World Competitiveness Report* Executive Opinion Survey. Based on an examination of Arab world FDI flows from 1985 to 2000 and an assessment of the recent reforms undertaken by specific countries to improve their respective investment environments, this chapter finds that barring a heightening of political instability in the region, the Arab world is likely to see an improvement in FDI flows. But sustained growth in, and increased effectiveness of, FDI rests in large part on the ability of governments to effect improvements in three areas: public institutions, physical infrastructure, and human resource development.

Five Defining Features of FDI in the Arab World, 1985 to 2000

Assessing the Arab world FDI flows from 1980 to 2001 reveals five key features. The first feature is that flows of FDI into the region have increased, but have not kept pace with world FDI flows. The inability to match the rate of increase in world FDI flows is depicted in the second feature, which is that the region's FDI flows have been lower than that of most other regions. The third feature reflects the concentration of FDI flows, showing how most FDI flows go only to a handful of countries and specific sectors. Further, at the country level, the flows and stock of FDI remain a small part of the respective economies, both in terms of the gross fixed capital formation and the gross domestic product. Finally, although intra-Arab investment is likely to be understated in international FDI statistics, it comprises a significant proportion of FDI inflows.

Feature 1: Regional stocks and flows have increased but not in pace with world FDI flows

Based on figures from UNCTAD, global FDI inflows soared by 605 percent, from an average US$180.0 billion in the 1985 to 1995 period to US$1.27 trillion in 2000. The growth in global FDI inflows is attributed mostly to flows among developed countries, and this is reflected in the slower, but nonetheless remarkable,

Table 1. FDI Inflows, 1985–2000 (in US$ million)

	1985-1995	1996	1997	1998	1999	2000
Arab World	2,185	3,309	6,825	7,481	2,221	4,570
All Developing Countries	50,745	152,495	187,352	188,371	222,010	240,167
World	180,300	384,910	477,918	692,554	1,075,049	1,270,764

Source: UNCTAD 2001

Table 2. Arab World FDI Inflows 1985–2000 (in Percent)

	1985–1995	1996	1997	1998	1999	2000
As % of Flows to Developing Countries	4.3	2.2	3.6	4.0	1.0	1.9
As % of Total World FDI Flows	1.2	0.9	1.4	1.1	0.2	0.4

Source: UNCTAD 2001

surge of 373.3 percent in developing country FDI inflows during the same period. Arab world FDI inflows for the same period failed to expand at the same rate as either global FDI or developing country FDI inflows, with an even slower growth rate of 109.1 percent.

Accordingly, the percentage of total world FDI flows going to the Arab world fell from 1.2 percent in the 1985 to 1995 period, to 0.4 percent in 2000. As a percentage of the total flows to developing countries, Arab FDI inflows constitute a smaller share, at 1.9 percent in 2000 from an average of 4.3 percent in the 1985 to 1995 period.

In the last five years, average annual FDI inflows to the region amounted to US$4.9 billion, a 103 percent increase over the 1985 to 1995 average. However, during the period 1996 to 2000, FDI flows varied considerably, rising as high as US$7.5 billion in 1998, then falling 70.3 percent to US$2.2 billion in the following year.

Throughout the 1985 to 2000 period, net flows to the region as whole has been consistently positive, resulting in a buildup of FDI stock. In 2000, the region's FDI stock amounted to US$85.3 billion, a 118 percent increase from the 1985 stock of US$39.2 billion.

Feature 2: The Arab world has received less FDI stocks and flows relative to most other regions

In the last five years, FDI inflows to the Arab world comprised 1 percent to 4 percent of total inflows to developing countries. In 2000, the region captured 1.9 percent of the total developing country FDI inflows of US$2402 billion, only slightly more than the developing countries in Europe, which together have

Figure 1. Arab World FDI Stock, 1985–2000 (in US$ billion)

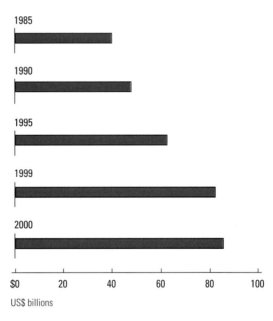

US$ billions

Source: UNCTAD 2001

the smallest share (0.8 percent). All other regions, however, had significantly larger shares compared to the Arab world. FDI inflows to the Latin America and the Caribbean region, for instance, account for 35.9 percent of the total, or nineteen times higher than the Arab world inflows. Similarly, but on a larger scale, FDI inflows to the Asia-Pacific region account for 58.9 percent of total inflows to developing countries, equivalent to thirty-one times the Arab world inflows.

Understanding the determinants of such low FDI flows to the Arab world requires a highly rigorous empirical analysis that is beyond the scope of this chapter. Broadly speaking however, many countries in the region have faced internal and external challenges that

Figure 2. FDI Inflows to Developing Countries, 2000

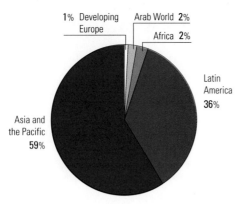

Source: Author's calculations based annex tables B.1 and B.2, UNCTAD 2001, World Investment Report 2001: Promoting Linkages, pp. 291-296

Tunisia, Bahrain, and Morocco. Of these countries, the first three account for nearly 70 percent of total FDI stock; Saudi Arabia and Egypt alone account for more than half of the total stock in the region. Not counting Libya, for which there is no available data, countries on the lowest end of the range include Mauritania, Kuwait, and Yemen, at 0.1 percent, 0.6 percent and 1.0 percent shares of the total stock in the region, respectively.

In terms of net FDI flows over the last five years, the same five countries with the highest FDI stock also have the highest average annual net FDI flows, albeit in a slightly different order. Saudi Arabia and Egypt still take the lead, with annual average net flows of US$1.1 billion and US$962 million, respectively. Bahrain however, has

have deterred FDI. Lebanon, Algeria, Kuwait, and Libya, for instance, have had periods of political instability over the past two decades that have discouraged investors. Moreover, until recently, many countries restricted foreign investment to very few sectors; even then, allowable investment was capped at only 49 percent, preventing a majority ownership and requiring a venture with a local partner. Another factor is the relatively slow pace of privatization; given the extent of government ownership prevalent in most economies in the region, FDI inflows for some countries have been closely linked to the pace and breadth of the privatization process, and as the process has encountered delays and significant opposition in many countries, so too, have inflows of FDI been impeded.

Feature 3: Arab world FDI stocks and flows are concentrated in a few countries and sectors

More than 80 percent of FDI stock in the Arab world is concentrated in five countries: Saudi Arabia, Egypt,

Figure 3. Arab World FDI Stock, 2000

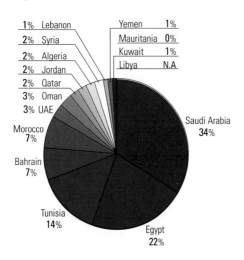

Source: UNCTAD 2001

Figure 4. Average Annual Net FDI Flows, 1996–2000 (in US$ million)

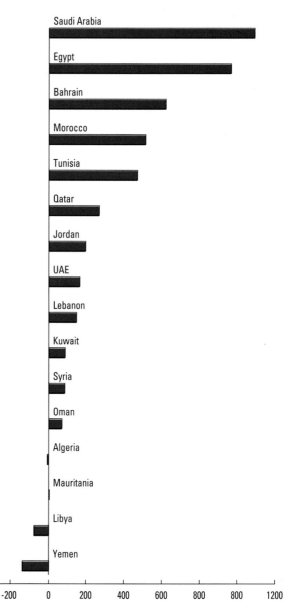

Source: UNCTAD 2001

received higher average annual net flows in the last five years, relative to Morocco and Tunisia. Among the countries at the bottom end of the range, five countries posted an annual average net flow of less than US$100 million: Kuwait, Syria, Oman, Algeria, and Mauritania; the latter two received average annual net flows of less than US$10 million. Notably, Libya and Yemen actually experienced negative average annual net outflows of US$79 and US$141, respectively.

Saudi Arabia, which accounts for a third of the region's FDI stock, received the bulk of their FDI stock between 1981 and 1984, indicating that growth in the country's net FDI flows have decelerated for over a decade. During this four-year period, cumulative net FDI flows amounted to US$27.4 billion, equivalent to 95.1 percent of the present stock. Net FDI flows to Saudi Arabia peaked in 1981, when US$11.1 billion was invested in the country. After 1984, flows languished at low levels for more than a decade, only to pick up again in 1997 and 1998 with flows of US$3.0 and 4.3 billion, respectively. Net FDI flows for the country, however, have been negative in the last two years.

Most of the region, in contrast to Saudi Arabia, received the bulk of their FDI inflows only over the last decade. Egypt, which has the second highest FDI stock, totaling US$19 billion, received net flows in the last five years that amount to nearly a quarter of the existing stock.

Tunisia, which has the third largest amount of FDI stock in the region (a total of US$11.6 billion), received 15 percent of this stock in the last three years alone. Meanwhile, Morocco, with a stock of US$5.8 billion, received 41 percent of its total stock in the last four years. Flows to Bahrain, which has an FDI stock of US$5.9 billion, peaked in 1996 with a net inflow of US$1.7 billion in a single year. Jordan, with FDI stock of US$1.8 billion, is particularly notable for receiving slightly less than half of that stock in the US$751 million of FDI flows that were registered in 2000.

In terms of sector distribution, the bulk of the region's FDI is directed predominantly to petroleum-related and other primary activities. Because of the extensive orientation towards natural resource activities, the inflows of FDI into the region have been historically volatile (Figure 5) due to vulnerability to commodity price changes (Fujita 2001). Although regional sector breakdowns of FDI flows are not available because of the paucity of data, country-level analyses confirm that for countries such as Saudi Arabia, Algeria, Oman, Qatar, Kuwait, Libya, and Yemen, the overwhelming majority of FDI is channeled to the hydrocarbon sector. Other countries, however, such as Bahrain, Egypt, Morocco, Tunisia, and Lebanon, have witnessed FDI flows into various sectors such as tourism, banking, telecommunications, manufacturing, and construction.

Figure 5. Volatility of Net Foreign Direct Investment Flows, (in Current US$), 1970–2000

Source: World Bank, World Development Indicators Database 2002

Table 3. FDI flows from Mergers and Acquisitions, Including Privatizations, 1996–2000

US $ millions	1996 Priv.	1996 M&A	1997 Priv.	1997 M&A	1998 Priv.	1998 M&A	1999 Priv.	1999 M&A	2000 Priv.	2000 M&A
Algeria	—	—	—	—	—	—	—	42	105	127
Bahrain	—	—	—	—	—	—	7	36	—	161
Egypt	89	171	—	102	—	48	123	738	242	528
Jordan									567	567
Kuwait	—	—	—	—	—	—	—	—	—	—
Lebanon	—	—	163	168	—	11	—	—	—	54
Libya	—	—	—	—	—	—	—	—	—	—
Mauritania	—	—	—	—	—	—	—	—	—	—
Morocco	9	40	544	578	—	5	113	123	—	—
Oman	—	7	—	—	—	—	—	28	—	—
Qatar	—	—	—	—	—	—	—	—	—	—
Saudi Arabia	—	26	—	—	—	—	—	—	—	2
Syrian AR	—	—	—	—	—	—	—	3	—	—
Tunisia	—	—	—	—	172	402	—	11	286	301
U.A.E.	—	—	—	56	—	—	—	200	—	4
Yemen, Rep.	—	—	—	—	—	—	—	—	—	—
Arab World Total	**98**	**244**	**707**	**904**	**172**	**467**	**243**	**1,181**	**1,200**	**1,744**

Source: UNCTAD, Cross-Border M&A Database, as cited in Fujita 2001

Some of these non-hydrocarbon sector FDI flows were ushered by cross-border mergers and acquisitions (M&A), particularly of privatized firms. Between 1996 and 2000, seven of the sixteen Arab world countries received FDI flows through privatizations, while thirteen countries received FDI inflows from to M&A in general. Cumulative 1996 to 2000 FDI inflows through M&A amounted to US$4.5 billion, equivalent to 20 percent of the region's net flows. Of the US$4.5 billion in flows accrued over this period, more than half is attributed to privatizations. Out of the total 1996 to 2000 FDI inflows, privatization accounts for only slightly less than 10 percent, or US$2.4 billion. Countries that have received a considerable amount of FDI through privatization over the last five years include: Jordan, Morocco, Egypt, and Tunisia. In the last five years, Morocco has received the highest FDI inflows from privatization, amounting to US$666 million, followed by Jordan with US$567 million, and Tunisia and Egypt with US$458 million and US$454 million, respectively. It is particularly notable that inflows from the 2000 privatization of the Telecommunications Corporation of Jordan alone, accounts for 28 percent of the existing FDI stock in Jordan, highlighting the role that the privatization process plays in facilitating inflows of foreign direct investment.

Table 4. Largest Cross-Border M&A (Privatization) Deals in the Arab World, 1996–2000

Acquired Company	Target Country	Acquiring Company	Country of Acquiring Company	Year of Transaction	Value (in US$ million)
Telecomm.Corp of Jordan	Jordan	Investor Group	France	2000	508.0
Assiut Cement	Egypt	Cemex	Mexico	1999	373.0
Societe Marocaine de L'Industrie	Morocco	Corral Petroleum Holdings AB	Sweden	1997	372.5
Societe des Ciments de Gabes	Tunisia	Secil (Semapa-Sociedade)	Portugal	2000	251.0
Al-Ameriya Cement Corporation	Egypt	Lafarge Titan	France	2000	249.0
Societe des Ciments de Jbel	Tunisia	Cimpor-Cimentos de Portugal EP	Portugal	1998	229.9
Alexandria Portland Cement (EG)	Egypt	Blue Circle Industries PLC	United Kingdom	2000	196.0
Societe des Ciments d'Enfidha	Tunisia	Uniland Cementera SA	Spain	1998	169.1
Credit Libanais (Lebanon)	Lebanon	Investor	Saudi Arabia	1997	163.0

Source: UNCTAD, Cross-Border M&A Database, as cited in Fujita 2001

FDI inflows in the region indicate that Morocco, Tunisia, Jordan, and Egypt are making the most progress in privatization. Saudi Arabia and the remaining GCC countries have made initial steps in their privatizing efforts, but work on the process remains. Lebanon's privatization program has been in the works for a few years, but has been stalled by politics. Syria has postponed privatization for the time being, while public enterprises undergo restructuring.

Feature 4: FDI plays a small part in most of the economies in the region

FDI flows in the Arab world account for a small percentage of gross capital formation in the region as a whole.[4] According to UNCTAD data, FDI flows comprised approximately 5 percent of the region's gross capital formation in the year 2000. In other developing countries, particularly those that have been successful in attracting foreign investment, FDI flows as a percentage of gross capital formation tend to be higher. In Singapore, for instance, FDI flows accounted for 26.1 percent of gross capital formation in 1999. For most countries in the region, FDI flows comprise less than 10 percent of gross domestic caital formation, with a few notable exceptions such as Bahrain, Jordan, and Tunisia, where FDI flows account for nearly 46.5 percent, 17.7 percent, and 15.2 percent, respectively, of gross domestic capital formation.

As a percentage of GDP, FDI stock in the region amounted to 14 percent in 2000, lower than the 16.5 percent average for developing countries (UNCTAD 2001). For thirteen countries in the Arab world, FDI stock comprises less than 20 percent of GDP, with ratios as low as 3.9 percent, 2.6 percent, and 1.4 percent for the United Arab Emirates, Algeria, and Kuwait, respectively. Only Bahrain and Tunisia have proportions of FDI stock comparable with developing countries that are successful in attracting FDI, such as China and Singapore.

Table 5. FDI Stock as Percent of GDP, 2000

	As % of GDP
Bahrain	74.0
Tunisia	59.6
Jordan	21.3
Egypt	19.2
Morocco	17.4
Saudi Arabia	16.6
Oman	12.6
Qatar	11.9
Mauritania	11.2
Yemen, Rep.	9.9
Syrian AR	7.3
Lebanon	6.1
U.A.E.	3.9
Algeria	2.6
Kuwait	1.4
Libya	n.a.
memorandum:	
Singapore	96
South Africa	41
China,P.R.: Mainland	32
Poland	23
Mexico	16

Source: UNCTAD 2001

Feature 5: Intra-Arab investment is a significant proportion of FDI flows

Foreign direct investment statistics that are available for the Arab world potentially understate the amount of total FDI flows if they are unable to fully capture the extent of intra-Arab trade. Not only are detailed country-level foreign direct investment statistics rare, in some cases intra-Arab investment is considered domestic investment in some national statistics.[5]

Significantly, the flow of intra-Arab investment is estimated to have increased by US$2.4 billion in 2001,[6] which is equivalent to more than half of the total FDI inflows to the region in 2000. Cumulative stock of intra-Arab investment from 1985 to 2001 is estimated to be US$17 billion, which is a tiny fraction of total overseas Arab investment, indicating significant potential for expansion. Overseas Arab investments in the OECD countries are estimated to be in excess of US$1.3 trillion (cited in the chapter by Wilson).

Also notable is the considerable amount of outward FDI flows and stock in the Arab world, as captured by UNCTAD data. As of 2000, at least four countries in the region have more than US$1 billion in outward FDI stock: Kuwait, Bahrain, Libya, and Saudi Arabia. Remarkably, Kuwait has a much higher outward FDI stock (US$1.98 billion) than inward FDI stock (US$527 million).

The Changing Investment Landscape

Although the examination of Arab world FDI in the 1985 to 2000 period reveals relatively low and declining FDI flows, recent structural reforms undertaken by several Arab economies augur well for the prospects of increased investment into the region. With a detailed study of structural reforms in the region available in another chapter in the Report (see the chapter by Page), this discussion will highlight only countries that have recent reforms that depict the changing investment landscape in the region.

Recent country-level institutional reforms relevant to FDI comprise five main categories: (1) new or revamped investment legislation; (2) incentives, including tax and custom duty breaks; (3) relaxed restrictions, including on foreign ownership limits, local content requirements, domestic labor floors and repatriation of capital; (4) privatization, and; (5) capital market reform.

Almost all Arab countries passed new investment legislation during the 1990s. Among the most recent

Box 1. Promoting FDI in the Arab World: The Missing Link

To capture FDI flows, developing countries either have to have markets deep and large enough to attract market-seeking FDI, or they have to be in close proximity and have a workforce that is skilled and productive enough to attract efficiency-seeking FDI (Moosa, 2002). The Arab region does not score well on either count. Despite their combined size of 270 million consumers, Arab markets are "small" because they do not constitute a free-trade area, and the individual economies remain largely outside the production chain of major direct investors. The question then arises: How can the region be made more attractive for investment?

Aside from the reforms mentioned in the paper, there is a complementary way to strengthen current efforts to attract FDI. This "complementary" approach becomes even more compelling when we consider that many of the conditions necessary to attract higher levels of FDI to the Middle East are likely to take time to materialize for structural and geopolitical reasons. Reforms have been steady but slow, and the passage of time incurs increasingly high opportunity costs for countries with large proportions of unemployed youth, a good number of them fairly well skilled.

Given that most of global FDI has been of the M&A type, which in turn is a function of "acquirable" or "mergeable" firms, the task at hand entails leveraging the largely untapped potential of entrepreneurs to build a critical mass of competitive small and medium sized firms. If not, the Arab world might continue to see the bulk of FDI flows go to limited opportunities in a few capital-intensive sectors, and to sporadic privatization offers---at the cost of foregoing the opportunity to develop a whole range of new products in export sectors, such as information and communication technology, light manufacturing, and services.

The confluence of the following four developments make this task more viable than before: (1) the increase in portfolio flows to Arab countries over the past decade; (2) the "first generation" institutional and incentive reforms described in the paper; (3) the recent developments in financial instruments that can leverage entrepreneurial capacity where there are pockets of private sector innovation; and, (4) firm-level innovation from Arab countries. These four developments are key components of a new set of institutions needed for a largely unexplored strategy to attract higher levels of FDI to the region: the creation of competitive firms that have potential as joint ventures, mergers, or acquisitions.

The steady ten-year increase in portfolio flows to the region reflects an increased sophistication in Arab capital markets, and presents opportunities for the creation of new instruments that can complement FDI. "First generation" institutional reforms, especially in the areas of repatriation restrictions, tax incentives, and conversion and transfer policies, have been important steps toward liberalizing domestic financial markets. However, leveraging the knowledge from recent developments in international financial markets to increase FDI activity will require a set of "second generation" institutions in Arab countries. These have to do with legislation and regulation for new financial instruments. The demand for such institutions is becoming pressing because of the knowledge gained by investors and entrepreneurs from recent experiences on capital markets (Eid, Industry Interviews June to August 2002). In recent years there has also been a surge in investor appetite for various types of new financial instruments, most notably private equity funds. This appetite comes from young Arab professionals who studied and worked in the West during the recent market boom, and saw the potential of such instruments in more sophisticated markets. Coupled with the current reluctance to invest in capital markets, this appetite is translating into a series of new private equity initiatives throughout the region, including initiatives in Jordan, Egypt, Lebanon, Saudi Arabia, United Arab Emirates, Tunisia, and Morocco (Eid, Industry Interviews, June to August 2002). The fourth factor is the growth of entrepreneurial Arab companies, many of which started fairly small and achieved a global scale over the past ten to fifteen years. Examples include Aramex, which became the only Arab company listed on the NASDAQ in 1999, and regional companies such as the Al-Mabani Group in Lebanon, the Juffali Group in Saudi Arabia, and the Atlas Group in Jordan and Palestine. Other examples on a smaller scale include Cyberia.com, Maktoob.com, and CareersMiddleEast.com, which have been launched by dynamic young entrepreneurs. The growth of such firms can serve to deepen Arab markets and make them more attractive to efficiency-seeking FDI, especially on counts such as skill level, product differentiation, and export potential.

Increasing the number of competitive firms entails leveraging local entrepreneurial talent. In economies like Tunisia, Lebanon, Jordan, and increasingly the U.A.E., entrepreneurs abound who seek to "make it" and get "bought out," largely inspired by the U.S. venture start-up culture of the last few years. Moreover, innovations in information and communication technology have ushered the emergence of some small firms as perfectly viable and competitive dealers on the regional/global business scene, thanks to irreversible economies of scale and efficiency gains (in marketing, distribution, advertising, inventory management, and access to larger markets). What the firms typically lack is the capital necessary to get them to the stage attractive for acquisition. In this regard, it is notable that recent innovations in financial instruments have created ways of channeling international finance directly to dynamic entrepreneurial firms that are privately held. Through private equity funds, portfolio investment can be promoted without going through the Arab world's relatively inactive stock markets for the time being.

Box 1. Promoting FDI in the Arab World: The Missing Link (continued)

The single most crucial missing element in Arab financial markets today is financing for start-up firms. The financial sector remains fairly limited to traditional collateral-backed bank lending that precludes cash-strapped, unconnected innovators. A critical mass of firms supported through private funds would then serve to create new opportunities and increase investment volume, both for Arab stock markets and for FDI. The missing link is the institutional structure necessary to support entrepreneurial firms. [9]

Attracting more capital to the region will entail creating new institutions with at least four components: the promotion of entrepreneurship, the creation of new financial instruments, a role for multilateral agencies in supporting the effort, and finally, a role for knowledge management.

Promoting entrepreneurship. Government, and in particular investment promotion agencies (IPAs), have an important role to play in marketing small businesses both as investment opportunities and in terms of their products, and putting them in touch with sources of FDI. This type of service is a public good, and requires scale and continuity, but has not traditionally been the purview of IPAs, nor does the current institutional structure reflect this function. Mechanisms such as business plan competitions [10] are excellent ways of encouraging innovation as well as supporting those with the highest chances of succeeding and adding value to the economy. Significantly, various Arab countries have sought help in creating a competition similar to the one in Lebanon.

Creating new financial instruments. The only truly new aspect of private equity instruments is their popularization and increased availability and accessibility. With regard to the Middle East in particular, the region has created a handful of funds and the experience to date has underscored their importance. [11] While investment bankers and venture capitalists from throughout the region recognize the importance of such funds to mobilize investment in the region, they also point to the institutional lacunae in investment laws when it comes to private equity instruments. [12] One simple example is capital market legislation that distinguishes between various types of funds (e.g. closed, privately held funds vs. open-ended, publicly listed ones). Another pressing example is a new set of incentives including tax breaks for private equity funds, investors, and companies drawing on such funds (Interview information from Atlasinvest, Jordan 2002 and Upline IT Management, Morocco 2002). Given the consensus on their importance, a region of 270 million inhabitants should contain at least fifty funds by now, not five or six. To make some conservative estimates, in ten years, once each fund has spawned five to ten successful firms that create an average of twenty jobs each, we might begin to see an impact both on the economies of the region, and on the level of FDI the region attracts. In Lebanon today, given the right institutional support, we are more likely to see the creation of fifty successful small companies that employ ten workers each than we are likely to see one large (typically "lumpy") FDI investment that creates 500 jobs. [13]

The role of multilateral organizations. Multilateral organizations lend expertise and credibility to operations in most countries, certainly in developing countries. For instance, the presence of the International Finance Corporation (IFC) as a shareholder in a private equity fund targeting start-up firms in Lebanon, for example, is likely to improve the chances of its creation because other investors would be willing to participate. The presence of IFC as an investor would also make it possible to receive multilateral and bilateral grants that are being used to subsidize the operating costs of equity funds. From their perspective, multilateral organizations such as the World Bank Group could, in general, devise a new type of private sector conditionality through such instruments, by linking financing to microeconomic financial fundamentals and "good business" practices, including environmental friendliness.

The role of knowledge management. Ranging from the research and teaching of entrepreneurial economics and finance, to creating programs that encourage new firm creation, universities have a key role to play in attracting FDI. Universities can act as clearinghouses of information in developing regions, a role that might be undervalued at present because it is taken for granted. An important factor in the rapid development of the agricultural sector in the U.S. Midwest was the Agricultural Extension Offices created at the Land Grant Colleges throughout the country in the mid-1800s. These centers essentially turned a group of "sod busters" into a highly educated and mechanized agricultural sector. A modern equivalent of this program in the Arab world could be just as important. [14] An equivalent could take the form of local/regional centers created for small businesses to get help on accounting practices, marketing, and so on, and would have a large impact on the economies of the region. Equity funds that tie their loans to firms that participate in education programs could yield positive externalities the region does not seem to have obtained from FDI.

All markets, including the traditional Arab souk, are governed by institutions that determine production relations and their economic benefits. Markets evolve as new institutions supplement or replace old ones to accommodate new production technologies, along with the updated financial, labor, and property rights relations that they entail. The Arab world's economic link to the new century must begin with institutions that allow the region to leverage its potential and create more competitive investment opportunities in nontraditional sectors, such as the venture start-up sector. Promoting entrepreneurship through the creation of new financial instruments and with the support of multilateral organizations and universities are key components of the new institutions necessary to support an evolving market.

and notable changes are those limiting foreign ownership in Saudi Arabia, Qatar, and Kuwait. Saudi Arabia established the Saudi General Investment Authority in 2000 and adopted a new foreign direct investment law in the same year, which states that foreigners are able to invest in all sectors except for about twenty activities on the "negative list." Likewise, Qatar passed a new investment law in 2000, which will allow 100 percent, up from 49 percent, foreign investment ownership in selected sectors such as agriculture, industry, health, education, and tourism. More recently, Kuwait adopted a new foreign investment law in March 2001, which allows foreign majority ownership and, under certain conditions, authorizes 100 percent ownership.

While many Arab countries have introduced legislation easing foreign investment limits, the range of investment incentives offered varies significantly from country to country. Within countries, incentives also differ between export-oriented FDI and domestic market-oriented FDI. Morocco, Lebanon, Jordan, Egypt, Bahrain, and the United Arab Emirates offer some of the strongest and most detailed sets of incentives for FDI. These include free-trade zones, with preferential treatment for foreign investors, which are expected to boost the region's position as an export platform (Azzam 1999).

Most countries have also significantly relaxed restrictions on the operations of foreign firms. Morocco and Lebanon are among the most open, with virtually no foreign ownership, local content, domestic labor, or capital repatriation limits. Local labor requirements remain high in some GCC countries (such as Saudi Arabia) and land ownership is restricted to nationals or GCC citizens (in nearly all GCC countries), but there are no local content and capital repatriation restrictions. In Tunisia and Egypt, some local content requirements are applied to certain sectors, and capital repatriation restrictions are somewhat of a constraint, but are not major obstacles. In Syria, on the other hand, repatriation restrictions are highly constraining, while local content and labor requirements are nonexistent.

Significantly, of more than 280 bilateral agreements signed in the 1990s to encourage and guarantee investments, sixty-one are between Arab countries, and half of these include Egypt, Libya, Morocco, and Tunisia. In addition, sixty-five double-taxation agreements were forged, and most of these involve developed countries. Many Arab countries also signed multinational agreements, such as with the

International Center for the Settlement of Investment Disputes and the Arab Investment Guarantee Corporation. The Multilateral Investment Guarantee Agency (MIGA) holds the signature of seventeen Arab countries, a slightly higher proportion than for Latin America and the Asia-Pacific region.

Capital market reform is also slowly sweeping through the region. Morocco has gone as far as privatizing its stock market—the most active in the Arab world. Tunisia also has a fairly active stock market. In Jordan, Lebanon, Egypt, and the GCC countries, stock markets are less active, and will probably remain so until markets have deepened. In general, capital market legislation and regulation in North Africa has outpaced the rest of the Arab world, particularly with regard to provisions for new financial instruments such as venture capital and private equity funds. These reforms are an integral part of a new set of institutions the Arab region must establish in order to encourage the creation of more competitive businesses and jobs, deepen financial markets, and attract higher levels of FDI (see Box 1).

Prospects for Enhanced FDI Flows

That many countries have instituted significant structural reforms intended to create a more favorable investment environment augurs well for the prospects of greater FDI flows into the region. The impact of these reforms however, ultimately rests on a government's ability to sustain the pace of these reforms and execute them effectively. While there is clearly pressure for reform from a variety of sources, including rising unemployment, the reform process in some of the countries is often complex and fraught with opposition from powerful domestic interests.

Although they are absolutely necessary, structural reforms alone are not sufficient to ensure greater and more effective FDI flows. After all, many developing countries are also going through, or have gone through, a structural reform process, including liberalizing their economies and offering fiscal and nonfiscal incentives to encourage foreign direct investment. To successfully attract greater flows of FDI, particularly the export-oriented variety, the policymakers in the region need to focus on three critical areas: improving the quality of public institutions, investing in physical infrastructure, and finally, investing in human development. The quality of a country's public institutions, particularly the transparency of the regulatory process, the protection of property rights, the effective resolution of disputes, and the business costs of corruption are important variables assessed by prospective investors. Likewise, the quality of transportation and communications infrastructure is a key factor considered by export-oriented investors because of its implications to trade logistics and costs. Finally, and perhaps one of the most important considerations, is the availability of a skilled, productive, and flexible workforce. Indeed, addressing these three areas will define the competitive advantages of a country as an investment destination.

The urgency and importance of addressing these three critical areas is underscored by the findings of the *Arab World Competitiveness Report* Executive Opinion Survey. When the Survey, which was conducted from October 2001 to March 2002 with over 240 respondents from ten countries,[7] is juxtaposed with the *Global Competitiveness Report*'s Executive Opinion Survey, the findings depict a tentative, yet instructive picture of the ranking of the region's investment environment relative to seventy-three of the world's leading economies analyzed in the *Global Competitiveness Report 2001-2002* (see Part 3: The Executive Opionion Survey).[8]

The results reveal that in terms of the quality of public institutions, several Arab economies have room for significant improvement. Lebanon and Saudi Arabia, for instance, would place 79th and 83rd out of eighty-three countries in an assessment of the burden of administrative regulation in the country. In terms of the costs of corruption to businesses, Saudi Arabia and Egypt would have ranked 64th and 65th, respectively. Tunisia and Egypt would have ranked 82nd and 83rd in terms of the length of time senior management spends with government agencies. Lebanon would have ranked 61st in terms of the independence of the judiciary from interference from government, and 52nd for intellectual property protection.

Likewise, several countries in the region need to enhance the quality of their infrastructure. Egypt and Lebanon rank the lowest in the region in terms of overall infrastructure quality. With regard to availability of telephones, Tunisia and Saudi Arabia would have ranked 65th and 66th, respectively. Saudi Arabia also rates fairly low in the sufficiency of competition (to ensure high quality and low prices) in both the communications and transportation sectors. In terms of electricity prices, Lebanon is perceived to have among the highest, at 81st place out of eighty-three countries.

In terms of human resource development, the quality of public schools in Saudi Arabia, Lebanon, and Egypt were rated below average. The quality of math and science education in Saudi Arabia is also perceived by survey respondents to lag behind most other countries in the world. In the region, Oman and Saudi Arabia received low scores in terms of the availability of scientists and engineers, while Jordan and Lebanon are perceived to have the highest incidence of brain drain, with scientists and engineers normally leaving to pursue opportunities in other countries.

While the three areas—quality of public institutions, infrastructure, and human resource development—are all critical to improving the investment environment, it is the latter that is most important in defining and sustaining a long-term competitive advantage. A country can increase investment flows by improving the quality of its public institutions and physical infrastructure, but unless human resource skills are developed and enhanced, it is difficult for a country to attract FDI engaged in higher value-added activities, much less establish the linkages that will enable the country to more fully reap the benefits of FDI.

Conclusion

The examination of investment flows from 1985 to 2000 reveal five key features of FDI in the Arab world: first, regional stocks and flows have increased, but have not kept pace with world FDI flows; second, the region has received less FDI flows relative to other regions; third, FDI flows to the Arab world are concentrated in five countries and directed mostly to the hydrocarbon sector, and to a lesser extent, the manufacturing and services (tourism, telecommunications, banking) sectors; fourth, FDI flows still play only a small part in the economies of the region; and fifth, intra-Arab investment is a significant proportion of FDI flows in the region and is likely to play an even greater role as regional integration and cooperation deepens.

Barring a heightening of political instability in the region, the prospects of improved FDI flows into the region are favorable because of the increased commitment by governments as manifested in the recent reforms undertaken to improve their respective investment environments. Prospects will be enhanced further, however, only if governments in the region build upon the momentum of the reform process (especially privatization) and effect more improvements in three critical areas: public institutions, physical infrastructure, and human resource development. Indeed, only by continuing the reform process and addressing these three critical areas, can the region successfully increase investment flows and more effectively seize its long-term benefits.

References

Album, Andrew. "Investing in Middle East equities." *The Middle East* 262 (December 1996):22–23.

Album, Andrew. "More Investment Choices Than Ever in Middle East Equities." *The Middle East* 263 (January 1997):29–30.

Azzam, Henry T. "Foreign Direct Investment Inflow to Arab Countries on the Decline." *Jordan Times* Amman edition. (9 December 1999).

Blair, Edmund. "Finance: Quenching the Thirst for Capital." *Middle East Economic Digest* 40, 1 (5 January 1996):5.

Butler, David. "Foreign Finance Fuels Projects." *Middle East Economic Digest* 39, 51 (22 December 1995):2–4.

Cattanash, Katherine A., Mary Frances Kelley, and Gail Marmorstein Sweeney. "Hidden Treasure: A Look into *Private Equity's History, Future, and Lure.*" In *Private Equity and Venture Capital: A Practical Guide for Investors and Practitioners*, edited by Lake, Rick, and Ronald A. Lake. London: Euromoney Books, 2000:ch.1.

De Mello, L.R. "Foreign Direct Investment-led Growth: Evidence from Time Series and Panel Data." *Oxford Economic Papers* 51 (1999):133–351.

Driffield, N., and Taylor, K. "FDI and the Labor Market: A Review of the Evidence and Policy Recommendations." *Oxford Review of Economic Policy* 16 (2000):90–103.

El-Erian, Mohamed A. "Middle Eastern Economies' External Environment: What Lies Ahead?" *Middle East Policy* 4, 3 (March 1996):137–147.

Fitzgerald, John M., and Ribar, David C. "Does a Rising Tide of Small Business Jobs Lift All Boats?" Washington, D.C.: The Office of Advocacy, U.S. Small Business Administration, July 2001.

Fujita, M. "FDI Flows in the League of Arab States: Some Recent Statistics and a Brief Overview of the Current Legal Framework for Investment." *The Arab Bank Review* 3, 2 (October 2001):16–19.

International Monetary Fund. *Balance of Payments Manual.* 5th ed. Washington, D.C. September 1993.

Joel Popkin and Company. "Small Business Share of Economic Growth." Washington, D.C.: U.S. Small Business Administration, 14 December 2001.

Kirchhoff, Bruce. *Entrepreneurship and Dynamic Capitalism.* Westport, CT: Quorum Books, 1994.

Middle East Economic Digest. "Equity investment funds develop despite Gulf." *Middle East Economic Digest* 38, 19 (13 May 1994):4.

Onyeiwu, Steve. "Foreign Direct Investment, Capital Outflows and Economic Development in the Arab World." *Journal of Development and Economic Policies* 2, 2 (June 2000):27–57.

Sadik, Ali T., and Ali A Bolbol. "Capital Flows, FDI, and Technology Spillovers: Evidence from Arab Countries." *World Development* 29, 12 (2001):2111–2125.

Smarzynska, Beata K., and Shang-Jin Wei. "Corruption and Composition of Foreign Direct Investment: Firm-Level Evidence." NBER Working Paper w7969.

Stone, S.F., and B.N. Jeon. "Foreign Direct Investment and Trade in the Asian-Pacific Region: Complementarity, Distance and Regional Economic Integration." Journal of Economic Integration 15 (2000):460–485.

The Heritage Foundation and Wall Street Journal. The Index of Economic Freedom. Washington D.C.: The Heritage Foundation, 2001. Accessed at <http://cf.heritage.org/index/country.cfm?ID=85> on 30 July 2002.

The HSBC Group. *Business Profile Series.* 2nd ed. Lebanon: HSBC, Third Quarter 2000. Accessed at <http://www.hsbc.com.hk/pdf/corp/lbm.pdf> on 20 July 2002.

U.S. Department of Commerce, National Trade Data Bank. "Saudi Arabia Investment Climate Statement." (3 September 1999). Accessed at <http://www.tradeport.org/ts/countries/saudiarabia/climate.html> on 7 August 2002.

UNCTAD. *Handbook of Statistics 2001.* Geneva: United Nations, 2001.

UNDP. *Arab Human Development Report 2002.* Geneva: United Nations, 2002.

The World Bank Group. *Global Development Finance 2001.* Washington D.C. 2001.

Xu, B., and J. Wang. "Trade, FDI and International Technology Diffusion." *Journal of Economic Integration* 15 (2000):585–601.

Yabuuchi, S. "Foreign Direct Investment, Urban Unemployment and Welfare." *Journal of International Trade and Economic Development* 8 (1999):359–371.

Endnotes

1. Arab Human Development Report, UNDP, page 87

2. Where the capital consists of any combination of equity, re-invested earnings and intra-company loans, and involves varying degrees of control over the recipient enterprise (IMF 1993; UNCTAD 2001).

3. Naturally, the distinction between FDI and portfolio investment is not a clear-cut one. Some FDI involves very low levels of control and is reversible in many ways including intra-firm financial transactions (Loungani & Razin 2001). And some portfolio investment can involve a significant controlling interest and can be fairly lasting in duration—features made possible by innovations in international financial instruments over the past decade, such as closed private equity and venture capital funds (Album 1997; Cattanach, Kelley & Sweeney 2000).

4. Echoes the observation of Fujita, page 17.

5. Other problems with FDI statistics in general include double counting, historical versus market valuation, accounting for domestic financing by foreign firms and capturing disguised investment and profit reinvestments.

6. Estimate from Abdul Rahman Sabri, representative of the Arab League Secretary General, as cited in "Intra-Arab Investments up $2.4 billion in 2001) Gulf News Online Edition, August 20, 2002.

7. Bahrain, Egypt, Jordan, Kuwait, Lebanon, Morocco, Oman, Qatar, Saudi Arabia, Tunisia, and United Arab Emirates

8. The Global Competitiveness Report 2001–2002 covers seventy-five countries but two of these countries are also part of the Arab World Competitiveness Report Executive Opinion Survey.

9. In the United States firms employing 100 people or less account for approximately 50% of jobs in the economy and for 60% of net jobs created annually (Fitzgerald & Ribar 2001; Joel Popkin & Co. 2001). These firms accounted for 50% of the share of non-farm GDP in the United States in 1997, and they are known to be more resilient to business cycles than large firms (Kirchhoff 1994). The experience appears to be similar in many countries at various levels of industrialization including several in the Arab world.

10. Such as the one launched in Lebanon in the year 2001. See www.enetworklebanon.org.

11. The design of appropriate private instruments requires further research, but their creation could include an important role for multilateral organizations such as the IMF or the World Bank to act as "clearing houses" that underwrite exchanges where derivatives on funds are traded. Derivative instruments could serve to diversify the risk on funds once a critical mass of them is created.

12. The design of appropriate private instruments requires further research, but their creation could include an important role for multilateral organizations such as the IMF or the World Bank to act as "clearing houses" that underwrite exchanges where derivatives on funds are traded. Derivative instruments could serve to diversify the risk on funds once a critical mass of them is created.

13. This is for the simple reason that entrepreneurs starting small firms already reside, work and have their capital in Lebanon, and therefore face a different risk-return trade-off than any foreign investor.

14. An example is the entrepreneurship program launched in 2001 in Lebanon.

The Arab World in the Global Market:
What the Trade Data Reveal

**Friedrich von Kirchbach, Fiona Paua,
Mondher Mimouni, and
Jean-Michel Pasteels**

In a region with remarkable yet varying factor endowments, the question of the role of natural resources to Arab world development inevitably arises. Many empirical studies, including Sachs and Warner (1995), have noted a negative relationship between natural resource abundance and long-run economic growth, fueling the concern that a rich natural resource endowment is a "curse."[1] Reservations regarding resource-based development have long prevailed in development literature. Such reservations arise partly out of considerations of resource sustainability and price volatility, but mostly out of concern that the declining relative prices of raw materials, relative to manufactures, would have an adverse impact on the terms of trade as well as on overall development prospects (Prebisch 1950; Singer 1950). This concern continues to be echoed even in the recent *Trade and Development Report* (UNCTAD 2002), which asserts that with the exception of a few east Asian economies, "developing country exports are still concentrated on products derived essentially from the exploitation of natural resources and the use of unskilled labor, which have limited prospects for productivity growth and lack dynamism in the world markets."

With the advent of the Doha Development Round of multilateral negotiations it is fitting that trade is more than ever in the forefront of the development agenda, particularly in the Arab world. Trade plays an important role in the economies of the region and is essential in facilitating the transition to higher stages of development. Trade, along with foreign direct investment, ushers in the technology and resources necessary to promote the levels of productivity required for a country to shift from factor-driven development, whereby growth is determined by the mobilization of the primary factors of production, to investment-driven development, whereby growth is increasingly achieved by harnessing global technologies to local production; and, then finally, to innovation-driven development, whereby global competitiveness is linked to high rates of social learning and the rapid ability to shift to new technologies (Porter et al. 2001).[2]

The new round of multilateral negotiations, according to the recent study *Harnessing Trade for Development and Growth in the Middle East* (Hoekman and Messerlin 2002), provides an opportunity "to identify options to use trade more effectively as an instrument of growth." But rather than assess trade and investment policies, as the study suggests, this chapter seeks to contribute to the discussion by examining what the trade data reveal about the Arab world's trade performance. How is the Arab world integrated in the international trading system? What does the region specialize in and how are the various economies performing in those markets? How are its resources allocated and how efficiently are the resources used? Most importantly, how can the region improve its overall trade performance, and in so doing, improve its prospects for development?

Using COMTRADE,[3] the world's largest trade database (covering more than 180 countries and 5000 traded products), this chapter assesses the trade performance of the Arab world, focusing on the trade of goods, which comprises 88 percent of the region's total trade.[4] The chapter begins with an overview of trade patterns and developments within the region, placing the Arab world in the context of global trade. The analysis is then conducted at the country and sector level, with the use of the Trade Performance Index (TPI), an analytical framework developed by the International Trade Centre.[5] The TPI calculates two composite rankings: *current* TPI, which is a snapshot of the overall trade position of a country in a sector for a particular year; and *change* TPI, which captures the evolution of a country's trade performance for a given sector over a five-year period. The TPI framework is intended to provide new insights into the competitive advantages of countries in specific sectors, but is not intended to provide an alternative measure of competitiveness (Cornelius et al. 2001).

Building on the TPI country and sector assessments, the analysis of the region's trade performance is then conducted at the level of individual companies, examining how the quality of the national business environment affects trade performance. The qualitative nature of this assessment complements the purely quantitative approach of the TPI. The analysis incorporates the perceptions of key business leaders in the region as captured by the Arab World Competitiveness Report (AWCR) Executive Opinion Survey, which was conducted from October 2001 to March 2002 and which had more than 240 respondents from ten countries.[6] Juxtaposing the Arab world survey results with findings of the *Global Competitiveness Report 2001–2002* (GCR) Executive Opinion Survey produces a tentative, yet very instructive, picture of the ranking of the region's trade environment relative to seventy-three of the world's leading economies.[7]

The final part of the chapter distills the findings of the trade performance assessment and asserts that while there have been, to varying degrees, improvements in the trade performance of the countries in the Arab world, significant challenges remain that need to be addressed if the region is to transition to higher levels of development. In particular, two policy imperatives emerge: improving the operating environment for exporters in the immediate to near term; and, in the medium- to long-term, building on the region's current trading advantages in order to diversify into higher value-added exports and gain increasing shares of markets that are not only expanding, but that also have room for substantial productivity growth.

Regional Trade in the Global Context

As of 2001, the Arab world, with an economy comprising 1.9 percent of the world's GDP, exports goods amounting to 3.5 percent of total world exports. In terms of imports, the region's weight is smaller, at 2.5 percent of total world imports; in value terms, combined imports of the sixteen countries in this Report amount to US$164 billion, and combined exports amount to US$225 billion, which places the region in the same export category as China. Two countries alone, Saudi Arabia and the United Arab Emirates, account for more than half of the region's total exports. Together with Algeria and Kuwait, the four countries account for 70 percent of the region's total exports (Table 1).

Significantly, the expansion of exports in the region has not kept pace with world export growth; rather, it correlates with changes in oil prices.

Table 1. National Exports as a Percent of Total Regional Exports, 2001

	Exports (US$ millions)	As Percent of the Region's Total Exports
Algeria	19,070	8.5
Bahrain	5,545	2.5
Egypt	4,123	1.8
Jordan	2,293	1.0
Kuwait	16,173	7.2
Lebanon	889	0.4
Libya	11,996	5.3
Mauritania	280	0.1
Morocco	7,116	3.2
Oman	11,072	4.9
Qatar	10,247	4.5
Saudi Arabia	73,032	32.4
Syrian AR	4,536	2.0
Tunisia	6,505	2.9
U.A.E.	49,196	21.8
Yemen, Rep.	3,205	1.4
Arab world	**225,278**	**100.0**

Sources: Authors' calculations based on data from the International Financial Statistics database, World Development Indicators 2002 database, United Nations Monthly Bulletin of Statistics, World Trade Organization, Food and Agriculture Trade Yearbook and Database and Economist Intelligence Unit

Twenty-one years ago, in 1981, the Arab world accounted for as much as 10.7 percent of world exports. Over two decades, the region's exports surpassed 1981 levels by only 4.4 percent; during the same period, however, world exports increased by 216.6 percent. Notably, the region's performance has been dragged down by two countries that experienced very sharp declines during this period: Libya, which had a drop in exports of 23.0 percent, and Saudi Arabia, which had a decline in exports of 39.1 percent. The rest of the countries in the region actually posted increases over 1981 levels, but mostly at a slower rate than world exports, with the exception of Yemen, which saw its exports grow by 390.0 percent (Figure 1).

In the last five years, all the major oil-exporting countries posted above-average growth rates, mostly attributed to favorable movements in the price of oil. Of particular note is Qatar, which increased its exports by 166.0 percent during the five-year period. The most recent data, however, reveals that a marked deceleration occurred last year for most Arab countries, primarily reflecting the decrease in oil prices since 2000.

Figure 1. Arab World Exports Relative to Total World Exports, 1980–2001 (in US$ million)

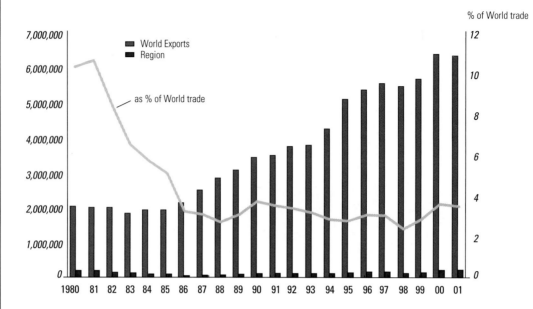

Sources: Authors' calculations based on data from the International Financial Statistics database, World Development Indicators 2002 database, United Nations Monthly Bulletin of Statistics, World Trade Organization, Food and Agriculture Trade Yearbook and Database, and the Economist Intelligence Unit

Changes in the terms of trade, however, were favorable for most of the economies in the region during the last five years. Using 1990 as the base year, the 2001 ratio of the export price index to the import price index mostly reflect increases, ranging from 144.8 for Algeria and 137.6 for Kuwait, to export revenues 8.1 for Morocco and 105.3 for Egypt. Less favorable terms of trade were posted by Tunisia, Yemen, Libya, and Oman. Of the countries in the region, Syria's terms of trade deteriorated the most in 2001, to 58.4 percent of its 1990 level (Table 3).[8]

Relative to its trade balance, the region is in a net surplus position, a reflection of the abundance of the oil sector. The 2001 trade statistics show the trade surplus of the Arab world to be US$61.6 billion, about a tenth of the region's GDP. Saudi Arabia alone accounts for 67.9 percent of the total, with a surplus of US$41.8 billion. Seven other countries are in a surplus position—the United Arab Emirates, Algeria, Kuwait, Qatar, Oman, Libya, and Bahrain—and notably, all are oil-exporting countries. For these countries, the surplus accounts for a significant portion of GDP. Qatar's trade surplus, for instance, is equivalent to 43.4 percent of its GDP. Also substantial, but of smaller proportion to GDP, are the trade surpluses of Oman, Kuwait, and Saudi Arabia, which are 27.3 percent, 24.8 percent, and 25.1 percent of GDP, respectively. Not all Arab world countries,

Table 2. Annual Export Growth Rates, 1997–2001 (in Percent)

	1997	1998	1999	2000	2001
Algeria	5	-27	21	76	-12
Bahrain	-7	-25	27	38	-3
Egypt	11	-20	14	32	-12
Jordan	1	-2	2	4	21
Kuwait	-4	-33	28	59	-17
Lebanon	-14	13	-5	6	24
Libya	1	-31	16	84	-16
Mauritania	-12	-15	5	-1	-24
Morocco	2	1	5	-1	-4
Oman	4	-28	31	56	-2
Qatar	1	30	37	68	-12
Saudi Arabia	0	-36	31	53	-6
Syrian AR	-2	-26	20	35	-3
Tunisia	1	3	3	-1	11
U.A.E.	8	-11	18	27	-3
Yemen, Rep.	0	-34	65	65	-22

Sources: Authors' calculations based on data from the International Financial Statistics database, World Development Indicators 2002 database, United Nations Monthly Bulletin of Statistics, World Trade Organization, Food and Agriculture Trade Yearbook and Database and Economist Intelligence Unit

Table 3. Terms of Trade (1990=100), 1997–2001

	1997	1998	1999	2000	2001
Algeria	123.2	88.0	99.2	169.4	144.8
Bahrain	—	—	—	—	—
Egypt	91.6	65.5	77.6	113.5	105.3
Jordan	118.5	122.1	126.9	109.4	118.5
Kuwait	102.1	63.6	97.0	163.3	137.6
Lebanon	40.4	43.8	—	—	—
Libya	115.9	73.1	103.3	92.2	92.2
Mauritania	—	—	—	—	—
Morocco	104.6	117.4	125.8	110.8	108.1
Oman	79.3	57.3	77.7	109.4	91.8
Qatar	49.4	52.2	104.4	133.3	132.5
Saudi Arabia	—	—	—	—	—
Syrian AR	63.7	44.8	53.9	71.2	58.4
Tunisia	96.0	94.2	97.1	97.0	99.9
U.A.E.	—	—	—	—	—
Yemen, Rep.	67.2	49.2	81.4	117.9	99.4

Source: Economist Intelligence Unit, 2002

however, are in trade surplus positions. Jordan, Tunisia, Morocco, Lebanon, and Egypt—all nonmajor oil exporters—have posted negative trade balances. Their trade deficits range from 38.3 percent of GDP, as in the case of Lebanon, to 7.2 percent of GDP, as in the case of Mauritania. Within a narrower range are the trade deficits of Tunisia, Morocco, and Egypt, which are 15.0 percent, 11.5 percent, and 8.9 percent of GDP, respectively (Table 4).

In terms of export structure, petroleum and other minerals comprise the predominant export sector of the region, accounting for 82 percent of total exports. For eight of the sixteen countries covered in this Report, the minerals sector comprises at least 80 percent of total exports, and for six of these eight countries—Algeria, Kuwait, Libya, Yemen, Qatar, and Saudi Arabia—the sector comprises at least 90 percent of total exports (Table 5).

Chemicals and clothing comprise the second and third largest export groups in the region, at US$7.8 billion and US$6.3 billion, respectively. The region's performance in the latter is significant, because it is the world's eighth largest exporter of clothing. The clothing sector is also notable for being the only major non-oil export group with positive net exports. When aggregating textiles and clothing,

Table 4. Trade Balance, 2001

	Trade Balance (in US$ million)	Trade Balance (Percent of GDP)
Algeria	8,904	16.2
Bahrain	1,282	16.0
Egypt	-8,657	-8.9
Jordan	-2,513	-28.5
Kuwait	8,848	24.8
Lebanon	-6,402	-38.3
Libya	2,764	9.7
Mauritania	-70	-7.2
Morocco	-3,842	-11.5
Oman	5,275	27.3
Qatar	7,203	43.4
Saudi Arabia	41,833	25.1
Syrian AR	-133	-0.7
Tunisia	-2,988	-15.0
U.A.E.	9,538	14.1
Yemen, Rep.	553	6.3
Arab World	**61,596**	**10.2**

Sources: Authors' calculations based on data from the International Financial Statistics database, World Development Indicators 2002 database, United Nations Monthly Bulletin of Statistics, World Trade Organization, Food and Agriculture Trade Yearbook and Database and Economist Intelligence Unit

Table 5. Minerals as Percentage of National Exports, 2000

	in Percent
Algeria	98
Bahrain	49
Egypt	37
Jordan	14
Kuwait	96
Lebanon	24
Libya	95
Mauritania	43
Morocco	11
Oman	59
Qatar	93
Saudi Arabia	92
Syrian AR	81
Tunisia	14
U.A.E.	81
Yemen, Rep.	95

Source: Authors' calculations based on data from the International Trade Centre

however, Arab countries remain net importers since a large proportion of fabrics have to be imported to produce the clothing (Box 1). The other major export groups are, in descending order, non-processed food, basic manufactured goods, electronic components, other (miscellaneous) manufacturing, non-electrical machinery, and processed food (Table 6).

Table 6. World Market Share of Major Exports of the Arab World, 2000

Sector	Exports (US$ billion)	World Market Share (in Percent)
Minerals	197.0	24.1
Chemicals	7.8	1.3
Clothing	6.3	3.4
Non-processed food	2.8	1.2
Basic manufacturing	2.7	0.6
Electronic components	1.6	0.3
Miscellaneous manufacturing	1.4	0.3
Non-electrical machinery	1.3	0.2
Processed food	1.1	0.5
Textiles	1.1	0.7

Source: Authors' calculations based on data from the International Trade Centre

The leading destinations for the region's exports vary significantly from country to country, but are mostly determined by geographic proximity (see Part 2: Country Profiles and Data Presentation). The European Union (EU), for instance, is a major export destination, particularly for Tunisia, Morocco, and Algeria. For the Gulf countries, Asia is also a major destination, specifically Japan, Singapore, South Korea, India, and China. Most countries also have significant trade with the United States.

Intra-Arab trade, however, is relatively small, despite several attempts to promote regional integration (Box 2). Over the last thirty years, intraregional exports have fluctuated between 4 percent and 8 percent, with the fluctuations accounted for mainly by changes in oil prices. According to the International Monetary Fund, in 1998 when oil prices were very low, intra-Arab trade was about 8 percent. Conversely, when oil prices significantly increased in 2000, the level of intraregional trade dropped to 4 percent. This 4 percent to 8 percent level of intraregional trade is marginal relative to other regions: intra-EU trade is estimated to be around 60 percent of total trade, intra-NAFTA trade is about 55 percent and intra-Southeast Asian trade at 23 percent (Table 7).

Table 7. Intra-Regional Trade, 1970–2000

Regional Trade Blocs	Merchandise Exports within Bloc (US$ million)					
	1970	1980	1985	1990	1995	2000
Arab Common Market	102	661	504	911	1,368	1,238
Gulf Cooperation Council	156	4,632	3,101	6,906	6,832	8,561
ASEAN	1,456	13,350	14,343	28,648	81,911	100,818
NAFTA	22,078	102,218	143,191	226,273	394,472	676,440

Source: World Development Indicators, 2002
ASEAN: Association of Southeast Asian Nations
NAFTA: North American Free Trade Area

In terms of trade orientation, the average trade-to-GDP ratio for the region is 64.6 percent, but there is great variation within the region. The disparity is quite evident between, for example, the United Arab Emirates and Bahrain with ratios greater than 100 percent and, on the other extreme, Egypt, with a 17.5 percent trade-to-GDP ratio and a 4.3 percent exports-to-GDP ratio.[9] There is an even wider divergence in per capita export revenues. Qatar has the highest export revenues per capita at US$17,078, and Egypt has the lowest at US$63 (Table 8).

Table 8. Trade Orientation, 2001

	Trade to GDP (in Percent)	Exports to GDP (in Percent)	Exports/ Capita
Algeria	53.3	34.7	621
Bahrain	122.6	69.3	7,921
Egypt	17.5	4.3	63
Jordan	80.4	26.0	441
Kuwait	65.7	45.2	7,032
Lebanon	49.0	5.3	247
Libya	74.2	41.9	2,181
Mauritania	64.9	28.9	104
Morocco	54.0	21.2	244
Oman	87.3	57.3	4,429
Qatar	80.1	61.7	17,078
Saudi Arabia	62.5	43.8	3,478
Syrian AR	47.1	23.2	265
Tunisia	80.1	32.6	671
U.A.E.	131.7	72.9	14,908
Yemen, Rep.	67.0	36.7	169

Sources: Authors' calculations based on data from the International Financial Statistics database, World Development Indicators 2002 database, United Nations Monthly Bulletin of Statistics, World Trade Organization, Food and Agriculture Trade Yearbook and Database and Economist Intelligence Unit

Box 1. Impact of Trade Liberalization in Textiles and Clothing for the Arab World

The dismantling of the Multi-Fiber Agreement (MFA) by 2005 and China's accession to the WTO will profoundly alter international competition in textiles and clothing. Many experts, based on the increasing number of studies that measure its impact on different economies, concur on this evaluation. The impact for Mediterranean countries such as Syria, Morocco, Tunisia, or Egypt has been investigated recently by Chaponnière (2002) and is summarized below.

Liberalization will imply that most exporting countries, such as LDCs, economies in transition, or Mediterranean countries, will lose their privileged market access to the EU. It will also mean for them that they would need to open their own markets, as foreseen by Article VII of the Agreement on Textiles and Clothing.

Import duties for apparel are very high in most Arab exporting countries, such as Jordan (34 percent on average), Tunisia (42 percent), Egypt (42.7 percent), and Morocco (49 percent). For textiles, applied tariffs are slightly lower, at 24 percent in Jordan, 38 percent in Morocco and Tunisia, and 49 percent in Egypt. Tunisia is the only country to have really started the liberalization process. Morocco only slowly initiated the process in 2001. Assuming that companies targeting only the local market will be more severely hit than those targeting exporting ones, Chaponnière comes to the conclusion that Egypt will be severely hit by this shock. The situation is less worrying for Tunisia, where around 10 percent of the labor force works in inward-oriented companies. For Morocco, a stronger impact is also expected, with 200 companies employing 50,000 persons (one-quarter in textiles), no longer generating any revenues from exports.

According to experts, the loss of preferential market access will be less painful for countries that have invested in downstream activities (local production of fabrics) than those that essentially assemble imported fabrics. Most Arab countries, as opposed to other countries such as Turkey, are in a difficult position since their exporting firms primarily use imported fibers. The cover rate (ratio of exports-to-imports) is particularly low for Egypt and Jordan. Egypt, known for its high-quality cotton, does not transform this into a high value-added product, and instead uses fibers imported "under temporary admission" for most of its exports.

The pattern of trade in textiles and clothing tends to be regional, owing in part to preferential market access schemes. However, other factors also influence trade flows, such as the proximity to the target market for fashion articles. Fashion houses and distributors run tight just-in-time stock control, where suppliers must respond quickly to orders. Tunisia and Morocco are well positioned on short distribution channels. Proximity may not be a sufficient determinant for the location of production in the future, and competition from China is already increasing in the mid-range market segment, which is one that can absorb air transportation costs.

Arab countries also present differences in terms of productivity and the participation of the state in the textiles and clothing sector. Productivity is higher in countries, such as Tunisia, that have invested in training centers specialized in textiles or clothing. State-owned companies are numerous in the textile sectors of many Arab countries, despite efforts at privatization. The state still plays a predominant role in Syria and Egypt, while they are less active in Morocco and Tunisia. Private investors have shown little interest in acquiring state-owned companies, where productivity is judged low according to international standards.

In this context, exporting countries in the Arab region may opt for two strategic responses that would each require increasing financial resources. The first response is to develop industrial linkages in the country and invest in high-quality machinery; this follows the example of Turkey, which has a cover ratio of 300 percent in the sector and has become a successful producer of synthetic fibers (9th worldwide). The second strategic option is to develop services in the country, such as managing inventories, and to sell products under their own brands.

As a whole, the region has made significant strides towards greater integration in the multilateral trading system. Between 1995 and 2000, as many as ten countries from the Arab world joined the World Trade Organization (WTO), while four others have attained observer status and another two countries have established accession working parties (Table 9).

There have also been numerous trade agreements on a bilateral and multilateral basis, the most notable being the Euro-Mediterranean Partnership (EMP) as discussed in the chapter by Ghoneim, et al. At the subregional level there are also multilateral free-trade initiatives, and these are discussed in Box 3.

Box 2. Regional Integration

When the Arab countries are divided into different subregions, namely the Maghreb countries (Algeria, Libya, Mauritania, Morocco, and Tunisia), the Mashreq countries (Egypt, Jordan, Lebanon, Syria, and Sudan) and the Gulf Cooperation Council countries (Bahrain, Kuwait, Oman, Qatar, Saudi Arabia, and the United Arab Emirates), the patterns change. The share of trade within the three subcategories is considerably higher than overall intra-Arab trade, indicating that obstacles to trade are fewer for the subregions than for the Arab region as a whole, and suggesting that there are specific subregional conditions. For example, Maghreb exports to the Arab world are predominantly exported to Maghreb countries, and GCC exports to Arab countries are highly concentrated in GCC countries.

Using a gravity model specifically designed to measure the "expected" level of trade in the Arab region, Al-Atrash and Yousef (2000) obtain very interesting results. First, Arab exports to the rest of the world are lower than the levels of exports simulated in the model, indicating the low level of integration in the multilateral trading system. More interestingly, the model suggests that the share of intra-Arab trade should be around 9 to 10 percent, instead of the present share. When looking at trade within the subgroups, the Mashreq shows the highest degree of economic integration, exhibiting a higher level of trade than what the model simulates. For the GCC and the Maghreb, the converse is true—the level of intraregional trade is below what the model predicts.

These results should be interpreted carefully, since the model used by the authors suffers from an "oil bias."[11] However, results obtained by Fontagné et al. (2002), using a gravity model designed specifically to capture south-south trade and excluding trade in raw materials, are similar those for intra-Arab trade. In the case of Egypt for instance, the International Trade Centre's calculations (based on the TradeSim model) show that current trade, particularly with Saudi Arabia and the United Arab Emirates, is far below potential. In 1999, Egypt's trade (excluding crude oil) with Saudi Arabia totaled US$100 million, but its potential is US$251 million. Similarly, Egypt's trade with the United Arab Emirates amounted to US$33 million in 1999, but potential trade is in the order of US$155 million.

Constraints to intra-Arab trade have been summarized recently in Al-Atrash and Yousef (2000). They include the lack of product complementarity, differences in trade policy and economic strategy (Allum 1998), political factors (including economic sanctions against Iraq), high transportation costs, and differences in per capita income.

The lack of product complementarity—in other words, the specialization in similar products (and in particular oil)—should not be understated. It explains, for example, the low level of intra-Arab trade between oil-exporting countries, and the positive correlation between the share of nonfuel products in national exports and the level of intra-Arab trade. However, it does not explain why countries such as Tunisia and Morocco exhibit low levels of intra-Arab trade, or the relatively high level of trade within subregions such as Mashreq, where the lack of product complementarity is supposed to be higher than in the whole Arab region. High transport costs between the Maghreb and the other Arab subregions provides a supplementary explanation to that of economic policy, since Tunisia and Morocco became highly specialized in sectors, such as textiles and clothing, where they benefit from a substantial preferential margin in the EU.

Differences in per capita income explain to some extent the relatively low level of Arab exports to GCC countries. As suggested by Fischer (1993), richer countries from the Gulf prefer to import high quality goods, which are more likely to be produced by industrialized nations. Equipment used in the oil industry, which accounts for a large part of imports, is also being produced in industrialized nations.

Economic and trade policy is another crucial factor (see El-Erian and Fischer 1996 and El-Naggar 1992). While GCC countries (in particular the United Arab Emirates) present a relatively flat import tariff structure, others such as Egypt, Algeria, and Syria have imposed important barriers to trade. In addition, nontariff barriers, such as restrictive licensing and restrictive foreign exchange allocation, are widely used in the region. This imposition of extensive barriers to trade is a legacy of the import substitution strategies adopted in the 1960s and the 1970s.

Box 3. Multilateral Free Trade Initiatives at Subregional Levels

In an attempt to boost subregional trade flows, a number of free-trade agreements have been established, each with varying degrees of relevance and success. There are four major multilateral initiatives at the subregional level, namely the Greater Arab Free Trade Area (GAFTA), the Gulf Cooperation Council (GCC), the Arab Maghreb Union (AMU) and the Mediterranean Arab Free Trade Area (MAFTA).

The most successful regional free-trade area is the Gulf Cooperation Council, which numbers six countries of the Gulf. The GCC was established in 1981, and after three years of drafting an agreement, the Unified Economic Agreement was submitted to the General Agreement on Tariffs and Trade. The GCC's objectives include the coordination, integration and cooperation of national policies in economic, social, and cultural fields. Trade among member countries is less than 10 percent, but there has been a strong desire to boost intraregional trade. In November 1999, GCC countries approved the establishment of a customs union by 2005. Duty on imports will fall to 7.5 percent by 2005, with the tariff on essential goods scheduled to drop to 5.5 percent during the same period. In December 2001, leaders of the GCC decided to reduce all tariff rates on nonessential goods to 5 percent by January 2003. Countries will retain nontariff protection measures in order to shelter key industries from competition in the region. With regard to rules of origin, duty-free access is provided to products originating in GCC countries if 40 percent of value added is from the GCC region, and if a citizen or entity from the GCC area owns 51 percent or more of the exporting enterprise.

The Greater Arab Free Trade Area extends from the Gulf region to North Africa and includes eighteen member countries. It was established in 1997 with the objective of eliminating all tariffs, nontariff barriers, taxes, and other distortion effects by 2007. All tariff rates are to be reduced at an annual rate of 10 percent. Specific items have been exempt from tariff reductions, namely those pertaining to health, religious, and security concerns, as well as those deemed essential to national development priorities. The list of exempted products ranges from as high as 800 products for Morocco to as little as thirty-five products for Jordan. The rules of origin for GAFTA stipulate that 40 percent of the value added must originate from the region.

In reality, the existence of nontariff barriers and distorting measures undermine the effectiveness of the free-trade area. In particular, impediments that exist at the GAFTA level include the complexity and lack of clarity regarding tax and charge structures. These charges are extra duties imposed by countries above the usual tariff rates. The countries in this study that do not impose such charges include Bahrain, Kuwait, Oman, Qatar, and Saudi Arabia.

In May 2001 there emerged a vision for creating a Mediterranean Arab Free Trade Area between four Mediterranean Arab countries, namely Egypt, Jordan, Morocco, and Tunisia. MAFTA is to launch its first regional economic program in 2002, and is due to discuss rules on trade competition, measures to prevent monopolistic competition, and the formation of political institutions necessary for implementing the program. The Arab Maghreb Union was established in 1989, and comprises Algeria, Libya, Mauritania, Morocco, and Tunisia. The aim of the AMU is to coordinate macroeconomic policies and liberalize trade. However, it has been confronted with a number of political setbacks and has had little impact on intraregional trade flows.

The European Union's sheer economic weight, together with the legacy of colonial trading links, have encouraged Arab countries to seek avenues for maintaining or increasing trade ties with the EU, sometimes at the expense of subregional integration. The Euro-Mediterranean Partnership (EMP) arose from the 1995 Barcelona conference, and is a pact between the EU and seven Arab countries. The EMP intends to set a free-trade area between the EU and these countries by 2010. This would create a major market place for international trade. The dismantling of tariffs on EU products entering Arab countries will take place within a ten- to twelve-year transition period. So far, the free-trade area is in force for only four countries (Jordan, Morocco, the Palestinian Authority, and Tunisia). Other countries have signed the agreements but ratification by all fifteen member-states of the EU is pending. Libya has an observer status at certain meetings of the EMP, while Syria is a likely contender to becoming an observer.

Table 9. WTO Accession History and Status*

Bahrain	Member since January 1, 1995
Kuwait	Member since January 1, 1995
Morocco	Member since January 1, 1995
Tunisia	Member since March 29, 1995
Mauritania	Member since May 31, 1995
Egypt	Member since June 30, 1995
Qatar	Member since January 13, 1996
U.A.E.	Member since April 10, 1996
Jordan	Member since April 11, 2000
Oman	Member since November 9, 2000
Algeria	Working party established, June 17, 1987 (observer status)
Saudi Arabia	Working party established, July 21, 1993 (observer status)
Lebanon	Working party established, April 14, 1999 (observer status)
Yemen, Rep.	Working party established, July 17, 2000 (observer status)
Syrian AR	Formal request for accession filed on October 30, 2001
Libya	Formal request for accession filed on December 10, 2001

Source: World Trade Organization, (WTO) website www.wto.org
*As of July 2002

Findings from the Trade Performance Index

The composite rankings of the TPI capture the multifaceted dimensions of export performance and competitiveness. The rankings facilitate comparative assessments of export and import performance, benchmarking countries against structure and trends in world trade. The *current* TPI and the *change* TPI are therefore presented as a ranking compared to all other countries, with 1 being the most desirable position. How the rankings are calculated is outlined in Appendix 1 of this chapter.

The *current* TPI is comprised of five criteria: the value of net exports, per capita exports, the world market share, the diversification of products, and the diversification of markets. The first criterion, value of net exports (defined as exports less imports), is an important indicator for several reasons, but most important, because it shows the fact that a growing share of inputs for exports is imported and often belong to the same product category. The second criterion, per capita exports, is a significant indicator because it is independent of the size of the economy and reveals the degree of outward orientation of an economy as well as the per capita revenue derived

Table 10. Rankings: Current TPI and Change TPI*

Country	Minerals		Chemicals		Clothing		Textiles		Fresh Food		Processed Food		Basic Manufacturing	
	Current TPI	Change TPI	Current TPI	Change TPI	Current TPI	Change TPI	Current TPI	Change TPI	Current TPI	Change TPI	Current TPI	Change TPI	Current TPI	Change TPI
Number of Countries Ranked	137	137	123	123	114	114	107	107	163	163	139	139	127	127
Algeria	6	13	91	68	—	—	—	—	—	—	—	—	97	79
Bahrain	13	2	69	104	70	7	50	6	143	19	—	—	28	13
Egypt	81	106	82	103	75	78	33	107	86	102	95	132	78	60
Jordan	80	44	56	20	80	34	79	14	111	43	86	22	76	36
Kuwait	11	76	41	2	—	—	—	—	—	—	—	—	—	—
Lebanon	102	111	98	46	91	60	86	20	102	30	89	6	80	24
Libya	27	38	59	76	—	—	—	—	—	—	—	—	83	25
Mauritania	93	97	—	—	—	—	—	—	50	15	123	8	—	—
Morocco	73	35	66	91	15	1	69	74	35	61	57	53	73	35
Oman	74	129	88	48	86	96	92	37	113	70	94	78	94	58
Qatar	28	1	38	6	71	27	—	—	—	—	—	—	—	—
Saudi Arabia	7	53	16	52	—	—	—	—	—	—	—	—	62	42
Syrian AR	45	105	—	—	62	9	66	10	59	80	105	75	—	—
Tunisia	77	90	47	82	11	54	74	44	100	109	53	38	65	91
U.A.E.	10	25	46	31	42	18	44	43	56	9	61	1	44	30
Yemen, Rep.	46	49	—	—	—	—	—	—	137	151	—	—	—	—

* Based on year 2000 data
Source: International Trade Centre

The third criterion, share of world exports, complements per capita exports by taking an aggregated national approach and capturing the overall competitive position of the country under review. The fourth criterion, product diversification, reflects the sector's vulnerability to product-specific shocks in external markets, and is measured in terms of the equivalent number of products of equal value and by the spread of export markets. The fifth criterion is market diversification, and like the product diversification variable, is measured in terms of the equivalent target markets and the spread of export markets.

Table 10 shows *current* TPI rankings of the sixteen countries across fourteen sectors. Not surprisingly, the rankings reveal that the strongest performance of Arab world is in its minerals sector. None of the countries in the region, however, appear in the top five places in the minerals sector: the highest ranked, in descending order, are Algeria, Saudi Arabia, United Arab Emirates, and Bahrain at 6th, 7th, 10th and 13th, respectively.

Outside of the minerals sector, the *current* TPI rankings reveal lackluster trade performance. In all of the fourteen remaining sectors, there are only three cases when a country has received a rank higher than 30th place: Tunisia, 11th place in clothing; Morocco, 15th place also in clothing; and Saudi Arabia 16th place for chemicals. Notably, the rankings also reveal that for the rest of the sectors, the *current* TPI the countries are below the median ranking.

The *current* TPI also reveals the striking lack of diversification in the overall export structure of most countries. Eight of the sixteen countries have exports belonging to less than six sectors. Notably, the least diversified tend to be major oil-exporting countries: Yemen and Kuwait have exports belonging only to two sectors; while Algeria, Libya, and Qatar have exports belonging to only three sectors. Conversely, the nonmajor oil-exporting countries have relatively diversified export structures; Tunisia is the foremost example, with exports spanning all fourteen sectors (Table 11).

Like the *current* TPI, the *change* TPI is also based on five criteria, but focused on indicators depicting changes in export performance. The five criteria are: change in the world market share, change in the cover ratio (exports divided by imports), the level

Table 10. Rankings: Current TPI and Change TPI* (continued)

Country	Misc. Manufacturing		Non Electrical-Machinery		Electronic Components		Consumer Electronics		Transport Equipment		Leather Products		Wood Products	
	Current TPI	Change TPI	Current TPI	Change TPI	Current TPI	Change TPI	Current TPI	Change TPI	Current TPI	Change TPI	Current TPI	Change TPI	Current TPI	Change TPI
Number of Countries Ranked	122	122	95	95	90	90	66	66	83	83	85	85	110	110
Algeria	—	—	—	—	—	—	—	—	—	—	—	—	—	—
Bahrain	92	114	70	53	—	—	55	38	72	68	—	—	—	—
Egypt	74	103	—	—	—	—	—	—	—	—	71	85	—	—
Jordan	78	8	76	2	71	17	—	—	—	—	—	—	75	9
Kuwait	—	—	—	—	—	—	—	—	—	—	—	—	—	—
Lebanon	85	32	65	42	78	16	—	—	—	—	75	81	80	20
Libya	—	—	—	—	—	—	—	—	—	—	—	—	—	—
Mauritania	—	—	—	—	89	54	—	—	—	—	—	—	—	—
Morocco	90	34	—	—	53	1	—	—	73	55	36	55	69	13
Oman	83	79	78	7	72	37	52	44	48	65	—	—	—	—
Qatar	—	—	—	—	—	—	—	—	—	—	—	—	—	—
Saudi Arabia	87	74	75	24	—	—	—	—	—	—	—	—	—	—
Syrian AR	108	101	—	—	—	—	—	—	—	—	63	37	—	—
Tunisia	59	66	63	35	38	8	56	63	56	5	31	13	61	15
U.A.E.	46	60	46	27	—	—	29	46	35	46	—	—	—	—
Yemen, Rep.	—	—	—	—	—	—	—	—	—	—	—	—	—	—

* Based on year 2000 data
Source: International Trade Centre

Part 1 The Arab World in the Global Market: What the Trade Data Reveal

Table 11. Export Categories by Country (Percent of National Exports)*

	Algeria	Bahrain	Egypt	Jordan	Kuwait	Lebanon	Libya	Mauritania	Morocco	Oman	Qatar	Saudi Arabia	Syrian AR	Tunisia	U.A.E.	Yemen, Rep.
Minerals	98	49	37	14	96	24	95	43	11	59	93	92	81	14	81	95
Chemicals	1	6	5	26	3	9	3	—	12	3	5	6	—	11	2	—
Clothing	—	7	10	11	—	3	—	—	32	3	1	—	4	38	2	—
Textiles	—	3	14	3	—	1	—	—	2	1	—	—	3	3	1	—
Fresh food	—	0	17	11	—	14	—	53	17	4	—	—	9	3	1	3
Processed food	—	1	2	5	—	7	—	1	6	6	—	—	0	6	2	—
Basic manufacturing	0	28	11	7	—	10	1	—	3	4	—	1	—	3	4	—
Misc manufacturing	—	1	3	6	—	24	—	—	2	2	—	1	—	2	2	—
Non electrical machinery	—	1	—	4	—	3	—	—	—	3	—	1	—	1	—	—
Consumer electronics	—	1	—	—	—	—	—	—	—	3	—	—	—	1	2	—
Electronic components	—	—	—	3	—	2	—	0	10	2	—	—	—	11	0	—
Leather products	—	—	0	2	—	1	—	—	3	—	—	—	1	6	—	—
Transport equipment	—	1	—	—	—	—	—	—	0	10	—	—	—	1	1	—
Wood products	—	1	—	6	—	2	—	—	2	—	—	—	—	1	—	—
Number of Export Sectors	3	12	9	12	2	12	3	4	12	12	3	5	6	14	11	2
Percent of Trade Captured	99	99	99	99	99	97	100	98	99	100	99	99	97	100	97	98

* Based on year 2000 data; marginal world market shares (<0.5%) are not displayed
Source: International Trade Centre

of specialization in dynamic products, change in product diversification, and the change in market diversification.

The first criterion, change in world market share, shows to what extent countries are gaining or losing in global markets. To calculate the percentage change in market share, it is divided into four elements; their total is the total change in world market share. The first element, the competitiveness effect, records gains in market share caused by increased competitiveness. It is calculated as the change in the exporting country's share in target-market imports multiplied by the initial share of the partner countries' imports in world trade. The second element, initial geographic specialization, measures the benefits associated with the initial specialization of domestic exports on dynamic markets and is calculated as the initial market share of the exporting country in partner countries, multiplied by the change in the share of partner countries in world trade. The third element, initial product specialization, captures the benefits associated with the initial sector specialization of the exporting country on products facing a dynamic demand. And the fourth element, the adaptation effect, captures the ability to adjust the supply of exports to changes in world demand. The ranking for the change in market share is calculated as the simple average of the rankings for these four items.

The second criterion is the trend in the coverage of imports by exports. This

Kuwait's export performance for its leading exports, crude petroleum oils and petroleum gases, is mostly in line with world market growth. Its other exports, however, such as noncrude petroleum oils, have shown much stronger growth, reflecting the expansion of the country's refining capacities. Other dynamic export groups include petrochemicals and plastics; these show strong development in recent years and the international demand for them is very dynamic in volume terms.

Unlike Kuwait, Libya is underperforming relative to the world export growth of its largest export groups, crude petroleum exports, noncrude petroleum exports, and petroleum gases. Crude oil is by far Libya's major export item, with noncrude oil and petroleum gases together accounting for around 15 percent of crude oil exports. Dynamic export groups include primarily petrochemicals, such as acyclic hydrocarbons and plastics (polymers of ethylene). These have shown strong development in recent years and international demand for them is very dynamic in volume terms. However, like Kuwait, the export turnover generated by these sectors remains modest.

As has the United Arab Emirates, Oman positioned itself as a major re-export platform. The corresponding national export portfolios should, therefore, be interpreted carefully since many products, such as vehicles, consumer electronics, or machinery are not produced locally but are only moving through the country. Oman hardly has any strong outperformers except for exports of noncrude petroleum oils, which have grown at the rate of 39 percent per annum. However, export of refined petroleum products only account for 4 percent of crude oil exports. The latter have kept pace with world market growth. Oman has also several exports (and re-exports) that are doing well in declining markets, such as cigarettes, wheat and meslin flour, palm oil, milk powder, and air conditioning units.

Qatar has posted a strong export performance in the oil sectors, with its three largest export groups outpacing world export growth. Specifically, Qatar's exports of crude petroleum oils, petroleum gases, and noncrude petroleum oils have registered growth rates of 18 percent, 76 percent and 13 percent per annum, respectively. Other champion products include clothing, specifically pullovers and women's clothing, and petrochemicals. Qatar's achievers in adversity include its fifth leading export, chemical fertilizers. Qatar also has underperformers in declining export markets, such as other bars and rods of iron.

Saudi Arabia's exports of crude petroleum oils have slightly outperformed the world market. And like many other Arab countries, the country's exports of petrochemicals such as cyclic hydrocarbons have also grown rapidly. But Saudi Arabia's exports of noncrude petroleum oils, however, have been stagnating and export performance remains mixed. Sectors and products of showing export underperformance are polymers and ethylene, which has contracted by 10 percent per annum, and insulated cables, a high-growth sector with international trade growing at 8 percent per year. Saudi Arabia has also an important number of achievers in adversity such as plastics, chemicals, and fruit and vegetable juices. It also has a few losers in declining markets, such as chemical fertilizers and sodium hydroxide.

Syria is losing its market share in crude petroleum, which is its leading export product. Increases in market share are, however, registered for refined petroleum oils, whose exports still account for less than 10 percent of crude petroleum exports. As opposed to most Arab oil-exporting countries, Syria has not developed export activities in petrochemicals and plastics. Its non-oil exports account for 20 percent of total exports, and are mainly distributed in the achievers in adversity quadrant. The cotton sector (cotton lint, yarn, sewing, and waste) has demonstrated remarkable export performance in an adverse context. Other achievers in adversity include calcium phosphates, women's clothing, vegetables, aluminum structures, and sheep leather. Apart from refined petroleum oils, Syria export champions are limited to pullovers, men's clothing, and electric transformers.

In terms of trade performance and specialization, the United Arab Emirates is a special case in the Arab world because of the differences in factor endowments and the trade development strategies in the different Emirates (Box 4). Dubai, for instance, has become the major regional re-exporting center. The United Arab Emirates has registered relatively lackluster growth in its largest export, crude petroleum oils, but export performance of its other major exports, such as petroleum gases, noncrude petroleum oils, and unwrought aluminum, have significantly outpaced world growth.

Yemen's largest mineral export groups have outpaced world export growth: its crude oil exports have grown by 9 percent per annum, and noncrude petroleum oil exports have expanded by 21.0 percent. Like Syria,

criterion assesses the ability of exporters in the sector to increase the sectoral trade surplus or reduce the deficit of exports over imports. The third criterion is specialization in the most dynamic products within a sector; this measures the specialization in products for which world demand is rapidly growing. The fourth criterion is the change in product diversification, which is measured as the average annual variation in the number of equivalent exports products and the spread of export products. The fifth and last criterion is the change in market diversification, which is measured as the average annual variation in the number of equivalent export markets and the spread of target markets.

The results of the *change* TPI, as depicted in Table 10, show that for the minerals sector the results are, at best, mixed. While Qatar is ranked 1st in the world and Bahrain 2nd, other major exporters like Saudi Arabia are ranked 53rd, denoting the deterioration of the latter's export performance in the minerals sector over the last five years.

Although there have been very poor *change* TPI scores in nearly all sector groups (barring the minerals sector), there are a few notable exceptions that suggest dramatic improvements over the last five years in export performance and competitiveness in certain export sectors. Morocco, for instance, is ranked number 1 in both the clothing and electronics sectors, and the United Arab Emirates is number 1 in the processed food sector. Kuwait is 2nd in the chemicals sector, and Bahrain is 2nd in wood products and 3rd in textiles. Jordan is 2nd in nonelectrical machinery and 8th for miscellaneous manufacturing, while Lebanon is 6th in processed food, and Syria is 9th in clothing. Finally, Tunisia is 5th in transport and 8th in electronic components, while Yemen is 15th in the fresh food sector. These significantly high *change* TPI ranks, particularly in non-oil sectors, confirm promising improvements in export performance.

Disaggregating the *change* TPI rankings to focus on changes in market share at the product level bears important findings to the question: how is the country's export performance relative to the changes in international demand? Specifically, is the country exporting in growing markets or declining markets? Moreover, is the country able to keep pace with market growth or is it falling behind? Based on average annual percentage growth of export values over the 1996 to 2000 period, country export performance relative to international demand fall into any one of four categories: winners in growth markets, losers in growth

markets, winners in declining market[...] declining markets.

The performance of oil exporting cou[...]

Petroleum oil can be considered a high [...] over the 1996 to 2000 period; during th[...] world trade grew by 7 percent on averag[...] However, because oil prices are volatile, [...] in oil fluctuates significantly. Consequen[...] accurate to look at changes in internatior[...] volume terms; in this respect, oil would b[...] moderate-growth sector. Indeed, internati[...] in volume terms of crude oil is rather stabl[...] at 1 percent per year on average. Trade in [...] petroleum has been more dynamic, with in[...] demand volumes growing at 4.3 percent pe[...]

Among oil-exporting countries, only a few [...] countries have managed to decrease their [...] on oil (see Box 4). Algeria's achievements i[...] diversification are very limited. It has expan[...] its petroleum sector to the extent that expor[...] crude petroleum oils, petroleum gases, and [...] petroleum oils have expanded faster than th[...] in international demand. Growth in exports [...] petrochemicals has recently accelerated, alth[...] export turnover had been very low at the start[...] Prospects for export diversification remain pr[...] in view of the recent trade liberalization, such [...] the elimination of importers' professional crite[...] requirements and the expected free-trade agree[...] under the EU's EMP, which will open the way fo[...] increased economic assistance and privileged ac[...] for Algerian goods.

Like Algeria, Bahrain's export performance has al[...] exceeded the growth in international demand for [...] its two largest exports: noncrude petroleum oil and[...] crude petroleum oils. Bahrain exports more refine[...] petroleum than crude oil; moreover, it imports [...] significant volumes of crude oil that is refined local[...] and mostly re-exported, demonstrating that develop[...] countries can also have value added in petroleum. [...] Bahrain's export success is not limited to petroleum [...] oils. The country is one of the major global players [...] in aluminum (unwrought and processed), with a 1[...] percent market share in aluminum bars, rods, and [...] profiles. (However, over the 1996 to 2000 period, [...] Bahrain's exporters have lost their market share in [...] aluminum bars.) Bahrain is also an active exporter [...] in other sectors such as clothing (exports have more [...] than doubled in the last five years), textiles, fertilizer[...] (in spite of shrinking international demand), plastics[...] paper and paperboard, and seafood.

Yemen does not export petrochemicals and plastics, and its non-oil exports are limited to unprocessed agricultural commodities such as coffee, bananas, cotton, live animals, fish, and crustaceans. For most of these commodities, Yemen is gaining world market share in an adverse context.

Performance of nonmajor oil exporters

Egypt's trade performance varies significantly across sectors, doing well in low-growth sectors and less well in high-growth sectors. Oil still accounts for more than one-third of total exports, but crude oil exports have declined significantly in recent years. Champion products include marble as well as miscellaneous clothing such as pullovers. Egypt has a large number of achievers, such as carbon, aluminum plate, fertilizers, cotton, rice and clothing and apparel that are performing well in adverse markets. The tourism industry is another pillar of the economy, generating usually as much income as total merchandise exports. However, the performance of the tourism industry is highly volatile, depending strongly on political stability in the region and on Western tourists' perception of the country.

Jordan has one of the most diversified export portfolios among Arab countries (see Box 4). The corresponding "bubble chart" shows a predominance of champions and declining sectors, which is an atypical pattern for a developing country (they usually have more achievers in adversity and underachievers). Champion export products include bulk medicament, dosage medicament, and women's clothing. Losers in declining markets include chemical fertilizers, which is the country's largest export product group, and cement.

Lebanon has a diversified export portfolio both in terms of product and performance. They have a slight predominance of achievers in adversity. Champion export products include aluminum bars, furniture, car seats, t-shirts, insulated cables, and electric transformers. Lebanon has several remarkable export performers in declining markets. For instance, the country's exports of diphosphorous pentaoxide, tobacco, fruits, wine, books, sugar confectionery, and raw hides have been gaining market share in an adverse context. Underperformers in high-growth sectors include pullovers and aluminum waste and scrap. Lebanon also has several losers in declining markets, such as ferrous and copper waste and scrap, phosphatic fertilizers, and grapes.

Globally, Mauritania has been maintaining its world market share for its two leading export sectors: iron ores and seafood. Those two sectors are characterized by low-growth in international demand, explaining the global decline of Mauritania's share in world trade. In terms of seafood exports, the country's performance is mixed, outperforming the world market in the exports of fresh fish, fish fillets, and smoked fish, but underperforming in the exports of frozen fish and mollusks. Mauritania is also exporting fertilizers and fish flour in small amounts. Both products are also characterized by a low-growth in international demand.

Morocco is notable among the countries in the Arab world for showing an increase in market share in most of its export products, resulting in an overall export growth of 15 percent per year over the 1996 to 2000 period against 4.5 percent for world exports in the same period. Champion products include refined petroleum oils, transistors, insulated cable, wood pulp, and several clothing items such as t-shirts, women's clothing, and pullovers. Other exports of Morocco that are performing relatively well in adverse markets are mollusks, chemical exports, clothing items, and tomatoes. Like Tunisia, the major problem faced by the Moroccan economy is its reliance on imported raw materials used in its major exporting industries. Consequently, any expansion in its exports implies a rise in its imports; this partly explains Morocco's persistent trade deficit. In the medium run, the erosion of preferential market access in the EU in textiles and clothing is also a major concern for Morocco (Box 1).

Like Morocco, Tunisia now has one the most diversified export portfolios in the Arab world. Twenty-five years ago, Tunisia exported predominantly raw materials (oil and mining products). Tunisia's achievements in export diversification are discussed in detailed in Box 4. Like Morocco, Tunisia has a predominance of champions and achievers in adversity. There are, however, numerous underperformers, such as petroleum products and clothing items, which explain the overall decrease of Tunisia's world market share.

Findings From the Executive Opinion Survey

While it is most useful in assessing trade performance using quantitative data, the TPI does not capture the qualitative aspects of trade performance. By revealing the perceptions of key business leaders in the region, the Executive Opinion Survey fills this gap, providing a qualitative assessment of the respective operating environments as it affects their trade performance. This section analyzes the findings of

Box 4. Product Diversification

The Arab countries are remarkably heterogeneous in terms of economic strategy and export diversification. In Gulf countries, petrochemicals dominate economic activity. As shown in the different national export portfolios of GCC countries, hydrocarbons account for a substantial share of their exports. Crude oil is not the only product exported, with liquefied natural gas and refined petroleum products registering major growth in most GCC countries.

Within the GCC, Oman and the United Arab Emirates have positioned themselves as major re-export platforms. Hence, the corresponding national export portfolios should be interpreted carefully since many products, such as rice, vehicles, or consumer electronics, are not produced locally but only pass through the country.

The profile of the different emirates is very interesting and appears symptomatic to what happens in the Arab world as a region. Since oil resources are unequally distributed among the different emirates, each emirate has pursued different trade development strategies. Oil-rich Abu Dhabi has focused its strategy on the development of the hydrocarbon sector and has invested a large proportion of its revenue from oil exports into assets held overseas. In an effort to diversify its foreign exchange earnings, Abu Dhabi has established a number of free-trade zones (FTZs), targeted at financial services and real estate. The emirate of Dubai, which lacks resources in hydrocarbons, has opted for the development of transportation, telecommunications, and trade services. Dubai is the region's largest re-export center and is continuously expanding its shipping capacities. The United Arab Emirates has the highest number of Internet users in the region, and the recent development of the Dubai Internet City has been highly successful, attracting many Internet startups as well as large information technology companies such as Microsoft, Oracle, or Hewlett Packard. Dubai had also been successful in developing trade zones. By the end of 2000, around 2,000 businesses were located in the Jebel Ali FTZ across a wide range of industries. Examples of foreign companies operating in the FTZs include Daimler Chrysler, Goodyear, and Bayer. Companies located in FTZs are taking advantage of the local market as well as regional markets such as Saudi Arabia, Bahrain, and Oman. Food products (such as frozen meat, vegetable preparations, and soybean cake), paper articles, chemicals, iron and steel, and electrical and electronic products are primarily oriented toward the local market, and constitute examples of successful import substitution strategies. These examples may serve as reference points for the new free zones established in other

emirates, such as Ajman, Fujairah, Sharjah, Umm al-Qaiwain, and Ras al-Khaimah, but also to other zones in development in the Arab world.

Chemicals represent an area where the United Arab Emirates has developed competitive advantage and where it is exporting to global markets. In particular, exports of plastics, ether, perfumes, and soaps have been following an upward trend in recent years, while the recent production facilities of Bayer (pharmaceuticals) in Jebel Ali will significantly broaden supply capacities and expand the range of products.

In North Africa, there is a more prominent manufacturing sector. Tunisia undoubtedly has one the most diversified export portfolios in the Arab world. Twenty-five years ago, Tunisia exported predominantly raw materials (oil and mining products). Today, Tunisia exports manufactured goods and processed goods and has also developed a successful tourism industry. Textiles and apparel (in particular jeans) are the main export items and have shown the most impressive growth in recent years. (Potential risks arising from the liberalization of textiles and clothing in the medium term are highlighted in Box 1.) Exports of electrical and mechanical equipment have become increasingly important, accounting for 11.5 percent of its exports in 2000. Other major export items include shoes and leather goods, chemicals, fertilizers, and olive oil. The major problem faced by the Tunisian economy is its reliance on imported raw materials used in its major exporting industries. Textiles, leather, mechanical and electrical industries both transform raw and semiprocessed imports into finished products for re-export. Consequently, any expansion in its exports implies a rise in its imports; this partly explains the country's persistent trade deficit. Another challenge facing the Tunisian manufacturing industry is the upgrading of its entire infrastructure in order to meet the challenge of competing with European and advanced economies. This process was launched following the signing of the Association Agreement with the EU in 1995, which will lead to free bilateral trade in industrial goods by 2008. Firms undertaking the program have seen promising results so far, with their turnover increasing by 15 percent, exports by 13 percent, and their staff base by 6.6 percent. This modernization process implies new equipment, reorganizing production systems, staff training, and implementing quality controls. These upgrades are very costly, and most of the domestic investment originally envisaged for them has not reached government targets.

East Mediterranean-based Arab countries have large manufacturing sectors, and services constitute a major source of foreign exchange earnings. Jordan's exports appear to be relatively well diversified in comparison to most Arab countries. Since the 1980s debt crisis, successive Jordanian governments have attempted to alter the legislative regime to promote private sector investment. Tourism-related services are the country's main income source. The downturn in tourist arrivals from Western (and Asian) countries post-September 11 was largely compensated by an increased influx of tourists from Arab countries. Further, the chemical, pharmaceutical, and textile industries have benefited from stronger regional demand. In addition, oil exploration is being actively undertaken, and in the long run, the country could become a net exporter of hydrocarbons. Notably, the pharmaceutical sector is one of the success stories of Jordan's industrial development, recording more than US$150 million in export revenues in 2000. Apart from pharmaceuticals, private investment is concentrated in light manufacturing, such as food processing, consumer goods, construction materials, and textiles.

East Asian investors have recently been active in the development of a qualifying industrial zone, which allow goods, currently predominantly textiles, duty-free access to the United States provided that 8 percent of the value added is produced in Israel. In the medium-term, prospects for textiles and apparel are not very promising (see Box 1). Jordan's trade performance across all sectors depends strongly on the political climate in neighboring Iraq, Israel, and Palestine. Prior to 1990, Iraq used to be Jordan's main export market. In addition, the political tensions in Israel and Palestine are perceived as an important risk by foreign investors. For example the Aqaba special economic zone, launched in January 2001, is an ambitious project, which has not yet attracted much investment, in spite of many expressions of interest from foreign firms. The free trade agreement with the United States came into effect on December 2001, and is expected to boost trade to that country. Jordan is the fourth country after Canada, Mexico, and Israel to benefit from such an agreement with the United States.

the AWCR Executive Opinion Survey, and compares the results with that of the GCR Executive Opinion Survey, which was conducted a few months earlier, from February to June of 2001. While the results are not directly comparable given the differences in time periods of the surveys, juxtaposing the results reveals an estimation of the likely ranking of Arab world countries among the countries included in the GCR. This gives a sense of the competitive position of the countries in the global economy (more details are in Part 3: The Executive Opinion Survey).

While the Executive Opinion Survey contains over a hundred items that span a range of macroeconomic and microeconomic competitiveness issues, several items are particularly relevant in depicting the operating environments of exporting companies. The selected survey items discussed below are particularly instructive in highlighting the policy challenges that need to be addressed. A rank of 1 indicates the most competitive position.

On the survey item about the ease of obtaining a loan with only a good business plan and no collateral, most countries in the Arab world scored below the sample mean for the GCR countries, with the exception of Bahrain. When asked whether in the past year obtaining credit for the company has become more difficult, Egypt posted the worst score in the region, in both the GCR and the AWCR surveys.

On the issue of whether government subsidies artificially keep uncompetitive businesses alive, or at best, improve the productivity of industries, four countries would have made it in the top ten of the combined sample: Oman, Qatar, Tunisia, and the United Arab Emirates, occupying the 5th, 6th, 7th, and 8th slots, respectively. Lebanon, however, would have placed near the bottom, ranking 72nd out of eighty-three countries.

Regarding the question of whether government officials are neutral or whether they favor well-connected firms and individuals when deciding upon policies and contracts, Saudi Arabia and Lebanon would have ranked poorly, at 72nd and 73rd places, respectively. Both countries would have also fared among the worst on the issue of whether unfair or corrupt activities of other firms impose costs on the respondent's firm: Lebanon and Saudi Arabia would have ranked 61st and 64th, respectively. Lebanon, moreover, has the worst score in the region on the question of the frequency of which firms make irregular extra payments or bribes connected with import and export permits. In terms of hidden import barriers (i.e., barriers other than published tariffs and quotas), Egypt has the worst score in the region on both surveys.

In terms of the regulatory burden to business, the United Arab Emirates and Bahrain would have been among the top ten countries in this criterion, at 4th and 6th places, respectively. It is notable that both Saudi Arabia and Lebanon ranked very near the bottom, with the latter being ranked last and given the worst assessment of eighty-three countries. Significantly, when respondents were asked how much time the senior management of the company spends working with government agencies, three Arab world countries also placed very near the bottom of the list: Kuwait is in 77th place; Saudi Arabia, in 80th; and Tunisia, in 82nd place.

Remarkably, the findings of a survey included in the recent study by Hoekman and Messerlin (2002) corroborate our survey results. The Hoekman and Messerlin study highlights problems of bureaucracy and red tape, citing that nontariff related trading costs average 10 percent of the value of goods shipped and that the average company spends ninety-five days of labor per year resolving problems with customs and other government officials. Moreover, the study authors note that although the average payment associated with customs clearance reported by respondents is only around 1 percent of the value of shipments, one-fifth of the managers report paying between 2 and 17 percent.

Regarding the ease and facility of starting a new business, several countries in the Arab world also fared poorly. When respondents were asked about the typical number of days required to start a new firm in the country, the average response from Saudi Arabia was 109.4 days, the longest time of all; the combined sample had a mean of 40.2 days. Oman, Kuwait, and Lebanon also fared poorly at 73rd, 74th, and 76th places, respectively. In terms of the number of permits to start a firm, the average cited by respondents from Kuwait is 14.7 permits, placing the country at the very bottom of the combined sample, which had a mean of 4.2 permits.

These results pertaining to entry regulations are strikingly similar to the findings of the World Bank's "Doing Business" database (Table 12), which covers ten of the sixteen countries of the Arab world.[10] As in the findings of the Executive Opinion Surveys, the World Bank cited that it takes ninety-nine days to start a firm in Saudi Arabia, the longest time in the region. Next to Saudi Arabia in this regard is Jordan, where it takes ninety days, eighteen times longer than it takes to start a firm in the United States.

Table 12. Entry Regulations

Country	Number of Procedures	Duration (Days)	Cost (US$)	Cost (Percent of GDP Per Capita)
Algeria	18	29	559.16	35
Egypt	13	52	908.40	61
Jordan	14	90	806.48	47
Lebanon	6	46	4,596.79	115
Morocco	13	76	216.85	18
Saudi Arabia	13	99	10,799.98	149
Syrian AR	10	42	161.06	17
Tunisia	9	57	438.63	21
U.A.E.	10	29	4,982.64	18
Yemen, Rep.	13	13	811.39	219
United States	5	5	210.00	1

Source: World Bank website, "Doing Business," http://rru.worldbank.org/DoingBusiness/default/aspx

Improving the Trade Performance of the Arab World

The findings of the Executive Opinion Surveys, combined with the results of the TPI, reveal that there have been, to varying degrees, improvements in the trade performance of the countries in the Arab world. However, significant challenges remain, and these need to be addressed if the region is to transition to higher levels of development. In particular, two policy imperatives emerge: the urgency to improve the operating environment for exporting companies in the immediate to near term (highlighted by the findings of the Executive Opinion Surveys); and the longstanding challenge of diversifying into higher value-added exports and gaining increasing shares of markets that are not only expanding, but also have room for substantial productivity growth (from the results of the TPI).

For the near term, the task is to provide a competitive and supportive operating environment for exporters. This task requires improvements on four fronts: trade facilitation, trade-related infrastructure, access to trade finance, and provision of marketing assistance.

Efforts to improve trade facilitation are, to a large degree, about reducing transaction costs and turnaround time. Trade facilitation involves the streamlining and harmonizing of overall trade procedures, including customs. While there are multilateral initiatives to harmonize and streamline procedures, individual governments need to invest in building capacity, upgrading technology, and simplifying customs and transport procedures—for these, investments will ultimately redound to cost savings and enhanced trade performance. Regulatory burdens need to be assessed to ensure no overlap and to eliminate any unintended distortions. Red tape must be eliminated or minimized, and as much relevant information as possible must be given to exporting companies regarding trade regulations of other countries and the respective customs procedures. The latter, in addition to providing useful information, also addresses the concerns that may prevail regarding a lack of transparency and clarity with the requirements.

Governments must also increase investments so as to improve trade-related infrastructure such as roads, ports, airports, and loading and storage facilities. The latter is particularly important to the exporters of agricultural products, where considerable losses are often incurred from spoilage and damage in the course of transport. Unless it is addressed, poor and suboptimal infrastructure will continue to increase costs and cause unnecessary delays, thereby putting local exporters at an immediate disadvantage against their competitors in other countries. Indeed, for many developing countries there are tremendous gains to be had from improving transport and handling alone.

In terms of access to finance, governments need to assist exporters, particularly those with small and medium enterprises, because they often do not have the resources to increase their scale of trading transactions. Access to credit must be available and, equally important, it must also be at a reasonable rate. Jordan is a useful case in this regard, as the country has initiated several facilities that will improve access to trade finance; for example, a low-interest financing facility for selected exports, a loan guarantee corporation, and an export and finance bank.

The fourth and last task in the immediate term is the provision of marketing assistance. Although many countries have trade promotion agencies that assist exporters, the breadth of services offered need to be broadened in order to address critical areas of improvement, such as quality control. More important, and beyond providing trade support services, governments should take the lead in improving the country's image and increasing its visibility overseas. It is becoming more common for governments of emerging markets to undertake international road shows to meet with prospective foreign investors.

In the longer term, improving trade performance in the region requires a continual upgrading of exports. This task entails building upon current trading advantages and increasing shares in existing markets. It also requires investing in human resource development and encouraging foreign direct investment so as to enable entry and penetration of new and dynamic markets.

The task of export diversification to higher value-added goods and services is perhaps the most important trade policy challenge facing policymakers in the Arab world. Several countries in the region, such as the United Arab Emirates, have already embarked on diversification of their economy and an upgrading of its exports (Box 4). But as the TPI analysis reveals, the export structure of the region as a whole is still primarily based either on its absolute advantage in petroleum products, as in the case of the major oil-producing countries like Kuwait and Qatar, or on its comparative advantage in labor-intensive manufactures, as in the case of Morocco and Tunisia.

While the resource-rich countries have been served well, in varying degrees, by basing their trade advantage solely on factor endowments, such a strategy is not the most optimal over the long-term. Trading based on advantages in resource endowments leads to depletion of natural resources. It also leaves a country vulnerable to the vagaries of the commodities markets. Many Arab world countries can attest to this; they each have experienced volatile oil-price movements that reverberate throughout the economy, leading to unpredictable government finances, balance of payments, and overall growth prospects. Basing trade advantages solely on low-cost labor is also not advisable in the long-term, because cheap labor does not necessarily lead to higher levels of productivity, and higher levels of productivity are critical if higher standards of living are to be achieved and sustained.

The task, however, does not necessarily entail a shift away from resource-based exports; but rather, it requires building on current strengths and expanding the current export portfolio. This is an important clarification, because resource-based exports do not necessarily have to be low-value added exports. According to a recent World Bank study: "Natural resource-based activities can be knowledge-industries. Mining was the 'national learning experience' in the United States that led to building a strong technological system from which modern manufacturing developed" (Ferranti et al. 2002:4). The study further cites supporting evidence from the development history of other natural resource-rich developed countries, such as Australia, Finland, and Sweden, emphasizing how these economies continue to be significant net exporters of natural resource-based products, along with high-tech products.

As demonstrated by the experience of these natural resource-rich developed countries, the Arab world must strive to shift to higher value added exports. Otherwise, the region will have great difficulty in making the transition to higher levels of development. To achieve higher rates of growth, the region needs to shift from trading on advantages based primarily upon factor endowments towards trading based more on unique products and processes; this entails competing not solely on low prices made possible by low-cost inputs, but instead, competing on quality and innovation. The latter requires improved productivity, which is the ability to obtain more output from given inputs, usually achieved by upgrading technology and improving the efficiency of the use and allocation of resources. Improved productivity is essential if countries are to meet the challenge of gaining increasing shares in dynamically expanding markets.

The question of how the region can diversify its exports, producing high value products and services that meet the test of world markets, remains. For the Arab world region, successful export diversification requires a long-term strategy anchored on two pillars: the promotion of domestic entrepreneurship, and, the encouragement of foreign direct investment (and further integration into the international production system).

The task of promoting entrepreneurial dynamism in the region requires creating an environment that fosters enough freedom to allow entrepreneurs to seize opportunities. The environment must also have enough stability to lend confidence as well as a degree of predictability that will facilitate long-term investment decision making. The environment must also have enough flexibility for new companies to enter and expand, and for inefficient companies to contract or go out of business. Indeed, entrepreneurship flourishes best in environments that allow market forces to work,[12] and in this regard, the pervasive role of the state needs to be examined in several economies in the region.

One of the most direct and effective ways to promote entrepreneurship is to ease the process of registering a new business. This is particularly relevant in the Arab world, as the results of the Executive Opinion

Surveys indicate. What is implied, but not captured in the responses to the Surveys, is the cost associated with registering a new business. The World Bank has calculated this cost, and the data reveal hefty costs of business registration in several countries in the region. Based on data from the World Bank, Saudi Arabia imposes the highest costs, in the order of US$10,780, or 149 percent of the GNP per capita. This figure is in stark contrast with the United States, where business registration costs US$210, equivalent to only 0.69% percent of GNP per capita (Table 12).

The other pillar, the promotion of foreign direct investment, addresses the region's weak integration in the international production system outside of the oil industry. As noted in a recent study of regional trade, most countries in the Arab world do not produce intermediate inputs that are sold on world markets (Hoekman and Messerlin 2002). Moreover, the region has also received only a small fraction of global investment flows relative to other regions, which is a source of concern because foreign direct investment, in particular, serves as one of the most effective vehicles for linking a country with the international trading and production systems (Table 13).

An outward orientation to both international trade and investment is absolutely essential if the Arab world is to close its productivity gap and increase its share of international trade and investment flows. Only by opening itself to the flow of goods and services, skills, and capital can the region receive the necessary technologies that will allow it to improve upon its use of its resources. While the region can also develop indigenous technology through its own research and development efforts, such initiatives require a long-term outlook, and entail significant risk and diversion of resources from other development priorities. Moreover, empirical studies have demonstrated that a country achieves the fastest rates growth by adapting technologies—copying, reverse engineering, and innovating upon existing technologies (McArthur and Sachs 2002).

One of the direct ways that the region can increase its integration in the global production system is further trade liberalization. The Gulf countries already have relatively low tariff rates, but the recent study by the Council on Foreign Relations reveals that tariffs, both unweighted and applied, are still very high in relative terms (Hoekman and Messerlin 2002). The average unweighted tariff rates in non-Gulf states may have fallen to 19.3 percent from the 1978—1980 level of 29.6 percent, but even at the

Table 14. Tariff Levels (in Percent)

Country	Year	All Products	Primary Products		Manufactured Products	
		Simple mean tariff	Simple mean tariff	Weighted mean tariff	Simple mean tariff	Weighted mean tariff
Algeria	1998	24.6	18.1	14.6	25.4	18.7
Egypt	1998	20.5	22.5	7.5	20.2	17.5
Jordan	2000	22.8	26.2	16.9	22.3	19.8
Lebanon	2000	17.9	23.9	24.3	16.9	16.0
Libya	1996	27.3	24.8	9.6	27.7	25.7
Morocco	2000	33.6	42.4	27.1	32.3	25.3
Oman	1997	4.8	4.0	3.1	4.9	5.0
Saudi Arabia	2000	12.3	11.9	7.9	12.4	10.9
Tunisia	1998	30.0	28.7	21.2	30.2	30.2

Source: World Development Indicators Database, 2002

reduced rate it is still higher than the average tariff rate of all other regions in the world, with the sole exception of south Asia (Table 14). Average customs duty collected is also high at 10 to 15 percent of the value of imports. In addition, nontariff barriers, such as quotas, subsidies, technical product standards, and licensing requirements are also prevalent. For several countries, import licenses are only granted to local residents, or in some cases, to foreign investors with local joint venture partners—such restrictions discourage foreign investment.

Since higher value-added exports tend to require importation of inputs, as well as machinery and equipment, import restrictions—both tariff and nontariff—must be reviewed and eventually minimized. While local producers may clamor for protection and customs duties may comprise a significant source of government revenue, tariff and nontariff barriers will eventually have to be reduced in the longer-term, as countries abide by their commitments to multilateral and bilateral trade agreements and prepare local producers for the pressures of greater competition.

Policymakers also need to have a more pro-investment stance. Beyond incentives and one-stop processing centers and free-trade zones, the government must also focus on the quality of its respective public institutions and legal systems, as well as its macroeconomic and political environment. In particular, governments must be prudent in its use of resources, taking care not to crowd out business access to finance and raise the cost of borrowing. It is also important that governments

implement the necessary structural reforms in order to minimize distortions in the economy, allowing the price mechanism to serve its signaling function in allocating resources.

Finally, and perhaps most importantly, policymakers must focus on labor and education policies in order to encourage foreign investment and diversify export portfolios. After all, the level of skill and education in the labor force ultimately determines the ability to absorb, use, transform, and innovate upon the technologies that are either developed locally, or harnessed from the international production system. Although the yields on investment in education are fairly long-term, it is imperative that governments allocate sufficient resources in the immediate term, because only by enhancing human resources can a country truly sustain higher levels of development.

Conclusion

This assessment of the trade performance of the Arab world reveals that despite signs of progress in overall regional trade performance, many fundamental challenges remain. The *current* TPI shows that most of the economies rank highest in the world in trade from the minerals sector, reflecting a prevailing resource-based orientation. In the nonminerals sectors, most of the economies rank highest in the chemicals and clothing sectors, the latter emphasizing the comparative advantage of many of the economies in labor-intensive manufactures. Meanwhile, the *change* TPI puts a more positive cast to the inroads being made in certain sectors, such as electronics and electronic components.

The findings of the TPI analysis, combined with the results of the Executive Opinion Surveys reveal that for the region to improve its trade performance and achieve higher levels of development, it must address two imperatives: enhancing the operating environment for exporters in the immediate to near term; and, in the medium- to long-term, building on its current trading advantages in order to diversify into higher value-added exports and gain increasing shares of markets that are not only expanding, but that also have room for substantial productivity growth.

The enhancement of the trading environment entails a focus on facilitating trade, enhancing trade-related infrastructure, improving access to trade finance, and providing marketing assistance. The other imperative, the need to upgrade existing exports and expand into new markets, entails a two-pronged strategy: one focused on promoting domestic entrepreneurship, and the other focused on encouraging foreign direct investment. Underpinning both imperatives is the need for macroeconomic and political stability, high-functioning public institutions and legal systems and, perhaps most important, investments in human resource development focusing on education and labor skills development.

For the Arab world, trade has played and continues to play, a vital role in its economy. Our analysis of the trade data reveals that the region has great potential to improve upon its trade performance by building upon its resource-based strengths and continuing its efforts to diversify and upgrade into higher-value added activities. Given its endowments, the region's development prospects look promising, but for the region to fully seize the benefits of trade and unleash its growth potential, it must pursue reforms.

References

Allum, P. "Intra-Arab Trade: Constraints and Prospects." Paper presented at the Sectoral Meeting on Trade and Development between the League of Arab States and the United Nations, Cairo. 8–11 June 1998.

Al-Atrash, H., and Yousef T. "Intra-Arab Trade: Is it Too Little?" IMF Working Paper no. WP/00/10. 2000.

Chaponnière J.-R. "Les Enjeux du Secteur Textile-habillement en Méditerranée." Information Economique, Direction des Relations Economiques Extérieures de la France, 2002.

Cornelius, P.K., F. von Kirchbach, M. Mimouni, J-M. Pasteels, S. Phadke. "Sectoral Trade Performance." *In Global Competitiveness Report 2001–2002.* New York: World Economic Forum; Oxford University Press, 2002.

de Ferranti, D., G. Perry, D. Lederman, William F. Maloney. *From Natural Resources to the Knowledge Economy: Trade and Job Quality.* Washington, D.C.: World Bank, 2002.

Economic and Social Commission for Western Asia. *Survey of Economic and Social Developments in the ESCWA Region.* New York: ESCWA, 2001.

El-Erian, M. Fischer S. "Is MENA a Region? The Scope for Regional Integration." IMF Working Paper no. 96/30. 1996.

El-Naggar S. "Foreign and Intra-Trade Policies of the Arab Countries." Washington, D.C.: International Monetary Fund, 1992.

Frankel, J. and D. Romer. "Does Trade Cause Growth?" *American Economic Review, 89*: 379–99 (1999).

Fischer S. "Prospects for Regional Integration in the Middle East." In *New Dimensions in Regional Integration*, edited by de Melo, J., and A. Panagariya. Cambridge: Cambridge University Press, 1993.

Fontagné L., Pajot M., Pasteels, J.M. "Potentiels de commerce entre économies hétérogènes: un guide a l'usage des modèles de gravité. " In *Economie et Prévision.* Forthcoming, 2002.

Hoekman, B., and P. Messerlin. *Harnessing Trade for Development and Growth in the Middle East.* Report by the Council on Foreign Relations, 2002.

Hoekman, B., A. Mattoo, and P. English. *Development, Trade and the WTO: A Handbook.* Washington, D.C.: World Bank, 2002.

International Trade Centre UNCATAD/WTO. "United Arab Emirates, Matrix of Tradable Goods." ITC project UAE/99/005, in conjunction with the ministry of economy and commerce, Abu Dhabi, U.A.E. 2002.

Leite, C. and J. Weidmann, "Does Mother Nature Corrupt? Natural Resources, Corruption, and Economic Growth." International Monetary Fund, July 1999.

Madani, D., and J. Page. "Challenges to Firm Competitiveness and Opportunities for Success." In *Globalization and Firm Competitiveness in the Middle East and North Africa Region,* edited by Fawzy, Samiha. Washington: D.C.: World Bank, 2002.

Mansour, A. "Support Services and the Competitiveness of Small and Medium Enterprises in the MENA Region." In *Globalization and Firm Competitiveness in the Middle East and North Africa Region,* edited by Fawzy, Samiha. Washington, DC: World Bank, 2002.

"Arab States Embrace Free Trade Pacts." *Middle East Economic Survey* (MEES) XLV, 13 (1 April 2002).

McArthur, J., and J. Sachs. "The Growth Competitiveness Index: Measuring Technological Advancement and Stages of Development." *In Global Competitiveness Report 2001–2002.* New York: World Economic Forum; Oxford University Press, 2002: 28–51.

Porter, M. E. *The Competitive Advantage of Nations.* New York: The Free Press; London: Macmillan Press, 1990.

Porter, M., J. Sachs, and J. McArthur. "Competitiveness and Stages of Economic Development." *In Global Competitiveness Report 2001–2002.* New York : World Economic Forum; Oxford University Press, 2002:16–25.

Sachs J., and A. Warner. "Natural Resource Abundance and Economic Growth." NBER Working Paper no. 5398. Cambridge, MA: National Bureau of Economic Research, 1995. Subsequently published in *Leading Issues in Economic Development*, edited by Meier, Gerald, and James Rauch. New York: Oxford University Press, 2000.

Sachs, J., and A. Warner: "The Big Push, Natural Resource Booms, and Growth." *Journal of Development Economics* (1999).

United Nations Conference on Trade and Development. *Trade and Development Report*, 2002. New York; Geneva: UNCTAD, 2002.

Endnotes

1. Often attributed to "Dutch Disease," so named from the recession caused by large discoveries of natural gas in the Netherlands

2. Refers to the stages of national competitive development in Michael E. Porter, *The Competitive Advantage of Nations.* New York: The Free Press; London: Macmillan Press, 1990

3. Several of the countries covered in this study do not report exports and imports. For these nonreporting countries, the export and import values are estimated on the basis of partner country data (mirror approach). The data for the *current* TPI refer to 2000 data while the data for the *change* TPI cover the years 1996 to 2000

4. The exclusion of the services sector is largely due to a lack of comparable data and this is unfortunate given the dynamism and increasing role of the services sector in some countries, such as Bahrain and United Arab Emirates.

5. International Trade Centre UNCATAD/WTO, a joint subsidiary organ of the United Nations Conference for International Trade and Development and the World Trade Organization.

6. Bahrain, Egypt, Jordan, Kuwait, Lebanon, Morocco, Oman, Qatar, Saudi Arabia, Tunisia, and United Arab Emirates

7. The *Global Competitiveness Report 2001–2002* covers seventy-five countries, but two of these countries are also part of the Arab World Competitiveness Report Executive Opinion Survey.

8. There were no available terms of trade data for Bahrain, Lebanon, Saudi Arabia, and United Arab Emirates.

9. Trade-to-GDP ratio has been calculated as the sum of exports and imports of goods divided by GDP.

10. Arab world countries included in the World Bank business environment database are: Algeria, Egypt, Jordan, Lebanon, Morocco, Saudi Arabia, Syria, Tunisia, the United Arab Emirates, and Yemen.

11. For reasons of data availability, their bilateral trade flows include oil, which may result both "in exaggerating the level of the region's trade with the rest of the world and also in underestimating the potential for intra-Arab given the similar structure of the oil economies" (Al-Atrash and Yousef 2000, p. 13). In fact, trade in raw materials and in particular oil do not obey to the main models of international trade: neither the Heckscher-Olin model that predicts that trade reflects different factor endowments or comparative advantages, not the intra-industry models which explain bilateral trade patterns based on product differentiation. Trade in oil is rather determined by "absolute advantages." Using bilateral data excluding oil might be an alternative. This would imply that explanatory variables used in the model such as GDP, should also be adjusted from revenues generated by the oil sector. In short, it is hard to estimate accurately the potential intra-Arab trade for oil exporting countries.

12. Pursuing privatization efforts would allow greater private participation in the economy. In other words, for reasons of data availability, their bilateral trade flows include oil, which may result both "in exaggerating the level of the region's trade with the rest of the world and also in underestimating the potential for intra-Arab given the similar structure of the oil economies" (Al-Atrash and Yousef 2000:13). In fact, trade in raw materials and, in particular, oil does not obey the main models of international trade (i.e., neither the Heckscher-Olin model that predicts that trade reflects different factor endowments or comparative advantages, nor the intraindustry models that explain bilateral trade patterns based on product differentiation). Trade in oil is rather determined by "absolute advantages." Using bilateral data that exclude oil might be an alternative. This would imply that explanatory variables used in the model, such as GDP, should also be adjusted from revenues generated by the oil sector. In short, it is hard to estimate accurately the potential intra-Arab trade for oil-exporting countries.

Appendix 1. Trade Performance Index
General Indicators (G1–G7), Current Index (P1–P5), and Change Index (C1–C5)

Indicators	What does it mean?	How is it calculated?	Ranking	Weight in the Ranking
General				
G1 Value of exports	Importance of the sector considered	Exports in 2000	no	—
G2 Trend of exports	Development of exports	Growth of exports over the period 1996–2000 (based on the least- squares method)	yes	—
G3 Share in national exports	Importance of the sector in national exports	Exports in the group of products divided by total exports	no	—
G4 Share in national imports	Importance of the sector in national imports	Imports in the group of products divided by total imports	no	—
G5 Average annual change in per capita exports	Evolution in the outward orientation of the economy	Percentage change in the ratio of exports to population	no	—
G6 Relative unit value	Standard of quality (or market segment) targeted by country exports	Unit value (value divided by quantity) of country relative to the world unit value	no	—
G7 Average annual change in relative unit value	Change in the quality standard (or market segment) targeted	Percent change of relative unit values	no	—
Current TPI				
P1 Value of net exports	Importance of the trade balance in the sector considered	Exports less imports in 2000	yes	1.00
P2 Per capita exports	Extent to which the labor force produces for the world market	Exports divided by population	yes	1.00
P3 Share in world market	Success on the world market	Exports as percentage share of world imports	yes	1.00
P4 Product diversification, measured by:	Number and weight of relative contribution of exported products	See cells below		(1.00)
P4-a Equivalent number of products	Number of export products of equal size that would lead to the observed concentration of exports	Inverse of the Herfindhal index	yes	0.50
P4-b Product spread	Spread of export markets for products	Weighted standard error	yes	0.50
P5 Market diversification, measured by:	Number and weight of partner countries	See cells below	yes	(1.00)
P5-a Equivalent number of markets	Number of markets of equal size that would lead to the observed concentration of exports	Inverse of the Herfindhal index	yes	0.50
P5-b Market spread	Spread of destination markets	Weighted standard error	yes	0.50

Appendix 1. Trade Performance Index (continued)
General Indicators (G1–G7), Current Index (P1–P5), and Change Index (C1–C5)

Indicators	What does it mean?	How is it calculated?	Ranking	Weight in the Ranking
C1 Percentage annual change in world market share explained by:	Change in global performance	Change in the world market share	no	(1.00)
Change in competitiveness	Gain (loss) in market share due to increased (worsened) competitiveness	Change in the exporting country's share in destination markets' imports weighted by the initial share of partner countries' imports in world trade (weighted average of the variation in the country's position in elementary markets*)	yes	0.25
Initial geographic specialization	Benefits associated with the initial specialization of domestic exporters on dynamic markets	Initial market share of the exporting country in partner countries weighted by the dynamics of their imports (weighted average of variations in the relative importance of export markets)	yes	0.25
Initial product specialization	Benefits associated with the initial export specialization on products characterized by dynamic demand	Change in the share of elementary markets in world trade weighted by the difference between: the initial share of the exporting country in elementary markets*, and the initial market share of the exporting country in destination markets, all products	yes	0.25
Adaptation to changes in world demand	Ability to adjust export supply to changes in world demand	Change in the share of the elementary markets* in world trade weighted by the change in the exporting country's market share in these elementary markets*	yes	0.25
C2 Trend of import coverage by exports	Development of sectorial surplus or deficit of exports over imports	Growth trend of the coverage ratio (exports divided by imports) over the period 1996–2000 (based on the least- squares method)	yes	1.00
C3 Matching with the dynamics of world demand	Similarity between the composition of national exports and product-specific dynamics of world demand	Spearman's rank correlation between the country's share of export products in national exports and the respective trends in world demand	yes	1.00
Change in product diversification measured by:	Ability to develop new export products	See cells below	yes	(1.00)
C4-a Change in the equivalent number of products	Change in the number of export products of equal size that would lead to the observed concentration of exports	Variation in the inverse of the Herfindhal index	yes	0.50
C4-b Change in the product spread	Change in the concentration of the export markets for products	Variation in the weighted standard error	yes	0.50
Change in the diversification of markets measured by:	Ability to penetrate new markets	See cells below	yes	(1.00)
C5-a Change in the equivalent number of markets	Change in the number of markets of equal size that would lead to the observed concentration of exports	Variation in the inverse of the Herfindhal index	yes	0.50
C5-b Change in market spread	Change in the concentration of the distribution of export markets	Variation in the weighted standard error	yes	0.50

Notes: All absolute values refer to 2000; growth rates to the period 1996–2000. World trade is calculated on the basis of some 100 reporting countries, which cover more than 90% of actual world trade. Coverage of nonreporting countries: the trade of nonreporting countries is reconstituted on the basis of partner country statistics (mirror statistics). This approach does not capture trade among nonreporting countries.

* An elementary market refers to one country's export of a specific product to a specific market.

Trade Relations Between the EU and North Africa

Ahmed Farouk Ghoneim, Jürgen von Hagen, and Susanna Wolf

Introduction

The European Union (EU) has had a comprehensive trade policy with North Africa for more than 25 years. This policy was initially based on a series of bilateral Association and Cooperation Agreements. Today, the EU's policy vis-à-vis the region is part of the broader Euro-Mediterranean Partnership (EMP) between the EU and twelve non-EU Mediterranean countries. The EMP Partnership has a much broader scope than just trade policy. Formally inaugurated by the EU with the Barcelona Declaration of 1995, it consists of intensified trade and development cooperation between the members, with the aim of shared prosperity. A key part of the EMP Partnership is the progressive establishment of a free trade area (FTA) between the EU and its partners in the Mediterranean. This is accompanied by substantial funding from the EU under the MEDA Program,[1] the EU's principal instrument for financial support to the region. MEDA offers technical and financial assistance to support economic and social reforms in the partner countries. By the year 2010, the FTA is expected to be the largest in the world, covering between 600 and 800 million people and some thirty to forty countries (European Commission 1995).

This paper reviews and discusses the trade relations between the EU and four North African countries: Algeria, Egypt, Morocco, and Tunisia.[2] All four have signed Euro-Mediterranean Association Agreements (EMAs). The agreements with Tunisia and Morocco were signed in 1995 and 1996 respectively and came into force in 1998 and 2000. The agreements with Egypt and Algeria, which were signed in 2001 and 2002 respectively, await ratification and are not yet in force.

We begin with a brief overview of the economic situation of the four North African countries. Next we review the trade and direct investment developments in the region and between these countries and the EU. In the section that follows, we consider the trade policies between the EU and North Africa. We identify the main factors governing this trade relationship, assess the effectiveness of the trade relationship, and provide some insights into its future outcomes. Next, we consider the competitiveness of the four countries, and discuss their potential for attracting foreign direct investment (FDI) and boosting exports, issues that are important, not only for the North African countries, but also for their European partners. A conclusion is offered in the final section.

Regional Economic Development

Table 1 lists a number of social and economic development indicators for the four North African countries. Altogether, we are looking at a region of 122 million people. Egypt has the largest population of the four countries (65.3 million), more than twice the population of Algeria (30.7 million) and Morocco (29.2 million), and almost seven times the population of Tunisia (9.7 million). Population growth in the region has declined, and has been well below 2 percent on average for the past decade. Today's total fertility rates are around 3.5 percent each in Algeria, Egypt, and Morocco, and 2.3 percent in Tunisia. However, rapid population growth in earlier years has resulted in labor force growth rates that are around 3 percent per annum; this contributes to high unemployment rates. Life expectancy is lowest in Egypt and highest in Tunisia. Algeria, Egypt, and Morocco have relatively low urbanization rates, while urbanization in Tunisia has reached 60 percent. As indicated by the Arab Human Development Report (2002) published by the United Nations Development Program (UNDP), health conditions in the four North African countries correspond to the average of the Arab region. Adult illiteracy rates vary between 24.9 percent (Tunisia) and 52 percent (Morocco), indicating relatively low levels of education. The secondary school enrollment rate is highest in Egypt (almost 75 percent), compared to almost 65 percent in Tunisia and Algeria and only 40 percent in Morocco.

Of the four North African countries, Morocco has the lowest per capita GDP—only US$1,147 per annum. Per capita income is considerably higher in Tunisia (US$2,062), while Egypt (US$1,482) and Algeria (US$1,788) fall in the middle. On the UNDP's Human Development Index, a summary statistic of human development that rates economic, social, health, and environmental conditions (with a score of 1 being the most developed), Algeria scores 0.69, Egypt 0.63, Morocco 0.58, and Tunisia 0.71.[3] Tunisia and Egypt enjoyed the highest GDP growth rates over the last decade, reaching 4.7 percent and 4.6 percent respectively. In Algeria, GDP growth was even lower than population growth, which means that GDP per capita declined.

Compared to other developing countries, the share of agriculture in GDP is relatively low in North Africa, and it has decreased slightly in the past decade. Agricultural GDP ranges from 17 percent (in Egypt) to 10 percent (in Algeria). Despite its small share in GDP and in exports, agriculture and fishing employ a large part of the working population, especially in rural areas. The services sector employs the majority of workers in urban areas, and contributes more than 50 percent to GDP in all North African countries (with the exception of Algeria, where services account for only 21 percent of GDP). Manufacturing GDP is almost 20 percent in Egypt and 18 percent in Tunisia and Morocco, but in Algeria it is quite low (9 percent) and, in recent years, has been falling. Overall, the composition of GDP in all four countries has not changed much over the past decade.

In recent years, economists and policymakers have increasingly recognized the importance of good government institutions (that is, governance) for strong and sustainable economic development. Governance determines the conditions under which economic transactions evolve, business contracts are made, and commitments to invest capital are entered into. Kaufmann et al. (2002) present an extensive database that allows international comparisons in this regard; the data are based on surveys and polls. They look at governance in six dimensions: voice and accountability, political stability, government

Table 1. Socioeconomic Indicators of Four North African Countries

	Algeria	Egypt	Morocco	Tunisia
Population, 2001 (million)	30.7	65.3	29.2	9.7
Population growth, 1990–2000 (average annual % growth)	2.00	1.99	1.64	1.68
Total fertility rate (%)	3.25	3.40	3.40	2.31
Life expectancy (years)	68.9	66.3	66.6	69.5
Percentage of urban population	50	44	47	60
GDP per capita, 2001 (US$)	1788	1482	1147	2062
GDP growth, 1990–2000 (average annual % growth)	1.9	4.6	2.3	4.7
Human Development Index, 2000	0.69	0.63	0.58	0.71
Agriculture, value-added, 2000 (% of GDP)	9.98	16.84	12.59	12.18
Manufacturing, value-added, 2000 (% of GDP)	9.26	19.68	17.90	18.47
Services, value-added, 2000 (% of GDP)	21.05	49.90	54.01	59.36
Secondary school enrollment, 1996 (% gross)	63.3	74.9	39.1	64.6
Secondary school enrollment female, 1996 (% gross)	61.7	69.9	33.7	63.2
Secondary school enrollment male, 1996 (% gross)	64.8	79.6	44.3	66.0
Exports of goods and services, 2000 (% of GDP)	40.91	16.10	31.18	43.79
Exports of goods and services, 1990–2000 (average annual % growth)	3.17	4.87	5.53	4.95
Imports of goods and services, 2000 (% of GDP)	21.76	22.80	37.47	46.34
Imports of goods and services, 1990–2000 (average annual % growth)	-1.89	3.85	6.30	4.62
Foreign direct investment, net inflows, 1999 (% of GDP)	0.01	1.19	0.01	1.67
Aid per capita, 1999 (current US$)	2.97	25.20	24.01	25.85
EC aid, 1990–2000 (% of total aid, average)	15.08	5.44	26.13	40.49

Sources: World Bank, World Development Indicators, 2001, and DAC, 2002; UNDP, Arab Human Development Report 2002

Table 2. Governance Indicators

	Algeria	Egypt	Morocco	Tunisia	Hungary	Mexico	Base Countries
Voice, Accountability	-1.64	-0.65	-0.23	-0.61	1.19	0.12	Albania, Georgia, Honduras
Political Stability	-2.06	0.21	0.16	0.82	0.75	0.06	Bahrain, Bosnia-Herzegowina, Cuba
Government Effectiveness	-1.23	0.27	0.10	1.30	0.60	0.28	Ghana, Guyana, Lebanon
Regulatory Quality	-0-79	0.13	0.54	0.81	0.88	0.58	Bangladesh, Colombia, Gambia
Rule of Law	-0.97	0.21	0.46	0.81	0.76	-0.41	Dominican Republic, Gambia, Lebanon
Control of Corruption	-0.62	-0.16	0.10	0.86	0.65	-0.28	Bahrain, Brazil, Croatia

Source: Kaufmann et al. (2002). Governance indicators are defined on a range of −2.5 to 2.5, higher numbers indicating better governance. Base countries are countries with values very close to zero

effectiveness, regulatory quality, rule of law, and control of corruption (see Table 2).[4] All the North African countries perform poorly in all areas of governance. Democracy is particularly weak in all the countries; Algeria stands out for its exceptionally poor performance overall. Political stability, government effectiveness, and regulatory quality in Egypt and Morocco are weaker than in Mexico. Only Tunisia has a quality of governance that is comparable on most scores to that achieved in Hungary.

With regard to macroeconomic developments, Morocco and Tunisia performed relatively well in recent years. These two countries had lower rates of inflation, more sustainable central government balances, and more stable real effective exchange rates. Egypt had both higher inflation and a higher budget deficit in the past, but has made significant progress towards macroeconomic stability in recent years. With low inflation, comfortable external reserve positions, and substantially reduced government debt, basic investment conditions are currently favorable in Morocco, Tunisia, and, although somewhat less, in Egypt.

Most North African countries have adopted managed floating exchange rate regimes, with Morocco and Tunisia pegging their currency mainly to the euro, Egypt pegging to the US dollar, and Algeria maintaining a balance between the two currencies. This reflects, to some extent, the greater importance of the United States as trading partner for the latter countries, although the EU is the dominant trading partner for all of them (see Figure 6). During 2000 and 2001 the Egyptian pound was devalued in several steps by about 35 percent, and the exchange rate system switched to a more flexible one with a band of 3 percent. Overall, the real effective exchange rates are rather high for most North African countries and have even increased for Morocco.

The economic fallout from the events of 11 September 2001 affected the economic performance of the North African countries. Earnings from tourism declined, especially in Egypt, but also in Tunisia and Morocco. Although they began to recover in early 2002, GDP growth will decline in 2002 compared to 2001 in all four countries. Although rising oil prices led to higher

Figure 1. Real Effective Exchange Rate

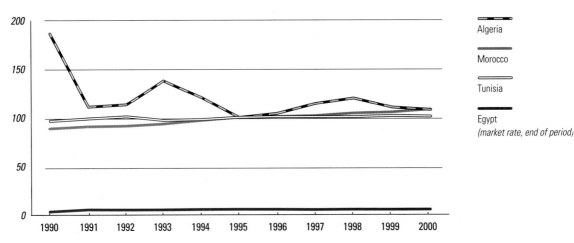

Source: World Bank, World Development Indicators, 2002

Figure 2. GDP and Current Account Forecasts, 2000–2003

Real GDP (Annual Change)

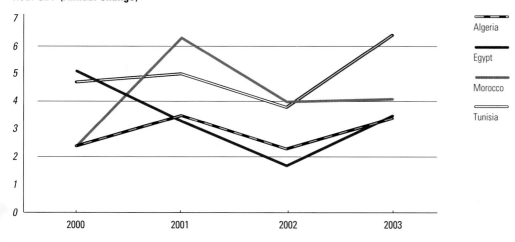

Current Account Balance (in Percent of GDP)

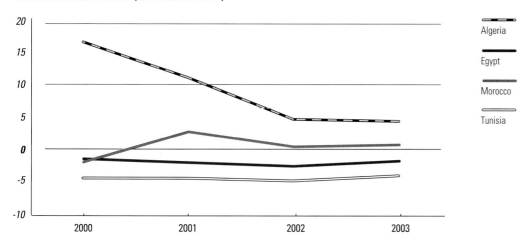

Source: IMF, World Economic Outlook 2002

growth in Algeria, this country's growth rate is also expected to decrease in 2002 because of cuts in oil output. Current account balances of all four countries are expected to worsen in 2002 and improvements are predicted only for 2003 (IMF 2002). Furthermore, unemployment and income inequalities are increasing, especially in Morocco and Egypt, causing a rise in social tensions (OECD and AfDB 2002)

Patterns of Trade and Foreign Direct Investment

The EU is the world's largest exporter and second largest importer. Its share of world trade is around 18 percent. In 2000 the EU had a trade deficit, especially in energy, and a large surplus in chemicals. Machinery and vehicles account for the largest share of EU exports and imports and, in general, EU trade is mainly intraindustry trade. Currently, the EU's main trading partners are industrial countries,

but the importance of other countries to EU trade is growing. This is especially true for the east and central European candidate countries for the next EU enlargement, which is expected to take place in 2003. The fourth largest trading partner of the EU in 2000 was China; trade with the four North African countries together account for only 3 percent of EU exports and imports.

Over the past few years, the trade performance of the North African countries has differed widely. Algeria's exports increased massively due to its concentration on petroleum, and with 0.4 percent of total world trade, it has the largest share in world trade of any North African country. Morocco and Tunisia were each able to increase nominal exports with a growth rate of around 5 percent in the last decade; at the same time they managed to reduce export concentration. Egypt's

Figure 3. Macroeconomic Stabilization in North Africa

Overall Budget Deficit (in Percent of GDP)

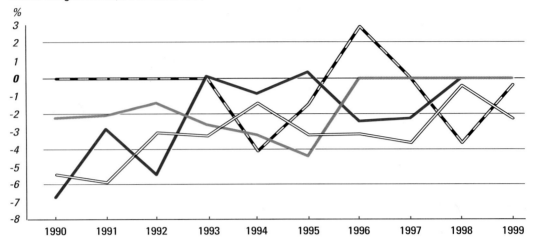

Inflation, Consumer Prices (Annual Percentage Change)

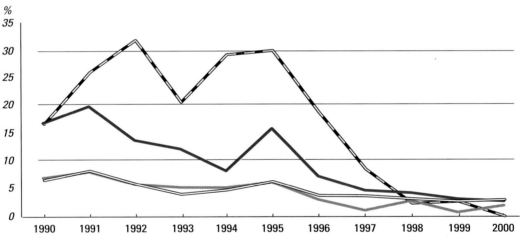

Source: World Bank, World Development Indicators 2001

exports fluctuated around a constant level in the first half of the 1990s, and only in recent years has it showed an increase. Tunisia is the most export oriented of the four countries, with exports of goods and services amounting to 44 percent of GDP, followed by Algeria with 41 percent and Morocco with 31 percent. Egypt has a much lower share, with exports comprising only 16 percent of GDP (see Table 1).

The composition of exports also differs across the North African countries. Fuels, manufactured goods such as textiles and clothing, and agricultural products (i.e., food items and agricultural raw materials, especially cotton) dominate Egypt's trade in goods. Algeria has a world market share of 9 percent in gas and its exports are further dominated by petroleum; fuels accounted for 97.1 percent of exports in 1999.

Tunisia's main exports are manufactured goods, especially textiles, fertilizers, electricity distributing equipment, and chemicals (which account for 80 percent); food items (vegetable oils) and fuels are also important exports. The types of goods Morocco exports are similar to that of Tunisia, with a dominant share of exports in manufactured goods (e.g., textiles, chemicals, transistors, fertilizers) and the second largest export sector in food items (fish, fruits, and nuts) (see Figure 5 and UNCTAD 2001a).

The share of commercial services in total exports of the four countries has been increasing in recent years, and these countries are gaining an increasing share in world markets for these services. For example, Egypt ranked thirty-second among the world's largest exporters of commercial services in 1999. These exports

Figure 4. Exports and Imports of Goods and Services, 1980–2000 (Constant 1995 US$ million)

Exports of Goods and Services

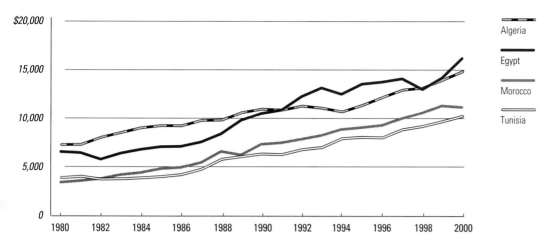

Imports of Goods and Services

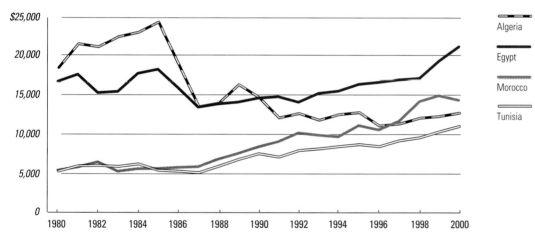

Source: World Bank, World Development Indicators 2001

include transport services to Suez Canal traffic. In 2000, Egypt had a share of 0.67 percent of the total world market for such services, while Tunisia and Morocco each had market shares of about 0.2 percent. All three countries enjoy comparative advantages in areas such as construction, travel, and audiovisual services.[5]

EU-North African trade

The EU is the largest trade partner for all North African countries. Trade in both directions has grown by more than 120 percent between 1990 and 2000. In 2000, Tunisia had the highest concentration of EU trade, with 76 percent of total exports going to the EU, followed by Algeria (65 percent) and Morocco (62 percent). For Egypt, the share of EU trade is only 43 percent. The figures for all four fluctuate to some extent, but no trend is observable.

North African exports to the EU are mainly in primary products and consumption goods, while most imports are intermediate goods and equipment. Crude and refined petroleum products account for more than 60 percent of Egypt's exports to the EU, whereas textiles and apparel account for only 15 percent and agriculture for 5 percent. Algeria's exports to the EU consist almost entirely of petroleum products; these products have an EU market share of around 8 percent. In contrast, apparel is the main export to the EU for both Tunisia and Morocco; these countries have 3.9 percent and 3.6 percent of the EU apparel market, respectively. In the past, exports of these goods were subject to quotas, which, however, were generally not binding. For Tunisia, other important exports to the EU are chemicals, crude petroleum, electrical machinery, leather, and footwear. For Morocco, other important exports are chemicals, food and beverages, agricultural products, and radio, television, and communication equipment. In recent

Figure 5. Composition of Total Goods Exports for Four North African Countries, 2000

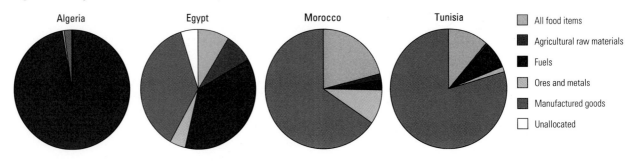

Source: UNCTAD 2001a

Figure 6. North African Exports by Destination

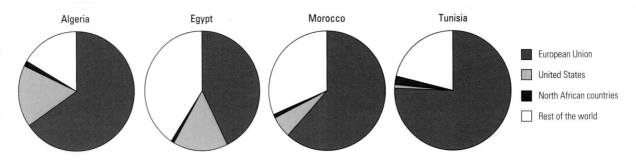

Source: UNCTAD 2001a

years, there has been a change in the composition of exports to the EU towards more consumption goods and capital goods for Morocco, Tunisia, and Egypt (European Commission 2001).

Overall, it seems that the preferential access of industrial products from North Africa to the EU market has not delivered the results hoped for. Instead, market shares of the North African countries have declined since 1980. This is due in part to an export structure that is not geared towards sectors in which there is growing demand in the EU and worldwide. However, it is also due to the various restrictions that are attached to the preferential access; for example, agricultural products from North African countries that are under the EMAs face several nontariff barriers when entering the EU market.

In general terms, exports from the North African countries to the EU was better for those products where preferential access was provided, such as electrical goods (from Morocco), leather products and engines (Tunisia), and coke and carpets (Egypt); these exports achieved annual growth rates of more than 20 percent. However, there were a number of years where Egypt was not able to fill its quota for textiles allowed in the EU. This suggests that supply side

problems restrict Egypt's export capacity (Chevallier and Freudenberg 2001).

A large part of North Africa's imports originates in the EU, although the EU's shares are slightly lower than those for exports. In 2000, Tunisia had the highest concentration with 72 percent of total imports coming from the EU, followed by Morocco (62 percent) and Algeria (58 percent). Egypt, again, had the lowest share, with only 36 percent.

The composition of imports from the EU has remained largely unchanged over the years. However, Morocco and Tunisia have each had a considerable increase in imports of consumption goods, especially clothing. This might be attributable to trade liberalization, as the textiles and clothing sector had been one of the most protected in both countries. Machinery and transport equipment account for the largest share of Moroccan, Tunisian, and Egyptian imports. Chemical products are also important for Egypt, while agricultural products are important import items for Algeria (Chevallier and Freudenberg 2001; European Commission 2001).

In sum, interindustry trade dominates the trade between the EU and North Africa. Trade between the EU and the North African countries largely conforms

Figure 7. North African Imports by Country of Origin, 2000

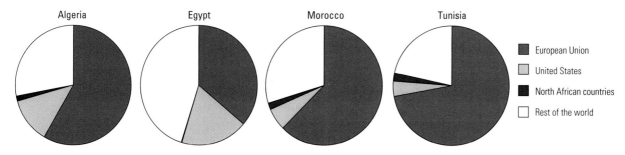

Algeria   Egypt   Morocco   Tunisia

■ European Union
□ United States
■ North African countries
□ Rest of the world

Source: UNCTAD 2001a

to the traditional, international division of labor between countries with widely differing income levels. In contrast, other trade partners of the EU, especially the central and east European countries, have much larger shares of intraindustry trade in their exchanges (Chevallier and Freudenberg 2001:55, see Table 3.3; European Commission 2001).

A recent study by Stengg (2001) provides some interesting insights into the trade in textiles and clothing between the EU and the Maghreb countries, which include Algeria, Morocco, and Tunisia. According to this study, the EU had a trade balance surplus in textiles of 661 million euros against the Maghreb. This surplus rose to 1.8 billion euros in 1995 and 2.6 billion euros in 2000. Meanwhile, the Maghreb countries had a trade surplus in clothing against the EU that amounted to 1.2 billion euros in 1988, 2.9 billion euros in 1995, and 4.1 billion euros in 2000. These figures indicate the existence of outward processing; that is, EU textile producers ship their products to the Maghreb, where they are made into clothing. Stengg notes that recently, 82 percent of the trade in clothing has been in the medium quality segment and only 12 percent in the high quality segment, down from 21 percent in 1988. For comparison, 63 percent of clothing imported by the EU is in the medium quality segment, and 25 percent in the high quality segment. This indicates that the North African countries currently have a bias against high quality in their exports.

Intraregional trade

Intraregional trade in North Africa is low compared with other regions in the world. In the Maghreb subregion, intraregional trade averages less than 4 percent of total external trade, and even this share has declined in recent years. The main reasons for this lack of trade are complementary production structures, inadequate infrastructure, and instability in political relations. Furthermore, high tariff barriers, and especially nontariff barriers, that continue to exist between most North African countries despite the conclusion of several partial preferential agreements, restrict intraregional trade. Since the 1980s, oil has been less important in intraregional trade, but non-oil intra-Arab trade still accounts for less than 2 percent of GDP.

Tunisia receives more than 2 percent of its imports from the three other Northern African countries, and only Tunisia also ships more than 2 percent of its own exports to them. For the other three countries, trade with the North African region is even lower (see Figures 6 and 7).

Tunisia is also the only country for which the Arab region as a whole is the second most important trading partner; for the three other countries, that partner is the United States. However, for specific products, the Arab countries play a bigger role in all North African countries. Egypt's shares of exports to Arab markets are greater than 50 percent of total exports in a number of product categories, such as processed foodstuffs, wood products, paper and printing, glass and mineral products, and transport equipment. In contrast, Egypt imports little from the Arab countries, mainly petroleum products, beverages, and textiles and clothing. While Egypt depends relatively heavily on Arab markets for its non-oil exports (20 percent), these markets are much less important for Morocco and Tunisia (Devlin and Page 2001).

In general, nontraditional exports make up most intraregional trade in North Africa, a pattern similar to other developing country regions. The main export products of North Africa are chemicals, iron and steel shapes, aluminum, fruits and vegetables, lime, and cement and other building materials. This means that their share of intraindustry trade is significantly higher in intraregional trade than in trade with the EU (Devlin and Page 2001).

The service sector represents an increasingly important component of intraregional trade. On a global scale, North African countries are significant importers of services, and as proximity of supply plays an important role, labor-related net flows account for a high share in intraregional trade. Egypt, Morocco, and especially Tunisia provide tourism and travel services to their neighboring countries (Hoekmann et al. 2001:170; Devlin and Page 2001:190). Although citizens of North African countries do not generally enjoy the right to move and work in neighboring countries, there is a high level of labor mobility in the region. This is reflected in the significant share of remittances in the balance of payments of these countries. For Egypt, remittances are almost as important as export revenues in the balance of payments (see Table 3).

Table 3. Ratio of Remittances to Exports, 1992–1997

	Egypt	Morocco	Tunisia
1992	2.00	0.54	0.14
1993	2.52	0.64	0.12
1994	1.06	0.33	0.14
1995	0.94	0.29	0.12
1996	0.88	0.31	0.13
1997	0.94	0.27	0.12
1998	1.08	0.28	0.12
1999	0.91	0.26	0.13

Source: Nassar and Ghoneim 2002

Comparative advantages

The index of revealed comparative advantage (RCA) is used to investigate the competitive position of a country in a certain product and market. It is based on the idea that a country's comparative advantages reveal themselves in the process of international trade, as the country is likely to export relatively more of those goods in which it has comparative advantages than of goods where it has comparative disadvantages. RCA indexes are computed relative to the total imports of a reference region. For example, an RCA greater than one for a given product relative to world imports indicates that the share of this product in a country's total exports is more than this product's share in world trade. Note that the observed RCAs are conditional on existing trade barriers. Table 7 reports the ten highest RCA indexes in 1996 for Egypt, Morocco, and Tunisia with respect to their exports to three regions: North Africa, the EU, and the world. No comparable data exists for Algeria.

Consider the North African regional market. RCA indexes indicate moderate levels of complementarity among the North African countries. For exports to the region, Egypt has the highest comparative advantages in vegetable fibers, radioactive material, briquettes and coke, cocoa, and natural rubber. Morocco's comparative advantages for exports to the region are highest in pulp and waste paper, fabrics and textile articles, leather, lead, and fish. For Tunisia, fabric waste material, inorganic chemicals, iron and steel, rubber tires, and agricultural machinery are the most competitive exports. Overall, RCAs within the region are on nontraditional goods and intermediate inputs, which tend to be more intensive in capital, knowledge, and research and development.

Regarding RCAs in the EU market, Egypt's most competitive exports are briquettes and coke, vegetable fibers, and cotton. Morocco's highest RCAs are in crude fertilizers, men's outerwear, and lead, while Tunisia's largest RCAs are in men's and women's outerwear and leather manufactures. In world markets, Egypt's most important RCAs are largely the same as those in the EU market. For Morocco, inorganic elements and frozen shellfish play a larger role in the world market than in the EU market, while for Tunisia, crude fertilizers play a large role in the world market.

Countries with broadly similar production possibilities should have broadly similar RCAs in markets outside their own region. Table 7 suggests that RCAs for Morocco and Tunisia overlap; they compete in EU and world markets in the production of fertilizers, inorganic elements, cork, and clothing. In contrast, except for clothing, complementarities of efficient productive capacities seem to be much more limited between these countries and Egypt. The fact that Morocco and Tunisia have very different regional market RCAs from their EU and world market RCAs suggests that there are rather restrictive regional trade policies on inorganic elements, fertilizers, and clothing.

Overlap of the sectors with RCAs in the regional and the EU markets indicates a potential for developing global competitiveness and diversification at the regional level. This is the case for vegetable fibers and briquettes from Egypt, as well as for fish and lead exports from Morocco. There is also some scope for developing a regional comparative advantage, because Morocco has an RCA for leather in the regional market and Tunisia has an RCA in leather manufactures in the EU market. This suggests that these countries could benefit from greater regional cooperation and division of labor, allowing them to better use specialized capital equipment and technical

Table 4. Top Ten 1996 RCA Non-Oil Sectors (Exports) for North African Countries (by Export Region)

Egypt

RCA Indexes (Region)		RCA Indexes (EU15)		RCA Indexes (World)	
Commodity		Commodity		Commodity	
072 Cocoa	16.3	054 Vegetables, fresh	5.2	042 Rice	5.4
074 Tea and mate	8.6	075 Spices	4.3	054 Vegetables, fresh	6.4
098 Edible products,	8.2	263 Cotton	7.8	075 Spices	6.8
232 Natural rubber, gums	15.0	265 Veg fibre	13.2	245 Fuel wood, charcoal	6.8
245 Fuel wood, charcoal	11.0	323 Briquets, coke	14.2	263 Cotton	8.4
265 Veg. fiber	18.7	651 Textile yarn	4.9	265 Veg fibre	18.1
322 Coal, lignite and peat	14.1	652 Cotton fabrics, woven	5.8	323 Briquets, coke,	18.3
323 Briquets, coke,	18.4	658 Textile articles	6.5	658 Textile articles	5.7
524 Radioactive material	18.6	846 Under garments knitted	4.1	659 Floor coverings	6.9
696 Cutlery	12.2	941 Zoo animals, pets	5.5	941 Zoo animals, pets	5.3

Morocco

RCA Indexes (Region)		RCA Indexes (EU15)		RCA Indexes (World)	
Commodity		Commodity		Commodity	
024 Cheese and curd	17.0	036 Shell fish fresh, frozen	14.0	036 Shell fish fresh, frozen	22.3
037 Fish	20.6	037 Fish	11.8	037 Fish	12.7
251 Pulp and waste paper	42.0	056 Vegetables prepared	11.6	056 Vegetables prepared	15.2
611 Leather	24.4	244 Cork	12.0	244 Cork	23.3
654 Woven textile fabric	20.7	271 Fertilizers, crude	113.0	271 Fertilizers, crude	167.0
655 knitted, etc fabrics	26.4	562 Fertilizers, manufactured	13.8	522 Inorganic elements,	24.2
658 Textile articles	21.7	685 Lead	15.3	562 Fertilizers, manufactured	12.9
685 Lead	22.8	842 Men's outerwear	17.5	685 Lead	17.0
774 Medical equipment	16.1	843 Women's outerwear	14.4	842 Men's outerwear	15.4
847 Textile accessories	17.6	844 Under garments	13.9	843 Women's outerwear	12.2

Tunisia

RCA Indexes (Region)		RCA Indexes (EU15)		RCA Indexes (World)	
Commodity		Commodity		Commodity	
269 Waste of textile fabrics	37.0	269 Waste of textile fabrics	7.1	244 Cork	10.4
515 Org-inorg compounds	17.5	271 Fertilizers, crude	10.6	271 Fertilizers, crude	29.1
523 Other inorg chemicals	32.9	423 Vegetable oils	16.1	423 Vegetable oils	15.0
625 Rubber tyres, tubes	27.2	562 Fertilizers, manufactured	14.8	522 Inorganic elements	12.7
628 Rubber articles nes	14.1	612 Leather etc manufactures	19.9	562 Fertilizers, manufactured	14.3
677 Iron, steal wire	13.5	773 Electronic equipment	6.5	612 Leather manufactures	17.9
679 Iron, steal castings	31.0	842 Men's outerwear	31.2	842 Men's outerwear	32.0
721 Agricultural machinery	20.9	843 Women's outerwear	18.7	843 Women's outerwear	18.1
749 Machine parts	10.8	844 Under garments	12.7	844 Under garments	10.1
776 Transistors, valves	16.2	846 Under garments, knitted	9.9	846 Under garments, knitted	10.1

Source: Devlin and Page 2001

or marketing knowledge, and to develop a common physical and marketing infrastructure with positive externalities for the development of transportation and communications networks.

Foreign direct investment

Compared to other developing countries, the economic importance of FDI is relatively small in North Africa; its contribution to gross fixed capital

Figure 8. FDI Flows and Stocks

FDI Inflows to North Africa, 1995–2000 (in US$ million)

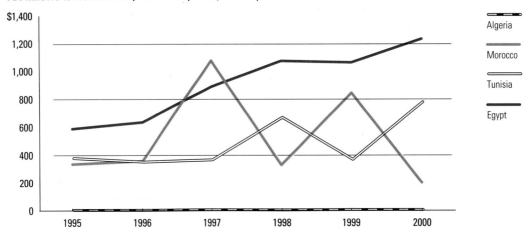

FDI Inward Stock in North Africa, 1980–2000 (in US$ million)

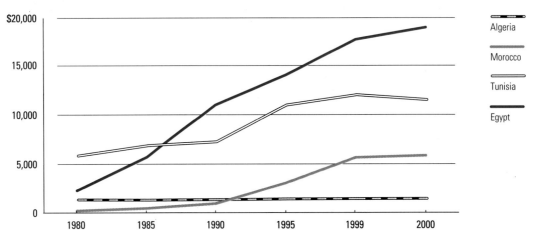

Source: UNCTAD 2001b

formation is a mere 5 percent. FDI remains especially small in Algeria and Morocco, where it was almost negligible in recent years. The regions' share in global FDI inflows fell from 0.7 percent between 1988 and 1990 to only 0.2 percent in the years 1998 to 2000; in contrast, developing countries in general increased their share. Egypt, which is the main recipient of FDI in North Africa, has experienced a continuous increase in FDI stocks over the past 20 years, but FDI flows have been characterized by declining growth rates. FDI inflows to Morocco and Tunisia increased since 1996, but they are rather volatile. The EU accounts for more than half of the FDI inflows to North Africa in general and as much as 75 percent in Tunisia. These inflows can, at least partly, be attributed to increased liberalization and to integration with the EU (UNCTAD 2001b; Lahouel 2001).

So far, most FDI to North Africa has gone to tourism, the energy sector, and low-skill light manufacturing. This suggests that the availability of natural resources and low labor costs have been main attractions for foreign capital. In Tunisia, FDI was attracted mainly by the energy sectors, where two large projects dominated in 1997, namely an extension of the national gas pipeline and the Miskar natural gas project. In Egypt, FDI the petroleum sector has received most FDI; nevertheless, the financial sector attracted one-fourth of total FDI inflows. In Morocco, however, two-thirds of FDI was directed towards the services sector, especially finance and tourism. Reflecting export opportunities created by the trade agreements with the EU, textiles, clothing, and footwear industries in Tunisia and Morocco have attracted European export-oriented direct investment flows in recent years. In addition, the continuing privatization of state-owned enterprises offers opportunities for European investors (OECD and AfDB 2002).

In most North African countries, investment regulations have been simplified and foreign firms can benefit from tax exemptions. Nevertheless, weak legal systems, bureaucratic red tape, barriers to capital flows, inadequate protection of property rights, restrictions to banking and finance, and the poor state of infrastructure remain the main factors behind the weak performance of FDI in North African states. On economic and political freedom indicators, Algeria scores best of all four North African countries, but because of its high incidence of violence, FDI in Algeria also remains low (see Table 5). Djankov et al. (2001) estimate that the cost of setting up a standardized firm is 1.7 percent of its start-up capital in Tunisia, 2.1 percent in Morocco, and 9.7 percent in Egypt.[6] Accounting for time spent with bureaucracies and administrative work, these costs rise to 3.4 percent in Tunisia, 4.4 percent in Morocco, and 11.7 percent in Egypt. In this regard, Tunisia is comparable to the Czech Republic and Germany, Morocco to Poland and Brazil, and Egypt to Hungary and Indonesia. Based on a similar methodology and including the cost of registering an export and import business, Morisset and Neso (2002) estimate set-up costs of 23 percent of per capita GDP for Tunisia, 59 percent for Egypt, and 197 percent for Morocco. According to their estimates of absolute dollar costs, Tunisia falls between costs in Burkina Faso and Argentina, Egypt between Argentina and the Czech Republic, and Morocco between Lesotho and Malawi. In all three North African countries, set-up costs for import-export businesses are significantly larger than those for comparable, domestic firms.

Table 5. Economic and Political Freedom Indicators, 2000

	Algeria	Egypt	Morocco	Tunisia
Capital Flow & Foreign Investment (barriers)	2.0	3.0 S	2.0 S	2.0
Banking/Finance (restrictions)	3.0	4.0 S	3.0 S	3.0
Wages/Prices (intervention)	3.0	3.0 S	2.0 B	2.0
Property Rights (protection)	4.0	3.0 S	4.0 W	3.0
Regulation	3.0	4.0 S	3.0 S	3.0
Overall Verdict	mostly free	mostly unfree	mostly free	mostly free

Source: Heritage Foundation 2002
Notes: S—same, B—better, W—worse

Foreign firms remain shut out of many activities, especially in the services sector, and privatization of infrastructure is also less advanced than in competing countries. In Tunisia, FDI is only unrestricted in manufacturing activities that are geared primarily toward producing for export and some services sectors. Otherwise, government approval is required. Furthermore, public utilities and telecommunications are still government owned, and land ownership of foreigners is restricted. In Morocco and Egypt, investors frequently complain about impediments such as customs clearance of goods, inefficient port services, inconsistent tax administration, inefficient commercial dispute settlement, high telecommunication costs, and inadequate skills.

Significant positive changes have occurred in government attitudes towards the private sector in recent years, such as the removal of investment licensing for most activities, simplification of administrative procedures, improvement of port and customs services, and so on. Further liberalization of the services sector will help to increase the attractiveness for foreign capital, because the transportation, telecommunications, and the financial sectors have a strong impact on production costs in other sectors (Lahouel 2001; Chabrier 2001). There have been several positive developments in telecommunications sectors, particularly in Egypt, Morocco, and Tunisia. A number of institutional and regulatory reforms that induce competition and raise efficiency were enacted in these countries. Private firms were allowed to enter the mobile services field in Egypt, Algeria, and Morocco, but mobile services still remains a public monopoly in Tunisia. Morocco and Tunisia have made General Agreement on Trade in Services (GATS) commitments regarding their telecommunications sectors, while Egypt is in the process of joining the basic telecommunications agreement (Lahouel 2002).

Trade Policy

In the 1970s and 1980s, North Africa was a politically volatile region in which the USSR was trying to develop its influence. To maintain political stability and strengthen its own influence, the EU adopted a global Mediterranean policy in 1972 to promote trading and financial relations between the EU and the Mediterranean states (Wolf 2001). The EU formalized and intensified its cooperation with the North African countries on a bilateral basis through Association and Cooperation Agreements. These agreements were open-ended, but confined to trade concessions for industrial exports from the North African countries to the EU. No trade concessions for EU exports to the region were implied. The agreements were accompanied by Financial Protocols, which were renewed every five years, and set the framework for financial aid to the region. Each of the cooperation agreements was negotiated separately in an ad hoc manner, and the trade concessions the EU granted were much less generous than for other partners (such as the states belonging to the African, Caribbean and Pacific group) and excluded almost all agricultural products. When Greece, Spain, and Portugal joined the EU in the 1980s, the North African countries lost considerable EU market shares for such goods as wine, fresh vegetables and fruits, and olive oil (Parfitt 1997).

Based on the Financial Protocols of 1976, 1981, and 1986, the EU's total financial aid to Algeria amounted to 504 million euros from 1976 to 1991. Morocco received a total of 653 million euros, and Tunisia a total of 458 million euros (European Commission 2002). Most of these funds were used for rural and agricultural development and to promote the development of fisheries. A shift in emphasis occurred with the Financial Protocols of 1991. While these protocols increased the volume of transfers, they also shifted the emphasis of funding objectives in the recipient countries from traditional development projects to promoting economic reform, enabling regional cooperation, and to environmental projects.

In the 1990s, as part of its broad process of enlargement (which includes the accession of some new member states and the creation of free trade areas with a large number of nonmembers), the EU decided to overhaul its relationship with the Mediterranean region, including North Africa. A new approach was adopted. It was based on reciprocal free trade agreements and promotion of regional cooperation among the partner countries, and went beyond narrow trade issues to cover cooperation in areas such as the fight against crime, money laundering, drug trafficking, and terrorism. From the EU perspective, external policy considerations, like regional peacekeeping and reducing pressures of migration to the EU, have as much weight as enhancing trade relations between the EU and its Mediterranean partners.

The Barcelona Declaration of 1995 identified three areas of activity that now constitute the core elements of the EMP Partnership:

1. **Political dialogue and security partnership.** Signatory states commit to developing the rule of law and democracy and respect for human rights;

they are also duty-bound to respect the equal rights of peoples and their right to self-determination. Furthermore, there is a scheme to promote regional security through arms control and weapons reduction.

2. **Economic and financial partnership.** The establishment of industrial free trade areas that have been agreed upon by all four North African countries and that will be implemented over twelve years. These countries have, therefore, already started to transform their trade relations with the EU from preferences to reciprocity. The EU has increased its financial assistance under the MEDA program in order to increase the competitiveness of the partner countries. A growing share of aid is therefore used for structural adjustment support.

3. **Social, cultural, and human cooperation.** This serves to increase of employment; this is another fundamental aim of the EU, which wants to prevent illegal migration into the Common Market. This activity also aims to promote understanding between cultures and rapprochement of the peoples in the Euro-Mediterranean region, in addition to developing free and flourishing civil societies.

Euro-Mediterranean Association Agreements

The EMAs with Algeria, Egypt, Morocco, and Tunisia consist of the following elements.

Free movement of manufactured goods

Liberalization on the North African side will take place over twelve years, with reductions on final consumer products back-loaded. Capital and intermediate goods not produced in any of the four North African countries are to be liberalized at a faster pace and starting directly after the agreements are enforced. Capital goods and raw inputs are to be liberalized over the first four years, followed by intermediate inputs over the second four years, and ending with final goods. Since North African manufactured goods already had nontariff access to EU markets, the implementation of the EMAs primarily puts pressure on these countries to liberalize their own import regimes. Since the average tariffs imposed by these countries are high by developing countries' norms, this liberalization will be quite significant for market developments even if the transition phase is long.

Cooperation in trade related areas

North African-EU trade will be subject to the rules of the EU's competition policy starting five years

Table 6. North African Countries' Trade and Financial Obligations within the Context of EMAs

Area/Field	Condition	Timing	Remarks	Europe Agreements
Industry	Opening up of the Northern-African countries market	Over 12 years	Safeguard measures allowed. Textiles quotas liberalized in line with GATT obligations	Over 10 years, textile quotas abolished on a faster track than GATT
Agriculture	Status quo as under the GCA, with few extra concessions	Issue reviewed 5 years after entry into force		
Services	Obligations of GATS only	Reviewed 5 years after entry into force of the Agreement		Temporary movement of natural persons allowed. Specific provisions for air and maritime services
FDI	No commitments for right of establishment	Reviewed 5 years after entry into force of the Agreement		Right of establishment for some sectors included within 3 years from entry into force of the agreement
Competition Policy	Required to adopt EU's competition policy	Within 5 years from entry into force	Antidumping and countervailing duties apply. State aid allowed within the first 5 years	Antidumping and countervailing duties apply
Rules of Origin	Defined on product by product basis		Possibility for cumulative rules of origin with other North African countries as long as they have the same set of rules of origin and have free trade area among them	Possibility for cumulation with other CEECs as long as they have the same set of rules of origin and have free trade area among them
Dispute Settlement Mechanism	Association Council			
Role of the Government	No special commitments		Liberalization of government procurement not required	
Regional of Cooperation	Decentralized MEDA programs		Covering different fields	
	Required for regulatory regimes and institutions		Mentioned as an aim without specific commitments	

Source: Authors' compilation

Note: GCA–General Cooperation Agreements

after the agreements enter into force. Parties to the EMAs maintain the right to undertake antidumping initiatives against other EMA parties (under World Trade Organization [WTO] rules and regulations). Furthermore, the EMAs seek to harmonize product standards and market rules and regulations in the North African countries with those in the EU to reduce nontariff barriers and promote mutual recognition. To help with implementation, an association council that deals with disputes is established for each EMA.

Financial cooperation

The primary aims of financial cooperation are fostering the development of the private sector and supporting reforms that restructure the economy

(to ensure that the North African countries are able to benefit from preferential access to the EU). Moreover, the system of financial cooperation has changed drastically. The new MEDA program increased the amount of money allocated to EMA countries and identified market reforms as the main objectives of aid disbursement. However, the mode of disbursement remains vague.

The task of ensuring that the goals of the Euro-Mediterranean Partnership are met lies with the Barcelona Committee. The Committee consists of the EU-Troika (the current EU president, as well as the previous and the upcoming one); twelve Mediterranean countries; and the Council Secretariat and European Commission representatives. Technical and financial programming is prepared by the Commission and then presented to the Committee.

Individual trade issues

Since free trade area (FTA) members only eliminate trade restrictions among themselves and retain their individual trade policies vis-à-vis third countries, rules of origin are necessary in order to make a free trade agreement viable. The restriction of preferential access to imports originating in partner countries prevents third-country imports from entering the FTA through the country with the lowest barriers, which would make different trade policies of FTA members obsolete. Rules of origin are used to determine the share of value-added in a product that was produced in a member country of the FTA, the remainder being subject to tariffs. For products that are wholly produced in one country, this distinction is quite obvious. But in a globalizing world where products often incorporate offshore components and different production steps take place in different countries, rules of origin become a difficult matter; products containing non-FTA components limit the trade advantages to those parts of a product produced within the FTA. Rules of origin applied by the EU tend to be restrictive and the procedures to prove origin complicated and, therefore, costly. Thus, the benefits of tariff preferences can be eroded by the administrative cost associated with rules of origin requirements.[7] Such costs can prevent exporters from benefiting from the FTA and might even prevent investment in North African countries if all required inputs are not available locally.

The issue of rules of origin is closely connected to the larger problem of the EU's traditional approach to forming FTAs with other regions. This is the "hub and spokes" approach practiced by the EU in the past (Baldwin 1994). The EU, as the hub, can export and import without restrictions with all its partners, the spokes. But as long as there is no integration between the spokes, only the EU becomes a more attractive location for production, because only from the EU can all the markets in the spokes be served without being subject to tariffs. This puts the spokes at a disadvantage in attracting capital investment.

The EU has asserted its interest in overcoming the hub and spokes approach by encouraging the North African countries to establish a free trade area among themselves. Furthermore, the EU permits the accumulation of inputs among North African countries; that is, the value-added content produced in all North African countries is exempt from tariffs when the product is exported to the EU by one of these countries. This should facilitate intraregional

trade and enhance market access of North African exports to the EU. Dessus et al. (2001) estimate that the accumulation of origin will increase intraregional trade among Mediterranean countries by 40 percent and FDI substantially.

Nevertheless, there remain practical difficulties. The accumulation of origin is subject to the condition that the North African states use identical rules of origin in their trade relations. Today, Tunisia and Morocco use identical rules of origin but these differ significantly from those adopted by Egypt. Given the low volume of intraregional trade between Egypt and the other countries, this provision is likely to remain idle in practice. However, this problem does not affect the relatively higher share of intraregional trade between Morocco, Tunisia, and Algeria, because they have adopted the same rules of origin. Recently, the Agadir Declaration, which foresees the establishment of an FTA between Egypt, Morocco, Tunisia and Jordan, has initiated a new investigation into the possibility of harmonizing rules of origin between these countries. So far, the investigation has produced no tangible results.

Standards and antidumping measures as nontariff barriers

Product standards and regulations prevailing in the EU represent major problems for exporting countries in North Africa. Exporters complain that EU standards are high, and that meeting them is very costly (Ghoneim 2000b). Other nontariff barriers that the EU has been using extensively are antidumping measures. The EU is one of the major users of the antidumping tool in the world, topped only by the United States and India. In the first half of the 1980s the antidumping measures constituted about 69 percent of the administrative protection tools used by the EU, which included antidumping measures, safeguards (Article XIX of the GATT) and countervailing actions (Finger 1990). During the period 1995 to 2001, the EU initiated six antidumping measures against Egypt (e.g., against cotton fabrics and bed linen) and one against Algeria (WTO 2002).

Financial assistance

The increased political relevance of Euro-Mediterranean cooperation has meant increased funding for countries MEDA. EU aid to Egypt, Morocco, and Tunisia has increased over the past decade; they, as well as Algeria, receive a substantial share of their total aid from the EU (see Table 1). Disbursements, however, fluctuate dramatically.

Figure 9. Aid Disbursements by the European Commission, 1990–2000 (in US$ million)

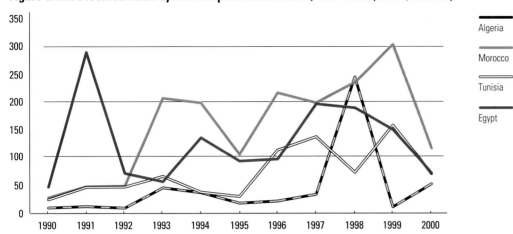

Source: OECD-DAC, 2002

For several decades, Egypt was the major recipient of total EU aid.[8] However, EU aid to Egypt has declined in recent years, and accounts now for only 5 percent of total aid received by Egypt. The four North African countries together receive 11 percent of all EU aid. Since 1993, Morocco has been the largest recipient of EU aid in absolute terms; EU aid totaled US$303 million in 1999. Tunisia ranks first in terms of total per capita aid, and the EU has the highest share of its total aid—more than 40 percent over the past decade. For Morocco, Tunisia, and Egypt, transfers from the EU are important sources of revenue; however, because of its critical geopolitical strategic position, the North African region is also a major recipient of aid from other donors. Total per capita aid from all countries is around US$25 in Egypt, Morocco, and Tunisia, but only US$3 in Algeria (see Table 1).

EU aid is provided mainly for social infrastructure and services. Support for structural adjustment that might also enable the North African countries to benefit from reciprocal free trade has increased over the last two decades. Financing of infrastructure has mostly been directed towards banking, finance, and business services, which are essential for increasing productivity and efficiently allocating resources. Recently, support for the development of the regional transport infrastructure, which should help increase intraregional trade, has been increased. Investment promotion by the European Commission has been negligible so far—only 0.6 percent of the total budget was allocated between 1986 and 1998. However, since the signing of the EMAs, trade enhancement and investment support have become more important.

Therefore the EU not only provides market access for North African products, but also helps to enhance the supply capacity of North African countries so that the preferred status can be used effectively. The EU also has participated in strengthening the social safety net that is affected by market reforms. In Egypt, for example, the EU has been a major donor for the Social Fund for Development, a project directed at reducing unemployment and alleviating poverty (Cox and Chapham 1999).

Agriculture

Trade in agricultural products is not liberalized by the EMAs. Most agricultural products are subject to various kinds of quotas when entering EU markets. The EMAs have increased some of the existing quotas; however, quotas are not the same for all the North Africa countries. Negotiations on further liberalization of agricultural trade was set to take place five years after the EMAs came into force.

Still, trade in agricultural products plays an important role in overall trade between the EU and North Africa. The EU's protectionist common agricultural policy (CAP) has been facing increasing criticism from other trading partners, mainly the United States and the Cairns Group. Developing countries that depend on agricultural products as their main export goods face multiple restrictions entering the EU markets, including tariff peaks, nontariff barriers, import levies, and so on. Since agricultural products constitute a large share of their export capacity, North African countries are hurt significantly by the EU's protectionist policy in this area; CAP prevents them from fully utilizing their comparative advantages and prohibits them from lowering their terms of trade for major exports in the world market.

The EU has discussed a major overhaul of CAP for years, prompted by external complaints as well as the increasing dissatisfaction of European consumers with high priced (and often low quality) agricultural goods. However, as the most recent EU Summit in Sevilla has shown, country particularism continues to block the road to far-reaching reforms. Significant reforms are now envisaged for 2007 and beyond. A CAP reform would, in fact, have ambiguous effects on the North African countries. While it could improve chances of export to the EU and promote growth in agricultural incomes, net food importing countries, such as Egypt, are likely to face a negative impact. When the EU becomes a larger importer of agricultural products, world prices for food will increase and, therefore, food imports to countries like Egypt will become more expensive. In the medium and long run, however, the positive effects following from the ability to better exploit comparative advantages and improve terms of trade, should dominate for the North African countries.

Services and investment

Negotiations regarding the liberalization of trade in services were deferred for five years after the agreements came into force. Meanwhile, the EU and North African countries have made commitments under the GATS that are also applicable to their trade with each other. The sectoral coverage of the North African commitments is still relatively small: 0.7 percent for Algeria, 8.4 percent for Tunisia, 16.8 percent for Egypt, and 23.2 percent for Morocco,[9] and in practice, their commitments are still severely limited by restrictions on market access and national treatment rules. Counting only the commitments where there are no such restrictions, sectoral coverage falls to 0.5 percent for Algeria, 1.5 percent for Tunisia, 7.9 percent for Egypt, and 6.5 percent for Morocco. This compares to an average 10 percent for large developing countries and 28 percent for high-income developed countries; the EU's coverage rate is 63 percent. Trade in services between the EU and North African countries is problematic, mainly because the services in which the latter four countries enjoy comparative advantages are highly labor intensive.

Regarding direct investment, the EMAs also deferred negotiations over the right of establishment to five years after the agreement is to be enforced. While EMAs have dealt explicitly with shallow integration

matters concerning tariffs and nontariff barriers, issues of deep integration have either been only vaguely tackled or left to future negotiations. The EMAs are, therefore, more limited in the coverage of issues it undertakes compared to other regional agreements, such as NAFTA, that produce compromises between developed and developing nations.

With the prospect of an integrated market among all Mediterranean countries and the EU, investors will locate in the most stable and dynamic Mediterranean countries. Given Tunisia's strong economic growth over the last decade and its relatively stable political environment, it has a good chance of benefiting from additional investment. At the very least, Morocco and Egypt could benefit in those sectors where they are more competitive than other suppliers. In general, EMAs may induce more technology-intensive FDI to the region because of the secured market access to the EU (Page and Underwood 1997).

Economic impact on the North African region

Opening the North African markets to imports from the EU will, first of all, make imports of machinery and upstream supplies cheaper, with the result that industrial and agricultural production costs in the North African countries are likely to fall. The lower costs of inputs imported from the EU may also increase the share of high quality inputs and, therefore, enhance the quality of production and exports. Both effects, in turn, should improve the competitiveness of North African products in EU markets. When tariffs on consumer good imports begin to fall, consumers in the North African states will also benefit from lower prices and, thus, enjoy higher real incomes.

More intense competition in the North African markets due to cheaper imports from the EU will also challenge incumbent producers in the region. This may become a problem especially for state owned enterprises, which still constitute a large share of the economies in the four North African countries and are generally considered less efficient than their counterparts in the private sector of the EU. The gradual phasing in of tariff reductions and their long anticipation, together with substantial financial aid from the EU aimed specifically at strengthening private sector competitiveness, should ease such adjustment costs. Ultimately, an improved exploitation of comparative advantages between the EU and North Africa through more intense trade and competition will have positive income effects in North Africa.

Table 7. Sectoral Coverage of Specific GATS Commitments (in Percent)

	High-Income Countries	Other Countries	Large Developing	Selected Arab Countries			
				Algeria	Egypt	Morocco	Tunisia
Market Access							
Average count (sectors/model listed as a share of maximum possible)	53.3	15.1	29.6	0.65	16.77	23.23	8.39
Average coverage (sectors/modes listed as a share of total GATS classif-ication, weighted by openness and binding scale factors)	40.6	9.4	17.1	0.48	10.48	11.21	3.71
Coverage/count (average coverage as a share of average count)	76.2	62.3	57.7	73.9	62.5	48.3	44.2
"No Restrictions" as a share of total offer made (no scaling)	56.4	47.3	36.7	75.0	47.1	28.5	23.1
"No Restrictions" as a share of total GATS classification	30.5	6.7	10.9	0.48	7.9	6.6	1.9
National Treatment							
Average count (sectors/modes listed as a share of maximum possible)	53.3	15.1	29.6	0.65	16.77	23.23	8.39
Average coverage (sectors/modes listed as a share of total GATS classification, weighted by openness and binding scale factors)	42.4	10.2	18.8	0.48	11.69	15.65	3.55
Coverage/count (average coverage as a share of average count)	79.5	67.5	63.5	73.9	69.7	67.4	42.3
"No Restrictions" as a share of total offer made (no scaling)	65.1	60.4	49.3	75.0	61.5	64.6	40.4
"No Restrictions" as a share of total GATS classification	35.3	8.5	14.6	0.48	10.3	15.0	3.4
Memorandum							
No restrictions on market access and national treatment as a share of total GATS classification	28.0	6.4	10.0	0.48	7.9	6.5	1.5

Source: Hoekman, Bernard and Carlos A. Primo Braga "Trade in Services, the GATS and the Arab Countries", in Saied El-Naggar, The Uruguay Round and The Arab Countries" International Monetary Fund,1996

The FTA will also have a serious effect on tariff revenues in the four North African states. Because half of their imports originate in the EU there will be a perceptible loss of customs duties; this will impose a considerable burden on national budgets as import duties still account for between 10 and 20 percent of tax revenue. Such a burden would aggravate the financial constraints of North African governments whose resources for social services (e.g., education and health) are already very limited. This suggests that the EU might be advised to support efforts for improving national tax systems in the region to ensure that free trade does not lead to a decline in public education, health, and other programs. If regional governments revert to raising national value-added taxes, the benefits from free trade to the consumer would be reduced and the effects of trade smaller than expected (Wolf 2001).

A number of empirical studies have recently tried to quantify the effects of the FTA between the EU and Morocco, Tunisia and Egypt (Testas 1999; Rutherford et al. 1997; Stern 2001). They conclude that trade liberalization in the North African countries against imports from the EU will increase economic welfare in North Africa by 1.5 to 3.3 percent. Since an FTA will initiate substantial structural change, an important condition for realizing these welfare gains is that capital is mobile across sectors. This points to the importance of reducing regulatory rigidities and, in particular, obstacles against capital inflows.[10]

For Morocco, an increase in the export price for fruit and vegetables is expected because of the more favorable treatment given these exports in the EMAs. An extended FTA that substantially covers all sectors would raise employment in fruit and vegetable production, as well as in the mining and the leather sectors. Empirical studies predict an increase in the combined imports of Algeria, Morocco, and Tunisia by approximately 40 percent, due to the FTA with the EU. About half of this trade expansion would occur because imports of manufactures were liberalized.

The dynamic effects of regional integration are likely to be even more important in practice than the aforementioned static efficiency gains. Larger market size increases incentives for investment because of the potential to exploit economies of scale and the need to react to more intense competition by modernizing capital equipment. Capital inflows to the region will again play a critical role by contributing substantially to the modernization of economies through access to modern technology and management techniques, marketing networks, and high quality inputs. This will increase the productivity of domestic firms. As the perception of a country by foreign investors depends not only on its own performance, but also on the stability and prosperity of neighboring countries, regional integration could help to improve the area's ability to attract foreign capital.

"New regional economics" puts a special emphasis on the dynamic gains to be had from reduced administrative and transaction costs due to improved institutions (Lawrence 1996). Increased internal competition will lead to higher competitiveness and decreased production costs and monopoly rents; it will also stimulate exports to the rest of the world. In terms of new regional economics, the EMAs can be characterized as an example of deep integration (dealing with behind-the-border issues including domestic rules and regulations) as opposed to shallow integration (which deals only with border issues). By going far beyond reciprocal free trade and aiming at harmonizing laws and regulations, EMAs may improve foreign investors' perception of the stability and openness of the North African countries. As a result, Euro-Mediterranean integration is expected to increase FDI, as it did in other North-South agreements. However, the impact of these increased capital flows will depend, crucially, on financial markets and other domestic reforms.

North African trade policy

The EMAs are not the only regional agreements in which the North African countries are engaged. These countries are also members of the Greater Arab Free Trade Area (GAFTA) and a number of bilateral agreements with Arab states. GAFTA aims at creating a free trade area over a ten-year period, which started in 1998. Moreover, Algeria, Morocco, and Tunisia are members of the Maghreb Union. Closer economic cooperation among African states is also a key goal of the New Partnership for Africa's Development (NEPAD) that was launched in 2001 and formally endorsed by the G8 countries in July 2002. On the multilateral level, the North African countries are full members of the WTO (with the exception of Algeria, which is still an observer). They are complying or trying to comply with all WTO measures. Of the four countries, only Egypt initiated antidumping measures, four of them against EU imports.

The four North African countries have implemented different trade policies in recent years. Whereas Egypt and Morocco have reduced their average tariff rates significantly (simple and weighted), Tunisia and Algeria have increased their average tariff rates. The reduction of the average tariff rates in Egypt has been accompanied by increased tariff dispersion. This is because of the presence of prohibitive tariffs on a number of commodities such as alcoholic beverages. Morocco and Algeria have experienced a reduction in tariff dispersion, implying positive developments in that area, while Tunisia has increased its tariff dispersion in addition to the increase in its average tariff rates.

Such developments in trade policy tools have been reflected in the degree of openness of the four countries concerned. Morocco, which has reduced its average tariff rate and tariff dispersion significantly over the 1990s, has enjoyed an increase in the ratio of exports and imports to GDP from 60 percent in 1990 to 70 percent in 2000. In contrast, this ratio has fallen in Tunisia and also especially in Egypt (see also Figure 10); these two countries did not change average tariff rates or tariff dispersions much over the last decade.

Can EU Policy Improve North Africa's Competitiveness?

Attention to three policy issues is critical if the competitiveness of North Africa is to improve and, with it, the potential for stronger economic development in the region.

Figure 10. Mean Tariff Barriers

Simple Mean Tariff %

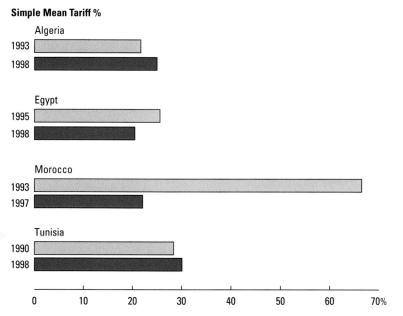

Weighted Mean Tariff %

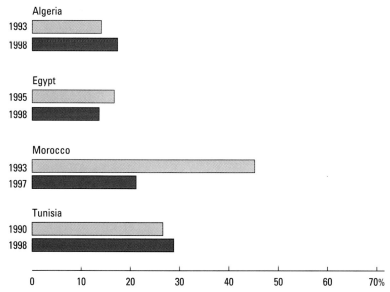

Source: World Bank, World Development Indicators 2001

The first issue is governance. Inefficient and ineffective government contributes to slow economic development through excessive costs of transactions and high set-up costs for new businesses. Reforming and improving domestic government institutions is critical in order for North African countries to provide environments that are more attractive for capital inflows and that stimulate domestic capital formation.

The second issue is human potential and its use in economic development. The poor performance of the region in terms of human development indicates an environment in which many human resources are left unused and human capital formation is discouraged. As a result, the more active and aspiring wish to leave the region for other countries, where they may use their potentials more fully. Improving health and education systems is one important way of developing human potential. Other important ways are to encourage greater participation in production by including women in the labor market and by strengthening the development of the private sector as an engine of growth and development.

The third issue is trade and economic cooperation among countries in the region. Given the wide variation in resource endowments, there is a potential for trade creation among Arab states. Deeper regional integration

Table 8. Standard Deviation of Tariff and Tariff Peaks (in Percent)

		Standard Deviation of Tariff Rates	Share of Lines with Int. Peaks Tariffs
Algeria	1993	16.9	44.2
	1998	16.4	52.2
Egypt	1995	33.2	53.1
	1998	39.5	47.4
Morocco	1993	29.5	96.8
	1997	19.3	61.8
Tunisia	1990	10	97.3
	1998	13.1	90.5

Source: World Bank, World Development Indicators 2001

among the North African and Mediterranean countries, as envisaged under GAFTA, could help them develop common comparative advantages and prepare their economies for integration with Europe and further multilateral liberalization in the WTO. Intensified Arab integration could lead to raised productivity growth rates, because import competition in the region would increase; increased competition could be expected to speed the adoption of new technologies and increase productivity at the plant level. Trade creation could also provide opportunities for businesspeople to learn about exporting by exporting on a regional level; especially for nontraditional exports, the markets of neighboring countries with similar levels of development and similar cultural backgrounds are easier to serve. This experience could then help firms to later enter the European market. Furthermore, intensified regional integration among Arab states could significantly reduce transaction costs through the harmonization of standards, the reduction of barriers to labor and capital mobility, and the development of trade-related infrastructure. A rise in productivity and a greater potential for using economies of scale would encourage Arab entrepreneurship. An integrated Arab market with nearly 300 million consumers would give investors the opportunity to make use of a relatively well educated labor force that is substantially cheaper than EU labor. Moreover, having a cheap labor force is likely to compensate for the disadvantages of the hub and spokes effect described above, and therefore to increase the gains from EMAs. Of course, deeper integration requires strong political support, significant efforts to harmonize regulatory policies, and the improvement of cross-border infrastructure.

The EU's new trade policy under the EMP Partnership addresses these issues explicitly. Regional integration is encouraged, and reform programs strengthening private sector development and domestic institutions are the main targets for financial aid. In this regard, the EMP Partnership ties in with the NEPAD, which gives private sector and institutional development similar priorities for development aid. To make it work effectively, these funding goals must not be sacrificed for short-run considerations of international politics and particularism.

Conclusions

The EMAs are challenges, rather than panaceas, for the North African countries; they are a new form of cooperation that North African countries have never experienced before. Differences between the EMAs and previous cooperative agreements include: the call for reciprocal treatment in trade relations, in contrast to the old, nonreciprocal trade relations; institutional changes, thereby reaching the roots of domestic regulations and national sovereignty, in contrast to the previous shallow integration that dealt only with border issues; and finally, the encompassing of political, cultural and social dimensions, in contrast to former agreements that were limited to trade and financial relations.

The North African countries should use the EMAs as vehicles of reform; they should use them to anchor otherwise tough reform decisions, especially as they are backed up by financial support and technical assistance. This would help the North African countries to overcome the many supply side problems that have kept their integration in the world economy and the EU markets low in the past, and enhance the openness of their economies.

Management of the EMAs requires a prudent approach on behalf of the North African countries. To exploit the secured market access in Europe, the North African countries must improve factor productivity and diversify their export capacity towards processed foods, basic manufactures, and services. Additional investment will be needed for this. Balancing the short and medium costs of implementation with the potential long-term gains should motivate policymakers to stick to the reforms initiated.

In the coming decade, however, the economic value of the EMAs is likely to decline, as general trade liberalization will proceed under the Doha round of trade negotiations. Preferential access to EU markets will be less valuable when liberalization takes place on a global scale. This could reduce the incentive for EMA reforms and lead to a return to old modes of trade in the region. To avoid this, the EU should be encouraged to target its financial aid even more effectively to countries and governments pursuing reform policies.

For the EU, closer cooperation with North African countries is also of great importance. As EMAs have the potential to increase growth in North Africa, at least in the longer run, these countries offer significant market opportunities for European firms. In the short to medium run, European firms could benefit from increasing investment opportunities in the North African countries due to the secured market access in Europe, overall improvements in macroeconomic policies, and improving institutional environments.

Finally, to make the EMP Partnership a worthwhile undertaking for all parties, it is important to extend the agreements, in a timely fashion, to the areas of agriculture and services. The EU should have an interest in liberalizing trade in these sectors, not the least because this will benefit the urban and rural poor and reduce incentives for migration.

References

Baldwin, Richard. *Towards an Integrated Europe*. London: CEPR, 1994.

Chabrier, Paul. "Growth Strategy for North Africa: A Regional Approach." In *Finance and Development*, 38, 2001.

Chevallier, Agnes, and Michael Freudenberg. "The Nature of Euro-Mediteranean Trade and the Prospects for Regional Integration." In *Towards Arab and Euro-Med Regional Integration*, edited by Dessus, Sebastien, Julia Devlin, and Raed Safadi. OECD, 2001.

Cox, Aidan, and Jenny Chapham. *The European Community External Cooperation Programmes: Policies, Management and Distribution*. London: ODI, 1999.

Djankov, Simeon, Rafael La Porta, Florencio Lopez de Silanes, and Andrej Shleifer. The Regulation of Entry. World Bank, working paper. World Bank, 2001.

Dessus, Sebastien, Julia Devlin, and Raed Safadi, eds. *Towards Arab and Euro-Med Regional Integration*. OECD, 2001.

Devlin, Julian, and John Page. "Testing the Waters: Arab Integration, Competitiveness, and the EMP Agreements." In *Towards Arab and Euro-Med Regional Integration*, edited by Dessus, Sebastien, Julia Devlin, and Raed Safadi. OECD, 2001.

European Commission. "Strengthening the Mediterranean Policy of the European Union: Establishing a Euro-Mediterranean Partnership." Bulletin of the European Union, Supplement 2/95. Luxembourg: Office for Official Publications of the European Communities, 1995.

European Commission. "Evaluation of Aspects of EU Development Aid to the MED Region." Final Synthesis Report. Brussels: EC, November 1998.

European Commission. *Bilateral Trade Relations: Algeria, Egypt, Morocco, Tunisia*. DG Trade A2/CG/SG/RQ. Brussels: EC, July 2001.

European Commission. *Union Européenne—Maghreb. 25 Ans de Coopération, 1976–2001*. Brussels: DG External Relations, 2002.

Finger, J. Michael. "The GATT as International Discipline Over Trade Restrictions: A Public Choice Approach." World Bank, policy research working paper no. 402. World Bank, 1990.

Ghoneim, Ahmed. "Antidumping Practice Under the GATT and the European Union Rules: Prospects for the Egyptian-European Partnership Agreement." In *The Egyptian Exports and the Challenges of the Twenty First Century*, edited by Nassar, Heba, and Alfons Naeim. Cairo: Center for Economic and Financial Research and Studies, 2000a.

Ghoneim, Ahmed Farouk. "Institutional Reform to promote Exports: Egypt and the EU." In *Institutional Reform and Economic Development in Egypt: Which Institutions and Why*, edited by Handoussa, Heba, and Noha El-Mikawy. Bonn: Center for Development Research, Bonn University. Republished by the American University in Cairo (AUC), 2000b.

Heritage Foundation. *The Index of Economic Freedom*. Washington D.C., 2002.

Hoekman, Bernard, and Carlos A. Primo Braga. "Trade in Services, the GATS and the Arab Countries." In , *The Uruguay Round and the Arab Countries*, edited by Saied El-Naggar . International Monetary Fund, 1996.

International Monetary Fund. *World Economic Outlook*. April 2002.

Kaufmann, Daniel, Aart Kraay, and Pablo Zoido-Lobatón. "Governance Matters II. Updated Indicators for 2000/01." World Bank, policy research paper no. 2722. Washington D.C.: World Bank, 2002.

Morisset, Jacques, and Olivier Lumenga Neso. "Administrative Barriers to Foreign Investment in Developing Countries." World Bank, policy research working paper. Washington DC: World Bank, 2002.

Nassar, Heba, and A. Ghoneim. "Trade and Migration, Are They Complements or Substitutes: A Review of Four MENA Countries." Paper presented at the University of European Union Annual Meeting, Florence Italy, 19–24 March 2002.

Lahouel, El Hedi Mohamed. "Foreign Direct Investment, the European Mediterranean Agreements and Integration Between Middle East and North African Countries." In *Towards Arab and Euro-Med Regional Integration*, edited by Dessus, Sebastien, Julia Devlin, and Raed Safadi. OECD, 2001.

Lahouel, Mohamed. "Telecommunications Services In the MENA Region. Country Case Analysis of Markets, Liberalization and Regulatory Regimes: Morocco, Tunisia and Egypt." Paper presented at the International Affairs Institute and the World Bank Institute Workshop, Tunisia, 5–6 April 2002.

Lawrence, Robert Z. *Regionalism, Multilateralism, and Deeper Integration*, Washington D.C.: The Brookings Institution, 1996.

OECD-DAC. *International Development Statistics*. Paris, 2002.

OECD/AfDB. *African Economic Outlook*. 2002.

Page, John, and John Underwood. "Growth, the Maghreb and Free Trade with the European Union." In Regional Partners in Global Markets: Limits and Possibilities of the EMP Agreements," edited by Galal, A., and B. Hoeckmann. CEPR London; ECES Cairo, 1997.

Parfitt, Trevor. "Europe's Mediterranean Designs: An Analysis of the Euromed Relationship with Special Reference to Egypt." *Third World Quarterly* 18 (1997):865–881.

Rutherford, Thomas F., E. Elisabeth Rutström, David Tarr. "Morocco's Free Trade Agreement with the EU: A quantitative Assesment." *Economic Modelling* 14 (1997): 237–269.

Stengg, Werner. The textile and clothing industry in the EU—A survey. European Commission Enterprise Papers 2–2001. Brussels: EC, 2001.

Stern, Robert M. "Dynamic Aspects of Euro-Mediterranean Agreements for the Middle East and North African Economies." In *Towards Arab and Euro-Med Regional Integration*, edited by Dessus, Sebastien, Julia Devlin, and Raed Safadi. OECD, 2001.

Testas, Abdelaziz. "The European Union's Global Approach to the Mediterranean Area." *Development Policy Review* 17 (1999):25–41.

United Nations Conference on Trade and Development. *Handbook of Statistics*, 2001. New York; Geneva. 2001.

United Nations Conference on Trade and Development. World Investment Report 2001. *Promoting Linkages*. New York; Geneva. 2001.

United Nations Development Program. *Arab Human Development Report*. New York. 2002.

Waer, Paul. "European Community Rules of Origin." In *Rules of Origin in International Trade: A Comparative Study,* edited by Vermulst, Edwin, Paul Waer, and Jacques Bourgeois. Ann Arbor: University of Michigan Press, 1992.

Wolf, Susanna. "The European Union and Africa: From Post-Colonialism towards Partnership?" In *Africa Contemporary Record, 1994–1996*. Vol. XXV, edited by Legum, Colin. New York; London: Holmes and Meier, 2001.

World Bank. *World Development Indicators*. Washington, D.C. 2001.

World Trade Organization. "Anti-Dumping Measures: By Reporting Party." Geneva, 2002.

Endnotes

1. MEDA means "financial and technical measures to accompany the reform of social and economic structures in the Mediterranean nonmember countries."

2. Libya has no special trade relations with the EU and there is only very limited data for that country. Therefore, we do not include Libya in our analysis, although it is part of the North African region.

3. Human Development Index scores are between 0 and 1, with 1 indicating the most advanced development. According the UNDP (2002), countries in the Arab region score an average of 0.64; this compares to 0.69 for Southeast Asia and the Pacific region, and 0.76 for Latin America and the Caribbean.

4. Voice and accountability refers to the ability of citizens to participate in the selection of their governments. Political stability indicates perceptions of the likelihood that a government will be overthrown by unconstitutional means. Government effectiveness refers to the perceptions of the quality of the bureaucracy and public service provision, while regulatory quality measures the quality of regulatory policies in terms of market friendliness and regulatory burden. Rule of law indicates the extent to which agents have confidence in the rules of society, and control of corruption measures the perception of how prevalent corruption is in society. See Kaufmann et al. (2002).

5. According to the IMF Balance of Payments Classification, commercial services constitute transportation (sea, air, and other); travel (business and personal); other services (communications, construction, insurance, financial, computer and information, royalties and license fees, other business services, and cultural and recreational and governmental services not identified elsewhere).

6. These authors account for all required administrative costs of setting up a firm. A standardized firm is defined as one that performs general industrial or commercial activities, operates in the largest city, and does not engage in foreign trade. It is not subject to special industry or environmental regulations and does not trade in goods subject to excise taxes. Its capital, which amounts to ten times per capita GDP in 1999, is domestically owned and subscribed in cash. Data for Algeria are not provided.

7. For example, a study of the former European Commission European free trade area agreement suggests that the cost of the border formalities to determine the origin of products amounted to at least 3 percent of the value of the goods concerned. This compared to an EU average of 6 percent MFN tariff rate (Waer 1992).

8. EU aid refers only to aid provided by the European Commission not aid provided by the individual member states.

9. There are 155 sectors and subsectors defined in GATS and four modes of supply, namely cross-border services, consumption abroad, commercial presence (FDI), and temporary entry of natural persons. Sectoral coverage is calculated as 100 times the number of sectors and subsectors for which a country has made a commitment divided by the total number of sectors, and multiplied by four.

10. Testas (1999), Rutherford et al. (1997), and Stern (2001) all agree that the North African countries would benefit even more from unilaterally liberalizing trade with all partners.

The Hydrocarbon Sector

Paul Tempest

Overview

All Arab states derive income from the hydrocarbon industry, either directly from oil, natural gas, and condensate production or indirectly through intra-Arab investment, intra-regional petroleum-related commerce, and remittance flows, which can be substantial. This phenomenon makes the Arab region quite different from any other large grouping of states. Despite national rivalries, the major Arab oil and gas producing and exporting states enjoy a degree of cohesion that also impacts the governance of all the other Arab states.

Petroleum activity in the region profoundly affects the economic performance, administrative efficiency, and technological adaptability of the twenty-two states of the Arab League to the extent that League nations' responses to other international market pressures and challenges are often modified, distorted, or disguised. There are some beneficial aspects of this petroleum activity; for example, access to the advanced technology used by extremely efficient multinational oil and gas operating and service companies. There are also, however, inherent disadvantages. For example, the multinationals attract and divert the very best in local human resources and skills. By and large also, oil- and gas-derived or related revenue is a financial and economic cushion that shields these Arab countries from some of the harsher aspects of cyclical fluctuations in international trade, yet this revenue often makes the group less flexible in responding to changing market conditions.

Arab states' relative regional isolation in the global economy is, therefore, both their strength and their weakness. This paper aims first to determine the weight today of the Arab states—individually and in aggregate—in global energy and, by implication, in the global economy. From this an assessment can be made of their prospects and potential for economic growth and development of their resources.

For over half a century, the leading Arab oil and gas producers have been pivotal to the course of the global economy. This paper will look at the energy-related problems, challenges, and issues that the Arab states are likely to face over the next decade. Finally, in light of that assessment and the evidence of the last two decades, we seek to identify how key Arab oil and gas producers may be able to maintain their competitive advantage over the next half-century, and how they may continue to play a role as a most useful economic regulator at the heart of the global economy.

Three Largely Separate Groups of Countries

While all twenty-two members of the Arab League enjoy strong sociological and linguistic ties to each other, reinforced by Islam and the strong heritage of a common Arab culture, they can be divided in energy orientation and economic national interest terms into three distinct groupings.

1. The North African states

The North African states look predominantly and increasingly toward southern Europe. These links have been strongly reinforced by the new gas pipelines to Italy and Spain. For southern Europe, Algerian, Libyan, and Egyptian natural gas as well as Libyan and Algerian oil offer distinct cost advantages, greater security of energy supply, and an abundant resource in a part of the world where such abundance appears to be diminishing. Looking in the other direction, the North Africans are most conscious of the energy-poor areas of the sub-Saharan states and their own role as a bridge and channel between energy-poor Africa and industry-rich Europe.

2. The Levantine states

Historically a vital northern corridor between the Mediterranean and the Gulf states, Syria, Lebanon, and Jordan have long earned a good living from the transit trade to Iraq and the Gulf. The value of this trade has been greatly inflated by the UN sanctions imposed on Iraq since 1990. Among the three countries, Syria's ample oil and gas resources stand in marked contrast to Lebanon and Jordan's almost total dependence on an external energy supply. Jordan has found an energy solution in its close relationship with Iraq; this has supplanted an earlier dependence on Saudi oil. The responses of all three Levantine Arab states to external economic and technological stimuli are inevitably colored by the shifting politics of the continuing Palestine/Israel conflict on their doorstep.

3. The Gulf/Arabian states

Saudi Arabia, Iraq, United Arab Emirates (U.A.E.), and Kuwait are among the giants in global oil. All look across the Gulf at the fifth Gulf giant, revolutionary Iran, with some trepidation. Iran has already pressed claims on the U.A.E. concerning the sovereignty of various islands. There are significant populations of Shi'ite Muslims in southern Iraq, the Eastern Province of Saudi Arabia, Bahrain, and in several of the U.A.E. states. Further, neither the combined Arab Gulf population nor the various local Arab defence forces begin to match those of Iran.

Increasingly, Gulf exports of oil and natural gas are targeting the Southeast/Pacific markets, with much less petroleum flowing around the Cape to Europe and North America. This change is beginning to have a profound effect on established relations between Gulf exporters and their major trading partners in Europe and the U.S. New entrants to the Pacific/ Southeast Asia gas market, such as Qatar and Oman, send substantial flows of liquefied natural gas (LNG) to Japan and Korea, increasing competition among the Gulf states. On the other hand, proposals for gaslines from Qatar to Kuwait and from Qatar through the U.A.E. to Oman are also new cohesive forces on the Arab side of the Gulf.

In purely economic and commercial terms, none of the Arab states are heavyweights on the global scale; some are very lightweight. To the extent that economic, commercial, and political cohesion can be established between them, mainly through the hydrocarbon sector, their separate and aggregate ability to compete is likely to be enhanced.

Small, Divided, and Isolated Energy Consumers

The total population of the twenty-two Arab states is about 290 million, 4.8 percent of the global total. Some of the more populous states, such as Egypt and Algeria, have quite low GDP per capita incomes, while Qatar, U.A.E., and Kuwait, with very small populations and very high oil and gas income, are at the very top of the GDP per capita income tables. Within many of the Arab states there are very wide ranges of income, with the lowest tier including many temporary immigrant

workers on minimal wages and pockets of isolated rural poverty. The strong drift to the towns has also posed some extremely difficult problems for adequate housing, employment, and the provision of an efficient infrastructure.

It is not surprising, therefore, that the aggregate demand for energy from the twenty-two Arab states (see Table 1) is, at 4.5 percent, less than the population share in the global total. Moreover, it is concentrated predominantly on oil and gas, with Arab use of hydro less than 0.8 percent, coal less than 0.4 percent, and nuclear 0.0 percent of the global totals.

Table 1. Arab Primary Energy Consumption, 2001

	Arab Total (mtoe)	% Global Total
Oil	217.2	6.2
Gas	181.1	7.5
Coal	9.2	0.4
Nuclear	0.0	0.0
Hydro	4.5	0.8
Total	412.0	4.5

Source: International Energy Agency; Oil and Gas Journal; PTA London
Note: mtoe—million tons of oil equivalent

Nonetheless, those lead Arab states that have developed their own oil and gas resources (see Table 2) do enjoy a competitive advantage. This is because they have been able to draw on these resources for their own needs at costs related to the cost of production rather than the costs imposed by competitive international markets. The availability of natural gas, often regarded as a free by-product of oil production, has greatly enhanced the economic viability of many new electricity generating, desalination, and petrochemical projects.

Table 2. Major Arab Consumers of Oil, 2001

	(000 mbd)	% Global Total
Gulf		
Saudi Arabia	1347	1.8
U.A.E.	318	0.4
Kuwait	72	0.3
North Africa		
Egypt	551	0.7
Algeria	200	0.3

Sources: British Petroleum Statistical Review of World Energy, June 2002; Oil and Gas Journal
Note: mbd—million barrels per day

More recently, the development of vast resources of natural gas primarily for export by pipeline or as LNG has tempted domestic Arab economic planners to take what gas they have needed for new domestic projects—often only a small part of the total volume of gas produced.

Such cost benefits bring in their train an unwelcome isolation from world markets. In almost all the Arab oil producing states, little attempt has been made, as in Europe, Japan, and North America, to restrain demand by imposing various consumer taxes. Prices of gasoline and diesel to the end-user in these Arab states are extremely low. There is, therefore, little incentive for the consumer to seek improved efficiency in new technology (e.g., in doubling miles per gallon by switching to hybrid fuel-cell technology in automobiles or by pioneering pollutant-free hydrogen-driven fleets of urban trucks or buses); vehicles and refuelling infrastructure still have high initial capital costs. The fuel savings of such a switch mean very little to the operator or consumer and, in a small economy, are unlikely to attract much support or interest from government.

The Arab states are, however, world leaders in several areas. Their vigorous economic growth and ability to pay in hard currency has kept many of them close to the technological frontier in desalination and electricity generation, and in ammonia, urea, and other aspects of petrochemical production. The new well-planned and efficiently administered cities of, Qatar, Bahrain, the U.A.E., and Oman, all founded on oil wealth, stand as valuable small-state development models (and are a source of envy) for the more populous Islamic neighbours (notably Iraq, Iran, and Pakistan) as well as for the entire developing world. The success is clearly visible in extensive new public sector housing projects, well-run public services and public works, and health care and hospitals of high quality. The transformation into clean, tidy, safe, and above all, verdant cities with considerable tourism potential has been principally achieved by the efficient deployment of government oil revenue and a willingness to harness expatriate labour, enterprise, and skills.

Another very strong competitive advantage becomes evident in times of supply crisis. At such times, energy consumers in Arab oil producer countries can derive immense benefit from ample availability of fuel at home, while elsewhere fuel shortages caused by the interruption of external supply might be bringing much more sophisticated industrial economies as well

as many energy-importing developing countries to their knees.

In summary, the Arab states, as consumers of energy, are small, weak, isolated, and divided. Even in aggregate, their leverage as energy consumers in the world markets is very limited. Their energy pricing policy subsidises the domestic consumer and, in a minor way, distorts international trade. Nonetheless, instant access to their own resources or, if energy-poor, access (on preferential terms) to richer fellow-Arab states lends greater energy security in times of regional or global turmoil.

Primary Energy Production

The energy production mix of the Arab countries is heavily skewed to oil and gas (see Table 3). There is negligible coal production, no nuclear power, and only a modest amount of hydro power in a few locations. The lack of coal, nuclear, and hydro makes the Arab world increasingly vulnerable to fluctuations in global demand for oil and gas. Indeed, the lack of energy substitution options is a considerable weakness in the wider prospects for the Arab economies. As far as alternative energy is concerned, some progress has been made with solar voltaics, favored by long hours of daily sunlight, and with wind power in a number of windy locations. These alternatives are particularly attractive in remote mountain and desert locations, but in aggregate add up to less than 1 percent in the total primary energy mix. There is little prospect of a change in this energy mix, certainly not in the next two decades; the future prosperity of the Arab world rests firmly on the continued production and export of oil, natural gas, and condensates.

High dependence on oil and gas production poses another problem for the Arab states: it makes them particularly vulnerable to global environmentalist pressures. Arab states have difficulty in formulating a common response to allegations that they are a major source of carbon dioxide and therefore partly accountable for global warming, a principal source of air pollution in urban environments, despoilers of natural landscape and creators of toxic industrial waste. However strenuous their efforts to answer these critics, governments often find the task of justification a most difficult and time-consuming part of their activities and responsibilities.

The greatest competitive strength of the Arab states lies in their 30 percent share of global oil production (see Tables 3 and 5), which is reinforced by an even

Table 3. Total Arab Primary Energy Production, 2001

	Arab Total (mbdoe)	% Global Total
Oil	22.3	29.9
Gas	5.0	11.1
Coal	**	**
Nuclear	**	**
Hydro	**	0.7
Total	27.3	14.8

**Nil or very small

Source: British Petroleum Annual Statistical Energy Review; PTA London, June 2002

Note: mbdoe—million barrels of oil equivalent per day

larger share of global oil reserves (60 percent) and a very strong position in international trade in oil (44 percent). With a buoyant and growing gas production (11 percent of the global total), Arab primary energy production has risen to almost 15 percent of the global total. As indicated later in this paper, this energy intensity is most likely to continue to rise and provide a rich source of future prosperity.

Dominant Arab Oil Reserves

The Arab states account for over 60 percent of total proven oil reserves (see Table 4). Compared with

Table 4. Total Arab Oil Reserves, 2001

	At End-2001 (000 mb)	% Global Total	Reserves/Production Ratio (Years)
Major Gulf			
Saudi Arabia	261.8	24.9	85.0
Iraq	112.5	10.7	>100.0
Kuwait	96.5	9.2	>100.0
U.A.E.	97.8	9.3	>100.0
Minor Gulf/ Arabia			
Qatar	15.2	1.4	55.5
Oman	5.5	0.5	15.8
Yemen	4.0	0.4	24.2
Levant			
Syrian AR	2.5	0.2	12.5
North Africa			
Libya	29.5	2.8	57.3
Algeria	9.2	0.9	17.6
Egypt	2.5	0.2	22.8
Tunisia	0.3	—	—
Total Arab States	86.6	60.5	49.6

Sources: British Petroleum Statistical Review of World Energy, June 2002; International Energy Agency; Oil and Gas Journal; PTA London

Note: mb—million barrels

most non-Arab producers, production costs are still low, and advancing technology, bringing hitherto uneconomic oil resources within reach, point to probable producible resources at least double and possibly four times the current level of proven reserves. It is generally assumed that within fifty years, global oil supplies will be vastly increased by extensive production from heavy oils, tar-sands, and shales. Already, Canada and Venezuela are the leaders in the field. The problem lies in the capital-intensive nature of extraction and high running costs. However fast these heavy oils and high-cost deep-water oil resources are developed, it can be assumed that the Arab states will be able to bring new supply into production at less cost. A more immediate problem for Arab producers is that of being left (as at present) as the "swing" supplier in an over-supplied market. This, together with the medium- and long-term prospects for global oil and energy production, is examined in detail later in this paper.

Within the total Arab oil resource, Saudi Arabia, with one quarter of global proven oil reserves, holds the strong lead position. Nonetheless, this lead is outweighed by the combined total of Iraq, U.A.E., and Kuwait with almost 30 percent of global reserves between them. The North African and other Gulf producers all have much smaller reserves. Two countries, Iraq and Libya, claim that they have significantly larger reserves than those generally used and widely accepted by the oil industry, banks, and the global stock markets (see discussion above and Table 3). Among the geological community and exploration departments of the leading multinationals, there is a very strong body of opinion that Iraq and Libya may well be right in their optimism.

Dominant Arab Oil Production

For calendar year 2001, Saudi Arabia stood head and shoulders above the rest of Arab oil producers, with an average of 8.8 million barrels per day (mbd) or some 11.8 percent of total global oil production (see Table 5). This total and share is almost exactly matched at present by the combined total of Iraq, Kuwait, U.A.E., Oman, and Qatar. The combined production and share of the three large North African producers, Libya, Algeria, and Egypt, is only 40 percent of the Saudi level and global share. In aggregate, therefore, the Arab share of total global oil production (30 percent) cannot be matched by any other regional grouping.

Table 5. Arab Oil Production, 2001

	(mbd)					% Global Total
	1991	1996	1999	2000	2001	
Major Gulf						
Saudi Arabia	8.8	9.0	8.5	9.1	8.8	11.8
Iraq	0.3	0.6	2.6	2.6	2.4	3.3
Kuwait	0.2	2.1	2.0	2.2	2.1	2.9
U.A.E.	2.6	2.5	2.2	2.5	2.4	3.2
Minor Gulf/ Arabia						
Oman	0.7	0.9	0.9	1.0	1.0	1.3
Qatar	0.4	0.6	0.7	0.8	0.8	1.0
Yemen	0.2	0.4	0.4	0.4	0.5	0.6
Levant						
Syrian AR	0.5	0.6	0.6	0.6	0.6	0.8
North Africa						
Libya	1.4	1.5	1.4	1.5	1.4	1.9
Algeria	1.4	1.4	1.5	1.6	1.6	1.8
Egypt	0.9	0.9	0.8	0.8	0.8	1.0
Tunisia	0.1	0.1	0.1	0.1	0.1	0.1
Total Arab States	**17.1**	**20.6**	**21.7**	**23.2**	**22.5**	**30.2**

Source: British Petroleum Statistical Review of World Energy, June 2002
Note: mbd—million barrels per day

High Arab Reserves and Production Ratios

When reserve levels are set against current (average 2001) production levels, all the major Arab producers have very high ratios. In Iraq, Kuwait, and the U.A.E., reserves will last more than 100 years; in Saudi Arabia, 85 years; and in Qatar and Libya, more than 50 years.

Taking the totals for all the Arab states in 2001, the reserves will last 49.6 years. This compares with 13.5 for North America (10.7 years for the U.S.); 7.8 for Europe; 21.1 for the Former Soviet Union (19.1 for the Russian Federation); and 15.6 for the Asian Pacific countries (19.9 for China).

Dominant Arab Position in International Oil Trade

Globally, the bulk of energy produced is consumed within the country of origin. Coal is largely consumed at home. Nuclear generation of electricity is also primarily for home consumption. The U.S. and China are major examples of countries where almost all energy produced is consumed at home.

Oil and, more recently, gas are the exceptions to this pattern. Easily transportable and tradable, oil can cross frontiers easily. It is easily distributed and enjoys

a high value/weight ratio. Oil has long been the largest single commodity in international trade and is therefore a vital component of the global economy. Gas offers considerable economies of scale as soon as the up-front capital has been mobilised, and adequate markets created and dedicated to long-term supply contracts.

Table 6. Arab International Oil Trade Movements, 2001

	1991	1996	1999	2000	2001
Total Arab Exports (mbd)	14.1	17.2	18.5	18.9	19.1
Total Global Exports (mbd)	32.3	38.3	40.7	42.4	43.8
Arab Share of Global Exports (%)	43.6	44.9	45.5	44.6	44.0

Sources: Petroleum Intelligence Weekly; PTA London
Note: mbd—million barrels per day

Table 7. Gross Value of Arab Oil Exports, 2001

	1991	1996	1999	2000	2001
Total Arab Crude Exports (mbd)	14.1	17.2	18.5	18.9	19.1
Average Dubai Oil Price dollars per barrel	16.56	18.56	17.30	26.24	22.80
Gross Value $bn	85.3	116.6	116.9	181.0	159.3

Sources: Petroleum Intelligence Weekly; PTA London
Note: mbd—million barrels per day

Only 41.3 percent of oil produced is consumed within the country of production; oil that is traded across international frontiers is therefore almost 60 percent of total oil production. In 2001, the Arab countries had a dominant share of 44 percent (see Table 6) of the total global exports of crude oil and oil products. This dominance gives the Arab states a major voice and vital role in oil price determination (see Table 7 and later section on OPEC and OAPEC).

A Significant Niche-Market Share in Oil Refining

The Arab states have worked hard to add value to their oil industry by investing in refining capacity to meet their own needs and offering oil product for export. Their total refining capacity stands at approximately 6.2 mbd, about 8.8 percent of the global total (see Table 8).

Although the totals and shares might seem modest, the Arab refining capacity led by Saudi Arabia (with 1.8 mbd, or 2.2 percent of the global total) has strengthened Arab competitiveness downstream. This has been supplemented by substantial investment in refineries overseas, most notably by Saudi Arabia, Kuwait, and U.A.E. in Japan, Korea, the U.S., and Western Europe.

Table 8. Arab Crude Oil Refining Capacities, end-2001

	(b/d)	% Global Total
Gulf/Arabia		
Saudi Arabia	1,745,000	2.1
Kuwait	773,300	0.9
U.A.E.	514,750	0.6
Iraq	417,500	0.5
Bahrain	248,900	0.4
Yemen	130,000	0.2
Oman	85,000	0.1
Qatar	57,500	0.1
North Africa		
Egypt	726,000	0.9
Algeria	450,000	0.5
Libya	343,400	0.4
Morocco	154,901	0.2
Sudan	121,700	0.1
Tunisia	34,000	—
Levant		
Syrian AR	242,140	0.3
Jordan	90,400	0.1
Lebanon	37,500	—
Total Arab Crude Refining Capacity	**6,172,240**	**8.8**

Note: The principal accepted sources of this information differ in a number of details: for Iraq British Petroleum quotes 720 000 bd whereas the Oil and Gas Journal (in its Annual Review of Refining dated 24.12.01) has 417 500 bd. Similarly for Kuwait British Petroleum uses 720 000 bd compared with 773 000 in the OGJ.

Sources: British Petroleum Annual Statistical Review of Energy, June 2002 ; Oil and Gas Journal, December 2001 Survey; Middle East Economic Survey and PTA London

Note: b/d—barrels per day

In the Asia/Pacific market, the Gulf refiners have provided a strong challenge to Japanese and Korean refiners as well as to the large, balancing export refiners in Singapore. In the Mediterranean, the short-haul of product to Western Europe and refinery imbalances in France, Spain, and Italy have offered significant niche markets for North African refiners. Further penetration of North African products into the U.S. and northwestern Europe via Rotterdam has also been achieved.

A Strong and Growing Share of Global Natural Gas

The Arab states account for 25 percent of global gas reserves (see Table 9) and 11.1 percent of global gas production (see Table 10). These volumes are increasing steadily and the Arab market share in the global total is likely to continue to rise.

Table 9. Arab Natural Gas Reserves, 2001

	(tcf)	(tcm)	% Global Total
Gulf/Arabia			
Qatar	508.5	14.4	9.3
Saudi Arabia	219.5	6.2	4.0
U.A.E.	212.9	6.0	3.9
Iraq	109.8	3.1	2.0
Kuwait	52.7	1.5	1.0
Oman	29.3	0.8	0.5
Yemen	16.9	0.5	0.3
Bahrain	3.2	0.1	0.1
North Africa			
Algeria	159.7	4.5	2.9
Libya	46.4	1.3	0.8
Egypt	35.2	1.0	0.6
Other Arab States	**10.2**	**0.3**	**0.2**
Total Arab States	**1403.6**	**39.8**	**25.6**

Sources: British Petroleum Annual Statistical Review of World Energy, June 2002; Oil and Gas Journal; International Energy Agency

Note: tcf—trillion cubic feet; tcm—trillion cubic meters

Table 10. Arab Natural Gas Production, 1991–2001

	(bcm)				
	1991	1996	1999	2000	2001
Gulf/Arabia					
Saudi Arabia	35.2	44.4	46.2	49.8	53.7
U.A.E.	23.8	33.8	38.5	39.8	41.3
Qatar	7.6	13.7	22.1	29.1	32.5
Oman	2.6	4.4	5.5	8.4	13.4
Kuwait	0.5	9.3	8.6	9.6	9.5
Bahrain	5.5	7.4	8.7	8.8	8.9
North Africa					
Algeria	53.2	71.8	86.0	84.4	78.2
Egypt	7.8	11.5	14.7	18.3	21.0
Libya	5.9	5.8	5.5	5.4	5.4
Other Arab States	**3.9**	**6.5**	**8.4**	**8.4**	**8.6**
Total Arab States	**146.0**	**208.6**	**244.2**	**262.0**	**272.5**

Source: British Petroleum Annual Statistical Review of World Energy, June 2002; Oil and Gas Journal; PTA London

Note: bcm—billion cubic meters

Until only 10 or 15 years ago, much of the gas discovered in the Gulf states and in North Africa was shut-in as stranded gas or used as re-injection gas to boost oil production. The advent of major gas pipelines across the Mediterranean and the development of new LNG routes between the Gulf and Asia-Pacific, together with new gas-based manufacturing projects in all the gas-producing states, have since completely transformed development and the prospects for continuing expansion of Arab gas supply.

Qatar heads the list of gas reserve majors with 9.3 percent of the global total, and Saudi Arabia and U.A.E. each have a further 4 percent.

In 2001, Algeria was the top producer of natural gas with 3.2 percent of the global total, followed by Saudi Arabia (2.2 percent), U.A.E. (1.7 percent), and Qatar (1.3 percent). These shares do not add up to a major global Arab share (11.1 percent) when compared to the U.S. (22.5 percent) and Russia (22.0 percent). However, given the wide geographical scatter of gas development, the Arab grouping produces gas roughly equal to that of all Europe and the entire Asia/Pacific region.

One-third of all gas produced by Arab states is exported. The new pipeline gas exports from Algeria to Italy (21.85 billion cubic meters [bcm] in 2001) and Spain (6.45 bcm in 2001) represent 44 percent of Italian pipeline gas imports and 84 percent of Spanish pipeline gas imports.

Gulf exports of LNG reached 31.05 bcm in 2001, of which Qatar exported 16.54 bcm, Oman 7.43 bcm, and U.A.E. 7.08 bcm. The principal markets were Japan (15.19 bcm) and Korea (11.97 bcm).

Algeria exported 25.54 bcm of LNG in 2001, of which 9.80 bcm went to France and 5.20 bcm to Spain. Libya exported 0.77 bcm, all of which went to Spain.

In summary, Arab gas prospects have been enhanced by many new pipeline and LNG export projects and by a wide range of gas manufacturing projects targeting export markets. Domestic consumption (Table 11) is also growing.

Higher Levels of Arab Oil and Gas Revenue

Fluctuations in global oil prices and variations in demand have led to major and unpredictable fluctuations in Arab oil and gas revenue, giving Arab governments complex budgetary problems. After the two oil-price discontinuities of 1973/1974 and 1979/1980, demand for OPEC oil fell back sharply, and through the eighties revenue from oil sagged. In 1999 revenue was, in nominal terms, at almost exactly the level of 1996 (i.e., US$117 million). The year 2000 brought a massive improvement in revenue of 55 percent, to US$181 billion.

The U.S. Department of Energy assessment as of June 2002 indicates that OPEC oil revenue held up well in

Table 11. Arab Natural Gas Consumption, 1991–2001

	(bcm)				
	1991	1996	1999	2000	2001
Gulf/Arabia					
Saudi Arabia	35.2	44.4	46.2	49.8	53.7
U.A.E.	20.4	27.2	31.4	32.9	34.3
Qatar	7.6	13.7	14.0	15.1	16.0
Kuwait	0.5	9.3	8.6	9.6	9.5
North Africa					
Algeria	17.0	21.4	21.2	21.0	21.6
Egypt	7.7	11.3	14.3	18.3	21.0
Other Arab States	13.5	19.2	23.4	24.2	25.0
Total Arab States %	101.9	146.5	159.1	170.9	181.1
Global Market Share %	5.1	6.6	6.9	7.1	7.5

Source: British Petroleum Annual Statistical Review of World Energy, June 2002; International Energy Agency; Oil and Gas Journal

Note: bcm—billion cubic meters

Table 12. Projected Financial Requirement for Maintenance and Expansion of Arab Oil Sector, 2002–2006 (in US$ billion)

	Cost of Maintenance	Cost of Expansion	Total
Gulf/Arabia			
Saudi Arabia	9.3	5.2	14.5
Iraq	2.5	3.0	5.5
Kuwait	2.3	0.9	3.2
U.A.E.	2.8	2.1	4.9
Oman	1.5	0.2	1.7
Qatar	1.0	0.1	1.1
Yemen, Rep.	0.8	0.7	1.5
Bahrain	0.1	—	0.1
North Africa			
Libya	2.5	4.5	7.0
Algeria	2.7	3.0	5.7
Egypt	1.1	—	1.1
Sudan	0.2	1.1	1.3
Tunisia	0.1	—	0.1
Levant			
Syrian AR	0.9	—	0.9
Total Arab States	28.8	20.8	49.6

Source: APICORP/OAPEC Report of April 2002

2001 (US$191 billion) and is likely to be in the order of US$178 billion in 2002; further, given the buoyancy of oil prices in the first half of 2002, oil revenue is well on track to exceed this level in 2002.

The boost in oil revenue over the past two and a half years has not been evenly shared, but in profitable periods such as these, there is a spillover effect of investment which affects the less fortunate Arab states.

In addition to oil revenue, gas revenue has been accelerating sharply, notably in Qatar, Oman, and Egypt.

Buoyant oil and gas revenues have given considerable impetus and dynamism to new projects in the main Arab producer states, prompting strong entrepreneurial activity and a common desire to update petroleum capacity and other associated technology (see Tables 12 and 13). Government budgets indicate a desire to plan for growth, particularly in the areas of electricity generation, desalination, and public works; there is also interest in using government subsidies and fiscal incentives to further diversify industry.

Table 13. Projected Investments in Arab Natural Gas, Refining and Petrochemical Projects, 2002–2006 (in US$ billion)

	Natural Gas	Refining	Petro-chemicals	Total
Gulf/Arabia				
Qatar	9.4	0.4	2.8	12.6
Saudi Arabia	5.0	1.5	5.1	11.6
U.A.E.	3.4	0.9	—	4.3
Oman	1.0	0.9	2.1	3.9
Kuwait	—	0.1	3.5	3.6
Bahrain	—	0.6	—	0.6
Yemen , Rep.	—	0.4	—	0.4
North Africa				
Egypt	7.6	0.6	3.0	11.2
Algeria	5.1	—	2.9	8.0
Libya	4.5	0.6	0.4	5.5
Levant				
Syrian AR	0.2	0.5	—	0.7
Total*	**36.4**	**7.2**	**19.8**	**63.4**

Source APICORP/OAPEC Report to Arab Governments April 2002

*This report was not able to include estimates for Iraq, Sudan, Tunisia or the other smaller Arab countries

The Roles of OPEC and OAPEC

The Organisation of Petroleum Exporting Countries (OPEC) was founded in Baghdad in 1960. Its headquarters are now located in Vienna. OPEC objectives, as defined in its charter documentation, were to:

1. co-ordinate and unify petroleum policies among member countries;

2. secure fair and stable prices for petroleum producers;

3. ensure an efficient, economic and regular supply of petroleum to consuming nations; and

4. ensure a fair return on capital to those investing in the industry.

There have been many quibbles over the years on what is meant by a fair price and a fair return, but the original objectives have survived intact and still appear appropriate to current needs, and they remain as good a basis as any for the next few years.

There has, however, been a fundamental change in the character and stance of OPEC. Founded as a vehicle for joint producer confrontation with the major oil multinationals (led by Shell, British Petroleum, and Exxon), OPEC found in the seventies that it was locked into conflict on oil supply and price with the leading consumer governments: the U.S., Germany, and Japan. To the surprise of many, OPEC evolved in the eighties into a much more cooperative entity, seeking pragmatic dialogue between oil consumers and producers.

The five founding members—Iran, Iraq, Kuwait, Saudi Arabia, and Venezuela—have today six other full members with them: Qatar (from 1961); Indonesia (1962); Libya (1962); U.A.E. (1973, from Abu Dhabi joining in 1967); Algeria (1969); and Nigeria (1971). Ecuador joined in 1973 and left in 1992, and Gabon joined in 1975 and left in 1995.

Within OPEC, the superior capacity and reserves of Saudi Arabia has given the Kingdom first voice. Originally conceived by Saudi Arabia and Venezuela, OPEC leadership rested principally with Saudi Arabia and Iran until 1979; after the Iranian Revolution of that year, Saudi Arabia, initially guided by the capable hand of Ahmed Zaki Yamani (Saudi oil minister, 1962–1986), retained control. Supported reliably by three of the five other Gulf members,

Kuwait, Qatar, and U.A.E., they have today only to secure the support of Iraq and either Libya or Algeria to have a numerical Arab majority (six out of a total membership of eleven). Even with Iraq partially sidelined by UN sanctions, the Arab Gulf and North African votes constitute a majority within OPEC. Decisions in OPEC are only rarely decided by member-vote: unanimity is sought if at all possible. Nonetheless, the alphabetical seating of the member-countries around the conference table gives credence to the concept of each member-country having its own independent voice in the proceedings and decisions.

The non-Arab members of OPEC have certainly added a great deal to OPEC's credibility and influence, extending the membership spread to Latin America, Southeast Asia, and West Africa. OPEC has therefore provided a most valuable model to the developing world—a genuinely successful, international, cross-culture organisation that has survived and prospered for over forty years, and that has been able to stand up to considerable "demonization" in the U.S. and Western Europe. OPEC has also learned how to work effectively with the international oil industry and to play a valuable neutral and reconciliatory role in the geo-politics of energy and the politics of the Middle East.

The value of OPEC to the smooth working of the global economy has been demonstrated several times in the last three years. Prompted by Saudi Arabia both to increase production to moderate prices and then, within a few months, to cut production and restore very low prices to an agreed target level, OPEC has managed its quota system with higher degrees of compliance than before. (The current OPEC quotas as at mid-July 2002 are given in Table 14). Recently, OPEC has had 100 percent success in helping to keep oil prices within its guidelines of US$22–28 per barrel. This delicate and painful balancing act of stabilising the world oil market has been accompanied by much stronger links with other international agencies. Such an agency is the International Energy Agency in Paris, which has as its prime function the representation of industrial countries' oil consumer interests.

The value of OPEC as an ad hoc price-regulator during emergencies within the oil market is now becoming more widely appreciated. OPEC can be expected to continue to fulfil this function, although its scope for action is hampered by the prospect of a

Table 14. OPEC Oil Quotas for Arab Member-States at end-June 2002

	(mbd)
Saudi Arabia	7.053
U.A.E.	1.894
Kuwait	1.741
Libya	1.162
Algeria	0.693
Qatar	0.562
Total Arab	
Less Iraq	13.105
Total OPEC	**21.700**
Share of Arab State Members Less Iraq	60.4%

Source: Petroleum Industry Weekly, July 2002
Note: At the OPEC meetings, the Arab states including Iraq occupy 7 of the 11 seats, a 63.6% majority in terms of the total number of members; mbd—million barrels per day

declining market share which may persist for one to three years (but certainly not much longer).

The Arab members of OPEC, most significantly together with Egypt and Oman, have another international organisation of considerable potential value to the global economy: the Organisation of Petroleum Arab Exporting Countries (OAPEC), headquartered in Kuwait. Like OPEC, OAPEC controls funds used for investment in other Arab states and as seed-money in intra-Arab trade, government, and commercial investment. It already possesses a formidable statistical and forward planning function. Yet OAPEC's greatest value may lie in the future: it is well equipped to evolve into a Pan-Arab central bank or similar regional industry planning and investment finance organisation.

At the political level, the Arab League, based in Cairo, is firmly established with its own diplomatic representation in the principal world centres.

The Medium and Long-Term Outlook

The central question for the medium- and long-term is: How long will the widely-expected transition from fossil fuels to hydrogen and other non-fossil alternative energy take? Will the new energies rapidly eclipse the old, assisted by global concerns for global warming, fossil-fuel pollution of the air, and the environmental damage caused by large-scale extraction, processing, and transportation of petroleum? Should the Arab states be planning for expanding or diminishing levels of oil and gas production?

Table 15. Arab Oil Prospects
Plausible Medium-Term Assumptions, 2006–2010

	2006	2008	2010
Business-as-Usual			
Global Energy Demand	+2–3%	+2–3%	+2 –3%
Global Oil Demand	+1–2%	+ 1%	+1%
Call on OPEC	Rising	Rising	Rising
Call on Arab States	Rising	Rising	Rising Fast
Likely Oil Price Range (US%/barrel)	15–25	20–30	25 –35
Disruptions			
Global Energy Demand	Falling	Falling	Flat
Call on OPEC	Falling	Flat	Rising
Call on Arab States	Flat	Rising	Rising
Likely Oil Price Range (US%/barrel)	15–60	15–60	15–60

Source: PTA London

Oil Prospects for the Period 2006–2010

Table 15 gives an outline of how the markets might evolve in the period 2006–2010 under two scenarios: "business as usual" and "disruptions," the latter involving a high degree of price volatility.

In both scenarios, global oil demand will begin to outstrip supply, most probably before 2008; there is no chance that alternative energy will have made an adequate impact within that time frame. From current investment planning in the petroleum industry in non-Arab sources, we can safely conclude that, despite some early lean years, and whether or not the global economy passes through a period of turmoil, the bulk of incremental oil demand will fall on the Arab states. Given the long time lags in oil and gas development, there will not be enough time for the non-OPEC and the non-Arab OPEC oil and gas producers to remedy that shortfall.

One of the points that clinches this conclusion is that, with huge reserves of oil and gas, the Arab producers can today bring in new supplies easily and quickly at US$5 per barrel. In contrast, the equivalent cost of oil from new deepwater offshore and new marginal fields in the North Sea are US$17 per barrel, with very high up-front capital cost at the technological frontier, where, of course, there are much higher risks.

Oil Prospects for the Period 2010–2050

For the purpose of this paper, I have taken three scenarios (Table 16): a stable globalized world (business-as-usual), a gas/nuclear/renewables acceleration, and a divided world.

Table 16. Arab Oil Prospects
Plausible Long-Term Assumptions, 2010–2050

	2010	2020	2030	2040	2050
Business-as-Usual					
Global Energy	doubles within period				
Global Oil Supply	peaks at 2030				
Global Gas Supply	buoyant throughout				
Arab Competitiveness	strengthening for major producers				
Gas/Nuclear/Renewables Acceleration					
Global Energy	triples within period				
Global Oil Supply	plateau from 2020				
Global Gas Supply	accelerates sharply				
Arab Competitiveness	gains linked increasingly to gas				
A Divided World					
Global Energy	rises slowly by 50% within period				
Global Oil Supply	non-OPEC oil begins to dry up				
Global Gas Supply	a much slower development				
Arab Competitiveness	marked gains are sustained by oil				

Source: PTA London

A stable, globalized world

In this scenario, we assume fairly steady globalization of economic activity, with strong growth in all world markets. We assume no major setbacks.

Global energy demand doubles within the period with strong expansion of natural gas production and much more varied use. Oil production peaks about 2030 and then begins a gentle decline. Arab states stand to prosper throughout this scenario.

A gas/nuclear/renewables acceleration

In this scenario, there are further technological breakthroughs in the gasification and liquefaction of in situ coal; new and cost-competitive gas to liquids technology; or a massive swing back to mass produced nuclear, both large and small-scale; or major technology breakthroughs in alternative energy, probably in battery design, improved fuel-cells, hydrogen distribution, and cheap photo-voltaics; or a mix of the above that can be manufactured cheaply and replicated quickly world-wide.

If such a fast-stream technology begins to take over by 2020, gas production and use are likely to accelerate, boosting energy demand to triple its present level by 2050. Global oil supply may not be able to keep up and may peak, possibly as early as 2020.

Arab competitiveness would still gain a boost from increased oil supply early on, but increasingly, the new opportunities to develop Arab gas would begin to take over as prime economic driver.

A divided world

This scenario takes account of some of the grim lessons learned from the September 11, 2001 terrorist attacks. Far from globalizing, the global economy begins to fragment. Regional and bilateral supply solutions are favored in preference to reliance on access to world markets. The scramble for scarce oil supplies results in local disputes and, in some areas, hostilities; old enmities are revived. Governments intervene with systems of rationing, more often than not with disastrous consequences.

Under this scenario, global economic growth is repeatedly halted in its tracks with energy demand gaining only perhaps 50 percent in forty years. Non-OPEC oil begins to dry up. The lack of trust and cooperation puts a stop to many of the projected major new gas projects, resulting in much slower growth in gas production capacity. In such circumstances, the Arab states will still be well-placed to sell their oil at high prices to the highest bidder. They will inevitably be drawn into schemes to alleviate the position of those developing countries that are hardest hit.

Conclusions

Based on the foregoing economic analysis, all the conclusions from this paper are geo-political in nature. In the Middle East, more than elsewhere, it makes no sense to look simply at the industry numbers and to ignore the often complex politics of the region.

Communication and cooperation between the twenty-two Arab states is a most significant phenomenon. It is valuable to all these states, helping to distribute the vast revenues of the lead-producer governments and spreading the benefits, (albeit sometimes only thinly) to all parts of the Arab world. There is a well-developed institutional framework, a cohesion founded on 1,400 years of Islam, a vibrant common culture, education, and language, and ancient ties of blood and kinship. It expresses itself in substantial flows of students, migrant workers, technicians, merchants, lawyers, doctors and nurses, teachers and scholars, as well as pilgrims and tourists around the Arab world. It also carries, in that great trading crossroads between Europe and the East and between Africa and Central Asia, the accumulated trading instincts of several millennia, a ferment of creative activity, and an acute awareness of the need

to respect, trade with, work with, and thoroughly understand many different peoples. These are just the qualities needed for the increasingly globalized societies of the twenty-first century.

On the ground today, the immediate prospects for Arab energy are clouded by an over-supply situation and a sharp fall in global investor confidence. The prospect of another military intervention in the area casts a further cloud over otherwise bright prospects.

While the going might be rough in the short-term (up to 2005), it is very hard to reach any other conclusion than that the Arab competitive position will begin to strengthen. With 60 percent of global oil reserves, 25 percent of global gas reserves, a 44 percent share in the global trade in oil, and some of the lowest oil and gas production costs in the world, the Arab states are already in an unassailable position. It is already clear that the transition to a non-hydrocarbon global economy is on the way; it is also clear that, for the next ten years, progress is likely to be slow.

Meanwhile, new trading alliances, based on a shift in the marketing of the bulk of Gulf oil and gas to Japan, Korea, China, and other Asia/Pacific markets, are bringing the Gulf states into a new long-term relationship with those eastern countries. Similarly, the growing trans-Mediterranean interdependence of the North African states and the countries of southern Europe in terms of oil and gas trade also have a new and strong political dimension which may begin to erode some of the territorial rivalries and conflicts of the past.

Challenges for Information and Communication Technology Development in the Arab World

Soumitra Dutta, Charles El-Hage, Karim Sabbagh, and Paola Tarazi

The Information and Communication Technology (ICT) sector has become one of the core foundations underpinning knowledge economies and sustainable social and economic development. Governments around the world are called on to develop ICT strategies in order to narrow the existing digital divide between the "connected" and the "unconnected" populations, and to place themselves on a competitive platform.

This paper examines the challenges faced by the Arab world in effectively developing and leveraging ICT. A close assessment of the three layers that underline ICT development (Environment, Readiness and Usage) provides new evidence on further gaps within the Arab world itself, emanating from countries' diverse efforts to develop their ICT potential and to bridge the digital divide with the developed world.

In this paper, we have identified three sets of challenges underpinning the significant role for ICT advancement in the economic development of the Arab World. We have also recommended a set of policy initiatives that can enhance the functioning of markets and alleviate the risks of ICT-marginalization and the consequent poor economic and social development of the Arab world:

Environment • Devise a clear and comprehensive ICT development plan, supported by the highest political constituencies

• Incorporate ICT skills and knowledge into the educational system

• Enact telecom laws and regulations to introduce competition through deregulation, privatization and sector liberalization

Readiness • Drive literacy and comfort with the ICT field through the promotion of awareness, trust, training and comfort

• Promote access device penetration among citizens, businesses (particularly SMEs) and governments, as well as employee training schemes to improve the readiness of market players to take advantage of ICT benefits

• Devise appropriate strategies for governments to deliver e-government services and participate in e-commerce

Usage • Tackle the digital divide by taking positive actions among population groups less likely to use the Internet

• Promote purposeful uptake of Internet technologies in the business community

• Promote online public services through strategic government policies in order to increase Internet usage among citizens, businesses and governments

These challenges and enablers for ICT growth are discussed in a more comprehensive manner in this paper, with the use of extensive references and examples from the region and best practices from international markets.

Review of ICT Developments

Global perspectives on ICT development [1]

In 2001, the global information and communication technology (ICT) market soared to more than US$2.3 trillion, with an average compounded annual growth rate of 9.7 percent over the 1998 to 2001 period. The United States led the competitive ICT regions and countries, claiming 36 percent of the world market (with a compounded growth rate of 8.2 percent), followed by 29 percent for Europe and 11 percent for Japan.

Given the current gaps between the ICT market share in the United States, Europe,[2] and Japan, market analysts anticipate that the United States will continue to lead the global ICT market. It is forecasted that each region, with the exception of Japan, will maintain the same market share in 2002, with slight decreases in year-to-year growth figures; Japan is expected to see growth of more than 6 percent.

he penetration of personal computers (PCs) is nsidered to be the main cause of the gap in ICT arkets between the United States, Europe, Japan and e rest of the world. In 2001, there were more than .25 PCs per 100 people in the United States, whereas Europe, there were only 17.94 PCs per 100 people.[3] 2002, worldwide PC sales are estimated to reach 4 million units,[4] 83 percent of which are in North nerica, Western Europe, and the Asia-Pacific regions. 2004, world PC sales are expected to reach 159 illion units. Furthermore, according to International elecommunications Union (ITU) statistics, the total umber of PCs worldwide currently stands at 495 illion units, 88 percent of which are located in the nited States, Europe, and Asia.

he World Wide Web has become a global medium r communication and information exchange and s, consequently, become an important indicator ICT development among regions. According to TU statistics, world Internet users amounted to 0 million people at the end of the year 2001. The nited States and Europe hold almost three-fifth of e world's Internet users (58 percent), although eir combined populations represent less than 18 rcent of the world's population. The Arab region, th 5 percent of world population, represents less an 1 percent of the world Internet population igure 1).

ith the substantial growth of e-commerce over e past few years, the Internet has become the ost advanced commercial tool. The days when ternet usage was merely limited to e-mail and trieving information from the World Wide Web ive long gone. The emergence of e-commerce tivities has greatly impacted the scale of the gital divide. According to Forrester Research, orld e-commerce transactions amounted to S$1,233 billion[5] in 2001, 98 percent of which were nducted in the regions of North America, Asia-cific, and Western. In the Arab world, the commerce market is estimated at US$3 billion .e., only 0.2 percent of world market), and is pected to grow to US$5 billion in 2005.

summary, ICT usage worldwide has witnessed traordinary growth. A closer look at the data shows marked digital divide among nations and geographic gions. This so-called digital divide is, in some part, reflection of deeper socio-economic inequalities tween countries and regions of the world, as is strongly related to the gap in world income stribution.

Figure 1. Breakdown of World Internet Users by Region, 2001

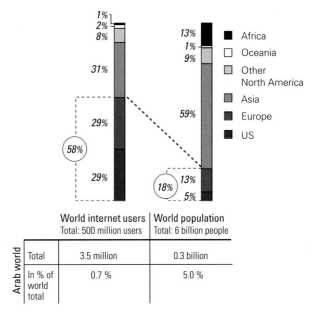

Arab world	World internet users Total: 500 million users	World population Total: 6 billion people
Total	3.5 million	0.3 billion
In % of world total	0.7 %	5.0 %

Note: In the chart, the Arab world's total population and Internet users are split between Asia and Africa

Source: ITU 2002

Figure 2 suggests that 34 percent of the world population comprises more than 75 percent of the world's Internet users. When considering the combined incomes of those 34 percent, they represent over 81 percent of the world's GDP. In other words, the holders of 81 percent of the world's income account for more than 75 percent of the world's Internet users. This is a strong evidence of the direct relationship between income and ICT penetration. The remaining 25 percent of Internet users are in the lower income group of countries that constitute more than two-thirds of the world population.

Figure 2. Global Digital Divide, 2002

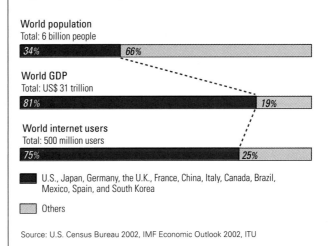

Source: U.S. Census Bureau 2002, IMF Economic Outlook 2002, ITU

It is important to keep in mind that the Arab world accounts for 5 percent of the world's population and 2 percent of the world GDP. Despite its relatively high average GDP per capita by international standards, the Arab world still accounts for less than 0.7 percent of the world's Internet users. Hence, the traditional digital divide barrier of lower income per capita does not appear to be the major impediment for ICT development in that region. This leads to the early suggestion that bridging the divide in the Arab world requires a multifaceted intervention by key stakeholders, in an even more pronounced fashion than in developing economies.

Figure 3. Selected ICT Indicators in the Arab World, 2001

Country	Internet Hosts per 10,000 Inhabitants	Internet Users per 10,000 Inhabitants	Estimated PCs per 100 Inhabitants
Egypt	0.3	92.9	1.5
Jordan	4.2	409.1	3.3
Kuwait	17.4	1,014.7	13.2
Lebanon	19.9	858.0	5.6
Morocco	0.8	131.5	1.3
Oman	17.8	457.5	3.2
Saudi Arabia	5.1	134.4	6.3
Syrian AR	0.01	36.1	1.6
U.A.E.	288.5	3,392.4	15.8

Source: ITU 2002

Amidst the emerging digital divide, it is important to note the prevailing gaps between countries in the Arab world (Figure 3). There are marked variances between countries in their efforts to adopt ICT tools and grow their networked economies. Therefore, Arab countries can build on each other's experiences and learnings to develop and implement their individual ICT agenda as well as an integrated regional ICT market. Arab countries, by working together to position themselves on a common competitive platform, can improve their combined standing in the world ICT market.

In the remainder of this paper, we have profiled Arab countries using similar indicators in order to compare their performance. We then identified a matrix of the most significant challenges and enablers to ICT development, and looked at various ways in which countries in the region are addressing these challenges. At the end of the paper, policy recommendations are outlined to enable Arab states to create a connected environment that better supports their agendas for sustainable economic growth.

ICT maturity evaluation

In order to assess the ICT maturity of Arab states, we have compiled a detailed quantitative and qualitative evaluation underscoring three layers of ICT development environment, readiness, and usage (Figure 4a).

Figure 4a. ICT Maturity Evaluation

Environment → "**Environment**" describes the conduciveness of the environment for ICT development. This encompasse the level of political leadership, regulatory openness, innovation, capability, IT skills within the population, and the cost and availability of access

Readiness → "**Readiness**" describes the ability of a country's economic stakeholders—individuals, businesses and governments—to capitalize on the opportunitie that a strong environment brings. Readiness requires appropriate access ICT devices, be it PC, DTV or even a mobile device, plus the skill and the desire to use it

Usage → "**Usage**" describes the uptake of online services, and the volume and sophistication of use. For individuals, the sophistication of use ranges from surfing and e-mailing through transactions like online banking and shopping, through to publication of their own web pages. For businesses and governments, basic use is the publication of a website, more sophisticated use is characterised by transactional e-commerce applications and the integration of other business processes online

Each of the three evaluation parameters was further divided into subparameters. These subparameters are defined by a set of structured criteria that drove the selection of data indicators. In other words, the three evaluation parameters—environment, readiness, and usage—were built up from relevant explanatory data points collected for each profiled country (Figure 4b).

We have profiled nine Arab countries for our benchmarking exercise on the basis of:

- Subregional representativeness (Levant, North Africa, and the Gulf)[6]

- Reliable and comprehensive data availability

Our findings have allowed the grouping of the nine countries into three clusters based on their overall performance (countries per cluster are listed in alphabetical order):

Figure 4b. Evaluation Layers and Criteria for Data Selection

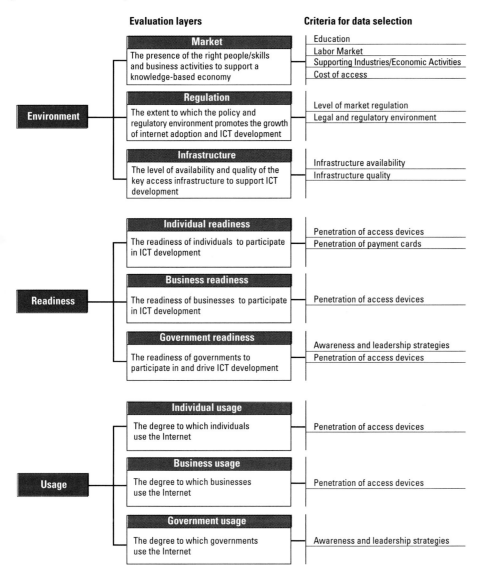

| Evaluation layers | Criteria for data selection |

Environment

Market
The presence of the right people/skills and business activities to support a knowledge-based economy

- Education
- Labor Market
- Supporting Industries/Economic Activities
- Cost of access

Regulation
The extent to which the policy and regulatory environment promotes the growth of internet adoption and ICT development

- Level of market regulation
- Legal and regulatory environment

Infrastructure
The level of availability and quality of the key access infrastructure to support ICT development

- Infrastructure availability
- Infrastructure quality

Readiness

Individual readiness
The readiness of individuals to participate in ICT development

- Penetration of access devices
- Penetration of payment cards

Business readiness
The readiness of businesses to participate in ICT development

- Penetration of access devices

Government readiness
The readiness of governments to participate in and drive ICT development

- Awareness and leadership strategies
- Penetration of access devices

Usage

Individual usage
The degree to which individuals use the Internet

- Penetration of access devices

Business usage
The degree to which businesses use the Internet

- Penetration of access devices

Government usage
The degree to which governments use the Internet

- Awareness and leadership strategies

Fast-Track — Kuwait, United Arab Emirates (U.A.E.)

Countries with a fast-track performance are those with an already clearly developed ICT growth agenda; they have consequently achieved adequate levels of readiness to absorb further ICT developments, as well as significant usage penetration levels.

Emerging — Egypt, Jordan, Lebanon, Saudi Arabia

Emerging ICT markets are those with either a well-developed environment for ICT growth but that have not yet acquired high levels of readiness and usage penetration, or those with significant readiness and usage patterns in an environment not predisposed to active ICT growth and development.

Developing — Morocco, Oman, Syrian AR

Developing markets are those still lagging behind other countries in the region in their efforts to bridge the digital divide. Some have already rolled-out successful ICT initiatives despite the absence of a national integrated framework for ICT development, while others have more recently introduced ICT tools in the market and are still developing ICT policies and national plans.

Figure 5 shows the performance of countries for each evaluation parameter and subparameter according to the aforementioned cluster. Note that the clustering of ICT performance in the Arab world is valid relative to the countries chosen for the exercise, and not in absolute terms.

In the following section, we have provided an abstract on a country-by-country basis of the main drivers and initiatives that are leading ICT development. The abstracts highlight countries' performances for each evaluation parameter.

Figure 5. Arab Countries ICT Maturity Clustering

ICT Maturity Clustering	
Fast-track	Kuwait U.A.E.
Emerging	Egypt Jordan Lebanon Saudi Arabia
Developing	Morocco Oman Syrian AR

Environment

Fast-track	Kuwait U.A.E.
Emerging	Egypt Jordan Lebanon Saudi Arabia
Developing	Morocco Oman Syrian AR

	Market	Regulation	Infrastructure
Fast-track	Kuwait U.A.E	Morocco Saudi Arabia	Kuwait U.A.E.
Emerging	Egypt Jordan Lebanon Saudi Arabia	Egypt Jordan Kuwait U.A.E.	Jordan Lebanon Oman Saudi Arabia
Developing	Morocco Syrian AR Oman	Lebanon Oman Syrian AR	Egypt Morocco Syrian AR

Readiness

Fast-track	Kuwait U.A.E.
Emerging	Jordan Lebanon Oman Saudi Arabia
Developing	Egypt Morocco Syrian AR

	Individual readiness	Business readiness [a]	Government readiness
Fast-track	Kuwait U.A.E.	Kuwait U.A.E.	Kuwait U.A.E.
Emerging	Jordan Lebanon Oman Saudi Arabia	Egypt Lebanon Saudi Arabia	Egypt Jordan Morocco Saudi Arabia
Developing	Egypt Morocco Syrian AR	Jordan Oman	Lebanon Oman Syrian AR

Usage

Fast-track	Kuwait U.A.E.
Emerging	Egypt Lebanon Oman Saudi Arabia
Developing	Jordan Morocco Syrian AR

	Individual use	Business use	Government use [b]
Fast-track	Kuwait U.A.E.	Kuwait U.A.E.	U.A.E.
Emerging	Egypt Lebanon Oman Saudi Arabia	Egypt Jordan Lebanon Morocco	Egypt, Jordan Kuwait, Lebanon Morocco Saudi Arabia
Developing	Jordan Morocco Syrian AR	Oman Saudi Arabia Syrian AR	Oman Syrian AR

Notes: a: There are no available data for Syria and Morocco
b: Countries were ranked based on qualitative assessment of usage. Quantitative data are not available
c: Countries within each cluster are listed in alphabetical order

We have used a symbol scheme to differentiate countries' performance within each layer:

● indicates that a country has a "fast-track" performance

◐ indicates that a country has an "emerging" performance

○ indicates that a country has a "developing" performance

(Countries are listed in alphabetical order)

Egypt

Environment

Market ◐
Regulatory ◐
Infrastructure ○

The Egyptian environment exhibits mixed elements for ICT development. On the one hand, Egypt stepped ahead of other Arab countries in defining a comprehensive national ICT development plan and phasing it in. On the other hand, Egypt continues to suffer from relatively high illiteracy rates. Access to capital remains limited due to a slow-moving, state-dominated banking system and a relatively small private sector.

Readiness

Individuals ○
Businesses ◐
Governments ◐

PC penetration in Egypt remains low at 2 percent. This is partly due to high import duties and sales taxes on computer hardware (15 percent in total). A vibrant export-oriented software industry is expected to set the stage for a regional role in the Arabization of Internet content.

Usage

Individuals ◐
Businesses ◐
Governments ◐

Low Internet penetration rates (0.9 percent) are attributed to high illiteracy rates and lack of Internet awareness. Government's support for setting up information technology (IT) "interest groups" in various regions of the country should encourage ICT uptake in the future.

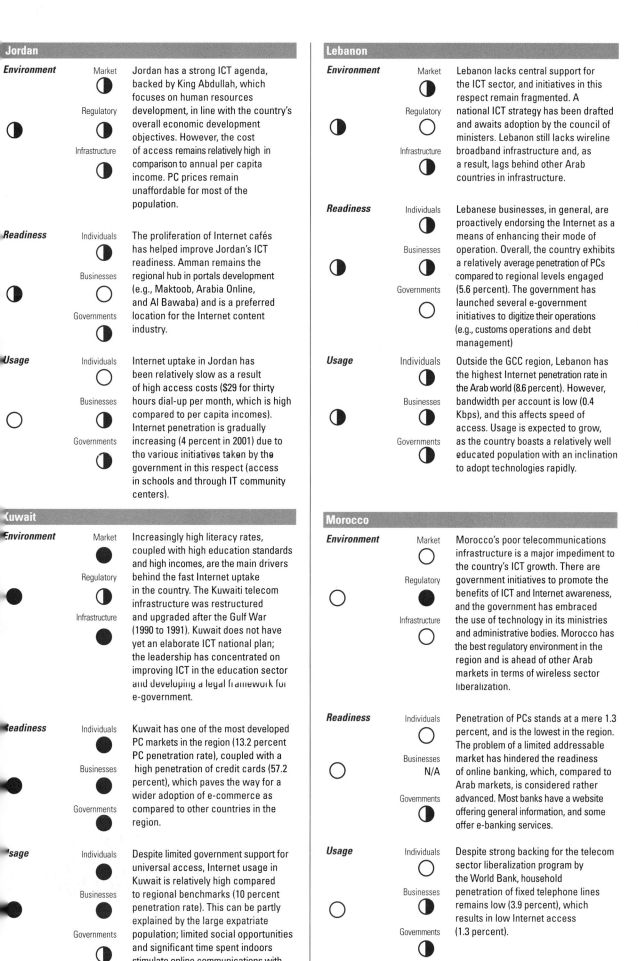

Jordan

Environment

Market
Regulatory
Infrastructure

Jordan has a strong ICT agenda, backed by King Abdullah, which focuses on human resources development, in line with the country's overall economic development objectives. However, the cost of access remains relatively high in comparison to annual per capita income. PC prices remain unaffordable for most of the population.

Readiness

Individuals
Businesses
Governments

The proliferation of Internet cafés has helped improve Jordan's ICT readiness. Amman remains the regional hub in portals development (e.g., Maktoob, Arabia Online, and Al Bawaba) and is a preferred location for the Internet content industry.

Usage

Individuals
Businesses
Governments

Internet uptake in Jordan has been relatively slow as a result of high access costs ($29 for thirty hours dial-up per month, which is high compared to per capita incomes). Internet penetration is gradually increasing (4 percent in 2001) due to the various initiatives taken by the government in this respect (access in schools and through IT community centers).

Kuwait

Environment

Market
Regulatory
Infrastructure

Increasingly high literacy rates, coupled with high education standards and high incomes, are the main drivers behind the fast Internet uptake in the country. The Kuwaiti telecom infrastructure was restructured and upgraded after the Gulf War (1990 to 1991). Kuwait does not have yet an elaborate ICT national plan; the leadership has concentrated on improving ICT in the education sector and developing a legal framework for e-government.

Readiness

Individuals
Businesses
Governments

Kuwait has one of the most developed PC markets in the region (13.2 percent PC penetration rate), coupled with a high penetration of credit cards (57.2 percent), which paves the way for a wider adoption of e-commerce as compared to other countries in the region.

Usage

Individuals
Businesses
Governments

Despite limited government support for universal access, Internet usage in Kuwait is relatively high compared to regional benchmarks (10 percent penetration rate). This can be partly explained by the large expatriate population; limited social opportunities and significant time spent indoors stimulate online communications with relatives and friends back home.

Lebanon

Environment

Market
Regulatory
Infrastructure

Lebanon lacks central support for the ICT sector, and initiatives in this respect remain fragmented. A national ICT strategy has been drafted and awaits adoption by the council of ministers. Lebanon still lacks wireline broadband infrastructure and, as a result, lags behind other Arab countries in infrastructure.

Readiness

Individuals
Businesses
Governments

Lebanese businesses, in general, are proactively endorsing the Internet as a means of enhancing their mode of operation. Overall, the country exhibits a relatively average penetration of PCs compared to regional levels engaged (5.6 percent). The government has launched several e-government initiatives to digitize their operations (e.g., customs operations and debt management)

Usage

Individuals
Businesses
Governments

Outside the GCC region, Lebanon has the highest Internet penetration rate in the Arab world (8.6 percent). However, bandwidth per account is low (0.4 Kbps), and this affects speed of access. Usage is expected to grow, as the country boasts a relatively well educated population with an inclination to adopt technologies rapidly.

Morocco

Environment

Market
Regulatory
Infrastructure

Morocco's poor telecommunications infrastructure is a major impediment to the country's ICT growth. There are government initiatives to promote the benefits of ICT and Internet awareness, and the government has embraced the use of technology in its ministries and administrative bodies. Morocco has the best regulatory environment in the region and is ahead of other Arab markets in terms of wireless sector liberalization.

Readiness

Individuals
Businesses
N/A
Governments

Penetration of PCs stands at a mere 1.3 percent, and is the lowest in the region. The problem of a limited addressable market has hindered the readiness of online banking, which, compared to Arab markets, is considered rather advanced. Most banks have a website offering general information, and some offer e-banking services.

Usage

Individuals
Businesses
Governments

Despite strong backing for the telecom sector liberalization program by the World Bank, household penetration of fixed telephone lines remains low (3.9 percent), which results in low Internet access (1.3 percent).

Oman

Environment

Market / Regulatory / Infrastructure

Oman signed the World Trade Organization (WTO) agreement in 2000, and is expected to liberalize its telecommunications sector soon. This will likely impact telecommunications tariffs. Nonetheless, the Sultanate continues to lack an explicit agenda for ICT development. According to Omantel, the state-owned incumbent operator, ADSL and ATM are being introduced to allow the development of broadband multimedia services, as well as e-commerce and high speed Internet.

Readiness

Individuals / Businesses / Governments

Oman has a relatively low PC penetration rate (3.2 percent) and lacks Internet services. In fact, 78 percent of businesses are estimated to have a dial-up Internet connection and only 8 percent have leased lines connections. Omantel has recently encouraged the licensing of Internet cafés in order to increase access.

Usage

Individuals / Businesses / Governments

Oman has a relatively high Internet penetration despite its overall low ranking on ICT maturity (it is a "developing" market). The young and highly educated population is expected to spur demand in the future.

Saudi Arabia

Environment

Market / Regulatory / Infrastructure

Saudi Arabia is one of the first Arab countries to develop a strong regulatory environment, setting a regulatory authority to oversee the telecommunications sector. A national committee for ICT policy has recently been created to draft a comprehensive ICT plan for the Kingdom. The competitive ISP market has led to recent consolidations, which is expected to improve service provision and quality.

Readiness

Individuals / Businesses / Governments

PC penetration in Saudi Arabia is equivalent to that of Lebanon (6 percent), but remains low compared to other GCC countries like the U.A.E. (16 percent) and Kuwait (13 percent). The government has introduced PCs in its ministries and is planning to provide information on government services, as well as online services to citizens, in the foreseeable future.

Usage

Individuals / Businesses / Government

Internet penetration in Saudi Arabia remains low compared to regional levels (1.3 percent). The Ministry of Planning is seeking to articulate national policies and initiatives to promote Internet penetration and usage.

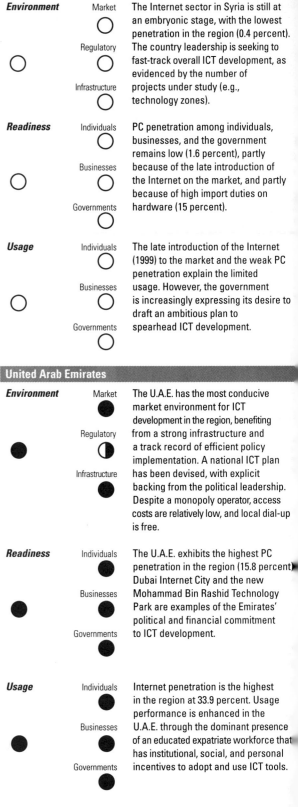

Syria

Environment

Market / Regulatory / Infrastructure

The Internet sector in Syria is still at an embryonic stage, with the lowest penetration in the region (0.4 percent). The country leadership is seeking to fast-track overall ICT development, as evidenced by the number of projects under study (e.g., technology zones).

Readiness

Individuals / Businesses / Governments

PC penetration among individuals, businesses, and the government remains low (1.6 percent), partly because of the late introduction of the Internet on the market, and partly because of high import duties on hardware (15 percent).

Usage

Individuals / Businesses / Governments

The late introduction of the Internet (1999) to the market and the weak PC penetration explain the limited usage. However, the government is increasingly expressing its desire to draft an ambitious plan to spearhead ICT development.

United Arab Emirates

Environment

Market / Regulatory / Infrastructure

The U.A.E. has the most conducive market environment for ICT development in the region, benefiting from a strong infrastructure and a track record of efficient policy implementation. A national ICT plan has been devised, with explicit backing from the political leadership. Despite a monopoly operator, access costs are relatively low, and local dial-up is free.

Readiness

Individuals / Businesses / Governments

The U.A.E. exhibits the highest PC penetration in the region (15.8 percent). Dubai Internet City and the new Mohammad Bin Rashid Technology Park are examples of the Emirates' political and financial commitment to ICT development.

Usage

Individuals / Businesses / Governments

Internet penetration is the highest in the region at 33.9 percent. Usage performance is enhanced in the U.A.E. through the dominant presence of an educated expatriate workforce that has institutional, social, and personal incentives to adopt and use ICT tools.

Assessment of the Key Challenges to ICT Development

In the previous section we assessed ICT development along three layers: environment, readiness, and usage. Based on international benchmarks of ICT strategies and the particular needs of the ICT market in the region, we have identified the main challenges under each layer in Figure 6.

Figure 6. Enablers of ICT Development in the Arab Region

① Environment	② Readiness	③ Usage
• **Political/Regulatory Leadership** – Existence & leadership of a national ICT agenda – Level of integration of initiatives – Responsibility for ICT agenda • **Market** – Privatization & competition landscape	• **Access Affordability** – Cost of PCs – Connection costs • **Infrastructure** – Availability and quality of ICT access tools	• **Awareness and Universal Access** – Knowledge about ICT – Comfort with ICT usage • **Compelling Content** – Language familiarity – Content relevance

Note: We have used "access affordability" and "infrastructure" criteria to ICT development as challenges to driving forward ICT "readiness," rather than "environment," as these challenges will directly affect the readiness of stakeholders to take advantage of ICT benefits.

Environment

Political and regulatory agenda

The development of ICT in the Arab world is unlikely to be solely determined by market-led logic. It is important for countries to articulate their national ICT strategies. Such an effort entails the assessment of opportunities for and challenges to future development, and the definition of a policy framework to take advantage of the opportunities and overcome prevailing challenges.

Governments in the Arab world have not all been proactive in formulating their ICT agendas. Some countries, for example, the U.A.E., Egypt, and Jordan, are at the forefront of ICT leadership policy, while other countries lag behind.

The U.A.E. government ICT policies aim to encourage investors to establish their enterprises in the U.A.E. and assist local businesses. An elaborate national ICT plan has been devised and is explicitly backed by the political leadership. It is a regional reference in ICT development, with proven results in creating technology parks, attracting leading companies in the ICT sector, and implementing e-government and e-learning initiatives.

Egypt has also defined a comprehensive ICT national plan. In September 1999, the government announced that the development of the information and telecommunications technology industry was a national priority. This led to the creation of a separate ministry for communications and information technology in October 1999. Realizing how a strong ICT sector could contribute to high and sustainable economic growth for the Egyptian economy, the Ministry of Communications and Information Technology has set the long-term objective of creating an export-driven, private sector-led ICT market. A three-year national plan for the development of the ICT industry has been designed, in close collaboration with the private sector and industry experts.

Jordan has also embarked on an ambitious plan to make full use of the ICT potential to support the national program for economic growth. In 1999, King Abdullah launched the REACH Initiative to bolster the country's ICT sector and maximize its ability to compete in local, regional, and global markets. This initiative aims to achieve full-scale Internet access within five years. The King's vision is to "...ensure that every citizen is computer-literate and that every single school and community will be wired… simply because this is the type of quality talent that we want in our workforce."

At the regional level, ICT leadership could be developed by intercountry cooperation. Regional cooperation could be considered for:

• Setting up multipurpose information and telecommunications centers

• Establishing technology incubation schemes and providing support for start-up enterprises

• Building networks of partner institutions

A recent project has been proposed by the United Nations Development Program to address the ICT agenda at a regional level. The project, called Information and Communication Technology for Development in the Arab Region (ICTDAR), would form a number of bilateral and multilateral joint ventures with some countries, international organizations, banks, multinational companies, and other organizations for the purpose of financial, technical, and advisory assistance. The aim of ICTDAR is to bring information technology to less developed areas in member countries and introduce enhanced IT education. Helping small companies improve their IT systems and assisting in widening the application of member countries' e-government, are other objectives of the ICTDAR.

Market

Another way to develop the ICT environment is to create a competitive market, where access to higher quality and lower cost ICT services stimulates ICT uptake.

A closer look at the state of telecommunications in the region reveals that all local, domestic long distance (DLD) and international long distance (ILD) voice markets are monopolies (except for the Kuwaiti ILD voice market). The mobile market has been partially liberalized in most markets except for Oman, Saudi Arabia, and the U.A.E. (Figure 7).

Figure 7. Level of Competition in the Telecommunications Market

Country	Local Voice	DLD Voice	ILD Voice	Mobile	Data	Internet
Egypt	M	M	M	D	C	C
Jordan	M	M	M	P	C	C
Kuwait	M	M	C	D	C	D
Lebanon	M	M	M	D	C	C
Morocco	M	M	M	C	C	C
Oman	M	M	M	M	M	M
Saudi Arabia	M	M	M	M	M	C
Syrian AR	M	M	M	P	M	C
U.A.E.	M	M	M	M	M	M

M=Monopoly D=Duopoly P=Partial Competition C=Competition
Source: ITU 2001

The Internet and data markets reveal the monopoly markets of higher income countries like the U.A.E. and Oman. However, lower income markets like Egypt, Morocco, Lebanon, and Jordan exhibit some form of managed competition, whereas some higher income markets appear to have partial or limited competition.

There have been several ISP mergers in the region, and balancing healthy margins with reliable high quality service remains a challenge. In Egypt, Africa Online purchased Mena Net, while Batelco Middle East Company bought 48 percent of Soficom. Link Egypt and In Touch communications merged under the guidance of Orascom Telecom, and in Lebanon, Cyberia merged with IntraCom. In Jordan, NETS and FirstNet merged and allowed Batelco Middle East Jordan to own 51 percent of the merged company, and Jordan Telecom acquired Global One-Jordan.

The Saudi ISP market has, very recently, experienced a wave of mergers. There are around thirty private ISPs in the country, five of which have already merged into two larger firms. Naseej, Awal-Net, and Alamiyah merged in April 2002, and it is said that the alliance

captured around 30 percent of Internet users, while Trinet and Dallah recently revealed that they are merging to become a larger ISP. The merger will not affect the subscribers of either firm, and the aim is to improve the quality of service.

In monopolistic, high-income countries, the incumbent telecommunications operator remains the sole Internet access supplier. Operating alone in high-income markets with high PC penetrations and a well-educated population of nationals and expatriates has allowed for healthy margins.

Competition remains imperative if prospects for better service and higher Internet penetration at lower costs are to improve. The region is moving towards liberalizing the telecommunications sector based, among other things, on WTO requirements.

In fact, several countries in the region have been taking steps toward telecommunications market reform. For example, Morocco's communications market is undergoing a major liberalization drive. L'Agence Nationale des Reglementations de Télécommunications (ANRT), Morocco's telecommunications sector regulator, is in the process of launching a tender for a second fixed license—including data and international gateway components. This would place Morocco as one of the first Arab countries to have two fixed line operators.

Saudi Arabia's telecommunications law was published in mid-2001, and it made explicit reference to market regulation and liberalization. The national regulatory authority, known as the Saudi Communications Commission, was set up later in the year and work is already underway to define secondary legislation and draw the liberalization path. Expectations are that a managed liberalization with data and mobile licenses will be issued in 2003 or 2004. In the meantime, the incumbent operator has been undergoing major restructuring after being incorporated in 1998, in preparation for the scheduled partial privatization in late 2002.

The U.A.E. is a member of the WTO and, accordingly, the telecommunications segment has a liberalization deadline of 2005. However, as yet no explicit date has been set for liberalization.

The Kuwaiti parliament's finance and economic committee approved a draft bill to sell state-run services to the private sector in February 2001. Later, in January 2002, the minister of telecommunications announced that a law for the privatization of fixed telephone services is likely to pass during the course of 2002.

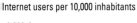

Figure 8. Internet Penetration Versus Cost of Access, 2001

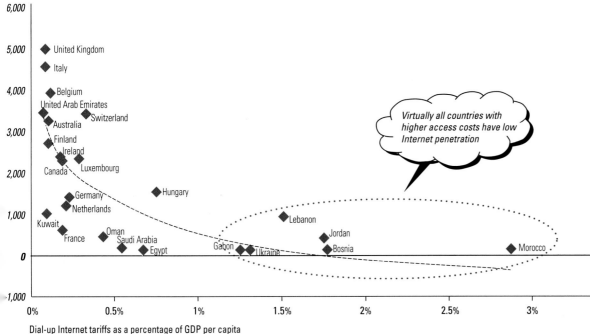

Source: ITU 2002

Readiness
Access affordability

The first enabler of ICT readiness is cost; cost plays an instrumental role in influencing ICT penetration. Taking the Internet as indicative of the ICT sector, an analysis of different ICT markets suggests that the lower the access cost, the higher Internet penetration (Figure 8).

The main elements of cost are the PC acquisition price, and connection charges. Most PCs in the Arab world are imported. According to ITU, Egypt, Morocco, and Syria have the highest duties and taxes on PCs (amounting to a 15 percent additional levy on the basic PC price)—(Figure 9).

Consequently, Morocco, Egypt, and Syria have the lowest PC penetration rates (Figure 10). The U.A.E. and Kuwait, on the other hand, impose only a 4 percent import duty (with no sales tax), the lowest in the Arab world. Consequently, these two markets have the highest PC penetrations in the region (16 percent and 13 percent respectively)—(Figures 9 and 10).

Figure 9. Import Duties and Sales Tax on Hardware in the Arab World, 2002

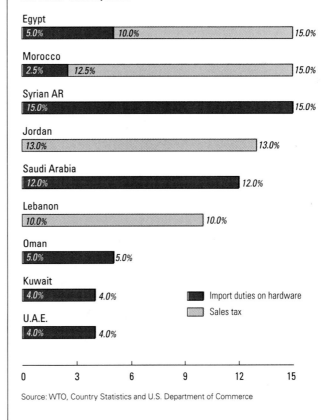

Source: WTO, Country Statistics and U.S. Department of Commerce

Figure 10. Personal Computer Penetration, 2001

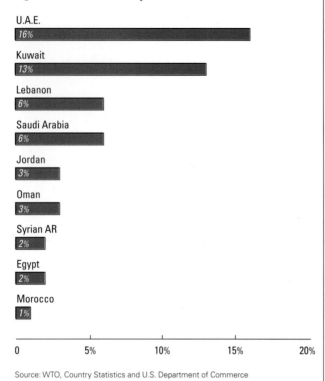

Source: WTO, Country Statistics and U.S. Department of Commerce

The second element of cost is connection charges. For example, an Internet dial-up account costs US$29 for 30 hours of use in Jordan. In Egypt, the monthly rate is as low as US$10, while in Syria, prices are still as high as US$47 per month (Figure 11).

Figure 11. Dial-Up Costs for 30 Hours of Use per Month, 2001 (in US$)

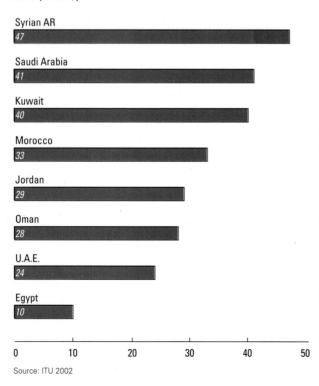

Source: ITU 2002

Governments are working to alleviate the digital divide by managing cost barriers. In fact, average ISP rates have fallen across the region, and preferred telephone rates have been established for Internet use in some countries. The dominance of monopolies in the region's telecommunications markets makes the supply of quality services at lower costs a challenging task.

Infrastructure

The second enabler of ICT readiness is an adequate infrastructure. The availability and adequate quality of ICT infrastructure are prime prerequisites for network access and the creation of an online market. The degree of ICT infrastructure availability and quality influences the potential for communities to access the new resources and leverage their benefit.

The availability of infrastructure varies from one country to another in the Arab world. For example, there is an average of more than 100 residential main lines per 100 households in Kuwait and the U.A.E., compared to less than 50 lines per 100 households in Syria, Egypt, Oman, and Morocco. Cellular line penetration also varies widely between countries in the Arab world. While the U.A.E. has a cellular penetration of 72 percent, Egypt has only a 4 percent penetration and Syria, 1 percent (Figure 12).

The growth rates in residential fixed line penetration reveal that fast-track countries have remained rather stable, whereas emerging and developing markets (with the exception of Oman and Morocco) have grown by more than 10 percent over the 1995 to 2000 period (Figure 12).

Cellular line penetration rates grew substantially in all markets between 1997 and 2000, again at a more pronounced pace in Syria, Morocco, Egypt, and Jordan, where penetration rates have more than doubled (Figure 12)

Because of the lack of other types of services, most users in the Arab world access the Internet via a dial-up service from home (Figure 13). This fact emphasizes the importance of telecommunications infrastructure availability as a factor affecting the degree of Internet uptake.

The number of faults per 100 fixed lines is an indicator used to determine the quality of a telecommunication system in a country. In the Arab world, the U.A.E., Oman, and Saudi Arabia each have below three faults per 100 fixed lines, comparable to Singapore, South Korea, and Mexico. Syria, Morocco, and Jordan each

Figure 12. Penetration of Residential Main Lines and Cellular Lines, 2001

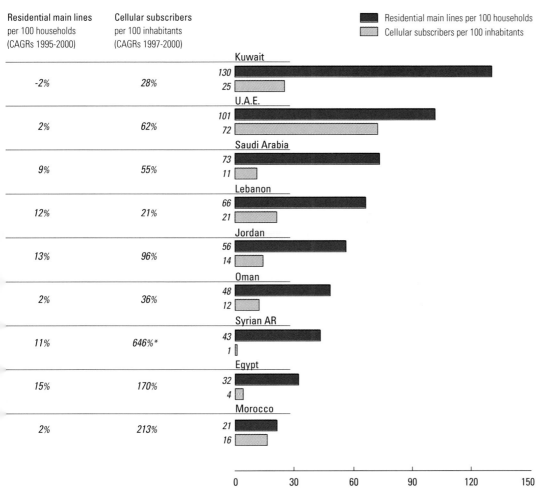

Residential main lines
per 100 households
(CAGRs 1995-2000)

Cellular subscribers
per 100 inhabitants
(CAGRs 1997-2000)

■ Residential main lines per 100 households
▢ Cellular subscribers per 100 inhabitants

Kuwait
-2% 28% 130 / 25

U.A.E.
2% 62% 101 / 72

Saudi Arabia
9% 55% 73 / 11

Lebanon
12% 21% 66 / 21

Jordan
13% 96% 56 / 14

Oman
2% 36% 48 / 12

Syrian AR
11% 646%* 43 / 1

Egypt
15% 170% 32 / 4

Morocco
2% 213% 21 / 16

0   30   60   90   120   150

CAGR for 1999 to 2000, as data prior to 1999 are not available

Source: ITU 2002

Figure 13. Internet Place of Access in the Arab World, 2001

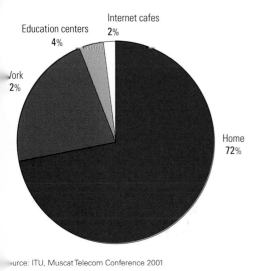

Education centers
4%

Internet cafes
2%

Work
2%

Home
72%

Source: ITU, Muscat Telecom Conference 2001

have more than eighteen faults per 100 lines; in fact, Syria has as many as fifty faults per 100 lines (Figure 14).

Total country bandwidth per account indicates the speed of Internet access. Morocco, Egypt, and Lebanon were among the first to introduce the Internet to the region (1992, 1993, and 1993 respectively). However, Lebanon's country bandwidth remains much lower than that of Egypt and Morocco because it failed to expand its network capacity. In fact, bandwidth capacity did not expand with the growth in the subscriber base, resulting in a relatively low bandwidth per account (0.38 Kbps) (Figure 15). On the other hand, Oman introduced the Internet to its market in 1996, and has managed to deliver higher bandwidth than Lebanon and Jordan.

The bandwidth per account indicates the Internet capacity per account and, hence, the quality of access. An escalating Internet subscriber base coupled with slow network capacity expansion will result in low bandwidth per account.

Figure 14. Faults per 100 Fixed Lines, 2000

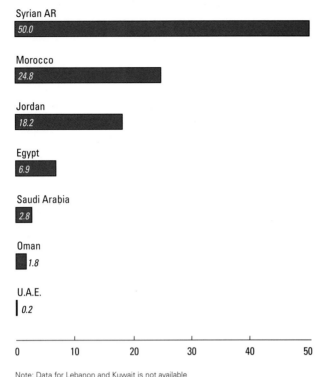

Syrian AR
50.0

Morocco
24.8

Jordan
18.2

Egypt
6.9

Saudi Arabia
2.8

Oman
1.8

U.A.E.
0.2

| 0 | 10 | 20 | 30 | 40 | 50 |

Note: Data for Lebanon and Kuwait is not available

Source: ITU 2002

Figure 15. Total Country Bandwidth, 2001

Country	Year of Internet Introduction	Total Bandwidth (in Mbps)	Internet Subscribers (in Thousands)	Bandwidth per Account (in Kbps)
Egypt	1993	450	145	3.75
Jordan	1996	127	60	2.12
Kuwait	1994	—	170	—
Lebanon	1993	45	120	0.38
Morocco	1992	155	44	3.52
Oman	1996	156	33	4.67
Saudi Arabia	1999	155	425	0.36
Syrian AR	1999	12	30	0.40
U.A.E.	1995	620	251	2.47

Source: Arab Advisors Group

In Saudi Arabia, low bandwidth is the result of an inefficient intermediation framework governing bandwidth supply. In fact, the regulated market structure stipulates that the incumbent telecommunications operator provides bandwidth on demand to the Internet regulator (KACST);[7] the latter re-sells it at a premium to ISPs.

Bandwidth utilization tracking, as published by KACST, suggests that some ISPs are underbuying bandwidth capacity and underallocating it. The result is that end

users experience slow transmission rates. In fact, 40 percent of the incumbent operator's bandwidth supply is not used by KACST and, similarly, 40 percent of the bandwidth made available by KACST is not used by ISPs (through end 2001).

The growing need for high speed Internet access is encouraging countries to expand their broadband capacity. For example, Oman's telecommunications operator, Omantel, has recently commissioned the supply and installation of an ADSL broadband network in order to ensure higher speed Internet access. It is expected that by the end of 2002, the total country bandwidth of 155 Mbps will almost double.[8]

To further illustrate the point, Jordan launched a new data communications and IP offering package, which gave ISPs the opportunity to achieve a 60 percent saving on end-to-end circuits. Prior to the launch of this offering, the total bandwidth for the country did not exceed 34 Mbps, and this was virtually saturated because most traffic was routed through the United States.

Usage
Awareness and universal access

Some of the challenges facing ICT development are related to its tangible dimensions, namely hardware, software, and costs. Conversely, ICT development also faces significant nontangible challenges in the form of education, language, and culture.

There is a broad consensus that schools and the education system are the basic tools needed to provide gradual greater comfort with the digital environment. Governments can advance policies to increase Internet awareness and literacy through initiatives to include IT courses in school curricula.

In the Arab world, the Saudi Watani project is the most prominent initiative of its kind in the region. The aim of the project is to exploit ICT in the education process by connecting all Saudi schools and educational directorate districts by means of a wide local area network; in fact, covering the entire Kingdom of Saudi Arabia. This would provide every student, teacher, parent, and educator with a multitude of services and a huge source of reference information.

In Egypt, the Ministry of Communications and Information Technology concentrated on the development of human resources necessary for the telecommunications and IT sectors. A professional development program was initiated, with the aim of training 5,000 professionals per year. The ministry plans to open a national information technology institute through which it will plan and prioritize the training programs required for the development of IT skills in Egypt. It is also seeking to set up technological universities, send young professionals abroad for training, and develop a communications and information technology curriculum in Egyptian faculties.

In Kuwait, the Ministry of Education launched a recent program to provide Internet access to 300 government schools; to start, the ministry issued a tender to the three ISPs. Quality Net won the tender to install the necessary infrastructure, connections, and so on in the schools. In addition, the three private ISPs in the country give various discounts to private schools. For example, Quality Net provides special discounts on monthly Internet charges and leased circuits to the American and English schools in Kuwait.

In the U.A.E., the Ministry of Education and Youth, together with Etisalat, have launched the Smart Schools project with the aim of promoting Internet use in schools and an interactive learning environment. The initiative includes free installation in government and private schools, with a discounted usage fee. To date, 100 of the 1,111 schools in the U.A.E. have subscribed to the service.

Jordan is also very active in developing its human resources in the IT sector. Within the overall REACH initiative, the government of Jordan has a specific human resources development agenda that has the following aims:

- initiating a training program by IT industries to benefit IT students

- helping universities focus on critical IT skills for all students

- strengthening the links between IT industries and universities

- promoting collaboration with overseas universities

- establishing a "center of excellence" training institute for the software industry

Many IT companies relocating in the region choose Egypt and Jordan as their regional headquarters, mainly because of these countries' human capital. Recent studies have suggested the liberalization of both countries' labor laws in order to combine their pool of IT workers.

In addition to creating an awareness of Internet usage, Internet access initiatives are required to alleviate barriers to access for specific segments of the population. Such universal access initiatives are used worldwide, and target poor income segments and geographic areas that have less infrastructure and fewer IT facilities.

For instance, in the U.A.E., several initiatives have been launched to increase Internet access in schools and via the education system. The IT Education Project, as it is called, is subdivided into several initiatives: PC laboratories in schools, an IT academy, an IT portal, an e-store, and Internet cafés. The overall aim is to provide students with cutting-edge technology and to increase Internet access among youth.

In Saudi Arabia, the aim of the Watani project is to enhance Internet access in schools. To parallel the focus of the project, the Ministry of Planning is formulating a series of initiatives, in coordination with the incumbent telecommunications operator, to provide financial incentives for schools to access the Internet.

The Jordan IT Community Centers (JITCC) initiative was launched in 1999 to harness the power of information technology to support a sustainable development strategy for Jordan. The aim of the initiative is to install sixty JITCCs using a three-phase approach. A network of JITCCs will serve as a platform for enhancing technological literacy, sustainable livelihoods, and equity and human development among the remote, poor, and information deprived segments of Jordan's population.

Compelling content

The lack of online content in Arabic is another factor deterring ICT usage in the Arab world, as language is a key enabler for creating compelling Internet content. In fact, Arabic is the sixth most widely spoken language in the world, with 175 million speakers, but the share of Arabic content on the Internet remains as low as 1 percent (Figure 16).

In an effort to combat these obstacles, many Arab countries have undertaken initiatives to widen the Arabic web-user base by developing new portals with Arabic content. For example, maktoob.com, launched in October 1998, was the first Arabic web-based e-mail solution on the Internet. Another Arabic based website is BBCarabic.com, which came as a result of Microsoft Middle East's cooperation with BBC world service to bring the world news, translated into Arabic, online for Arabic Internet users.

Figure 16. Population per Language (in Millions) Versus Percentage of Language Online

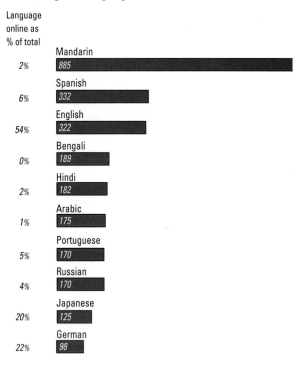

Language online as % of total

2%	Mandarin 885
6%	Spanish 332
54%	English 322
0%	Bengali 189
2%	Hindi 182
1%	Arabic 175
5%	Portuguese 170
4%	Russian 170
20%	Japanese 125
22%	German 98

Source: ITU 2001

The innovative Arabization software industry is a promising value-added activity that will indirectly stimulate ICT development in the Arab world and create employment for Arab IT skilled labor. A growing number of international companies see the potential of the software Arabization industry in Egypt, and many have begun subcontracting Egyptian software developers in a bid to gain a share of the lucrative Middle East market. IBM, for example, has its Arabic development software offices in Egypt, and all the support for its Arabic software products is based there.

With almost 80 percent of its software exported to the Arab world, Egypt is slowly emerging as a regional software development hub. A five-year plan to promote the software industry in Egypt aims at growing the existing software market, estimated at US$50 million, to a market of US$2 billion. The five-year plan has received backing from international software companies as well as local software industries.

Governments can lead the market in the creation of more compelling and useful content for users, as they provide many services well suited for the online world (e.g., passport renewal applications, medical care, benefits administration). By transferring core public services to the Internet, the government will encourage take-up across the population.

By developing online provision of its services, the government can—through partnership with private enterprises—help to develop skills and assets in the commercial sector. This will create opportunities to promote entrepreneurship so that innovative new applications are launched quickly and successfully.

For example, in the U.A.E., the federal government issued a resolution for the development and implementation of a national e-government project; the Ministry of Finance was appointed to direct it. The aim of the project is to improve the effectiveness and efficiency of administrative delivery of services in all government entities. In light of this resolution, two e-government portals have been developed (Dubai and Abu Dhabi), and a third is under construction (Fujairah). The portals are interactive platforms that offer a rich source of information on each Emirate, and they also offer online services, such as trade licenses, commercial permits, and fine settlement.

Policy Recommendations to Support ICT Development

Going forward, Arab countries have the opportunity to fast-track their ICT development program by enacting a selected set of critical policies, as presented hereafter. Our recommendations draw on international best practice policies stemming from nine ICT-developed countries, namely: the United Kingdom, Sweden, Canada, Australia, the United States, Italy, Japan, Germany, and France. The findings are based on 150 face-to-face policy interviews, as well extensive benchmarking. Importantly, we have focused on policies that have had success and have impacted their home market.[9]

Best practice ICT development policies

For the sake of clarity, we have structured the following write-up along the same framework used to analyze the performance of Arab countries, specifically, environment, readiness, and usage. Each of these dimensions is analyzed in detail (Figure 17), to maximize what can be learned and the insights that can be gained so that Arab countries can effectively leverage the policies.

Figure 17. Best Practice Policy Analysis Framework

Environment	Readiness	Usage
• Political/Regulatory Leadership	• Individuals	• Individuals
	• Businesses	• Businesses
• Market		
	• Governments	• Governments
• Infrastructure		

Environment—political and regulatory leadership

Political and regulatory leadership describes the extent to which governments have effectively driven the ICT agenda. Such leadership is best manifested by providing strong, high profile political momentum, setting clear strategies and targets, establishing dedicated delivery organizations, and creating a regulatory framework that fosters ICT development.

Our study of ICT-developed markets confirms that political leadership is strong, and the regulatory environment is generally open in all. Specifically, Germany, the United States, the United Kingdom, and Canada have strong political leadership, each with different styles. In the United States, the leadership is primarily treasury-based. The United Kingdom uses a cabinet office leadership, and Germany follows a home office approach for leadership.

Canada has followed a more informal approach through its e-Business Round Table. Under this policy, the private sector led an initiative to improve Canada's environment for e-commerce. The forum included representatives from across many industries, leading to credibility and distancing the initiative from a "lobby" group. The round table suggested politically safe, actionable recommendations that could benefit the entire economy, but would likely have the largest impact on the ICT sector. The impact of this initiative was a marked improvement in the Canadian environment for investment.

Environment—market

Fostering a strong market environment for ICT development requires building the skills of the population by promoting ICT in education, supporting cluster industries, and promoting low access cost for the Internet. Our research suggests three main trends:

- best practice approaches—Canada, the United Kingdom, and Sweden have best practice approaches in promoting ICT in education

- cluster industries—the United States has most successfully promoted cluster industries, with strong emphasis on venture capital

- low-cost access—approaches to creating low cost access vary with local competitive conditions

The United Kingdom National Grid for Learning Initiative (NGFL) provides a best practice to promote ICT in education. Specifically, the program provides funding for ICT equipment and Internet connections in schools. It also focuses on providing ICT training for teachers. Results to date show that 98 percent of schools are linked to the Internet, up from 28 percent in 1998 when NGFL began. Additionally, 84 percent of teachers have signed up for ICT training, and 190,000 having completed it.

In the same vein, the aim of ITiS program in Sweden was to bring ICT advancements to all schools (all levels). Key targets included the accessibility to e-mail addresses for all pupils and teachers, high speed Internet access to all schools, and Internet availability in every classroom. The ITiS enabled up to 90 percent of municipalities to achieve their goals. For example, there has been an increase in Internet connectivity to 78 percent of all available computers, up from 57 percent in 1999.

Last, but not least, the Connecting Canadians program has delivered strong results. The initiative seeks to ensure that all Canadians have access to the Internet; the program is an example of early action by the Canadian government. As a result, 100 percent of schools and public libraries have been connected to the Internet since 1999. Additionally, roughly 10,000 rural and remote communities have access points.

In terms of promoting cluster industries, the United States has the most successful model, as evidenced by the advent and role of venture capital. One of the most prominent initiatives has been the Small Business Investment Company (SBIC) Act, which was introduced in 1958 to fill the gap between the availability of venture capital and the needs of small businesses in start-up and growth situations. Once funded, SBICs are able to borrow from the federal government at preferential rates (approximately 2.5 percent above ten-year bond rate) over the long term (e.g., five years), which enables so-called "patient capital." SBIC ICT successes include Intel, AOL, Apple, Sun Microsystems, Sage, and Peoplesoft.

Environment—infrastructure

Policymaking to promote the development of infrastructure can encompass multiple approaches: setting a competitive market framework to boost competition among private sector players or lean on a strong incumbent; and investing public funds to provide infrastructure as a necessary public good, or attempting to provide incentives to the private sector to encourage them to lead.

Canada has effectively created a competitive market framework. Again, the key feature of the Canadian program has been its early start; its program can also be replicated in other markets. Beginning in 1998, cable companies were exposed to broadcast competition from telecommunications companies, and to broadband access competition from third party ISPs. Similarly, beginning in 1997 and 1998, telecommunications companies were exposed to competition from both cable companies and CLECs in the local loop. The prospect of increased competition drove investment by cable companies and telecommunications companies ahead of deregulation; investors sought to secure market share as a defensive measure, and cultivate a new revenue stream. Canada presently boasts the lowest business and individual broadband rates among the benchmark group, and has one of the highest availability levels.

In similar moves to Canada, Japan forced the incumbent NTT to open up facilities to competitors through "local loop unbundling" in August 1999, and followed with a series of regulatory actions, namely: leaning on the NTT to upgrade exchanges beyond metropolitan areas in 2000 by revising the provision of NTT connectivity, and forcing the NTT to offer wholesale DSL in June 2001.

Australia exhibits best practice policies in investing public funds to close the urban-rural digital divide. Specifically, the Networking the Nation program aimed to: (1) enhance telecommunications infrastructure and services in nonurban areas; (2) increase access to, and promote the use of, services available through telco networks; and (3) reduce disparities in access to services and facilities. The Australian government has committed funds for this strategy and is in the process of implementing related projects. Ten rounds of funded projects were executed with more than AUD200 million invested. Additionally, Australia extended the universal service obligation in 1997 to include a digital data service obligation (DDSO), which requires the digital service provider to set out plans for how 100 percent of Australians will be served. As a result, regional Internet connectivity has more than doubled to 36 percent in the past two years.

Readiness—individuals

Policymaking to boost citizen readiness encompasses measures to promote access device availability, to boost or encourage the development of skills, as well as measures to boost broader confidence in ICT media.

Sweden has achieved high citizen readiness, having acted to promote PC uptake for households. In 1998, the Swedish government reformed the tax system to enable employees to purchase PCs tax-free from their employer. The employer administers the scheme, typically providing the machine to the employee, who then repays it over a period of three years. Payments are deducted from gross salary. All employees were eligible, even those who did not need a machine for work purposes. Financing for the initial capital outlay was provided by banks, which took advantage of the security of a government guarantee. As a result, PC penetration in Sweden increased the most of all European countries between 1997 and 1999, despite starting at an already high level.

Italy has been prominent in supporting the European Computer Driving License (ECDL) as a common training standard. The ECDL is a common European qualification, but the government of Italy has done the most to promote this qualification as a standard. The most prominent facets of the program are: (1) public sector staff will be trained for ECDL, (2) an e-learning course will be provided to promote ECDL among teachers and students, (3) ECDL training will form part of military service, and (4) further initiatives to train unemployed people to ECDL standard. A fiscal bonus is provided for companies employing staff with an ECDL.

Readiness—businesses

Policymaking to promote business readiness involves the promotion of access device penetration among businesses, designing incentives for businesses to train their staff, as well as addressing business concerns over, for example, the security of the online medium. It can also potentially involve positive action to enhance the value-for-money of online versus offline commerce.

Germany has strong business readiness, because it has concentrated on ensuring that adequately trained staff is available. The government engaged industry and unions to agree on an action plan—Innovation and Jobs for the Information Society—to attract 250,000 IT jobs by 2005 and eliminate skills shortages. The plan included a short-term emergency measure to alleviate the acute near-term shortage: 20,000 green cards for non-EU specialists over two years. Longer-term measures included EUR1 billion for training courses from the Federal Labor Office, a commitment from industry to increase training places by 50 percent, and an additional EUR50 million to create new computer science courses. Recent progress reports suggest that the target of 250,000 specialists will be reached, as 160,000 were attracted by end of 2001 alone.

U.K. Online for Business is the most successful business support network model. The program is a government-industry partnership to support businesses in making the best use of ICT. With a budget of £67 million, the scheme represents a considerable investment. Help and support are provided through a variety of contact points: (1) a network of 400 advisers in over 100 contact centers nationwide, (2) Internet portals with access to information and e-business planning tools; (3) call centers and helplines, and (4) a partnership program to help spread best practices among SMEs. The support network was promoted by a marketing campaign in mass media (TV, radio, trade press). In terms of impact, the project exceeded its target of getting 1 million SMEs online.

Readiness—governments | 3

Government readiness policies foster a government's ability to deliver e-government services and to participate in e-commerce. For a government to be ready, it must have the appropriate strategies in place, a sufficient level of equipment and, very importantly, progress should be made towards establishing common standards and architectures for cross-departmental service delivery, such as a public key infrastructure. Cases in point are government initiatives in Germany and the United Kingdom to establish common ICT related standards across agencies.

The aim of the BundOnline program in Germany is to put all priority services of the federal government online by 2005. Project planning includes very definite linkages between the development of back-office capability and front-end service delivery. Although it may take longer to get services online, they will have robust back-office foundations at delivery time, and this stability will promote user confidence. Progress to date includes a detailed implementation plan with a clear timeline and prioritization for services provided by federal agencies. The federal cabinet has accepted the plan, including funding of EUR1.65 billion through 2005.

The Government Gateway Initiative in the United Kingdom provides a secure interface enabling any department to offer a service through it and to use it as an "authentication engine." It was launched in January 2001, at a cost of £16 million; five pilots were complete by December 2001. The service is far ahead of similar schemes in other countries because it is operational; progress so far includes 390,000 registered users.

Usage—individuals | 1

Promoting citizen usage involves tackling issues of the digital divide and potentially taking positive action among population groups less likely to use the Internet. It also involves taking action to increase the incentives for use, by improving, for example, the quality of broadband content. And it involves measures to encourage citizens up the "adoption ladder" of usage sophistication, although few governments have been active in this area.

Germany's Women to the Web campaign has reduced the digital divide between genders. The program is part of a series called the Internet for All programs. Training was offered at over 200 cites across the country on a subsidized basis—the fee was EUR28 per course. The initiative was supported by Brigitte magazine, a popular women's magazine, and the program was made successful by most women's ability and willingness to pay a small fee for training. Additionally, the scheme's impact was enhanced by imaginatively leveraging the private sector through exposure in magazines. Sponsorship from DTAG also extended the reach of the scheme. This far, 100,000 women have been trained and 200,000 enrolled for future courses. Importantly, 98 percent of course attendees intend to continue using the Internet.

The Canadian government has helped numerous voluntary organizations get online. The VolNet initiative offered Internet skills and equipment to voluntary organizations. The scheme makes available resources such as a basic Internet account for one year, a discount of 50 percent on the cost of access devices, and training in basic Internet skills for general use and website publishing. Additional support takes the form of applied learning, such as online discussion groups, and support from IT volunteers. The 50 percent discount on computer equipment was a substantial incentive to organizations usually cash constrained. Additionally, the comprehensiveness of the scheme, including ongoing support, made it a complete package for volunteer groups. Progress to date includes the training and online presence of 10,000 voluntary organizations. In the process, 17,000 staff and volunteers were trained.

Usage—businesses | 2

In business usage policymaking, the general level of purposeful uptake and use of Internet technologies by a nation's businesses is promoted. Strong uptake is characterized by high levels of use at several levels of sophistication, from basic use to trading online, and by high levels of use by small as well as large businesses.

Australia's Information Technology Online (ITOL) grants have facilitated industry cooperation for a small outlay. Grants are provided to projects, which broker industry collaboration to either develop common standards within and across industries, and/or bring whole industries online through collaborative projects. Only AUD2 million are available annually (a deliberately small amount to ensure that they play only a facilitation role). Eighty-one awards, with a total value of AUD7.3 million, have been made to at least fifteen different sectors. Among other initiatives, the ITOL program has enabled Australia to achieve one of the highest proportions of small businesses that trade online.

Canada's Student Connection Program creates IT specialists and places them in SMEs. Launched in 1996, the program provides students interested in IT (though not necessarily studying it) with IT training. Students then provide training within the center, or more intensively through a placement. Some students are subsequently hired for permanent positions. The scheme operates from fifteen centers within universities and colleges. Among the key success factors is the low risk and high return for businesses in placing student trainers or in taking a course themselves—both are virtually free. Additionally, the government lends its brand and trusted status to students who would not otherwise be hired in an ICT role. So far shows more than 85,000 small businesses have used the scheme, and more than 3,500 young people have been placed on the scheme.

Usage—governments

Government usage policies promote purposeful uptake and use of Internet technologies by the public sector in general. Strong uptake is characterized by a large proportion of services offered online, particularly those that are more transactional, and by the services being used by a large proportion of the nation's citizens and businesses.

Germany adopted a three-pronged approach to encourage state and local government service delivery, specifically: (1) competition to encourage innovation at a local level; (2) shared resources, such as creating procurement platforms and authentication engines, which are open to local governments; and (3) direct cooperation where services allow this. Interestingly, the German federal government has no authority over state and local governments in determining the means of service delivery. Both these approaches apply the strategy of creating an incentive for local governments to buy into online service delivery and common standards.

Canada was among the first governments to offer services through "user-centric" interfaces, rather than interfaces corresponding to traditional government departments. The redesigned website was launched in February 2001. Canadians can access 450 websites through three user-specific gateways and thirty-five service clusters. Canada has begun to move to the next stage of e-government, where services are redesigned around this customer centric delivery process. Not only are Canadian government services delivered through customer centric portals, but also the choice of services and the means of delivery are shaped by extensive customer research. For example, fifty focus groups were used in advance of the re-launch of the main website in 2001. As a result of this work, Canada's e-government service was ranked number one in an international survey in both 2000 and 2001, due to both its extensiveness and sophistication.

Policy recommendations for Arab countries

Our policy recommendations for ICT development in the Arab world echo the proven principles and guidelines implemented in international markets and in some Arab countries with a fast-track record. Specifically, we have formulated the proposed policies along the three pillars: environment, readiness, and usage.

Environment—political and regulatory leadership

We believe that the first imperative to ICT development is the formulation of a clear national plan, supported by the highest political constituencies. Cases in point from the Middle East region are the Jordanian and Egyptian programs, which have benefited from strong advocacy at the highest national level.

The ICT development plan must formulate specific strategies, goals, and targets. As demonstrated in many ICT advanced nations and the fast-track Arab markets such as the U.A.E., initiatives are better when prioritized and paced for timely roll-out (e.g., the U.A.E.'s e-government program roll-out spans three to five years).

Critical to the success of a top-down national ICT development initiative is the governance model that defines roles and responsibilities in the design and execution, as well as performance management. International practices in governance structure vary greatly, ranging from a highly centralized set-up where a common set of ICT objectives is acknowledged in a unified master plan, to a decentralized structure where national level initiatives are not necessarily coordinated under a common umbrella.

In most developing and developed economies we have benchmarked, allowing market forces to lead the way towards higher ICT advancement—without any government interference—has not been common. Even in countries where the private sector leads the majority of initiatives towards ICT universality, the government leads the definition of a national agenda and rolls out regulation and policies that create the right environment to enable ICT advancements. Additionally, governments must set up a highly visible entity (e.g., e-Envoy in the U.K.) to establish a sustainable and accountable institutional structure.

In tandem with the ICT leadership agenda, governments should outline a clear roadmap for developing support clusters, mainly in telecommunications and e-commerce. For telecommunications, there must an explicit roadmap for sector deregulation and liberalization. This is particularly relevant to Arab countries where most telecommunications sectors remain dominantly monopolistic and with a marked absence of market-driven regulatory framework. Deregulation and liberalization, when adequately managed, can considerably improve quality of service and added value to end-users.

Milestones for the support of e-commerce include ICT security as well as trust. This applies particularly to laws that manage the trade of goods and services through electronic means, along with laws to combat computer related crimes. The latter laws remain underdeveloped in the Arab world, with varying levels of progress. The overriding finding is that there is increasing awareness and effort to develop cyber-laws; to these activities are added proponents of unifying such laws at a regional level, for example, within Gulf countries. The initial emphasis appears to be on combating unlawful activities through electronic means in the areas of privacy offenses, content-related offences, economic crimes, unauthorized access and sabotage, as well as intellectual property offences.

Environment —market `2`

At the market level, the number one imperative is incorporating ICT skills and knowledge into the educational system.

A number of Arab countries have initiated the design of national programs for building ICT skills in schools and universities. However, the general observation is that there is relative slowness in executing the envisaged plans; senior stakeholders must press on with these initiatives and instill a sense of urgency. A case in point

is the Watani project in Saudi Arabia, which presents one of the most comprehensive plans for an electronic educational network in the region since 1999, but which appears to advance at a slower pace than was envisaged.

Arab governments can also play an instrumental role in stimulating the development of support clusters. The most prominent manifestation of such a policy is the creation of economic zones focusing on ICT subsectors. Dubai pioneered the design and fast-track implementation of related concepts with the advent of the Dubai Internet City and Dubai Media City. These clusters have attracted world-class players in their related fields (e.g., Microsoft and Oracle). Jordan, Egypt, and Syria are seeking to make use of comparable potential in their countries, with plans to create new media and Internet zones. Saudi Arabia is also entertaining the idea of creating IT parks.

Conditions for ICT development are also enhanced by accessibility to capital markets. The equity market in most Arab nations continues to be underdeveloped; funding mechanisms are primarily managed through commercial banks. Further developments are required at national and regional levels to ensure that capital is available, particularly for emerging ICT related industries. Specifically, Arab markets must provide adequate capital instruments ranging from venture capital to funding through public offerings. An example of such an instrument is the recent development of the Dubai International Financial Center, which is to provide, among other things, a world-class capital market for the region—from North Africa to east and central Asia, and encompassing the Middle East. Another development is the upcoming capital market reforms in Saudi Arabia, following the successful launch of the Tadawul electronic trading platform for the local stock market.

Environment—infrastructure

The key requirement at the level of the infrastructure for Arab countries is the expeditious enactment of telecommunications laws and regulations that are geared toward introducing competition. As mentioned earlier in this report, the region is dominantly monopolistic. Much remains to be done in terms of enacting new telecommunications laws that call for deregulation, privatization of incumbent operators, and sector liberalization.

In addition to the core objective of enabling infrastructure development through market forces, Arab governments may have to pursue targeted initiatives, such as the Networking the Nation initiative in Australia, to secure the connectivity required for ICT-related activities. Such programs would support infrastructure advancement and services in nonurban areas and reduce prevailing gaps. An immediate application would be the set-up of Universal Internet Access funds, targeting groups with constrained economics (e.g., public schools, rural areas, low income households, and so on).

Readiness—individuals

Arab government policies in the area of citizen readiness should drive literacy and comfort with the ICT field. Our research in Arab countries suggests that these elements represent the most significant barriers to ICT adoption today. Initiatives in this vein can evolve with two themes: awareness and trust, and training and comfort.

Awareness and trust represent the first hurdle, particularly in relatively conservative Arab societies. While not insurmountable, these elements require significant up-front management by the government to set the stage among the rural and urban societies for ICT development. The task can be achieved through public information and educational programs, as well as by targeted programs in schools. The objectives are to demonstrate the imperative and benefits of ICT—that is, what's in it for citizens to use the Internet and acquire computer skills—as well as to underscore ICT compatibility with social and cultural norms.

Once the initial hurdles are removed, Arab governments must play an active role in bringing citizens gradually up to speed with ICT skills. Training programs can, and must, be established at the level of educational institutions. Training activities can also be set up to support groups that are not naturally driven to embrace ICT skills, for example, young housewives. The German Women to the Web program provides a good reference in this area.

Readiness—businesses

The challenges for achieving business readiness in Arab countries, especially among SMEs, are comparable to the ones for citizens. On the one hand, governments need to drive awareness and trust. On the other hand, a certain level of training and comfort must be achieved to pave the way for ICT endorsement.

In line with best practice policies in ICT-developed markets, in the Arab world there have been high-potential initiatives to advance the level of readiness among SMEs. A case in point is the Dubai Sheikh Mohammed Business Support and Development Establishment, which was developed to provide business support and tools, including ICT enabled ones such as e-government and e-procurement, to SMEs.

At a grass-roots level, initiatives driving awareness of the benefit of ICT-enabling businesses as well as providing initial consulting and help-desk support, are emerging in some market such as Saudi Arabia. Such initiatives can also be extended to encompass training and accessibility. For example, subsidized training programs in nationally accessible centers can be offered at no, or limited, fee for SMEs. Creating common platforms (e.g., e-procurement portals) and tools (e.g., standard business support applications for SMEs, with customization capabilities) can also improve accessibility.

For both citizens and businesses, readiness-driven policies must also address the issue of language barrier. As most Arab populations are not conversant in English, providing ICT content in Arabic is critical and requires dedicated attention. It is unlikely that such an Arabization effort could yield, in all cases, commercially viable ventures. Therefore, governments must be ready to invest directly in this vein, and to secure funding for related service providers.

Readiness—governments

At the level of government, readiness efforts must focus, again, on awareness and trust and on training and comfort. Policies must also promote and develop e-government organizations that would define strategies and targets for implementing e-government services.

As observed in ICT-developed markets, and apparent already in some Arab countries, the biggest obstacle to achieving government readiness will be inter-departmental coordination. Policies dealing with this obstacle must ensure that lines of accountability are clearly defined, and at the same time encourage participation across government departments to yield resource efficiency and effectiveness. The absence of such policies may lead to situations of conflicting agendas, undue competition across complementary entities, and inefficient use of public resources.

Usage—individuals

Policies to promote citizen usage should aim to create as many "contact points" as possible between ICT tools and prospective users in order to increase confidence, comfort, and adoption.

Initially, contact points could focus on training opportunities in schools, community centers, or other for-profit centers, with financial backing from public funds. The objective is to make resources available to those who would not otherwise be exposed to them.

Usage, of course, would follow a systematic buildup of readiness levers such as awareness, trust, and comfort. Therefore, Arab governments, along with national support groups, should view usage on a continuum that starts with the creation of an ICT favorable environment.

Usage—businesses `| | 2 |`

Business usage could be stimulated through policies that would promote the diffusion of ICT tools as well as the buildup of skills readiness. Through such policies, Arab governments can pursue a series of programs that would enhance accessibility to public telecommunications networks, ICT hardware and software and, most importantly, skills. At the simplest level, usage can be encouraged through supportive funding, creation of a competitive environment, and learning incentives. Importantly, governments must recognize the role of SMEs in the national economy, and aim to target them directly through ICT-usage building programs.

Usage—governments `| | 3 |`

Policies to promote ICT usage among government agencies should have as their aim the offering of a large number of online services that are accessible by a large proportion of citizens and businesses.

Typically, the application of these policies calls for a prioritization of the services to be offered online. Government agencies must also create tangible incentives to end users for the endorsement of online services over traditional services. Such incentives could underscore the internal benefits to government agencies and be a self-reinforcing mechanism that offers new services online, while improving the format and delivery of existing services.

Conclusion

Our work is not intended to provide a long-range roadmap for all ICT related initiatives and policies. Rather, our aim is to outline the short- to medium-term policies that can positively impact ICT development in the Arab world. Many of these ideas have been seen in practice in one or more of the Arab countries referred to throughout this report, as well as in ICT-developed countries.

We believe that a series of multiple measures, with clear and consistent policies, can deliver the best results; this is why we have designed this approach in a policy framework to guide ICT advancement.

In the end, each Arab country will need to develop its own policies, which should be driven by the local conditions (infrastructure, IT skills, education, and so on). It is key, however, to understand that the "window of opportunity" for catching up with developed economies is limited, hence the need for Arab governments to act quickly to boost ICT advancement in their countries.

References

American University. "Information Technology Landscape in Nations." Country reports on Egypt (1999), Lebanon (2001), Saudi Arabia (1998), and the United Arab Emirates (2000). Washington D.C.

Arab Advisors Group. "Communications Projections Country Reports." Research on Egypt, Jordan, Kuwait, Lebanon, Morocco, Oman, Saudi Arabia, Syria, and the United Arab Emirates.

Arab Advisors Group. "GCC E-Commerce Primer." 2000.

Arab Advisors Group. "Internet and Datacomm Landscape Country Reports." Research on Egypt, Jordan, Kuwait, Lebanon, Morocco, Oman, Saudi Arabia, Syria, and the United Arab Emirates.

Arab Advisors Group. "ISPs in the Arab World." 2001.

Arab Information Project. "Studying the Information Revolution in the Arab World." Georgetown University. <http://www.georgetown.edu/research/arabtech/>

Booz Allen Hamilton. "The World's Most Effective Policies for E-Commerce." July 2002.

Ein-Dorr, Philipp, Seymour Goodman, and Peter Wolcott. The Global Diffusion of Internet Project. The Hashemite Kingdom of Jordan, 1999.

ETForecasts. "PC Sales Growth: Slow and Jagged." <http://www.etforecasts.com/> (May 2002).

E-Readiness Guides. <http://www.ereadinessguide.org/>

European Information Technology Observatory. Annual Reports. 2001, 2002.

Fahmy, Miral. "Dubai IT Hub Seen as Mid East Answer to Silicon Valley." <http://www.arabia.com> (August 2001).

The Heritage Foundation, and the Wall Street Journal. The Index of Economic Freedom Report. 2002.

Human Rights Watch. The Internet in the Middle East and North Africa. 1999.

International Telecommunications Union. The Arab Region Internet and Telecom Summit. Muscat, Oman, May 2001.

International Telecommunications Union. Yearbook of Statistics 1991–2000.

Jordan IT Community Centers. "The REACH Initiative: Launching Jordan's Software and IT Services Industry." <http://www.jitcc.gov.jo/>

Kirkman, Geoffrey S., Peter K. Cornelius, Jeffrey D. Sachs, Klaus Schwab. The Global Information Technology Report 2001-2002: Readiness for the Networked World. New York: World Economic Forum, Oxford University Press, 2002.

McArthur, John, and Jeffrey Sachs. The Growth Competitiveness Index: Measuring Technological Advancement and the Stages of Development. Harvard University, Center for International Development.

UN Commission for Science and Technology for Development. ICT Development Indices.

UNDP. E-Government: Considerations for Arab States. 2001.

UNDP, and Arab Fund for Economic and Social Development. Arab Human Development Report 2002: Creating Opportunities for Future Generations. 2002.

UNESCO Observatory on the Information Society. Internet in the Arab World. 2002.

U.S.-Arab Tradeline, and Joseph Braude. Free Internet to Provide a Boost to ISPs and Telecom Egypt. March 2002.

U.S. Department of Commerce, Technology Administration. Technology Competitiveness.

WITSA. The Digital Planet 2002: The Global Information Economy.

World Bank Information for Development Program (infoDev). E-Readiness as a Tool for ICT Development.

Endnotes

1. Based on statistics from the European Information Technology Observatory (EITO) Report (2002).

2. Western Europe plus the following countries: Czech Republic, Hungary, Poland, Russia, Slovakia, and Slovenia.

3. Based on ITU Statistics (2002).

4. World PC sales are based on etforecasts estimates 2001. etforecasts. "PC Sales Growth: Slow and Jagged." <http://www.etforecasts.com/> (May 2002).

5. Estimates of e-commerce transactions vary widely from one source to the other, ranging from as low as $345 billion (Ovum), to $740 billion (Goldman Sachs), to $953 billion (Gartner Group), among others.

6. Countries selected in those three subregions are: Jordan, Lebanon, and Syria (Levant); Egypt and Morocco (North Africa); Kuwait, Oman, Saudi Arabia, and the U.A.E. (Gulf).

7. The current Internet regulator in Saudi Arabia (i.e., the Internet Service Unit [ISU] of King Abdulaziz City for Science and Technology [KACST]) is responsible for preparing policies and regulations regarding the use of the Internet in the Kingdom. The regulator also gives ISPs with access to the Internet international backbone by buying bandwidth from Saudi Telecom and re-selling it at a premium to service providers. The recently appointed Saudi Communications Commission is expected to take over Internet regulatory responsibility in the near future.

8. Based on Arab Advisors Group forecast.

9. Based on Booz Allen Hamilton report, "The World's Most Effective Policies for E-Commerce." July 2002.

A Review of Telecommunications and Networked Readiness in the Arab World:
Capturing the Opportunity

Scott Beardsley, Kito de Boer, Gassan al-Kibsi, and Luis Enriquez

Introduction

This chapter briefly summarizes the state and performance of the telecommunications sector in the Middle East region and its impact on "Networked Readiness."[1] Networked Readiness refers to the availability and the use of telecommunications infrastructure and services that allow a community to participate in the networked world. It ranges from basic voice services to the availability and use of narrowband and broadband Internet. Three key messages emerge from this chapter.

- *Reform can be a powerful tool for improving the performance of the telecommunications sector and, hence, improving Networked Readiness.* A global review of telecommunications reform suggests that intelligent, well-managed reform can drive large improvements in the performance levels of the telecommunications sector and can, therefore, be a powerful tool for encouraging Networked Readiness. However, this review also identifies differing policy imperatives for countries at different income levels. Poorer countries have focused on encouraging infrastructure deployment. At the other end, developed countries have been, until recently, focused on increasing competition and lowering prices to encourage usage of (mostly) existing infrastructure. However, because broadband upgrades and deployments of advanced services in mobile and fixed networks require large infrastructure investments, the emphasis on lower prices has been inconsistent with deployment

objectives. Middle-income countries have essentially been somewhere in between, managing tradeoffs between the need for the telecommunications industry to fund infrastructure and give incumbents the time to improve efficiency, and the desire to transfer some of the industry's surplus to consumers in the form of lower prices.

- *Compared to the rest of the world, the Middle East has low access to and (in particular) low penetration of telecommunications, partly because of the limited efforts at reform in the region.* When measured by the number of subscribers as a percent of population, the telecommunications sector in the Middle East appears to be underperforming compared to other regions around the world. This pattern holds for all clusters and income levels in the region. Although the causes for this gap are multiple and complex, a key driver appears to be slower progress towards creating competitive telecommunications markets where new entrants can find niche-market opportunities and accelerate their development. Today, however, single, often state-owned telecommunications operators are the prevalent service provision models in most countries in the region. In addition, there appear to be unique elements in the region that create additional challenges. These challenges range from relatively small market sizes in the high-income Gulf Cooperation Council (GCC) countries, to the need to build regulatory institutions to support the sector's potential attractiveness to investors.

- *Tailoring reform to individual countries and managing regulation at a detailed level will be critical to success.* There is significant value at stake both in terms of unlocking value in incumbent operators and in funding (or failing to fund) significant infrastructure upgrades for the region. A clear understanding of the potential objectives and how to translate those objectives into reality through detailed regulation will be critical to capturing that value and improving Networked Readiness.

The primary focus of this chapter is to provide insight into the key factors required to manage sector reform in support of Networked Readiness in the Middle East. This chapter is structured in three sections. The first section will draw relevant lessons from global experience. In the second, challenges in the Middle East will be summarized. The final section discusses what sector reforms will be needed to improve Networked Readiness in the region.

Networked Readiness and Telecommunications Sector Reform

Networked Readiness includes the availability and use of telecommunications infrastructure and services that allow a community to participate in the Networked World. It ranges from basic voice services to the availability and use of narrowband and broadband Internet; therefore, it means networking through telecommunications systems and access to information digitally stored in networks such as the Internet. Networked Readiness shows a close correlation with the growth of per capita income. While telecommunications is not the only enabler for Networked Readiness, it plays an important role in supporting it.

Figure 1. Impact of Telecommunications on Networked Readiness

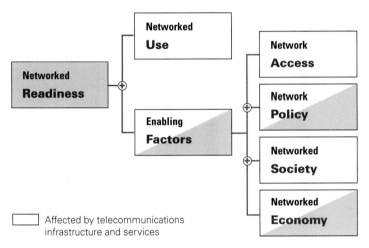

Sources: World Economic Forum; Harvard University; McKinsey

At the core of our discussion is the belief that telecommunications sector reform, done correctly, can accelerate the development of networked infrastructure and services and is, therefore, a strong tool for promoting GDP growth. However, at lower levels of GDP, this relationship is weaker. Although well-executed market reform still confers benefits to poorer countries, it appears to be most effective among wealthier countries. This suggests that ensuring that regulation supports sustainable business models is critical to the success of reform. At lower income levels, the market may be too small to support multiple operators unless regulation is clearly tailored to that situation. Simply transferring models developed in richer countries may not work.

Amid a general spread of telecommunications sector reform around the world, policymakers have typically pursued three options: privatization of the incumbent telephone operator, full and unimpeded opening of the fixed market (including the award of additional fixed and mobile licenses), or privatization and liberalization. We will see later that separating these options is relevant when assessing the effectiveness of telecommunications sector reform.

Translating policy objectives into regulation

Global experience suggests that intelligent reform is key to overcoming the multiple challenges that countries face. While the details of each country vary, several elements are common to successfully managed reform. First, there needs to be a clear understanding of the objectives of reform and the tradeoffs that must be made to achieve these objectives. The second step is to translate these objectives into policy through transparent regulatory tools. A clear understanding of the economics of market players is critical to ensuring that reform creates working markets with stable, and financially viable, players. Finally, reform must iterate this process and regulations must be updated as objectives either change or are fulfilled.

Objectives

Countries have pursued several different objectives as they initiate reform. The first objective is typically to focus on delivering benefits to customers by increasing choice and lowering service prices overall. The second is to create an efficient industry, which encourages an innovative and competitive industry that is a cost and service leader. A third, obvious objective is delivering proceeds to government; this often shapes the tradeoffs in many developing countries where proceeds from privatization are often a key tool for closing budget gaps or providing foreign exchange. A fourth objective is to promote universal service, and this relates to the desire to ensure that access to the telecommunications network is available to a broad segment of the population. The fifth objective, attracting investments, often revolves around creating conditions in which the incumbent and/or entrants can deploy investments in the sector. And finally, reforms promoting Networked Readiness are focused around encouraging the deployment and adoption of information and Internet-based services.

Figure 2. Objectives of Reform

	Examples **Country**	Benefits to customers	Efficient industry	Proceeds for government	Universal service	Attract investments	Networked Readiness	
Developed countries	Germany		✓		✓			Broadly favored market efficiency and competition
	France	✓	✓					
	U.K. (1)			✓				
	U.K. (2)	✓	✓					
	Sweden	✓	✓		✓			
	U.S.	✓	✓			✓		
	Australia	✓	✓					
	New Zealand	✓	✓					
	Japan		✓					
	South Korea	✓	✓		✓			
Emerging countries	Argentina (1)			✓				Compromised between efficiency, privatization proceeds and teledensity
	Argentina (2)		✓					
	Brazil		✓					
	Chile (1)							
	Chile (2)	✓	✓	✓				
	Mexico (1)		✓	✓				
	Mexico (2)		✓					
	Czech Republic		✓	✓	✓	✓		
	Hungary	✓	✓	✓	✓			
	Poland		✓	✓	✓			
	Russia		✓					
	Malaysia		✓				✓	
	South Africa			✓	✓			
Developing countries	China	✓	✓		✓	✓		Promoted teledensity and additional investments
	India	✓	✓		✓	✓		
	Indonesia				✓	✓		
	Philippines				✓	✓		

Similar emphasis

*Qualitative evaluation of objectives based on observed regulatory outcomes

Sources: Espicom; International Telecommunications Union; national policy statements and legislation; press clippings; McKinsey

These objectives can be conflicting. For example, creating immediate benefits to consumers through lower prices would lower the privatization price that could be obtained by the government. Therefore, tradeoffs must be made according to the priorities set by the political process.

With at least these six objectives, therefore, deciding how to prioritize is clearly linked to the tradeoffs that are made at the time of reform. These tradeoffs have varied by country, reflecting the different pressures that stakeholders put on the reform process. We have attempted to discern country objectives from a survey of speeches, press releases, and articles, objectives stated in the telecommunications law, and in licensing and other government documents. The survey results for selected countries are summarized in Figure 2.

Bearing in mind the shortcomings of such a survey—not least that stated objectives are not always translated into the appropriate regulation—three major tendencies emerged. In developed countries, the focus tends to be on benefits to customers and creating competitive, efficient industries. Developing countries as a group have tended to focus on access and teledensity issues, although India and China have clearly also worried about creating efficient industries that would bring benefits to customers. Finally, those in the middle, the emerging countries, have pursued a combination of multiple objectives, making tradeoffs between promoting access, obtaining proceeds for government, and developing efficient industries.

In pursuing reform, it is clear that countries need to continuously evaluate the appropriateness of prioritizing objectives at various stages of the sector reform process. This becomes important, for example, in supporting broadband deployment, because it is a fundamentally different type of challenge in developing countries from the challenge that developed countries have so far faced. Broadband requires infrastructure, a challenge that is much more similar to the teledensity challenges of developing countries rather than the competition challenges that have been the focus in most advanced countries.

Detailed regulation

Translating high-level objectives into actual market incentives and rules is critical to successfully implementing reform. The key tools for doing this are multiple regulatory levers. For simplicity, regulatory levers have been grouped into six categories. These are industry structure, pricing, interconnection, customer access, universal service, and performance levels. The details of these levers will not be discussed in this chapter, but it is critical to note that successful reform must be executed through these levers. This

Figure 3. Regulatory Levers

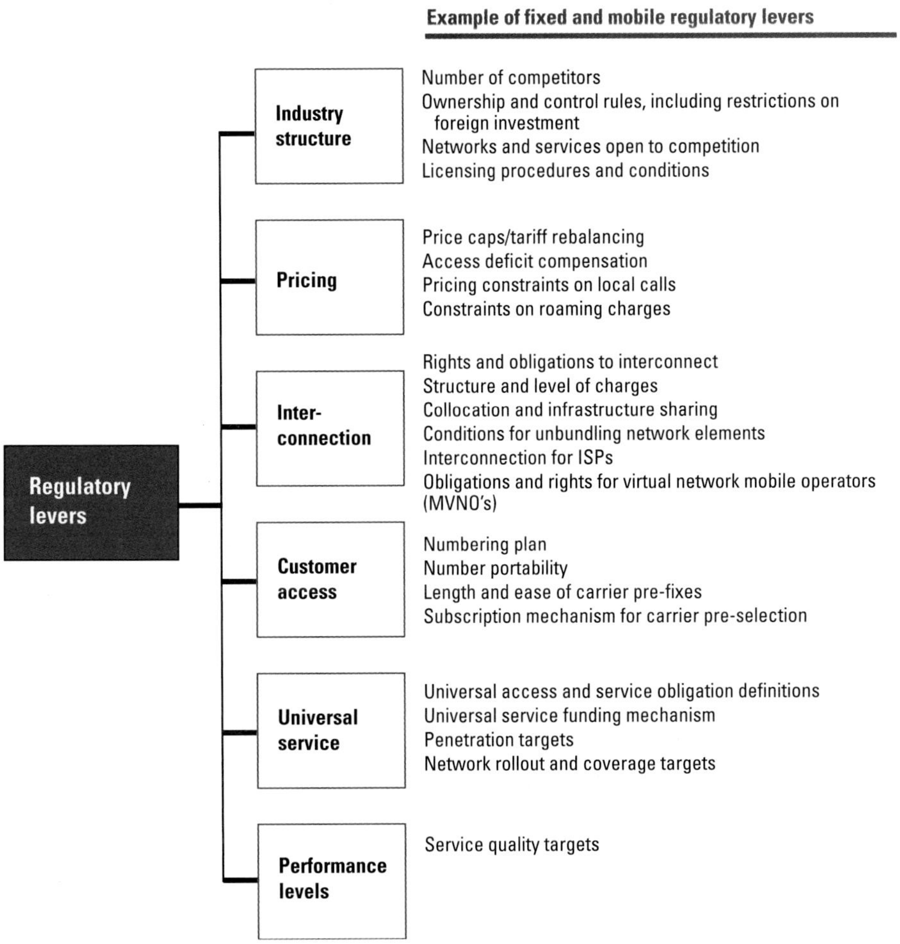

Example of fixed and mobile regulatory levers

Industry structure
- Number of competitors
- Ownership and control rules, including restrictions on foreign investment
- Networks and services open to competition
- Licensing procedures and conditions

Pricing
- Price caps/tariff rebalancing
- Access deficit compensation
- Pricing constraints on local calls
- Constraints on roaming charges

Inter-connection
- Rights and obligations to interconnect
- Structure and level of charges
- Collocation and infrastructure sharing
- Conditions for unbundling network elements
- Interconnection for ISPs
- Obligations and rights for virtual network mobile operators (MVNO's)

Customer access
- Numbering plan
- Number portability
- Length and ease of carrier pre-fixes
- Subscription mechanism for carrier pre-selection

Universal service
- Universal access and service obligation definitions
- Universal service funding mechanism
- Penetration targets
- Network rollout and coverage targets

Performance levels
- Service quality targets

will require a thorough understanding of the detailed policy options and tools that can be deployed in each category and the impact that those levers will have on the business models of both the incumbent operator and new entrants.

Figure 3 provides some examples of the detail that must be considered to support successful reform. Not all tools need to be used at once, and different combinations can be used to support multiple objectives. Furthermore, the economic impact, importance, and critical role of potential tools vary significantly among countries, and depend on a country's market structure and prime objectives. These levers must be thought of holistically, as many of them are interdependent.

It is critical to understand how regulatory details affect market structure and the economics of competitors. For example, subtle differences in the interconnection regulation pursued by France and Germany led to dramatically different outcomes, even though both countries were compliant with European Union (EU) directives. Both countries opened their national public fixed telephony markets to competition on 1 January 1998. Germany adopted an approach to liberalization that sought to rapidly lower prices, while France focused on requiring upfront infrastructure investments from potential entrants. This difference in approach led to differences in how each country managed key details of the interconnection regime.

Several interconnection factors were involved: what services were offered by the incumbent, what criteria new entrants had to satisfy to qualify for the lowest interconnection tariffs, and what prices were charged by incumbents to carry traffic on their networks. Germany set relatively low infrastructure requirements for new entrants to qualify for cost-based interconnection from the incumbent Deutsche Telecom (DT). In line with its focus on infrastructure, French service providers had to meet minimum deployment levels in order to qualify for France Telecom's cost-oriented tariffs. The impact was significant. Operators in Germany could rapidly enter the German market with minimal infrastructure and offer a national service by "piggy-backing" on DT's network. In France, however, an operator who wished to offer a countrywide service had to connect multiple times to France Telecom points of presence.

Germany went further on several other levers. On customer access, Germany introduced carrier pre-selection and number portability in 1998, in addition to call-by-call carrier selection. (France, on the other hand, introduced pre-selection and number portability only in time to meet the 2000 EU deadline.) In addition, Germany required DT to provide ancillary support services, such as billing, for entrants.

A critical feature of the German model, however, was the interconnection services offered by the incumbent. DT had to effectively offer access to the whole country in order to both terminate and, crucially, originate calls for entrants. This double tandem origination service allowed an operator to establish only one connection with DT, but still reach the entire country. This tilted entry strategies away from network building and infrastructure and towards marketing and branding. As a result, German network operators and resellers had conditions that were significantly more favourable for entry. (Eventually, however, this was not necessarily an attractive outcome for entrants, as prices would erode rapidly.) This allowed new entrants to make larger market share gains than in France. Although German regulators were aware that their policies would encourage entry, the extent of the market share loss and price declines were surprising—long distance prices fell by 60 percent within the first year of liberalization.

Measuring impact

The global review looked at several measurable factors that could reveal a focus on specific objectives: teledensity and Internet penetration were expected to reflect a focus on universal access and investments; declines in price levels, an emphasis on benefits to consumers; and incumbent financial performance, a focus on government proceeds, because this factor would impact the sale values of tranches a government could obtain after privatization. Finally, this section provides some evidence of the significant value that has been unlocked through privatization of telecommunications operators.

Increases in fixed and mobile penetration

Using fixed and mobile penetration as a measure of teledensity, we can see that upper high-income countries—all of which have pursued reform—had an increase of fifty-four fixed and mobile lines per 100 people between 1996 and 2000.

In contrast, countries that have not reformed (see Figure 4) had a significantly smaller increase in teledensity. Countries that pursued privatization alone

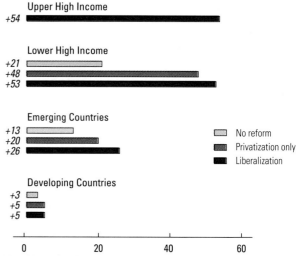

Figure 4. Teledensity Growth, 1996–2000
Change in Teledensity*

Upper High Income
+54

Lower High Income
+21
+48
+53

Emerging Countries
+13
+20
+26

- No reform
- Privatization only
- Liberalization

Developing Countries
+3
+5
+5

Note: All upper high income countries have pursued reform. Teledensity in those countries has grown from 70% to 123% from 1996 to 2000
*Fixed plus mobile lines per 100 population
**Includes countries that have privatized and liberalized
Sources: International Telecommunications Union; EMC; WEFA; McKinsey

had higher growth rates in teledensity, concentrated on mobile access (not illustrated in Figure 4); this reflects the rapid adoption and growth of those networks. Countries that pursued full reform had even more dramatic increases. For lower high-income and emerging countries, teledensity growth rates were nearly double the no-reform increases over this period. For developing countries, the increase was negligible. These facts infer important implications for lower income countries. The surplus available in lower income countries is limited. If a country aggressively tries to use reform to drive prices lower or to generate privatization revenues, its goals on infrastructure and teledensity may be compromised.

Increases in Internet penetration

Reform clearly increases Internet penetration. Figure 5 shows that although Internet penetration increased in those countries with no reform, growth rates have been far more rapid in countries that privatized, and those that pursued full reform enjoyed the most significant increases. It is interesting to note that the patterns of increase mirror those seen in teledensity, despite the fact that Internet penetration is actually a more complex adoption process. Figure 5 reinforces the belief that a "digital divide" is emerging.

The research suggests that emerging and developing countries should certainly follow privatization reform, as this has a positive impact on penetration. This positive impact may potentially take place

Figure 5. Increase in Internet Penetration, 1996–2000*

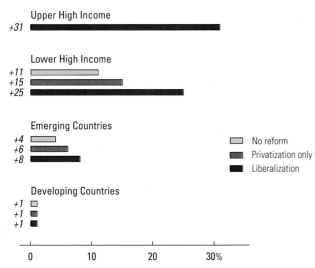

Upper High Income
+31

Lower High Income
+11
+15
+25

Emerging Countries
+4
+6
+8

No reform
Privatization only
Liberalization

Developing Countries
+1
+1
+1

0   10   20   30%

Note: All upper high income countries have pursued reform. Internet penetration in these countries has grown from 7% to 38% of the population from 1996 to 2000
*Percentage change of Internet users per 100 inhabitants
**Includes countries that have privatized and liberalized
Source: International Telecommunications Union; EMC; WEFA; McKinsey

Figure 6. Benefits to Consumers (in Percent)
Long Distance Cumulative Price Change*

Countries that emphasized benefits to customers

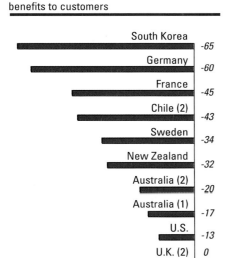

South Korea -65
Germany -60
France -45
Chile (2) -43
Sweden -34
New Zealand -32
Australia (2) -20
Australia (1) -17
U.S. -13
U.K. (2) 0

Countries that did not emphasize benefits to customers

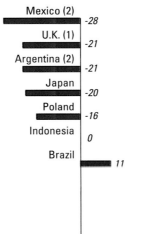

Mexico (2) -28
U.K. (1) -21
Argentina (2) -21
Japan -20
Poland -16
Indonesia 0
Brazil 11

*Based on tariffs of incumbent operators, three years post-reform
Source: International Telecommunications Union; McKinsey

because privatization may bring in more professional management and create a sense of urgency, and remove funding constraints often associated with government activity. However, further reform through liberalization does not appear to help significantly, if at all, in the poorest countries. In order for competition to work, entrants need sustainable business models; in developing countries there may not be enough market potential to make

this work. Bridging the digital divide, therefore, will likely require a combination of privatization and policies that encourage direct investment and detailed understanding of the viability of potential competitors that may enter through reform.

Reduction in prices
Countries that emphasized benefits to customers appear to have larger service-price reductions than countries that did not, although significant differences in the rates of price declines among countries are noticeable. A large part of the difference is driven by the details of regulation. Germany, for example, took a very aggressive approach to liberalization, and this is reflected in price declines.

Incumbent performance and value
Finally, those countries that emphasized incumbent value (which went hand in hand with government proceeds) did relatively better than those countries that did not.

Using the earnings before interest, taxes, depreciation, and amortization (EBITDA) margin of the incumbent at the start of reform as a proxy for value creation, those incumbents in the group with no priority on earnings actually started from a slightly better position than those in countries that had that emphasis. Within three years, however, positions were reversed, with incumbent performance in those countries that did encourage value creation for the incumbent surpassing those in the other group. In those countries where incumbent value was not a priority, performance actually deteriorated. The situation is similar when looking at earnings before interest and taxes.

A company's position on value creation clearly has had an effect on its stock market valuation. Telecom incumbents generally trade at a premium price-to-earnings multiple higher than the valuation levels of other companies in a country's major stock market index. At the time of reform, this premium was comparable in both groups of countries, although still slightly lower in countries that did not emphasize value

Figure 7. Incumbent Performance and Valuation
Change in Perfomance and Relative Value (in Percent Median Values)

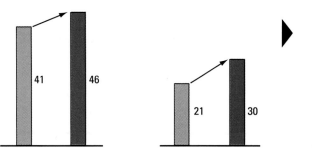

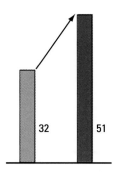

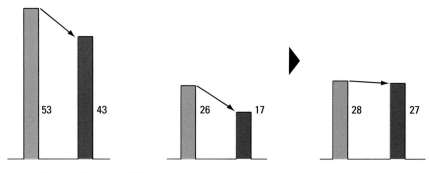

Sources: Bloomberg; Datastream; McKinsey
* Based on flotation dates of incumbents from 19 countries

Figure 8. Value Unlocked

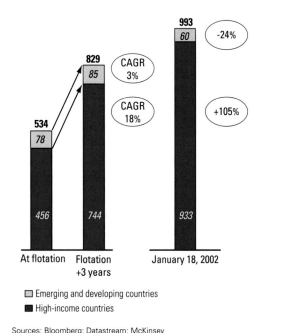

Emerging and developing countries
High-income countries

Sources: Bloomberg; Datastream; McKinsey

*In cases where floatation dates less than 3 years, market capitalization of August 31, 2001 was used

Note: Based on 42 countries where information on market capitalization was available

(despite higher operating margins). Three years into reform, the premium had risen significantly (to 50 percent above the average values for the market as a whole) in countries that focused on incumbent value creation. In countries that did not emphasize value, this premium had dropped slightly.

A major source of this difference is re-balancing, which eliminated cross subsidies and raised local access prices. Countries with improved performance raised prices by an average of 100 percent in the three years after reform started; the other group kept local access prices fairly constant. This process has succeeded in unlocking significant value that was previously hidden in government accounts. The impact of this additional liquidity into financial markets and the effect it may have had on foreign investors' perception of a country's investment climate have been significant.

Reform has unlocked significant value, approximately US$1/2 trillion at the time of privatization. This figure had grown by approximately 60 percent three years after privatization in developed countries and had still managed to rise in developing countries. Although value creation has continued, even after accounting for the recent boom and bust in share prices, most of this value was unlocked in developed counties. In fact, current market capitalization of incumbents outside the developed world is actually below the privatization price. This has two major implications: first, countries cannot take foreign investors for granted, given the historical performance of incumbent valuations in developing countries; and second, small or poorer markets must certainly focus on how to create market rules that support sustainable business models for all operators.

Reform priorities going forward

Reform will continue to matter. Our global review summarized three themes that will drive the focus of reform going forward: access, usage, and quality.

First, delivering universal access cost-efficiently will continue to be a major challenge for more than half of the world. Some 800 million households lack access to communications infrastructure today. While many of these households have more pressing concerns such as education, health, and basic living conditions, as these households become richer, their ability to be connected and participate in a country's economy and society will depend on the success of policies that address access issues.

Second, there is wide variation among countries in the usage and intensity of usage of the existing infrastructure, even among countries that had pursued reform. Many of those differences are partly or wholly driven by variations in the details of regulation among countries. This means that significant revisions and iterations to regulatory approaches must still take place to encourage more use of the network. In addition, 5.7 billion people worldwide are not using the Internet, and for them, reform will be a primary means of delivering Internet access and encouraging use. The same dynamics apply to data networks, telephony networks, and a myriad of other services and applications; the debate in this area will continue.

With the right policy approach, the combined market capitalization at stake is as much as US$150 to 200 billion, not including the remaining tranches of Deutsche Telekom, France Telecom, and other former monopolies in liberalized markets. This is a significant amount, given that most of this unlocked value creation will occur in emerging and developing countries. However, it is important to remember that the incumbent is not a cash cow, but rather a mechanism for filling the access gap, one that will require incentives to do so. In 80 percent of developing countries, the conditions for further investment are relatively unfavorable due to market constraints.

Finally, there are vast differences in the quality of access in individual countries (e.g., third generation mobile [3G] and broadband). If one thinks of broadband as providing a qualitatively different user experience than narrowband, then the deployment of broadband capabilities is very limited—even in advanced countries—and steps must be taken to reach the projected 190 million connections (and perhaps 400 million users) in 2005. Furthermore, 3G mobile networks will require another US$200 billion just to build the networks and upgrade the handsets in Europe alone. To put this in perspective, this is equivalent to spending, in the next five to ten years (including the license fees), an amount that dwarfs the Marshall Plan to rebuild Europe after World War II.

The Middle East Appears to Have an Access Gap When Compared to Countries With Similar Profiles

The Middle East region comprises a large and diverse group of countries with a combined population of approximately 145 million, a per capita gross national income of approximately US$10,800 (measured on a purchasing power parity basis) and a surface area larger than that of continental Western Europe. As of the end of 2001, total fixed and mobile lines amounted to approximately 25 million lines, which translates into a combined teledensity of about 18 percent.

Despite this diversity, the challenges faced by the region mirror those observed in other parts of the

Figure 9. Key Characteristics of the Middle East Region

11 countries: Bahrain, Egypt, Jordan, Kuwait, Lebanon, Oman, Qatar, Saudi Arabia, Syrian AR, U.A.E. and Yemen, Rep.

Total area covered (million square kilometers) = 4.3

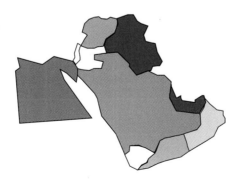

Total population (millions) = 144
Weighted CAGR, 1998-2001 = 2.41%
Average GNI per capita PPP*** (US$) = 5,300

Average household size* (number of persons) = 5.7

Population under 14 years of age = 38%
Population of foreign nationals** = 10%
Population in rural areas = 43%

Total fixed lines*** = 15
Total mobile subscribers (millions) = 10
Internet subscribers per 100 inhabitants (weighted average) = 2.1

*1998 data
**1990 data
***2001 data

Source: U.S. Census Bureau; WEFA-WMM; World Development indicators, World Bank; UN population division; All figures for end of year 2001 unless stated

Figure 10. Country Clusters

	Number of countries	Total population, 2001 (million)	GNI per capita PPP, 2000 (US$000)	Fixed lines per 100 population	Mobile subscribers percent of population
Upper High Income Countries	3	5	22,600	32	50
Lower High Income Countries	2	23	11,100	14	13
Emerging Countries	5	98	3,800	10	5
Developing Countries*	1	18	800	2	1

*Includes Yemen only

Source: International Telecommunications Union

Figure 11. Teledensity and Penetration Indicators

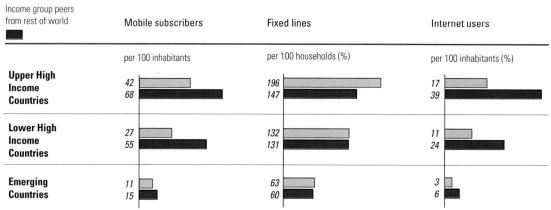

Income group peers from rest of world

	Mobile subscribers per 100 inhabitants	Fixed lines per 100 households (%)	Internet users per 100 inhabitants (%)
Upper High Income Countries	42 / 68	196 / 147	17 / 39
Lower High Income Countries	27 / 55	132 / 131	11 / 24
Emerging Countries	11 / 15	63 / 60	3 / 6

Source: International Telecommunications Union

world, except that the region's diversity makes those challenges different for each country.

Clusters of countries
Regional averages hide wide disparities among countries in the region. The countries can really be grouped into three clusters:

- Small oil-rich states, which includes GCC countries (except Saudi Arabia and Oman). These countries have incomes that match those in the richest economies in the world.

- Two lower high-income countries, which include Saudi Arabia and Bahrain

- A group of emerging middle income countries, which include Egypt, Jordan, Lebanon, Oman, and Syria

Yemen is in its own category, classified as a developing country with a per capita income below US$3,000. More detailed descriptions of the clusters (and Yemen) are included in Figure 10.

Apparent penetration "gaps" for all clusters
Each cluster appears to achieve lower measures of teledensity and penetration than comparable countries outside the region. Although overall teledensity lags that observed in other countries, fixed penetration appears more or less in line with levels observed in other countries, but both mobile and Internet penetration are far below levels achieved in other countries. For the richer GCC countries, this gap is about 20 percentage points of penetration, a significant amount, although on a small scale, due to those countries' small size.

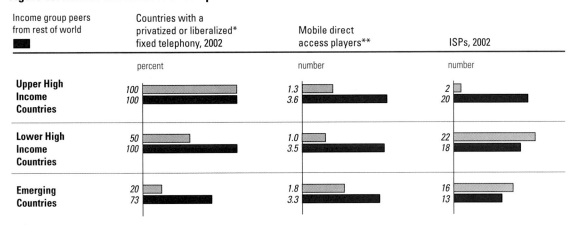

Figure 12. Penetration and Pricing of Selected Data Services

Income group peers from rest of world ■	Number of residential broadband connections, 2001*	Number of broadband connections (residential and business), 2001*	Rental cost 2mb/s 200 km circuit p.a., May 2000
	per 1000 households	per 1000 inhabitants	US$000/annum
Upper High Income Countries	3.8 / 95.3	2.6 / 36.3	56.6 / 17.7
Lower High Income Countries	0 / 3.7	0.2 / 2.1	83.5 / N/A
Emerging Countries	N/A / 1.2	N/A / 0.5	87.6 / 36.3

*Number of benchmark countries = 11; number of Middle East countries = 2 (United Arab Emirates and Saudi Arabia)
Source: Ovum estimates; IDC

Figure 13. Reform and Number of Competitors

Income group peers from rest of world ■	Countries with a privatized or liberalized* fixed telephony, 2002	Mobile direct access players**	ISPs, 2002
	percent	number	number
Upper High Income Countries	100 / 100	1.3 / 3.6	2 / 20
Lower High Income Countries	50 / 100	1.0 / 3.5	22 / 18
Emerging Countries	20 / 73	1.8 / 3.3	16 / 13

*Includes partial privatization, privatization in progress, liberalisation only, and full reforms
**Does not include players who have licenses but are not yet operating
Sources: International Telecommunications Union, EMC, ISP Planet, Jamaican Government, African Internet Connectivity Website, NSRC

Internet penetration also is much lower in each cluster than in countries with comparable per capita incomes. These figures are summarized in Figure 11.

This pattern is mirrored in data access and availability. This review uses broadband deployment as a proxy for the availability of higher quality data services for consumers and small businesses. In addition, prices for 2 Mbps lines for business services are compared with benchmark prices outside the region. The 2 Mbps circuit is a basic building block for advanced data connections, and although lower bandwidths would be used by most businesses, prices for this type of circuit can be compared relatively easily across countries. A higher price would discourage the penetration

of advanced data services. On both bandwidth and price issues, countries in the region appear to show differences with levels observed in other countries.

The causes of these observed gaps in data penetration are multiple and complex. Among these factors are the penetration and availability of PCs; the availability of Internet content in Arabic; the degree of Arab economies' foreign trade; the share of the economy that uses information-intensive industries; and finally, the performance and customer-responsiveness of local telecommunications operators. However, a clear reason for the gap is the region's lag in introducing and managing a gradual process of reform.

When measured by the number of operators in a given market, the region lags behind world levels of competition in both fixed and mobile markets. Only in Internet service provisioning does the region match the rest of the world. Figure 13 details the degree of reform and the number of competitors that an average country in a cluster has in both mobile and Internet service provisioning. These figures are compared with the rest of the world.

Implications for Middle East Sector Reform Agenda

Policymakers in most Middle Eastern countries have recently started to seriously assess what is the most appropriate sector reform agenda going forward. They recognize the importance of Networked Readiness to their national development program, and see a great opportunity in using sector reform to accelerate the closing of the gap with peer country groups. Several conclusions emerge from the foregoing analysis that policymakers should consider. These can be summarized as follows:

• Reform must manage the significant value at stake. The value that could be created by more effective sector reform policies is significantly larger than that created by less effective reform.

• Policymakers must prepare to manage conflicting objectives. Reform policies should be based on a clear understanding of sector objectives and actively balance likely tradeoffs. This is a difficult task, and reform is an inherently political process with multiple stakeholders involved in shaping the direction, pace, and eventual outcome of reform.

• Translating objectives through detailed implementation of regulatory levers will be critical to effectively managing these tradeoffs. Regulators must make sure that reform regulations produce sustainable, attractive business models for entrants and incumbents alike.

Significant value at stake

There is significant value at stake. The following are rough estimates of the value derived from only: (1) current value in the sector today; (2) potential growth opportunities; and (3) likely funding needs for the sector over the next three to four years.

First, public ownership in telecommunications providers in the Middle East is significant and increasing as a result of recent and ongoing privatization programs. Nongovernment shareholders

own about US$10 to 12 billion of telecommunications stock in operators around the region, mostly privatized incumbents in the GCC (although the overall market capitalization is larger). Ongoing reform, with efforts such as the privatization of Saudi Telecom and Telecom Egypt, is expected to increase public holdings by an additional US$4 to 5 billion. Many of the region's governments view the success of privatization projects for shareholders as critical to maintaining support for and credibility of the remaining projects in the program. Further privatization could boost this figure. However, there is a risk that privatization could be derailed or proceeds from it reduced if reform goes awry; this can happen if the impact of regulation on market players and potential investors is not taken into consideration.

The second value element is the significant potential in additional growth, particularly in wireless (GSM) and data. A rough estimate of the value of additional subscribers to mobile services is US$10 billion (approximately a 25 percent growth if current levels if the gap with the rest of the world were to be closed). The risk of reform discouraging additional investment or the competition for customers could reduce this opportunity. The impact on future products, such as 3G, will likely add to this value. Similarly, the potential value of opportunity in the data market is US$1 to 2billion.

Third, policies must ensure that funds are provided for critical infrastructure needs. The region has significant infrastructure needs, and investment will be needed not only to close this obstacle to access but also to enhance the quality of service to the existing subscriber base (e.g., with broadband or 2.5G/3G). Naturally, quality is much more a concern of the more wealthy countries in the region. In total, approximately US$2.5 to 3 billion of capital expenditure would be required annually to build both fixed and wireless access. To the extent that policymakers view these figures as a major infrastructure challenge, they must tailor reform to address that challenge.

Managing conflicting objectives

Reform of the telecommunications sector is a priority for most of the region's governments. Several countries, such as Jordan and Egypt, have been vocal about their commitment to sector reform and its importance to their national development agenda. A country's approach to reform will have a material impact on the sector's development and the ultimate national objectives. This section will outline potential objectives from reform, highlight conflicts that may arise in managing these objectives, and illustrate potential risks.

Expected gains from reform are specific to each country group, but could include the following:

- **Attracting investment in infrastructure.** This includes investment in basic access and universal service obligations in low-income countries as well as investments in higher quality advanced services for more developed countries. This may involve foreign investment in countries where domestic governments or local capital markets cannot deliver the required sums;

- **Lowering selective prices for customers and potentially re-balancing price.** In all countries, there is continuous pressure to reduce product prices. Low-income countries focus on basic voice services to encourage usage. In high-income countries, the focus is increasingly on advanced broadband services. While the efforts of policymakers have succeeded in reducing prices in smaller markets, competition through new entries has been introduced in several markets and is considered seriously in most other large and small markets;

- **Improving performance levels.** Reform will require incumbents to demonstrate rapid and significant improvements in operating performance, service quality, and availability of services. In other regions, reform has been managed so as to allow incumbents the opportunity not only to improve performance, but also to re-balance prices. This is important, because the incumbent accounts for most of the sector in the early stages of reform, and has significant influence on the pace of change in the sector and plays a key role in its development even after liberalization;

- **Generating revenue for the government.** In some cases, governments view sector reform (liberalization) as a way to extract additional value from the telecommunications sector through privatization, taxation, and/or licensing.

All the above must be pursued in a manner that allows entrants to build sustainable business models, and developed in the context of a political process with multiple stakeholders. In addition, reform must reflect country-specific conditions. For example, due to their limited market size, the smaller but wealthy GCC countries aspiring to liberalize the telecommunications sector will have to carefully manage reform in order to attract new entrants. In Saudi Arabia and Egypt, reformers must consider how to build regulatory institutions and capabilities to support entrants but at the same time, must be careful that the incumbent is allowed the opportunity to achieve operational efficiencies and price re-balancing.

The devil is in the details

This review highlighted the point that minor differences in how policy objectives are translated into regulation can have significant impacts on market outcomes. Understanding the effect of each regulatory lever on the economics and incentives of market players is critical to the correct management of reform. In general, the clear lesson of this chapter is that bold objectives for telecommunications sector reform must be accompanied by thoughtful and detailed regulations that reinforce the intent of the objectives. It is the details of regulation that largely determine the economic viability and funding model of the industry. Therefore, knowing the details will be critical to understanding the impact of regulation on the business models of both entrants and incumbent operators as competition develops. Fifty percent or more of the incumbent's value—in either a positive or negative sense—will be at stake as the region pursues further liberalization.

Conclusion

The Middle East has significant potential for intelligently managing reform to deliver on the aspirations of the people in the region, to improve the region's connectivity and Networked Readiness, and to close the gap with the rest of the world. Although the region has lagged in the speed with which reform is undertaken, there are already signs of movement in that direction. For example, Saudi Arabia, the largest economy in the region, has already created a separate regulator and intends to introduce additional mobile competition in the coming year. The region has an opportunity to learn from the processes undertaken elsewhere and to tailor a local solution.

This chapter identified several elements that must be considered for reform to be successful:

- Clear objectives and the tradeoffs that will be necessary to achieve the objectives. For example, if a country wishes to improve its quality of data services, it may be better off trading intense short-term competition for a regime that encourages a limited number of infrastructure entrants and that allows the incumbent operator to take the necessary operational and pricing improvements to adequately face competition;

- A technical understanding of the regulatory levers through which those objectives will be translated into policy;

- A clear understanding of the economic impact of reform choices on the multiple stakeholders involved in the process and the market constraints that the region faces (for example, a recognition of the limitations that the smaller GCC countries may have in attracting new entrants and the steps that can be taken to mitigate the market size constraint);

- A process that encourages the creation of sustainable business models for all players, entrants, and incumbents alike and gradually seeks to reduce the degree of regulatory intervention in key markets.

There is significant opportunity to create a dynamic telecommunications sector in the region and to capture the value at stake due to reform to support all key stakeholders. Given the huge amounts of capital investment required, a detailed understanding of the economic viability and funding of the industry and its direct link to regulatory decisions will be critical. The benefits of getting it right will be huge, but the devil will be in the details.

Endnote

1. The Arab world in this paper includes all countries in the Gulf Cooperation Council, Egypt, Jordan, Syria, and Lebanon. It excludes Iran, the Arabic speaking North African countries west of Egypt, and Iraq and Palestine (the last two are excluded mostly because of lack of reliable data and clear political constraints that make their evaluation difficult).

Education in the Arab States:
Preparing to Compete in the Global Economy

Thomas J. Cassidy, Jr.[*]

The Arab countries of the Middle East and North Africa region have made significant progress in expanding access to and improving the quality and equitable distribution of education resources in their countries during the last half of the twentieth century. Much remains to be done, however, and significant new challenges threaten to erode many of the advances that have been made and marginalize many Arab countries as players in the global economy.

The social, political, and economic contexts in all of the countries in the region, and globally, are very different from what they were forty to fifty years ago. The frequency and complexity of the interactions taking place across national and cultural boundaries have grown exponentially. The nations of the world are more connected economically and technologically than ever before, and as the current global economic crisis highlights, the fate of many countries is inextricably bound to economic events beyond their boundaries. Countries that do not do all that they can to understand and prepare for involvement in the changing global economy risk being left behind for years to come.

In recent years, international conferences have heralded the importance of education in preparing for participation in the increasingly competitive and global "knowledge-based" economy. It is now widely held that a country's investments in human capital are at least as important as their stock of physical capital and their natural resource endowments, although the links between education, technology, and other education inputs to a country's competitiveness ranking have yet to be fully understood (Levinson 2000).

At the same time, the alarming inability of many countries' education systems to effectively and efficiently support economic development and participation in the global economy, and the limited success of their reform efforts, have received widespread attention. It is now widely believed that countries that do not take actions to improve the efficiency and quality of the education offered in their K-12 and tertiary institutions, and to better align the knowledge and skill outputs of their education systems with the changing and evolving needs of the global economy, will not become and/or remain competitive players.

The Arab countries of the Middle East and North Africa are among those at considerable risk of being left behind—a point made in numerous forums in recent years. Most recently it was highlighted in the United Nations Arab Human Development Report 2002, which concluded that ". . . a mismatch between educational output on the one hand and labor-market and development needs on the other could lead to Arab countries' isolation from global knowledge, information, and technology at a time when accelerated acquisition of knowledge and formation of human skills are becoming prerequisites for progress" (UNDP 2002:51).

Although the nations of the Arab world vary in terms of available resources and differ in many of the specific economic and social challenges that they face, all must begin in earnest to redefine the learning objectives they will pursue, and thoughtfully consider how education can be better organized to assure the development of a sustainable capacity to compete in a changing and evolving global economy.

A Brief Overview of the State of Education in Arab Countries

The recently published AHDR 2002 provides a thorough and useful analysis of the performance of Arab countries by using a set of standard educational indicators to compare education development in the Arab states with other countries and regions of the world. In summary, the authors of the AHDR 2002 conclude that while "Arab countries have made

* The author wishes to thank James Difrancesca for invaluable research assistance.

great strides in education…nevertheless educational achievement in Arab countries as a whole, judged even by traditional criteria, is still modest when compared to elsewhere in the world, even in developing countries." A comparison of the analyses presented in the AHDR 2002 with data available from recent World Bank sources and the "popular wisdom" of numerous other reports and commentaries on the state of education in Arab countries, confirms this conclusion.

Access to education, based on 1998 data

Significant strides have been made in increasing access to all levels of education in Arab countries as a group, but enrollments continue to lag behind those reported in more developed countries and there is considerable variation in current enrollment rates for each level across countries in the region. There are indications that rates may be slipping in some countries. (See Appendixes 2, 3, and 4 for a complete listing of enrollment rates for all of the Arab countries and comparison of Arab countries with other regional and economic country groupings).

On average, for boys and girls combined, gross enrollment rates at the primary levels are estimated at 97 percent, a rate considerably above that found in the least developed countries as a group (89 percent), but also considerably below that reported for middle- and upper-middle-income countries (111 to 127 percent), and well below the rates reported for the countries of Latin America and the Caribbean (130 percent). But comparisons of averages mask a marked disparity in the rates reported for the twenty countries that constitute the group of Arab states. In Arab countries for which data are available, primary level gross enrollment rates range from a low of 56 percent in Sudan to a high of 119 percent in Tunisia.

On average, gross enrollment rates at the secondary levels are estimated to be in the range of 60 percent, a rate considerably above that reported for the least developed countries (29 percent), but also below that reported for middle- and upper-middle-income countries with reported rates ranging from 67 to 81 percent. Across Arab countries, rates range from 25 percent in Comoros and 29 percent in Sudan to a high of 93 percent in Bahrain.

At the tertiary level, gross enrollment rates are estimated to be 22 percent, a rate suggesting a dramatic and laudable increase in enrollments from the reported 1990 rate of 12 percent. With an enrollment rate of 22 percent, Arab countries stand slightly above the rate of 20 percent reported for upper-middle-income countries, but significantly lag behind the reported 1990 rate of 37 percent reported for the more industrialized nations of Europe and Central Asia.

Gender issues

While considerable progress has been made over the past ten years in providing access to education for girls, persistent inequities exist between the enrollments of boys and girls within specific countries, and in the rates reported for girls in Arab countries compared to rates in most other parts of the world. At the primary level, girls in the Arab region continue to be enrolled at rates below that of boys (90 percent vs 103 percent), but a comparison of rates in individual countries suggests that while individual patterns of enrollment are consistent with regional patterns, some countries have made greater progress than others in closing the gap.

At the secondary level also, enrollment rates for girls in Arab countries as a group are below that reported for boys (56 percent vs 64 percent). Interestingly, however, rates for girls are appreciably higher in some countries.

Over and above the imperative to fulfill girls' basic rights to education, the social and economic benefits of educating girls provide a compelling motivation to pursue strategies to close the gender gap in the Arab countries. Studies continue to point to the benefits of educating girls in terms of improvements in public health, as well as to other social and economic advantages, particularly for girls and women in rural areas.[1]

The continuing challenge of access

Early successes of Arab countries in increasing access to all levels of education, coupled with projected further increases in the school age population over the next ten, fifteen, and 20 years and apparent declining resources, means that access will continue to present a significant challenge to many countries in the region, and may continue to be the dominant concern in some. As noted, increasing the enrollment of girls must continue to be a central focus of educational policy in Arab countries.

Ironically, governments can expect increased pressure to expand opportunities for access to educational services at all levels in part because of their successes in providing access to primary, secondary, and tertiary education in recent years (UNESCO 2000). As efforts continue to achieve universal primary education, parents and students will increasingly come to expect access to secondary and then tertiary education.

But while there is significant unmet demand in some countries, it is the increasing school age population that presents the greater problem to countries in the region. UN projections suggest that, for the region as a whole, the population of young people ages one to seventeen could increase by as much as 50 percent by 2015, with many countries experiencing significantly greater increases and school-age populations doubling in some countries. For many countries in the region, this will have enormous short-term financial and resource implications. Significant numbers of schools and classrooms will need to be built, teachers recruited and trained, and materials and supplies purchased and distributed. All of this will have to be accomplished in unison with efforts to improve quality and assure the relevance of what students learn and are able to do upon graduation. (See Appendix 1 for a table of projected population increases by country).

Financing education

As reported in the UNDP Arab Human Development Report 2002, Arab countries as a group have historically, at least since 1980, spent slightly more per capita on education than other developing nations. They have spent significantly less than the more industrialized countries of the world, however, and expenditures on education seem to be leveling off and may be declining in some countries (UNDP 2002: 53). By the mid-1990s, per capita expenditure on education in Arab countries was reportedly only about 10 percent of the levels of expenditure per capita in the more industrialized countries. This prevailed even while percentages of public expenditure on education reportedly increased from the 1970s into the 1990s in both oil-producing and non-oil producing Arab countries as a group (Sherbiny), from 8.3 percent to 14 percent and 11.9 percent to 14 percent, respectively.

Difficult choices lie ahead. Meeting the combined demands of increasing access, assuring relevance and improving quality in the face of diminishing relative resources will severely test governments and educators in most Arab countries. Governments that have not yet begun to do so must give immediate attention to defining and implementing measures to increase efficiency, and simultaneously seek alternative sources of financing for all levels of education. Clearly, political pressures recommend against any relative increase in the private costs of education; however, even with the promise of distance education for reducing total costs

of education, most countries simply will not be able to finance the changes necessary for competition in the global economy without changes in the structure of public subsidies. It is proving a difficult pill to swallow, but more countries will need to explore cost recovery schemes at the tertiary level, at least for students from the higher income brackets.[2]

Quality

Quality is an elusive and debatable term in education. For current purposes we will consider quality in two dimensions: internal efficiency and learning outcomes.

By internal efficiency we mean a system's or institution's abilities to keep students enrolled and move them along in a timely manner. More efficient systems and institutions have both low dropout and low repetition rates. Unfortunately, the data required to conduct a meaningful assessment of the internal efficiency of education systems in most Arab countries are woefully inadequate to the task. Data on repetition and dropouts are generally not available, and when data are available, they are of suspect quality.[3] What data are available suggest that internal efficiency is not good, and there are many signs that internal efficiency may even be declining (UNDP 2002:54). Clearly, in light of the challenges facing countries in the region (highlighted above and elaborated later in this paper), governments will have to take actions to improve the quality of education data to more effectively understand and target needed interventions.

By learning outcomes, we mean primarily the extent to which systems produce graduates who possess the knowledge and skills required for effective participation in the economy and society. Despite a lack of empirical studies, it is widely held that educational systems and institutions in Arab countries are not, in general, producing graduates with the knowledge and skills required to meet the needs of business and industry, and that this mismatch threatens to limit countries' abilities to participate meaningfully in the evolving global and knowledge-based economy. What little empirical evidence does exist, often in the form of participation by a very small number of Arab countries in international education assessments, supports this widely held belief. Only three countries in the region— Jordan, Tunisia, and Morocco—participated in the 1999 Trends in Mathematics and Science Study.[4] The tests in the study sought to assess the relative science and mathematics performance of eighth grade students. All three countries scored significantly below the international average and very significantly lower than the highest performing countries. Jordan scored highest of the three countries.

Generally, discussion of the mismatch of educational outputs with the needs of the labor market centers on the strength of the outputs of tertiary institutions, but increasingly, and as the performance of Jordan, Tunisia, and Morocco may hint, the preparedness and "quality" of the graduates of one level can significantly influence the abilities of institutions at higher levels to produce graduates with the skills needed to move effectively and efficiently through the system and into the marketplace. When, for example, secondary school graduates are not sufficiently prepared to undertake university level studies immediately upon entry, as is the case in a number of countries, costs associated with strengthening the basic skills of new university entrants can consume a significant share of education budgets and compromise the overall capacity and efficiency of higher level institutions to produce qualified graduates.[5] Efforts to strengthen education systems must then include efforts to understand the linkages between various levels and efforts to redress observed misalignments.

Linking Education with the World of Work[6]

What then should the graduates of Arab tertiary educational institutions know and be able to do to participate productively in the emerging global, knowledge-based economy?[7] Generalizing the needs of a diverse array of educational institutions across a number of countries is, of course, an impossible task and not our intent. What is outlined below is a set of knowledge and skills that, to varying degrees, those responsible for organizing and delivering education services should endeavor to inculcate in all their graduates. It is understood that there will always be a need for highly educated and skilled graduates at various levels and in very specific disciplines. Demands for specialized skills will vary somewhat with the economic and social context in which institutions operate. In fact, a strategy that promotes or directly facilitates the differentiation and alignment of the various types of educational institutions and programs that countries offer with the emerging needs of "knowledge-based" firms, should be encouraged. For example, while there are some very high-quality technical universities in Arab states, the global and local economic environments demand many more specialists and workers in science and technology than are currently being produced. In many Arab nations, too few students are being trained at higher levels in science and technology disciplines while gluts exist in the supply of humanities and social

science graduates (Fergany 2000); in such a lack of alignment of production with needs, everyone loses. Over-enrollment of students in nonscience disciplines does permit many potential students access to higher education by substituting the cheaper input cost of nonscience education for the more expensive teaching and research costs of science education. However, this imbalance results in chronic "educated unemployment" and represents a poor match between the technical skills demanded in the labor market and the supply of graduates.

Additionally, with the exception of countries like the United Arab Emirates, Bahrain, and Saudi Arabia, there is little capacity to train the semi-skilled workers and technicians needed in Arab countries (Al-Sulayti 1999:275). Increased vertical differentiation of institutions of higher education is also necessary, then, to better meet the labor needs of firms. In addition to providing the theoretical training, which now dominates university programs, Arab nations must be able to train, in two-year and other shorter-length programs of study, graduates whose technical skills match the needs of the market for semi-skilled labor (Fergany 2000:8).[8]

Governments and institutions must continue to consider their local context and needs as they shape their choices about the types of programs that their school systems offer. At the same time, if they are to attract and secure longer-term commitments from non-national firms to locate in their countries and communities, they must encourage the establishment of programs that will prepare graduates to work with regional as well as multi- and transnational firms.

Increasingly, it is becoming clear that there is not only a need for students to acquire new areas of knowledge and specific types of skills that knowledge-based firms require. Equally, and arguably more important, students need understand new forms[9] of learning; that is, models of learning that will prepare graduates to approach new and evolving challenges that they will face in later stages of schooling, their communities, and work environments (UNESCO 2000a:34–35). The core capacities that students must possess to meet the demands of new-economy firms have been researched and discussed in numerous forums around the world in recent years. A consensus is beginning to emerge.[10] The following list is not meant to be exhaustive, but rather to provide a summary of emerging wisdom about the types of knowledge and skills widely in demand by global, knowledge-based firms (Murnane and Levy 1996; UNESCO 2000a):

- **The ability to locate, evaluate, and use relevant information.** Students and graduates must be able to undertake problem-solving projects; evaluate the appropriateness, accuracy and usefulness of information of various types and from a variety of information resources; to develop inquiry strategies; think critically, but constructively; and develop and communicate results and solutions (Al-Sulayti 1999: 274; Badran 1999:116).

- **The capacity to use both current and emerging information and communications technologies.** Students and graduates must be able to actively and appropriately use information technology, broadly conceived, in the process of problem solving and in their work.[11]

- **The ability to work collaboratively with others.** The knowledge economy requires specialists in many areas who are able to work effectively with others, often across lines of cultural and geographic difference, to complete projects and solve problems as well as to communicate results, findings, and opinions.[12]

- **A capacity to think systemically.** Thinking systemically involves building a capacity to understand problems and challenges in all their complexity; to understand how and why systems work (i.e., to see not only system components, but to also understand how components are connected and interact); to see problems not merely as a series of unrelated events but rather to see the patterns of interactions and interdependencies in the challenges one faces. It is about possessing an ability to anticipate future needs and adapt to meet new challenges and navigate effectively in changing conditions.[13]

- **A solid foundation of basic knowledge education.** The "knowledge economy" still needs workers who are specialists in very specific disciplines, professions, and fields. But at the same time, it requires workers with broader foundations of knowledge to serve as springboards for future learning and as a base for adapting to the ever-changing state of knowledge. Increasingly, employers also want workers who possess a broad awareness of the economic, social, political, humanistic, and ethical dimensions of good corporate and social citizenship.

- **A commitment to life-long learning.** The phrase "lifelong learning" is often used as shorthand for a new attitude toward learning. It implies a commitment to keeping ones knowledge and skills current and to seek the acquisition of new knowledge. It implies both a commitment to gather and upgrade knowledge and skills for and by oneself, but also a commitment, willingness, and capacity to return comfortably to institutional learning situations throughout one's life (UNESCO 2000a:35).

Cooperation with the World of Work

Given the demands of the knowledge economy, it is more important than ever that educational institutions work closely and cooperatively with employers and firms in the communities they serve. Ultimately, this is likely to be the only way that Arab institutions of learning will be able to adjust and align the character of their programs to the changing demands of the market. There are a number of credible and time-tested options for bringing about such alignments. Governments should encourage and create incentives for institutions to enter into such cooperative arrangements.

Educational institutions in the Arab states must be more directly but flexibly linked to the workplaces of employers (Bubtana 1998). Internship programs are one example of a learning experience for students that may also serve as a feedback loop to institutions, providing an evaluation of and communication about how well an institution is doing in training its students for the real demands of work. Joint advisory boards, composed of higher education institutions and industry officials, by offering input to faculty and institutions of higher education on curriculum, can be another structural mechanism for this sort of needed feedback. Increasing the use of "practitioner-faculty" is yet another possible means of linking firms and educational institutions, particularly in technical colleges. Such faculty would offer the benefit of their own continued immersion in their professional context. Project-based research and development activities supported by firms can also provide educational benefits for students in the form of research training and applied problem-solving opportunities, even as such activities strengthen universities' contributions to the economy. Forward-thinking institutions might also establish an administrative culture of "external leadership;" that is, leadership that seeks and encourages political and substantive engagements with stakeholder constituencies in the community, government, and private sector firms.[14]

The Implications for Learning and Teaching

"Learning and teaching" are widely understood to be the core elements of education. The creation of education experiences that will lead to the knowledge and skill outcomes outlined above will require a major shift in the processes of teaching and learning, with consequent wide-reaching implications for how education is organized and delivered at the classroom level.

Unlike memorizing "facts," helping students to use specific skills and integrate their knowledge will require the use of a broader set of complementary instructional methods than has been the case in the past. It will require engaging students with more complex problem-solving techniques and approaches to knowledge discovery. To breed comfort and instinctive facility with using information technology to solve problems, instructors must be capable of integrating technology into their own teaching and into the tasks required of students. If students are to learn skills of collaboration, opportunities must be provided for students to participate in more collaborative learning projects (Wallis and Mitchell 1985). To develop skills in complex problem solving, students must be introduced to methods and contexts that encourage critical inquiry and the application of theory to practical situations.

Incorporating new knowledge and skill needs into current learning and teaching activities will require a significant shift from current and long-standing learning and teaching practices. Practices based on the individual pursuit of rote learning and memorization must give way to practices that encourage teamwork, critical thinking, and problem-solving; methods that assume that all people learn in similar ways must also give way to methods that understand that people often learn in very different ways.

Educators at all levels will be challenged by efforts to reform education systems to incorporate new knowledge and skills, but it is teachers, in particular, who face a daunting task. Simultaneously, teachers will be expected to change what they teach and how they teach, use time and classroom space differently, allow and create opportunities for children to learn at their own pace and in their own ways while at the same time creating opportunities for meaningful group work, learn to use computers themselves and to incorporate technology use in their classroom and lesson plans, change the ways that they assess student development and achievement, and invite parents into the classroom as partners in the learning-teaching process.

In a nutshell, the challenge for government and education leaders will be how to provide teachers with the substantial resources they will require to successfully produce graduates with the requisite knowledge and skills to move to higher levels in the education system, and then on to productive employment.

Reforming education to accommodate changes in modes of learning and teaching is a significantly more complex undertaking than is generally understood, even by many educators. Figure 1 provides a systemic overview of many of the challenges facing educators as they endeavor to reconfigure institutions in ways that will insure that they are producers of knowledge and skills, in the form of human capital, to serve the needs of the labor market and the goals of society at large. Learners are understood to be the central focus of the model. More effective institutions are those that produce graduates whose knowledge and skills are closely aligned with the needs of labor and society.

As the model highlights, the more critical elements at the school level are that educational leaders must attend to: (1) leadership, (2) teachers, (3) curriculum and materials, (4) new forms of teaching and learning and student assessment, (5) school and classroom design, and (6) educational technologies (with an emphasis on information and communications technologies). Although it is the school-level staff who must be prepared to maintain and use these elements in productive ways, it is the responsibility of sector officials to assure the delivery of quality components to the school in the form of effective leaders, a coherent curriculum, teachers qualified to implement the curriculum, adequate facilities, and necessary educational technologies.

Although a simplification, Figure 1 is sufficiently detailed to highlight the interrelationships of the various system elements and to suggest how changing any one element in the system can have significant implications for other elements. The process typically begins with a redefinition of learning standards and targets for what is taught and how. Standards and targets can, in turn, can have broad implications for curriculum design and development, the choice and mix of education technologies, facilities design, teacher preparation, the development of systems for assessing the performance of students, teachers, principals and other education professionals, for redefining how students and teachers are evaluated, and for changing how education systems are managed and monitored. For example, pursuing the objective of producing graduates with higher levels of computer skills has implications for each and all of the other components in the model. Curriculum units must be redesigned, facilities rearranged and modified, teachers trained, new forms of assessment developed, and so on.

One of the most critical elements to assuring successful reforms will be the establishment of considerable and on-going professional development opportunities for teachers. If teachers are to be prepared to implement new learning objectives and standards, professional development opportunities will need to include attention to a host of important issues, including the following:

- Strategies and methods for ensuring high quality teaching-learning including: interdisciplinary instruction; differentiated instruction; and group-based cooperative learning;

- Expanding personal knowledge and skill in the appropriate use of emerging technologies;

- Integrating information technologies in academic programs;

- Understanding emerging theories and "best practice'" in teaching and learning, particularly vis-à-vis understanding new knowledge and skill targets;

- Understanding the meaning of "learner-centered learning";

- Understanding how to structure lessons, and how to use and manage groups, time, and space effectively;

- Understanding how to use equipment and materials effectively;

- Knowing how to assess student achievement effectively and in multiple ways.

Similarly, the leaders of education institutions face significant challenges. The challenge of changing learning and teaching will require a change in the roles that school leaders play. Managing schools will be more interesting, but more challenging than it has ever been. The model of a principal as primarily an administrator who manages centralized policy and a highly prescribed education model, if ever accurate, will no longer be valid as principals' work is transformed to that of an instructional leader. In the schools envisioned for the future, principals as instructional leaders will need to serve multiple roles as:

1. visionaries and leaders, who inspire their teachers and students;

2. hands-on managers, who work as partners with other professional staff and teachers to set institutional goals and objectives and administer education programs effectively and efficiently;

3. master teachers, who are up-to-date with current thinking and knowledgeable about current "best practices," who are well-versed on the impacts and use of emerging technologies and the proliferation of new sources and methods for accessing information, and who work with teachers to set learning goals and objectives and constantly improve classroom practice; and

4. master communicators capable of managing the involvement of a diverse array of community and business leaders, parents and teachers, while at the same time serving as the primary link with ministry and regional office leadership.

Preparing to Compete: The Challenge of Shifting the Focus of Education Systems from Administration, Maintenance, and Control to Management, Quality, and Performance

While some countries have already begun to reform elements of their education systems to meet the changing knowledge and skill needs of organizations operating in the global, knowledge-based economy, much remains to be done. For many countries, becoming and/or remaining competitive will require a more significant and systemic rethinking and reorganization of their education systems and institutions and a greater emphasis on capacity-building than has yet been attempted. What is required is a significant and fundamental shift in the organizational and structural underpinnings of education systems; a shift from systems originally organized primarily to facilitate expansion and focused on the administration, maintenance, and control of educational inputs, to systems with an explicit emphasis on improving quality, increasing performance, and assuring the on-going relevance of system output.

Systems of education in most Arab countries and in many other countries around the world can trace their core organizational structures and operational practices to a time, not long ago, when the primary emphasis in education was on planning for expansion; that is, on increasing access and the opportunity for schooling to areas beyond cities and large towns. With the singular goal of expansion, the work of

Figure 1. Selected Key Elements Challenging Efforts to Reform Education

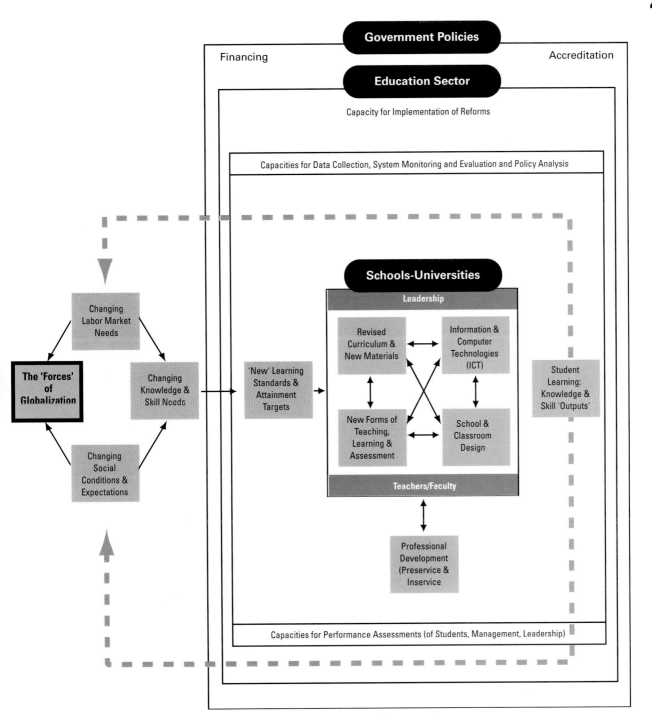

ministries was well defined. The objective was to deliver educational inputs—classrooms, teachers, accommodations, books and materials—to those locations that required them, and to then maintain the inputs. The model was very much an industrial one, with schooling conceived of as something that would happen if only we assemble all the component parts in one place. The emphasis was on inputs. Outcomes were assumed. Processes were virtually ignored. To accomplish the goal, structures and processes were

put in place to facilitate the delivery of the identified components. Separate divisions and units were established at the ministerial level, sometimes with subunits at the regional and district levels, to deal with teachers, facilities, textbooks, materials, and so on. There was little, if any, formal interaction or integration across these divisions. Only the most senior administrators and decision makers had formalized access across divisions and units. Communication systems were hierarchical. Planning and decision-making were largely tactical. Data gathering and maintenance was largely the task of individual units, and little integration of data was attempted or possible. Data on personnel, examinations, and costs were rarely available for review or independent analysis. What statistics were made available to others was largely confined to counts of students, teachers, classrooms, and schools. In such an environment, monitoring involves little more than tracking the distribution of inputs and reporting them on an annual basis, usually aggregated at the national and regional levels. The primary indicators of concern are enrollment ratios. The emphasis from the top level of the ministry and within divisions is on maintenance and control of a well, if narrowly, defined operational mission (Ross and Mahlck 1990; Davis 1980).

An organizational emphasis on management, quality, and performance will require significant changes in how education systems are organized and how they operate. A system focusing on management, quality, and performance must be more agile—better prepared to respond and adapt to the continually changing knowledge and skill needs—than has historically been the case. There must be a greater emphasis on the integration of system inputs and on understanding the processes of learning and teaching. Communication systems must be more open and vertical. Planning and decision-making must become more strategic. Monitoring, evaluation, and analysis must become a more serious activity and more integrated in decision-making processes. Information systems must be significantly upgraded to include not only the collection and maintenance of enrollment data, but also collection and access to data on performance, teachers and other education personnel, examination results, and costs.

Facilitating the achievement of the goals and objectives of the reforms meant to change learning and teaching will also significantly impact the work of central education agencies. The nature of the relationships between central units and schools will need to change in some very significant ways. As the focus of the education system shifts to child-based learning and a clearly articulated organizational focus on the centrality of the classroom and teaching-learning processes, old bureaucratic systems will need to be replaced with new more agile and responsive service-based systems. The design and development systems and processes of old will need to give way to more creative and responsive models. Many central units will need to remake themselves; to transform themselves from being viewed as cumbersome, outdated mazes of bureaucratic inertia

to become a source of responsive proactive support and quality services for schools and teachers. Ministerial units must become the sources of up-to-date information, ideas, methods, and examples of effective practice. They must be able to provide relevant and timely services and materials to schools; they must become a source of new ideas, for example, on new and multiple approaches to assessing student achievement and new and constantly evolving ways to integrate the use of computers in classrooms. This will be a significant challenge.

Assuring Success

Obviously, governments can play an important role in assuring the success of efforts to reform education. They can promote the creation of policies and regulations that will contribute to the success of efforts to change the outputs of education, by creating, for example, systems of accreditation for educational institutions or changing the terms of service for education sector employees. However, at the same time, government policies and regulations—particularly the continuation of highly centralized, unaligned planning mechanisms—will likely impede the education system's ability to respond to changing knowledge and skill demands, and thus not contribute to any significant increase in a country's capacity to compete in the global knowledge-based economy.

There are a number of things that governments can and, as Figure 1 suggests, must, attend to in order to promote and assure sustained delivery of educational services that will lead to the attainment of the knowledge and skills objectives discussed above. Some, but not all, of these are highlighted in Figure 1. Among the more critical issues that governments must consider is the establishment of policies and mechanisms that will lead to the elimination of significant weaknesses in centralized administration, maintenance, and control-based systems—weaknesses that, if not addressed, could compromise their reform efforts. These include consideration of policies and mechanisms that will ensure: (1) the building of higher levels of capacity to implement reforms at the national, regional, and local levels; (2) the development of rigorous systems of institutional accreditation; (3) the development of standards for assessing system performance; (4) the strengthening of capacities for data collection, system monitoring and evaluation, and policy analysis; (5) the development of new sources of financing and/or strategies for improving efficiency in education; and (6) the development of new, shared, and decentralized forms of decision making and governance.

The building of higher levels of capacity to implement reforms at the national, regional, and local levels is essential. This does not mean hiring large numbers of new staff; rather, it requires establishing substantive professional development programs and other learning opportunities that will ensure that educators have opportunities to develop the same types of skills needed in the graduates of their institutions. An important objective of these programs will be to turn career administrators into system managers and more active participants in the design and provision of educational services. Of course, more than professional development will be required. A number of long-standing formal and informal processes will need to be rethought. For example, historically hierarchical channels of communication must be streamlined and replaced with more open, distributed systems, and ways must be found to promote more integrated management and planning. Promotion schemes based primarily on age and years of service, and a belief in educators as generalists, must be reconsidered to recognize good performance and encourage the development of educational specialties.

The development of rigorous systems of accreditation must be developed and capacities for enforcement quickly established. Accreditation will be an important element in assuring quality at all levels, but the need for a system of accreditation is particularly acute in higher education in many countries in the region. Escalating demand for seats in higher education institutions has given rise to a proliferation of foreign institutions, many of questionable quality. To assure that the objectives of such institutions are indeed aligned with the development needs in the countries in which they operate, governments must define the standards that guide these 'guest' institutions and develop mechanisms for accreditation. The lack of cross-institutional standards also must be addressed. Presently, there are no well-established accreditation system for colleges and universities in most Arab countries (Badran 1999:112). Without mechanisms for ensuring the comparable minimum quality of institutions and programs within nations and across the region, private institutions are not subject to the sort of oversight that could identify "diploma mills" or other forms of exploitive educational enterprise. Additionally, lack of an effective accreditation process discourages the kind of horizontal differentiation of institutions that might permit more high-quality private institutions to arise. The lack of a system of educational transferability of credit – a by-product of

lack of overall accreditation – is simply inefficient and poses practical barriers to the sort of lifelong learning demanded by the knowledge economy (Cassidy and Miller 2002).

The development of standards for assessing system performance and increasing efforts to strengthen capacities for data collection, system monitoring, and evaluation, and policy analysis, are closely linked. The difficulty in attaining relevant, reliable, and timely education system data from many of the Arab countries has been well documented and cited (most recently in the UN's Arab Human Development Report 2002). Significant skills and resources are required to monitor and evaluate the introduction and distribution of inputs, changes in processes and, more importantly, the impacts of changes in inputs and processes on outputs in such a complex, multifaceted undertaking as the reform of an education system. The statistics units in most countries are ill-prepared to meet the growing demands for the more comprehensive sets of data and information that will be required to monitor, evaluate, and plan educational development and assure a continuing alignment of system outputs against social and economic goals. Additionally, a shift to concerns for quality and performance, coupled with concerns for equity and efficiency, will require a capacity to identify both well-performing schools, to learn what they are doing so that others may learn, as well as identifying schools that are not performing to standards, so that interventions can be targeted to improve their performance. Current data systems are not prepared to support such sophisticated forms of analysis, and the staff in many units are not sufficiently skilled to perform the analysis if the data were they available.

Research and evaluation at the level of the college or university, and broad-scale educational research on higher education at the national and regional levels, must be central to the agenda for higher education reform. Institutional research and planning units are not generally found in universities in the region, and educational research conducted at national and regional levels has an international outlook; the data are, therefore, devoid of much that is of practical application to institutional planning. Capacities for evaluation, research, and assessment must be developed at the institutional level. On the descriptive level, leaders and constituents of higher education institutions must have accurate, meaningful, and interinstitutionally comparable data about such matters as the composition of the faculty, the demographics and achievement of students, finances and budgeting, and more. Reliable institutional research data can then support more robust governance and decision-making models and processes at an institution. For example, programs can be reviewed more rationally—and continued, discontinued, or modified—in light of educational and labor-market attainment by graduates or other measures, than has historically been the case. Moreover, to institute the sort of education reforms we have been discussing, schools and universities alike must have the means to measure how student outcomes and instructional inputs align with educational goals. Finally, at the national and regional levels, support for comparable data across institutions and the related capacity for sector-wide educational research offer an important mechanism for formulating and assessing institutional, national, and regional policies. Such capacities are not well developed in any of the Arab states, although the United Arab Emirates has made considerable efforts to support evaluation and assessment in its national education plan (Mograby 1999).[6]

Conclusion

The challenge of preparing education systems and institutions in the Arab countries of the Middle East and North Africa is going to be considerable. This is in part due to past successes, which have given rise to increasing demand for access to institutions at all levels of education; but it is also more a function of declining financial resources, increasing population growth, and the complexity of the reforms required.

Efforts to address many of the concerns that have been raised are already underway in many countries in the region. Some of them are very good. There are many outstanding schools, colleges, and universities in each country in the region. We need to find ways to identify these institutions, and create opportunities for people to share the wisdom of their experiences and identify best practices. But, generally, the results of reform efforts have been less dramatic than hoped, and more taxing on the capacities of education professionals than anticipated. It is one thing to redefine standards, curriculums, and rehab facilities and install computers and computer networks in schools, but it can be quite another matter to change what people do and how they do it. Experience and research tell us that changing people's behavior takes time, sustained effort, and lots of support. Change is never easy, and education systems can be quite

resistant to it, but the costs to countries in the region of not changing, soon and fast, could be very high.

Last, it is ironic and profound that a lack of the very knowledge and skills that we are seeking to produce as the output of education systems in the region, is very likely a critical factor limiting the success of current efforts to organize education to better prepare graduates to compete in the knowledge economy. Thus one of the keys to the success of current efforts is certainly the establishment of significant, substantive, and on-going professional development activities for educators working at all levels; activities that by design will result in the preparation of education professionals with the knowledge and skills that make them good models for the students they teach.[15]

Appendix 1. Pre-School Through Secondary School Population (000)

Age	1990 (0-4)	(5-14)	(15-17)	Total	2000 (0-4)	(5-14)	(15-17)	Total	2015 (0-4)	(5-14)	(15-17)	Total
Algeria	3,654	6,766	1,690	12,110	3,519	7,035	2,103	12,657	3,298	6,880	2,071	12,249
Bahrain	58	97	21	176	57	124	32	213	57	103	33	193
Comoros	92	155	36	283	117	187	52	356	152	272	70	494
Egypt	8,414	14,035	3,275	25,724	8,011	15,993	4,658	28,662	7,411	15,285	4,750	27,446
Iraq	2,996	4,639	1,188	8,823	3,556	5,998	1,549	11,103	4,288	8,011	2,147	14,446
Jordan	579	944	242	1,765	761	1,206	329	2,296	897	1,719	465	3,081
Kuwait	304	481	111	896	144	455	159	758	266	451	92	809
Lebanon	344	603	185	1,132	335	753	206	1,294	331	674	197	1,202
Libya	619	1,264	299	2,182	643	1,152	420	2,215	667	1,477	398	2,542
Mauritania	353	542	129	1,024	470	706	177	1,353	674	1,113	266	2,053
Morocco	3,473	6,326	1,659	11,458	3,596	6,759	1,947	12,302	3,385	7,207	2,119	12,711
Oman	342	486	101	929	404	715	173	1292	651	1,056	247	1,954
Qatar	52	78	16	146	53	98	25	176	54	103	32	189
Saudi Arabia	2,669	3,950	861	7,480	3,187	5,548	1,300	10,035	4,516	7,746	1,947	14,209
Somalia	1,429	1,997	463	3,889	1,787	2,422	579	4,788	2,939	4,507	1049	8,495
Sudan	3,965	6,484	1,672	12,121	4,728	7,746	2,004	14,478	5,247	9,792	2,697	17,736
Syrian AR	2,297	3,625	827	6,749	2,239	4,373	1,233	7,845	2,782	5,188	1,359	9,329
Tunisia	1,046	2,022	525	3,593	832	1,976	629	3,437	979	1,811	483	3,273
U.A.E.	244	354	82	680	199	479	130	816	231	451	123	805
Yemen, Rep.	2,303	3,355	810	6,468	3,909	5,278	1,108	10,295	6,312	9,875	2,368	18,555
TOTALS	35,233	58,203	14,192	107,628	38,547	69,003	18,821	126,371	45,137	83,721	22,913	151,771

Sources: Population Division of the Department of Economic and Social Affairs of the United Nations Secretariat, World Population Prospects: The 2000 Revision; World Urbanization Prospects: The 2001 Revision

Appendix 2. Gross and Net Primary School Enrollment Ratios

	(% Gross)		(% Net)		Female (% Gross)		Female (% Net)		Male (% Gross)		Male (% Net)	
	1990	1998	1990	1998	1990	1998	1990	1998	1990	1998	1990	1998
Algeria	100	109	93	94	92	104	87	92	108	114	99	96
Bahrain	110	104	99	97	110	104	99	98	110	104	99	96
Comoros	75	76	—	50	63	70	—	46	87	82	—	54
Egypt	94	100	—	92	86	96	—	89	101	104	—	95
Iraq	111	88	—	80	102	80	—	74	120	96	—	85
Jordan	71	69	66	64	71	69	66	65	71	68	66	63
Kuwait	60	—	—	—	59	—	—	—	62	—	—	—
Lebanon	120	110	—	78	118	108	—	77	123	113	—	79
Libya	105	—	—	—	102	152	—	—	108	154	—	—
Mauritania	49	83	—	60	41	81	—	58	56	86	—	62
Morocco	67	97	58	79	54	87	48	73	79	107	68	85
Oman	86	75	70	66	82	72	68	65	90	77	73	67
Qatar	97	96	87	86	94	93	86	85	101	98	87	86
Saudi Arabia	73	71	59	59	68	70	53	57	78	73	65	61
Somalia	11	—	—	—	7	—	—	—	14	—	—	—
Sudan	53	56	—	46	45	51	—	42	60	60	—	50
Syrian AR	108	104	98	93	102	99	93	89	114	109	103	96
Tunisia	113	119	94	98	107	116	90	96	120	123	97	99
U.A.E.	104	94	94	83	103	92	93	82	106	96	95	83
West Bank and Gaza	—	—	—	—	—	—	—	—	—	—	—	—
Yemen, Rep.	58	78	—	61	33	55	—	44	83	100	—	77
East Asia & Pacific	120	107	98	91	116	108	96	91	124	106	100	91
Europe & Central Asia	98	—	—	—	98	—	—	—	99	—	—	—
Latin America & Caribbean	106	130	89	97	105	128	—	98	107	131	—	99
Least Developed Countries (UN Classification)	67	89	—	63	60	83	—	59	75	96	—	67
Low & Middle Income	102	104	—	—	96	100	—	—	108	107	—	—
Low Income	89	96	—	—	79	88	—	—	98	103	—	—
Lower Middle Income	116	106	96	91	112	107	94	91	120	106	98	91
Middle East & North Africa	96	97	—	83	87	90	—	79	104	103	—	87
Middle Income	114	111	95	92	110	111	—	92	117	111	—	92
South Asia	90	101	—	—	77	93	—	—	103	109	—	—
Sub-Saharan Africa	74	78	—	—	67	72	—	—	82	85	—	—
Upper Middle Income	105	127	91	97	103	126	—	96	106	128	—	98
World	102	104	—	—	97	101	—	—	108	107	—	—

Source: World Bank, World Development Indicators 2002

Appendix 3. Gross and Net Secondary Enrollment Ratios

	(% Gross)		(% Net)		Female (% Gross)		Female (% Net)		Male (% Gross)		Male (% Net)	
	1990	1998	1990	1998	1990	1998	1990	1998	1990	1998	1990	1998
Algeria	61	66	54	58	54	67	48	59	67	66	60	58
Bahrain	100	93	85	80	101	98	86	85	98	89	84	76
Comoros	18	25	—	—	14	22	—	—	21	27	—	—
Egypt	76	81	—	—	68	78	—	—	84	84	—	—
Iraq	47	—	—	31	36	14	—	25	57	25	—	38
Jordan	45	66	—	60	46	67	—	62	44	65	—	58
Kuwait	43	—	—	—	43	—	—	—	43	—	—	—
Lebanon	73	89	—	76	75	94	—	79	70	85	—	72
Libya	86	77	—	71	87	81	—	76	85	73	—	67
Mauritania	14	18	—	—	9	15	—	—	19	21	—	—
Morocco	35	40	—	—	30	35	—	—	41	44	—	—
Oman	46	67	—	58	40	67	—	58	51	68	—	57
Qatar	81	79	67	67	85	90	70	69	77	68	64	65
Saudi Arabia	44	66	31	—	39	62	28	47	49	70	34	50
Somalia	6	—	—	—	4	—	—	—	8	—	—	—
Sudan	24	29	—	—	21	28	—	—	27	30	—	—
Syrian AR	52	42	46	38	44	39	39	36	60	44	52	39
Tunisia	45	73	—	55	40	73	—	56	50	72	—	54
U.A.E.	67	78	59	70	72	80	63	73	63	75	56	68
West Bank and Gaza	—	—	—	—	—	—	—	—	—	—	—	—
Yemen, Rep.	58	45	—	35	19	24	—	20	94	66	—	50
East Asia & Pacific	48	62	—	51	43	59	—	49	53	65	—	52
Europe & Central Asia	85	—	—	—	85	—	—	—	85	—	—	—
Latin America & Caribbean	49	75	29	—	51	78	—	—	46	71	—	—
Least Developed Countries (UN Classification)	18	29	—	—	13	26	—	—	23	32	—	—
Low & Middle Income	48	56	—	—	43	52	—	—	52	60	—	—
Low Income	37	42	—	—	30	35	—	—	44	49	—	—
Lower Middle Income	56	63	—	—	51	60	—	50	60	66	—	53
Middle East & North Africa	57	60	—	—	49	56	—	—	66	64	—	—
Middle Income	56	67	—	—	53	66	—	—	59	69	—	55
South Asia	40	48	—	—	29	40	—	31	49	56	—	46
Sub-Saharan Africa	23	—	—	—	20	—	—	—	26	—	—	—
Upper Middle Income	58	81	41	—	59	83	—	—	57	79	—	—
World	55	65	—	—	51	60	—	—	59	69	—	—

Source: World Bank, World Development Indicators 2002

Appendix 4. Gross Tertiary Enrollment (in Percent)

Country	1990	1998
Algeria	11	15
Bahrain	18	26
Comoros	0	1
Egypt	16	39
Iraq	13	13
Jordan	16	—
Kuwait	0	—
Lebanon	29	38
Libya	15	57
Mauritania	3	6
Morocco	11	9
Oman	4	—
Qatar	27	26
Saudi Arabia	12	19
Somalia	3	—
Sudan	3	7
Syrian AR	18	6
Tunisia	9	17
U.A.E.	9	13
West Bank and Gaza	—	—
Yemen, Rep.	4	10

Region	1990	1998
East Asia & Pacific	6	8
Europe & Central Asia	34	—
Latin America & Caribbean	17	20
Least Developed Countries (UN Classification)	2	3
Low & Middle Income	10	—
Low Income	7	—
Lower Middle Income	11	11
Middle East & North Africa	12	22
Middle Income	13	13
South Asia	5	—
Sub-Saharan Africa	3	4
Upper Middle Income	18	20
World	16	—

Source: World Bank, World Development Indicators 2002

References

Al-Sulayti (1999:275).

Arab Regional Conference on Higher Education. "Beirut Declaration on Higher Education in the Arab States." 5 March 1998.

Badran In *Education in the Arab World: Challenges of the Millennium.* Emirates Center for Strategic Studies and Researcher. Abu Dhabi, United Arab Emirates. 1999:116.

Bahgat, Gawdat. "Education in the Gulf Monarchies: Retrospect and Prospect." *International Review of Education* 45, 2 (1999):127–136.

Bruhn, Christa. "Higher Education in Transition: Current Realities in Palestinian Universities." Paper presented at MESA, November 2000.

Bubtana, Abdalla. "Higher Education and Graduate Employment in the Arab States: A Regional Perspective." In *Graduate Prospects in a Changing Society*, edited by Ronning, Anne Holding, and Mary-Louise Kearney. Paris: UNESCO Publishing, 1998.

Cassidy, Thomas J. "A Framework of Salient 'Local' Institutional Challenges and Issues: Arab and Gulf States." A PPE (Programs in Professional Education) working paper. March 2000.

Cassidy, Thomas J., and Matthew Miller. "Higher Education in the Arab States: Responding to the Challenges of Globalization." Discussion paper. AMIDEAST Conference on Higher Education in Arab Countries, Marrakech, Morocco, October 2002.

Christensen, C. Roland, David A. Garvin, and Ann Sweet, eds. *Education for Judgment: The Artistry of Discussion Leadership.* Boston, MA: Harvard Business School Press, 1992.

Coffman, James. "Current Issues in Higher Education in the Arab World." *International Higher Education* Boston, MA: Boston College, 1996.

Committee for Economic Development. *A Shared Future: Reducing Global Poverty.* New York. 2002.

"Self-Doomed to Failure: Arab Development." *The Economist* Special Report (1) (6 July 2002):24–26.

Emirates Center for Strategic Studies and Researcher. *Education in the Arab World: Challenges of the Millennium.* Abu Dhabi, United Arab Emirates. 1999.

Fiormica, Piero, Tayeb A. Kamali, and John Metzner. *Spinoffs from Innovative Learning Environments: Doing Business in the Knowledge Economy.* Abu Dhabi, United Arab Emirates. 1999.

Fergany, Nader. "Arab Higher Education and Development: An Overview." Paper presented at the Third Mediterranean Development Forum, March 2000. Available at <http://www.worldbank.org> (2000).

Gibbons, Michael. "Higher Education Relevance in the 21st Century." Paper presented at the UNESCO World Conference on Higher Education, Paris, 1998.

Gill, Indermit, Fred Fluitman, and Amit Dar. *Vocational Education and Training Reform: Matching Skills to Markets and Budgets*. Cary, N.C.: Oxford University Press, 2000.

Global Information Infrastructure Commission. *Building the Global Information Economy*. Washington, D.C. 1998.

Kader, Abdullah. "Transformation of Information Technology Into Information Resources in the 21st Century in the GCC." Paper presented at the TEND 2000: "Crossroads of the New Millennium." Abu Dhabi, United Arab Emirates, 8 April 2000.

Kearney, Mary-Louise. "Graduate Employment in a Changing Society: A Social Responsibility for Higher Education." In *Graduate Prospects in a Changing Society*, edited by Ronning, Anne Holding, and Mary-Louise Kearney. Paris: UNESCO Publishing, 1998.

Kapiszewski, Andrzej. „Population, Labour and Education Dilemmas Facing GCC States at the Turn of the Century." Paper presented at the TEND 2000: "Crossroads of the New Millennium." Abu Dhabi, United Arab Emirates, 9 April 2000.

Levinson, Macha. "Education for Technology or Technology for Education: The Dilemma of the New Economy." In *The Global Competitiveness Report 2000*. New York: World Economic Forum; Oxford University Press, 2000.

Mazawi, Andre Elias. "The Contested Terrains of Education in the Arab States: An Appraisal of Major Research Trends." *Comparative Education Review* 43, 3 (1999):332–352.

Mograby In *Education in the Arab World: Challenges of the Millennium*. Emirates Center for Strategic Studies and Researcher. Abu Dhabi, United Arab Emirates, 1999.

Murnane, Richard J. and Frank Levy. *Teaching the New Basic Skills*. New York: The Fress Press, 1996.

Rassekh, Shapour, and Jeannine Thomas. *The Management of Curriculum Change in the Gulf Region*. Final report of the Seminar, Muscat, Oman, 17–21 February 2001. Paris: UNESCO Publishing, 2001.

Sanyal, Bikas C. "Diversification of Sources and the Role of Privatization in Financing of Higher Education in the Arab States Region." Working document in the series: IIEP Contributions 30. Paris: International Institute for Educational Planning, UNESCO, 1998.

Senge, Peter M. *The Fifth Discipline: The Art and Practice of the Learning Organization*. New York: Doubleday, 1990.

Schön, Donald. *Educating the Reflective Practitioner*. San Francisco, CA: Jossey Bass, 1990.

Sherbiny, Naiem A." Guns or Butter? Public Expenditure in Arab Countries."

United Nations Economic and Social Commission for Western Asia. *Survey of Economic and Social Developments in the ESCWA Region 1999–2000*. New York: United Nations, 2000.

United Nations Development Program. *Arab Human Development Report 2002: Creating Opportunities for Future Generations*. New York: United Nations Development Program, 2002.

United Nations Development Program. The Human Development Report. New York: United Nations Development Program, 1999.

United Nations Education, Scientific, and Cultural Organization. *Higher Education in Developing Countries: Peril and Promise*. Paris. 2000a.

United Nations Education, Scientific, and Cultural Organization. *World Education Report 2000*. Paris. 2000.

United Nations Education, Scientific, and Cultural Organization. *World Education Report 2000*. Paris. 2000b.

Vandewalle, D. "Higher Education and Development in Arab Oil Exporters: The UAE [United Arab Emirates] in Comparative Perspective." Paper presented at the TEND 2000: "Crossroads of the New Millennium." Abu Dhabi, United Arab Emirates, 10 April 2000.

Wallis, Barbara and Kenneth Mitchell, "The Teaching of Group Process Skills as a Basis for Problem-Based Learning in Small Task-Oriented Groups." In *Problem-Based Learning in Education for the Professions*, edited by Boud, David. Sydney: HERDSA, 1985:171–176.

World Bank. *Claiming the Future: Choosing Prosperity in the Middle East and North Africa*, Washington, D.C. 1995.

World Bank. *Will Arab Workers Prosper or Be Left Out in the Twenty-First Century?* Washington, D.C. 1995.

World Bank. *World Development Indicators*. Washington, D.C. 2002.

Zahlan, A. B. "Knowledge and Development in the Arab World." Paper presented at the Third Mediterranean Development Forum, March 2000.

Endnotes

1. See "A Shared Future: Reducing Global Poverty." 2002. A statement by the Research and Policy Committee for Economic Development.

2. Jordan and Bahrain are two countries that are making substantial efforts to introduce fees at the tertiary level. Lessons being learned in both countries may provide clues for others seeking this strategy.

3. Here I draw primarily on my extensive personal experience working with the statistical and planning departments in a number of countries in the region.

4. The Trends in Mathematics and Science Study, or TIMSS, was a study conducted in 1995 and 1999 by the International Association for the Evaluation of Educational Achievement.

5. For example, by some estimates, 30 to 40 percent of the higher education budget in the U.A.E. is reportedly spent on remedial and foundation programs.

6. Cassidy and Miller first presented a version of this discussion in a paper written for presentation at the AMIDEAST conference in Marrakech, October 2001.

7. Here we use the term "tertiary institutions" generally, referring not only to universities but also to all institutions from which graduates leave to seek employment.

8. Nader Fergany (2000:8) cites UNESCO's 1998 *World Statistical Outlook on Education: 1980-1995* thus: "Compared to advanced countries and even to developing countries combined, enrollment in the first university degree...in Arab countries is much higher at the expense of shorter period higher education, normally in the shape of 'technical institutes'..."

9. We follow Harvard psychologist Robert Kegan in distinguishing between educational "content" and "form"— that is, between *what* we learn or know and *how* we learn or know.

10. A particularly interesting and relevant discussion can be found in the final report of the UNESCO-sponsored Seminar on The Management of Curriculum Change and Adaptation in the Gulf Region, held in Muscat, February 2001.

11. Our discussion of technology is limited in this paper, as it is addressed in another paper in this Report.

12. This collaboration construct is related to "social aptitude" identified as three key skill types ("basic knowledge," "technical knowledge," and "social aptitude") by the influential Delors Commission Report.

13. For more on learning organizations, see Senge (1990).

14. We are indebted to Richard Elmore of Harvard University for this conception of higher education leadership.

15. Notably, institutionalization of professional development has been a long-standing component in Malaysia's strategy for strengthening administration and management in its education system. Professional development is also an important component in Jordan's strategy, and there are indications that it is having a significant impact.

Environmental Sustainability in the Arab World

Daniel C. Esty, Marc A. Levy, and Andrew Winston

Arab states face profound sustainability challenges that will influence their ability to achieve lasting economic, social, and environmental goals. This chapter analyzes the most important environmental sustainability trends in the region, discusses their long-term implications, and suggests strategies for improving performance. While there are some signs of progress and reasons for hope, in general the Arab states are lagging behind in many important environmental areas. Unless measures are undertaken to address the challenges of environmental sustainability, major problems—with serious economic and social consequences—are likely in the future. In addition to the problem of water scarcity, which is endemic to much of the region, there are alarming trends concerning air pollution, greenhouse gas emissions, population growth, and urbanization. Our analysis makes it especially clear that the Arab states lag behind the rest of the world in the core domestic institutions that make basic environmental governance possible, and in their contributions to global processes of shared environmental management.

The analysis in this chapter draws heavily on the 2002 Environmental Sustainability Index (ESI) and the collection of data and indicators created for the ESI (World Economic Forum [WEF] et al. 2002a). The ESI quantifies various dimensions of environmental sustainability, benchmarks national conditions and progress, and facilitates empirical assessment of environment-economy tradeoffs. At the most aggregate level, the ESI is best thought of as a

measure of the ability of a society to preserve critical environmental conditions several generations into the future (Esty and Cornelius 2002; Levy 2002). At a more disaggregated level it permits cross-national comparisons on a number of the most critical environmental aspects of sustainability. The ESI also highlights relative environmental performance and provides a mechanism for identifying "best practices," and thus opportunities, for improved pollution control and natural resource management.

The 142 countries in the 2002 ESI include sixteen of the twenty-two Arab League members. Bahrain, Comoros, Djibouti, Qatar, the West Bank and Gaza, and Yemen were omitted.[1] Each of these countries fell short of the required variable coverage. In addition, Bahrain and Comoros fell below both the population and area limits of the ESI, and Djibouti and Qatar fell below the population threshold.

Background

As the world community focuses on sustainable development objectives in the context of the World Summit on Sustainable Development in Johannesburg, with considerable emphasis being placed on quantifiable metrics of performance, the Arab world finds itself far behind on many aspects of environmental sustainability.

Environmental sustainability has been understood as a fundamental aspect of development for some time, going back at least as far as the Brundtland Commission Report (World Commission on Environment and Development 1987). At the international level, environmental performance is now an uncontroversial component of the Millennium Development Goals, representing the latest in a long series of global consensus documents urging such a focus. At the private-sector level, firms, investors, and consumers now routinely consider environmental issues to have a far higher priority than they did in the past, recognizing the impact that environmental performance may have on financial performance.

Quantifying environmental performance has been difficult, though recent advances now make it possible to offer useful comparative metrics (Esty 2002). The ESI is only one such measure. Other cross-national measures include the "Wellbeing Index" (Prescott-Allen 2001) and the Index of the Consultative Group on Sustainable Development Indicators (CGSDI) (2002). Despite their different assumptions and emphases, all three of these recent measurement efforts agree that Arab states are in significant environmental trouble compared to the rest of the world. Arab states are, on average, 11 points lower than other countries on Prescott-Allen's "Environmental Wellbeing Index" (which ranges from 20 to 72) and 178 points lower than other countries on the CGSDI Environmental Index (which ranges from 87 to 763). For its part, the ESI ranks the average Arab country slightly more than 10 points below other countries (the ESI ranges from 24 to 74). Each of these differences is statistically significant (at the 0.002 level or greater). It is also striking that for each of these indicators the lowest worldwide scores are found in Arab countries.

Table 1. Arab Countries in Comparison to Rest of World, Three Sustainability Indicators

	ESI		Wellbeing Index		Consultative Group Overall Index	
	Arab countries	Rest of world	Arab countries	Rest of world	Arab countries	Rest of world
Minimum	24	32	25	27	218	238
Maximum	52	74	41	64	476	740
Average	41	51	32	43	412	495

Sources: Environmental Sustainability Index 2002; Prescott-Allen 2001; CGSDI 2002

These differences are independent of the level of income per capita. Thus, even when differences in per capita income are controlled for, Arab states still have significantly sub-par levels of environmental sustainability across each of these three aggregate sustainability indicators. This pattern holds whether one takes the more narrow environmental formulations of these indexes or the broader formulations that combine human and environmental aspects of sustainability.

Of course, the Arab world faces some unique challenges based on the geography and climate of the region. The indices surveyed above may not fully reflect these circumstances.[2] But one can only conclude that there is a distinctive Arab pattern to dynamics of environmental sustainability and that this pattern reveals a number of critical issues that deserve attention. In the following sections we analyze this pattern in more detail.

Situational Constraints

Because Arab states lie predominantly in extremely arid regions, and because water is such a fundamental aspect to environmental sustainability, it is logical to suspect that the low sustainability scores found in Arab states are a function of location. When we test this proposition empirically we find that, at the highest level of aggregation, the degree to which a country is arid does correlate significantly with sustainability measures, controlling for per capita income and population density.[3] However, even when this measure of aridness is included as a control in the analysis, scores of Arab states remain significantly below other states. Geography, therefore, appears to matter, but not enough to account for the systematic under-performance observed among Arab states. This reality clearly emerges in Table 2. Only five Arab countries score above their peers (defined according to per capita income levels), and then by very small increments. The rest score below their peers, some quite severely.

Table 2. ESI Scores and Desert Extent of Arab League Members

Country	ESI	Peer-Group ESI	Percent of Territory Desert
Algeria	49.4	48.2	86.4
Egypt	48.8	48.2	92.3
Iraq	33.2	48.2	76.4
Jordan	51.7	48.2	76.4
Kuwait	23.9	54.5	100.0
Lebanon	43.8	48.2	0.0
Libya	39.3	53.5	95.9
Mauritania	38.9	47.3	63.7
Morocco	49.1	48.2	51.2
Oman	40.2	53.5	91.7
Saudi Arabia	34.2	53.5	100.0
Somalia	37.1	44.2	19.0
Sudan	44.7	47.3	29.2
Syrian AR	43.6	48.2	29.1
Tunisia	50.8	48.2	39.8
U.A.E.	25.7	54.5	100.0

Sources: Environmental Sustainability Index 2002; SEDAC's Population, Landscape, and Climate Estimates (PLACE) Data Set

Note: ESI scores are presented as percentiles, which in theory range from 0 to 100; in practice global ESI scores range from 23.9 to 73.9. Peer group ESI is the average ESI score for countries within the same GDP per capita quintile.

It is important to keep in mind that the purpose of the ESI and other efforts to quantify environmental sustainability is to facilitate more effective decision-making. Assigning blame or praise is not the goal. Thus, even if it is true that geographic constraints account for some part of Arab countries' low scores, what matters (from the perspective of supporting more effective decision-making) is better understanding the nature of the challenges facing each country and the opportunities available within each country to better address these issues.

When one goes through the exercise of assessing the more specific nature of the challenges and the readiness to cope with them, a number of striking facts emerge. Arab countries score below average on seventeen of the ESI's twenty indicators, as summarized in the following table.

Table 3. Arab League ESI Indicator Scores as Compared to Rest of World

Indicator	Average Arab League Member Score	Average Rest of World Score
Air quality	-0.28	0.04
Water quantity ***	-0.58	0.07
Water quality ***	-0.54	0.07
Biodiversity	-0.12	0.01
Terrestrial systems **	0.54	-0.07
Reducing air pollution	-0.14	0.02
Reducing water stress ***	-0.76	0.12
Reducing ecosystem stress ***	0.54	-0.07
Reducing waste & consumption pressures	-0.14	0.14
Reducing population growth **	-0.63	0.08
Basic human sustenance	0.22	-0.03
Environmental health	-0.06	0.01
Science and technology	-0.23	-0.19
Capacity for debate ***	-0.43	0.05
Environmental governance ***	-0.61	-0.02
Private sector responsiveness	-0.28	-0.12
Eco-efficiency **	-0.52	0.07
Participation in international cooperative efforts *	-0.33	0.02
Reducing Greenhouse Gas Emissions *	-0.44	0.06
Reducing Transboundary Environmental Pressures	0.03	0.04

Source: Environmental Sustainability Index 2002
*** = statistically significant at 0.001 level or greater.
** = statistically significant at 0.01 level or greater.
* = statistically significant at 0.05 level or greater.
Note: These indicator scores are presented as the average of standardized "z-scores," which range from about –3 to about +3.

The Arab states are, in general, far below average on measures of environmental systems (the quality of air and water, for example) and on measures of social and institutional capacity and global stewardship. By contrast, they score above average on preserving

land from human influence and in reducing human vulnerability to environmental harms. The above-average performance in reducing human vulnerability is especially notable.

This broad picture is on balance consistent with other regional assessments. In both 1997 and 2000, the United Nations Environment Program (UNEP) Global State of the Environment Report identified water, contamination and waste, land degradation, and coastal degradation as the most critical problems in west Asia, and classified air pollution and habitat fragmentation as less severe (UNEP 1997, 2000). Similarly, the Arab Declaration to the World Summit on Sustainable Development drew special attention to problems associated with population growth, water scarcity, and limitations in social and governmental capacity (United Nations Economic and Social Council 2001). The Abu Dhabi Declaration of 2001 emphasized water shortages, land degradation, inefficient resource use, urbanization problems, and coastal degradation (Global News Wire 2001a).

In the media, the discussion of environmental issues is less balanced than these expert assessments. Issues of water and of biodiversity and habitat conservation receive almost all the attention. The following table summarizes the relative frequency of broad categories of environmental concern in the region as reflected in the regional press:

Table 4. Relative Frequency of Mention of Environmental Issues in Gulf News, 2001–2002

Issue	Number of Mentions	Proportion of Total
Biodiversity and Habitat Conservation	346	48.2%
Water	310	43.2%
Air Pollution	39	5.4%
Climate Change	23	3.2%

Source: Lexis-Nexis Academic Universe was used to identify *Gulf News* articles.
Note: Analysis was performed during June 2002, covering period 1 January 2001 through 31 May 2002. Some double counting resulted from press reports that mentioned multiple terms.

Critical Issues

To provide a more detailed understanding of the region's environmental situation, we discuss below some of the most critical challenges facing the Arab world.

Water

Water shortages are serious in many Arab countries. With 10 percent of the world's land, the Arab region controls only 1.2 percent of the global water reserves and relies on imports from outside the region for 60 percent of its needs.[4] By 2025, the shortage is expected to reach 30 billion cubic meters (Gulf News May 2002).

For the measure of water stress used in the ESI (the percent of territory in which water consumption exceeds availability by 40 percent or more), the average Arab state had a value of 71 percent as compared to 20 percent for other states. African members of the Arab League countries fare better on water issues than do the Arabian Peninsula and West Asian countries.

Table 5. Water Indicators

Country	Water Quantity	Water Quality	Reducing Water Stress
Algeria	-1.04	-0.18	-0.18
Egypt	-0.27	-0.55	-0.82
Iraq	-0.08	-0.66	-0.47
Jordan	-0.70	-0.53	-0.45
Kuwait	-1.09	-1.10	-2.79
Lebanon	-1.07	-0.79	-1.48
Libya	-0.66	-0.75	-0.61
Mauritania	0.14	-0.53	0.59
Morocco	-1.07	-0.69	-0.27
Oman	-1.06	-0.05	-1.54
Saudi	-1.08	-0.56	-0.59
Somalia	-0.08	-0.25	0.26
Sudan	-0.01	-0.75	0.45
Syrian AR	-0.18	-0.40	-0.76
Tunisia	-0.64	0.05	-0.62
U.A.E.	-0.36	-0.92	-2.87
Arab average	-0.58	-0.54	-0.76
World average	0.00	0.00	0.11

Source: Environmental Sustainability Index 2002
See Annex 1 for variable details. Units are averages of z-scores across multiple variables.

For countries where water inflows and groundwater resources are far below levels needed to support basic human needs and economic growth, greater desalination capacity is required. Some countries are already investing in ambitious infrastructure development along these lines, but there are signs that demand is exceeding supply (Middle East Economic Digest 2001). More troubling is the acknowledged failure to integrate planning for meeting water needs with other aspects of social and resource planning. The 2002 Arab Development Report draws attention to the weak conservation and reuse programs; the failure to come to grips with tradeoffs among agriculture, industrial, and human water needs; and the lackluster attention paid to the challenges of managing transboundary freshwater resources (United Nations Development Program [UNDP] 2002). Regional assessments increasingly raise concerns about the ability of the region to meet freshwater needs over the coming decades in the absence of effective integrated planning (*Middle East Economic Digest* 2001).

These interdependencies lead us to think that the countries with the most severe long-term vulnerability from water problems are those that have highest water scarcity, most rapid population growth, and lowest levels of governmental capacity. Among Arab League members, Iraq, Libya, and the Syrian AR have especially worrisome combinations of these three factors.

Air pollution

Air pollution receives far less attention among Arab countries than issues of water scarcity, although it now receives more attention than it used to. Our ability to quantify air quality problems and to understand opportunities for progress is limited by the extremely poor state of global air quality monitoring. Given the limited data on ambient concentrations, we can more reliably compare Arab countries in terms of emissions of air pollutants, which are relatively well quantified. On this score, the Arab countries generally exhibit higher levels of emissions than other countries, particularly of oxides of nitrogen and volatile organic compounds. We anticipate the most severe problems where emissions and vehicle densities are highest, governmental response capacity is lowest, and growth is fastest. Accordingly, Libya, Kuwait, and Egypt are especially likely to experience ever more serious air pollution problems in the coming decades in the absence of significant change.

Wildlife, habitat, and biodiversity conservation

Wildlife conservation is the most frequently discussed environmental sustainability issue among Arab states. Arab states are stewards to unique landscapes and rare species—they account for 35 percent of the world's desert biome,[5] for example—and this has clearly generated a special sense of responsibility among elites in the region. A number of Arab countries take wildlife stewardship seriously and have launched programs to protect species and habitat.[6]

The ESI indicators pertaining to anthropogenic impact on the land show very strong scores for Arab states. Satisfaction with this apparent success must be tempered by the realization that settlement patterns in desert areas may naturally lead to relatively low human impact. Nevertheless, the habitat restoration and wildlife conservation programs that have been implemented have been impressive and deserve praise. We do not anticipate major problems in this area over the next two or three decades.[7]

The great importance assigned to wildlife conservation by Arab leaders could be seen, however, as out of sync with the region's priorities as identified by environmental experts. With the exception of coastal environments, which major regional assessments agree deserve greater attention, regional expert assessments do not draw special attention to issues of wildlife and habitat preservation. The 2001 Abu Dhabi Declaration on the Future of the Arab Environment Program, for example, conspicuously ignores wildlife conservation and instead draws quite explicit attention to other more pressing issues as follows:

[The] major environmental problems of priority faced by the Arab countries at the beginning of the twenty-first century are:

- severe shortage of water resources, both in quantity and quality;

- limitation of available lands and deterioration of available land resources;

- unsustainable consumption of natural resources;

- rapid rates of urbanization and associated problems;

- deterioration of coastal and marine areas.

For wildlife and habitat protection to receive almost as much attention in the press as freshwater issues, and almost ten times as much as either air pollution or climate change (as reflected in Table 4), may reflect an imbalance in priorities. It will be important for Arab societies to have an open and informed debate about the relative importance of wildlife conservation versus other issues in the coming years.

Table 6. Wildlife, Habitat, and Biodiversity Conservation Indicators (in Percent)

Country	Percentage of mammals endangered	Percentage of Birds Endangered	Percentage of Territory with Very Low Human Influence	Percentage of Territory with Very High Human Influence	Percentage of CITES reporting Rrequirements Met	Percentage of Territory Protected
Algeria	14.1	3.1	80.4	0.5	60.0	2.4
Egypt	12.2	4.6	70.1	2.4	19.0	0.1
Iraq	12.3	6.4	3.7	1.2	0.0	0.0
Jordan	11.3	5.7	2.1	1.0	35.0	3.1
Kuwait	4.8	28.0	0.1	7.0	0.0	1.0
Lebanon	10.5	4.5	0.0	14.5	0.0	0.5
Libya	11.8	1.1	80.4	0.1	0.0	0.1
Mauritania	16.4	0.7	79.5	0.0	0.0	0.5
Morocco	15.2	4.3	17.5	1.5	60.9	0.7
Oman	16.1	9.3	54.0	0.8	0.0	12.5
Saudi Arabia	9.1	9.7	44.3	0.4	0.0	29.6
Somalia	11.1	2.4	17.7	0.1	7.7	0.3
Sudan	9.0	0.9	41.4	0.2	56.3	4.9
Syrian AR	6.3	3.9	0.1	2.0	0.0	0.0
Tunisia	14.1	2.9	26.2	4.3	100.0	0.3
U.A.E.	12.0	11.9	0.2	2.6	66.7	0.0
Arab average	11.7	6.2	32.3	2.4	25.4	3.5
World average	13.0	4.2	18.6	7.1	57.0	8.4

CITES is the Convention on International Trade in Endangered Species

Source: Environmental Sustainability Index 2002

Climate change

For some scholars and policymakers, a country's approach to climate change is the acid test of its approach to sustainability. In a world in which billions face present-day crises concerning food, water, shelter, and fuel, we believe that such a singular focus cannot be justified. Nevertheless, one can make a strong case that the nations of the Arab world are slighting the problem of climate change. The lack of focus on greenhouse gas emissions may, over the coming decades, appear to be short sighted.

Table 7. Climate Change Indicators

Country	CO$_2$ Emissions per Capita*	CO$_2$ Emissions per Unit GDP**	Energy Consumption per GDP***	Renewable Energy as Percent of Total Energy****
Algeria	1.0	2.0	8.6	0.2
Egypt	0.4	1.5	9.4	7.8
Iraq	1.0	3.2	20.6	0.5
Jordan	0.6	2.2	11.5	0.1
Kuwait	5.1	2.9	15.3	0.0
Lebanon	1.4	2.4	12.2	3.1
Libya	1.9	2.8	12.2	0.0
Mauritania	0.3	2.0	11.5	0.6
Morocco	0.3	0.9	4.3	3.7
Oman	2.3	2.3	13.6	0.0
Saudi Arabia	3.8	3.6	19.9	0.0
Somalia	0.0	0.1	3.3	0.0
Sudan	0.0	0.2	4.8	14.4
Syrian AR	0.9	2.7	15.8	9.7
Tunisia	0.7	1.2	5.2	0.3
U.A.E.	10.2	4.9	23.0	0.0
Arab average	1.6	2.2	11.9	2.5
World average	1.1	1.5	9.1	16.6

Source: Environmental Sustainability Index 2002
*Metric tons of carbon per person
**Metric tons per US$ GDP
***Billion BTU/US$ million GDP
****Renewable energy production as a percent of total energy consumption

For each of the core climate change indicators, the Arab League average exceeds world averages. And these averages mask dramatic extremes within the Arab world. The United Arab Emirates has almost double the per capita carbon dioxide emissions of the United States, for example; and Kuwait's emissions are only slightly less than those of the United States. If it were not for the extremely low-emission countries such as Somalia and Sudan, the Arab average on greenhouse gas emissions would be far higher.

Arab League members are not playing a leading role in the world community's response to climate change. Only three have signed or ratified the Kyoto Protocol, although eighteen of twenty-two have ratified the Climate Change Convention (United Nations Framework Convention on Climate Convention 2001, 2002). The reluctance to participate in the Kyoto Protocol is especially striking, since Kyoto requires no specific action on the part of Arab states. Moreover, very few Arab states have made concrete greenhouse gas reduction targets outside the framework of the Kyoto Protocol, although even countries that have backed away from the Kyoto approach, such as the United States, have taken that step.

Taking into account the energy-related issues involved, the lack of focus among Arab states on the climate change problem—and even hostility in some quarters—may not be surprising. It seems clear, however, that over multiple decades such opposition is not sustainable. We expect that Arab states that find productive ways to contribute to more effective management of the global climate change problem will be better positioned competitively and with regard to environmental well-being. As Sheik Hamdan bin Zayed Al Nahyan of the United Arab Emirates put it, "The stakes are high for us, and high for our planet" (Global News Wire, February 2002).

Driving Forces

Many of the data points collected for the purposes of creating the ESI cut across multiple environmental domains because they contribute to a range of environmental sustainability challenges. Chief among these multidimensional issues are population and consumption.

Arab League countries have among the highest population growth rates in the world. Part of the rise in population can be attributed to declining infant mortality and increased lifespans—both of which reflect successful investments in nutrition and healthcare. But regardless of the reason, fertility rates remain high, and as a result the pressure on environmental systems remains serious.

As many regional assessments have observed,[8] these population growth rates pose extraordinary challenges for Arab governments. In the words of the 2001 Abu Dhabi Declaration, "the relentless increase in population is a major long-term threat" (Gulf News 5 February 2001). High fertility rates contribute to countries having disproportionately high youth

Table 8. Population Indicators

Country	Total Fertility Rate*	Projected Change in Population by 2050 (%)
Algeria	3.1	66.2
Bahrain	2.8	300.4
Comoros	6.8	207.9
Djibouti	6.1	67.1
Egypt	3.5	64.3
Iraq	5.3	127.1
Jordan	3.6	128.5
Kuwait	4.2	180.7
Lebanon	2.5	35.4
Libya	3.9	106.4
Mauritania	6.0	207.9
Morocco	3.4	66.0
Oman	6.1	218.0
Qatar	3.9	45.3
Saudi Arabia	5.7	185.4
Somalia	7.3	240.5
Sudan	4.9	99.9
Syrian AR	4.1	105.9
Tunisia	2.3	46.5
U.A.E.	3.5	53.6
West Bank and Gaza	5.9	239.4
Yemen	7.2	295.0
Arab country average	4.6	140.3
World average	3.4	66.2

Source: 2002 ESI; original data from Population Reference Bureau, 2001 World Population Data Sheet

*Total fertility rate: number of children born per woman

Table 9. Ecological Footprint per Capita

Country	Ecological Footprint per Capita
Algeria	1.8
Egypt	1.7
Iraq	1.7
Jordan	1.7
Kuwait	10.1
Lebanon	3.2
Libya	4.4
Mauritania	1.2
Morocco	1.6
Oman	3.4
Saudi Arabia	6.2
Somalia	1.0
Sudan	1.1
Syrian AR	2.6
Tunisia	2.3
U.A.E.	10.1
Arab county average	3.4
World average	3.1

Source: World Wide Fund for Nature, Living Planet Report 2000

populations, which puts a burden on social services and heightens the need for employment growth as youth seek to enter the work force. High total growth rates (which take into account migration) present challenges for managing development across numerous dimensions. One recent global study concluded that high rates of population growth significantly dampen prospects for lasting economic development (Birdsall et al. 2001).

Rapid urbanization is also endemic throughout the region. The United Nations Population Division reports that on average, urban areas in the Arab world are growing a percentage point faster than in the rest of the world. Some of the poorest countries, such as Comoros, Mauritania, and Somalia, have rates of urbanization in excess of 4 percent per year, which puts tremendous strains on urban water supplies and sanitation. Cairo, the

largest Arab city with a population of 10.6 million, has significant air quality and sanitation problems. Casablanca, a city of 3.3 million, properly disposes of only 10 percent of household waste through sanitary landfills and incineration. Sana'a (Yemen), with 1.2 million people, effectively has no sanitary waste disposal facilities (Global Urban Indicators Database 2 1998). The proportion of household wastes that are processed range from only 3 percent in Damascus to 83 percent in Tunisia. Once again, despite the salience of the issue, Arab countries are largely absent from international processes aimed at improving urban environmental quality, such as the International Center for Local Environmental Initiatives' (ICLEI) Local Agenda 21 Campaign.

Consumption pressures are also high across the region, especially in the oil-producing states. Arab states have weak recycling and resource conservation programs, in part because energy has been so inexpensive for many of them. The measure in the ESI that best captures overall consumption pressures is the per capita Ecological Footprint, calculated by the Redefining Progress Institute and World Wide Fund for Nature. The Ecological Footprint is a measure of the implicit land area required to support a country's levels of natural resource consumption. Although the Arab states as a whole have a Footprint measure close to the world average, a few states are markedly above this average. As conclusions from many regional assessments indicate, such resource profligacy is not likely to be sustainable in the long term. Even if energy is inexpensive in the region, it comes with a significant set of spillovers in the way of water and air pollution and pressures on climate change. Countries that fail to find effective strategies to use natural resources more efficiently are likely to face more significant sustainability challenges than they would otherwise. Moreover, low resource productivity detracts from competitiveness (Porter and van der Linde 1995).

Global Engagement

Achieving lasting improvement in the most fundamental aspects of environmental sustainability will almost assuredly require greater engagement in global processes of environmental management. There are very few purely local environmental problems. We live in an era of profound global connections that require interconnected processes of governance. Yet it is precisely on measures of global engagement that Arab League members have especially low ranks.

environmental agreement also rises, reflecting both a greater interest in global environmental management and greater capacity to participate in international initiatives. Yet among Arab League members this relationship does not hold. The wealthiest Arab countries do not participate any more actively than the poorest. When they do become parties to multilateral environmental agreements, Arab countries are significantly more likely to do so after the treaty has already entered into force (on average 62 percent of the time) than other countries (on average 54 percent of the time). Again, this difference is accentuated when differences in income are taken into account. What this suggests is that Arab League members are significantly less likely to be among the leaders in negotiating multilateral environmental agreements.

Figure 1. Multilateral Environmental Agreements

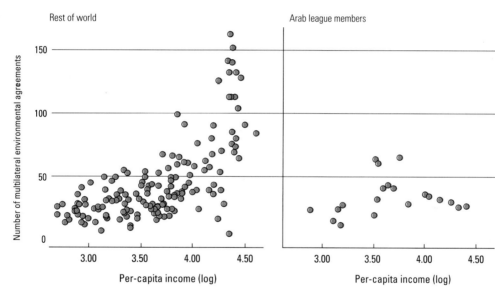

Source: 2002 Environmental Treaties and Resource Indicators (ENTRI)

The sixteen Arab League members represented in the ESI are absent from significantly more of the global data sets that make up the ESI than other countries. On average they are missing from 31 percent of the ESI's global data inputs, as compared to 22 percent among other countries. Only one Arab state participates in the Global Environmental Monitoring System's air quality program, for example, and only four participate in its water quality program.

The average Arab League member is a party to only thirty multilateral environmental agreements, as compared to an average of thirty-nine for other countries.[9] This difference is much more profound when one takes into account differences in per capita incomes. In general, as per capita income rises, participation in

Not a single Arab League member contributes payments to the Global Environmental Facility (GEF). This is true even for those members whose per capita income is equal to or higher than many other large GEF contributors.

This pattern of environmental disengagement is paralleled within the private sector of the Arab world. A corporation based in an Arab League member state is 65 percent less likely to obtain ISO 14001 (environmental management) certification than corporations based elsewhere. Arab-based corporations are 85 percent less likely to join the World Business Council on Sustainable Development (WBCSD). While ISO 14001 and the WBCSD are admittedly not the only routes to corporate environmental progress, the large gap reflects a fundamental difference in the degree of engagement between Arab commercial enterprises and their counterparts elsewhere.

Environmental Governance

Managing the challenges of environmental sustainability over the long run requires an ability to monitor and assess complicated dynamics, balance competing social priorities, set realistic and useful goals, and implement measures effectively and flexibly. All of this makes an institutional commitment to environmental governance extremely important. Collectively, the world's governments are searching for mechanisms that will achieve these functions. Creating regulatory systems and the other institutional structures that support sound environmental decision-making requires great effort. In this regard there are no shortcuts or magic bullets. Yet there are some generalizations that support a conclusion that the need for reform among Arab countries is acute.

As these indicators show, Arab League members lag world averages on most measures of environmental governance. The area of scientific and technical

Table 10. ESI Governance Indicators

Country	Scientific and Technical Capacity	Capacity for Public Debate	Environmental Governance	Private Sector Innovation
Algeria	-0.53	-0.57	-0.93	0.02
Egypt	-0.48	-0.91	-0.29	-0.12
Iraq	-0.32	-0.85	-1.31	-0.41
Jordan	0.37	0.41	-0.33	0.14
Kuwait	0.10	0.04	-0.65	-0.41
Lebanon	0.42	0.55	-0.59	-0.27
Libya	0.42	-0.59	-1.03	-0.41
Mauritania	-1.51	-0.19	-0.47	-0.41
Morocco	0.26	-0.55	-0.14	-0.38
Oman	0.45	-0.37	-0.28	-0.35
Saudi Arabia	0.09	-0.74	0.05	-0.40
Somalia	-1.10	-0.55	-0.71	-0.41
Sudan	-1.58	-1.04	-0.88	-0.41
Syrian AR	-0.39	-0.94	-0.81	-0.38
Tunisia	-0.50	-0.38	-0.53	-0.38
U.A.E.	0.57	-0.21	-0.80	0.09
Arab country average	-0.23	-0.43	-0.61	-0.28
World average	-0.19	0.00	-0.09	-0.14

Source: Environmental Sustainability Index 2002

capacity is a partial exception, with many Arab countries possessing significant capacity. For other capacity measures, however, the record is consistently more problematic. In general, Arab countries are relatively closed to effective public debate about environmental problems, their governments are prone to the kind of distortions (such as subsidies and corruption) that make efficient resource management more difficult, and their industries are not actively engaged in environmental innovation.

We know that these patterns of capacity and governance have a strong influence on environmental outcomes (Esty and Porter 2002). In an analysis of quantitative measures of environmental performance that took into account cross-national differences in air and water pollution, land protection, and greenhouse gas emissions, as well as rates of change in these measures, we found that measures of environmental capacity and governance had a far stronger correlation with environmental outcomes than any other measure, including per capita income (WEF 2002b). Countries that invest in social, commercial, and public sector capacities, and that deploy their abilities to address the complex problems of sustainability, benefit from more effective environmental outcomes.

Although there is some risk of embedding a Western bias in measures of capacity and governance, we find it quite striking that regional assessments carried out among Arab states are increasingly reaching very similar conclusions. The 2001 Abu Dhabi Declaration referred to the need to expand the involvement of civil society in governance, for example. More starkly, in the 2002 Arab Human Development Report it was concluded that:

The way forward involves tackling human capabilities and knowledge. It also involves promoting systems of good governance, those that promote, support and sustain human well-being, based on expanding human capabilities, choices, opportunities and freedoms (economic and social as well as political).

The most important of state institutions is that of representation and legislation which provides the basic link between the governance regime and the people. Liberating human capabilities in Arab countries requires comprehensive political representation in effective legislatures based on free, honest, efficient and regular elections. Reforming public administration is also a central and urgent task for Arab countries. Governments need to perform their functions as providers of public services and enforcers of contracts, in an effective, efficient and transparent manner. Public sector institutions need to be reformed to encourage private sector investment and growth, to curb monopolies and to end graft and cronyism

Conclusions

Arab countries face serious threats to their environmental sustainability. There are strong reasons to believe that if these threats are not effectively managed, broad social and economic harm will result. Likewise, there is reason to believe that countries that do effectively manage these challenges will reap benefits including improved competitiveness (Esty and Porter 2001). The 2002 Arab Human Development Report draws explicit linkages between human development and the environment. The evidence presented in this chapter lends further support to the significance of this relationship.

There is no single blueprint for environmental progress. Although some countries perform better than others, all face issues that need to be addressed forthrightly. The most broad-reaching deficiencies in the Arab world have to do with systems of environmental capacity and governance. We see no foundation for thinking that Arab countries will be able to manage the challenges they face in the way of water scarcity, pollution levels, climate change, and population growth in the absence of major institutional reform. But the Arab world also has great strengths. Many countries have resources and capacities that make better environmental performance a very real possibility—if a commitment to greater environmental sustainability is made.

References

"Abu Dhabi Declaration on the Future of the Arab Environment Programme." Global News Wire. (5 February 2001a).

Birdsall, Nancy, Allen C. Kelley, and Steven W. Sinding. *Population Matters: Demographic Change, Economic Growth, and Poverty in the Developing World*. Oxford: Oxford University Press, 2001.

Consultative Group on Sustainable Development Indicators. "Dashboard of Sustainable Development Indicators." Dataset dated 9 January 2002.

"Environment Officials to Meet," *Gulf News*, 5 February 2001.

Esty, Daniel C., and Michael Porter. "Ranking National Environmental Performance: A Leading Indicator of Future Competitiveness?" In World Economic Forum, *The Global Competitiveness Report 2001*. New York: Oxford University Press, 2001:78–101.

Esty, Daniel C., and Peter Cornelius, eds. *Environmental Performance Measurement: The Global Report 2001–2002*. New York: Oxford University Press, 2002.

Esty, Daniel C.. "Why Measurement Matters." In *Environmental Performance Measurement: The Global Report 2001–2002*, edited by Daniel C. Esty and Peter Cornelius. New York: Oxford University Press, 2002:2–10.

Esty, Daniel C., and Michael Porter. "National Environmental Performance Measurement and Determinants." In *Environmental Performance Measurement: The Global Report 2001–2002*, edited by Daniel C. Esty and Peter Cornelius. New York: Oxford University Press, 2002:24–43.

Levy, Marc A. "Measuring Nations' Environmental Sustainability." In *Environmental Performance Measurement: The Global Report 2001–2002*," edited by Daniel C. Esty and Peter Cornelius. Oxford: Oxford University Press, 2002: 12–23.

Global Urban Indicators Database 2, United Nations Human Settlement Program, http://www.unchs.org/programmes/guo/guo_indicators.asp.

"Middle East Should Pay Attention to Global Warming: Hamdan." Global News Wire. (10 February 2001b).

Porter, Michael, and Claas van der Linde. "Toward a New Conception of the Environment-Competitiveness Relationship." *The Journal of Economic Perspectives* 9, 4 (Fall 1995).

Prescott-Allen, Robert. *The Wellbeing of Nations*. Washington D.C: Island Press, 2001.

"Saudi Arabia: Water Privatization." Quarterly Report, *Middle East Economic Digest* (3 September 2001).

"Study Warns of Water Crisis," *Gulf News*, 27 May 2002.

United Nations Environment Program. Global State of the Environment Report 1997 <http://www.grida.no/geo1/exsum/ex3.htm> (1997).

United Nations Environment Program., "Global Environmental Outlook." <http://www.unep.org/geo2000/english/0105.htm> (2000).

United Nations Economic and Social Council. "The Arab Declaration to the World Summit on Sustainable Development (WSSD)." E/CN.17/2002/PC.2/. 1 December 2001. <http://www.johannesburgsummit.org/html/documents/westasiaministerial.pdf> (2001).

United Nations Development Program. *Arab Human Development Report.* New York: UNDP, 2002.

World Commission on Environment and Development. *Our Common Future.* Oxford: Oxford University Press, 1987.

World Economic Forum, Yale University, and Columbia University. *2002 Environmental Sustainability Index.* <http://www.ciesin.columbia.edu/indicators/ESI/> (2002a).

World Economic Forum, Columbia University, and Yale University. *Pilot Environmental Performance Index.* <http://www.ciesin.columbia.edu/indicators/ESI/EPI2002_11FEB02.pdf> (2002b).

Endnotes

1. The ESI does not contain data on all countries; countries that were very small in size or population, or that were not well-represented in major global data sets, were omitted.

2. Efforts are underway to develop a set of regional indicators that might help to create a more rounded picture of the environmental scene in the Arab world.

3. The measure of aridity used was "percent of area classified within the biome 'desert and xeric shrubs' in the Population, Landscape, and Climate and Estimates (PLACE) data set, version 1.1. <http://beta.sedac.ciesin.columbia.edu/plue/nagd/place.html>.

4. Turkey and Ethiopia are the most important exporters of water to the Arab world.

5. Calculated using PLACE data set (endnote 3), which contains variables measuring the extent of each country's territory occupied by the world's biomes.

6. See, for example, Environmental Research and Wildlife Development Agency, "Environmental Strategic Plan for the Emirate of Abu Dhabi 2000–2004," which documents significant successes in habitat restoration and species conservation.

7. However, an occasional controversy is inevitable even where the overall pattern is strong, as the recent dispute between the Convention on International Trade in Endangered Species and the United Arab Emirates (which has been resolved successfully) illustrates.

8. "The Arab Declaration to the World Summit on Sustainable Development (WSSD) Johannesburg, South Africa," . The Arab Ministers Responsible for Development, Planning, and Environment, in their meeting held at the League of Arab States in Cairo, on 24 October 2001 (8th Shaaban 1422 Hijri) in preparation for the WSSD.

9. The data reported in this paragraph were calculated using the Environmental Treaties and Resource Indicators database, Center for International Earth Science Information Network, revised beta version, July 2002. <http://sedac.columbia.edu/entri/> (2002).

Annex 1: Data Sources

Except where otherwise noted, the data used in this chapter come from the 2002 Environmental Sustainability Index. Complete documentation and data sets are available for download at http://www.ciesin.columbia.edu/indicators/ESI/. The following table lists the variables included.

Table 11. ESI Building Blocks

Component	Indicator	Variable
Environmental Systems	Air quality	Urban SO2 concentration
		Urban NO2 concentration
		Urban TSP concentration
	Water quantity	Internal renewable water per capita
		Per capita water inflow from other countries
	Water quality	Dissolved oxygen concentration
		Phosphorus concentration
		Suspended solids
		Electrical conductivity
	Biodiversity	Proportion of mammals threatened (%)
		Proportion of breeding birds threatened (%)
	Land	Proportion of land area having very low anthropogenic impact (%)
		Proportion of land area having high anthropogenic impact (%)
Reducing Stresses	Reducing air pollution	NOx emissions per populated land area
		SO2 emissions per populated land area
		VOCs emissions per populated land area
		Coal consumption per populated land area
		Vehicles per populated land area
	Reducing water stress	Fertilizer consumption per hectare of arable land
		Pesticide use per hectare of crop land
		Industrial organic pollutants per available fresh water
		Proportion of country's territory under severe water stress (%)
	Reducing ecosystem stresses	Change in forest cover 1990–2000 (%)
		Proportion of territory experiencing acidification exceedence (%)
	Reducing waste and consumption pressures	Ecological footprint per capita
		Radioactive waste
	Reducing population growth	Total fertility rate
		Change in projected population between 2001 and 2050 (%)
Reducing Human Vulnerability	Basic human sustenance	Proportion of undernourished in total population
		Proportion of population with access to improved drinking-water supply (%)
	Environmental health	Child death rate from respiratory diseases
		Death rate from intestinal infectious diseases
		Age 5 and younger mortality rate

Source: Environmental Sustainability Index 2002

Table 11. ESI Building Blocks (continued)

Component	Indicator	Variable
Social and Institutional Capacity	Science and technology	Technology achievement index
		Technology Innovation Index
		Mean years of education
	Capacity for debate	IUCN member organizations per million population
		Civil and political liberties
		Democratic institutions
		Proportion of ESI variables in publicly available data sets (%)
	Environmental governance	WEF Survey Questions on Environmental governance
		Land area under protected status (%)
		Number of sectoral EIA guidelines
		FSC accredited forest area (as a % of total forest area)
		Control of corruption
		Price distortions (ratio of gasoline price to international average)
		Subsidies for energy or materials usage
		Subsidies to the commercial fishing sector
	Private sector responsiveness	Number of ISO14001 certified companies per million US$ GDP
		Dow Jones Sustainability Group Index
		Average Innovest EcoValue rating of firms
		World Business Council for Sustainable Development members
		Private sector environmental innovation
	Eco-efficiency	Energy efficiency (total energy consumption per unit GDP)
		Renewable energy production (as a % of total energy consumption)
Global Stewardship	Participation in international collaborative efforts	Number of memberships in environmental intergovernmental orgs.
		Proportion of CITES reporting requirements met (%)
		Levels of participation in the Vienna Convention/Montreal Protocol
		Levels of participation in the Climate Change Convention
		Montreal protocol multilateral fund participation
		Global environmental facility participation
		Compliance with Environmental Agreements
	Greenhouse gas emissions	Carbon lifestyle efficiency (CO2 emissions per capita)
		Carbon economic efficiency (CO2 emissions per US$ GDP)
	Reducing transboundary environmental pressures	CFC consumption (total times per capita)
		SO2 exports
		Total marine fish catch
		Seafood consumption per capita

Source: Environmental Sustainability Index 2002

Part 2

Country Profiles and Data Presentation

How Country Profiles Work

By Jennifer Blanke, Friedrich von Kirchbach, and Jean-Michel Pasteels

This section includes four-page country profiles for sixteen Arab world countries. Each profile summarizes important data for a country. It displays major economic, financial, social, and trade data from published sources. Country profiles are laid out as follows: the first page presents basic indicators for the country in order to give a general overview of its present situation in terms of economic and social development; the second page covers exchange and capital restrictions, providing a snapshot of the country's financial openness; and the third and fourth pages provide a detailed analysis of the country's export profile in the form of a detailed trade table and an accompanying chart.

Page 1:
Key Indicators

This page presents recent economic data such as the size of the economy and the volume of trade and foreign direct investment, as well as a number of social development indicators such as literacy rates and life expectancy. The primary data sources used are the World Bank, World Development Indicators 2002; the International Monetary

Fund (IMF) International Financial Statistics; the IMF World Economic Outlook Database 2002; The Heritage Foundation 2002 Index of Economic Freedom; United Nations Conference on Trade and Development (UNCTAD) FDI statistics; and the Economist Intelligence Unit. In some cases and for some countries, these sources did not provide recent data, in which case national sources were also checked and used when possible.

Page 2:
Exchange Rate and Capital Restrictions

This page presents information related to a country's financial openness and recent exchange rate fluctuations. The table at the top of the page presents general information on exchange rate arrangements, and specifies the particular exchange and capital restrictions in place. The graph

at the bottom of the page shows the evolution of the real effective exchange rate since 1995 for most of the countries, providing a relative measure of competitiveness. In those cases where the real effective exchange rate is not available, the nominal effective exchange rate or the real exchange rate relative to the U.S. Dollar is presented instead.

Pages 3 and 4:
Export Performance Trade Tables and Trade Charts

These two pages present information on national export performance by country, both in graphical and table format. These tables and charts have been developed by the International Trade Centre UNCTAD/WTO (ITC) (www.intracen.org). They address the following questions:

1. What are the leading export products of each country? How concentrated or diversified is each country's export portfolio in terms of products?

2. In what products has the country performed better than other countries and increased its international market share? Which export products are falling behind?

3. To what extent are the leading export products positioned in growing or declining markets?

Each assessment is based on trade data for the years 1996 to 2000 reported to the COMTRADE database of the United Nations Statistics Division.

When a country's export data are not available, mirror statistics are used; these are amounts reported by the importing rather than exporting country. This approach has the advantage of covering the nonreporting countries. At the same time, mirror statistics have some shortcomings that must be taken into account. First, contrary to international convention, these export data are expressed in CIF terms (i.e., cost, insurance, and freight are

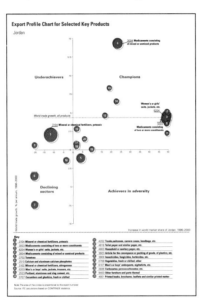

included). As a general rule, CIF values tend to be about 10 percent higher than the free-on-board (FOB) values normally used for exports. Second, mirror statistics only capture those exports of nonreporting countries that are imports of the reporting countries. As a result, a major share of trade among developing countries is excluded. More generally, trade statistics have a number of weak points of which readers should be aware. Nondeclared and informal trade, for instance, have reached significant volumes in a number of countries, but these statistics are not included.

Page 3: How to Read the Trade Tables

The export performance tables present major indicators on a country's export performance. A footnote indicates whether the indicators are derived from that country's export statistics or from partner countries.

The indicators included in the tables are defined as follows.

All goods
The top line gives value, growth, and growth pattern information for a country's total merchandise exports. In the case of mirror statistics, export value is estimated according to the import data of the major trading nations.

All goods (WTO)
The second line indicates the value of national exports according to national sources (as reported in the WTO's Annual Report publication). The comparison of this figure with total exports as derived from partner country data indicates the level of export flows covered by mirror statistics. In a few countries, mirror statistics are actually larger than statistics in the national data. This may reflect the CIF-FOB difference in valuation and the nonreporting of exports in the country under review.

Rank
This section ranks up to forty leading merchandise export product groups of the country under review for 2000.

HS Code and product label
This section uses the Harmonized System (HS Code), an internationally recognized system of specific identifiers for every commodity. The data are arranged by HS product item followed by an abbreviated product description. The original (1988) version of the HS is used.

Exports in 2000 (USD m)
Export values for 2000 are reported here in USD million. For nonreporting countries this is calculated as the sum of imports from that country by all reporting countries.

Net exports in 2000 (USD m)
Net export values (i.e., export value minus import value) for 2000 are reported here in USD million. For nonreporting countries, mirror estimates are used and net exports should be considered as indicative only. Negative values mean that the country is a net importing country (i.e., imports are higher than exports).

Export growth for 1996 to 2000, percent per annum, value
The average annual percentage growth of export values are calculated for the 1996 to 2000 period, based on the least-squares method. For nonreporting countries, the value is calculated on the basis of mirror statistics. The growth rate is only displayed if the corresponding partner countries have consistently reported trade data to COMTRADE over the previous five years. For countries that report trade data in 2000 but not systematically for the four previous years, such as Bahrain, mirror estimates are used, provided that there is no significant discrepancy between the country's statistics and mirror estimates in 2000.

Export growth for 1996 to 2000, percent per annum, quantity
The average annual percentage growth of export quantities are reported for the 1996 to 2000 period, based on the least-squares method. For nonreporting countries, this figure is not calculated due to problems of aggregation and the possibility of unreliable data.

World trade growth 1996 to 2000, percent per annum, value
The average annual percentage growth of world imports (1996 to 2000) are reported for the product under review based on their least-squares fit.

World trade growth 1996 to 2000, percent per annum, quantity
The average annual percentage growth of volumes of world imports (1996 to 2000) of the product under review are calculated based on their least-squares fit. The world trade growth of unit values (average prices) can be calculated approximately as the difference between the growth rate in value and the growth rate in quantity. For example, for most of the primary products listed, world trade in value has been decreasing over the 1996 to 2000 period in spite of increasing volumes.

Export share in world, in percent
This is the percentage share of exports of the corresponding country in total world exports, based on 2000 export values. For example, if the world market share of a country was estimated at 3.8 percent in 1999 and 4.0 percent in 2000, the change in market share is equal to 5 percent.

Leading markets
This lists the two largest markets for a country's year 2000 exports and their share in that country's exports. The table below provides the key to the three-letter codes for countries listed in the last columns of the tables. This information is not available for some countries, due to unreliable or incomplete data.

Bottom of the table: data on exports of services
Earnings in USD millions from services sold internationally in 2000, when available, are presented at the end of the table for goods. These are divided into three categories: transportation services; travel; and other services (including finance, insurance, communications, computing, and construction). Service categories are not represented on the graph, to avoid inappropriately comparing services with more narrow goods categories. The source is the WTO Annual Report on International Trade Statistics. (See www.wto.org for more information.)

Page 4: How to Read the Trade Charts (see Figure 1)

The chart presents the performance of selected key export product groups of a country, which are listed in the key at the bottom of the chart in order of export value. A number of products listed in the trade table are not displayed in the corresponding chart. This is due to missing or incomplete data, which makes a calculation of the increase in market share impossible. In addition, some products such as re-exports or special transactions have been omitted since they are less interesting in terms of trade performance and commercial policy.

The chart shows the export value of the product group under review (delineated by the size of the "bubbles") and compares the national increase in world market share (on the horizontal axis) to the growth of international demand (on the vertical axis). It also indicates the average nominal growth of world imports over the same period, which was 4.5 percent per annum (horizontal reference line). Moreover, the vertical line (i.e., the line of constant world market share) divides the chart into two parts. Exports of product groups to the right of this line have grown faster than world imports and have thereby increased their share in the world market. Conversely, product groups to the left of the vertical line have seen a decrease in their world market share.

The vertical and the horizontal reference lines are of particular interest from a trade development perspective, since they divide the chart into four quadrants with different characteristics. For ease of reference, each of these quadrants has been given a name.

Champions—winners in growth markets (upper right quadrant). These are the export products for which the country under review has performed very well, increasing its share of world imports. They are comprised of products that are growing faster than world trade in general, and for which the country has been able to outperform world market growth. Exporters of these products proved their international competitiveness during the late 1990s. Trade promotion efforts for these products are less risky, as there are national success stories that can serve as reference points.

Promotional efforts should aim at broadening the supply capacity.

Underachievers—losers in growth markets (upper left quadrant). These products represent particular challenges for trade promotion efforts in the country under review. While international demand has been growing at above-average rates, the country has been falling behind. Its exports have either declined or grown less dynamically than world trade. As a result, the country under review has been losing international market share. In general, the bottleneck is not international

Figure 1. How to Read the Export Profile Charts for Selected Key Products

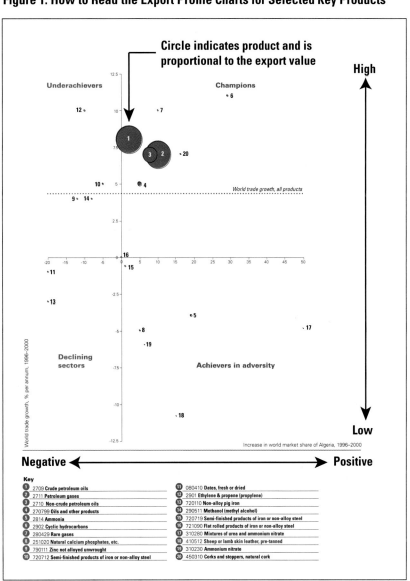

demand, but supply factors. For these products, it is essential to identify and remove the specific bottlenecks that impede a more dynamic expansion of exports.

Decling sectors—losers in declining markets (lower left quadrant). The export prospects for these products tend to be bleak. World imports of the product concerned have been stagnating or have actually declined, and the market share of the country under review has gone down. Trade promotion efforts for product groups in this category face an up-hill task. They need to adopt an integrated approach to take into account bottlenecks both on the supply and on the demand side.

Achievers in adversity— winners in declining markets (lower right quadrant). Products in this quadrant are characterized by growing shares of the country's exports in world import markets that are declining or growing below average. From a trade promotion perspective, niche-marketing strategies are required to isolate the positive trade performance from the overall decline in these markets.

It should be noted that the criterion for distinguishing growing and declining products is the average nominal growth rate of total world imports from 1996 to 2000, which was at 4.5 percent annually. Products that have world import growth below this rate (e.g., at 1 percent annually) are classified as declining products, because their share in world trade is declining.

The charts also provide an overview of the concentration of exports; the appearance of one or a few comparatively large circles shows that exports are highly concentrated.

Below is a list of national websites that provide primary statistical information on the countries listed.

Algeria
National Office of Statistics
www.ons.dz

Ministry of Finance
membres.lycos.fr/mfdgep

Central Bank
www.bank-of-algeria.dz

Bahrain
Government Statistics
www.bahrain.gov.bh/english/stats/index.asp

Ministry of Finance and National Economy
www.mofne.gov.bh/english/index.htm

Monetary Agency
www.bma.gov.bh

Egypt
Ministry of Economy
www.interoz.com/economygoveg/index.htm

Central Bank
www.cbe.org.eg

Jordan
Department of Statistics
www.dos.gov.jo

Ministry of Finance
www.mof.gov.jo/english/inside.asp

Central Bank
www.cbj.gov.jo/index.html

Kuwait
Ministry of Finance
www.mof.gov.kw

Central Bank
www.cbk.gov.kw

Lebanon
Central Administration for Statistics
www.cas.gov.lb

Ministry of Finance
www.finance.gov.lb

Ministry of Economy and Trade
www.economy.gov.lb

Central Bank
www.bdl.gov.lb

Libya
Central Bank
www.cbl-ly.com/eng/about.html

Mauritania
National Office of Statistics
www.ons.mr

Morocco
Ministry of Economy and Finance
www.finances.gov.ma

National Bank
www.bkam.ma

Oman
Ministry of Finance
www.mof.gov.om

Ministry of National Economy
www.moneoman.gov.om

Central Bank
www.cbo-oman.org

Qatar
Ministry of Finance (Under Construction as of July 2002)
www.qatar.net.qa/customs

Central Bank
www.qcb.gov.qa

Saudi Arabia
Ministry of Finance and National Economy
www.mof.gov.sa/index_e.html

Monetary Agency
www.sama.gov.sa

Syrian Arab Republic
Ministry of Economy and Foreign Trade
www.syrecon.org/

Central Bank
www.syrecon.org

Tunisia
Government Website
www.ministeres.tn/html/ministeres.html

Central Bank
www.bct.gov.tn

United Arab Emirates
Ministry of Economy and Commerce
www.economy.gov.ae

Ministry of Finance and Industry
www.uae.gov.ae/mofi

Central Bank
www.cbuae.gov.ae

Yemen
Central Bank
www.centralbank.gov.ye

Ministry of Planning and Development
www.mpd-yemen.org

ISO Codes List

ISO Code	Statistical Territory	ISO Code	Statistical Territory	ISO Code	Statistical Territory	ISO Code	Statistical Territory
ABW	Aruba	DEU	Germany	KAZ	Kazakstan	PRK	Korea, Dem. People's Rep. of
AFG	Afghanistan	DJI	Djibouti	KEN	Kenya	PRT	Portugal
AGO	Angola	DMA	Dominica	KGZ	Kyrgyzstan	PRY	Paraguay
ALB	Albania	DNK	Denmark	KHM	Cambodia	PYF	French Polynesia
AND	Andorra	DOM	Dominican Republic	KIR	Kiribati	QAT	Qatar
ARE	United Arab Emirates	DZA	Algeria	KOR	Korea, Republic of	ROM	Romania
ARG	Argentina	ECU	Ecuador	KWT	Kuwait	RUS	Russian Federation
ARM	Armenia	EGY	Egypt	LAO	Lao People's Democratic Rep.	RWA	Rwanda
ATG	Antigua and Barbuda	ERI	Eritrea	LBN	Lebanon	SAF	South Africa
AUS	Australia	ESH	Western Sahara	LBR	Liberia	SAU	Saudi Arabia
AUT	Austria	ESP	Spain	LBY	Libya	SDN	Sudan
AZE	Azerbaijan	EST	Estonia	LKA	Sri Lanka	SEN	Senegal
BDI	Burundi	ETH	Ethiopia	LSO	Lesotho	SGP	Singapore
BEL	Belgium-Lux	FIN	Finland	LTU	Lithuania	SLE	Sierra Leone
BEN	Benin	FJI	Fiji	LUX	Luxemburg	SLV	El Salvador
BFA	Burkina Faso	FRA	France	LVA	Latvia	SOM	Somalia
BGD	Bangladesh	fzz	FREE ZONES	MAC	Macau	STP	Sao Tome and Principe
BGR	Bulgaria	GAB	Gabon	MAR	Morocco	SUR	Suriname
BHR	Bahrain	GBR	United Kingdom	MDA	Moldova, Republic of	SVK	Slovakia
BHS	Bahamas	GEO	Georgia	MDG	Madagascar	SVN	Slovenia
BIH	Bosnia and Herzegovina	GHA	Ghana	MDV	Maldives	SWE	Sweden
BLR	Belarus	GIB	Gibraltar	MEX	Mexico	SWZ	Swaziland
BLZ	Belize	GIN	Guinea	MHL	Marshall Islands	SYC	Seychelles
BMU	Bermuda	GMB	Gambia	MLI	Mali	SYR	Syrian Arab Republic
BOL	Bolivia	GNB	Guinea-Bissau	MLT	Malta	TCD	Chad
BRA	Brazil	GNQ	Equatorial Guinea	MMR	Myanmar	TGO	Togo
BRB	Barbados	GRC	Greece	MNG	Mongolia	THA	Thailand
BRN	Brunei Darussalam	GRD	Grenada	MOZ	Mozambique	TJK	Tajikistan
BTN	Bhutan	GRL	Greenland	MRT	Mauritania	TKM	Turkmenistan
bun	BUNKERS	GTM	Guatemala	MUS	Mauritius	TON	Tonga
BWA	Botswana	GUF	French Guiana	MWI	Malawi	TTO	Trinidad and Tobago
CAF	Central African Rep.	GUM	Guam	MYS	Malaysia	TUN	Tunisia
CAN	Canada	GUY	Guyana	NAM	Namibia	TUR	Turkey
CHE	Switzerland	HKG	Hong Kong	NCL	New Caledonia	TWN	Taiwan (PoC) and Other Asia
CHL	Chile	HND	Honduras	NER	Niger	TZA	Tanzania
CHN	China	HRV	Croatia	nes	Areas not otherwise specified	UGA	Uganda
CIV	Côte d'Ivoire	HTI	Haiti	NGA	Nigeria	UKR	Ukraine
CMR	Cameroon	HUN	Hungary	NIC	Nicaragua	URY	Uruguay
COD	Congo, Dem. Rep.	IDN	Indonesia	NLD	Netherlands	USA	United States of America
COG	Congo	IND	India	NOR	Norway	UZB	Uzbekistan
COK	Cook Islands	IRL	Ireland	NPL	Nepal	VEN	Venezuela
COL	Colombia	IRN	Iran, Islamic Republic of	NZL	New Zealand	VNM	Viet Nam
COM	Comoros	IRQ	Iraq	OMN	Oman	VUT	Vanuatu
CPV	Cape Verde	ISL	Iceland	PAK	Pakistan	YEM	Yemen , Rep.
CRI	Costa Rica	ISR	Israel	PAN	Panama	YUG	Yugoslavia
CUB	Cuba	ITA	Italy	PER	Peru	ZAF	Southern African Customs Union
CYM	Cayman Islands	JAM	Jamaica	PHL	Philippines	ZMB	Zambia
CYP	Cyprus	JOR	Jordan	PNG	Papua New Guinea	ZWE	Zimbabwe
CZE	Czech Republic	JPN	Japan	POL	Poland		

Algeria

Key Indicators

Surface area (thousand sq. km.)	2,382
Population (millions), 2001	30.7
Population (average annual percent growth), 1980–2000	2.4 %
Life expectancy at birth, 2000	
Male (years)	69
Female (years)	73
Adult illiteracy rate (percent), 2000	
Male	24 %
Female	43 %
Gross tertiary enrollment ratio, 1998 or most recent year	15 %

Gross domestic product (US$ billion), 2001	54.9
Gross domestic product (average annual percent growth), 1990–2000	1.9 %
Gross national income per capita (US$, PPP), 2000	5,040
Growth of output (average annual percent growth), 1990–2000	
Agriculture	3.6 %
Industry	1.8 %
Manufacturing	-2.1 %
Services	1.9 %
Inflation (annual percentage change), 2001	4.1 %

Unemployment (percent of total labor force), 2001	28.5 %
Gross national savings rate (percent of GDP), 2001	34.4 %
Gross capital formation (percent of GDP), 2000	23.8 %
Household final consumption (percent of GDP), 2000	41.7 %

Current government revenue (ex grants, percent of GDP), 2001	32.7 %
Total government expenditure (percent of GDP), 2001	31.1 %
Overall budget deficit/surplus (percent of GDP), 2001	1.6 %
Highest marginal tax rate, 2001	
Individual	50 %
Corporate	30 %

Money and quasi money (annual percent growth), 2000	13.2 %
Domestic credit provided by the banking sector (percent of GDP), 2000	32 %

Stock market capitalization (US$ million), end 2001	—

Exports of goods (US$ million), 2001	19,070
Imports of goods (US$ million), 2001	10,166
Net energy imports (percent of commercial energy use), 1999[2]	-405 %
Current account balance (percent of GDP), 2001	12.3 %
Foreign direct investment inward stock (US$ million), 2000	1,407
Foreign direct investment (percent of gross capital formation), 2000	0.1 %
Total international reserves minus gold (US$ million), end 2001	18,081.0
Total international reserves minus gold (months of import coverage), 2001	21.3
Total foreign debt (US$ million), 2001	22,789
Long-term debt (US$ million), 2001	20,931
Total debt service (percent of GDP), 2001	8.7 %
Total foreign debt service paid (percent of exports of goods), 2001	25.2 %
Sovereign long-term foreign debt ratings, July 2002	
Moody's	—
Standard and Poors	—
Real effective exchange rate (1997=100), 2001[3]	88.8

Sources: The Heritage Foundation 2002 Index of Economic Freedom; World Development Indicators 2002; IMF International Financial Statistics 2002; IMF World Economic Outlook Database, April 2002; Economist Intelligence Unit; UNCTAD FDI Statistics.

[2]A minus sign indicates that the country is a net energy exporter

[3]Values greater (less) than 100 indicate appreciation (depreciation)

Exchange Rate and Capital Restrictions
Algeria

Exchange rate arrangements

Currency	Algerian Dinar
Exchange rate structure	Unitary
Classification	Managed floating
Exchange tax	No
Exchange subsidy	No
Forward exchange market	Yes

Controls on current payments and transfers

	Controls in place?
Arrangements for payments and receipts	
Bilateral payments arrangements	
Payments arrears	
Controls on Payments for invisible transactions and current transfers	●
Proceeds from exports and/or invisible transactions	
Repatriation requirements	●
Surrender requirements	●

Capital controls

	Controls in place?
Capital market securities	●
Money market instruments	●
Collective investment securities	▲
Derivatives and other instruments	●
Commercial credits	●
Financial credits	●
Guarantees, sureties, and financial backup facilities	●
Direct investment	●
Liquidation of direct investment	
Real estate transactions	●
Personal capital movements	—
Provisions specific to commercial banks and other credit institutions	●
Provisions specific to institutional investors	

● = The specific practice is a feature of the exchange system and a control is in place.
▲ = The specific practice is not regulated.
— = Data not available.
Source: IMF Annual Report on Exchange Arrangements and Exchange Restrictions 2001

Real effective exchange rate

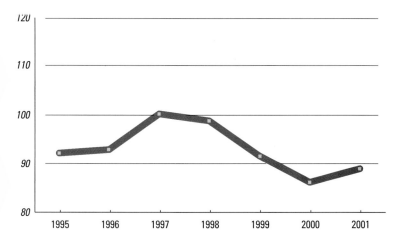

Index Numbers (1997=100): Period Averages
A higher (lower) exchange rate indicates an appreciation (depreciation) of the currency.

Source: Economist Intelligence Unit

Export Profile Table of Algeria

RANK	HS Code and Product Label		Exports 2000	Export Growth, 1996–2000 % per annum		World Trade Growth, 1996–2000 % per annum	Share in World
			US$ m	value	quantity	value	%
	All products		22,031	14	—	4	0
11	080410	Dates, fresh or dried	15	-28	-13	-1	9
27	151620	Vegetable fats and oils and their fractions	3	—	—	-3	0
28	220421	Grape wines	3	-6	4	5	0
8	251020	Natural calcium phosphates, aluminum calcium phosphates, etc.	21	0	-83	-5	9
4	270799	Oils and other products of high temperature coal tar distillation, etc.	190	10	6	5	17
1	2709	Crude petroleum oils	9,254	10	4	8	2
3	2710	Non-crude petroleum oils	3,146	15	8	7	4.3
2	2711	Petroleum gases	9,017	17	11	7	7.4
7	280429	Rare gases	21	20	22	10	8
5	2814	Ammonia	56	15	10	-4	2.9
12	2901	Ethylene & propene (propylene)	14			10	0
6	2902	Cyclic hydrocarbons	33	40	30	11	0.1
14	290511	Methanol (methyl alcohol)	12	-4	8	4	1
19	310230	Ammonium nitrate	7	—	—	-6	1
17	310280	Mixtures of urea and ammonium nitrate	8	65	83	-5	2
24	340111	Toilet soaps, etc.	5	—	—	-1	0
18	410512	Sheep or lamb skin leather, otherwise pre-tanned	7	4	11	-11	4
26	410519	Sheep or lamb skin leather, tanned or retanned, other	4	6	15	4	2
22	450200	Natural cork, debacked or roughly squared or in rectangular blocks, etc.	5	118	135	10	14
20	450310	Corks and stoppers, natural cork	6	23	27	7	1
13	720110	Non-alloy pig iron containing by weight 0,5 % or less of phosphorus	13	-31	-25	-3	1
10	720712	Semi-finished products of iron or non-alloy steel, rectangular or cross section (containing less than 0.25% carbon)	17	—	—	5	0
15	720719	Semi-finished products of iron or non-alloy steel (containing less than 0.25% carbon)	11	—	—	-1	2
23	720890	Flat-rolled products of iron or non-alloy steel, of a width of 600 mm or more, hot-rolled, not clad, plated or coated, other	5	11	15	-4	1
16	721090	Flat-rolled products of iron or non-alloy steel, of a width of 600 mm or more, clad, plated or coated	8	—	—	0	3
25	740400	Waste and scrap, copper or copper alloy	4	-21	-8	-5	0
9	790111	Zinc not alloyed unwrought	20	-8	-8	4	1
21	870190	Wheeled tractors	5	—	—	-6	0

Notes: Based on Algerian trade statistics.

Export Profile Chart for Selected Key Products

Algeria

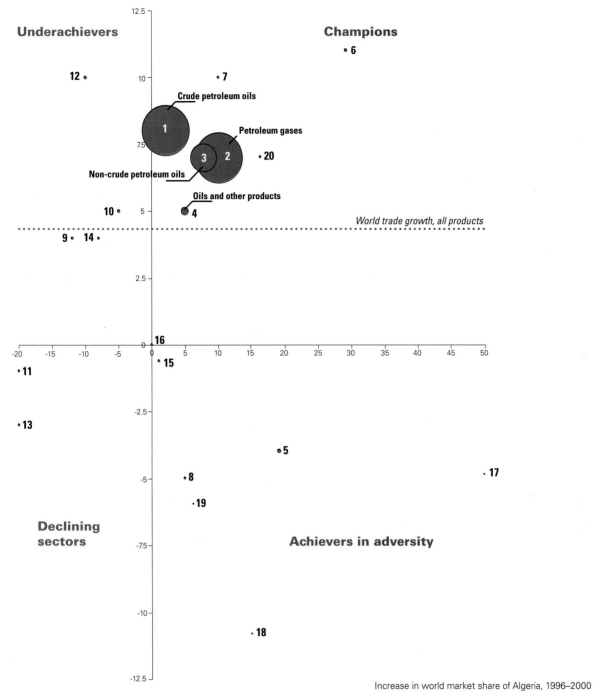

Underachievers

Champions

• 6

12 • 10 • 7

Crude petroleum oils

1

Petroleum gases

3 2 • 20

Non-crude petroleum oils

Oils and other products

10 • 5 • 4

World trade growth, all products

9 • 14 •

2.5

16

-20 -15 -10 -5 0 5 10 15 20 25 30 35 40 45 50

•11 • 15

-2.5

•13

• 5

-5 • 8 • 17

•19

**Declining
sectors**

-7.5

Achievers in adversity

-10

• 18

-12.5

Increase in world market share of Algeria, 1996–2000

World trade growth, % per annum, 1996–2000

Key

1	2709	**Crude petroleum oils**
2	2711	**Petroleum gases**
3	2710	**Non-crude petroleum oils**
4	270799	**Oils and other products**
5	2814	**Ammonia**
6	2902	**Cyclic hydrocarbons**
7	280429	**Rare gases**
8	251020	**Natural calcium phosphates, etc.**
9	790111	**Zinc not alloyed unwrought**
10	720712	**Semi-finished products of iron or non-alloy steel**

11	080410	**Dates, fresh or dried**
12	2901	**Ethylene & propene (propylene)**
13	720110	**Non-alloy pig iron**
14	290511	**Methanol (methyl alcohol)**
15	720719	**Semi-finished products of iron or non-alloy steel**
16	721090	**Flat rolled products of iron or non-alloy steel**
17	310280	**Mixtures of urea and ammonium nitrate**
18	410512	**Sheep or lamb skin leather, pre-tanned**
19	310230	**Ammonium nitrate**
20	450310	**Corks and stoppers, natural cork**

Note: The area of the circles is proportional to the export turnover
Source: ITC calculations based on COMTRADE statistics.

Bahrain

Key Indicators

Surface area (thousand sq. km.)	0.6
Population (millions), 2001	0.7
Population (average annual percent growth), 1980–2000	—
Life expectancy at birth, 2000	
Male (years)	71
Female (years)	76
Adult illiteracy rate (percent), 2000	
Male	9 %
Female	17 %
Gross tertiary enrollment ratio, 1998 or most recent year	26 %
Gross domestic product (US$ billion), 2001	8.0
Gross domestic product (average annual percent growth), 1990–2000	4.8 %
Gross national income per capita (US$, PPP), 2000	—
Growth of output (average annual percent growth), 1990–2000	
Agriculture	—
Industry	—
Manufacturing	—
Services	—
Inflation (annual percentage change), 2001	-0.2 %
Unemployment (percent of total labor force), 2000	4.0 %
Gross national savings rate (percent of GDP), 2001	22.9 %
Gross capital formation (percent of GDP), 2000	16.8 %
Household final consumption (percent of GDP), 2000	47.1 %
Current government revenue (ex grants, percent of GDP), 2001	28.3 %
Total government expenditure (percent of GDP), 2001	34.3 %
Overall budget deficit/surplus (percent of GDP), 2001	-6.0 %
Highest marginal tax rate, 2001	
Individual	0 %
Corporate	0 %
Money and quasi money (annual percent growth), 2000	10.2 %
Domestic credit provided by the banking sector (percent of GDP), 2000	63.3 %
Stock market capitalization (US$ million), end 2001	6,601
Exports of goods (US$ million), 2001	5,545
Imports of goods (US$ million), 2001	4,263
Net energy imports (percent of commercial energy use), 1999[2]	-19 %
Current account balance (percent of GDP), 2001	1.3 %
Foreign direct investment inward stock (US$ million), 2000	5,908
Foreign direct investment (percent of gross capital formation), 2000	—
Total international reserves minus gold (US$ million), end 2001	1,684.0
Total international reserves minus gold (months of import coverage), 2001	4.7
Total foreign debt (US$ million), 2001	2,903
Long-term debt (US$ million), 2001	2,202
Total debt service (percent of GDP), 2001	6.0 %
Total foreign debt service paid (percent of exports of goods), 2001	9.2 %
Sovereign long-term foreign debt ratings, July 2002	
Moody's	Ba1[1]
Standard and Poors	—
Real effective exchange rate (1997=100), 2001[3]	96.4

Sources: The Heritage Foundation 2002 Index of Economic Freedom; World Development Indicators 2002; IMF International Financial Statistics 2002; IMF World Economic Outlook Database, April 2002; International Labor Office LABORSTA; Economist Intelligence Unit; UNCTAD FDI Statistics.

[1]Issuer's rating

[2]A minus sign indicates that the country is a net energy exporter

[3]Values greater (less) than 100 indicate appreciation (depreciation)

Exchange rate arrangements

Currency	Bahrain Dinar
Exchange rate structure	Unitary
Classification	Conventional pegged
Exchange tax	No
Exchange subsidy	No
Forward exchange market	Yes

Controls on current payments and transfers

	Controls in place?
Arrangements for payments and receipts	
Bilateral payments arrangements	
Payments arrears	
Controls on Payments for invisible transactions and current transfers	
Proceeds from exports and/or invisible transactions	
Repatriation requirements	
Surrender requirements	

Capital controls

	Controls in place?
Capital market securities	●
Money market instruments	
Collective investment securities	
Derivatives and other instruments	
Commercial credits	
Financial credits	
Guarantees, sureties, and financial backup facilities	
Direct investment	●
Liquidation of direct investment	
Real estate transactions	●
Personal capital movements	
Provisions specific to commercial banks and other credit institutions	●
Provisions specific to institutional investors	

● = The specific practice is a feature of the exchange system and a control is in place.

▲ = The specific practice is not regulated.

—= Data not available.

Source: IMF Annual Report on Exchange Arrangements and Exchange Restrictions 2001

Real effective exchange rate

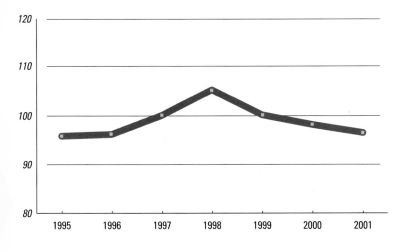

Index Numbers (1997=100): Period Averages
A higher (lower) exchange rate indicates an appreciation (depreciation) of the currency.

Source: Economist Intelligence Unit

Export Profile Table of Bahrain

RANK	HS Code and Product Label	Exports 2000 US$ m	Net Exports 2000 US$ m	Export Growth, 1996–2000 % per annum value	Export Growth, 1996–2000 % per annum quantity	World Trade Growth, 1996–2000 % per annum value	World Trade Growth, 1996–2000 % per annum quantity	Share in World %	Leading Markets 1st	%	Leading Markets 2nd	%
	ALL GOODS	5,622										
	ALL GOODS (WTO)	5,710	1,098									
27	0306 Crustaceans	8	7	-10		3.1	2.8	0.1	KOR	56	LAO	14
21	1515 Fixed vegetable fats and oils	13	6	8		0.0	1.3	1.2	SAU	49	ARE	22
25	1905 Bread, pastry, cakes, biscuits and other bakers' wares, etc.	9	-8	5					SAU	98	LBR	2
4	2601 Iron ores and concentrates; including roasted iron pyrites	197	125	1		-1.2	0.7	1.6	IDN	18	JPN	17
2	2709 Crude petroleum oils	1,435	-617	8		7.2	1.0	0.4	nes	100		
1	2710 Non-crude petroleum oils	2,556	2,547	11		6.9	4.3	1.9	nes	100	ARE	0
18	2814 Ammonia, anhydrous or in aqueous solution	16	16	-10		-4.4	1.2	0.8	THA	38	IND	30
12	2905 Acyclic alcohols and their halogenated, sulphonated, nitrated or nitrosated derivatives	39	39	-1		2.0	7.0	0.4	USA	41	LAO	21
8	3102 Mineral or chemical fertilizers, nitrogenous	69	68	120		-7.5	0.2	1.3	USA	49	NZL	18
29	3917 Tubes, pipes and hoses and fittings of plastics	7	2	-6		4.1	9.6	0.1	SAU	57	ARE	20
23	3923 Articles for the conveyance or packing of goods, of plastics, etc.	12	4	15		6.4	8.3	0.1	SAU	52	IND	25
16	4803 Household or sanitary paper, etc.	18	16	12		0.6	5.3	1.4	SAU	62	NRU	24
30	4818 Toilet paper and similar paper, used for household or sanitary purposes, etc.	6	-7	12		4.5	8.0	0.1	SAU	71	YEM	7
38	4819 Cartons, boxes, cases, bags and other packing containers, of paper, etc.	3	-3	87		2.3	4.7	0.0	SAU	91	JOR	2
20	5205 Cotton yarn (other than sewing thread), not for retail sale	13	-22	95		-0.3	4.7	0.2	USA	62	LBN	16
19	5208 Woven fabrics of cotton, weighing no more than 200 grams per meter squared	16	-16	65		-5.4	-1.2	0.2	USA	55	NLD	21
10	5209 Woven fabric of cotton, weighing over 200 grams per meter squared	43	8	27		0.8	5.9	0.6	NLD	30	ARB	25
11	6104 Women's suits, dresses, skirts and shorts (other than swimwear), knitted or crocheted	41	39	2		1.0	5.5	0.7	USA	97	SAU	2
31	6105 Men's shirts, knitted or crocheted	6	5	-10		-2.0	0.6	0.1	USA	100	cat	0
40	6108 Women's or girls' slips, panties, pyjamas, bathrobes etc., knitted or crocheted	3	1			5.4	8.3	0.0	USA	88	CAN	10
13	6203 Men's or boys' suits, jackets, trousers and shorts (other than swimwear), etc.	29	23	42		3.5	8.6	0.1	USA	98	OMN	1
5	6204 Women's or girls' suits, jackets, dresses skirts and shorts (other than swimwear)	146	139	33		4.4	7.9	0.5	USA	97	OMN	2
35	6205 Men's or boys' shirts	4	2			0.3	3.2	0.0	USA	99	cat	1
14	6206 Women's or girls' blouses, shirts and shirt-blouses	27	25	5		-1.1	3.2	0.4	USA	100	cat	0
39	6601 Umbrellas and sun umbrellas	3	3			0.1	4.3	0.2	SGP	84	SAU	14
26	7204 Ferrous waste and scrap; remelting scrap ingots of iron or steel	8	8			-0.8	5.8	0.1	IND	76	ARE	6
24	7303 Tubes, pipes and hollow profiles, of cast iron	11	8			-5.2	-0.8	2.3	SAU	65	IND	17
33	7304 Tubes, pipes and hollow profiles, seamless, iron or steel	5	-5			-6.5	-2.5	0.1	IND	77	SAU	18
6	7601 Unwrought aluminum	80	79	-5		3.3	4.3	0.3	JPN	24	TWN	24
36	7602 Aluminum waste and scrap	3	3			6.7	6.4	0.1	IND	38	ROM	19
17	7603 Aluminum powders and flakes	17	16			4.8	2.6	6.7	JPN	32	DEU	21
3	7604 Aluminum bars, rods and profiles	532	526	2		6.3	8.9	11.7	TWN	22	SAU	19
9	7605 Aluminum wire	64	63	6		4.7	6.7	5.7	SAU	56	SGP	8
7	7606 Aluminum plates, sheets and strip, exceeding 0.2 mm in thickness	79	77	13		3.7	6.1	0.7	ARB	26	NLD	16
32	7607 Aluminum foil not exceeding 0.2 mm in thickness	5	3			1.9	6.1	0.1	SAU	57	ARE	28
28	7616 Articles of aluminum, other	8	5			5.5	8.4	0.2	DEU	43	SAU	13
15	8415 Air conditioning machines*	24	-14	8		3.0	10.9	0.2	SAU	38	LBR	19
22	8708 Parts and accessories of large motor vehicles, tractors, etc.*	12	-2	-1		5.9	11.4	0.0	NLD	36	NOR	33
34	9403 Other furniture and parts thereof	5	-19			8.2	8.7	0.0	SAU	44	LBR	25
37	9405 Lamps and lighting fittings	3	-7			8.6	11.8	0.0	SAU	35	LBR	21
	Other services, credit	79	-19	3		4.0		0.0				
	Transport services, credit	281	-135	-3		1.5		0.1				
	Travel, credit	469	300	15		1.9		0.1				

Notes: The indicators are based on Bahrain's trade statistics except for the export growth rate, which is derived from mirror estimates.

*May include re-exports or ships registration.

Export Profile Chart for Selected Key Products

Bahrain

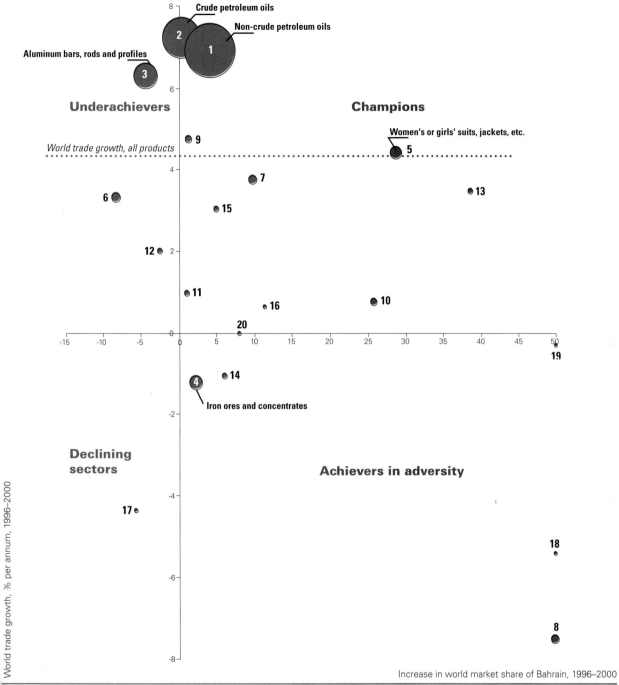

World trade growth, % per annum, 1996–2000

Increase in world market share of Bahrain, 1996–2000

Key

1 2710 **Non-crude petroleum oils**
2 2709 **Crude petroleum oils**
3 7604 **Aluminum bars, rods and profiles**
4 2601 **Iron ores and concentrates**
5 6204 **Women's or girls' suits, jackets, etc.**
6 7601 **Unwrought alumimum**
7 7606 **Aluminum plates, sheets and strip**
8 3102 **Mineral or chemical fertilizers**
9 7605 **Aluminum wire**
10 5209 **Woven fabrics of cotton,weighing over 200 grams**

11 6104 **Women's suits, dresses, knitted or crocheted**
12 2905 **Acyclic alcohols and their derivatives**
13 6203 **Men's or boys' suits, jackets, trousers, etc.**
14 6206 **Women's or girls' blouses, shirts and shirt-blouses**
15 8415 **Air conditioning machines***
16 4803 **Household or sanitary paper, etc.**
17 2814 **Ammonia, anhydrous or in aqueous solution**
18 5208 **Woven fabrics of cotton, weighing no more than 200 grams**
19 5205 **Cotton yarn, not for retail sale**
20 1515 **Fixed vegetable fats and oils**

Note: The area of the circles correponds to the export value of the product group for Bahrain.
Source: ITC calculations based on COMTRADE statistics.

Egypt

Key Indicators

Surface area (thousand sq. km.)	1,001
Population (millions), 2001	65.3
Population (average annual percent growth), 1980–2000	2.2 %
Life expectancy at birth, 2000	
Male (years)	66
Female (years)	69
Adult illiteracy rate (percent), 2000	
Male	33 %
Female	56 %
Gross tertiary enrollment ratio, 1998 or most recent year	39 %

Gross domestic product (US$ billion), 2001	96.8
Gross domestic product (average annual percent growth), 1990–2000	4.6 %
Gross national income per capita (US$, PPP), 2000	3,670
Growth of output (average annual percent growth), 1990–2000	
Agriculture	3.1 %
Industry	4.9 %
Manufacturing	6.3 %
Services	4.5 %
Inflation (annual percentage change), 2001	2.4 %

Unemployment (percent of total labor force), 1997	12.0 %
Gross national savings rate (percent of GDP), 2001	24.2 %
Gross capital formation (percent of GDP), 2000	23.9 %
Household final consumption (percent of GDP), 2000	73.0 %

Current government revenue (ex grants, percent of GDP), 2001	25.0 %
Total government expenditure (percent of GDP), 2001	30.6 %
Overall budget deficit/surplus (percent of GDP), 2001	-5.6 %
Highest marginal tax rate, 2001	
Individual	40 %
Corporate	40 %

Money and quasi money (annual percent growth), 2000	11.6 %
Domestic credit provided by the banking sector (percent of GDP), 2000	100.2 %

Stock market capitalization (US$ million), end 2001	24,168

Exports of goods (US$ million), 2001	4,123
Imports of goods (US$ million), 2001	12,780
Net energy imports (percent of commercial energy use), 1999[2]	-31 %
Current account balance (percent of GDP), 2001	-0.1 %
Foreign direct investment inward stock (US$ million), 2000	19,005
Foreign direct investment (percent of gross capital formation), 2000	5.2 %
Total international reserves minus gold (US$ million), end 2001	12,926.0
Total international reserves minus gold (months of import coverage), 2001	12.1
Total foreign debt (US$ million), 2001	28,625
Long-term debt (US$ million), 2001	24,934
Total debt service (percent of GDP), 2001	2.5 %
Total foreign debt service paid (percent of exports of goods), 2001	52.3 %
Sovereign long-term foreign debt ratings, July 2002	
Moody's	Ba1
Standard and Poors	BB+
Real effective exchange rate (1997=100), 2001[3]	102.8

Sources: The Heritage Foundation 2002 Index of Economic Freedom; World Development Indicators 2002; IMF International Financial Statistics 2002; IMF World Economic Outlook Database, April 2002; Economist Intelligence Unit; UNCTAD FDI Statistics.

[2]A minus sign indicates that the country is a net energy exporter

[3]Values greater (less) than 100 indicate appreciation (depreciation)

Exchange Rate and Capital Restrictions

Egypt

Exchange rate arrangements

Currency	Egyptian Pound
Exchange rate structure	Multiple
Classification	Pegged/ horizontal bands
Exchange tax	No
Exchange subsidy	No
Forward exchange market	Yes

Controls on current payments and transfers

	Controls in place?
Arrangements for payments and receipts	
Bilateral payments arrangements	●
Payments arrears	●
Controls on Payments for invisible transactions and current transfers	
Proceeds from exports and/or invisible transactions	
Repatriation requirements	
Surrender requirements	

Capital controls

	Controls in place?
Capital market securities	●
Money market instruments	
Collective investment securities	
Derivatives and other instruments	
Commercial credits	●
Financial credits	
Guarantees, sureties, and financial backup facilities	
Direct investment	●
Liquidation of direct investment	
Real estate transactions	●
Personal capital movements	
Provisions specific to commercial banks and other credit institutions	●
Provisions specific to institutional investors	●

● = The specific practice is a feature of the exchange system and a control is in place.

▲ = The specific practice is not regulated.

— = Data not available.

Source: IMF Annual Report on Exchange Arrangements and Exchange Restrictions 2001

Real effective exchange rate

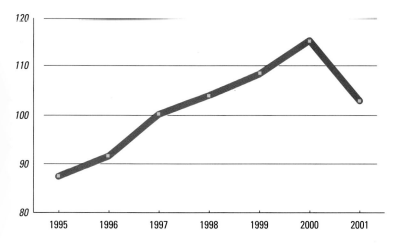

Index Numbers (1997=100): Period Averages
A higher (lower) exchange rate indicates an appreciation (depreciation) of the currency.

Source: Economist Intelligence Unit

Export Profile Table of Egypt

RANK	HS Code and Product Label	Exports 2000 US$ m	Net Exports 2000 US$ m	Export Growth, 1996–2000 % per annum value	Export Growth, 1996–2000 % per annum quantity	World Trade Growth, 1996–2000 % per annum value	World Trade Growth, 1996–2000 % per annum quantity	Share in World %	Leading Markets 1st	Leading Markets %	Leading Markets 2nd	Leading Markets %
	ALL GOODS	5,274		-1								
	ALL GOODS (WTO)	4,689	-9,321									
30	0701 Potatoes	28	4	-15		-1.7	1.4	2.2	ITA	40	GBR	32
40	0708 Leguminous vegetables, shelled or unshelled, fresh or chilled	22	22	-1		3.5	5.6	4.5	NLD	41	ITA	13
20	0805 Citrus fruit, fresh or dried	47	47			-4.5	0.5	1.0	SAU	72	HKG	8
25	1006 Rice	38	36	10		-6.1	3.9	0.8	TUR	52	ROM	16
35	1703 Sugar molasses	25	25	2		-15.9	-3.6	5.3	ESP	20	IDN	17
22	2106 Food preparations, other	44	18			-0.4	7.6	0.6	SAU	46	TUN	24
17	2515 Marble, travertine, ecaussine, etc., whether or not roughly trimmed or merely cut, etc.	57	46	104		7.9	12.9	12.2	CHN	82	ITA	12
18	2704 Coke and semi-coke of coal, lignite or peat, whether or not agglomerated; retort carbon	51	46	2		-0.9	2.7	2.3	FRA	32	TUR	22
1	2709 Crude petroleum oils	1,192	1,192	-10		7.2	1.0	0.3	ITA	47	GBR	17
2	2710 Non-crude petroleum oils	786	660	4		6.9	4.3	0.6	USA	15	FRA	14
32	2711 Petroleum gases	26	5	335		7.1	2.3	0.0	ITA	58	TUR	20
19	2803 Carbon (carbon blacks and other forms of carbon, other)	50	45	39		1.3	3.9	4.6	FRA	34	ESP	16
33	3004 Medicaments of mixed or unmixed products for therapeutic or prophylactic uses, in dosage	25	-198			14.2	10.2	0.0	SAU	50	ROM	23
13	3102 Mineral or chemical fertilizers, nitrogenous	78	73	96		-7.5	0.2	1.4	USA	30	FRA	30
38	3922 Baths, shower-baths, wash-basins, bidet and similar sanitary ware, of plastic	23	21	15		2.5	7.2	1.8	FRA	33	DEU	30
27	4104 Leather of bovine or equine animals	35	33	52		-0.2	2.0	0.3	ITA	49	ESP	35
3	5201 Cotton, not carded or combed	166	166	18		-13.7	-5.1	2.9	ITA	31	TUR	15
4	5205 Cotton yarn (other than sewing thread), not for retail sale	156	150	-8		-0.3	4.7	2.4	ITA	36	USA	15
24	5208 Woven fabrics of cotton, weighing no more than 200 grams per meter squared	39	20	-20		-5.4	-1.2	0.6	USA	36	ITA	25
16	5702 Carpets and other woven textile floor covering, including hand-woven rugs	61	61	11		-1.5	4.2	3.5	USA	65	GBR	12
34	5703 Carpets and other textile floor covering, tufted	25	24	9		-2.0	2.6	0.7	JPN	17	GBR	10
36	6104 Women's or girl's suits, dresses, skirt and shorts (other than swimwear), knitted or crocheted	25	4	8		1.0	5.5	0.4	USA	71	DEU	10
26	6105 Men's or boys' shirts, knitted or crocheted	36	34	-2		-2.0	0.6	0.8	USA	48	GBR	28
29	6107 Men's or boys' underpants, nightshirts, pyjamas, bathrobes, etc., knitted or crocheted	33	30	23		5.0	7.9	1.3	GBR	68	DEU	8
21	6108 Women's or girls' slips, panties, pyjamas, bathrobes, etc., knitted or crocheted	47	19	46		5.4	8.3	0.8	GBR	65	USA	18
8	6109 T-shirts, singlets and other vests, knitted or crocheted	107	99	7		9.9	11.5	0.8	DEU	22	USA	21
11	6110 Jerseys, pullovers, cardigans, waistcoats, etc., knitted or crocheted	81	71	15		7.9	9.5	0.3	USA	76	GBR	9
7	6203 Men's or boys' suits, jackets, trousers and shorts (other than swimwear), etc.	114	56	14		3.5	8.6	0.5	USA	75	GBR	12
6	6204 Women's or girls' suits, jackets, dresses skirts and shorts (other than swimwear), etc.	121	85	16		4.4	7.9	0.4	USA	91	ITA	6
23	6205 Men's or boys' shirts	39	20	-7		0.3	3.2	0.4	USA	75	FRA	10
9	6302 Bed, table, toilet and kitchen linens	94	93	7		4.2	7.6	1.4	GBR	30	USA	20
39	6910 Ceramic sink, wash basin, bath, bidet, urinals and similar sanitary fixtures	23	20	10		4.3	8.1	1.4	GBR	32	FRA	21
15	7208 Flat-rolled products of iron or non-alloy steel, of a width of 600 mm or more, hot rolled	62	25	76		-2.1	2.3	0.4	ITA	54	ESP	17
31	7213 Bars and rods, hot-rolled, in irregularly wound coils, of iron or non-alloy steel	28	27	-1		-4.0	1.9	0.7	USA	33	ESP	25
14	7601 Unwrought aluminum	74	73	-12		3.3	4.3	0.3	ITA	32	ESP	14
10	7606 Aluminum plates, sheets and strip, of a thickness exceeding 0.2 mm	82	75	82		3.7	6.1	0.7	ITA	34	DEU	19
12	8411 Turbo-jets*	79	-93	12		12.7	10.2	0.2	GBR	66	DEU	29
37	8544 Insulated wire or cable	24	-88	222		6.8	7.7	0.1	GBR	68	BEL	11
28	9403 Other furniture and parts thereof	35	0	10		8.2	8.7	0.1	USA	58	ITA	8
5	9999 Special Transaction Trade	126	-107	24		8.1		0.1	USA	91	GBR	3
	Other services, credit	2,697	-1,180	-4		4.0		0.4				
	Transport services, credit	2,645	433	0		1.5		0.8				
	Travel, credit	4,345	3,273	7		1.9		1.0				

Notes: The indicators are based on the partner countries' export statistics (mirror estimates).

*May include re-exports or ships registration.

Export Profile Chart for Selected Key Products

Egypt

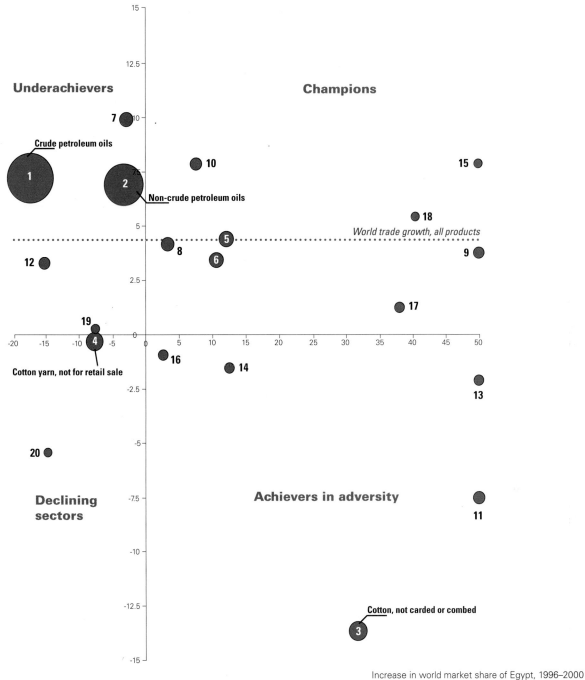

Underachievers

Champions

7 10

Crude petroleum oils

1

2

10

15

Non-crude petroleum oils

18

5 World trade growth, all products

8

12

6

9

17

19

4

16 14

Cotton yarn, not for retail sale

13

20

Declining sectors

Achievers in adversity

11

Cotton, not carded or combed

3

World trade growth, % per annum, 1996–2000

Increase in world market share of Egypt, 1996–2000

Key

1 2709 Crude petroleum oils	11 3102 Mineral or chemical fertilizers, nitrogenous
2 2710 Non-crude petroleum oils	12 7601 Unwrought alumimum
3 5201 Cotton, not carded or combed	13 7208 Flat-rolled products of iron or non-alloy steel
4 5205 Cotton yarn, not for retail sale	14 5702 Carpets and other woven textile floor covering
5 6204 Women's or girls' suits, jackets, etc.	15 2515 Marble, travertine, ecaussine etc.
6 6203 Men's or boys' suits, jackets, trousers, etc.	16 2704 Coke and semi-coke of coal, lignite or peat
7 6109 T-shirts, singlets and other vests	17 2803 Carbon (carbon blacks and other forms of carbon)
8 6302 Bed, table, toilet and kitchen linens	18 6108 Women's or girls' slips, panties, pyjamas, etc.
9 7606 Aluminum plates, sheets and strip	19 6205 Men's or boys' shirts
10 6110 Jerseys, pullovers, cardigans, waistcoats, etc.	20 5208 Woven fabrics of cotton

Note: The area of the circles is proportional to the export turnover
Source: ITC calculations based on COMTRADE statistics.

Part 2   Country Profiles and Data Presentation

Jordan

Key Indicators

Surface area (thousand sq. km.)	89.2
Population (millions), 2001	5.2
Population (average annual percent growth), 1980–2000	4 %
Life expectancy at birth, 2000	
Male (years)	70
Female (years)	73
Adult illiteracy rate (percent), 2000	
Male	5 %
Female	16 %
Gross tertiary enrollment ratio, 1998 or most recent year	19 %

Gross domestic product (US$ billion), 2001	8.8
Gross domestic product (average annual percent growth), 1990–2000	5.0 %
Gross national income per capita (US$, PPP), 2000	3,950
Growth of output (average annual percent growth), 1990–2000	
Agriculture	-2 %
Industry	4.7 %
Manufacturing	5.4 %
Services	5.0 %
Inflation (annual percentage change), 2001	1.8 %

Unemployment (percent of total labor force), 2001	14.7 %
Gross national savings rate (percent of GDP), 2001	27.8 %
Gross capital formation (percent of GDP), 2000	20.3 %
Household final consumption (percent of GDP), 2000	80.7 %

Current government revenue (ex grants, percent of GDP), 2001	25.6 %
Total government expenditure (percent of GDP), 2001	32.6 %
Overall budget deficit/surplus (percent of GDP), 2001	-7.0 %
Highest marginal tax rate, 2001	
Individual	30 %
Corporate	35 %

Money and quasi money (annual percent growth), 2000	7.6 %
Domestic credit provided by the banking sector (percent of GDP), 2000	90.6 %

Stock market capitalization (US$ million), end 2001	6,314

Exports of goods (US$ million), 2001	2,293
Imports of goods (US$ million), 2001	4,806
Net energy imports (percent of commercial energy use), 1999	94 %
Current account balance (percent of GDP), 2001	0.6 %
Foreign direct investment inward stock (US$ million), 2000	1,771
Foreign direct investment (percent of gross capital formation), 2000	33.0 %
Total international reserves minus gold (US$ million), end 2001	3,062.2
Total international reserves minus gold (months of import coverage), 2001	7.6
Total foreign debt (US$ million), 2001	8,005
Long-term debt (US$ million), 2001	6,927
Total debt service (percent of GDP), 2001	10.4 %
Total foreign debt service paid (percent of exports of goods), 2001	40.5 %
Sovereign long-term foreign debt ratings, July 2002	
Moody's	Ba3
Standard and Poors	BB-
Real effective exchange rate (1997=100), 2001[3]	114.8

Sources: The Heritage Foundation 2002 Index of Economic Freedom; World Development Indicators 2002; IMF International Financial Statistics 2002; IMF World Economic Outlook Database, April 2002; Economist Intelligence Unit; UNCTAD FDI Statistics; Department of Statistics of Jordan.

[3]Values greater (less) than 100 indicate appreciation (depreciation)

Exchange Rate and Capital Restrictions

Jordan

Exchange rate arrangements

Currency	Jordan Dinar
Exchange rate structure	Unitary
Classification	Conventional pegged
Exchange tax	No
Exchange subsidy	No
Forward exchange market	Yes

Controls on current payments and transfers

	Controls in place?
Arrangements for payments and receipts	
Bilateral payments arrangements	●
Payments arrears	●
Controls on Payments for invisible transactions and current transfers	
Proceeds from exports and/or invisible transactions	
Repatriation requirements	
Surrender requirements	

Capital controls

	Controls in place?
Capital market securities	
Money market instruments	
Collective investment securities	
Derivatives and other instruments	
Commercial credits	
Financial credits	
Guarantees, sureties, and financial backup facilities	
Direct investment	●
Liquidation of direct investment	
Real estate transactions	●
Personal capital movements	
Provisions specific to commercial banks and other credit institutions	●
Provisions specific to institutional investors	

● = The specific practice is a feature of the exchange system and a control is in place.

▲ = The specific practice is not regulated.

— = Data not available.

Source: IMF Annual Report on Exchange Arrangements and Exchange Restrictions 2001

Real effective exchange rate

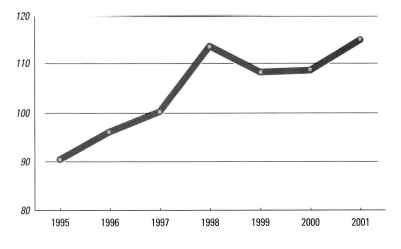

Index Numbers (1997=100): Period Averages
A higher (lower) exchange rate indicates an appreciation (depreciation) of the currency.

Source: Economist Intelligence Unit

Export Profile Table of Jordan

RANK	HS Code and Product Label	Exports 2000 US$ m	Net Exports 2000 US$ m	Export Growth, 1996–2000 % per annum value	quantity	World Trade Growth, 1996–2000 % per annum value	quantity	Share in World %	Leading Markets 1st	%	2nd	%
	ALL GOODS	928		-5								
	ALL GOODS (WTO)	1,897	-2,642									
39	0407 Birds' eggs, in shell	6	5	-23	-21.3	-6.9	1.1	0.6	IRQ	47	ARE	27
5	0702 Tomatoes	34	34	3		-1.3	-0.1	1.1	ARE	34	KWT	26
29	0704 Cabbages, cauliflowers, kohlrabi, kale and similar edible brassicas, fresh or chilled	8	8	10	11.2	-2.6	2.4	0.9	ARE	41	KWT	24
10	0707 Cucumbers and gherkins, fresh or chilled	15	15	-5		-1.5	-0.5	1.9	ARE	22	LBN	20
16	0709 Vegetables, fresh or chilled, other	13	13	5	0.1	2.7	5.2	0.3	LBN	25	KWT	17
30	0805 Citrus fruit, fresh or dried	7	-3	-28	-24.6	-4.5	0.5	0.2	SAU	33	KWT	23
27	1516 Animal or vegetable fats, oils and their fractions, hydrogenated, etc., not further prepared	8	6	-46	-12.6	-0.9	5.4	0.8	IRQ	85	SAU	8
28	2402 Cigars, cigarillos and cigarettes	8	-2	26	32.3	-3.7	0.5	0.1	nes	83	PAN	7
6	2510 Calcium and aluminum calcium phosphates, natural and phosphatic chalk	32	32	-31		-3.6	-4.0	3.0	TUR	25	THA	20
9	2523 Portland, aluminous and slag cement, supersulphate cement and similar hydraulic cements	17	17	-24	-24.6	0.5	3.2	0.4	EGY	33	SDN	31
25	2826 Fluorides, fluorosilicate, fluor aluminates and other complex fluorine salt	9	9	-4	3.3	4.4	3.5	1.5	ARE	62	EGY	23
18	2836 Carbonates; peroxocarbonates; commercial ammonium carbonate containing ammonium carbamate	12	12	3	7.7	0.4	5.1	0.6	SAU	30	ARE	24
2	3003 Medicaments consisting of two or more constituents, mixed together for therapeutic or prophylactic uses, in bulk	58	47	150	201.1	4.1	6.3	1.3	SAU	35	LBY	14
4	3004 Medicaments consisting of mixed or unmixed products for therapeutic or prophylactic uses, in dosage	41	-51	38	38.3	14.2	10.2	0.1	SAU	34	DZA	17
7	3102 Mineral or chemical fertilizers, nitrogenous	26	19	-28		-7.5	0.2	0.5	ETH	32	nes	26
1	3104 Mineral or chemical fertilizers, potassic	78	77	-9		1.9	0.4	2.0	IDN	14	PHL	11
33	3105 Mineral or chemical fertilizers containing nitrogen, phosphorus and potassium, etc.	7	2	-8		-4.4	0.7	0.1	SAU	50	LBN	13
40	3208 Paints and varnishes (including enamels and lacquers) based on synthetic polymers, etc.	5	4	57	72.2	1.9	4.9	0.1	ARE	26	nes	21
15	3808 Insecticides, fungicides, herbicides, etc. packed for retail sale	13	2	10	5.1	0.0	1.3	0.1	nes	57	SAU	16
36	3907 Polyacetals, other polyethers and epoxide resins, in primary forms, etc.	6	-2	-17	-14.5	4.8	8.9	0.0	nes	31	ARE	27
24	3917 Tubes, pipes and hoses and fittings of plastics	9	6	13	16.3	4.1	9.6	0.2	nes	40	TUN	14
14	3923 Articles for the conveyance or packing of goods, of plastics, etc.	13	5	30	28.6	6.4	8.3	0.1	nes	75	ISR	5
11	4202 Trunks, suitcases, camera cases, handbags, etc., of leather, plastic, textiles, etc.	15	11	153	148.1	2.1	8.9	0.1	USA	87	ISR	13
13	4803 Household or sanitary paper, etc.	14	14	3	2.9	0.6	5.3	1.1	SAU	66	ARE	18
12	4818 Toilet paper and similar paper, used for household or sanitary purposes, etc.	14	11	22	16.4	4.5	8.0	0.2	GBR	33	LBN	20
21	4819 Cartons, boxes, cases, bags and other packing containers, of paper, etc.	11	1	15	26.9	2.3	4.7	0.1	nes	49	SAU	26
32	4820 Registers, account books, notebooks, and other stationary articles of paper	7	6	32	8.5	4.3	6.9	0.3	nes	89	SAU	4
20	4901 Printed books, brochures, leaflets and similar printed matter	11	3	8	1.8	1.3	4.3	0.1	nes	82	LBY	8
38	5601 Wadding of textile materials and articles thereof; textile fibres, etc.	6	5	0	-1.4	-1.1	3.5	0.5	nes	68	ARE	21
17	6107 Men's or boys' underpants, nightshirts, pyjamas, bathrobes, etc., knitted or crocheted	13	11	129	125.3	5.0	7.9	0.5	ISR	100	USA	0
8	6203 Men's or boys' suits, jackets, trousers and shorts (other than swimwear), etc.	18	11	68	118.8	3.5	8.6	0.1	USA	61	ISR	15
3	6204 Women's or girls' suits, jackets, dresses skirts and shorts (other than swimwear), etc.	49	44	449	539.1	4.4	7.9	0.2	USA	49	ISR	47
26	7113 Articles of jewellery and parts thereof, of precious metals, etc.	8	2	20				0.1	ISR	51	USA	37
37	7308 Structures and parts of structures (i.e., bridges and bridge-sections, roofs, doors and windows, etc.)	6	-9	12	7.5	2.0	5.4	0.1	nes	78	ARE	11
31	7602 Aluminum waste and scrap	7	7	9	6.6	6.7	6.4	0.2	JPN	49	ARE	10
35	7604 Aluminum bars, rods and profiles	7	4	39	47.5	6.3	8.9	0.1	ISR	44	DZA	23
23	8413 Pumps for liquids, liquid elevators	10	-18	123	82.7	1.5	5.9	0.1	nes	97	TUN	3
22	8415 Air conditioning machines	10	1	33	33.5	3.0	10.9	0.1	ISR	26	SAU	22
34	8418 Refrigerators, freezers and other refrigerating or freezing equipment, etc.	7	-16	100	82.9	2.2	6.2	0.1	ISR	26	nes	25
19	9403 Other furniture and parts thereof	12	-7	28	47.3	8.2	8.7	0.0	SAU	42	nes	29
	Other services, credit	600	144	-3		4.0		0.1				
	Transport services, credit	301	-282	-7		1.5		0.1				
	Travel, credit	722	335	0		1.9		0.2				

Notes: The indicators are based on Jordan's export statistics.

*May include re-exports or ships registration.

Export Profile Chart for Selected Key Products

Jordan

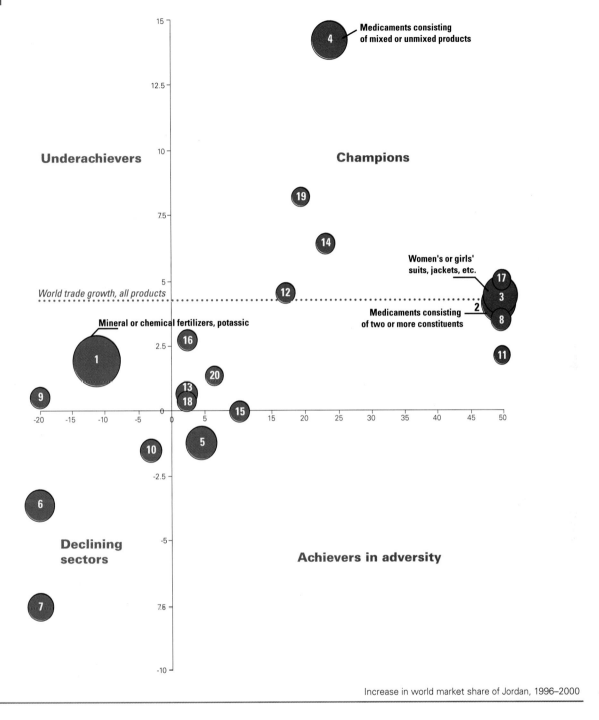

World trade growth, % per annum, 1996–2000

Increase in world market share of Jordan, 1996–2000

Champions

Underachievers

Declining sectors

Achievers in adversity

Medicaments consisting of mixed or unmixed products

Women's or girls' suits, jackets, etc.

Medicaments consisting of two or more constituents

Mineral or chemical fertilizers, potassic

World trade growth, all products

Key

1 3104 **Mineral or chemical fertilizers, potassic**
2 3003 **Medicaments consisting of two or more constituents**
3 6204 **Women's or girls' suits, jackets, etc.**
4 3004 **Medicaments consisting of mixed or unmixed products**
5 0702 **Tomatoes**
6 2510 **Calcium and aluminum calcium phosphates**
7 3102 **Mineral or chemical fertilizers, nitrogenous**
8 6203 **Men's or boys' suits, jackets, trousers, etc.**
9 2523 **Portland, aluminous and slag cement, etc.**
10 0707 **Cucumbers and gherkins, fresh or chilled**

11 4202 **Trunks, suitcases, camera cases, handbags, etc.**
12 4818 **Toilet paper and similar paper, etc.**
13 4803 **Household or sanitary paper, etc.**
14 3923 **Article for the conveyance or packing of goods, of plastics, etc.**
15 3808 **Insecticides, fungicides, herbicides, etc.**
16 0709 **Vegetables, fresh or chilled, other**
17 6107 **Men's or boys' underpants, nightshirts, etc.**
18 2836 **Carbonates; peroxocarbonates; etc.**
19 9403 **Other furniture and parts thereof**
20 4901 **Printed books, brochures, leaflets and similar printed matter**

Note: The area of the circles is proportional to the export turnover
Source: ITC calculations based on COMTRADE statistics.

Kuwait

Key Indicators

Surface area (thousand sq. km.)	17.8
Population (millions), 2001	2.3
Population (average annual percent growth), 1980–2000	1.8 %
Life expectancy at birth, 2000	
Male (years)	75
Female (years)	79
Adult illiteracy rate (percent), 2000	
Male	16 %
Female	20 %
Gross tertiary enrollment ratio, 1998 or most recent year	19 %

Gross domestic product (US$ billion), 2001	35.7
Gross domestic product (average annual percent growth), 1990–2000	3.2 %
Gross national income per capita (US$, PPP), 2000	18,690
Growth of output (average annual percent growth), 1990–2000	
Agriculture	—
Industry	—
Manufacturing	—
Services	—
Inflation (annual percentage change), 2001	2.5 %

Unemployment (percent of total labor force), 1998	0.7 %
Gross national savings rate (percent of GDP), 2001	34.7 %
Gross capital formation (percent of GDP), 2000	11.1 %
Household final consumption (percent of GDP), 2000	40.7 %

Current government revenue (ex grants, percent of GDP), 2001	68.6 %
Total government expenditure (percent of GDP), 2001	45.9 %
Overall budget deficit/surplus (percent of GDP), 2001	22.7 %
Highest marginal tax rate, 2001	
Individual	0 %
Corporate	0 %

Money and quasi money (annual percent growth), 2000	6.3 %
Domestic credit provided by the banking sector (percent of GDP), 2000	82.2 %

Stock market capitalization (US$ million), end 2001	—

Exports of goods (US$ million), 2001	16,173
Imports of goods (US$ million), 2001	7,325
Net energy imports (percent of commercial energy use), 1999[2]	-503 %
Current account balance (percent of GDP), 2001	26.1 %
Foreign direct investment inward stock (US$ million), 2000	527
Foreign direct investment (percent of gross capital formation), 2000	0.4 %
Total international reserves minus gold (US$ million), end 2001	9,897.3
Total international reserves minus gold (months of import coverage), 2001	16.2
Total foreign debt (US$ million), 2001	9,299
Long-term debt (US$ million), 2001	3,440
Total debt service (percent of GDP), 2001	2.9 %
Total foreign debt service paid (percent of exports of goods), 2001	5.9 %
Sovereign long-term foreign debt ratings, July 2002	
Moody's	A2
Standard and Poors	A+
Real effective exchange rate (1997=100), 2001[3]	111.6

Sources: The Heritage Foundation 2002 Index of Economic Freedom; World Development Indicators 2002; IMF International Financial Statistics 2002; IMF World Economic Outlook Database, April 2002; International Labor Office LABORSTA; Economist Intelligence Unit; UNCTAD FDI Statistics.

[2] A minus sign indicates that the country is a net energy exporter

[3] Values greater (less) than 100 indicate appreciation (depreciation)

Exchange Rate and Capital Restrictions

Kuwait

Exchange rate arrangements

Currency	Kuwaiti Dinar
Exchange rate structure	Unitary
Classification	Conventional pegged
Exchange tax	No
Exchange subsidy	No
Forward exchange market	Yes

Controls on current payments and transfers

	Controls in place?
Arrangements for payments and receipts	
Bilateral payments arrangements	
Payments arrears	
Controls on Payments for invisible transactions and current transfers	
Proceeds from exports and/or invisible transactions	
Repatriation requirements	
Surrender requirements	

Capital controls

	Controls in place?
Capital market securities	●
Money market instruments	●
Collective investment securities	●
Derivatives and other instruments	●
Commercial credits	
Financial credits	
Guarantees, sureties, and financial backup facilities	
Direct investment	●
Liquidation of direct investment	
Real estate transactions	●
Personal capital movements	
Provisions specific to commercial banks and other credit institutions	●
Provisions specific to institutional investors	

● = The specific practice is a feature of the exchange system and a control is in place.

▲ = The specific practice is not regulated.

— = Data not available.

Source: IMF Annual Report on Exchange Arrangements and Exchange Restrictions 2001

Real effective exchange rate

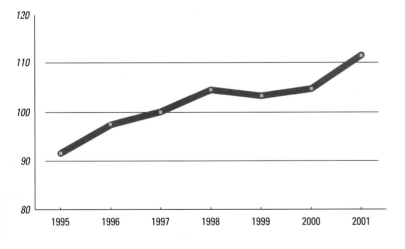

Index Numbers (1997=100): Period Averages
A higher (lower) exchange rate indicates an appreciation (depreciation) of the currency.

Source: Economist Intelligence Unit

Export Profile Table of Kuwait

RANK	HS Code and Product Label	Exports 2000 US$ m	Net Exports 2000 US$ m	Export Growth, 1996–2000 % per annum value	Export Growth, 1996–2000 % per annum quantity	World Trade Growth, 1996–2000 % per annum value	World Trade Growth, 1996–2000 % per annum quantity	Share in World %	Leading Markets 1st	Leading Markets %	Leading Markets 2nd	Leading Markets %
	ALL GOODS	16,861		10								
	ALL GOODS (WTO)	19,544	11,922									
23	0306 Crustaceans	4	4	2		3.1	2.8	0.0	JPN	94	SAU	5
30	1902 Pasta	2	0			-0.9	1.7	0.1	SAU	99	JOR	1
27	1905 Bread, pastry, cakes, biscuits and other bakers' wares, etc.	3	-17			1.7	5.6	0.0	SAU	96	USA	3
20	2009 Fruit and vegetable juices	5	2			0.2	3.7	0.1	SAU	93	JOR	7
13	2503 Sulphur of all kinds, other than sublimed, precipitated and colloidal	13	13	1		2.4	6.2	1.5	TUN	64	MAR	29
1	2709 Crude petroleum oils	11,300	11,300	8		7.2	1.0	3.2	JPN	32	USA	24
2	2710 Non-crude petroleum oils	3,899	3,883	16		6.9	4.3	3.0	JPN	23	IDN	19
3	2711 Petroleum gases	863	863	6		7.1	2.3	1.2	JPN	51	KOR	24
8	2713 Petroleum coke and bitumen, etc.	42	42	2		1.5	3.4	1.2	USA	97	IRN	2
5	2905 Acyclic alcohols and their halogenated, sulphonated, nitrated or nitrosated derivatives	117	117	352		2.0	7.0	1.3	IDN	50	ITA	21
11	2909 Ethers, ether-alcohols, etc., and their derivatives	14	13			7.1	4.7	0.3	ITA	61	ESP	30
18	3002 Human and animal blood for therapeutic use	6	-6			8.8	9.8	0.1	SAU	100	EGY	0
10	3102 Mineral or chemical fertilizers, nitrogenous	21	20	-29		-7.5	0.2	0.4	KOR	29	PHL	29
4	3901 Polymers of ethylene, in primary forms	255	252	569		3.9	5.6	1.4	CHN	43	HKG	17
9	3902 Polymers of propylene or of other olefins, in primary forms	26	25	579		1.9	6.4	0.3	SAU	28	CHN	21
29	3924 Tableware, kitchenware, and other household and toilet articles, of plastic	3	-4			3.8	11.3	0.1	SAU	99	GBR	1
24	4804 Uncoated kraft paper and paperboard	4	-9			0.1	2.8	0.1	SAU	95	JOR	5
21	4805 Uncoated paper and paperboard, in rolls or sheets, other	5	4			0.7	3.1	0.1	SAU	95	JOR	5
22	4819 Cartons, boxes, cases, bags and other packing containers, of paper, etc.	5	1			2.3	4.7	0.1	SAU	95	UGA	5
26	5101 Wool, not carded or combed	3	3	-6		-11.6	-4.1	0.1	ITA	66	TUR	17
14	6203 Men's or boys' suits, jackets, trousers and shorts (other than swimwear), etc.	12	-8	254		3.5	8.6	0.1	USA	99	ESP	0
25	6205 Men's or boys' shirts	3	-2	-2		0.3	3.2	0.0	USA	100	CAN	0
12	7019 Glass fibres (including glass wool) and articles thereof	13	10			3.4	7.8	0.3	SAU	96	JOR	2
19	7404 Copper waste and scrap	6	6	1		-4.7	1.6	0.1	KOR	66	JPN	34
16	7602 Aluminum waste and scrap	8	8	-5		6.7	6.4	0.2	KOR	55	JPN	18
7	8411 Turbo-jets*	44	4	34		12.7	10.2	0.1	GBR	100	ITA	0
28	9404 Mattress supports, mattresses, quilts, etc.	3	-3			7.7	12.1	0.1	SAU	100	JOR	0
17	9406 Prefabricated buildings	6	5			1.5	4.7	0.3	SAU	92	ETH	8
15	9706 Antiques more than one hundred years old	9	-1	129				0.3	GBR	92	CHE	8
6	9999 Special Transaction Trade	49	-139	21		8.1		0.0	USA	94	ESP	2
	Other services, credit	88	0	-3		4.0		0.0				
	Transport services, credit	1,607	68	9		1.5		0.5				
	Travel, credit	98	-2,354	-18		1.9		0.0				

Notes: The indicators are based on the partner countries' export statistics (mirror estimates).

*May include re-exports or ships registration.

Export Profile Chart for Selected Key Products

Kuwait

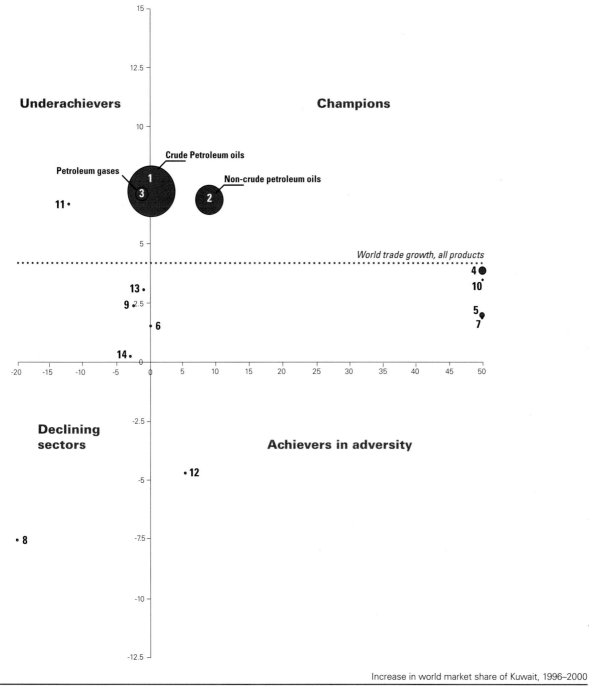

Increase in world market share of Kuwait, 1996–2000

World trade growth, % per annum, 1996–2000

Key

2709 **Crude Petroleum oils**	⑧ 3102 **Mineral or chemical fertilizers, nitrogenous**
2710 **Non-crude petroleum oils**	⑨ 2503 **Sulphur of all kinds, other than sublimed**
2711 **Petroleum gases**	⑩ 6203 **Men's or boys' suits, jackets, trousers, etc.**
3901 **Polymers of ethylene, in primary forms**	⑪ 7602 **Aluminum waste and scrap**
2905 **Acyclic alcohols and their derivatives**	⑫ 7404 **Copper waste and scrap**
2713 **Petroleum coke and bitumen, etc**	⑬ 0306 **Crustaceans**
3902 **Polymers of propylene or of other olefins, in primary forms**	⑭ 6205 **Men's or boys' shirts**

Lebanon

Key Indicators

Surface area (thousand sq. km.)	10.4
Population (millions), 2001	3.6
Population (average annual percent growth), 1980–2000	1.8 %
Life expectancy at birth, 2000	
Male (years)	69
Female (years)	72
Adult illiteracy rate (percent), 2000	
Male	8 %
Female	20 %
Gross tertiary enrollment ratio, 1998 or most recent year	38 %

Gross domestic product (US$ billion), 2001	16.7
Gross domestic product (average annual percent growth), 1990–2000	6.0 %
Gross national income per capita (US$, PPP), 2000	4,550
Growth of output (average annual percent growth), 1990–2000	
Agriculture	1.8 %
Industry	-1.6 %
Manufacturing	-4.3 %
Services	4.1 %
Inflation (annual percentage change), 2001	0

Unemployment (percent of total labor force), 1997	8.6 %
Gross national savings rate (percent of GDP), 2001	-2.7 %
Gross capital formation (percent of GDP), 2000	18.0 %
Household final consumption (percent of GDP), 2000	87.8 %

Current government revenue (ex grants, percent of GDP), 2001	18.6 %
Total government expenditure (percent of GDP), 2001	35.5 %
Overall budget deficit/surplus (percent of GDP), 2001	-16.9 %
Highest marginal tax rate, 2001	
Individual	20 %
Corporate	15 %

Money and quasi money (annual percent growth), 2000	9.8 %
Domestic credit provided by the banking sector (percent of GDP), 2000	183.4 %

Stock market capitalization (US$ million), end 2001	1,228

Exports of goods (US$ million), 2001	889
Imports of goods (US$ million), 2001	7291
Net energy imports (percent of commercial energy use), 1999	97 %
Current account balance (percent of GDP), 2001	-27.1 %
Foreign direct investment inward stock (US$ million), 2000	998
Foreign direct investment (percent of gross capital formation), 2000	10.0
Total international reserves minus gold (US$ million), end 2001	5,013.8
Total international reserves minus gold (months of import coverage), 2001	8.3
Total foreign debt (US$ million), 2001	15,143
Long-term debt (US$ million), 2001	12,167
Total debt service (percent of GDP), 2001	10.5 %
Total foreign debt service paid (percent of exports of goods), 2001	196.2 %
Sovereign long-term foreign debt ratings, July 2002	
Moody's	B2
Standard and Poors	B-
Real effective exchange rate (1997=100), 2001[3]	106.9

Sources: The Heritage Foundation 2002 Index of Economic Freedom; World Development Indicators 2002; IMF International Financial Statistics 2002; IMF World Economic Outlook Database, April 2002; Economist Intelligence Unit; UNCTAD FDI Statistics.

[3]Values greater (less) than 100 indicate appreciation (depreciation)

Exchange Rate and Capital Restrictions

Lebanon

Exchange rate arrangements

Currency	Lebanese Pound
Exchange rate structure	Unitary
Classification	Conventional pegged
Exchange tax	No
Exchange subsidy	No
Forward exchange market	Yes

Controls on current payments and transfers

Controls in place?

Arrangements for payments and receipts
  Bilateral payments arrangements
  Payments arrears

Controls on Payments for invisible transactions and current transfers

Proceeds from exports and/or invisible transactions
  Repatriation requirements
  Surrender requirements

Capital controls

Controls in place?

Capital market securities	●
Money market instruments	●
Collective investment securities	●
Derivatives and other instruments	●
Commercial credits	●
Financial credits	●
Guarantees, sureties, and financial backup facilities	
Direct investment	
Liquidation of direct investment	
Real estate transactions	●
Personal capital movements	
Provisions specific to commercial banks and other credit institutions	●
Provisions specific to institutional investors	

● = The specific practice is a feature of the exchange system and a control is in place.

▲ = The specific practice is not regulated.

— = Data not available.

Source: IMF Annual Report on Exchange Arrangements and Exchange Restrictions 2001

Real effective exchange rate

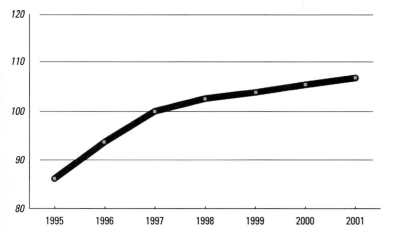

Index Numbers (1997=100): Period Averages
A higher (lower) exchange rate indicates an appreciation (depreciation) of the currency.

Source: Economist Intelligence Unit

Export Profile Table of Lebanon

RANK	HS Code and Product Label	Exports 2000 (US$ m)	Net Exports 2000 (US$ m)	Export Growth, 1996–2000 % per annum		World Trade Growth, 1996–2000 % per annum		Share in World %	Leading Markets			
				value	quantity	value	quantity		1st	%	2nd	%
	ALL GOODS	614		2								
	ALL GOODS (WTO)	714	-5,514									
12	0504 Guts, bladders and stomachs of animals (other than fish)	9	9	-12		-2.1	3.0	0.6	DEU	64	TUR	25
35	0701 Potatoes	3	-1	14		-1.7	1.4	0.3	JOR	57	BHR	27
9	0805 Citrus fruit, fresh or dried	9	9			-4.5	0.5	0.2	SAU	46	BHR	33
21	0806 Grapes, fresh or dried	6	6	-9		1.8	3.0	0.2	JOR	62	BHR	21
18	0808 Apples, pears and quinces, fresh	7	7	2		-5.2	0.5	0.2	JOR	84	SAU	12
10	0901 Coffee	9	-14			-7.0	2.3	0.1	ARM	44	GEO	37
26	1704 Sugar confectionery	5	-1	11		1.5	4.2	0.2	SAU	27	PRT	16
29	2005 Other vegetables prepared or preserved otherwise than by vinegar or acetic acid, not frozen	4	-3			-0.4	4.6	0.1	SAU	34	USA	19
30	2008 Fruits, nuts prepared or preserved	4	2	14		-0.8	3.5	0.1	USA	53	CAN	22
22	2204 Wine of fresh grapes	6	4	16		3.5	-2.6	0.0	GBR	31	FRA	28
4	2401 Tobacco unmanufactured; tobacco refuse	25	23	10		-2.5	-0.5	0.4	USA	74	ROM	12
6	2523 Portland, aluminous and slag cement, supersulphate cement and similar hydraulic cements	23	23			0.5	3.2	0.6	ESP	27	ITA	21
3	2809 Diphosphorus pentaoxide; phosphoric acid and polyphosphoric acids	26	26	405		-7.3	-5.4	2.8	BEL	41	FRA	27
17	3103 Mineral or chemical fertilizers, phosphatic	7	7	-25		-8.5	-3.4	1.3	ESP	44	ITA	34
19	4101 Raw hides and skins of bovine or equine animals	7	6	196		-4.2	0.2	0.2	HKG	60	ITA	17
36	4102 Raw skins of sheep or lambs	3	3	-9		-20.7	-3.5	0.4	ITA	63	TUR	36
5	4901 Printed books, brochures, leaflets and similar printed matter	24	6	3		1.3	4.3	0.2	MAR	24	DZA	18
28	5208 Woven fabrics of cotton, weighing no more than 200 grams per meter squared	5	1			-5.4	-1.2	0.1	BHR	100	SEN	0
25	5209 Woven fabric of cotton, weighing over 200 grams per meter squared	6	1			0.8	5.9	0.1	BHR	100	CAF	0
32	6109 T-shirts, singlets and other vests, knitted or crocheted	4	-3	12		9.9	11.5	0.0	DEU	59	FRA	18
39	6110 Jerseys, pullovers, cardigans, waistcoats, etc., knitted or crocheted	3	-7	2		7.9	9.5	0.0	FRA	82	USA	9
27	6203 Men's or boys' suits, jackets, trousers and shorts (other than swimwear), etc.	5	-10	-12		3.5	8.6	0.0	FRA	39	USA	25
40	6204 Women's or girls' suits, jackets, dresses skirts, etc. and shorts (other than swimwear)	2	-19			4.4	7.9	0.0	SAU	77	FRA	7
1	7102 Diamonds whether or not worked, but not mounted or set	79	19	4				0.2	CHE	66	BEL	31
8	7103 Precious stones (other than diamonds) and semi-precious stones	11	9	1				0.6	CHE	95	HKG	2
2	7113 Articles of jewellery and parts thereof, of precious metals, etc.	74	17	-6				0.5	CHE	60	USA	29
11	7204 Ferrous waste and scrap; remelting scrap ingots of iron or steel	9	9	-27		-0.8	5.8	0.1	TUR	91	NLD	5
13	7404 Copper waste and scrap	8	8	-4		-4.7	1.6	0.2	JPN	52	KOR	33
20	7503 Nickel waste and scrap	7	7			0.3	2.0	1.6	GBR	100		
15	7602 Aluminum waste and scrap	8	8	-1		6.7	6.4	0.2	KOR	38	GBR	27
7	7604 Aluminum bars, rods and profiles	15	10	26		6.3	8.9	0.3	FRA	55	BEL	28
37	8418 Refrigerators, freezers and other refrigerating or freezing equipment, etc.	3	-24	89		2.2	6.2	0.0	DZA	65	SAU	15
33	8438 Other machinery for the industrial preparation or manufacture of food or drink	4	-3	3		-7.2	0.8	0.1	TUN	19	SAU	16
31	8504 Electric transformers, static converters, etc.	4	-16	13		9.3	11.5	0.0	FRA	62	JOR	28
38	8544 Insulated wire or cable	3	-6	124		6.8	7.7	0.0	ESP	89	CYP	2
23	8901 Cruise ship, cargo*	6	6			-3.1	2.5	0.1	IDN	100	CYP	0
34	9401 Seats, whether or not convertible into beds, and parts thereof	4	-4	20		10.9	9.6	0.0	USA	83	SAU	7
16	9403 Other furniture and parts thereof	8	-21	49		8.2	8.7	0.0	USA	35	JOR	22
24	9706 Antiques more than one hundred years old	6	3	41				0.2	CHE	68	USA	31
14	9999 Special Transaction Trade	8	-21	8		8.1		0.0	USA	92	JPN	5

Notes: the indicators are based on the partner countries' export statistics (mirror estimates).

*May include re-exports or ships registration.

Export Profile Chart for Selected Key Products

Lebanon

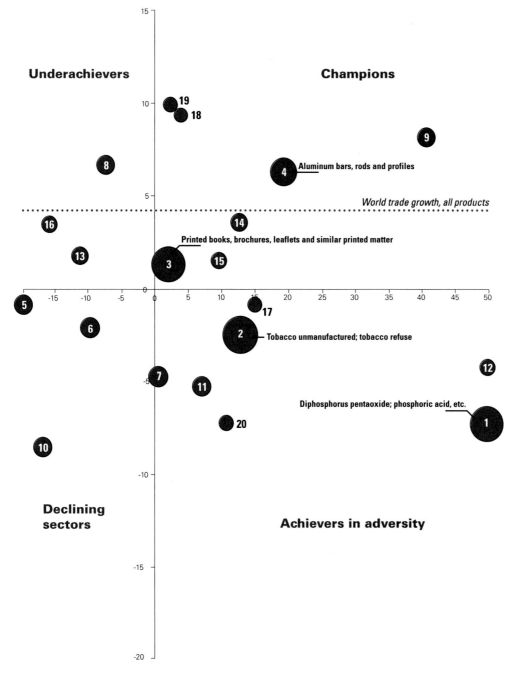

Underachievers

Champions

19
18

9

8

4 — Aluminum bars, rods and profiles

World trade growth, all products

16

14

13

Printed books, brochures, leaflets and similar printed matter

3

15

5

17

6

2 — Tobacco unmanufactured; tobacco refuse

12

7

11

Diphosphorus pentaoxide; phosphoric acid, etc.

1

20

10

Declining
sectors

Achievers in adversity

World trade growth, % per annum, 1996–2000

Increase in world market share of Lebanon, 1996–2000

Key

2809 Diphosphorus pentaoxide; phosphoric acid, etc.	11 0808 Apples, pears and quinces, fresh
2401 Tobacco unmanufactured; tobacco refuse	12 4101 Raw hides and skins of bovine or equine animals
4901 Printed books, brochures, leaflets and similar printed matter	13 0806 Grapes, fresh or dried
7604 Aluminum bars, rods and profiles	14 2204 Wine of fresh grapes
7204 Ferrous waste and scrap; remelting scrap ingots of iron or steel	15 1704 Sugar confectionery
0504 Guts, bladders and stomachs of animals	16 6203 Men's or boys' suits, jackets, trousers, etc.
7404 Copper waste and scrap	17 2008 Fruits, nuts prepared or preserved
7602 Aluminum waste and scrap	18 8504 Electric transformers, static converters, etc.
9403 Other furniture and parts thereof	19 6109 T-shirts, singlets and other vests, etc.
3103 Mineral or chemical fertilizers, phosphatic	20 8438 Other machinery, to manufacture food or drink

Note: The area of the circles is proportional to the export turnover

Source: ITC calculations based on COMTRADE statistics.

Libya

Key Indicators

Surface area (thousand sq. km.)	1,759
Population (millions), 2001	5.5
Population (average annual percent growth), 1980–2000	2.8 %
Life expectancy at birth, 2000	
Male (years)	69
Female (years)	73
Adult illiteracy rate (percent), 2000	
Male	9 %
Female	32 %
Gross tertiary enrollment ratio, 1998 or most recent year	57 %
Gross domestic product (US$ billion), 2001	28.6
Gross domestic product (average annual percent growth), 1990–2000	-0.5 %
Gross national income per capita (US$, PPP), 2000	—
Growth of output (average annual percent growth), 1990–2000	
Agriculture	—
Industry	—
Manufacturing	—
Services	—
Inflation (annual percentage change), 2001	-8.5 %
Unemployment (percent of total labor force)	—
Gross national savings rate (percent of GDP), 2001	24.2 %
Gross capital formation (percent of GDP), 2000	—
Household final consumption (percent of GDP), 2000	—
Current government revenue (ex grants, percent of GDP), 2001	33.7 %
Total government expenditure (percent of GDP), 2001	20.4 %
Overall budget deficit/surplus (percent of GDP), 2001	13.3 %
Highest marginal tax rate, 2001	
Individual	90 %
Corporate	35 %
Money and quasi money (annual percent growth), 2000	3.2 %
Domestic credit provided by the banking sector (percent of GDP), 2000	—
Stock market capitalization (US$ million), end 2001	—
Exports of goods (US$ million), 2001	11,996
Imports of goods (US$ million), 2001	9,232
Net energy imports (percent of commercial energy use), 1999[2]	-499 %
Current account balance (percent of GDP), 2001	6.6 %
Foreign direct investment inward stock (US$ million), 2000	—
Foreign direct investment (percent of gross capital formation), 2000	—
Total international reserves minus gold (US$ million), end 2001	14,800.0
Total international reserves minus gold (months of import coverage), 2001	19.2
Total foreign debt (US$ million), 2001	4,544
Long-term debt (US$ million), 2001	3,844
Total debt service (percent of GDP), 2001	2.8 %
Total foreign debt service paid (percent of exports of goods), 2001	6.5 %
Sovereign long-term foreign debt ratings, July 2002	
Moody's	–
Standard and Poors	–
Real effective exchange rate (1997=100), 2001[3]	62.6

Sources: The Heritage Foundation 2002 Index of Economic Freedom; World Development Indicators 2002; IMF International Financial Statistics 2002; IMF World Economic Outlook Database, April 2002; Economist Intelligence Unit; UNCTAD FDI Statistics.

[2]A minus sign indicates that the country is a net energy exporter

[3]Values greater (less) than 100 indicate appreciation (depreciation)

Exchange Rate and Capital Restrictions

Libya

Exchange rate arrangements

Currency	Libyan Dinar
Exchange rate structure	Dual
Classification	Conventional pegged
Exchange tax	Yes
Exchange subsidy	No
Forward exchange market	No

Controls on current payments and transfers

	Controls in place?
Arrangements for payments and receipts	
Bilateral payments arrangements	●
Payments arrears	
Controls on Payments for invisible transactions and current transfers	●
Proceeds from exports and/or invisible transactions	
Repatriation requirements	●
Surrender requirements	●

Capital controls

	Controls in place?
Capital market securities	●
Money market instruments	●
Collective investment securities	●
Derivatives and other instruments	—
Commercial credits	●
Financial credits	●
Guarantees, sureties, and financial backup facilities	●
Direct investment	●
Liquidation of direct investment	●
Real estate transactions	●
Personal capital movements	—
Provisions specific to commercial banks and other credit institutions	—
Provisions specific to institutional investors	—

● = The specific practice is a feature of the exchange system and a control is in place.

▲ = The specific practice is not regulated.

— = Data not available.

Source: IMF Annual Report on Exchange Arrangements and Exchange Restrictions 2001

Real effective exchange rate

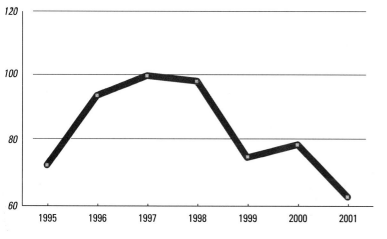

Index Numbers (1997=100): Period Averages
A higher (lower) exchange rate indicates an appreciation (depreciation) of the currency.

Source: Economist Intelligence Unit

Export Profile Table of Libya

RANK	HS Code and Product Label	Exports 2000 US$ m	Net Exports 2000 US$ m	Export Growth, 1996–2000 % per annum value	Export Growth, 1996–2000 % per annum quantity	World Trade Growth, 1996–2000 % per annum value	World Trade Growth, 1996–2000 % per annum quantity	Share in World %	Leading Markets 1st	%	2nd	%
	ALL GOODS	13,469		3								
	ALL GOODS (WTO)	14,200	6,460									
27	0302 Fish, fresh or chilled	1	1	5		1.6	3.3	0.0	TUN	55	JPN	26
13	0303 Frozen fish	9	8	267		1.6	2.2	0.1	JPN	93	KOR	7
28	0509 Sponges, natural of animal origin	1	1	0		0.7	1.3	5.7	JPN	57	ITA	43
33	0703 Onions, shallots, garlic	0	0	154		0.0	1.0	0.0	TUN	100		
15	1202 Ground-nuts, not roasted	8	8	39		-6.2	-1.4	0.9	TUN	100		
21	2002 Tomatoes prepared or preserved	3	-18			-3.7	1.7	0.2	TUR	53	ITA	47
7	2707 Oils and other products of the distillation of high temperature coal tar, etc.	54	52	54		7.2	6.2	1.8	ITA	100	IND	0
1	2709 Crude petroleum oils	11,022	11,022	3		7.2	1.0	3.1	ITA	42	DEU	24
2	2710 Non-crude petroleum oils	1,615	1,331	2		6.9	4.3	1.2	ITA	58	GBR	17
3	2711 Petroleum gases	220	220	0		7.1	2.3	0.3	ESP	46	ITA	18
23	2712 Petroleum jelly; paraffin wax	2	2	272		4.2	3.5	0.2	ITA	100	MAR	0
11	2814 Ammonia, anhydrous or in aqueous solution	20	20	-7		-4.4	1.2	1.0	TUN	50	MAR	24
19	2815 Sodium hydroxide; potassium hydroxide; peroxides of sodium or potassium	3	3	8		-5.8	1.3	0.2	ITA	63	TUN	25
4	2901 Acyclic hydrocarbons	173	173	19		9.6	5.9	2.8	ESP	30	ITA	20
5	2905 Acyclic alcohols and their halogenated, sulphonated, nitrated or nitrosated derivatives	98	98	-8		2.0	7.0	1.1	ITA	70	ESP	15
26	2914 Ketones and quinones and their derivatives	2	2			1.4	4.1	0.1	MAR	100		
6	3102 Mineral or chemical fertilizers, nitrogenous	64	63	-17		-7.5	0.2	1.2	ITA	36	ESP	31
8	3901 Polymers of ethylene, in primary forms	52	50	541		3.9	5.6	0.3	ITA	35	BEL	23
14	3904 Polymers of vinyl chloride or other halogenated olefins, in primary forms	8	8	-9		4.0	4.6	0.1	TUN	75	MAR	11
30	3915 Waste, parings and scrap, of plastics	1	1	32		11.5	13.2	0.0	TUN	90	MAR	10
22	4101 Raw hides and skins of bovine or equine animals	2	2	-11		-4.2	0.2	0.1	ITA	45	TUR	41
16	4102 Raw skins of sheep or lambs	7	7	-25		-20.7	-3.5	0.9	ITA	83	TUR	11
32	4105 Sheep or lamb skin leather, without wool	0	0	16		-3.8	7.0	0.0	ITA	100	FRA	0
24	7201 Pig iron and spiegeleisen in pigs, blocks or other primary forms	2	2			-3.5	1.4	0.1	IDN	100		
9	7203 Ferrous products obtained by direct reduction of iron ore and other spongy ferrous products	32	31			-7.5	5.6	5.7	ITA	47	ESP	23
18	7207 Semi-finished products of iron or nonalloy steel	4	4	15		-1.3	4.8	0.1	TUN	93	ALB	7
10	7208 Flat-rolled products of iron or non-alloy steel, of a width of 600 mm or more, hot rolled	28	26	-5		-2.1	2.3	0.2	ITA	62	TUN	17
31	7209 Flat-rolled products of iron or non-alloy steel wider than 600 mm, cold rolled	1	-1	-55		-1.1	4.8	0.0	MAR	82	TUN	18
17	7213 Bars and rods, hot-rolled, in irregularly wound coils, of iron or non-alloy steel	5	5			-4.0	1.9	0.1	TUN	100	NGA	0
12	7214 Other bars and rods of iron or non-alloy steel, not further worked than forged, etc.	10	8	-12		-3.0	3.7	0.2	TUN	100	MAR	0
25	7503 Nickel waste and scrap	2	2			0.3	2.0	0.4	GBR	100		
29	7601 Unwrought aluminum	1	1	-43		3.3	4.3	0.0	JPN	69	ITA	26
20	8411 Turbo-jets*	3	-43	15		12.7	10.2	0.0	GBR	69	ITA	28

Notes: The indicators are based on the partner countries' export statistics (mirror estimates).

*May include re-exports or ships registration.

Export Profile Chart for Selected Key Products

Libya

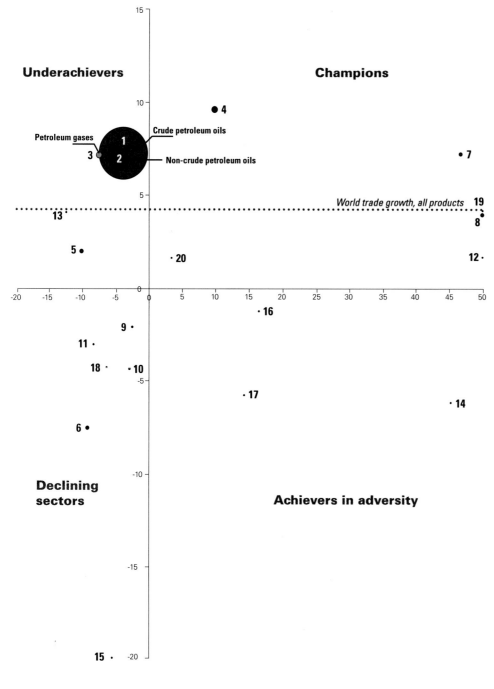

World trade growth, % per annum, 1996–2000

Increase in world market share of Libya, 1996–2000

Key

1	2709 Crude petroleum oils	11	7214 Other bars and rods of iron or non-alloy steel
2	2710 Non-crude petroleum oils	12	0303 Frozen fish
3	2711 Petroleum gases	13	3904 Polymers of vinyl chloride or other halogenated olefins
4	2901 Acyclic hydrocarbons	14	1202 Ground-nuts, not roasted
5	2905 Acyclic alcohols and their derivatives	15	4102 Raw skins of sheep or lambs
6	3102 Mineral or chemical fertilizers, nitrogenous	16	7207 Semi-finished products of iron or non-alloy steel
7	2707 Oils and other products of the distillation of coal tar, etc.	17	2815 Sodium hydroxide; potassium hydroxide; etc.
8	3901 Polymers of ethylene, in primary forms	18	4101 Raw hides and skins of bovine or equine animals
9	7208 Flat-rolled products of iron or non-alloy steel	19	2712 Petroleum jelly; paraffin wax
0	2814 Ammonia, anhydrous or in aqueous solution	20	0302 Fish, fresh or chilled

Note: The area of the circles is proportional to the export turnover
Source: ITC calculations based on COMTRADE statistics.

Mauritania

Key Indicators

Surface area (thousand sq. km.)	1,030
Population (millions), 2001	2.7
Population (average annual percent growth), 1980–2000	2.7 %
Life expectancy at birth, 2000	
Male (years)	50
Female (years)	53
Adult illiteracy rate (percent), 2000	
Male	49 %
Female	70 %
Gross tertiary enrollment ratio, 1998 or most recent year	6 %

Gross domestic product (US$ billion), 2001	1.0
Gross domestic product (average annual percent growth), 1990–2000	4.2 %
Gross national income per capita (US$, PPP), 2000	1,630
Growth of output (average annual percent growth), 1990–2000	
Agriculture	5.0 %
Industry	2.4 %
Manufacturing	-0.5 %
Services	4.9 %
Inflation (annual percentage change), 2001	4.7 %

Unemployment (percent of total labor force)	—
Gross national savings rate (percent of GNI), 2000	30.8 %
Gross capital formation (percent of GDP), 2000	30.1 %
Household final consumption (percent of GDP), 2000	67.7 %

Current government revenue (ex grants, percent of GDP), 2000	26.2 %
Total government expenditure (percent of GDP), 2000	27.9 %
Overall budget deficit/surplus (percent of GDP), 2000	-1.7 %
Highest marginal tax rate, 2001	
Individual	55 %
Corporate	40 %

Money and quasi money (annual percent growth), 2000	16.1 %
Domestic credit provided by the banking sector (percent of GDP), 2000	-2.7 %

Stock market capitalization (US$ million), end 2001	—

Exports of goods (US$ million), 2000	280
Imports of goods (US$ million), 2000	350
Net energy imports (percent of commercial energy use)	—
Current account balance (percent of GDP), 2001	—
Foreign direct investment inward stock (US$ million), 2000	—
Foreign direct investment (percent of gross capital formation), 2000	1.8 %
Total international reserves minus gold (US$ million), end 2001	—
Total international reserves minus gold (months of import coverage), 2001	—
Total foreign debt (US$ million), 2001	—
Long-term debt (US$ million), end 2000	2,150
Total debt service (percent of GNI), 2000	11.0 %
Total foreign debt service paid (percent of exports of goods and services), 2000	25.9 %
Sovereign long-term foreign debt ratings, July 2002	
Moody's	–
Standard and Poors	–
Real exchange rate Ouguiya to US$, (1997=100), 2001[3]	74.3

Sources: The Heritage Foundation 2002 Index of Economic Freedom; World Development Indicators 2002; IMF International Financial Statistics 2002; IMF World Economic Outlook Database, April 2002; Economist Intelligence Unit; UNCTAD FDI Statistics; National Statistical Office of Mauritania (ONS), International Trade Centre.

[3]Values greater (less) than 100 indicate appreciation (depreciation)

Exchange Rate and Capital Restrictions
Mauritania

Exchange rate arrangements

Currency	Mauritanian Ouguiya
Exchange rate structure	Unitary
Classification	Managed floating
Exchange tax	No
Exchange subsidy	No
Forward exchange market	No

Controls on current payments and transfers

	Controls in place?
Arrangements for payments and receipts	
Bilateral payments arrangements	●
Payments arrears	●
Controls on Payments for invisible transactions and current transfers	●
Proceeds from exports and/or invisible transactions	
Repatriation requirements	●
Surrender requirements	●

Capital controls

	Controls in place?
Capital market securities	●
Money market instruments	●
Collective investment securities	●
Derivatives and other instruments	●
Commercial credits	●
Financial credits	●
Guarantees, sureties, and financial backup facilities	●
Direct investment	●
Liquidation of direct investment	—
Real estate transactions	●
Personal capital movements	—
Provisions specific to commercial banks and other credit institutions	●
Provisions specific to institutional investors	—

● = The specific practice is a feature of the exchange system and a control is in place.

▲ = The specific practice is not regulated.

— = Data not available.

Source: IMF Annual Report on Exchange Arrangements and Exchange Restrictions 2001

Real exchange rate (Ouguiya to US$)

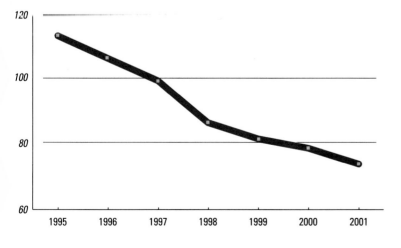

Index Numbers (1997=100): Period Averages
A higher (lower) exchange rate indicates an appreciation (depreciation) of the currency.

Source: IMF International Financial Statistics 2002

Export Profile Table of Mauritania

RANK	HS Code and Product Label	Exports 2000 US$ m	Net Exports 2000 US$ m	Export Growth, 1996–2000 % per annum value	Export Growth, 1996–2000 % per annum quantity	World Trade Growth, 1996–2000 % per annum value	World Trade Growth, 1996–2000 % per annum quantity	Share in World %	Leading Markets 1st	Leading Markets %	Leading Markets 2nd	Leading Markets %
	ALL GOODS	543.7		-4								
	ALL GOODS (WTO)	300.0	-40									
4	0302 Fish, fresh or chilled	23.2	23	12		1.6	3.3	0.4	PRT	43	ESP	20
2	0303 Frozen fish	135.4	135	-1		1.6	2.2	1.5	NGA	51	CIV	15
7	0304 Fish fillets, fresh, chilled or frozen	3.9	4	28		3.4	2.2	0.1	FRA	65	ESP	26
8	0305 Cured and smoked fish	3.0	3	15		-0.6	-1.5	0.1	HKG	53	ESP	36
6	0306 Crustaceans	5.4	5	2		3.1	2.8	0.0	ESP	85	PRT	15
3	0307 Molluscs	117.0	117	-12		-1.0	4.3	2.4	JPN	67	ESP	18
11	0511 Animal products not for human consumption, other	0.8	1	16		1.4	0.4	0.1	ESP	100	FRA	0
19	1301 Lac; natural gums, resins, gum-resins and oleoresins (for example, balsams)	0.2	0	-55		-3.7	1.5	0.1	FRA	100	DEU	0
21	1504 Fish or marine mammal fat, oils, etc. not chemically modified	0.1	0	123		-10.4	2.1	0.0	RUS	74	BLR	14
22	1605 Crustaceans, molluscs, prepared or preserved	0.1	0	96		4.0	6.5	0.0	JPN	100	KOR	0
5	2301 Flour, etc. of meat, fish, crustacean, etc., not for human consumption	5.6	6			-7.6	1.7	0.2	BLR	43	RUS	34
24	2520 Gypsum; anhydrite; plasters (consisting of calcined gypsum or calcium sulphate), etc.	0.1	0	122		-2.9	1.0	0.0	NGA	92	CIV	8
1	2601 Iron ores and concentrates	236.4	236	-2		-1.2	0.7	2.0	FRA	39	ITA	23
23	2710 Non-crude petroleum oils	0.1	-39	-71		6.9	4.3	0.0	RUS	100	BEL	0
9	3105 Mineral or chemical fertilizers containing nitrogen, phosphorus and potassium, etc.	2.5	3			-4.4	0.7	0.1	NGA	100	IDN	0
14	4102 Raw skins of sheep or lambs	0.3	0	-20		-20.7	-3.5	0.0	FRA	85	TUN	11
13	6109 T-shirts, singlets and other vests, knitted or crocheted	0.3	0	17		9.9	11.5	0.0	FRA	65	GBR	15
17	6110 Jerseys, pullovers, cardigans, waistcoats, etc., knitted or crocheted	0.2	0	-22		7.9	9.5	0.0	FRA	67	GBR	12
10	6203 Men's or boys' suits, jackets, trousers and shorts (other than swimwear), etc.	0.9	-1	63		3.5	8.6	0.0	FRA	93	SAU	5
15	6205 Men's or boys' shirts	0.3	-1	-17		0.3	3.2	0.0	FRA	79	JPN	8
20	6211 Track suits and swimwear; other garments	0.1	0			-2.4	3.6	0.0	GBR	98	FRA	2
25	7113 Articles of jewellery and parts thereof, of precious metals, etc.	0.1	0					0.0	GBR	100	BEL	0
18	7204 Ferrous waste and scrap; remelting scrap ingots of iron or steel	0.2	0	35		-0.8	5.8	0.0	ESP	76	JPN	24
16	7404 Copper waste and scrap	0.2	0	-4		-4.7	1.6	0.0	ESP	100	HKG	0
12	7606 Aluminum plates, sheets and strip, of a thickness exceeding 0.2 mm	0.6	1			3.7	6.1	0.0	NGA	100		

Notes: The indicators are based on the partner countries' export statistics (mirror estimates).

*May include re-exports or ships registration.

Export Profile Chart for Selected Key Products

Mauritania

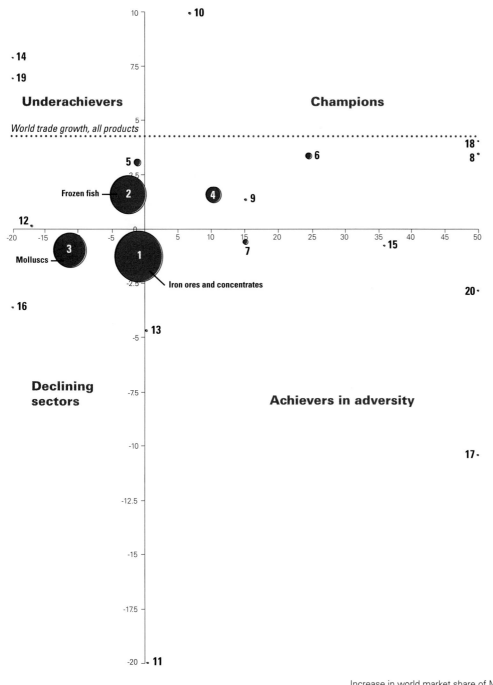

Underachievers

Champions

World trade growth, all products

Frozen fish

Molluscs

Iron ores and concentrates

Declining sectors

Achievers in adversity

World trade growth, % per annum, 1996–2000

Increase in world market share of Mauritania, 1996–2000

Key

1	2601 Iron ores and concentrates	**11**	4102 Raw skins of sheep or lambs
2	0303 Frozen fish	**12**	6205 Men's or boys' shirts
3	0307 Molluscs	**13**	7404 Copper waste and scrap
4	0302 Fish, fresh or chilled	**14**	6110 Jerseys, pullovers, cardigans, waistcoats, etc.
5	0306 Crustaceans	**15**	7204 Ferrous waste and scrap
6	0304 Fish fillets, fresh, chilled or frozen	**16**	1301 Lac; natural gums, resins, gum-resins and oleoresins
7	0305 Cured and smoked fish	**17**	1504 Fish or marine mammal fat, oils, etc.
8	6203 Men's or boys' suits, jackets, trousers, etc.	**18**	1605 Crustaceans, molluscs, prepared or preserved
9	0511 Animal products not for human consumption	**19**	2710 Non-crude petroleum oils
10	6109 T-shirts, singlets and other vests, etc.	**20**	2520 Gypsum; anhydrite; plasters, etc.

Note: The area of the circles is proportional to the export turnover
Source: ITC calculations based on COMTRADE statistics.

Morocco

Key Indicators

Surface area (thousand sq. km.)	446.6
Population (millions), 2001	29.2
Population (average annual percent growth), 1980–2000	2.0 %
Life expectancy at birth, 2000	
Male (years)	66
Female (years)	69
Adult illiteracy rate (percent), 2000	
Male	38 %
Female	64 %
Gross tertiary enrollment ratio, 1998 or most recent year	9 %
Gross domestic product (US$ billion), 2001	33.5
Gross domestic product (average annual percent growth), 1990–2000	2.3 %
Gross national income per capita (US$, PPP), 2000	3,450
Growth of output (average annual percent growth), 1990–2000	
Agriculture	-0.9 %
Industry	3.2 %
Manufacturing	2.7 %
Services	2.8 %
Inflation (annual percentage change), 2001	0.5 %
Unemployment (percent of total labor force), 2001	20.3 %
Gross national savings rate (percent of GDP), 2001	28.0 %
Gross capital formation (percent of GDP), 2000	24.4 %
Household final consumption (percent of GDP), 2000	62.6 %
Current government revenue (ex grants, percent of GDP), 2001	31.8 %
Total government expenditure (percent of GDP), 2001	34.3 %
Overall budget deficit/surplus (percent of GDP), 2001	-2.5 %
Highest marginal tax rate, 2001	
Individual	44 %
Corporate	35 %
Money and quasi money (annual percent growth), 2000	8.4 %
Domestic credit provided by the banking sector (percent of GDP), 2000	92.1 %
Stock market capitalization (US$ million), end 2001	9,140
Exports of goods (US$ million), 2001	7,116
Imports of goods (US$ million), 2001	10,958
Net energy imports (percent of commercial energy use), 1999	94 %
Current account balance (percent of GDP), 2001	2.9 %
Foreign direct investment inward stock (US$ million), 2000	5,848
Foreign direct investment (percent of gross capital formation), 2000	0.1 %
Total international reserves minus gold (US$ million), end 2001	8,474.0
Total international reserves minus gold (months of import coverage), 2001	9.3
Total foreign debt (US$ million), 2001	16,777
Long-term debt (US$ million), 2001	16,556
Total debt service (percent of GDP), 2001	9.6 %
Total foreign debt service paid (percent of exports of goods), 2001	44.6 %
Sovereign long-term foreign debt ratings, July 2002	
Moody's	Ba1
Standard and Poors	BB
Real effective exchange rate (1997=100), 2001[3]	95.3

Sources: The Heritage Foundation 2002 Index of Economic Freedom; World Development Indicators 2002; IMF International Financial Statistics 2002; IMF World Economic Outlook Database, April 2002; Economist Intelligence Unit; UNCTAD FDI Statistics.

[3]Values greater (less) than 100 indicate appreciation (depreciation)

Morocco

Exchange rate arrangements

Currency	Moroccan Dirham
Exchange rate structure	Unitary
Classification	Conventional pegged
Exchange tax	No
Exchange subsidy	No
Forward exchange market	Yes

Controls on current payments and transfers

	Controls in place?
Arrangements for payments and receipts	
Bilateral payments arrangements	●
Payments arrears	
Controls on Payments for invisible transactions and current transfers	●
Proceeds from exports and/or invisible transactions	
Repatriation requirements	●
Surrender requirements	●

Capital controls

	Controls in place?
Capital market securities	●
Money market instruments	●
Collective investment securities	●
Derivatives and other instruments	●
Commercial credits	●
Financial credits	●
Guarantees, sureties, and financial backup facilities	●
Direct investment	●
Liquidation of direct investment	
Real estate transactions	●
Personal capital movements	●
Provisions specific to commercial banks and other credit institutions	●
Provisions specific to institutional investors	●

● = The specific practice is a feature of the exchange system and a control is in place.

▲ = The specific practice is not regulated.

— = Data not available.

Source: IMF Annual Report on Exchange Arrangements and Exchange Restrictions 2001

Real effective exchange rate

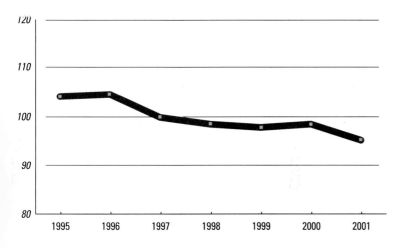

Index Numbers (1997=100): Period Averages
A higher (lower) exchange rate indicates an appreciation (depreciation) of the currency.

Source: Economist Intelligence Unit

Export Profile Table of Morocco

RANK	HS Code and Product Label	Exports 2000 US$ m	Net Exports 2000 US$ m	Export Growth, 1996–2000 % per annum value	quantity	World Trade Growth, 1996–2000 % per annum value	quantity	Share in World %	Leading Markets 1st	%	2nd	%
	ALL GOODS	7,426		15								
	ALL GOODS (WTO)	7,417	-4,067									
22	0302 Fish, fresh or chilled	68	68	2	7.8	1.6	3.3	1.1	ESP	37	ITA	18
31	0303 Frozen fish	41	39	19	11.3	1.6	2.2	0.4	ESP	70	ITA	9
26	0306 Crustaceans	56	53	12	24.5	3.1	2.8	0.4	ESP	83	NLD	15
2	0307 Molluscs	580	580	7	17.1	-1.0	4.3	12.0	JPN	42	ESP	33
19	0702 Tomatoes	82	82	3	4.4	-1.3	-0.1	2.7	FRA	90	CHE	4
11	0805 Citrus fruit, fresh or dried	193	193	-8	-3.8	-4.5	0.5	4.1	RUS	27	FRA	22
9	1604 Prepared or preserved fish	202	201	4	7.2	-1.7	4.3	3.6	FRA	17	USA	11
21	2005 Other vegetables prepared or preserved otherwise than by vinegar or acetic acid, not frozen	72	71	-9	-0.5	-0.4	4.6	2.1	FRA	48	USA	22
6	2510 Calcium and aluminum calcium phosphates, natural and phosphatic chalk	389	389	3	0.4	-3.6	-4.0	35.8	USA	16	ESP	14
28	2608 Zinc ores and concentrates	49	49	1	3.2	-0.9	-0.7	2.3	ESP	51	FRA	25
7	2710 Non-crude petroleum oils	272	101	39	47.3	6.9	4.3	0.2	FRA	43	ITA	23
3	2809 Diphosphorus pentaoxide; phosphoric acid and polyphosphoric acids	506	504	-1	0.2	-7.3	-5.4	53.3	IND	53	BEL	12
20	3103 Mineral or chemical fertilizers, phosphatic	76	74	-34	-25.3	-8.5	-3.4	13.3	IRN	38	FRA	19
8	3105 Mineral or chemical fertilizers containing nitrogen, phosphorus and potassium, etc.	247	237	62	76.2	-4.4	0.7	5.1	FRA	15	ITA	12
35	4105 Sheep or lamb skin leather, without wool	36	32	-16	-12.3	-3.8	7.0	2.5	ITA	57	CHN	13
25	4703 Chemical wood pulp, soda or sulphate, other than dissolving grades	59	51	14	9.3	5.8	3.8	0.3	ITA	28	TUR	25
38	6103 Men's or boys' suits, jackets, trousers and shorts (other than swimwear) knitted or crocheted	31	30	4	9.8	4.2	9.9	1.5	FRA	59	ESP	21
24	6104 Women's suits, dresses, skirts and shorts (other than swimwear), knitted or crocheted	64	61	54		1.0	5.5	1.1	FRA	36	GBR	33
23	6106 Women's or girls' blouses, shirts & shirt-blouses, knitted or crocheted	64	63	181	150.8	4.1	4.4	1.8	GBR	70	FRA	14
40	6107 Men's or boys' underpants, nightshirts, pyjamas, bathrobes, etc., knitted or crocheted	29	23	61	78.6	5.0	7.9	1.1	FRA	46	ESP	34
27	6108 Women's or girls' slips, panties, pyjamas, bathrobes, etc., knitted or crocheted	50	35	102	82.6	5.4	8.3	0.8	FRA	38	GBR	37
12	6109 T-shirts, singlets and other vests, knitted or crocheted	191	132	38	70.4	9.9	11.5	1.4	FRA	43	DEU	20
13	6110 Jerseys, pullovers, cardigans, waistcoats, etc., knitted or crocheted	179	175	8	13.8	7.9	9.5	0.6	FRA	75	DEU	10
32	6202 Women's or girls' overcoats, capes, wind-jackets, etc.	40	38	89	91.1	-2.4	3.0	0.8	FRA	47	ESP	28
4	6203 Men's or boys' suits, jackets, trousers and shorts (other than swimwear), etc.	477	474	29	26.0	3.5	8.6	2.0	FRA	32	GBR	25
1	6204 Women's or girls' suits, jackets, dresses skirts, etc. and shorts (other than swimwear)	612	583	94	79.9	4.4	7.9	2.0	FRA	36	GBR	23
15	6205 Men's or boys' shirts	110	108	34	33.0	0.3	3.2	1.2	FRA	57	GBR	21
16	6206 Women's or girls' blouses, shirts and shirt-blouses	107	104	163		-1.1	3.2	1.5	FRA	35	GBR	23
17	6211 Track suits, ski suits and swimwear; other garments	92	90	67	73.7	-2.4	3.6	1.8	FRA	46	GBR	40
14	6212 Brassieres, girdles, corsets, suspenders, etc.	131	69	72	74.1	7.4	8.0	2.5	GBR	51	FRA	22
18	6403 Footwear with outer sole of rubber, plastic, leather	82	81	14	25.2	-0.6	0.6	0.3	FRA	37	ITA	27
30	6406 Parts of footwear; removable in-soles, heel cushions	44	19	71	53.7	-4.1	0.4	1.0	FRA	86	LBY	6
29	7106 Silver (including silver plated with gold or platinum)	44	44	7				1.4	FRA	57	CHE	32
39	7210 Flat-rolled products of iron or non-alloy steel, of a width of 600 mm or more	30	6	21	30.4	3.5	8.4	0.2	ESP	39	FRA	22
36	8105 Cobalt mattes and other intermediate products of cobalt metallurgy	35	35	69	91.0	-7.1	4.8	3.0	BEL	54	JPN	21
33	8536 Electrical applications for switching (ie fuses, etc.)	39	-24	90	80.2	7.5	10.3	0.1	FRA	82	DEU	6
5	8541 Diodes, transistors and similar semiconductor devices, etc.	448	203	1,287		12.4	11.2	1.4	FRA	100	MLI	0
37	8542 Electronic integrated circuits and microassemblies	33	-12	1,449		11.6	9.7	0.0	FRA	100	DEU	0
10	8544 Insulated wire or cable	197	114	31		6.8	7.7	0.5	FRA	44	ITA	39
34	9032 Automatic regulating or controlling instruments and apparatus	38	23	760		6.5	10.3	0.3	FRA	100	MLI	0
	Other services, credit	414	-142	6		4.0		0.1				
	Transport services, credit	540	-210	6		1.5		0.2				
	Travel, credit	1,906	1,449	6		1.9		0.4				

Notes: The indicators are based on Morocco's trade statistics.

*May include re-exports or ships registration.

Export Profile Chart for Selected Key Products

Morocco

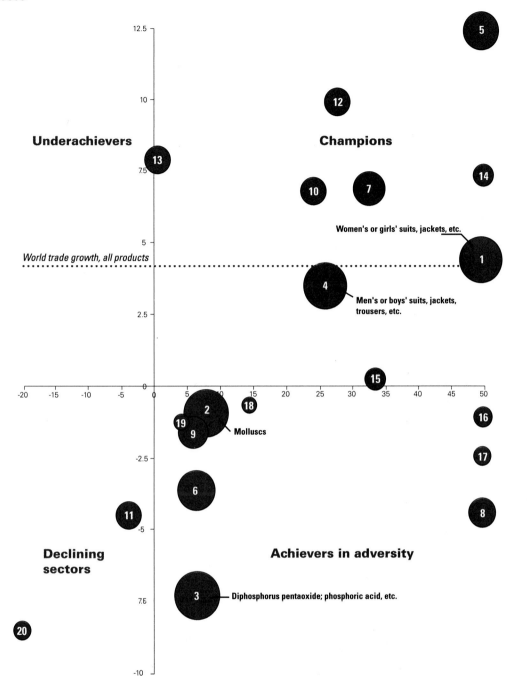

World trade growth, % per annum, 1996–2000

Underachievers

Champions

World trade growth, all products

Women's or girls' suits, jackets, etc.

Men's or boys' suits, jackets, trousers, etc.

Molluscs

Declining sectors

Achievers in adversity

Diphosphorus pentaoxide; phosphoric acid, etc.

Increase in world market share of Morocco, 1996–2000

Key

1. 6204 **Women's or girls' suits, jackets, etc.**
2. 0307 **Molluscs**
3. 2809 **Diphosphorus pentaoxide; phosphoric acid, etc.**
4. 6203 **Men's or boys' suits, jackets, trousers, etc.**
5. 8541 **Diodes, transistors and similar semiconductor devices, etc.**
6. 2510 **Calcium and aluminum calcium phosphates, etc.**
7. 2710 **Non-crude petroleum oils**
8. 3105 **Mineral or chemical fertilizers**
9. 1604 **Prepared or preserved fish**
10. 8544 **Insulated wire or cable**

11. 0805 **Citrus fruit, fresh or dried**
12. 6109 **T-shirts, singlets and other vests, etc.**
13. 6110 **Jerseys, pullovers, cardigans, waistcoats, etc.**
14. 6212 **Brassieres, girdles, corsets, suspenders, etc.**
15. 6205 **Men's or boys' shirts**
16. 6206 **Women's or girls' blouses, shirts and shirt-blouses**
17. 6211 **Track suits, ski suits and swimwear; etc.**
18. 6403 **Footwear with outer soles of rubber, plastic, leather**
19. 0702 **Tomatoes**
20. 3103 **Mineral or chemical fertilizers, phosphatic**

Note: The area of the circles is proportional to the export turnover
Source: ITC calculations based on COMTRADE statistics.

Oman

Key Indicators

Surface area (thousand sq. km.)	212.5
Population (millions), 2001	2.5
Population (average annual percent growth), 1980–2000	3.9 %
Life expectancy at birth, 2000	
Male (years)	72
Female (years)	75
Adult illiteracy rate (percent), 2000	
Male	20 %
Female	38 %
Gross tertiary enrollment ratio, 1998 or most recent year	8 %

Gross domestic product (US$ billion), 2001	19.3
Gross domestic product (average annual percent growth), 1990–2000	5.9 %
Gross national income per capita (US$, PPP), 2000	—
Growth of output (average annual percent growth), 1990–2000	
Agriculture	—
Industry	—
Manufacturing	—
Services	—
Inflation (annual percentage change), 2001	-2.6 %

Unemployment (percent of total labor force)	—
Gross national savings rate (percent of GDP), 2001	26.3 %
Gross capital formation (percent of GDP), 2000	—
Household final consumption (percent of GDP), 2000	—

Current government revenue (ex grants, percent of GDP), 2001	32.8 %
Total government expenditure (percent of GDP), 2001	36.1 %
Overall budget deficit/surplus (percent of GDP), 2001	-3.3 %
Highest marginal tax rate, 2001	
Individual	0 %
Corporate	12 %

Money and quasi money (annual percent growth), 2000	6.0 %
Domestic credit provided by the banking sector (percent of GDP), 2000	—

Stock market capitalization (US$ million), end 2001	3,391

Exports of goods (US$ million), 2001	11,072
Imports of goods (US$ million), 2001	5,798
Net energy imports (percent of commercial energy use), 1999[2]	-544 %
Current account balance (percent of GDP), 2001	11.5 %
Foreign direct investment inward stock (US$ million), 2000	2,517
Foreign direct investment (percent of gross capital formation), 2000	—
Total international reserves minus gold (US$ million), end 2001	2,364.9
Total international reserves minus gold (months of import coverage), 2001	4.9
Total foreign debt (US$ million), 2001	6,034
Long-term debt (US$ million), 2001	4,558
Total debt service (percent of GDP), 2001	5.7 %
Total foreign debt service paid (percent of exports of goods), 2001	10.2 %
Sovereign long-term foreign debt ratings, July 2002	
Moody's	Baa2
Standard and Poors	BBB
Nominal effective exchange rate (1997=100), 2001[3]	112.8

Sources: The Heritage Foundation 2002 Index of Economic Freedom; World Development Indicators 2002; IMF International Financial Statistics 2002; IMF World Economic Outlook Database, April 2002; Economist Intelligence Unit; UNCTAD FDI Statistics; Ministry of National Economy of Oman.

[2] A minus sign indicates that the country is a net energy exporter

[3] Values greater (less) than 100 indicate appreciation (depreciation)

Exchange Rate and Capital Restrictions

Oman

Exchange rate arrangements

Currency	Rial Omani
Exchange rate structure	Unitary
Classification	Conventional pegged
Exchange tax	No
Exchange subsidy	No
Forward exchange market	Yes

Controls on current payments and transfers

	Controls in place?
Arrangements for payments and receipts	
Bilateral payments arrangements	
Payments arrears	
Controls on Payments for invisible transactions and current transfers	●
Proceeds from exports and/or invisible transactions	
Repatriation requirements	
Surrender requirements	

Capital controls

	Controls in place?
Capital market securities	●
Money market instruments	
Collective investment securities	
Derivatives and other instruments	
Commercial credits	
Financial credits	
Guarantees, sureties, and financial backup facilities	
Direct investment	●
Liquidation of direct investment	
Real estate transactions	●
Personal capital movements	
Provisions specific to commercial banks and other credit institutions	●
Provisions specific to institutional investors	—

● = The specific practice is a feature of the exchange system and a control is in place.

▲ = The specific practice is not regulated.

— = Data not available.

Source: IMF Annual Report on Exchange Arrangements and Exchange Restrictions 2001

Nominal effective exchange rate

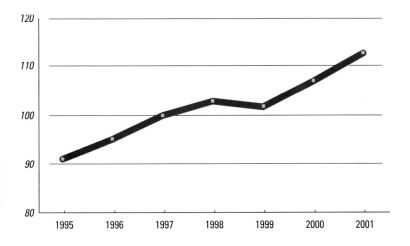

Index Numbers (1997=100): Period Averages
A higher (lower) exchange rate indicates an appreciation (depreciation) of the currency.

Source: IMF International Financial Statistics 2002

Export Profile Table of Oman

R A N K	HS Code and Product Label	Exports 2000 US$ m	Export Growth, 1996–2000 % per annum value	Export Growth, 1996–2000 % per annum quantity	World Trade Growth, 1996–2000 % per annum value	Share in World %
	All products	10,852	8		4	0
22	010420 Live goats	20	4	4	7	37
32	010600 Live animals, other	13	-5	-3	2	4
19	030229 Flatfish, fresh or chilled, other	23			-4	14
28	030239 Tunas, fresh or chilled, other	14			1	3
18	040221 Milk and cream powder, unsweetened, exceeding 1.5% fat	24	128	154	-1	1
23	040299 Milk and cream sweetened, other	18			-6	6
15	110100 Wheat or meslin flour	29	23	35	-15	2
37	151190 Palm oil and its fractions	10	860	863	-2	0
39	151529 Maize (corn) oil	10	-4	-1	6	2
47	210320 Tomato ketchup and other tomato sauces	7			0	1
5	240220 Cigarettes containing tobacco	133	5	-13	-4	1
17	252329 Portland cement, other	25	293	584	-1	1
1	2709 Crude petroleum oils	8,727	8	-99	8	2
2	2710 Non-crude petroleum oils	222	39		4	1
46	330300 Perfumes and toilet waters	8	9	26	4	0
16	340220 Organic surface-active agents (other than soap), etc. for retail sale	26			4	1
45	392111 Film and sheet, etc., cellular of polymers of styrene	8	596	552	-1	2
33	401110 Pneumatic new tires of rubber for motor cars	11	-9	-6	2	0
38	401120 Pneumatic new tires of rubber for buses or lorries	10	-11	-13	3	0
24	551329 Woven fabrics of synthetic staple fibres, containing less than 85% by weight of such fibres	16			10	15
10	620342 Mens/boys cotton trousers and shorts, not knitted	45			4	0
29	620349 Mens/boys trousers and shorts, of other textile materials, not knitted	14			1	2
42	620432 Womens/girls cotton jackets, not knitted	8			0	1
36	680221 Worked monumental or building stone and articles thereof, of marble, travertine and alabaster	10			1	2
35	721410 Bars & rods, of forged iron or non-alloy steel	11	33	38	-13	9
40	730531 Tubes and pipes of iron or steel, longitudinally welded, the external diameter of which exceeds 406.4 mm	9			-16	6
14	740312 Wire bars, copper, unwrought	32			-24	34
26	760611 Plate, sheet or strip aluminium, not alloyed, rectangular or square, exceeding 0.2 mm	14	258	289	1	1
49	841510 Air conditioning machines window or wall types, self-contained	7	4	5	1	0
44	841581 Air conditioning machines, other	8	256	203	12	1
12	843143 Parts of boring or sinking machinery, whether or not self-propelled	36	-7	-7	-2	1
31	850710 Lead-acid electric accumulators of a kind used for starting piston engines	13	-3	-3	1	1
48	852711 Radio-broadcast receivers capable of operating without an external source of power	7	56	65	-4	1
20	852990 Parts suitable for use solely or principally with the transition, reception and radar apparatus, etc.	22			10	0
25	854459 Electric conductors, for voltage greater than 80 V but not exceeding 1,000 V, other	15			3	0
43	870290 Buses with a seating capacity of more than nine persons	8	-39	-36	-5	1
8	870322 Automobiles with reciprocating piston engine displacing from 1000 cc to 1500 cc	58			-4	0
4	870323 Automobiles with reciprocating piston engine displacing from 1500 cc to 3000 cc	154			4	0
6	870324 Automobiles with reciprocating piston engine displacing more than 3000 cc	83			11	0
7	870390 Automobiles including gas turbine powered	68			-8	13
41	870422 Diesel powerd trucks of a gross vehicle weight exceeding 5 tons but not exceeding 20 tons	9			3	0
21	870431 Gas powered trucks with a gross vehicle not exceeding 5 tons	20	2	5	5	0
27	870490 Trucks	14			-7	11
3	870899 Motor vehicle parts	175			5	0
13	880330 Aircraft parts	33			9	0
11	880390 Parts of balloons, dirigibles, and spacecraft, other	40			-15	1
34	890590 Floating docks and vessels which perform special functions	11			23	1
30	940421 Mattresses of cellular rubber or plastics, whether or not covered	13	15	28	3	3
9	9999AA National Chapter 99 data	52	-5		7	0

Notes: Based on Oman trade statistics. Figures include re-exports from Oman.

Export Profile Chart for Selected Key Products

Oman

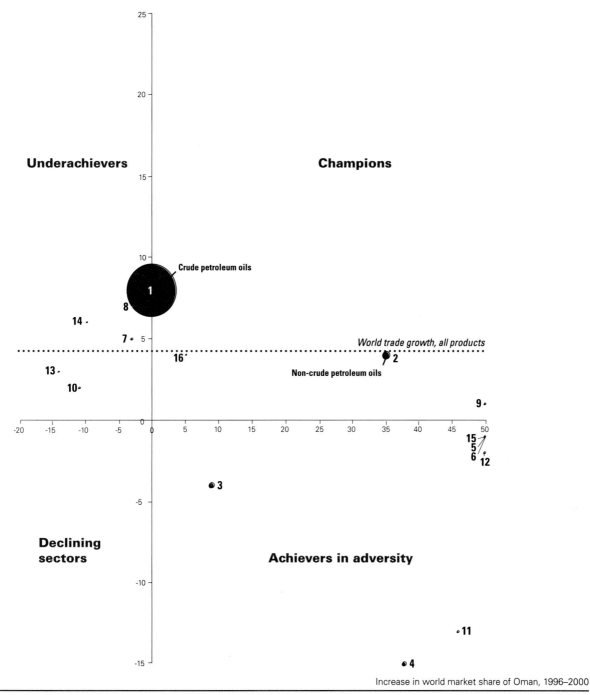

Underachievers

Champions

Crude petroleum oils

World trade growth, all products

Non-crude petroleum oils

Declining sectors

Achievers in adversity

World trade growth, % per annum, 1996–2000

Increase in world market share of Oman, 1996–2000

Key

1. 2709 **Crude petroleum oils**
2. 2710 **Non-crude petroleum oils**
3. 240220 **Cigarettes containing tobacco**
4. 110100 **Wheat or meslin flour**
5. 252329 **Portland cement, other**
6. 040221 **Milk and cream powder, unsweetened**
7. 870431 **Gas powered trucks**
8. 010420 **Live goats**
9. 760611 **Plate, sheet or strip aluminium, not alloyed**
10. 401110 **Pneumatic new tires of rubber for motor cars**

11. 721410 **Bars and rods, of forged iron or non-alloy steel**
12. 151190 **Palm oil and its fractions**
13. 401120 **Pneumatic tires new of rubber for buses etc.**
14. 151529 **Maize (corn) oil**
15. 392111 **Film and sheet, etc., of polymers of styrene**
16. 330300 **Perfumes and toilet waters**

 Note: The area of the circles is proportional to the export turnover
Source: ITC calculations based on COMTRADE statistics.

Qatar

Key Indicators

Surface area (thousand sq. km.)	11.4
Population (millions), 2001	0.6
Population (average annual percent growth), 1980–2000	—
Life expectancy at birth, 2000	
Male (years)	75
Female (years)	75
Adult illiteracy rate (percent), 2000	
Male	20 %
Female	17 %
Gross tertiary enrollment ratio, 1998 or most recent year	26 %

Gross domestic product (US$ billion), 2001	16.6
Gross domestic product (average annual percent growth), 1990–2000	3.6 %
Gross national income per capita (US$, PPP), 2000	—
Growth of output (average annual percent growth), 1990–2000	
Agriculture	—
Industry	—
Manufacturing	—
Services	—
Inflation (annual percentage change), 2001	-0.7 %

Unemployment (percent of total labor force)	—
Gross national savings rate (percent of GDP), 2001	45.3 %
Gross capital formation (percent of GDP), 2000	—
Household final consumption (percent of GDP), 2000	—

Current government revenue (ex grants, percent of GDP), 2001	47.6 %
Total government expenditure (percent of GDP), 2001	37.7 %
Overall budget deficit/surplus (percent of GDP), 2001	9.9 %
Highest marginal tax rate, 2001	
Individual	0 %
Corporate	35 %

Money and quasi money (annual percent growth), 2000	10.7 %
Domestic credit provided by the banking sector (percent of GDP), 2000	49.1 %

Stock market capitalization (US$ million), end 2001	—

Exports of goods (US$ million), 2001	10,247
Imports of goods (US$ million), 2001	3,044
Net energy imports (percent of commercial energy use), 1999[2]	-225 %
Current account balance (percent of GDP), 2001	26.6 %
Foreign direct investment inward stock (US$ million), 2000	1,987
Foreign direct investment (percent of gross capital formation), 2000	—
Total international reserves minus gold (US$ million), end 2001	1,312.7
Total international reserves minus gold (months of import coverage), 2001	5.2
Total foreign debt (US$ million), 2001	13,008
Long-term debt (US$ million), 2001	12,323
Total debt service (percent of GDP), 2001	13.3 %
Total foreign debt service paid (percent of exports of goods), 2001	21.1 %
Sovereign long-term foreign debt ratings, July 2002	
Moody's	Baa2
Standard and Poors	A-
Real effective exchange rate (1997=100), 2001[3]	110.2

Sources: The Heritage Foundation 2002 Index of Economic Freedom; World Development Indicators 2002; IMF International Financial Statistics 2002; IMF World Economic Outlook Database, April 2002; Economist Intelligence Unit; UNCTAD FDI Statistics.

[2] A minus sign indicates that the country is a net energy exporter

[3] Values greater (less) than 100 indicate appreciation (depreciation)

Qatar

Exchange rate arrangements

Currency	Qatar Riyal
Exchange rate structure	Unitary
Classification	Conventional pegged
Exchange tax	No
Exchange subsidy	No
Forward exchange market	Yes

Controls on current payments and transfers

	Controls in place?
Arrangements for payments and receipts	
Bilateral payments arrangements	—
Payments arrears	
Controls on Payments for invisible transactions and current transfers	
Proceeds from exports and/or invisible transactions	
Repatriation requirements	
Surrender requirements	

Capital controls

	Controls in place?
Capital market securities	
Money market instruments	
Collective investment securities	
Derivatives and other instruments	
Commercial credits	
Financial credits	
Guarantees, sureties, and financial backup facilities	
Direct investment	●
Liquidation of direct investment	
Real estate transactions	
Personal capital movements	●
Provisions specific to commercial banks and other credit institutions	
Provisions specific to institutional investors	

● = The specific practice is a feature of the exchange system and a control is in place.

▲ = The specific practice is not regulated.

— = Data not available.

Source: IMF Annual Report on Exchange Arrangements and Exchange Restrictions 2001

Real effective exchange rate

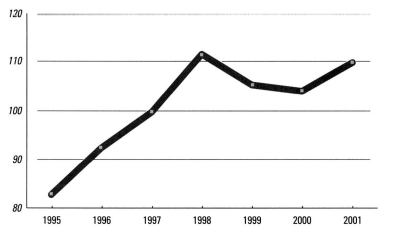

Index Numbers (1997=100): Period Averages
A higher (lower) exchange rate indicates an appreciation (depreciation) of the currency.

Source: Economist Intelligence Unit

Export Profile Table of Qatar

R A N K	HS Code and Product Label	Exports 2000 US$ m	Net Exports 2000 US$ m	Export Growth, 1996–2000 % per annum		World Trade Growth, 1996–2000 % per annum		Share in World %	Leading Markets			
				value	quantity	value	quantity		1st	%	2nd	%
	ALL GOODS	10,988		24								
	ALL GOODS (WTO)	9,378	6,038									
31	0302 Fish, fresh or chilled	1	1						SAU	100		
28	2520 Gypsum; anhydrite; plasters (consisting of calcined gypsum or calcium sulphate), etc.	2	2			-2.9	1.0	0.4	SAU	100	OMN	0
18	2523 Portland, aluminous and slag cement, supersulphate cement and similar hydraulic cements	8	5						SAU	100		
1	2709 Crude petroleum oils	7,148	7,148	18		7.2	1.0	2.0	JPN	58	KOR	18
3	2710 Non-crude petroleum oils	260	251	13		6.9	4.3	0.2	JPN	43	KOR	31
2	2711 Petroleum gases	2,723	2,723	76		7.1	2.3	3.7	JPN	59	KOR	33
10	2814 Ammonia, anhydrous or in aqueous solution	28	28	5		-4.4	1.2	1.4	AUS	82	JOR	18
13	2901 Acyclic hydrocarbons	16	16	-7		9.6	5.9	0.3	BEL	33	ESP	30
9	2905 Acyclic alcohols and their halogenated, sulphonated, nitrated or nitrosated derivatives	35	34			2.0	7.0	0.4	CHN	54	KOR	28
4	2909 Ethers, ether-alcohols, etc., and their derivatives	152	152			7.1	4.7	3.1	USA	100	BEL	0
5	3102 Mineral or chemical fertilizers, nitrogenous	139	139	2		-7.5	0.2	2.5	USA	32	AUS	22
6	3901 Polymers of ethylene, in primary forms	113	113	15		3.9	5.6	0.6	CHN	38	SAU	13
32	3904 Polymers of vinyl chloride/other halogenated olefins, in primary forms	1	1			4.0	4.6	0.0	SAU	95	IRN	2
20	3911 Petroleum resins, polyterpenes, polysulphides, etc., in primary forms	6	5			1.6	5.3	0.3	SAU	100	IND	0
30	4102 Raw skins of sheep or lambs	1	1	-15		-20.7	-3.5	0.2	TUR	100		
27	6104 Women's suits, dresses, skirts and shorts (other than swimwear), knitted or crocheted	2	1	131		1.0	5.5	0.0	USA	100	GBR	0
21	6105 Men's or boys' shirts, knitted or crocheted	5	5	-17		-2.0	0.6	0.1	USA	94	GBR	5
25	6109 T-shirts, singlets and other vests, knitted or crocheted	3	1	-11		9.9	11.5	0.0	USA	93	GBR	7
12	6110 Jerseys, pullovers, cardigans, waistcoats, etc., knitted or crocheted	17	15	68		7.9	9.5	0.1	USA	100	ESP	0
16	6201 Men's or boys' overcoats, capes, windjackets, etc.	11	11	73		-3.4	0.6	0.2	USA	100	DEU	0
29	6202 Women's or girls' overcoats, capes, wind-jackets, etc.	2	2	-15		-2.4	3.0	0.0	USA	100	CAN	0
11	6203 Men's or boys' suits, jackets, trousers and shorts (other than swimwear), etc.	24	23	18		3.5	8.6	0.1	USA	92	GBR	4
7	6204 Women's or girls' suits, jackets, dresses skirts, etc. and shorts (other than swimwear)	62	58	21		4.4	7.9	0.2	USA	99	CAN	0
15	6205 Men's or boys' shirts	14	13	-2		0.3	3.2	0.1	USA	100	FRA	0
23	6206 Women's or girls' blouses, shirts and shirt-blouses	4	3	3		-1.1	3.2	0.1	USA	100	DEU	0
26	6211 Track suits, ski suits and swimwear; other garments	2	0	10		-2.4	3.6	0.0	USA	97	FRA	2
22	7113 Articles of jewellery and parts thereof, of precious metals, etc.	4	-9	10			.	0.0	GBR	94	HKG	3
24	7114 Articles of goldsmith's or silversmith's wares, etc.	4	2	171				1.2	GBR	100	ITA	0
14	7207 Semi-finished products of iron or nonalloy steel	16	16			-1.3	4.8	0.2	CHN	100	OMN	0
8	7213 Bars and rods of alloy steel, in irregularly wound coils, of iron or non-alloy steel	36	36			-4.0	1.9	0.9	SAU	100	IDN	0
17	7214 Other bars and rods of iron or non-alloy steel, not further worked than forged, etc.	10	9	-9		-3.0	3.7	0.2	SAU	100	DEU	0
19	7228 Bars and rods of alloy steel, etc. and hollow drill bars and rods, of alloy or non-alloy steel	7	7						SAU	100		

Notes: The indicators are based on the partner countries' export statistics (mirror estimates).

*May include re-exports or ships registration.

Qatar

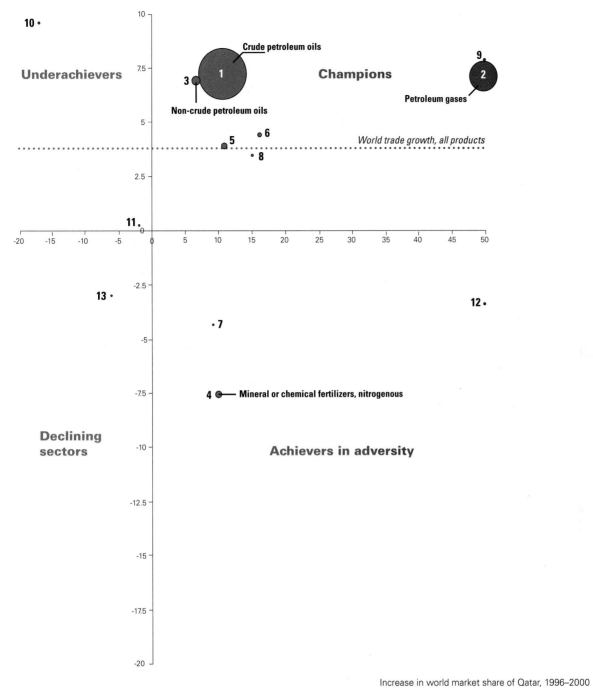

World trade growth, % per annum, 1996–2000

Increase in world market share of Qatar, 1996–2000

Key

1. 2709 **Crude petroleum oils**
2. 2711 **Petroleum gases**
3. 2710 **Non-crude petroleum oils**
4. 3102 **Mineral or chemical fertilizers, nitrogenous**
5. 3901 **Polymers of ethylene, in primary forms**
6. 6204 **Women's or girls' suits, jackets, etc.**
7. 2814 **Ammonia, anhydrous or in aqueous solution**
8. 6203 **Men's or boys' suits, jackets, trousers, etc.**
9. 6110 **Jerseys, pullovers, cardigans, waistcoats, etc.**
10. 2901 **Acyclic hydrocarbons**

11. 6205 **Men's or boys' shirts**
12. 6201 **Men's or boys' overcoats, capes, windjackets, etc.**
13. 7214 **Other bars and rods of iron or non-alloy steel, etc.**

Note: The area of the circles is proportional to the export turnover
Source: ITC calculations based on COMTRADE statistics.

Saudi Arabia

Key Indicators

Surface area (thousand sq. km.)	1,960.6
Population (millions), 2001	21.0
Population (average annual percent growth), 1980–2000	4.0 %
Life expectancy at birth, 2000	
Male (years)	71
Female (years)	74
Adult illiteracy rate (percent), 2000	
Male	17 %
Female	33 %
Gross tertiary enrollment ratio, 1998 or most recent year	19 %
Gross domestic product (US$ billion), 2001	166.7
Gross domestic product (average annual percent growth), 1990–2000	1.5 %
Gross national income per capita (US$, PPP), 2000	11,390
Growth of output (average annual percent growth), 1990–2000	
Agriculture	0.7 %
Industry	1.5 %
Manufacturing	2.7 %
Services	2.0 %
Inflation (annual percentage change), 2001	-1.4 %
Unemployment (percent of total labor force)	—
Gross national savings rate (percent of GDP), 2001	24.6 %
Gross capital formation (percent of GDP), 2000	16.3 %
Household final consumption (percent of GDP), 2000	32.9 %
Current government revenue (ex grants, percent of GDP), 2001	33.5 %
Total government expenditure (percent of GDP), 2001	37.1 %
Overall budget deficit/surplus (percent of GDP), 2001	-3.6 %
Highest marginal tax rate, 2001	
Individual	30 %
Corporate	45 %
Money and quasi money (annual percent growth), 2000	4.5 %
Domestic credit provided by the banking sector (percent of GDP), 2000	68.4 %
Stock market capitalization (US$ million), end 2001	73,207
Exports of goods (US$ million), 2001	73,032
Imports of goods (US$ million), 2001	31,199
Net energy imports (percent of commercial energy use), 1999[2]	-429 %
Current account balance (percent of GDP), 2001	8.4 %
Foreign direct investment inward stock (US$ million), 2000	28,845
Foreign direct investment (percent of gross capital formation), 2000	—
Total international reserves minus gold (US$ million), end 2001	17,596.0
Total international reserves minus gold (months of import coverage), 2001	6.8
Total foreign debt (US$ million), 2001	36,215
Long-term debt (US$ million), 2001	19,026
Total debt service (percent of GDP), 2001	1.8 %
Total foreign debt service paid (percent of exports of goods), 2001	4.4 %
Sovereign long-term foreign debt ratings, July 2002	
Moody's	Baa3[1]
Standard and Poors	—
Real effective exchange rate (1997=100), 2001[3]	100.5

Sources: The Heritage Foundation 2002 Index of Economic Freedom; World Development Indicators 2002; IMF International Financial Statistics 2002; IMF World Economic Outlook Database, April 2002; Economist Intelligence Unit; UNCTAD FDI Statistics.

[1] Issuer's rating

[2] A minus sign indicates that the country is a net energy exporter

[3] Values greater (less) than 100 indicate appreciation (depreciation)

Exchange rate arrangements

Currency	Saudi Arabian Riyal
Exchange rate structure	Unitary
Classification	Conventional pegged
Exchange tax	No
Exchange subsidy	No
Forward exchange market	Yes

Controls on current payments and transfers

	Controls in place?
Arrangements for payments and receipts	
Bilateral payments arrangements	
Payments arrears	
Controls on Payments for invisible transactions and current transfers	
Proceeds from exports and/or invisible transactions	
Repatriation requirements	
Surrender requirements	

Capital controls

	Controls in place?
Capital market securities	●
Money market instruments	●
Collective investment securities	●
Derivatives and other instruments	●
Commercial credits	●
Financial credits	●
Guarantees, sureties, and financial backup facilities	●
Direct investment	●
Liquidation of direct investment	
Real estate transactions	●
Personal capital movements	
Provisions specific to commercial banks and other credit institutions	●
Provisions specific to institutional investors	

● = The specific practice is a feature of the exchange system and a control is in place.

▲ = The specific practice is not regulated.

— = Data not available.

Source: IMF Annual Report on Exchange Arrangements and Exchange Restrictions 2001

Real effective exchange rate

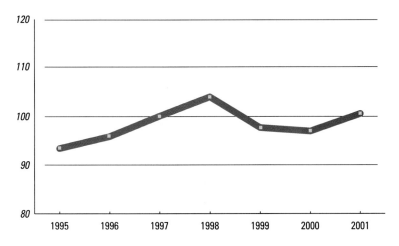

Index Numbers (1997=100): Period Averages
A higher (lower) exchange rate indicates an appreciation (depreciation) of the currency.

Source: Economist Intelligence Unit

Export Profile Table of Saudi Arabia

RANK	HS Code and Product Label		Exports 2000 US$ m	Net Exports 2000 US$ m	Export Growth, 1996–2000 % per annum value	Export Growth, 1996–2000 % per annum quantity	World Trade Growth, 1996–2000 % per annum value	World Trade Growth, 1996–2000 % per annum quantity	Share in World %
	ALL GOODS		77,207		3				
	ALL GOODS (WTO)		84,060	53,760					
32	0207	Meat and edible offal, of poultry, chilled or frozen	28	-340	6		-3.1	4.3	0.4
39	0401	Milk and cream, not concentrated nor sweetened	24	-1	-4		-1.3	4.5	0.9
36	0402	Milk and cream, concentrated or sweetened	26	-254	39		-2.1	2.8	0.5
19	0403	Buttermilk, cream, yogurt, etc.	62	57	10		4.1	10.0	5.4
24	1214	Swedes, mangolds, hay, etc.	43	40	8		-3.9	3.9	5.4
35	1905	Bread, pastry, cakes, biscuits and other bakers' wares, etc.	26	-59	2		1.7	5.6	0.4
22	2009	Fruit and vegetable juices	45	-47	11		0.2	3.7	0.7
11	2523	Portland, aluminous and slag cement, supersulphate cement and similar hydraulic cements	107	83	5		0.5	3.2	2.5
1	2709	Crude petroleum oils	61,397	61,397	8		7.2	1.0	15.8
2	2710	Non-crude petroleum oils	9,690	9,649	4		6.9	4.3	30.1
15	2815	Sodium hydroxide; potassium hydroxide; peroxides of sodium or potassium	87	86	-11		-5.8	1.3	6.2
31	2823	Titanium oxides	28	27	-16		0.3	0.5	4.8
8	2901	Acyclic hydrocarbons	157	146	-8		9.6	5.9	2.6
6	2902	Cyclic hydrocarbons	450	378	21		10.6	6.2	4.1
9	2903	Halogenated derivatives of hydrocarbons	119	96	7		1.1	2.5	2.6
3	2905	Acyclic alcohols and their halogenated, sulphonated, nitrated or nitrosated derivatives	1,058	1,038	2		2.0	7.0	11.9
25	2906	Cyclic alcohols and their derivatives	39	38	225		-1.7	7.6	6.6
4	2909	Ethers, ether-alcohols, etc., and their derivatives	716	712	11		7.1	4.7	14.8
7	3102	Mineral or chemical fertilizers, nitrogenous	229	225	-16		-7.5	0.2	4.2
28	3305	Hair preparations	34	-21	16		5.5	10.0	1.1
40	3401	Soap; organic surface-active products and preparations for use as soap	23	-8	-13		6.4	9.8	1.3
18	3402	Organic surface-active agents (other than soap); washing preparations, etc.	79	37	15		2.4	6.3	0.9
23	3814	Organic composite solvents and thinners	43	28	15		3.9	5.7	7.3
5	3901	Polymers of ethylene, in primary forms	634	547	-10		3.9	5.6	3.5
16	3902	Polymers of propylene or of other olefins, in primary forms	87	59	11		1.9	6.4	0.9
20	3903	Polymers of styrene, in primary forms	61	51	13		3.2	5.6	0.5
12	3904	Polymers of vinyl chloride or other halogenated olefins, in primary forms	102	90	16		4.0	4.6	1.2
33	3917	Tubes, pipes and hoses and fittings of plastics	27	-12	25		4.1	9.6	0.4
26	3923	Articles for the conveyance or packing of goods, of plastics, etc.	36	-5	18		6.4	8.3	0.2
13	4818	Toilet paper and similar paper, used for household or sanitary purposes, etc.	95	64	-2		4.5	8.0	1.2
34	4819	Cartons, boxes, cases, bags and other packing containers, of paper, etc.	27	-10	25		2.3	4.7	0.3
42	5503	Synthetic staple fibres, not processed for spinning	22	8	5		-3.9	1.9	0.5
37	5702	Carpets and other woven textile floor covering, including hand-woven rugs	26	-33	0		-1.5	4.2	1.5
30	7003	Cast glass and rolled glass, in sheets or profiles	32	30	60		4.3	2.4	9.6
27	7214	Other bars and rods of iron or non-alloy steel, not further worked than forged, etc.	36	12	-23		-3.0	3.7	0.9
14	7222	Bars and rods of other stainless steel	88	84	5		0.6	5.8	4.5
29	7306	Tubes, pipes and hollow profiles of iron or steel, other	33	-76	17		1.3	5.5	0.5
21	7308	Structures and parts of structures (i.e., bridges and bridge-sections, roofs, doors and windows, etc.)	59	-42	-1		2.0	5.4	0.7
41	7326	Articles of iron or steel, other	22	-22	0		8.0	9.1	0.2
38	7413	Stranded wire, cables, plaited bands, etc. of copper, not electrically insulated	25	24	34		0.5	9.1	7.4
17	8415	Air conditioning machines*	80	-114	-6		3.0	10.9	0.6
10	8544	Insulated wire or cable	113	13	-4		6.8	7.7	0.3

Notes: The indicators are based on the Saudi Arabia's trade statistics.
*May include re-exports or ships registration.

Export Profile Chart for Selected Key Products

Saudi Arabia

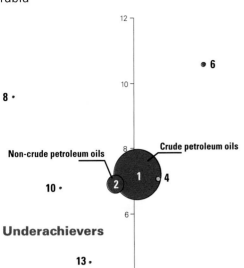

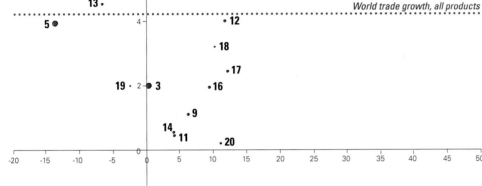
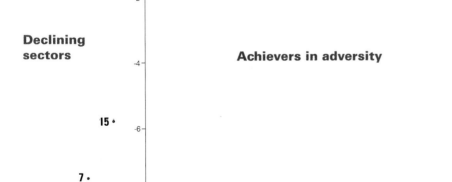

Increase in world market share of Saudi Arabia, 1996–2000

World trade growth, % per annum, 1996–2000

Key

1	2709 Crude petroleum oils		**11**	2523 Portland, aluminous and slag cement, etc.
2	2710 Non-crude petroleum oils		**12**	3904 Polymers of vinyl chloride or other halogenated olefins
3	2905 Acyclic alcohols and their derivatives		**13**	4818 Toilet paper and similar paper, etc.
4	2909 Ethers, ether-alcohols, etc., and their derivatives		**14**	7222 Bars and rods of other stainless steel
5	3901 Polymers of ethylene, in primary forms		**15**	2815 Sodium hydroxide; potassium hydroxide; etc.
6	2902 Cyclic hydrocarbons		**16**	3902 Polymers of propylene or of other olefins
7	3102 Mineral or chemical fertilizers, nitrogenous		**17**	3402 Organic surface-active agents (other than soap), etc.
8	2901 Acyclic hydrocarbons		**18**	3903 Polymers of styrene, in primary forms
9	2903 Halogenated derivatives of hydrocarbons		**19**	7308 Structures and parts of structures
10	8544 Insulated wire or cable		**20**	2009 Fruit and vegetable juices

Note: The area of the circles is proportional to the export turnover
Source: ITC calculations based on COMTRADE statistics.

Syrian Arab Republic

Key Indicators

Surface area (thousand sq. km.)	185.2
Population (millions), 2001	17.1
Population (average annual percent growth), 1980–2000	3.1 %
Life expectancy at birth, 2000	
Male (years)	67
Female (years)	72
Adult illiteracy rate (percent), 2000	
Male	12 %
Female	40 %
Gross tertiary enrollment ratio, 1998 or most recent year	6 %

Gross domestic product (US$ billion), 2001	19.5
Gross domestic product (average annual percent growth), 1990–2000	5.8 %
Gross national income per capita (US$, PPP), 2000	3,340
Growth of output (average annual percent growth), 1990–2000	
Agriculture	5.3 %
Industry	9.9 %
Manufacturing	10.8 %
Services	4.6 %
Inflation (annual percentage change), 2001	1.0 %

Unemployment (percent of total labor force)	—
Gross national savings rate (percent of GDP), 2001	—
Gross capital formation (percent of GDP), 2000	20.7 %
Household final consumption (percent of GDP), 2000	62.4 %

Current government revenue (ex grants, percent of GDP), 2001	—
Total government expenditure (percent of GDP), 2001	—
Overall budget deficit/surplus (percent of GDP), 2001	—
Highest marginal tax rate, 2001	
Individual	64 %
Corporate	—

Money and quasi money (annual percent growth), 2000	19.0 %
Domestic credit provided by the banking sector (percent of GDP), 2000	27.6 %

Stock market capitalization (US$ million), end 2001	—

Exports of goods (US$ million), 2001	4,536
Imports of goods (US$ million), 2001	4,669
Net energy imports (percent of commercial energy use), 1999[2]	-90 %
Current account balance (percent of GDP), 2001	1.1 %
Foreign direct investment inward stock (US$ million), 2000	1,338
Foreign direct investment (percent of gross capital formation), 2000	3.2 %
Total international reserves minus gold (US$ million), end 2001	—
Total international reserves minus gold (months of import coverage), 2001	—
Total foreign debt (US$ million), 2001	22,265
Long-term debt (US$ million), 2001	16,089
Total debt service (percent of GDP), 2001	2.5 %
Total foreign debt service paid (percent of exports of goods), 2001	10.8 %
Sovereign long-term foreign debt ratings, July 2002	
Moody's	—
Standard and Poors	—
Real exchange rate Pound to US$, (1997=100), 2001[3]	109.9

Sources: The Heritage Foundation 2002 Index of Economic Freedom; World Development Indicators 2002; IMF International Financial Statistics 2002; IMF World Economic Outlook Database, April 2002; Economist Intelligence Unit; UNCTAD FDI Statistics.

[2] A minus sign indicates that the country is a net energy exporter

[3] Values greater (less) than 100 indicate appreciation (depreciation)

Syrian Arab Republic

Exchange rate arrangements

Currency	Syrian Pound
Exchange rate structure	Multiple
Classification	Conventional pegged
Exchange tax	No
Exchange subsidy	No
Forward exchange market	No

Controls on current payments and transfers

	Controls in place?
Arrangements for payments and receipts	
Bilateral payments arrangements	●
Payments arrears	●
Controls on Payments for invisible transactions and current transfers	●
Proceeds from exports and/or invisible transactions	
Repatriation requirements	●
Surrender requirements	●

Capital controls

	Controls in place?
Capital market securities	●
Money market instruments	●
Collective investment securities	●
Derivatives and other instruments	—
Commercial credits	●
Financial credits	●
Guarantees, sureties, and financial backup facilities	●
Direct investment	●
Liquidation of direct investment	●
Real estate transactions	●
Personal capital movements	—
Provisions specific to commercial banks and other credit institutions	●
Provisions specific to institutional investors	—

● = The specific practice is a feature of the exchange system and a control is in place.

▲ = The specific practice is not regulated.

— = Data not available.

Source: IMF Annual Report on Exchange Arrangements and Exchange Restrictions 2001

Real exchange rate (Pound to US$)

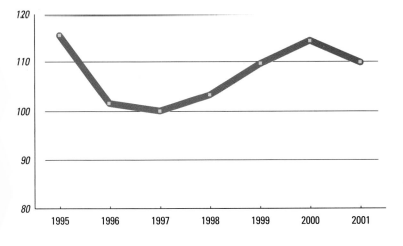

Index Numbers (1997=100): Period Averages
A higher (lower) exchange rate indicates an appreciation (depreciation) of the currency.

Source: IMF International Financial Statistics 2002

Export Profile Table of Syrian Arab Republic

R A N K	HS Code and Product Label	Exports 2000 US$ m	Net Exports 2000 US$ m	Export Growth, 1996–2000 % per annum value	Export Growth, 1996–2000 % per annum quantity	World Trade Growth, 1996–2000 % per annum value	World Trade Growth, 1996–2000 % per annum quantity	Share in World %	Leading Markets 1st	Leading Markets %	Leading Markets 2nd	Leading Markets %
	ALL GOODS	4,498		4								
	ALL GOODS (WTO)	4,250	390									
4	0104 Live sheep and goats	77	69			-7.8	-0.2	15.1	SAU	100	JOR	0
13	0504 Guts, bladders and stomachs of animals (other than fish)	16	16	-1		-2.1	3.0	1.1	DEU	73	DNK	11
8	0702 Tomatoes	41	41			-1.3	-0.1	1.4	SAU	92	RUS	3
18	0713 Vegetables, leguminous dried	11	9	-21		-4.3	1.7	0.6	TUR	45	JOR	39
14	0805 Citrus fruit, fresh or dried	16	16			-4.5	0.5	0.3	SAU	90	BHR	9
25	0806 Grapes, fresh or dried	7	7			1.8	3.0	0.2	SAU	75	JOR	22
38	0807 Melons, watermelons and papaws, fresh	4	4			1.2	3.4	0.3	SAU	64	BHR	30
34	0808 Apples, pears and quinces, fresh	5	5	111		-5.2	0.5	0.1	SAU	89	BHR	6
16	0809 Apricots, cherries, peaches, nectarines, fresh	13	13			-1.8	4.8	0.7	SAU	87	BHR	12
10	0909 Seeds of anise, badian, fennel, coriander, cumin, caraway or juniper	31	31	16		-1.8	-1.1	19.5	USA	25	BRA	12
35	1006 Rice	4	-9	328		-6.1	3.9	0.1	NGA	93	SEN	7
19	1404 Vegetable products, other	11	10	7		-1.1	7.1	3.4	USA	33	DEU	32
40	1512 Safflower, sunflower or cotton-seed oil and fractions	4	-1	185		-8.8	-3.1	0.3	TUR	85	JOR	15
11	2510 Calcium and aluminum calcium phosphates, natural and phosphatic chalk	20	20	4		-3.6	-4.0	1.8	PRT	20	ITA	19
1	2709 Crude petroleum oils	3,206	3,206	4		7.2	1.0	0.9	DEU	44	FRA	16
2	2710 Non-crude petroleum oils	295	224	11		6.9	4.3	0.2	ITA	42	USA	21
6	4105 Sheep or lamb skin leather, without wool	52	52	9		-3.8	7.0	3.5	ITA	93	KOR	6
3	5201 Cotton, not carded or combed	220	220	1		-13.7	-5.1	3.8	TUR	32	ITA	16
33	5202 Cotton waste (including yarn waste and garnetted stock)	5	5	-5		-8.6	1.5	2.0	TUR	39	ITA	34
23	5204 Cotton sewing thread, whether or not for retail sale	8	8	471		1.4	8.8	5.3	DEU	94	TUR	5
5	5205 Cotton yarn (other than sewing thread), not for retail sale	70	68	110		-0.3	4.7	1.1	ITA	47	PRT	31
21	5407 Woven fabrics of synthetic filament yarn	9	-30			-0.8	6.4	0.1	SAU	33	DZA	19
31	6103 Men's or boys' suits, jackets, trousers and shorts (other than swimwear), knitted or crocheted, etc.	5	5	39		4.2	9.9	0.2	USA	69	FRA	11
22	6104 Women's suits, dresses, skirts and shorts (other than swimwear), knitted or crocheted	8	8	31		1.0	5.5	0.1	USA	52	DEU	12
37	6105 Men's or boys' shirts, knitted or crocheted	4	4	68		-2.0	0.6	0.1	USA	34	FRA	25
26	6107 Men's or boys' underpants, nightshirts, pyjamas, bathrobes, etc., knitted or crocheted	7	7	8		5.0	7.9	0.3	DEU	65	JOR	24
24	6108 Women's or girls' slips, panties, pyjamas, bathrobes, etc., knitted or crocheted	7	7			5.4	8.3	0.1	SAU	42	DEU	36
9	6109 T-shirts, singlets and other vests, knitted or crocheted	36	36	2		9.9	11.5	0.3	DEU	35	USA	22
12	6110 Jerseys, pullovers, cardigans, waistcoats, etc., knitted or crocheted	20	19	33		7.9	9.5	0.1	USA	34	DEU	18
36	6111 Babies' garments and clothing access, knitted or crocheted	4	4	44		10.6	11.1	0.1	USA	47	DEU	24
15	6203 Men's or boys' suits, jackets, trousers and shorts (other than swimwear), etc.	13	13	6		3.5	8.6	0.1	USA	49	DEU	15
17	6204 Women's or girls' suits, jackets, dresses skirts, etc. and shorts (other than swimwear)	13	13	1		4.4	7.9	0.0	GBR	40	DEU	19
29	6205 Men's or boys' shirts	6	6	1		0.3	3.2	0.1	FRA	69	USA	12
20	6206 Women's or girls' blouses, shirts and shirt-blouses	9	9	-12		-1.1	3.2	01	GBR	60	DEU	16
27	6208 Women's or girls' singlets, slips, briefs, pyjamas, bathrobes, etc.	7	7	49		1.0	6.4	0.3	JOR	58	USA	25
39	6302 Bed, table, toilet and kitchen linens	4	3	5		4.2	7.6	0.1	JOR	44	DEU	28
32	7610 Aluminium structures and parts of structures (i.e., bridges and bridge-sections, roofs, doors and windows), etc.	5	5	351		1.2	5.9	0.2	GBR	100	JOR	0
30	8504 Electric transformer, static converter*	5	-20	149		9.3	11.5	0.0	NGA	98	JPN	1
7	9706 Antiques more than one hundred years old	43	42	40				1.6	USA	99	JPN	0
28	9999 Special Transaction Trade	6	-17	41		8.1		0.0	USA	76	GBR	10

Notes: The indicators are based on the partner countries' export statistics (mirror estimates).

*May include re-exports or ships registration.

Export Profile Chart for Selected Key Products

Syrian Arab Republic

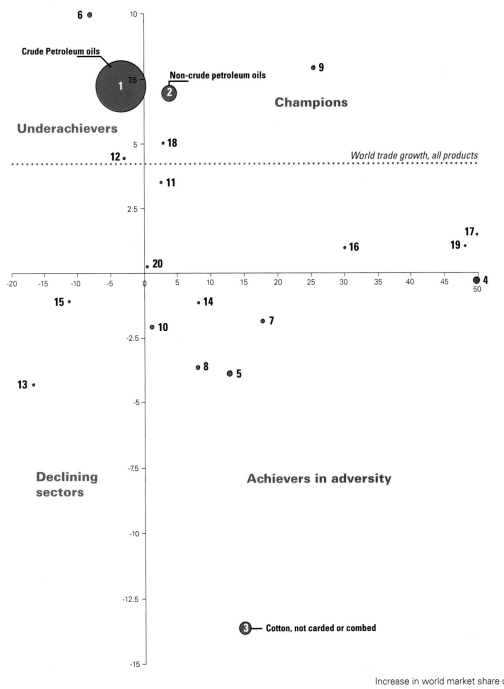

World trade growth, % per annum, 1996–2000

Increase in world market share of Syria, 1996–2000

Champions

Underachievers

Declining sectors

Achievers in adversity

World trade growth, all products

Crude Petroleum oils

Non-crude petroleum oils

3 — Cotton, not carded or combed

Key

1 2709 **Crude Petroleum oils**	11 6203 **Men's or boys' suits, jackets, trousers, etc.**
2 2710 **Non-crude petroleum oils**	12 6204 **Women's or girls' suits, jackets, etc.**
3 5201 **Cotton, not carded or combed**	13 0713 **Vegetables, leguminous dried**
4 5205 **Cotton yarn not for retail sale**	14 1404 **Vegetable products, other**
5 4105 **Sheep or lamb skin leather, without wool**	15 6206 **Women's or girls' blouses, shirts, etc.**
6 6109 **T-shirts, singlets and other vests, etc.**	16 6104 **Women's girls' suits, dresses, etc.**
7 0909 **Seeds of anise, badian, fennel, etc.**	17 5204 **Cotton sewing thread**
8 2510 **Calcium and aluminum calcium phosphates**	18 6107 **Men's and boys' underpants, nightshirts, etc.**
9 6110 **Jerseys, pullovers, cardigans, waistcoats, etc.**	19 6208 **Women's or girls' singlets, slips, etc.**
10 0504 **Guts, bladders and stomachs of animals**	20 6205 **Men's or boys' shirts**

Note: The area of the circles is proportional to the export turnover
Source: ITC calculations based on COMTRADE statistics.

Tunisia

Key Indicators

Surface area (thousand sq. km.)	163.6
Population (millions), 2001	9.7
Population (average annual percent growth), 1980–2000	2.0 %
Life expectancy at birth, 2000	
Male (years)	70
Female (years)	74
Adult illiteracy rate (percent), 2000	
Male	19 %
Female	39 %
Gross tertiary enrollment ratio, 1998 or most recent year	17 %

Gross domestic product (US$ billion), 2001	20.0
Gross domestic product (average annual percent growth), 1990–2000	4.7 %
Gross national income per capita (US$, PPP), 2000	6,070
Growth of output (average annual percent growth), 1990–2000	
Agriculture	2.4 %
Industry	4.6 %
Manufacturing	5.5 %
Services	5.3 %
Inflation (annual percentage change), 2001	1.9 %

Unemployment (percent of total labor force), 2001	15.6 %
Gross national savings rate (percent of GDP), 2001	22.6 %
Gross capital formation (percent of GDP), 2000	27.4 %
Household final consumption (percent of GDP), 2000	60.5 %

Current government revenue (ex grants, percent of GDP), 2001	30.3 %
Total government expenditure (percent of GDP), 2001	32.9 %
Overall budget deficit/surplus (percent of GDP), 2001	-2.6 %
Highest marginal tax rate, 2001	
Individual	35 %
Corporate	35 %

Money and quasi money (annual percent growth), 2000	14.1 %
Domestic credit provided by the banking sector (percent of GDP), 2000	73.2 %

Stock market capitalization (US$ million), end 2001	2,303

Exports of goods (US$ million), 2001	6,605
Imports of goods (US$ million), 2001	9,493
Net energy imports (percent of commercial energy use), 1999	7 %
Current account balance (percent of GDP), 2001	-4.8 %
Foreign direct investment inward stock (US$ million), 2000	11,566
Foreign direct investment (percent of gross capital formation), 2000	14.1 %
Total international reserves minus gold (US$ million), end 2001	1,989.2
Total international reserves minus gold (months of import coverage), 2001	2.5
Total foreign debt (US$ million), 2001	10,944
Long-term debt (US$ million), 2001	9,926
Total debt service (percent of GDP), 2001	8.2 %
Total foreign debt service paid (percent of exports of goods), 2001	24.7 %
Sovereign long-term foreign debt ratings, July 2002	
Moody's	Baa3[1]
Standard and Poors	BBB
Real effective exchange rate (1997=100), 2001[3]	96.7

Sources: The Heritage Foundation 2002 Index of Economic Freedom; World Development Indicators 2002; IMF International Financial Statistics 2002; IMF World Economic Outlook Database, April 2002; Economist Intelligence Unit; UNCTAD FDI Statistics.

[1] Issuer's rating

[3] Values greater (less) than 100 indicate appreciation (depreciation)

Tunisia

Exchange rate arrangements

Currency	Tunisian Dinar
Exchange rate structure	Unitary
Classification	Managed floating
Exchange tax	No
Exchange subsidy	No
Forward exchange market	Yes

Controls on current payments and transfers

	Controls in place?
Arrangements for payments and receipts	
Bilateral payments arrangements	
Payments arrears	
Controls on Payments for invisible transactions and current transfers	●
Proceeds from exports and/or invisible transactions	
Repatriation requirements	●
Surrender requirements	●

Capital controls

	Controls in place?
Capital market securities	●
Money market instruments	●
Collective investment securities	●
Derivatives and other instruments	●
Commercial credits	●
Financial credits	●
Guarantees, sureties, and financial backup facilities	●
Direct investment	●
Liquidation of direct investment	
Real estate transactions	●
Personal capital movements	●
Provisions specific to commercial banks and other credit institutions	●
Provisions specific to institutional investors	●

● = The specific practice is a feature of the exchange system and a control is in place.

▲ = The specific practice is not regulated.

— = Data not available.

Source: IMF Annual Report on Exchange Arrangements and Exchange Restrictions 2001

Real effective exchange rate

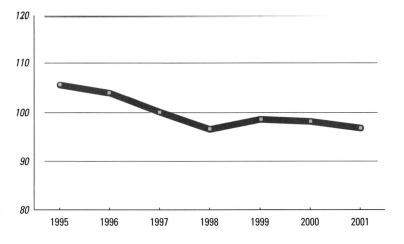

Index Numbers (1997=100): Period Averages
A higher (lower) exchange rate indicates an appreciation (depreciation) of the currency.

Source: Economist Intelligence Unit

Export Profile Table of Tunisia

R A N K	HS Code and Product Label	Exports 2000 US$ m	Net Exports 2000 US$ m	Export Growth, 1996–2000 % per annum value	quantity	World Trade Growth, 1996–2000 % per annum value	quantity	Share in World %	Leading Markets 1st	%	2nd	%
	ALL GOODS	5,845		2								
	ALL GOODS (WTO)	5,850	-2,710									
20	0306 Crustaceans	54	54	9	16.1	3.1	2.8	0.4	ESP	55	ITA	37
24	0804 Dates, figs, pineapples, etc.	39	38	-4	5.1	6.5	6.6	2.1	FRA	37	ITA	16
33	1101 Wheat or meslin flour	26	26	19	35.0	-6.8	2.9	3.3	LBY	95	nes	4
6	1509 Olive oil	193	192	12	35.0	-7.8	4.9	8.9	ITA	76	ESP	12
39	2002 Tomatoes prepared or preserved	20	19	34	40.4	-3.7	1.7	1.6	LBY	97	FRA	2
36	2402 Cigars, cigarillos and cigarettes	22	-1	-7	-12.9	-3.7	0.5	0.2	bun	27	nes	20
25	2510 Calcium and aluminum calcium phosphates, natural and phosphatic chalk	34	34	-4	-4.1	-3.6	-4.0	3.1	POL	30	TUR	20
34	2523 Portland, aluminous and slag cement, supersulphate cement and similar hydraulic cements	24	15	-15	-18.4	0.5	3.2	0.6	DZA	62	LBY	17
37	2608 Zinc ores and concentrates	21	21	30	32.3	-0.9	-0.7	1.0	RUS	27	BEL	24
2	2709 Crude petroleum oils	611	361	6	0.7	7.2	1.0	0.2	ITA	45	ESP	25
16	2710 Non-crude petroleum oils	96	-374	-16	-19.3	6.9	4.3	0.1	CHE	31	bun	15
7	2809 Diphosphorus pentaoxide; phosphoric acid and polyphosphoric acids	177	177	-6	-2.7	-7.3	-5.4	18.7	IND	61	IRN	11
31	2826 Fluorides, fluorosilicate, fluor aluminates and other complex fluorine salt	30	30	6	14.2	4.4	3.5	5.2	ZAF	22	BHR	20
19	2835 Phosphinates, phosphonates, phosphates and polyphosphates	57	55	0	6.1	-3.3	1.3	4.1	EGY	48	MAR	11
15	3103 Mineral or chemical fertilizers, phosphatic	108	108	-4	3.8	-8.5	-3.4	18.9	IRN	27	BRA	19
8	3105 Mineral or chemical fertilizers containing nitrogen, phosphorus and potassium, etc.	158	156	-3	6.6	-4.4	0.7	3.2	ITA	22	TUR	19
23	5209 Woven fabric of cotton, weighing over 200 grams per meter squared	49	-305	-4	-4.1	0.8	5.9	0.7	nes	42	FRA	33
38	6103 Men's or boys' suits, jackets, trousers and shorts (other than swimwear), knitted or crocheted	21	20	53	64.4	4.2	9.9	1.0	FRA	62	ITA	32
27	6104 Women's suits, dresses, skirts and shorts (other than swimwear), knitted or crocheted	34	32	5	7.3	1.0	5.5	0.6	FRA	47	DEU	46
28	6108 Women's or girls' slips, panties, pyjamas, bathrobes, etc., knitted or crocheted	33	14	-4	4.9	5.4	8.3	0.5	ITA	37	FRA	26
13	6109 T-shirts, singlets and other vests, knitted or crocheted	118	79	17	22.2	9.9	11.5	0.8	ITA	38	FRA	25
9	6110 Jerseys, pullovers, cardigans, waistcoats, etc., knitted or crocheted	144	98	10	17.9	7.9	9.5	0.5	ITA	68	FRA	18
32	6112 Track suits, ski suits and swimwear, knitted or crocheted	29	21	-5	2.1	-0.8	3.7	1.4	FRA	51	NLD	27
26	6201 Men's or boys' overcoats, capes, windjackets, etc.	34	30	-16	-7.7	-3.4	0.6	0.6	ITA	41	FRA	25
1	6203 Men's or boys' suits, jackets, trousers and shorts (other than swimwear)	642	620	-6	-0.2	3.5	8.6	2.7	FRA	37	ITA	19
4	6204 Women's or girls' suits, jackets, dresses skirts, etc. and shorts (other than swimwear)	356	347	-2	7.2	4.4	7.9	1.2	DEU	34	FRA	28
17	6205 Men's or boys' shirts	84	71	-6	-1.9	0.3	3.2	0.9	DEU	35	FRA	31
21	6206 Women's or girls' blouses, shirts and shirt-blouses	50	49	-8	0.4	-1.1	3.2	0.7	DEU	46	FRA	34
22	6208 Women's or girls' singlets, slips, briefs, pyjamas, bathrobes, etc.	49	29	0	2.9	1.0	6.4	2.2	FRA	46	ITA	30
3	6211 Track suits, ski suits and swimwear; other garments	356	307	7	10.6	-2.4	3.6	6.9	FRA	44	BEL	18
12	6212 Brassieres, girdles, corsets, suspenders, etc.	125	78	2	15.7	7.4	8.0	2.4	FRA	42	ITA	17
14	6403 Footwear with outer sole of rubber, plastic, leather	117	76	8	15.0	-0.6	0.6	0.4	ITA	46	DEU	24
11	6406 Parts of footwear; removable in-soles, heel cushions	130	84	5	9.8	-4.1	0.4	3.1	ITA	51	FRA	44
35	6908 Glazed ceramic flags and paving, tiles; glazed ceramic mosaic cubes, etc.	23	20	15	26.5	0.3	4.3	0.5	LBY	38	FRA	25
18	8504 Electric transformer, static converter	73	12	14	19.1	9.3	11.5	0.2	DEU	42	FRA	35
30	8534 Printed circuits	31	27	25	40.0	16.7	19.4	0.2	DEU	55	ITA	22
10	8536 Electrical applications for switching (i.e. fuses, etc.)	140	47	24	23.6	7.5	10.3	0.4	FRA	51	DEU	38
40	8538 Parts suitable for use with electrical apparatus	20	-81	96	84.4	5.8	6.7	0.2	ITA	79	FRA	11
5	8544 Insulated wire or cable	287	184	13	24.0	6.8	7.7	0.8	DEU	43	FRA	30
29	8708 Parts and accessories of large motor vehicles, tractors, etc.	33	-56	14	30.3	5.9	11.4	0.0	FRA	58	DEU	16
	Other services, credit	321	53	2		4.0		0.1				
	Transport services, credit	578	33	-3		1.5		0.2				
	Travel, credit	1,688	1,444	3		1.9		0.4				

Notes: The indicators are based on Tunisian trade statistics.

*May include re-exports or ships registration.

Export Profile Chart for Selected Key Products

Tunisia

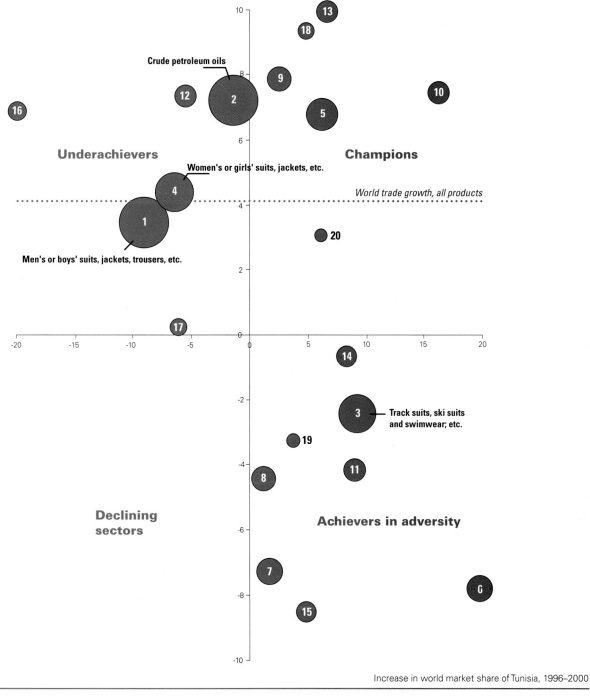

World trade growth, % per annum, 1996–2000

Crude petroleum oils

Underachievers

Champions

Women's or girls' suits, jackets, etc.

World trade growth, all products

Men's or boys' suits, jackets, trousers, etc.

Track suits, ski suits and swimwear; etc.

Declining sectors

Achievers in adversity

Increase in world market share of Tunisia, 1996–2000

Key

1	6203	**Men's or boys' suits, jackets, trousers, etc.**
2	2709	**Crude petroleum oils**
3	6211	**Track suits, ski suits and swimwear; etc.**
4	6204	**Women's or girls' suits, jackets, etc.**
5	8544	**Insulated wire or cable**
6	1509	**Olive oil**
7	2809	**Diphosphorus pentaoxide; phosphoric acid etc.**
8	3105	**Mineral or chemical fertilizers, phosphatic**
9	6110	**Jerseys, pullovers, cardigans, waistcoats, etc.**
10	8536	**Electrical applications for switching (i.e. fuses, etc.)**
11	6406	**Parts of footwear; removable in-soles, etc.**
12	6212	**Brassieres, girdles, corsets, suspenders, etc.**
13	6109	**T-shirts, singlets and other vests, etc.**
14	6403	**Footwear with outer sole of rubber, plastic, leather**
15	3103	**Mineral or chemical fertilizers, phosphatic**
16	2710	**Non-crude petroleum oils**
17	6205	**Men's or boys' shirts**
18	8504	**Electric transformer, static converter**
19	2835	**Phosphinates, phosphonates, etc.**
20	0306	**Crustaceans**

Note: The area of the circles is proportional to the export turnover
Source: ITC calculations based on COMTRADE statistics.

United Arab Emirates

Key Indicators

Surface area (thousand sq. km.)	82.9
Population (millions), 2001	3.3
Population (average annual percent growth), 1980–2000	5.1 %
Life expectancy at birth, 2000	
Male (years)	74
Female (years)	77
Adult illiteracy rate (percent), 2000	
Male	25 %
Female	21 %
Gross tertiary enrollment ratio, 1998 or most recent year	13 %

Gross domestic product (US$ billion), 2001	67.5
Gross domestic product (average annual percent growth), 1990–2000	2.9 %
Gross national income per capita (US$, PPP), 2000	—
Growth of output (average annual percent growth), 1990–2000	
Agriculture	—
Industry	—
Manufacturing	—
Services	—
Inflation (annual percentage change), 2001	2.2 %

Unemployment (percent of total labor force), 2000	2.3 %
Gross national savings rate (percent of GDP), 2001	34.8 %
Gross capital formation (percent of GDP), 2000	—
Household final consumption (percent of GDP), 2000	—

Current government revenue (ex grants, percent of GDP), 2001	27.1 %
Total government expenditure (percent of GDP), 2001	33.3 %
Overall budget deficit/surplus (percent of GDP), 2001	-6.2 %
Highest marginal tax rate, 2001	
Individual	0 %
Corporate	0 %

Money and quasi money (annual percent growth), 2000	15.3 %
Domestic credit provided by the banking sector (percent of GDP), 2000	—

Stock market capitalization (US$ million), end 2001	13,660

Exports of goods (US$ million), 2001	49,196
Imports of goods (US$ million), 2001	39,658
Net energy imports (percent of commercial energy use), 1999[2]	-383 %
Current account balance (percent of GDP), 2001	10.2 %
Foreign direct investment inward stock (US$ million), 2000	2,642
Foreign direct investment (percent of gross capital formation), 2000	—
Total international reserves minus gold (US$ million), end 2001	14,146.4
Total international reserves minus gold (months of import coverage), 2001	4.3
Total foreign debt (US$ million), 2001	18,513
Long-term debt (US$ million), 2001	7,204
Total debt service (percent of GDP), 2001	2.1 %
Total foreign debt service paid (percent of exports of goods), 2001	3.0 %
Sovereign long-term foreign debt ratings, July 2002	
Moody's	A2
Standard and Poors	—
Real effective exchange rate (1997=100), 2001[3]	112.2

Sources: The Heritage Foundation 2002 Index of Economic Freedom; World Development Indicators 2002; IMF International Financial Statistics 2002; IMF World Economic Outlook Database, April 2002; International Labor Office LABORSTA; Economist Intelligence Unit; UNCTAD FDI Statistics.

[2] A minus sign indicates that the country is a net energy exporter

[3] Values greater (less) than 100 indicate appreciation (depreciation)

Exchange rate arrangements

Currency	U.A.E Dirham
Exchange rate structure	Unitary
Classification	Conventional pegged
Exchange tax	No
Exchange subsidy	No
Forward exchange market	Yes

Controls on current payments and transfers

	Controls in place?
Arrangements for payments and receipts	
Bilateral payments arrangements	
Payments arrears	
Controls on Payments for invisible transactions and current transfers	
Proceeds from exports and/or invisible transactions	
Repatriation requirements	
Surrender requirements	

Capital controls

	Controls in place?
Capital market securities	●
Money market instruments	
Collective investment securities	●
Derivatives and other instruments	
Commercial credits	
Financial credits	
Guarantees, sureties, and financial backup facilities	
Direct investment	●
Liquidation of direct investment	
Real estate transactions	●
Personal capital movements	
Provisions specific to commercial banks and other credit institutions	●
Provisions specific to institutional investors	

● = The specific practice is a feature of the exchange system and a control is in place.

▲ = The specific practice is not regulated.

— = Data not available.

Source: IMF Annual Report on Exchange Arrangements and Exchange Restrictions 2001

Real effective exchange rate

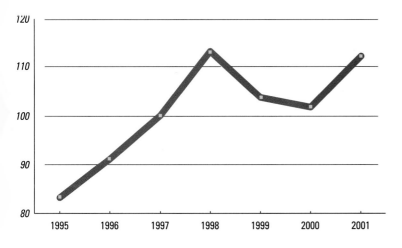

Index Numbers (1997=100): Period Averages
A higher (lower) exchange rate indicates an appreciation (depreciation) of the currency.

Source: Economist Intelligence Unit

Export Profile Table of United Arab Emirates

R A N K	HS Code and Product Label	Exports 2000 US$ m	Net Exports 2000 US$ m	Export Growth, 1996–2000 % per annum		World Trade Growth, 1996–2000 % per annum		Share in World	Leading Markets			
				value	quantity	value	quantity	%	1st	%	2nd	%
	ALL GOODS	30,237		6								
	ALL GOODS (WTO)	39,900	7,970									
12	0101 Live horses*	109	-82	19		12.8	14.6	6.2	GBR	94	IRL	5
16	0902 Tea*	82	58			0.8	0.5	4.0	SAU	70	IRN	19
39	1006 Rice*	32	30	28		-6.1	3.9	0.6	IRN	92	USA	2
15	1701 Cane or beet sugar*	91	-120	55		-11.0	-1.2	1.3	IRN	38	IDN	27
33	2523 Portland, aluminous and slag cement, supersulphate cement and similar hydraulic cements	38	34	14		0.5	3.2	0.9	BHR	35	SAU	24
1	2709 Crude petroleum oils	17,895	17,850	3		7.2	1.0	5.1	JPN	64	KOR	20
3	2710 Non-crude petroleum oils	2,972	2,756	22		6.9	4.3	2.3	JPN	34	KOR	21
2	2711 Petroleum gases	3,022	2,974	8		7.1	2.3	4.1	JPN	75	KOR	11
9	2909 Ether	134	127	-2		7.1	4.7	2.8	USA	78	NLD	21
32	3004 Medicaments of mixed or unmixed products for therapeutic prophylactic uses, in dosage	41	-138			14.2	10.2	0.1	SAU	86	BHR	4
28	3303 Perfumes and toilet waters	53	-175	25		5.0	7.9	1.2	SAU	24	BEL	20
21	4011 New pneumatic tires, of rubber	65	-194	7		2.8	8.3	0.3	IRN	52	BEL	11
36	5208 Woven fabrics of cotton, weighing no more than 200 grams per meter squared	36	-6	14		-5.4	-1.2	0.5	USA	36	DEU	17
24	5407 Woven fabrics of synthetic filament yarn	60	-517	10		-0.8	6.4	0.5	IRN	82	DZA	3
34	6105 Men's or boys' shirts, knitted or crocheted	36	26	-4		-2.0	0.6	0.8	USA	45	GBR	25
22	6109 T-shirts, singlets and other vests, knitted or crocheted	64	-12	-3		9.9	11.5	0.5	GBR	30	FRA	14
13	6110 Jerseys, pullovers, cardigans, waistcoats, etc., knitted or crocheted	99	67	15		7.9	9.5	0.3	USA	38	GBR	24
26	6203 Men's or boys' suits, jackets, trousers and shorts (other than swimwear), etc.	58	-41	20		3.5	8.6	0.2	GBR	33	USA	32
10	6204 Women's or girls' suits, jackets, dresses skirts, etc. and shorts (other than swimwear)	131	60	10		4.4	7.9	0.4	USA	77	GBR	6
29	6205 Men's or boys' shirts	52	8	-7		0.3	3.2	0.6	USA	63	DEU	12
25	6908 Glazed ceramic flags and paving, tiles; glazed ceramic mosaic cubes, etc.	58	23			0.3	4.3	1.1	SAU	53	DEU	5
38	7018 Glass beads, imitation pearls, imitation precious or semi-precious stones, etc.	34	-51	25		7.8	10.2	4.5	HKG	97	CZE	1
5	7102 Diamonds, not mounted or set*	319	-2	99				0.6	BEL	52	HKG	24
20	7108 Gold (including gold plated with platinum), unwrought or in semi-manufactured form*	66	-228	-5		-11.0	-5.0	0.4	SGP	59	SAU	17
8	7113 Articles of jewellery and parts thereof, of precious metals, etc.*	148	-553	2				1.1	GBR	53	SGP	12
31	7308 Structures and parts of structures (i.e., bridges and bridge-sections, roofs, doors and windows, etc.)	43	-18	41		2.0	5.4	0.5	GBR	34	SAU	14
40	7317 Nails, tacks, staples and similar articles, of iron or steel	31	27	37		3.5	5.5	2.8	USA	96	ETH	3
4	7601 Unwrought aluminum	668	658	13		3.3	4.3	2.8	JPN	26	USA	15
6	8411 Turbo-jets and other gas turbines*	295	-135	13		12.7	10.2	0.7	GBR	52	HKG	39
23	8415 Air conditioning machines*	62	-86	13		3.0	10.9	0.5	IRN	77	SAU	8
19	8431 Machinery parts*	68	-194	10		1.7	3.8	0.4	CAN	75	IRN	6
11	8471 Automatic data processing machines*	114	-415	27		7.7	13.4	0.1	IRN	46	GBR	30
17	8473 Machine parts and accessories*	75	-229	23		11.8	13.1	0.1	IRN	39	GBR	39
37	8521 Video recording or reproducing apparatus*	35	-211	22		7.4	10.6	0.2	HKG	56	GBR	17
14	8525 Television cameras, radios*	93	-688	48		23.6	19.5	0.2	HKG	60	GBR	20
30	8528 Television receivers*	48	-293	13		6.7	8.0	0.2	TKM	44	SGP	12
35	8529 Parts suitable for use solely or principally with the transition, reception and radar apparatus, etc.*	36	-85	20		10.8	9.0	0.1	TKM	76	IRN	8
27	8703 Motor vehicles designed for the transport of persons*	54	-1,267	-12		6.4	7.0	0.0	HKG	40	GBR	12
18	8708 Parts and accessories of large motor vehicles, tractors, etc.*	70	-225	17		5.9	11.4	0.1	IRN	49	HKG	20
7	9999 Special Transaction Trade	180	-188	3		8.1		0.1	USA	73	SGP	13

Notes: The indicators are based on the partner countries' export statistics (mirror estimates).

*Including re-exports Dubai is the major regional re-export center Around one third of UAE's imports are re-exportedto the region.

Export Profile Chart for Selected Key Products

United Arab Emirates

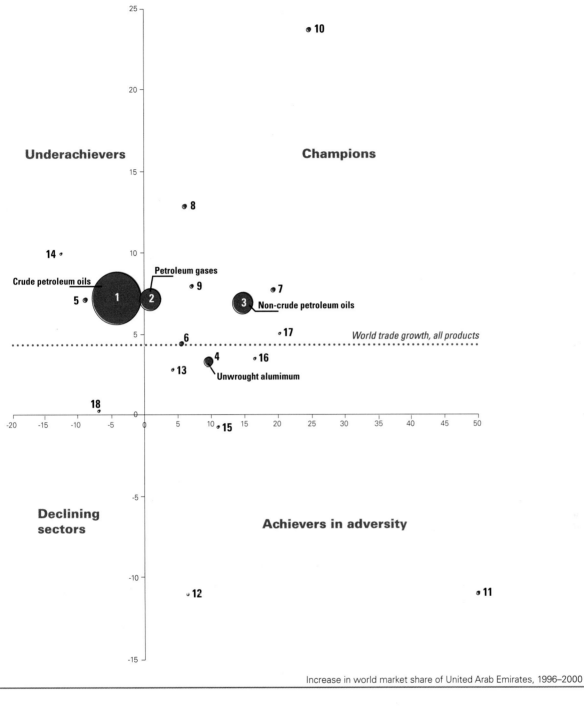

Underachievers

Champions

Crude petroleum oils

Petroleum gases

Non-crude petroleum oils

Unwrought alumimum

World trade growth, all products

Declining sectors

Achievers in adversity

World trade growth, % per annum, 1996–2000

Increase in world market share of United Arab Emirates, 1996–2000

Key

1. 2709 **Crude petroleum oils**
2. 2711 **Petroleum gases**
3. 2710 **Non-crude petroleum oils**
4. 7601 **Unwrought alumimum**
5. 2909 **Ether**
6. 6204 **Women's or girls' suits, jackets, etc.**
7. 8471 **Automatic data processing machines***
8. 0101 **Live horses***
9. 6110 **Jerseys, pullovers, cardigans, waistcoats, etc.**
10. 8525 **Television cameras, radios***

11. 1701 **Cane or beet sugar***
12. 7108 **Gold (including gold plated with platinum)***
13. 4011 **New pneumatic tires, of rubber**
14. 6109 **T-shirts, singlets and other vests, etc.**
15. 5407 **Woven fabrics of synthetic filament yarn**
16. 6203 **Men's or boys' suits, jackets, trousers, etc.**
17. 3303 **Perfumes and toilet waters**
18. 6205 **Men's or boys' shirts**

Source: ITC calculations based on COMTRADE statistics. Note: The area of the circles is proportional to the export turnover.

Including re-exports from Dubai, the major regional re-export center.

Around one third of UAE's imports are re-exported to the region.

Yemen, Rep.

Key Indicators

Surface area (thousand sq. km.)	528.0
Population (millions), 2001	19.0
Population (average annual percent growth), 1980–2000	3.6 %
Life expectancy at birth, 2000	
Male (years)	56
Female (years)	57
Adult illiteracy rate (percent), 2000	
Male	32 %
Female	75 %
Gross tertiary enrollment ratio, 1998 or most recent year	10 %

Gross domestic product (US$ billion), 2001	8.7
Gross domestic product (average annual percent growth), 1990–2000	5.8 %
Gross national income per capita (US$, PPP), 2000	770
Growth of output (average annual percent growth), 1990–2000	
Agriculture	5.1 %
Industry	7.9 %
Manufacturing	4.4 %
Services	5.1 %
Inflation (annual percentage change), 2001	11.9 %

Unemployment (percent of total labor force)	—
Gross national savings rate (percent of GDP), 2001	31.3 %
Gross capital formation (percent of GDP), 2000	19.2 %
Household final consumption (percent of GDP), 2000	57.8 %

Current government revenue (ex grants, percent of GDP), 2001	37.4 %
Total government expenditure (percent of GDP), 2001	36.3 %
Overall budget deficit/surplus (percent of GDP), 2001	1.1 %
Highest marginal tax rate, 2001	
Individual	35 %
Corporate	35 %

Money and quasi money (annual percent growth), 2000	25.3 %
Domestic credit provided by the banking sector (percent of GDP), 2000	5.2 %

Stock market capitalization (US$ million), end 2001	—

Exports of goods (US$ million), 2001	3,205
Imports of goods (US$ million), 2001	2,652
Net energy imports (percent of commercial energy use), 1999[2]	-545 %
Current account balance (percent of GDP), 2001	10.9 %
Foreign direct investment inward stock (US$ million), 2000	888
Foreign direct investment (percent of gross capital formation), 2000	-12.3 %
Total international reserves minus gold (US$ million), end 2001	3,658.1
Total international reserves minus gold (months of import coverage), 2001	16.6
Total foreign debt (US$ million), 2001	5,674
Long-term debt (US$ million), 2001	4,542
Total debt service (percent of GDP), 2001	3.0 %
Total foreign debt service paid (percent of exports of goods), 2001	8.3 %
Sovereign long-term foreign debt ratings, July 2002	
Moody's	—
Standard and Poors	—
Real effective exchange rate (1997=100), 2001[3]	132.8

Sources: The Heritage Foundation 2002 Index of Economic Freedom; World Development Indicators 2002; IMF International Financial Statistics 2002; IMF World Economic Outlook Database, April 2002; Economist Intelligence Unit; UNCTAD FDI Statistics.

[2]A minus sign indicates that the country is a net energy exporter

[3]Values greater (less) than 100 indicate appreciation (depreciation)

Exchange Rate and Capital Restrictions

Yemen, Rep.

Exchange rate arrangements

Currency	Yemeni Rial
Exchange rate structure	Unitary
Classification	Independently floating
Exchange tax	No
Exchange subsidy	No
Forward exchange market	No

Controls on current payments and transfers

	Controls in place?
Arrangements for payments and receipts	
Bilateral payments arrangements	
Payments arrears	●
Controls on Payments for invisible transactions and current transfers	
Proceeds from exports and/or invisible transactions	
Repatriation requirements	
Surrender requirements	

Capital controls

	Controls in place?
Capital market securities	
Money market instruments	
Collective investment securities	
Derivatives and other instruments	
Commercial credits	●
Financial credits	●
Guarantees, sureties, and financial backup facilities	●
Direct investment	
Liquidation of direct investment	
Real estate transactions	
Personal capital movements	
Provisions specific to commercial banks and other credit institutions	●
Provisions specific to institutional investors	

● = The specific practice is a feature of the exchange system and a control is in place.

▲ = The specific practice is not regulated.

— = Data not available.

Source: IMF Annual Report on Exchange Arrangements and Exchange Restrictions 2001

Real effective exchange rate

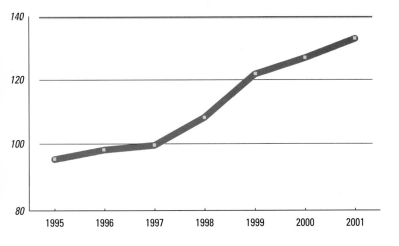

Index Numbers (1997=100): Period Averages
A higher (lower) exchange rate indicates an appreciation (depreciation) of the currency.

Source: Economist Intelligence Unit

Export Profile Table of Yemen, Rep.

RANK	HS Code and Product Label	Exports 2000 US$ m	Net Exports 2000 US$ m	Export Growth, 1996–2000 % per annum value	quantity	World Trade Growth, 1996–2000 % per annum value	quantity	Share in World %	Leading Markets 1st	%	2nd	%
	ALL GOODS	2,370		10								
	ALL GOODS (WTO)	4,200	1,320									
6	0104 Live sheep and goats	10	10			-7.8	-0.2	1.9	SAU	100	OMN	0
3	0302 Fish, fresh or chilled	21	21			1.6	3.3	0.3	SAU	88	JOR	7
23	0303 Frozen fish	1	1	3		1.6	2.2	0.0	FRA	34	SAU	29
13	0304 Fish fillets fresh, chilled or frozen	2	2			3.4	2.2	0.0	FRA	74	GBR	16
4	0305 Cured and smoked fish	15	15	17		-0.6	-1.5	0.6	HKG	97	SGP	1
8	0306 Crustaceans	5	5	-9		3.1	2.8	0.0	ESP	28	FRA	23
9	0307 Molluscs	5	5	7		-1.0	4.3	0.1	JPN	49	SGP	20
19	0409 Honey, natural	1	0						SAU	100		
12	0703 Onions, shallots, garlic	2	2						SAU	100		
7	0803 Bananas	8	7						SAU	100		
15	0806 Grapes, fresh or dried	2	1						SAU	100	SDN	0
24	0807 Melons (including watermelons) and papaws, fresh	1	1						SAU	100		
28	0810 Other fruits, fresh	1	1			2.4	4.2	0.0	SAU	100	ETH	0
5	0901 Coffee	11	10			-7.0	2.3	0.1	SAU	45	USA	30
16	1005 Maize (corn)*	1	-16						SAU	100		
30	1207 Oil seeds and oleaginous fruits, other	1	-1			-0.4	0.8	0.1	SAU	97	DZA	3
17	1517 Margarine; edible mixtures or preparations of animal or vegetable fats or oils, etc.	1	1	9		3.9	8.6	0.1	ETH	100	DZA	0
21	1905 Bread, pastry, cakes, biscuits and other bakers' wares, etc.	1	-4	9		1.7	5.6	0.0	ETH	92	GHA	4
26	2402 Cigars, cigarillos and cigarettes*	1	-4			-3.7	0.5	0.0	SAU	100	USA	0
20	2501 Salt	1	1	319		-4.2	0.5	0.1	ETH	98	SAU	2
1	2709 Crude petroleum oils	1,910	1,909	9		7.2	1.0	0.5	CHN	38	KOR	30
2	2710 Non-crude petroleum oils	317	307	21		6.9	4.3	0.2	ETH	74	KOR	7
10	2711 Petroleum gases	4	4	23		7.1	2.3	0.0	FRA	63	TUR	15
27	3401 Soap; organic surface-active products and preparations for use as soap*	1	-2	27		6.4	9.8	0.0	ETH	91	SAU	9
11	4102 Raw skins of sheep or lambs	3	3	-18		-20.7	-3.5	0.4	ITA	76	GBR	19
25	4820 Registers, account books, notebooks, and other stationary articles of paper	1	0	42		4.3	6.9	0.0	ETH	99	KEN	1
18	5201 Cotton, not carded or combed	1	1	4		-13.7	-5.1	0.0	KOR	49	PRT	35
14	7108 Gold (including gold plated with platinum), unwrought or in semi-manufactured form	2	2						SAU	100	NPL	0
29	7404 Copper waste and scrap	1	1	-21		-4.7	1.6	0.0	KOR	39	ITA	30
22	7602 Aluminum waste and scrap	1	1	-1		6.7	6.4	0.0	KOR	89	JPN	11

Notes: The indicators are based on the partner countries' export statistics (mirror estimates).

Export Profile Chart for Selected Key Products

Yemen, Rep.

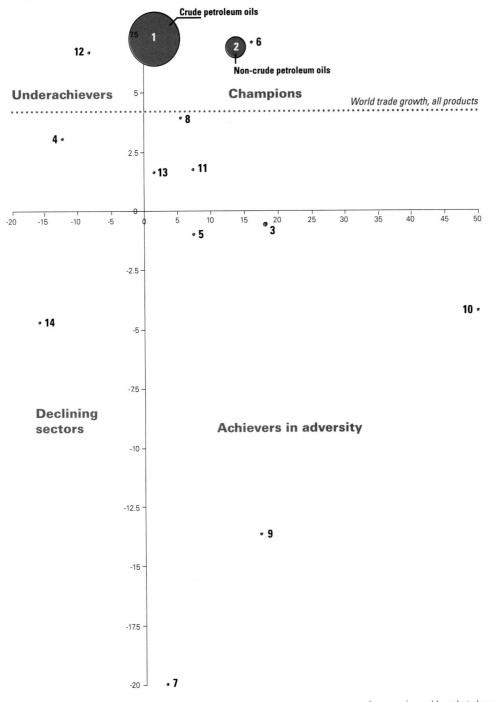

Crude petroleum oils

12 ·

Underachievers

Champions

World trade growth, all products

Non-crude petroleum oils

· **8**

4 ·

· **13** · **11**

· **5** 3

· **14**

10 ·

**Declining
sectors**

Achievers in adversity

· **9**

· **7**

World trade growth, % per annum, 1996–2000

Increase in world market share of Yemen, 1996–2000

Key

1	2709 **Crude petroleum oils**	**8**	1517 **Margarine, etc.**
2	2710 **Non-crude petroleum oils**	**9**	5201 **Cotton, not carded or combed**
3	0305 **Cured and smoked fish**	**10**	2501 **Salt**
4	0306 **Crustaceans**	**11**	1905 **Bread, pastry, cakes, etc.**
5	0307 **Molluscs**	**12**	7602 **Aluminum waste and scrap**
6	2711 **Petroleum gases**	**13**	0303 **Frozen fish**
7	4102 **Raw skins of sheep or lambs**	**14**	7404 **Copper waste and scrap**

Note: The area of the circles is proportional to the export turnover
Source: ITC calculations based on COMTRADE statistics.

Part 3

The Executive Opinion Survey

Interpreting the Executive Opinion Survey

By Jennifer Blanke

This section presents the responses by top business executives to our *Arab World Competitiveness Report 2002* Executive Opinion Survey, conducted in ten Arab world countries, Bahrain, Egypt, Jordan, Kuwait, Lebanon, Oman, Qatar, Saudi Arabia, Tunisia, and the United Arab Emirates (U.A.E.), between November 2001 and March 2002. The Survey records the perspectives of business leaders within the Arab world, asking them to compare aspects of their local business environment with global standards. The underlying premise of this approach is that the business leaders and entrepreneurs whose success depends on fair and efficient economies are those who are best placed to assess their own countries' business environments.

The usefulness of this unique Survey data is that it provides information on aspects of an economy's competitiveness for which no hard data sources exist. By capturing a broad array of intangible factors that cannot be found in official statistics, but that nonetheless affect a country's ability to achieve sustained economic growth, the Report's Survey provides an important instrument for assessing the macro- and micro-economic foundations of competitiveness. Such crucial underlying growth factors include hidden import and export barriers, quality of education, administrative red tape and corruption. In many cases the Survey provides unique insight into the gaps between economies' *de jure* regulatory frameworks and their *de facto* enforcement.

The rest of this section is organized as follows. First we will provide a short explanation on how to read the Survey data itself. We will then raise a number of caveats that must be taken into account when interpreting the results of this particular Survey. This includes the relatively small number of responses received and the timing of the Survey. Finally, a selection of the results will be juxtaposed with the results of the *2001–2002 Global Competitiveness Report* Executive Opinion Survey results, to provide a tentative picture of where these countries might be ranked in an international context.

How to Read the Survey Data

For each Survey variable, the original question is included in the description at the top of the table. This Survey followed the same methodology as past Competitiveness Report surveys. In most cases, the questions asked for responses on a scale from 1 to 7, where an answer of 1 corresponds to one end of a spectrum of responses (perception of very poor performance) and an answer of 7 corresponds to the other end (perception of very good performance). A typical question is presented in Box 1 for variable 6.04 on the soundness of banks.

Box 1. Typical Executive Opinion Survey Question

6.04 Soundness of Banks — Banks in your country are:		
Insolvent and may require bailout	1 2 3 4 5 6 7	**Generally healthy with sound balance sheets**
Circling 1	Means you agree wholeheartedly with the answer on the left-hand side	
Circling 7	Means you agree wholeheartedly with the answer on the right-hand side	
Circling 2	Means you largely agree with the left-hand side	
Circling 3	Means you agree somewhat with the left-hand side	
Circling 4	Means your opinion is indifferent between the two answers	
Circling 5	Means you agree somewhat with the right-hand side	
Circling 6	Means you largely agree with the right-hand side	

Specifically, variable 6.04 corresponds to the question about respondents' perceptions of the soundness of banks in their country, with higher scores corresponding to a higher estimated level of soundness. The corresponding chart in the Survey Responses section of this Report has been reproduced in Figure 1.

Looking at Figure 1, we see that the score given for Bahrain is 6.28, indicating the arithmetic mean of responses to this question from executives in Bahrain and a high average confidence in the banking system in that country.

Figure 1. Typical Survey Responses Chart

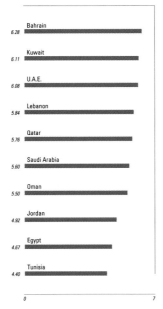

Exercising Caution in Interpreting the Results: The Number of Responses and Timing of the Survey

Having propounded the value of the Executive Opinion Survey, we must, however, urge significant caution in interpreting these Survey results. With survey data, it is critical that a sufficient number of senior business leaders participate and that the sample remain unbiased with regard to any particular business group. However, in the case of this particular survey, the responses we received were insufficient to allow for rigorous statistical analysis. For this reason, unlike in our past Competitiveness Reports, we have made no attempt to compile overall country rankings based upon this data. Table 1 reports the number of responses received from each Arab world country.

Table 1. Responses to the Survey

Country	Number of Responses
Bahrain	25
Egypt	28
Jordan	36
Kuwait	19
Lebanon	33
Oman	7
Qatar	26
Saudi Arabia	17
Tunisia	25
United Arab Emirates	25

While the responses may not be sufficient to establish rankings, they are useful in providing an informative snapshot of business executives' perceptions of their countries' competitive environments. For this reason we have chosen, nonetheless, to present the results of the Survey in this Report.

There is a further caveat we must mention with regards to interpreting the results: the reader should keep in mind that this Survey was carried out at a particularly difficult time for the Arab world. Throughout the past year there was a climate of tension in the Middle East, which became exacerbated after the events of September 11. This, in some cases, might have influenced the attitudes of the respondents.

Where Might These Countries Be Ranked on an International Scale?

Although the responses to the Survey may not be representative of business perceptions in the region for a variety of reasons, we nevertheless believe that it is informative to take a closer look at a selection of the Survey's results in key areas in order to observe where these Arab world countries would fall in the context of an international survey. In this respect we must reiterate that great caution must be taken by our readers when assessing the significance of the discussion to follow.

An international comparison has been accomplished by combining the responses from the *Arab World Competitiveness Report* (AWCR) Executive Opinion Survey with responses from the Executive Opinion Survey reported in the *Global Competitiveness Report 2001–2002* (GCR). It is important to mention that the two surveys were not carried out at the same point in time: the GCR Survey was carried out during the second quarter of 2001, approximately six months prior to the AWCR Survey. However, while the Survey responses are not directly comparable, juxtaposing their results provides an estimation of the probable ranking of Arab world countries.

We have combined the average responses (the means) of all of the countries in the two surveys: the responses of the ten countries covered in the AWCR Survey were merged with those of the seventy-five countries covered by the GCR Survey. Since two countries were covered in both surveys, Egypt and Jordan, this gave two possible rankings—one from each survey. (This, in itself, provided interesting information, since most responses were similar, but in a few cases responses in the two surveys were significantly different. Such differences might reflect a change in mood, for example, because of the backlash following September 11.) We re-ranked the entire list to create a possible ranking between 1 (being the highest) to 83 (being the lowest), factoring out the two "doubled" cases.

This section will take a brief look at the Survey responses in areas that are particularly important for national competitiveness: the macroeconomic environment, finance, institutions, and technology.

Macroeconomic environment, finance, and institutions
Responses to Survey questions on the macroeconomic environment, as well as on finance and institutions, give a sense of the atmosphere in which businesses are operating. It seems appropriate to begin an analysis by looking at the most general Survey question addressing the macroeconomic environment: perceptions about the likelihood of the country being in a recession by the following year (question 1.01). Responses to this question put most Arab world countries surveyed in the lower two-thirds on the international ranking. The only exception is Qatar, which would be at 18th place, between Romania and Greece; Kuwait is in 49th place (between Lithuania and Australia), followed by the U.A.E. in 54th place (between Portugal and Thailand). This suggests that many of the business leaders surveyed believe the spectre of recession will be hovering over their countries in 2003.

On the other hand, it is encouraging to note that there are a number of areas where some of the Arab world countries would be found at the very top of the international rankings. Turning to the burden of administrative regulations (question 1.02), some of the countries do very well. For example, the U.A.E. would be ranked 4th, just behind Hong Kong, Singapore, and Iceland. Bahrain would follow closely, with a ranking of 6, and Qatar with a ranking of 11. In these countries, business leaders surveyed consider that administrative regulations are not overly burdensome to carrying out their business activities. At the other end of the spectrum, a number of Arab world countries are at the bottom of the ranking. Such countries include Egypt, which comes in at 71st or 73rd place, depending on which of the two surveys is used; Saudi Arabia, ranked 79th; and Lebanon, which actually comes in 83rd, or last. This indicates that, of all the countries surveyed in both surveys, business leaders in Lebanon consider that their country has the most burdensome administrative requirements of all.

In the area of banking and finance, responses to the question of whether the banks in the country are sound (question 6.04) put a number of countries in the upper third of the international rankings. Bahrain is ranked 23rd; Kuwait 25th; and the U.A.E., 29th similar to countries such as Portugal, Austria, and Norway. Business leaders in these countries are rather confident about the health of the banking sector in their countries. Further, none of the Arab world countries surveyed fall at the bottom of the rankings in this area, demonstrating that the banking sector in the region is seen as in comparatively good health with respect to some other regions.

Several business leaders surveyed also believe that it has become easier for companies to obtain credit over the past year (question 6.09). Kuwait is ranked first overall before Italy and Taiwan, followed by Bahrain and the U.A.E., ranked 8th and 9th, respectively. This reflects the feeling that there has been an improvement in the functioning of the banking sector in a number of these countries.

However, in contrast to the question on availability of credit, access to local equity and bond markets are perceived as much more difficult. When business leaders were questioned about the level of difficulty in raising money by issuing shares on the local stock market (question 6.12), the only country to be found in the top third is Egypt, in 26th place, based on responses from the GCR Survey. However, this is contradicted by the responses to the AWCR Survey, which was carried out several months later; responses to the second Survey place Egypt all the way down to 51st place. This may indicate that there has been a change in mood over the months in between the two surveys, or that access to equity markets became more difficult over this period. It is most likely the latter given the negative performance of equity markets over the past year. The two Arab world countries falling lowest on the international list in this area are the U.A.E., at 61st place between Slovenia and Costa Rica, and Saudi Arabia, at 72nd place, between the Czech Republic and Argentina.

Access to bond markets is also seen as very difficult for companies (question 6.11). Kuwait, ranked 16th, is the only country surveyed to come in at the top half of the international ranking. Most of the other countries covered by the Survey are in the middle or lower third of the rankings. For example, the U.A.E. comes in 53rd between Trinidad and Tobago and Panama. Close to the bottom of the list is Saudi Arabia in 73rd place, and at the very bottom is Oman, in 83rd place. Just as access to equity markets is perceived to be difficult, bond markets do not seem to provide a readily available form of financing in these countries.

In other words, it is safe to say that, in general, bond and equity markets are not perceived as sufficiently developed in the region to provide adequate financing for companies.

On issues related to problems of corruption in the economic realm, many of the countries show great strength. For example, tax evasion (question 1.07) is an interesting area. Four of the countries literally top the list (the U.A.E., Qatar, Bahrain, and Oman), and five of them hold the top seven places (Kuwait is ranked 7th, after Singapore and Hong Kong). This demonstrates that business leaders in these countries consider that tax evasion is not at all a problem in their countries. This is not surprising given the low to nonexistent individual and corporate tax rates in these particular countries. On the other side of the spectrum is Lebanon, coming in well at the bottom of the list at 76th place, just after Guatemala and before Russia. These rankings hold for the question on irregular payments in tax collection (1.11), where the five top countries are once again quite high on the international list, and with Lebanon again coming in almost at the bottom, in 78th place.

This overall environment is echoed in the question on what is kept "off the books." When asked what amount of profits and wages they believed were unreported in their industry (question 2.07), Oman and Qatar ranked 3rd and 4th, after Belgium and Finland and before Denmark, Japan, and Norway. Bahrain and the U.A.E. are ranked 14th and 15th, just after the U.S. and before Australia and Ireland. In these countries, business leaders perceive that business dealings are relatively transparent. Similarly, when asked what percentage of businesses in the country are unofficial or not registered (question 2.08), Oman is ranked 1st, and Qatar 4th, just after Singapore and Japan. In other words, the informal sector is not perceived to be a large problem in these particular countries.

Technology

Since technology is an important potential driver of growth and competitiveness in the Arab world, it is also informative to look at where these countries would figure on an international scale in this area. With regard to the question of the country's overall technological sophistication (5.01), there is a very large range of perceptions among the countries surveyed. The U.A.E. does quite well, ranking 18th between Austria and Belgium, followed by Bahrain at 24th place, between Korea and New Zealand. At the other end of the spectrum we find Oman ranked 67th, between Ukraine and Colombia, and Saudi Arabia ranked 72nd, between El Salvador and Bulgaria.

Turning to the government's prioritization of information and communications technologies (ICTs) (question 1.16), some of the countries come in very high on the international ranking. The U.A.E. comes in first on the ranking, ahead of Singapore and Finland. This reflects the perception that the country's massive drive to become a high-tech hub has been a success. It is followed by Tunisia in 4th place and Bahrain in 8th place. Jordan is ranked 5th (AWCR) or 12th (GCR), perhaps reflecting the perception that ICTs became an even greater priority for the government between the two periods.

However, despite several governments' perceived prioritization of ICTs, responses from all the countries surveyed to questions about direct government intervention in the form of subsidies and tax credits for firm-level research and development (questions 5.05 and 5.06) were less positive. With the exception of Tunisia, which ranked relatively high on both questions, most business leaders responding to the Survey do not believe their governments are using these incentives to encourage innovation; these nine countries were placed from the middle to the very end of the rankings. Particularly negative responses were reported from Lebanon, which fell second to last in the rankings on both questions, and Saudi Arabia, which was third to last on the question of tax credits. It would seem that, in general, these types of incentives could be better used by all of the countries in question if, indeed, their governments are serious about prioritizing these new tools.

In terms of firm-level technology absorption (5.02), a number of the Arab world countries fall into the high to average range of countries in the international Survey. The U.A.E., Qatar, Kuwait, Bahrain, Tunisia, and Lebanon all ranged from 17th to 37th in the rankings. Business leaders in these countries perceive that firms in their countries absorb outside technologies reasonably well. On the other hand, business leaders from Jordan, Egypt, Saudi Arabia, and Oman were much less positive about their firms' interest in absorbing new technologies. Interestingly, respondents from Jordan were quite a bit less positive on this question in the AWCR than in the GCR Survey, taking Jordan from 52nd (GCR) to 67th (AWCR) in the international rankings. Conversely, Egyptian business leaders were more positive, moving Egypt up from 76th (GCR) to 56th (AWCR).

Questioned about the innovative capacity of their countries in terms of the availability of scientists and engineers so crucial for technological innovation (question 4.13), responses were mixed. While Jordan, Lebanon, Tunisia, and Egypt are all ranked in the top third of the countries surveyed, most countries were much lower on the international list. Kuwait, the U.A.E., and Qatar are all ranked quite low, at 60th, 63rd, and 71st, respectively. At the very bottom of the list are Saudi Arabia and Oman, in 77th and 82nd place, respectively. This seems to indicate that most Arab world countries surveyed lack the scientific talent needed to prosper in a knowledge-based economy.

The responses were also mixed on how well countries are able to retain those scientists and engineers that they do have. When asked about the problem of the "brain drain" from their countries (question 4.14) four of those surveyed, Kuwait, Qatar, the U.A.E., and Bahrain, are in the top eight of the ranking, along with countries such as the U.S., Finland, and Japan. These countries do not seem to be suffering an outflow of talent. However, for many of the other countries in the region, the brain drain is indeed seen to be an important problem. Jordan comes in 71st or 72nd depending on whether the GCR or AWCR Survey responses are taken, and Lebanon is ranked 82nd, or second-to-last.

In sum, it seems clear that there is a great diversity in the rankings of the countries covered in most of the areas investigated. A number of the countries figure near the bottom of the international list on many of the questions asked, demonstrating that a great deal will need to be done in these areas to create environments more conducive to growth and competitiveness. It is encouraging to note, on the other hand, that some of the countries are already making important progress in specific areas, such as technology. They can thus serve as critical benchmarks not only for the rest of the Arab world, but for other developing countries as well.

Index of Tables

Index of Tables

Survey Responses

Government and Country Performance

1.01
Recession expectations

The likelihood of your country's economy being in a recession next year is:

Scale   *1 = highly likely, 7 = not likely*

Qatar	
5.46	
Bahrain	
5.00	
Oman	
4.83	
Tunisia	
4.52	
Kuwait	
4.37	
U.A.E.	
4.13	
Jordan	
3.81	
Saudi Arabia	
3.19	
Egypt	
3.14	
Lebanon	
2.58	

0   7

1.02
Administrative regulations

Administration regulations in your country are:

Scale   *1 = burdensome, 7 = not burdensome*

U.A.E.	
5.33	
Bahrain	
4.92	
Qatar	
4.42	
Jordan	
3.83	
Tunisia	
3.72	
Oman	
3.50	
Kuwait	
3.11	
Egypt	
2.57	
Saudi Arabia	
2.31	
Lebanon	
2.00	

0   7

1.03
Composition of government spending

Government spending in your country is:

Scale *1 = wasteful, 7 = provides necessary goods and services that the market does not provide*

U.A.E.	5.56
Oman	5.20
Qatar	5.04
Bahrain	4.84
Tunisia	4.75
Kuwait	3.79
Saudi Arabia	3.65
Jordan	3.58
Egypt	3.48
Lebanon	2.15

0   7

1.04
Extent of distortive government subsidies

Government subsidies to business in your country:

Scale *1 = keep uncompetitive industries alive artificially, 7 = improve productivity of industries*

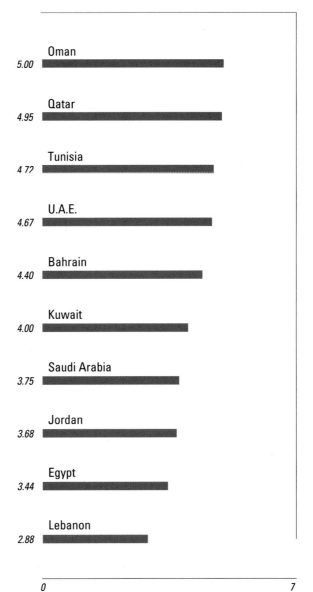

Oman	5.00
Qatar	4.95
Tunisia	4.72
U.A.E.	4.67
Bahrain	4.40
Kuwait	4.00
Saudi Arabia	3.75
Jordan	3.68
Egypt	3.44
Lebanon	2.88

0   7

Government and Country Performance

1.05

Favoritism in decisions of government officials

When deciding upon policies and contracts, government officials:

Scale   *1 = favor well-connected firms and individuals,*
7 = are neutral among firms and individuals

1.06

Competence of public officials

The competence of personnel in the public sector is:

Scale   *1 = lower than the private sector, 7 = higher than the*
private sector

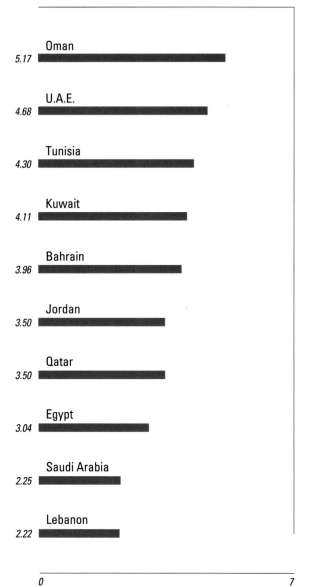

1.05

Oman	5.17	
U.A.E.	4.68	
Tunisia	4.30	
Kuwait	4.11	
Bahrain	3.96	
Jordan	3.50	
Qatar	3.50	
Egypt	3.04	
Saudi Arabia	2.25	
Lebanon	2.22	

0   7

1.06

Tunisia	3.32	
Qatar	3.08	
U.A.E.	3.04	
Bahrain	2.75	
Jordan	2.39	
Kuwait	2.26	
Egypt	2.11	
Saudi Arabia	2.06	
Oman	1.83	
Lebanon	1.34	

0   7

1.07
Tax evasion

Tax evasion is:

Scale *1 = common in your country, 7 = minimal in your country*

U.A.E.	
6.65	
Qatar	
6.54	
Bahrain	
6.44	
Oman	
6.33	
Kuwait	
6.06	
Saudi Arabia	
4.94	
Tunisia	
3.56	
Jordan	
3.03	
Egypt	
2.57	
Lebanon	
2.12	

0   7

1.08
Irregular payments in import & export permits

In your industry, how often would you estimate that firms make irregular extra payments or bribes connected with **import and export permits***:*

Scale *1 = common, 7 = never occurs*

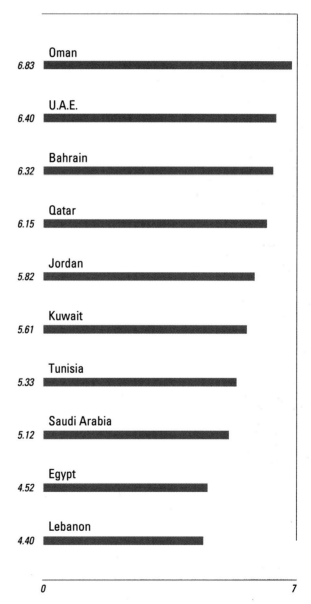

Oman	
6.83	
U.A.E.	
6.40	
Bahrain	
6.32	
Qatar	
6.15	
Jordan	
5.82	
Kuwait	
5.61	
Tunisia	
5.33	
Saudi Arabia	
5.12	
Egypt	
4.52	
Lebanon	
4.40	

0   7

Government and Country Performance

1.09

Irregular payments in public utilities

In your industry, how often would you estimate that firms make irregular extra payments or bribes connected with **connection to public utilities (e.g., telephone or electricity):**

Scale *1 = common, 7 = never occurs*

Oman
6.50

U.A.E.
6.00

Qatar
5.85

Bahrain
5.73

Jordan
5.66

Tunisia
5.08

Kuwait
5.05

Saudi Arabia
4.65

Lebanon
4.63

Egypt
4.42

0   7

1.10

Irregular payments in public contracts

In your industry, how often would you estimate that firms make irregular extra payments or bribes connected with the **awarding of public contracts (investment projects) and/or the initial acquisition of business licenses:**

Scale *1 = common, 7 = never occurs*

Oman
6.50

U.A.E.
5.24

Qatar
5.04

Jordan
5.03

Bahrain
4.64

Kuwait
4.47

Tunisia
4.38

Egypt
3.96

Saudi Arabia
3.76

Lebanon
3.44

0   7

1.11

Irregular payments in annual tax collection

In your industry, how often would you estimate that firms make irregular extra payments or bribes connected with **annual tax payments**:

Scale *1 = common, 7 = never occurs*

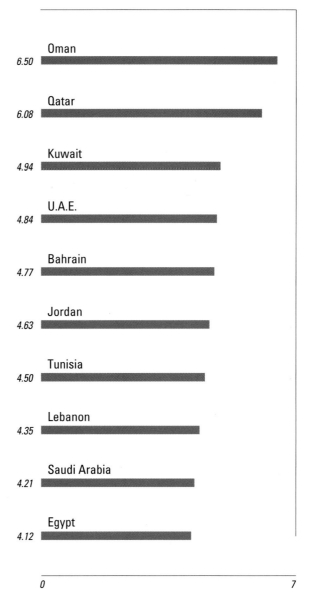

Bahrain	
6.88	
Oman	
6.67	
U.A.E.	
6.57	
Qatar	
6.30	
Kuwait	
5.60	
Saudi Arabia	
5.00	
Jordan	
4.77	
Tunisia	
4.12	
Egypt	
3.76	
Lebanon	
3.27	

0   7

1.12

Irregular payments in loan applications

In your industry, how often would you estimate that firms make irregular extra payments or bribes connected with **loan applications**:

Scale *1 = common, 7 = never occurs*

Oman	
6.50	
Qatar	
6.08	
Kuwait	
4.94	
U.A.E.	
4.84	
Bahrain	
4.77	
Jordan	
4.63	
Tunisia	
4.50	
Lebanon	
4.35	
Saudi Arabia	
4.21	
Egypt	
4.12	

0   7

1.13

Recent increase/decrease in irregular payments

In the past three years, the frequency of additional payments or bribes such as those listed in question 2.08 has:

Scale *1 = increased significantly, 7 = decreased significantly*

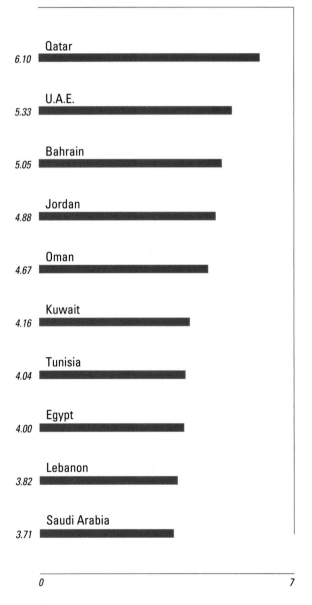

Qatar	6.10
U.A.E.	5.33
Bahrain	5.05
Jordan	4.88
Oman	4.67
Kuwait	4.16
Tunisia	4.04
Egypt	4.00
Lebanon	3.82
Saudi Arabia	3.71

0　　　　　　7

1.14

Future prospects for irregular payments

In the next three years, do you expect the overall level of payments or bribes to:

Scale *1 = increase significantly, 7 = decrease significantly*

Qatar	6.05
Bahrain	5.80
U.A.E.	5.08
Jordan	4.85
Oman	4.75
Tunisia	4.41
Kuwait	4.37
Saudi Arabia	4.21
Egypt	4.04
Lebanon	3.94

0　　　　　　7

1.15
Business costs of corruption

Do unfair (e.g., influence on government policies) or corrupt activities of other firms impose costs on your firm?

Scale *1 = impose large costs, 7 = impose no costs/not relevant*

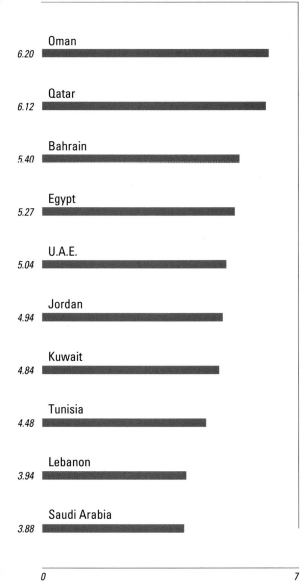

Oman	6.20
Qatar	6.12
Bahrain	5.40
Egypt	5.27
U.A.E.	5.04
Jordan	4.94
Kuwait	4.84
Tunisia	4.48
Lebanon	3.94
Saudi Arabia	3.88

0   7

1.16
Government prioritization of ICT

Information and communication technologies (ICT) are an overall priority for the government:

Scale *1 = strongly disagree, 7 = strongly agree*

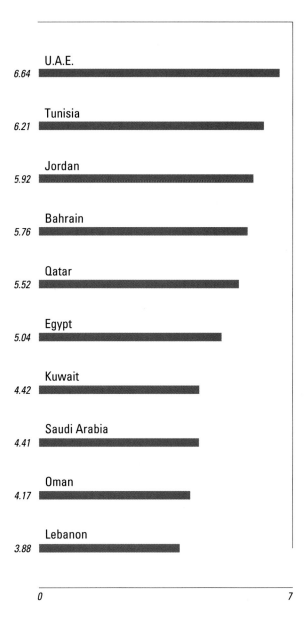

U.A.E.	6.64
Tunisia	6.21
Jordan	5.92
Bahrain	5.76
Qatar	5.52
Egypt	5.04
Kuwait	4.42
Saudi Arabia	4.41
Oman	4.17
Lebanon	3.88

0   7

1.17
Government success in ICT promotion

Government programs promoting the use of ICT are:

Scale *1 = not very successful, 7 = highly successful*

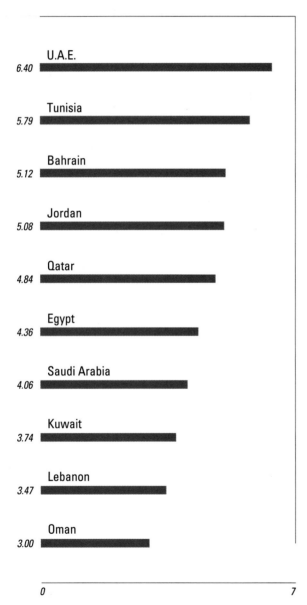

2.01
Legal and political reforms

To what extent are major legal and political reforms discussed in your country?

Scale   *1 = a great deal, 7 = very little*

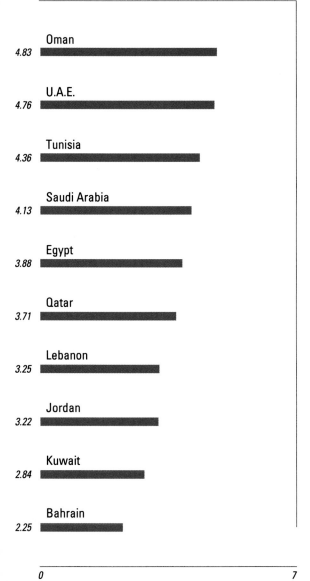

Oman	4.83
U.A.E.	4.76
Tunisia	4.36
Saudi Arabia	4.13
Egypt	3.88
Qatar	3.71
Lebanon	3.25
Jordan	3.22
Kuwait	2.84
Bahrain	2.25

0   7

2.02
Extent of bureaucratic red tape

How much time does the senior management of your company spend working with government agencies/ regulations?

Scale   *1 = less than 10% of its time, 2 = 10-20%, 3 = 21-30%,…, 8 = 71-80%*

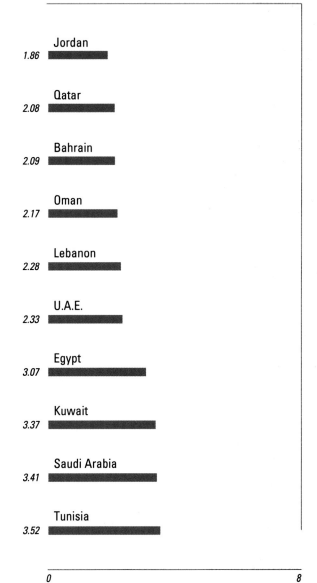

Jordan	1.86
Qatar	2.08
Bahrain	2.09
Oman	2.17
Lebanon	2.28
U.A.E.	2.33
Egypt	3.07
Kuwait	3.37
Saudi Arabia	3.41
Tunisia	3.52

0   8

2.03
Judicial independence

The judiciary in your country is independent and not subject to interference by the government and/or parties to the dispute:

Scale *1 = not true, 7 = true*

Kuwait	6.05
Qatar	5.58
U.A.E.	5.16
Bahrain	5.08
Oman	5.00
Jordan	4.97
Tunisia	4.75
Egypt	4.74
Saudi Arabia	4.50
Lebanon	3.35

0 — 7

2.04
Availability of legal framework for business

A trusted legal framework exists in your country for private businesses to challenge the legality of government actions and/or regulations:

Scale *1 = not true, 7 = true*

Kuwait	5.53
Qatar	5.52
Oman	5.33
Tunisia	5.13
Bahrain	4.74
Jordan	4.72
U.A.E.	4.63
Lebanon	3.97
Egypt	3.93
Saudi Arabia	3.50

0 — 7

Institutions

2.05
Reliability of police protection

Police services:

Scale *1 = cannot be relied upon to protect businesses from criminals, 7 = can be relied upon to protect businesses from criminals*

U.A.E.	6.56
Qatar	6.38
Bahrain	6.28
Jordan	6.19
Tunisia	5.75
Kuwait	5.68
Oman	5.67
Saudi Arabia	5.00
Lebanon	4.75
Egypt	4.58

0   7

2.06
Organized crime

Organized crime (racketeering, extortion) in your country:

Scale *1 = imposes significant costs on businesses, 7 = does not impose significant costs on businesses*

Jordan	6.69
Qatar	6.50
U.A.E.	6.43
Oman	6.25
Bahrain	6.04
Lebanon	5.97
Saudi Arabia	5.88
Egypt	5.74
Kuwait	5.68
Tunisia	5.57

0   7

2.07
Unreported profits and wages

Based on your experience, what amount of profits and wages does a company in your industry typically "keep off the books"?

Scale *1 = less than 5% of profits and wages, 2 = 6-10%, 3 = 11-20%,..., 10 = more than 80%*

Oman
1.00

Qatar
1.04

Bahrain
1.28

U.A.E.
1.29

Kuwait
1.31

Saudi Arabia
1.38

Jordan
2.42

Tunisia
2.55

Egypt
3.12

Lebanon
3.61

0   10

2.08
Informal sector

What percentage of businesses in your country would you guess are unofficial or unregistered?

Scale *1 = less than 5% of all businesses, 2 = 6-10%, 3 = 11-20%,..., 9 = more than 70%*

Oman
1.00

Qatar
1.36

U.A.E.
1.86

Kuwait
1.86

Jordan
2.29

Bahrain
2.3

Tunisia
2.39

Saudi Arabia
2.6

Lebanon
4.17

Egypt
4.24

0   9

2.09

Intellectual property protection

Intellectual property protection in your country is:

Scale *1 = weak or non-existent, 7 = equal to the world's most stringent*

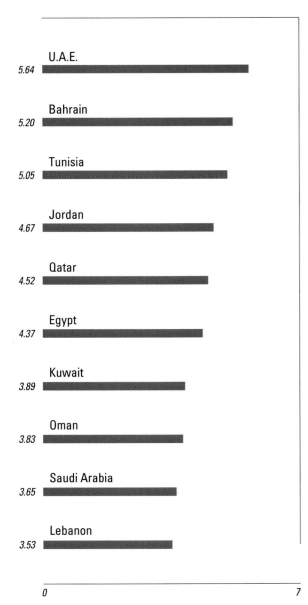

U.A.E.	
5.64	
Bahrain	
5.20	
Tunisia	
5.05	
Jordan	
4.67	
Qatar	
4.52	
Egypt	
4.37	
Kuwait	
3.89	
Oman	
3.83	
Saudi Arabia	
3.65	
Lebanon	
3.53	

0   7

Infrastructure

3.01
Overall infrastructure quality

General infrastructure in your country is:

Scale *1 = poorly developed and inefficient,*
7 = among the best in the world

U.A.E.	6.38
Kuwait	5.53
Bahrain	5.44
Qatar	5.27
Oman	5.00
Jordan	4.86
Saudi Arabia	4.35
Tunisia	4.24
Lebanon	3.88
Egypt	3.75

0 — 7

3.02
Railroad infrastructure development

Railroads in your country are:

Scale *1 = underdeveloped, 7 = as extensive and efficient*
as the world's best

Tunisia	3.52
Egypt	3.39
Qatar	2.67
Saudi Arabia	2.00
Bahrain	1.91
U.A.E.	1.69
Jordan	1.54
Lebanon	1.06
Kuwait	1.00
Oman	1.00

0 — 7

Infrastructure

3.03
Port infrastructure quality

Port facilities and inland waterways in your country are:

Scale *1 = underdeveloped, 7 = as developed as the world's best*

U.A.E.
6.64

Bahrain
5.64

Qatar
5.48

Saudi Arabia
5.06

Kuwait
5.06

Oman
4.40

Tunisia
3.96

Lebanon
3.88

Jordan
3.66

Egypt
3.57

0   7

3.04
Air transport infrastructure quality

Air transport in your country is:

Scale *1 = infrequent and inefficient, 7 = as extensive and efficient as the world's best*

U.A.E.
6.76

Qatar
5.77

Bahrain
5.76

Kuwait
5.58

Lebanon
5.28

Saudi Arabia
5.06

Jordan
5.06

Oman
5.00

Tunisia
4.88

Egypt
3.96

0   7

Infrastructure

3.05
Telephone/fax infrastructure quality

New telephone lines for your business are:

Scale *1 = scarce and difficult to obtain widely, 7 = available and highly reliable*

Qatar	6.85
U.A.E.	6.84
Bahrain	6.64
Jordan	6.22
Oman	6.17
Lebanon	6.06
Kuwait	6.00
Egypt	5.43
Tunisia	4.96
Saudi Arabia	4.82

0   7

3.06
Mobile phone infrastructure quality

Mobile or cellular telephones for your business are:

Scale *1 = not available, 7 = accessible and affordable as the in the world's most technologically advanced countries*

U.A.E.	6.92
Qatar	6.69
Kuwait	6.63
Bahrain	6.56
Lebanon	6.48
Jordan	6.47
Egypt	6.21
Oman	6.00
Saudi Arabia	5.71
Tunisia	4.60

0   7

Infrastructure

3.07

Quality of competition in telecommunications sector

Is there sufficient competition in the telecommunications sector in your country to ensure high quality, infrequent interruptions and low prices?

Scale *1 = no, 7 = yes, equal to the best in the world*

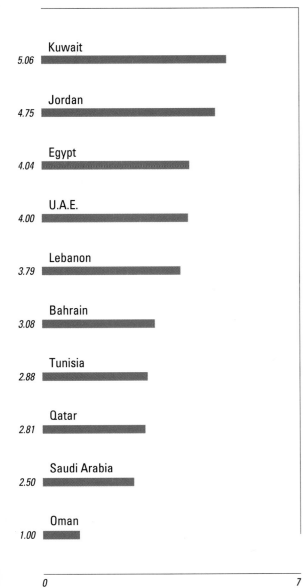

Kuwait	5.06
Jordan	4.75
Egypt	4.04
U.A.E.	4.00
Lebanon	3.79
Bahrain	3.08
Tunisia	2.88
Qatar	2.81
Saudi Arabia	2.50
Oman	1.00

0 7

3.08

Quality of competition in transportation sector

Is there sufficient competition in the transportation sector in your country to ensure high quality, infrequent interruptions and low prices?

Scale *1 = no, 7 = yes, equal to the best in the world*

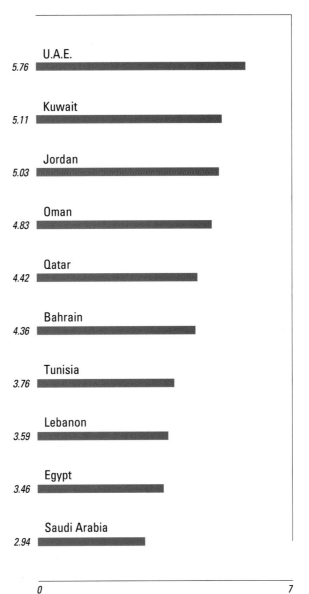

U.A.E.	5.76
Kuwait	5.11
Jordan	5.03
Oman	4.83
Qatar	4.42
Bahrain	4.36
Tunisia	3.76
Lebanon	3.59
Egypt	3.46
Saudi Arabia	2.94

0 7

Infrastructure

3.09

Quality of competition in the ISP sector

Is there sufficient competition in the Internet Service Provider sector in your country to ensure high quality, infrequent interruptions and low prices?

Scale *1 = no, 7 = yes, equal to the best in the world*

Jordan	5.50
Lebanon	5.22
U.A.E.	4.48
Egypt	4.36
Kuwait	4.26
Bahrain	3.84
Tunisia	3.79
Saudi Arabia	3.65
Qatar	3.19
Oman	2.40

0   7

3.10

Electricity prices

The price of electricity per kilowatt-hour in your country compared to the international standard is:

Scale *1 = much higher, 7 = among the lowest in the world*

Kuwait	6.79
Qatar	5.73
Bahrain	4.92
Egypt	4.79
Saudi Arabia	4.69
U.A.E.	4.04
Tunisia	3.88
Jordan	3.71
Oman	3.17
Lebanon	2.19

0   7

Infrastructure

3.11
Quality of electricity supply

The quality of electricity supply in your country (in terms of lack of interruptions and lack of voltage fluctuations) is:

Scale *1 = worse than most other countries, 7 = equal to the highest in the world*

Kuwait	6.63
U.A.E.	6.52
Qatar	6.35
Bahrain	6.16
Saudi Arabia	5.24
Oman	5.17
Jordan	4.97
Tunisia	4.88
Egypt	4.54
Lebanon	2.06

0   7

3.12
Public access to Internet

Public access to the Internet (through telecenters, libraries, post offices, etc.) is:

Scale *1 = very limited, 7 = pervasive, most people have frequent Internet access*

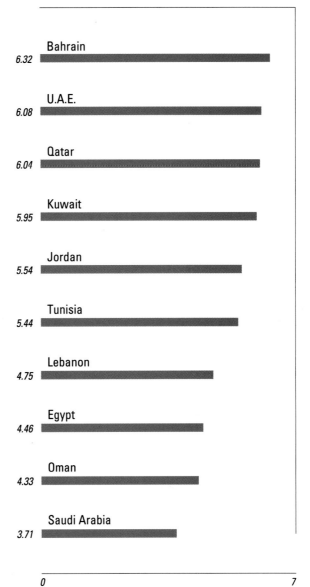

Bahrain	6.32
U.A.E.	6.08
Qatar	6.04
Kuwait	5.95
Jordan	5.54
Tunisia	5.44
Lebanon	4.75
Egypt	4.46
Oman	4.33
Saudi Arabia	3.71

0   7

Infrastructure

3.13
Internet access in schools

Internet access in schools is:

Scale *1 = very limited, 7 = pervasive, most children have frequent Internet access*

U.A.E.
4.52

Bahrain
4.42

Qatar
4.27

Kuwait
4.00

Tunisia
4.00

Jordan
3.74

Lebanon
3.50

Egypt
3.33

Saudi Arabia
3.06

Oman
1.50

0   7

3.14
Governmental restrictions on Internet content

Governmental restrictions on Internet content in your country are:

Scale *1 = rigid and strictly enforced by government agencies, 7 = non-existent*

Lebanon
6.09

Jordan
5.94

Egypt
5.39

Qatar
5.00

Kuwait
4.79

Bahrain
4.68

Tunisia
3.67

U.A.E.
3.32

Oman
3.17

Saudi Arabia
1.59

0   7

4.01
Quality of public schools

The public (free) schools in your country are:

Scale *1 = of poor quality, 7 = equal to the best in the world*

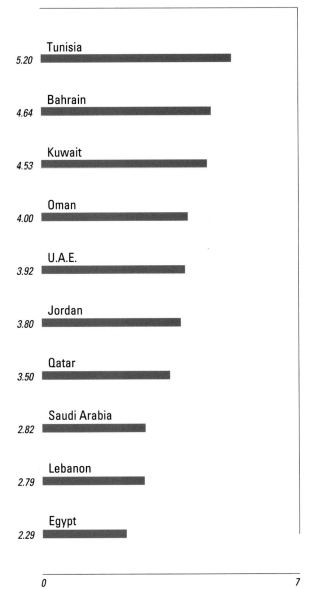

Tunisia
5.20

Bahrain
4.64

Kuwait
4.53

Oman
4.00

U.A.E.
3.92

Jordan
3.80

Qatar
3.50

Saudi Arabia
2.82

Lebanon
2.79

Egypt
2.29

0   7

4.02
Difference in quality of schools

The difference in the quality of the schools available to rich and poor children in your country is:

Scale *1 = large, 7 = small*

Tunisia
5.24

Kuwait
4.84

Oman
4.50

Bahrain
3.80

U.A.E.
3.80

Qatar
3.65

Saudi Arabia
2.59

Lebanon
2.42

Egypt
2.36

Jordan
2.20

0   7

Human Resources

4.03
Hiring and firing practices

Hiring and firing of workers is:

Scale *1 = impeded by regulations, 7 = flexibly determined by employers*

U.A.E.	5.64
Kuwait	4.95
Qatar	4.64
Jordan	4.03
Tunisia	3.72
Bahrain	3.60
Saudi Arabia	3.35
Lebanon	3.24
Oman	2.67
Egypt	2.64

0   7

4.04
Employment rules

Companies can cut back the hours of workers or get overtime labor without too much extra cost in your country:

Scale *1 = no, 7 = yes*

U.A.E.	5.20
Egypt	4.81
Oman	4.67
Tunisia	4.40
Bahrain	4.25
Jordan	4.19
Lebanon	3.77
Saudi Arabia	3.69
Qatar	3.62
Kuwait	3.53

0   7

4.05

Social welfare and incentives

Your country's social welfare and unemployment program:

Scale *1 = deters citizens from entering the workforce, 7 = strongly encourages and supports participation in the workforce*

Oman
6.25

U.A.E.
5.39

Jordan
5.26

Bahrain
4.95

Tunisia
4.84

Kuwait
4.65

Qatar
4.63

Egypt
4.52

Lebanon
4.29

Saudi Arabia
3.94

0   7

4.06

Women in the economy

Women's participation in the economy is:

Scale *1 = limited and usually takes place in less important jobs, 7 = equal to that of other groups*

Tunisia
5.24

Kuwait
4.95

Egypt
4.86

U.A.E.
4.80

Bahrain
4.72

Oman
4.33

Jordan
4.31

Lebanon
4.25

Qatar
3.00

Saudi Arabia
1.94

0   7

4.07
Minorities in the economy

Minority groups' participation in the economy is:

Scale *1 = limited and usually takes place in less important jobs,*
7 = equal to that of other groups

Tunisia	5.80
U.A.E.	5.65
Jordan	5.64
Oman	5.50
Kuwait	5.26
Bahrain	4.96
Lebanon	4.67
Egypt	4.50
Qatar	4.30
Saudi Arabia	3.59

0   7

4.08
Ethnic tension in the workplace

Workplace tensions between different ethnic groups in your company are:

Scale *1 = very high, 7 = very low*

Tunisia	6.69
Oman	6.33
Lebanon	6.31
Kuwait	6.26
Jordan	5.92
U.A.E.	5.92
Qatar	5.91
Bahrain	5.87
Egypt	5.48
Saudi Arabia	5.12

0   7

Human Resources

4.09

Quality of healthcare system

The overall quality of your country's healthcare system is:

Scale *1 = low, 7 = among the world's best*

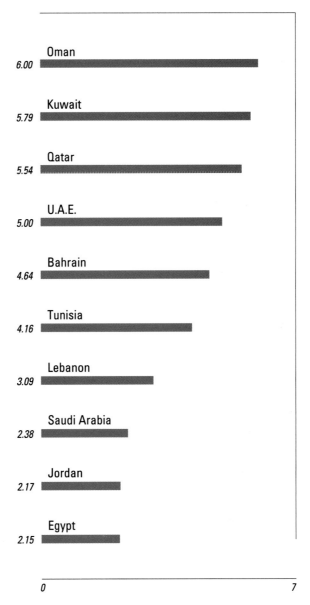

Bahrain	5.60
Oman	5.33
Qatar	5.24
Kuwait	5.21
U.A.E.	4.72
Tunisia	4.71
Saudi Arabia	4.27
Jordan	4.17
Lebanon	4.06
Egypt	3.29

0   7

4.10

Difference in quality of healthcare

The difference in the quality of healthcare available to rich and poor people in your country is:

Scale *1 = large, 7 = small*

Oman	6.00
Kuwait	5.79
Qatar	5.54
U.A.E.	5.00
Bahrain	4.64
Tunisia	4.16
Lebanon	3.09
Saudi Arabia	2.38
Jordan	2.17
Egypt	2.15

0   7

4.11
Public health agencies

Public health agencies in your country are able to deal with public outbreaks of disease (e.g. cholera, tuberculoses, etc.):

Scale *1 = barely at all, 7 = very effectively*

Oman	6.33
Bahrain	6.32
U.A.E.	6.25
Kuwait	6.05
Tunisia	6.04
Qatar	5.88
Jordan	5.64
Egypt	4.84
Saudi Arabia	4.35
Lebanon	4.16

0 — 7

4.12
Quality of math and science education

Math and science education in your country's schools:

Scale *1 = lags far behind most other countries, 7 = is among the best in the world*

Tunisia	5.92
Lebanon	5.53
Jordan	5.36
U.A.E.	5.12
Bahrain	4.80
Oman	4.67
Kuwait	4.63
Egypt	4.29
Qatar	4.27
Saudi Arabia	2.88

0 — 7

4.13
Availability of scientists and engineers

Scientists and engineers in your country are:

Scale *1 = non-existent or rare, 7 = widely available*

Jordan	6.11
Lebanon	5.91
Tunisia	5.76
Egypt	5.75
Bahrain	4.96
Kuwait	4.58
U.A.E.	4.44
Qatar	4.12
Saudi Arabia	3.59
Oman	3.17

0   7

4.14
Brain drain

Scientists and engineers in your country:

Scale *1 = normally leave to pursue opportunities in other countries,*
7 = almost always remain in the country

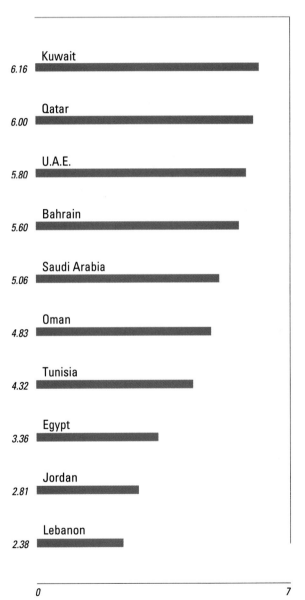

Kuwait	6.16
Qatar	6.00
U.A.E.	5.80
Bahrain	5.60
Saudi Arabia	5.06
Oman	4.83
Tunisia	4.32
Egypt	3.36
Jordan	2.81
Lebanon	2.38

0   7

Technology

5.01
Technological sophistication

Your country's position in technology:

Scale *1 = generally lags behind most other countries,*
7 = is among the world leaders

U.A.E.	5.64
Bahrain	4.84
Kuwait	4.32
Qatar	4.27
Jordan	4.08
Lebanon	4.00
Tunisia	4.00
Egypt	3.43
Oman	3.00
Saudi Arabia	2.63

0　　　　7

5.02
Firm-level technology absorption

Companies in your country are:

Scale *1 = not interested in absorbing new technology,*
7 = aggressive in absorbing new technology

U.A.E.	5.80
Qatar	5.50
Kuwait	5.47
Bahrain	5.36
Tunisia	5.20
Lebanon	5.16
Egypt	4.75
Jordan	4.50
Saudi Arabia	4.35
Oman	4.00

0　　　　7

Technology

5.03
Firm-level innovation

In your business, continuous innovation plays a major role in generating revenue:

Scale *1 = not true, 7 = true*

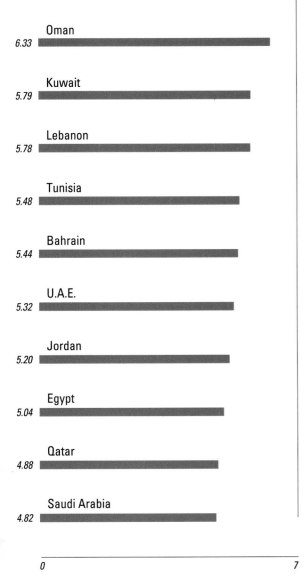

Oman	6.33
Kuwait	5.79
Lebanon	5.78
Tunisia	5.48
Bahrain	5.44
U.A.E.	5.32
Jordan	5.20
Egypt	5.04
Qatar	4.88
Saudi Arabia	4.82

0   7

5.04
Firm-level R&D spending

Companies in your country:

Scale *1 = do not spend money on R&D, 7 = spend heavily on R&D relative to international peers*

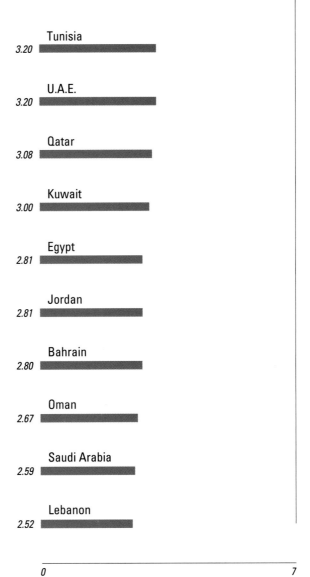

Tunisia	3.20
U.A.E.	3.20
Qatar	3.08
Kuwait	3.00
Egypt	2.81
Jordan	2.81
Bahrain	2.80
Oman	2.67
Saudi Arabia	2.59
Lebanon	2.52

0   7

5.05

Subsidies for firm-level research & development

Direct government subsidies to firms conducting research and development in your country:

Scale *1 = never occur, 7 = are widespread and large*

Tunisia	4.58
Kuwait	3.26
U.A.E.	2.91
Qatar	2.88
Saudi Arabia	2.67
Bahrain	2.61
Oman	2.33
Jordan	2.28
Egypt	2.15
Lebanon	1.42

0   7

5.06

Tax credits for firm-level research & development

Government tax credits to firms conducting research and development in your country:

Scale *1 = never occur, 7 = are widespread and large*

Tunisia	3.64
Jordan	2.94
U.A.E.	2.67
Bahrain	2.42
Oman	2.33
Kuwait	2.31
Egypt	2.19
Qatar	2.17
Saudi Arabia	1.50
Lebanon	1.35

0   7

6.01
Financial market sophistication

The level of sophistication of financial markets in your country is:

Scale   *1 = lower than international norms, 7 = higher than international norms*

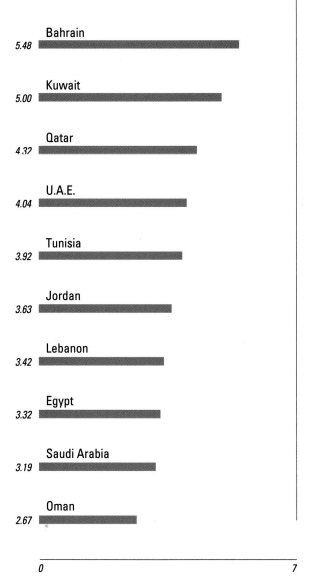

Bahrain	5.48	
Kuwait	5.00	
Qatar	4.32	
U.A.E.	4.04	
Tunisia	3.92	
Jordan	3.63	
Lebanon	3.42	
Egypt	3.32	
Saudi Arabia	3.19	
Oman	2.67	

0   7

6.02
Ease of access to loans

How easy is it to obtain a loan in your country with only a good business plan and no collateral?

Scale   *1 = impossible, 7 = easy*

Bahrain	4.04
Kuwait	3.95
U.A.E.	3.71
Tunisia	3.67
Qatar	3.15
Saudi Arabia	2.71
Egypt	2.46
Lebanon	2.41
Jordan	1.97
Oman	1.67

0   7

Finance

6.03
Venture capital availability

Entrepreneurs with innovative but risky products can generally find venture capital in your country:

Scale *1 = not true, 7 = true*

Kuwait	3.68
Qatar	3.56
Bahrain	3.36
U.A.E.	3.25
Tunisia	3.13
Jordan	2.64
Saudi Arabia	2.59
Lebanon	2.44
Egypt	2.32
Oman	2.17

0 — 7

6.04
Soundness of banks

Banks in your country are:

Scale *1 = insolvent and may require bailout, 7 = generally healthy with sound balance sheets*

Bahrain	6.28
Kuwait	6.11
U.A.E.	6.08
Lebanon	5.84
Qatar	5.76
Saudi Arabia	5.60
Oman	5.50
Jordan	4.92
Egypt	4.67
Tunisia	4.40

0 — 7

Finance

6.05
Entry into banking industry

The entry of new banks into the domestic banking industry is:

Scale *1 = very difficult or rarely allowed, 7 = easy and subject only to reasonable regulations*

Bahrain
5.29

Lebanon
4.23

Qatar
4.12

Jordan
4.06

Tunisia
3.75

U.A.E.
3.30

Egypt
2.90

Oman
2.50

Kuwait
2.26

Saudi Arabia
1.77

0   7

6.06
Interest rates

Interest rates on bank deposits or loans are:

Scale *1 = subject to government control, 7 = freely determined by the market*

Lebanon
5.84

U.A.E.
5.67

Bahrain
5.00

Saudi Arabia
4.86

Tunisia
4.38

Oman
3.83

Qatar
3.33

Jordan
3.17

Kuwait
3.05

Egypt
2.88

0   7

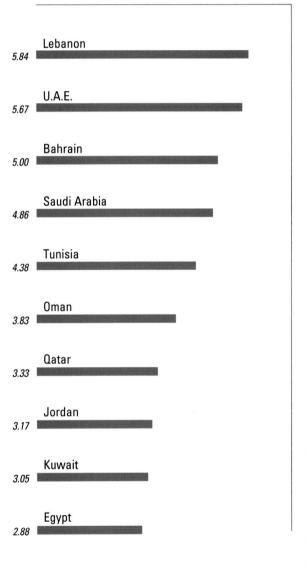

6.07
Financial regulation and supervision

The regulation and supervision of financial institutions are:

Scale *1 = inadequate for financial stability, 7 = among the world's most stringent*

Bahrain	
5.96	
Kuwait	
5.42	
Saudi Arabia	
5.40	
Lebanon	
5.03	
Oman	
5.00	
U.A.E.	
4.96	
Tunisia	
4.91	
Qatar	
4.83	
Jordan	
4.50	
Egypt	
4.00	

0   7

6.08
Perceived interest rate gap

The gap between interest rates for bank loans and interest rates for deposits is:

Scale *1 = greater than international norms, 7 = smaller than international norms*

Bahrain	
4.00	
Kuwait	
3.89	
Tunisia	
3.75	
U.A.E.	
3.75	
Egypt	
3.09	
Jordan	
2.97	
Qatar	
2.89	
Saudi Arabia	
2.85	
Oman	
2.50	
Lebanon	
2.35	

0   7

Finance

6.09
Access to credit

During the past year, obtaining credit for your company has become:

Scale   *1 = more difficult, 7 = easier*

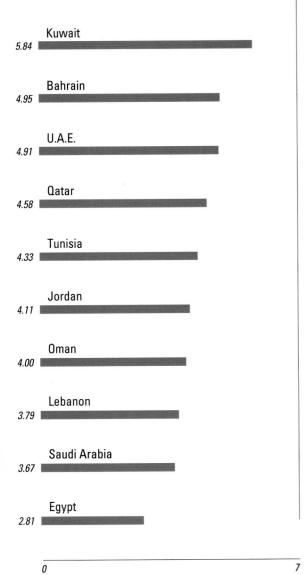

Kuwait	5.84
Bahrain	4.95
U.A.E.	4.91
Qatar	4.58
Tunisia	4.33
Jordan	4.11
Oman	4.00
Lebanon	3.79
Saudi Arabia	3.67
Egypt	2.81

0   7

6.10
Sources of investment finance

When financing investments, your company:

Scale   *1 = typically relies on its own retained earnings,*
7 = typically raises funds from banks or bond markets

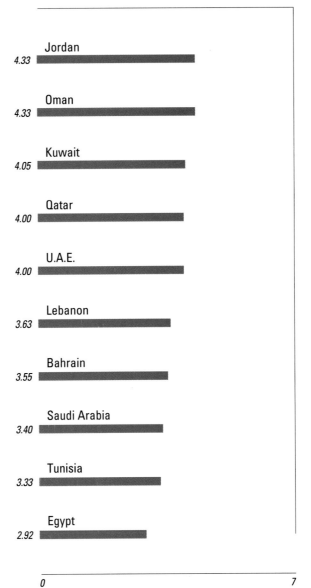

Jordan	4.33
Oman	4.33
Kuwait	4.05
Qatar	4.00
U.A.E.	4.00
Lebanon	3.63
Bahrain	3.55
Saudi Arabia	3.40
Tunisia	3.33
Egypt	2.92

0   7

Finance

6.11
Access to bond markets

Your company could borrow on the international bond market if necessary:

Scale *1 = not true, 7 = true*

Kuwait	5.50
Bahrain	3.65
U.A.E.	3.40
Egypt	3.12
Qatar	3.12
Tunisia	2.90
Lebanon	2.90
Jordan	2.76
Saudi Arabia	2.33
Oman	1.00

0   7

6.12
Local equity market access

Raising money by issuing shares on the local stock market is:

Scale *1 = nearly impossible, 7 = quite possible for a good company*

Kuwait	5.39
Tunisia	5.26
Bahrain	5.00
Egypt	4.69
Qatar	4.60
Jordan	4.50
Lebanon	4.20
Oman	4.17
U.A.E.	4.04
Saudi Arabia	3.25

0   7

6.13

Local investment in local e-commerce ventures

Domestic venture capital and private equity markets in your country are:

Scale *1 = unwilling to invest in local e-commerce ventures,*
7 = willing to invest in local e-commerce ventures

Kuwait	4.84
U.A.E.	4.67
Bahrain	4.20
Egypt	4.15
Jordan	3.97
Tunisia	3.90
Lebanon	3.87
Saudi Arabia	3.63
Qatar	3.12
Oman	2.67

0   7

6.14

Local investment in foreign e-commerce ventures

Domestic venture capital and private equity markets in your country are:

Scale *1 = unwilling to invest in e-commerce ventures in other countries, 7 = willing to invest in e-commerce ventures in other countries*

Kuwait	4.84
Bahrain	4.40
U.A.E.	4.25
Jordan	4.06
Lebanon	4.04
Oman	3.83
Qatar	3.76
Saudi Arabia	3.75
Egypt	3.73
Tunisia	3.22

0   7

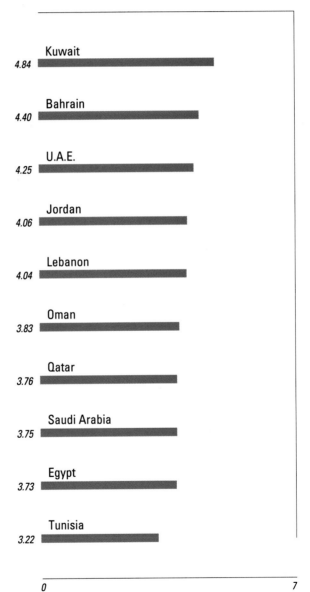

Finance

6.15
International investment in local e-commerce ventures

International venture capital and private equity markets are:

Scale *1 = unwilling to invest in e-commerce ventures in your country, 7 = willing to invest in e-commerce ventures in your country*

Tunisia
4.44

Bahrain
4.44

U.A.E.
4.29

Kuwait
4.26

Jordan
4.22

Oman
4.00

Egypt
3.37

Lebanon
3.26

Qatar
3.12

Saudi Arabia
2.81

0   7

6.16
Availability of online payment systems

Online Internet payment systems in your country are:

Scale *1 = not available, 7 = used by most people*

U.A.E.
4.38

Kuwait
4.16

Bahrain
3.88

Jordan
3.39

Egypt
3.36

Lebanon
3.21

Qatar
3.04

Saudi Arabia
2.69

Tunisia
2.30

Oman
2.20

0   7

6.17
Internet banking

Internet banking in your country is:

Scale *1 = not available, 7 = widely used at most banking institutions*

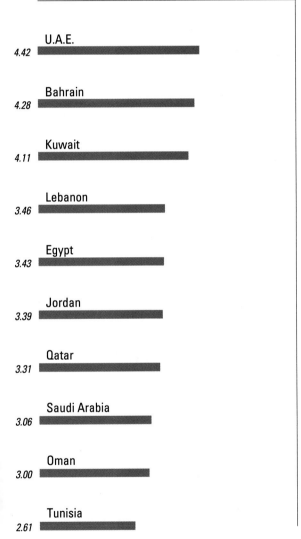

U.A.E.	
4.42	
Bahrain	
4.28	
Kuwait	
4.11	
Lebanon	
3.46	
Egypt	
3.43	
Jordan	
3.39	
Qatar	
3.31	
Saudi Arabia	
3.06	
Oman	
3.00	
Tunisia	
2.61	

0   7

7.01

Cost of importing foreign equipment

When your firm needs to import foreign equipment, the combined effect if import tariffs, license fees, bank fees and the time required for administrative red tape raises the cost by about:

Scale *1 = less than 10%, 2 = 11-20%, 3=31-40%,...,*
9 = greater than 80%

Oman	1.00
Qatar	1.17
U.A.E.	1.29
Kuwait	1.38
Tunisia	1.61
Bahrain	1.76
Saudi Arabia	1.93
Lebanon	1.97
Jordan	2.18
Egypt	3.76

0   9

7.02

Hidden import barriers

In your country, hidden import barriers (other than published tariffs and quotas) are:

Scale *1 = an important problem, 7 = not an important problem*

U.A.E.	6.46
Bahrain	6.21
Qatar	6.20
Kuwait	6.13
Oman	5.83
Lebanon	4.93
Saudi Arabia	4.87
Jordan	4.74
Tunisia	4.68
Egypt	2.71

0   7

Openness

7.03

Exchange rate premium

In order to obtain foreign currency, your firm must pay a premium over the official exchange rate of :

Scale *1 = 0%, 2 = 1-10%, 3=11-20%,..., 9 = greater than 70%*

Oman	1.00
Qatar	1.08
Lebanon	1.10
U.A.E.	1.14
Kuwait	1.25
Bahrain	1.26
Jordan	1.29
Saudi Arabia	1.33
Tunisia	1.35
Egypt	2.15

0 — 9

7.04

Exchange rate and exports

The current official exchange rate of your country is:

Scale *1 = highly appreciated and bad for exports,*
7 = highly depreciated and good for exports

U.A.E.	5.71
Bahrain	5.09
Tunisia	4.92
Kuwait	4.67
Qatar	4.64
Saudi Arabia	4.63
Oman	4.50
Egypt	4.41
Jordan	4.14
Lebanon	3.48

0 — 7

8.01
Intensity of local competition

In most industries, competition in the local market is:

Scale   *1 = limited and price cutting is rare, 7 = intense as market leadership changes over time*

U.A.E.	6.44
Oman	5.67
Kuwait	5.33
Lebanon	5.22
Jordan	5.17
Egypt	5.07
Bahrain	4.76
Saudi Arabia	4.63
Tunisia	4.54
Qatar	4.23

0   7

8.02
Administrative burden for startups

Starting a new business in your country is generally:

Scale   *1 = extremely difficult and time consuming, 7 = easy*

U.A.E.	5.76
Oman	5.17
Bahrain	4.96
Qatar	4.92
Tunisia	4.72
Jordan	4.58
Egypt	4.48
Kuwait	4.11
Lebanon	4.09
Saudi Arabia	3.94

0

Competition

8.03

Permits to start a firm

Approximately how many permits would you need to start a new firm?

Scale *open question: number of permits required*

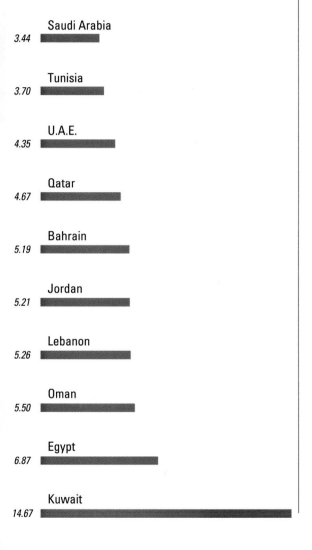

Saudi Arabia	*3.44*
Tunisia	*3.70*
U.A.E.	*4.35*
Qatar	*4.67*
Bahrain	*5.19*
Jordan	*5.21*
Lebanon	*5.26*
Oman	*5.50*
Egypt	*6.87*
Kuwait	*14.67*

0   *15*

8.04

Days to start a firm

Considering license and permit requirements, what is the typical number of days required to start a new firm in your country?

Scale *open question: number of days required*

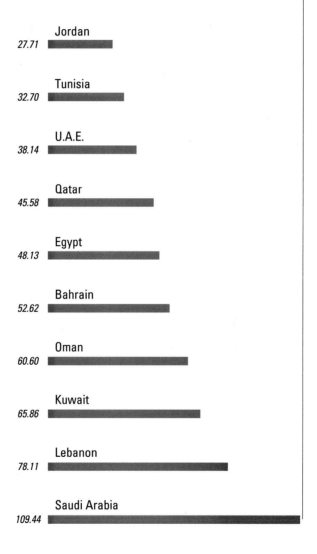

Jordan	*27.71*
Tunisia	*32.70*
U.A.E.	*38.14*
Qatar	*45.58*
Egypt	*48.13*
Bahrain	*52.62*
Oman	*60.60*
Kuwait	*65.86*
Lebanon	*78.11*
Saudi Arabia	*109.44*

0   *110*

Competition

8.05
Effectiveness of anti-trust policy

Anti-monopoly policy in your country:

Scale *1 = is lax and not effective at promoting competition,*
7 = effectively promotes competition

U.A.E.	4.71
Bahrain	4.32
Tunisia	4.32
Kuwait	4.17
Oman	4.17
Jordan	4.11
Qatar	4.08
Egypt	3.64
Lebanon	3.16
Saudi Arabia	2.75

0   7

8.06
Extent of market concentration

Corporate activity in your country is:

Scale *1 = dominated by a few business groups, 7 = spread among many firms*

Kuwait	5.11
U.A.E.	5.00
Tunisia	4.92
Egypt	4.50
Bahrain	4.36
Jordan	4.25
Lebanon	3.94
Qatar	3.88
Saudi Arabia	3.40
Oman	3.00

0

8.07
Extent of product and process collaboration

Product and process development in your country:

Scale *1 = is conducted within companies or with foreign suppliers,*
7 = involves intensive collaboration with local suppliers,
local customers and local research institutions

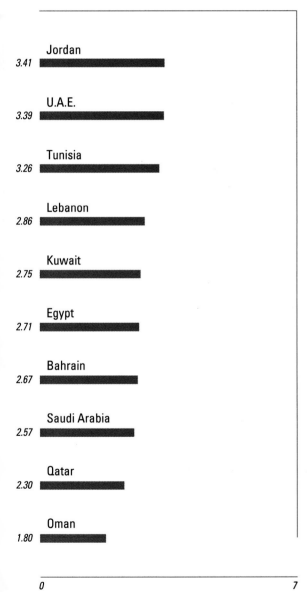

Jordan	3.41
U.A.E.	3.39
Tunisia	3.26
Lebanon	2.86
Kuwait	2.75
Egypt	2.71
Bahrain	2.67
Saudi Arabia	2.57
Qatar	2.30
Oman	1.80

0   7

Company Operations and Strategy

9.01
Extent of branding

Companies that sell internationally:

Scale *1 = sell commodities or market under foreign brands,*
7 = have developed their own international brands

Oman	5.00
Egypt	4.71
Lebanon	4.25
Saudi Arabia	3.87
Tunisia	3.82
Bahrain	3.76
Kuwait	3.64
U.A.E.	3.63
Jordan	3.52
Qatar	3.42

0   7

9.02
Degree of customer orientation

Firms in your country:

Scale *1 = generally treat their customers with no care,*
7 = pay close attention to customer satisfaction

U.A.E.	6.08
Kuwait	5.69
Oman	5.50
Tunisia	5.35
Bahrain	5.12
Qatar	5.04
Lebanon	4.81
Jordan	4.78
Saudi Arabia	4.00
Egypt	3.93

0   7

9.03

Control of international distribution

International distribution and marketing from your country:

Scale   *1 = takes place through foreign companies, 7 = is owned and controlled by local companies*

Kuwait	5.60
Jordan	5.06
U.A.E.	4.92
Lebanon	4.73
Bahrain	4.67
Egypt	4.64
Qatar	4.50
Oman	4.33
Saudi Arabia	4.06
Tunisia	4.05

0   7

9.04

Extent of regional sales

Exports from your country to surrounding regions are:

Scale   *1 = limited, 7 = substantial and growing*

U.A.E.	5.88
Oman	4.83
Jordan	4.74
Tunisia	4.74
Saudi Arabia	4.73
Qatar	4.73
Bahrain	4.56
Egypt	4.37
Lebanon	4.03
Kuwait	2.81

0   7

Company Operations and Strategy

9.05

Breadth of international markets

Exporting companies from your country:

Scale *1 = sell primarily in a few foreign markets, 7 = sell in virtually all international markets*

U.A.E.	4.67
Egypt	4.08
Bahrain	4.00
Qatar	4.00
Tunisia	3.95
Jordan	3.40
Lebanon	3.16
Kuwait	3.12
Saudi Arabia	2.88
Oman	2.80

0   7

9.06

Extent of staff training

The general approach of companies in your country to human resources is to:

Scale *1 = invest very little in training and employee development, 7 = invest heavily to attract, train and retain staff*

Tunisia	4.91
Bahrain	4.44
U.A.E.	4.29
Qatar	3.84
Oman	3.83
Saudi Arabia	3.75
Kuwait	3.35
Egypt	3.11
Lebanon	3.09
Jordan	3.08

0   7

9.07
Willingness to delegate authority

Willingness to delegate authority to subordinates is:

Scale *1 = generally low, 7 = generally high*

U.A.E.	4.17
Tunisia	4.14
Kuwait	3.94
Bahrain	3.76
Oman	3.50
Qatar	3.39
Saudi Arabia	3.25
Jordan	3.03
Egypt	3.00
Lebanon	2.75

0   7

9.08
Extent of incentive compensation

Compensation of management in your country:

Scale *1 = is based exclusively on salary, 7 = includes substantial incentives in the form of bonuses and stock options*

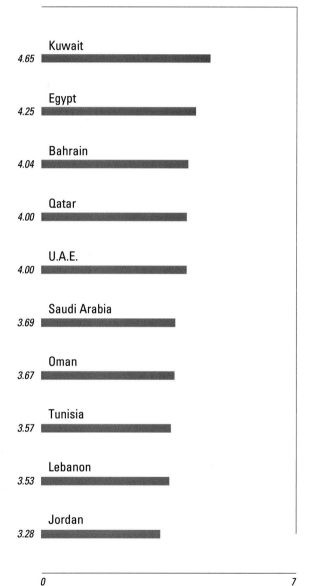

Kuwait	4.65
Egypt	4.25
Bahrain	4.04
Qatar	4.00
U.A.E.	4.00
Saudi Arabia	3.69
Oman	3.67
Tunisia	3.57
Lebanon	3.53
Jordan	3.28

0   7

Company Operations and Strategy

9.09

Reliance on professional management

Senior management positions in your country:

Scale   *1 = are often held by relatives, 7 = go only to skilled professionals*

9.10

Efficacy of corporate boards

Corporate boards in your country are:

Scale   *1 = controlled by management, 7 = powerful and represent outside shareholders*

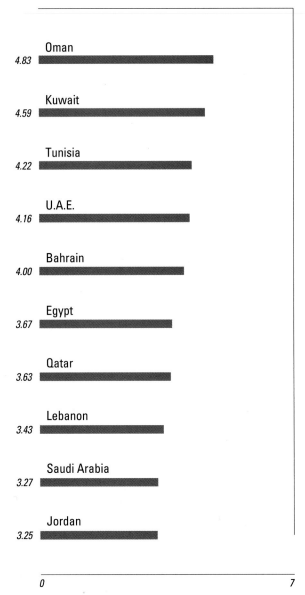

9.09		9.10	
Oman	4.83	Oman	4.50
Kuwait	4.59	Bahrain	4.46
Tunisia	4.22	Kuwait	4.35
U.A.E.	4.16	Qatar	3.91
Bahrain	4.00	Tunisia	3.70
Egypt	3.67	U.A.E.	3.68
Qatar	3.63	Lebanon	3.33
Lebanon	3.43	Jordan	3.29
Saudi Arabia	3.27	Saudi Arabia	3.21
Jordan	3.25	Egypt	2.80

0   7

0   7

Acknowledgments

INVESTCORP

Consolidated Contractors Company

Consolidated Contractors Company (CCC) is a leading international company, with diverse operations in such areas as construction, engineering, project management, procurement, development, and investment. CCC conducts much of its activities in the Middle East region. The company is committed to providing reliable, professional, and amicable service to its clients, and to being supportive of local businesses and social activities and the environment within which it operates. Meeting client requirements and ensuring high-quality work is the way CCC demonstrates its appreciation of client interests. CCC's growth and profitability are maintained through innovation, technical enhancements, and adaptability in all its markets. The company's profitability is directed towards sustaining growth and providing satisfactory returns to its shareholders. CCC's commitment to growth is firmly linked to its employees' continuous development in rewarding careers. Its strength emanates from its distinct culture, strong and close relationships with its clients, employees' competence and loyalty, entrepreneurial and flexible management teams, dynamism, focus on quality and safety, and commercial acumen. In all the above, CCC is and aims to continue to be second to none

Investcorp

Investcorp shares the vision that by empowering entrepreneurial talent and through the creative allocation of capital, it can generate wealth and contribute to economic and social progress, across national boundaries and continents. Investcorp, a management-driven global investment firm, operates out of New York, London and Bahrain. Over the past 20 years it has provided debt and equity capital of over US$20 billion to entities on both sides of the Atlantic. Participation in these investments has been offered to leading international financial institutions as well as to its select clients in the Arabian Gulf countries.

National Bank of Kuwait (NBK)

Since its inception in 1952 as the first indigenous bank in the Gulf, NBK has met the needs of Kuwaiti institutions and individuals with world-class financial services and customized solutions, while promoting economic development and growth in national wealth.

Aided by an international network in the major financial centers, NBK's focus on diversifying income and managing risk prudently has produced consistent growth in profitability and market capitalization and the highest credit rating from international agencies among Middle East and emerging market banks.

Our mission is to lead the way forward as a premier Arab institution supporting economic progress and integration within the region and helping revitalize the private sector as we expand our regional presence beyond Kuwait, Lebanon, and Bahrain to other countries in the Middle East.

Our belief and investment in technology and people permeates our vision for the provision of financial services in the future, while transparency and accountability continue to define our relationship with all stakeholders.

Osman Group

The Osman Group was founded in the early seventies and is considered to be one of the largest and best-established private groups in Egypt. It is composed of several specialized industrial, contracting, agricultural and general engineering companies with numerous offices and branches not only in Egypt, but worldwide. The labor force of the Osman Group has surpassed more than four thousand employees in the last few years, and is still growing.

The Osman Group acquires its strength from the experience, talent, skill, credibility and devotion of its human resources, either at the leadership or the shop floor level.

Our mission is to provide a range of high quality services in the field of industry, construction, real estate, agriculture, animal products, trading, information, and environmental conservation.

بنـك قطـر الوطـني

QATAR NATIONAL BANK ᴼˢᴄ

Qatar National Bank

Qatar National Bank (QNB) was incorporated in the
State of Qatar in 1964. The Government of Qatar owns
50 percent of its shares, while the rest is held by private
Qatari individuals and institutions. QNB is considered
today to be one of the premier banks in Qatar and the
Middle East. A closer look reveals an institution of great
integrity, with a proven track record spanning nearly
four decades. Known for its professional approach and
strong leadership, QNB plays a significant role in the
development of the Qatari banking system and economy.

The Bank's most important assets, of course, are its
employees. Many of the industry's finest are working
for QNB, providing a wealth of experience in all aspects
of banking. As part of the Bank's ongoing Corporate
Citizenship Philosophy, QNB provides generous support
to various projects and charitable organizations in the
areas of education, health, environment, humanities and
sports.

The Middle East is a region with enormous growth
potential and QNB is poised to play a significant role in
that growth.

Saudi Basic Industires Corporation (SABIC)

SABIC was established in 1976 to add value to Saudi
Arabia's natural hydrocarbon resources. Today we
are among the leading international petrochemical
companies in terms of sales and product diversity.
Headquartered in Riyadh, we are also the Middle East's
largest non-oil industrial company.

SABIC is owned by the Saudi Government (70%) and
the private sector (30%). Private sector shareholders
are from Saudi Arabia and other countries of the six-
nation Gulf Cooperation Council (GCC). Our businesses
are grouped into five core sectors: Basic Chemicals,
Intermediates, Polymers, Fertilizers and Metals. Each
sector consists of several Strategic Business Units (SBUs)
that are entirely dedicated to the customers they serve.
Our manufacturing network in Saudi Arabia consists of 18
world-scale industrial complexes operated by 16 affiliates.
Most of these affiliates are based in Jubail Industrial City
on the Arabian Gulf. Two are located in Yanbu Industrial
City on the Red Sea and one in the Eastern Province
city of Dammam. We are also partners in three regional
ventures based in Bahrain.

The vision that led to our creation was closely associated
with the aspirations of Saudi Arabia as a developing
nation. We continue to play an important role in
achieving some of those aspirations, including the
development of the country's human resources. We are
also committed to Saudi social and cultural values and
international business and environmental standards.

ارامكو السعودية
Saudi Aramco

Saudi Aramco

The Saudi Arabian Oil Company (Saudi Aramco) is the state-owned oil company of the Kingdom of Saudi Arabia. It ranks first among oil companies worldwide in terms of crude oil production and exports, and is among the leading producers of natural gas and natural gas liquids exports. Saudi Arabia is holder of the world's largest oil reserves—fully one-quarter—at more than 259.3 billion barrels. Saudi Aramco is a fully integrated oil company with operations in exploration, production, refining, marketing and international shipping.

Saudi Aramco employs approximately 56,000 workers and is headquatered in Dhahran, Saudi Arabia, in the Eastern Province. Operations span the Kingdom, with production and product distribution facilities linking all market areas. Major export shipping terminals are located at ports on the Arabian Gulf and Red Sea, while domestic demand for automotive and aviation products are met through strategic refineries.

Internationally, Saudi Aramco holds substantial joint venture interests in refining and marketing activities in the United States, the Republic of Korea, the Philippines and Greece. Key market service support offices are located in major cities in North America, Europe and the Far East. Saudi Aramco also operates a sizeable fleet of supertankers for shipping crude oil and product vessels serving all customer bases.

Domestically, expansion of the company's capability to discover, produce, process and transport natural gas is a major emphasis as Saudi Aramco moves into the 21st century. Increased efforts in exploration for non-associated gas reserves, along with extensive projects to handle increased gas production, are focused on supplying greater domestic demand for gas to fuel industries, provide petrochemcial feedstock, and serve such essential infrastructure needs as power generation and water desalination.

The company's more than six decades of operations have witnessed a steady yet dramatic rise in importance among world oil producers, and today is positioned to continue its prominence as a stable and reliable supplier of hydrocarbon resources well into the future.

Xenel Group

From its family roots in Saudi Arabia, the Xenel Group has grown on a global scale. Enterprises created include subsidiaries, foreign partnerships, and quoted companies in the manufacturing and service industries and in the provision of infrastructure.

Activities include the manufacture of power cables and fibre optics, steel products and petrochemicals, construction, operations and maintenance, healthcare, real estate, oil and gas, transportation and port operations, and provision of advanced video conferencing and telecommunication services. Total solutions include the first privately-owned petrochemical plant in the Middle East; the largest operating Build-Operate-Own power station in South Asia; hundreds of kilometers of transmission lines and the first commercial desalination plant in Saudi Arabia.

Xenel's vision is that by achieving growth through truly sustainable projects, bridges will be built between developed and developing countries, and that bonds between the Arab world and the rest of the international community will be strengthened.

Acknowledgments

Contributors

List of Contributors

Gassan al-Kibsi is a consultant in McKinsey & Company's Dubai Office. He joined the company in June 1997, first working in the company's North American offices in Washington DC and New York/New Jersey, he then joined the Dubai office in January 2000. Mr. al-Kibsi has worked in the areas of strategy, operations, organization, and mergers and acquisitions in various industries particularly energy, telecommunications, and media. Among his recent achievements is assuming leadership of an internal research initiative to assess the evolutionary path of the telecommunications sector in the Middle East. Prior to joining McKinsey, Mr. al-Kibsi was the director of strategy and business development at WorldSpace Management Corporation, a media and satellite company focusing on digital audio and multimedia via satellite, including Internet services, for the developing world. At WorldSpace, Mr. al-Kibsi was responsible for developing the company's content and acquisition strategy in the African, Latin American, and Middle Eastern markets. He also led negotiations with potential investors as well as regulators in target markets. He worked in Washington and London. Mr. al-Kibsi has a B.S. in industrial engineering from the Georgia Institute of Technology (valedictorian). In addition, he has a M.S. in operations research from Massachusetts Institute of Technology (MIT) and an M.B.A. in strategic management from the Sloan School of Management, MIT, both with highest honors.

Elsa V. Artadi is currently in the Department of Economics at Harvard University. Her research interests include public finance, economic development, and African economics. She earned her master of arts degree from Harvard University and a Master of Sciences from Universitat Pompeu Fabra in Barcelona.

Scott Beardsley is a director in McKinsey & Company's Brussels office. He is a global leader of McKinsey's telecommunications practice, has led the European wireline practice for five years, and is currently leading a global special initiative on broadband. Prior to joining McKinsey, Mr. Beardsley was an editor and marketing manager at the Sloan Management Review; he has also worked in strategic sales and product marketing for the semiconductor industry's Advanced Micro Devices and Analog Devices. Mr. Beardsley was recently honored as a fellow at the Institut d'Administration et de Gestion at the Université Catholique de Louvain in Belgium for outstanding contributions to management, and is a guest lecturer at the Business School. He was a Henry S. Dupont III Scholar (highest honors) at the MIT Sloan School of Management where he graduated with an M.B.A. in corporate strategy and marketing, and he holds a bachelor of science in electrical engineering, magna cum laude, from Tufts University where he was a Kodak Scholar, elected a member of Tau Beta Pi, and was president of Eta Kappa Nu.

Jennifer Blanke is an economist with the Global Competitiveness Programme at the World Economic Forum. Previously, she was senior program manager responsible for developing the business, management, and technology section of the World Economic Forum's Annual Meeting in Davos, from 1998 to 2001. Between 1995 and 1998, before joining the Forum, Blanke worked as a management consultant for Eurogroup, Mazars Group in Paris, France, where she specialized in banking and financial market organization. Blanke obtained a master of international affairs from Columbia University and an M.A. equivalent in international economics from the Graduate Institute of International Studies (Geneva), where she is currently pursuing her doctorate.

Kito de Boer is managing director of McKinsey & Company's Middle East office. He joined McKinsey in London in 1985, transferred to New Delhi in 1993 to help launch McKinsey in India, and moved to Dubai in 1999 to found and run McKinsey's Middle East office. He has substantial experience in serving the government sector both in terms of policy as well as strategy and organization. In the Middle East, de Boer has led several projects for government clients, including strategies for technology hubs and e-government. He is one of McKinsey's e-government experts and has led and participated in worldwide e-government benchmarking. In India, he has worked with the Confederation of Indian Industry, Ministry of Food Processing, Ministry of Finance, Ministry of Planning, and the Ministry of Railways. He is also a member of the Expert Committee on Railway Reform. Prior to joining McKinsey, de Boer worked for Shell in the Netherlands, Burroughs Computers in the United States, and Electrolux in Singapore, Malaysia, and Thailand. He has an M.B.A. from Cranfield and a B.Sc. in management science from Loughborough University.

Thomas J. Cassidy, Jr., is the director of the International Education Group at the Harvard Graduate School of Education (HGSE), where he also teaches two courses under the theme "Data for Decisions in Developing Education Systems" and serves as the chair of Harvard's annual international seminar, "Improving Quality in Education Systems." Dr. Cassidy has extensive experience working in the Middle East and the Gulf region. He was formerly the director of the Abu Dhabi Office of HGSE's Institutes for Higher Education and has served as a consultant in ministries of education in Egypt, Jordan, Lebanon, and Saudi Arabia, and as an advisor to UNESCO's Director of Education for the Middle East and North Africa Region on the Pan-Arab Education Decision Support Initiative (PAPED). Dr. Cassidy is an educational planner with particular expertise in education management information systems (EMIS) and organizational change and development. Over the past fifteen years, in addition to his work in Arab states, he has managed education development and capacity-building projects around the world, including in Pakistan, Malaysia, Jamaica, and Ghana. He is currently managing Harvard education projects in Latvia and Georgia. Dr. Cassidy holds a master's and doctorate degree from Harvard University.

Peter K. Cornelius is the director of the Global Competitiveness Programme at the World Economic Forum. Previously, he was the head of International Economic Research at Deutsche Bank and a senior economist of the International Monetary Fund (IMF), where he also served as the IMF's resident representative in Lithuania from 1993 to 1995. A former staff economist at the German Council of Economic Advisors and a former consultant to the United Nations Industrial Development Organization

and the European Union, Dr. Cornelius has also been an advisor to Deutsche Asset Management, an adjunct professor at Brandeis University, a visiting lecturer at Wissenschaftliche Hochschule für Unternehmensführung, School of Management, Koblenz, and a visiting scholar at the Harvard Institute for International Development at Harvard University. Dr. Cornelius studied economics and philosophy at the London School of Economics and Political Science, and received his doctorate in economics from the University of Göttingen.

Soumitra Dutta is the Roland Berger Professor of e-Business and Information Technology and dean for Executive Education at INSEAD. He is the faculty director of INSEAD's initiative in building a center of excellence in teaching and research in the digital economy in collaboration with leading international organizations such as Morgan Stanley, SAP, and Intel. Prior to joining the faculty of INSEAD, he was employed with Schlumberger in Japan and General Electric in the U.S. His research and consulting have focused on breakthrough approaches to the interrelationships between innovation, technology, and organizational design. His latest book is *The Bright Stuff: How Innovative People and Technology can make the Old Economy New* (Financial Times/Prentice Hall 2002). His previous books were *Embracing the Net: Get.Competitive* (Financial Times/Prentice Hall 2001) and *Process Reengineering, Organizational Change and Performance Improvement* (Mc-Graw Hill 1999). His next manuscript is entitled *The Global Information Technology Report: Readiness for the Networked Future* (Oxford University Press January 2003). In addition, he has published more than fifty articles in leading international journals. A fellow of the World Economic Forum, he has won several awards for research and pedagogy. His research has been showcased in the international media including CNN, BBC, and CNBC. He has taught in, and consulted with, leading international corporations across the world. Professor Dutta obtained his Ph.D. in computer science and his M.S. in business administration from the University of California at Berkeley.

Charles El-Hage is a vice president and partner of Booz Allen Hamilton, leading the firm's commercial consulting activities in the Middle East. Mr. El-Hage has wide experience in strategy, corporate transformation, privatization, organization, and new venture development work. Mr. El-Hage has led and participated in a large number of multifunctional assignments spanning various industries and continents, including preparing a number of companies and government entities for privatization in the Middle East, in the areas of telecommunications, energy, chemicals, metals, and consumer products; strategy and restructuring/turnaround work in banking, telecommunications, airlines, chemicals, automotive, railway, and heavy equipment industries in North America, Europe, and the Middle East; assisting a leading Gulf Cooperation Council country in the implementation of ambitious economic development programs; and assistance to a Middle Eastern country in the development and ongoing implementation of its national economic and public service turnaround program. Prior to joining Booz Allen Hamilton in Europe, Mr. El-Hage was organization and systems coordinator with the Abu Dhabi National Oil Company, where he led internal strategy, operations, and organization assignments. A dual Lebanese-French citizen, Mr. El-Hage is fluent in English, Arabic, and French. He holds a master of science degree in industrial engineering and a bachelor of science in industrial management obtained from Purdue University in Indiana, the United States.

Florence Eid teaches finance and economics at the Graduate School of Business and Management at the American University of Beirut. Dr. Eid returned to Lebanon after ten years in the United States where she worked for the World Bank and the Ford Foundation and pursued graduate studies at UCLA, MIT, and Harvard. She analyzed Lebanon's public hospital autonomy law and began the effort to amend key portions of the legislation. She is the founder of Lebanon's Entrepreneurship Network, a nonprofit association that organizes a nationwide business plan competition, which the prime minister of Lebanon supports. The competition's first year (2001/2002) has been extremely successful and is serving as a model for the region. Florence's Eid's interest in encouraging start-ups as a means of economic development is informed by her experience in development with the World Bank, and recent history in financial markets. Dr. Eid earned her Ph.D. in organization economics from MIT, where her dissertation research was in the area of contract theory.

Luis Enriquez is an associate principal in McKinsey & Company's London office. He has extensive experience serving cable, mobile, and fixed operators in the telecommunications industry in the U.S., Europe, and Latin America. He is one of the practice's global regulatory experts, and has led McKinsey's regulatory knowledge initiative. Prior to McKinsey, Mr. Enriquez worked extensively in regulation both in the U.S. and Latin America, and assisted Eastern European

governments with liberalization and European Union accession issues. Mr. Enriquez holds a bachelor of arts in economics, magna cum laude, from Harvard University and did his doctoral work in economics at the University of California at Berkeley.

Daniel Esty is professor of Environmental Law and Policy at Yale University. He teaches at both the Law School and the Environment School, where he also serves as Associate Dean. He is Director of the Yale Center for Environmental Law and Policy and of the Yale World Fellows Program. Prior to coming to Yale in 1994, Esty was a senior fellow at the Institute for International Economics. From 1989 to 1993, he served in a variety of senior positions in the U.S. Environmental Protection Agency. He is the author or editor of six books and numerous articles on environmental policy issues and the relationships between environment and trade, security, global governance, competitiveness, international institutions, and development. Esty holds degrees from Harvard College, Oxford University, and the Yale Law School.

Ahmed Farouk Ghoneim is currently an assistant professor, Faculty of Economic and Political Sciences, Cairo University. He is also an advisor on foreign trade issues to the Minister of Foreign Trade and is the Deputy Director of the Center for Economic and Financial Research and Studies, Cairo University. He is a research associate at the Economic Research Forum for Arab Countries, Iran, and Turkey (ERF) and a member of the economic committee of the National Democratic Party, Giza Governorate. He works as a consultant to several international organizations including the World Bank and the World Intellectual Property Organization (WIPO). Ghoneim holds a Ph.D. in economics and his special interests in research include trade policy, regional trade integration, and the multilateral trading system.

Jürgen von Hagen is a professor of economics and director of the Center for European Integration Studies, University of Bonn. He previously served as assistant and associate professor of Business Economics at Indiana University, and as professor of economics at the University of Mannheim. He is presently a research fellow of the Center for Economic Policy Research, London, and a member of the Comitee Economique de la Nation, Paris. Professor von Hagen was the winner of the first Gossen Prize of the Verein für Sozialpolitik (German Economics Association) in 1997. His main research topics are monetary economics, public finance, and European integration.

He has published more than sixty articles in leading international, refereed academic journals and more than 100 contributions to non-refereed journals and books. He serves as co-editor of *Perspektiven der Wirtschaftspolitik* and is a member of the editorial boards of *Open Economies Review*, the *Journal of International Finance and Economics*, the *Scottish Journal of Political Economy*, the *European Journal of Political Economy*, and the *European Economic Review*. Consulting activities include work for the IMF, the European Commission, the European Central Bank, the Federal Reserve Board, the Interamerican Development Bank, and several governments. He studied economics and political science at the University of Dortmund and the University of Bonn, and received his Ph.D. in economics from the University of Bonn.

Friedrich von Kirchbach is chief of the Market Analysis Section in the Geneva-based International Trade Centre of the United Nations Conference on Trade and Development/World Trade Organization. His team has developed a variety of Web-based tools for strategic market research, which are now being used around the world. He has been associated with several national and international institutions, including the United Nations Economic and Social Commission for Asia and the Pacific, INSEAD, the International Labor Organization, the Organization for Economic Cooperation and Development, and the Volkswagen Foundation. Von Kirchbach holds a Ph.D. in economics focusing on international investment and has written and lectured widely on trade-related issues.

Marc A. Levy is associate director of the Center for International Earth Science Information Network (CIESIN; www.ciesin.columbia.edu), in the Earth Institute at Columbia University. At CIESIN he is director of the Science Applications group, and oversees programs concerning indicators of environmental sustainability, measures of state capacity, information tools for international environmental agreements, and other work aimed at integrating natural and social science information on the environment. He is a project scientist for CIESIN's Socioeconomic Data and Applications Center, which is one of the primary liaisons between NASA's Earth Observing System and the social science and policymaking communities. He has taught political science and international environmental policy since 1987, including appointments at Princeton, Williams, and Columbia. He has published on environmental sustainability indicators, the effectiveness of international environmental institutions, social learning and environmental policymaking, and on

environment-security connections. Levy is co-editor (with Robert O. Keohane and Peter M. Haas) of *Institutions for the Earth* (MIT Press 1993) and co-editor (with Keohane) of *Institutions for Environmental Aid* (MIT Press 1996).

Mondher Mimouni is a market analyst with the International Trade Centre of the United Nations Conference on Trade and Development/World Trade Organization. As part of his work on international trade he has built a bilateral database on market access (MAcMap), and developed the Trade Performance Index for assessing and monitoring the multifaceted dimensions of the export performance and competitiveness of countries. He holds an M.Phil. equivalent in development economics from the Economic University of Montpellier, an M.S. in agricultural policy and development administration from the International Centre for Advanced Mediterranean Agronomic Studies (CIHEAM-Montpellier). He is currently completing a Ph.D. at the University of Paris I (Panthéon-Sorbonne).

Karim Nashashibi is senior resident representative of the IMF for the West Bank and Gaza. He advises on matters concerning the economies and economic policies of the twenty-four member countries, and assists in the formulation of IMF policies for these countries. He is responsible for IMF-supported economic programs in Algeria, and has recently headed missions to Morocco and Syria. Dr. Nashashibi has previously served as assistant director of the Fiscal Affairs Department of the IMF (1988 to 1993), and senior economist at the Center for Projections and Policies of the United Nations. He has written works on a wide range of macroeconomic issues, including *The Social Impact of Free Trade in the Euro-Mediterranean Regions* (November 1999), *Export Performance and Competitiveness in Arab Countries*, with Analisa Fedelino and Ward Brown (October 1999), and *Global Macroeconomic Consequences of the Euro for the Arab Economies*, with Peter Allum (May 1999). He received his doctorate from the University of California, Berkeley.

John Page is director for poverty reduction policy at the World Bank. He joined the Bank in 1980 and has undertaken a wide range of research, policy, and operational assignments. From 1985 to 1992 he was a divisional manager for operations in Latin America. In 1992 and 1993, he was senior economic advisor in the Policy Research Department and principal author of the Bank's East Asian Miracle study. He then served as chief economist of the Middle East and North Africa Region and director of its Social and Economic Development Group from 1993 to 1999. Before assuming his current position in March 2000, he was the Bank's director of economic policy. He has published several books and more than fifty papers on trade and industrial policy, growth and productivity change, and economic development. Dr. Page has written extensively and lectured widely on the economies of the Middle East, including at all four Middle East Economic Summits. He is also adjunct professor in the Middle East Program of the Paul Nitze School of Advanced International Studies of the Johns Hopkins University, and has taught economics at Stanford University and Princeton University. Dr. Page obtained his bachelor's degree in economics from Stanford University and his doctorate from Oxford University, where he was a Rhodes scholar.

Jean-Michel Pasteels is presently working with the International Trade Centre UNCTAD/WTO, Switzerland as a trade economist and contributes to studies on country-specific trade development strategies, trade policy issues, and trade performance. He also develops and maintains tools for market analysis, such as gravity models and tools for identifying products with intraregional trade potential. He has published articles in the *International Journal of Forecasting*, *Economie et Prévison*, and the *Global Competitiveness Report*. His research interests include national competitiveness, commercial policy, trade promotion strategy, trade negotiations, international business, market performance, time-series analysis, and economic forecasting. He obtained his Ph.D. in economics from Universite Libre de Bruxelles, where he contributed to the development of an expert system for economic forecasting.

Fiona Paua is an economist with the Global Competitiveness Programme at the World Economic Forum. Previously, she was the country head of research for Citibank Philippines and a financial analyst at Goldman Sachs in the U.S., Hong Kong, and Singapore. She has also served in various capacities at several institutions including the World Bank (Middle East and North Africa division), the United States Agency for International Development, and on technology-related projects at Harvard University. She is also the co-founder of b2bpricenow.com, recipient of the 2001 Development Marketplace Award of the World Bank. Paua is a graduate of Dartmouth College and Harvard University.

Karim Sabbagh is a principal with the communications, media, and technology practice at Booz Allen Hamilton, based in the firm's Riyadh and Dubai Offices. He has participated in a number of economic and business development assignments primarily in the context of large-scale privatization programs, and worked on a number of strategy-based transformation engagements focused on strategic planning, marketing, and business process re-design, with an emphasis on telecommunications. Overall, Sabbagh has acquired sixteen years of strategy and operation experience through various projects in the Middle East, Europe, and North America. His experience covers various sectors such as fixed, wireless, and mobile voice and data telecommunications, media, financial services, and consumer goods, and also encompasses the development of large-scale economic programs. He is currently focusing on his role as the handling officer for the restructuring of Saudi Telecom, in preparation for the company's privatization and the liberalization of the telecommunications sector in Saudi Arabia. A dual Lebanese-Canadian citizen, he is fluent in English, French, and Arabic. Sabbagh is pursuing graduate studies in Development Economics and Finance at the Center for Financial and Management Studies at the University of London. He holds a Ph.D. in strategic management (with honors) from Century New Mexico University, United States. He also earned an M.B.A., with a concentration in finance, and a B.B.A., with a concentration in marketing (with distinction) from the American University of Beirut.

Xavier Sala-i-Martin is a professor in the Department of Economics at Columbia University, and a visiting professor at Universitat Pompeu Fabra. He was previously an associate professor at the Department of Economics at Yale University. His research interests include economic growth, macroeconomics, public finance and social security, health and population economics and monetary economics. Professor Sala-i-Martin is a member of the Board of Editors of the *Journal of Economic Growth*, *Macroeconomics Dynamics*, *and Economics Letters*. He is also a research fellow at the CEPR and the NBER, and a consultant for the World Bank and the International Monetary Fund. He earned his Ph.D. in economics from Harvard University.

Paola Tarazi is a consultant with Booz Allen Hamilton, based in the firm's Beirut office. She has participated in various strategy, economic, and business development assignments. Her recent assignments include analyzing and validating the concept of introducing a Special Economic Zone with special emphasis on ICT and industry in the Levant region, developing a business plan for an e-commerce venture in the region that is part of a leading Technology Park in the Gulf, focusing on e-commerce start-up incubation, and formulating a development strategy for an ICT-related subsector in the Gulf region. Prior to joining Booz Allen Hamilton, Tarazi worked at the Central Bank of Lebanon. Her work involved various projects related to monetary policies and macroeconomic developments in Lebanon and the region. This included advising on the impact of changes in the international monetary environment on the Lebanese economy (such as EMU and financial crises), developing inflation indicators for assessing the impact of monetary policies, building estimates for FDI and portfolio investments in the banking sector, and designing sectoral business surveys to support conjuncture analyses. A dual British-Lebanese citizen, she is fluent in English, French, and Arabic. Tarazi has pursued intensive training at the IMF Institute in Washington and the Banque de France in Paris. She holds an M.Sc. in operational research from the London School of Economics and Political Science, and a B.Sc. in statistics and economics from the University College London in the United Kingdom.

Paul Tempest is vice president of the British Institute of Energy Economics and executive director of the Windsor Energy Group. He was director-general of the World Petroleum Council and Congresses from 1991 to 1999, and is a past president of the International Association for Energy Economics. Between 1985 and 1991, he attended fifteen OPEC meetings as the on-the-spot representative of the Shell Group. Tempest has been acquainted with OPEC since its founding in 1960/1961, when he worked at the Bank of England on the management of Kuwait's external reserves and later in Doha, Qatar from 1970 to 1971 as general manager of the Currency Authority covering seven of the Emirates of the Lower Gulf. Between 1973 and 1976, he was secretary of the Bank of England's Special Oil Committee, which handled several difficult oil-related issues, including the impact of the new oil surpluses on the London euro-dollar market and on London banks, recycling mechanisms in the industrialised world, debt and trade impacts at home and elsewhere, and specific infrastructure problems that emerged in Saudi Arabia and among OPEC producers. In 1990, OPEC published, in its *Thirtieth Anniversary Bulletin*, his paper, "OPEC—A View From the Deck" on the past, present, and future of OPEC.

He continued to write on this theme in articles in the *Oil and Gas Journal, Energy Policy, the Geopolitics of Energy*, the IAEE Newsletter, and in *The Politics of Middle East Oil* (Graham and Trotman 1993), which he also introduced and edited.

Andrew Warner is a research fellow at CID. His recent work has focused on the political economy of election results in Russia, the banking system in Russia, and an attempt to measure the impact of adverse climate and geography on national income levels using regional data for large countries. He has also helped develop a new methodology for ranking national competitiveness (jointly with Jeffrey Sachs), the results of which have appeared in several editions of the *Global Competitiveness Report* and the *Africa Competitiveness Report* of the World Economic Forum. His current activities include research on the fundamental driving forces behind economic growth, including new enterprise formation, the role of exports, legal institutions, and urbanization. He is also a part-time consultant with governments in Bulgaria, Central America, and Trinidad and Tobago. He received his Ph.D. in economics in 1991 from Harvard University.

Rodney Wilson is professor of economics at the Institute for Middle Eastern and Islamic Studies, University of Durham. He was chairman of the Council of the British Society for Middle Eastern Studies (1996 to 2000) and currently serves as chairman of the Academic Committee of the Institute of Islamic Banking and Insurance in London. In 1998, he was a visiting fellow at the Islamic Research and Training Institute of the Islamic Development Bank in Jeddah. His recent books include *Economic Development in the Middle East* (Routledge 1995); *Economics, Ethics and Religion: Jewish, Christian and Muslim Economic Thought* (Macmillan 1997; reprinted 1998 and 2001); and *The Political Economy of the Middle East*, edited with Tim Niblock and Edward Elgar (Cheltenham 1999). Recent articles include "The Interface Between Islamic and Conventional Banking," in *Islamic Banking and Finance: New Perspectives on Profit Sharing and Risk*, edited by Munawar Iqbal and David T. Llewellyn, Edward Elgar (Cheltenham 2002) and "The Challenges of the Global Economy for Middle Eastern Governments," in *Globalisation and the Middle East*, edited by Toby Dodge and Richard Higgott (Royal Institute of International Affairs 2002).

Andrew Winston has an extensive background in business, with over ten years of strategy and marketing experience in top consulting and media companies.

He received a B.A. in economics from Princeton University in 1991 and an M.B.A. from Columbia University in 1999. Andrew completed coursework for a certificate in conservation biology from the Columbia Consortium for Environmental Research and Conservation, and has completed the Sustainable Business Challenge, a certificate program from the World Business Council on Sustainable Development. In 2003 he will receive the master of environmental management degree from Yale University.

Susanna Wolf has been working as a research fellow at for the Center for Development Research (ZEF) at the Rheinische Friedrich Wilhelms University, Bonn, in the Department Economics and Technological Change, since December 1997. Dr. Wolf's research focuses on relations between the EU and Africa, including aid, trade, and investment relations. Her research interests also include the role of ICT in the development and competitiveness of small and medium enterprises. Following studies in economics and mathematics at Hamburg University, she received her Ph.D. from the University of the Federal Armed Forces in Hamburg in 1996. Her thesis was entitled: "Limited Success of the Lomé Conventions."